Xcode 5
Start to Finish

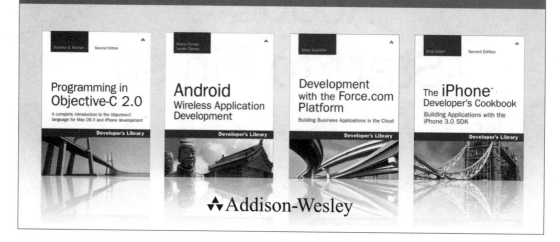

Xcode 5
Start to Finish

---

iOS and OS X
Development

Fritz Anderson

✦Addison-Wesley

Upper Saddle River, NJ • Boston • Indianapolis • San Francisco
New York • Toronto • Montreal • London • Munich • Paris • Madrid
Capetown • Sydney • Tokyo • Singapore • Mexico City

Many of the designations used by manufacturers and sellers to distinguish their products are claimed as trademarks. Where those designations appear in this book, and the publisher was aware of a trademark claim, the designations have been printed with initial capital letters or in all capitals.

The author and publisher have taken care in the preparation of this book, but make no expressed or implied warranty of any kind and assume no responsibility for errors or omissions. No liability is assumed for incidental or consequential damages in connection with or arising out of the use of the information or programs contained herein.

For information about buying this title in bulk quantities, or for special sales opportunities (which may include electronic versions; custom cover designs; and content particular to your business, training goals, marketing focus, or branding interests), please contact our corporate sales department at corpsales@pearsoned.com or (800) 382-3419.

For government sales inquiries, please contact governmentsales@pearsoned.com.

For questions about sales outside the United States, please contact international@pearsoned.com.

Visit us on the Web: informit.com/aw

Library of Congress Cataloging-in-Publication Data
Anderson, Fritz.
    Xcode 5 start to finish : iOS and OS X development / Fritz Anderson.
        pages   cm
    Includes index.
    ISBN 978-0-321-96720-6 (pbk. : alk. paper)—ISBN 0-321-96720-8
(pbk. : alk.paper)
    1. Mac OS. 2. iOS (Electronic resource) 3. Macintosh (Computer)—Programming. 4. iPhone (Smartphone)—Programming. 5. Application software—Development. I. Title.
    QA76.774.M33A53 2014
    005.3'82—dc23
                                                                    2014000229

ISBN-13: 978-0-321-96720-6
ISBN-10: 0-321-96720-8

Text printed in the United States on recycled paper at Edwards Brothers Malloy in Ann Arbor, Michigan.
First printing, May 2014

Editor-in-Chief
Mark L. Taub

Senior Acquisitions Editor
Trina MacDonald

Senior Development Editor
Chris Zahn

Managing Editor
John Fuller

Full-Service Production Manager
Julie B. Nahil

Copy Editor
Stephanie Geels

Indexer
Ted Laux

Proofreader
Andrea Fox

Technical Reviewers
Duncan Champney
Chuck Ross
Dan Wood

Editorial Assistant
Olivia Basegio

Cover Designer
Chuti Prasertsith

Compositor
LaurelTech

❖

For Magdalen Jeanette Anderson (1952–2013),
the mother of my children

❖

Contents at a Glance

Contents

Acknowledgments

Only part of the effort that went into putting *Xcode 5 Start to Finish* into your hands was spent at a text editor. I am indebted to those without whom this book could not have been made. Many of them appear in the formal production credits; they deserve better-than-formal thanks.

Trina MacDonald guided me through the from-scratch planning process that a new Xcode book required, and advocated for it when the need was not obvious.

Olivia Basegio made sure the contracts, correspondence, (and advance payments!) all got through. She herded the reviewers through their work while the book was still pieces lying on the ground.

The reviewers—Duncan Champney, Chuck Ross, and Dan Wood—were friends to the book even through the burden of trying to make sense of a work that spiraled, rather than marched, to its conclusion. They saved me much embarrassment, and made this a much better work than it started. Errors remain. Some are intentional, some not; they are all my own.

Julie Nahil, the production manager, and Stephanie Geels, the copy editor, made it exceptionally easy to give you a book that is as close as it can be to what I meant it to be. The process was never smoother.

A full-time day job is not an author's best friend (except for the part about paying the rent), but Emerging Technologies, in the IT Services department of The University of Chicago, was a friend to me. My boss, Alan Takaoka, got me three-day weekends while I wrote, even when I ran over by a couple of weeks. I promised to keep all my Monday meetings and deadlines while I worked on the book, but my colleague, Cornelia Bailey, made the deadlines on our projects disappear.

Bess and Kate bore more than daughters should of my doubts and frustrations, and were simply confident that I would do fine—which was all they needed to do.

About the Author

Fritz Anderson has been writing software, books, and articles for Apple platforms since 1984. He has worked for research and development firms, consulting practices, and freelance. He was admitted to the Indiana bar, but thought better of it. He is now a senior iOS developer for the Emerging Technologies and Communications division at The University of Chicago. He has two daughters.

Introduction

Welcome to *Xcode 5 Start to Finish*! This book will show you how to use Apple's integrated development environment to make great products with the least effort.

Xcode 5 is the descendant of a family of development tools dating back 20 years to NeXT's ProjectBuilder. It started as a text editor, a user-interface designer, and a front end for Unix development tools. It has become a sophisticated system for building applications and system software, with a multitude of features that leverage a comprehensive indexing system and subtle incremental parser to help you assemble the right code for your project, and get it right the first time.

That much power can be intimidating. My aim in *Xcode 5 Start to Finish* is to demystify Xcode, giving you a gradual tour through examples that show you how it is used day to day. Don't let the gentle approach fool you: This book will lead you through the full, best-practices workflow of development with Xcode 5. There are no "advanced topics" here—I'll show you version control and unit testing in their proper places in the development process.

How This Book Is Organized

First, a word on my overall plan for *Xcode 5 Start to Finish*. This is a book about developer tools. If it teaches you something about how to use the Cocoa frameworks, or something about programming, that's fine, but that's incidental to showing you the Xcode workflow. There are many excellent books and other resources for learning the frameworks; you'll find many of them listed in Appendix B, "Resources."

Every tour needs a pathway, and every lesson needs a story. The first three parts of this book demonstrate Xcode through three applications—a command-line tool, an iOS app, and an OS X application—that calculate and display some statistics in American football. None of the apps are very useful; the graphical apps run almost entirely on sample data. But they demand enough of the development tools to give you a solid insight into how to use them.

The full code for the example programs is available online from informit.com/9780321967206 (register your book to gain access to the code). In the interest of space, I'll be showing only excerpts.

Xcode supports some technologies, like Core Data and OS X bindings, that are *not* for beginners. *Xcode 5 Start to Finish* dives straight into those techniques, ignoring conceptually simpler approaches, so I can demonstrate how Xcode works. Other "advanced" techniques, like unit testing and version control, appear at the points where best practices require them. Again, I'll be showing you the workflow as Xcode supports it.

I'm using applications for iOS and OS X as examples, but read both Parts II and III, even if you're only interested in one platform. The applications are only *stories*; the techniques apply to both platforms.

First Steps

In Part I, I'll take you from installing Xcode and running your first project through basic debugging skills. You'll work through a small command-line application. The application may be simple, but you'll learn foundational skills you'll need before adding the complexity of graphical apps.

- **Chapter 1, Getting Xcode**—Some things to consider before you download Xcode 5; two ways to download and install it.
- **Chapter 2, Kicking the Tires**—Your first look at Xcode, setting up a trivial project and running it.
- **Chapter 3, Simple Workflow and Passive Debugging**—Write, build, and run a simple application, and respond to a crash.
- **Chapter 4, Active Debugging**—Take charge of debugging by setting breakpoints and tracing through the program. I'll show you how to organize your workspace.
- **Chapter 5, Compilation**—A pause for a description of the process of building an application.
- **Chapter 6, Adding a Library Target**—Add a library target to a project, and learn how to build a product from multiple targets.
- **Chapter 7, Version Control**—Why source control is important, and how to take advantage of Xcode's built-in support for versioning through Git and Subversion.

The Life Cycle of an iOS Application

Part II tells the story of a small iPhone app, and how to use Apple's developer tools to build it. It introduces you to the graphical editor for user interfaces, and shows how to profile an app to optimize its speed and memory burden.

- **Chapter 8, Starting an iOS Application**—You'll start by creating an iOS project, and learn the Model-View-Controller design at the core of Cocoa on iOS and OS X alike.
- **Chapter 9, An iOS Application: Model**—Design a Core Data schema and supplement it with your own code.
- **Chapter 10, An iOS Application: Controller**—Create a controller to link your model to the on-screen views. On the way, I'll tell you about refactoring, and Xcode's continual error-checking.
- **Chapter 11, Building a New View**—Design the user-interface views for your app with the integrated Interface Builder, and take advantage of source-code completion.

- **Chapter 12, Autolayout in a New View**—In Xcode 5, autolayout is more about getting things done than fighting the tools. Learn how to make Cocoa layout do what you want.
- **Chapter 13, Adding Table Cells**—While adding an in-screen component to your app, you'll debug memory management, and control how Xcode builds, runs, and tests your apps through the Scheme editor.
- **Chapter 14, Adding an Editor**—Add an editor view, and get deep into Storyboard.
- **Chapter 15, Unit Testing**—Unit testing speeds development and makes your apps more reliable. I'll show you how Xcode supports it as a first-class part of the development process.
- **Chapter 16, Measurement and Analysis**—Use Instruments to track down performance and memory bugs.
- **Chapter 17, Provisioning**—Behind the scenes, the process of getting Apple's permission to put apps on devices is complicated and temperamental. I'll show you how Xcode saves you from most of the pain, and give you a few tips on how to get out if it backs you into a corner.

Xcode for Mac OS X

Part III shifts focus to OS X development. Some concepts are more important to OS X than iOS, but you'll be learning techniques you can use regardless of your platform.

- **Chapter 18, Starting an OS X Application**—Carrying iOS components over to OS X; what the responder chain is, and how Interface Builder makes it easy to take advantage of it.
- **Chapter 19, Bindings: Wiring an OS X Application**—As you build a popover window, you'll use OS X bindings to simplify the link between your data and the screen. You'll also encounter autosizing, a legacy technique for laying out view hierarchies.
- **Chapter 20, A Custom View for OS X**—Add a custom view to your app, and see how Interface Builder can lay it out and configure it, even though it's not a standard Cocoa component.
- **Chapter 21, Localization**—How you can translate your Mac and iOS apps into other languages.
- **Chapter 22, Bundles and Packages**—You'll master the fundamental structure of most Mac and iOS products, and how both platforms use the `Info.plist` file to fit apps into the operating system.
- **Chapter 23, Frameworks**—Package and share a complete subprogram you can incorporate into any OS X application.
- **Chapter 24, Property Lists**—Learn the basic JSON-like file type for storing data in both OS X and iOS.

Xcode Tasks

By this point in the book, you'll have a foundation for digging into the details of the Xcode toolset. Part IV moves on to topics that deserve a more concentrated treatment than Parts II and III.

- **Chapter 25, Documentation in Xcode**—How Xcode gives you both immediate help on API, and browsable details on the concepts of Cocoa development. Find out how you can add your own documentation to the system.

- **Chapter 26, The Xcode Build System**—I'll show you the fundamental rules and tools behind how Xcode goes from source files to executable products.

- **Chapter 27, Instruments**—Using Apple's timeline profiler, you can go beyond basic performance and memory diagnostics to a comprehensive look at how your program uses its resources.

- **Chapter 28, Debugging**—How to use breakpoint actions and conditions to eliminate in-code diagnostics. You'll also find a tutorial on the `lldb` debugger command set, for even closer control over your code.

- **Chapter 29, Continuous Integration**—Mavericks Server complements Xcode 5 with a sleek continuous-integration system that can synthesize your code analysis, perform cross-platform unit tests, and generate product archives. I'll show you how to get started, and how to put it to best use.

- **Chapter 30, Snippets**—A roundup of tips, traps, and features to help you get the most from the developer tools.

Appendixes

The appendixes in Part V contain references to help you master the build system, and find help and support.

- **Appendix A, Some Build Variables**—The most important configuration and environment variables from Xcode's build system.

- **Appendix B, Resources**—A compendium of books, tools, and Internet resources to support your development efforts.

About Versions

This book was finished in the fall of 2013, shortly after Apple released iOS 7, OS X Mavericks, and Xcode 5 to the public. *Xcode 5 Start to Finish* is written to the first-bugfix versions of all three.

About the Code

Xcode 5 Start to Finish has many examples of executable code—it's about a system for creating code and running it. My goal is to teach *workflow*. What the code itself does is practically incidental. In particular, be aware: **Much of the code in this book will not run as initially presented.** *Xcode 5 Start to Finish* is about the development process, most of which (it seems) entails prosecuting and fixing bugs. You can't learn the workflow unless you learn how to respond to bugs.

So I'll be giving you buggy code. You may find it painful to read, and if you try to run it, it will be painful to run. Trust me: It's for a reason.

Also, sample code for this book is available at `informit.com/title/9780321967206` (register your book to gain access to the code). You'll find archives of the projects in this book as they stand at the end of each chapter. With very few exceptions—I'll make them very clear—if you want the project as it stands at the *start* of a chapter, you should use the archive for the *end* of the previous chapter.

The chapter archives do not include version-control metadata. If you are following along with the examples, and using Git (or Subversion) for your work, copy the changes into your own working directory. If you replace your directory with a sample directory, you'll lose your version history.

Conventions

This book observes a number of typographic and verbal conventions.

- Human-interface elements, such as menu items and button labels, are shown **like this**.
- File names and programming constructs are shown `like this`. This will sometimes get tricky as when I refer to the product of the "Hello World" *project* (plain text, because it's just a noun) as the *file* `Hello World`.
- Text that you type in will be shown **`like this`**.
- When I introduce a new term, I'll call it out *like this*.

I'll have you do some command-line work in the Terminal. Some of the content will be wider than this page, so I'll follow the convention of breaking input lines with backslashes (\) at the ends. I'll break long output lines simply by splitting them, and indenting the continuations. When that output includes long file paths, I'll replace components with ellipses (. . .), leaving the significant parts.

For many, many years the Macintosh had a one-button mouse. (Don't laugh—most purchasers didn't know what a mouse *was*; try pushing the wrong button on an old Mac mouse.) Now it has four ways to effect an alternate mouse click: You can use the right button on an actual mouse; you can hold down the Control key and make an ordinary click; you can hold down two fingers while clicking on a multi-touch trackpad (increasingly common even on desktop Macs); or you can tap at a designated corner of a multi-touch trackpad. And there are more variations available through System Preferences. Unless the distinction really matters, I'm simply going to call it a "right-click" and let you sort it out for yourself.

Part I

First Steps

1

Getting Xcode

If you want to use Xcode, you must install it. Developer tools were bundled into OS X in the early days, but now you must download it, drag the Xcode application into your /Applications folder, and start it up.

Before You Begin

Before you do anything, be sure you can use Xcode 5. There are two considerations.

Developing for Earlier Operating Systems

When Apple brings out a new version of Xcode, it includes software development kits (SDKs) for the latest versions of its operating systems, and only those. (As of Xcode 5.0.1, which can be used on OS X 10.8 Mountain Lion, these were OS X 10.8 and 10.9, and iOS 7.) In theory, that isn't much of a constraint: You can still target earlier OSes; the SDK does the right thing to adapt itself to the earlier versions.

However, there are some APIs that don't make the cut. (An earlier, incompatible version of libcrypto was dropped in OS X 10.6 after warnings more than a year in advance.) The same with PowerPC development: If you need to do that, get a Mac that can run 10.6 and use Xcode 3.2.6. I'll explain how use the xcode-select tool to switch your system between versions of Xcode in the "Command-Line Tools" section of Chapter 26, "The Xcode Build System."

Also, a strategy that used to work in Xcode 3 no longer does: With earlier SDKs available, you could temporarily drop back to the SDK for your earliest target system, and the compiler would tell you where you relied on newer API. Xcode doesn't afford that any more.

> **Note**
>
> People have asked whether they can pluck SDKs from earlier Xcode installations and drop them into Xcode 5. Ultimately it doesn't work: The older SDKs rely on compilers and runtime libraries that are simply not available in Xcode 5, and Xcode 5 assumes that its SDKs are built to support the tools it does have.

Requirements

Apple is cagey about what the operating requirements are for Xcode, and that's understandable, because it depends on your usage and preferences.

- Xcode 5 runs on OS X Mountain Lion (10.8) and Mavericks (10.9).

- The download will be about 2 GB.

- How much disk space the installed Xcode takes up depends on what documentation sets and supplementary tools you download. A fresh installation is about 6.5 GB; 9 GB is not uncommon with options.

- Xcode 5 can be *run* in 2 GB of memory, but don't expect to do much more than look at it. For the examples in this book, 4 GB should be enough, but for medium-sized projects, my rule of thumb is that you'll need about 3 GB, plus another 750 MB for each processor core in your machine. Get more RAM if you can; I don't know anybody who has reached the point of diminishing returns.

- Xcode is a 64-bit Intel application. The minima for this book are 64-bit, dual-core, and 1.8 GHz. More is better.

- Bigger—particularly, wider—displays are better. I'm writing on a MacBook Air with 1,440 pixels' horizontal resolution. With the display-management techniques I'll show you, it's comfortable most of the time. And with my 15" Retina MacBook Pro set to show the maximum content, I have no complaints.

The bottom-of-the-line Mac mini on sale as I write this ($599 in the U.S., plus display, keyboard, and mouse) is fine for the purposes of *Xcode 5 Start to Finish*, as are most Macs sold since 2010.

Installing Xcode

For most purposes, obtaining Xcode 5 is very easy: Find it in the Mac App Store (MAS), enter your Apple ID and password, and download it. It's free. See "Downloading Xcode," later in this chapter, for another option, and why you might need it.

The download is just over 2 GB. Once the download is complete, Xcode will be in your `/Applications` folder.

> **Note**
>
> Want to see what you got? Right-click the Xcode icon in `/Applications`, and select **Show Package Contents**. You'll see the directories and files behind the pseudo-file representing Xcode. Poke around all you like, but don't make any changes.

There is no step three. There are no installation options—there's no installer. In earlier versions, developer tools were put in a `/Developer` directory at the root of the boot volume (or the one you selected in the installer). No more: All the tools you need for basic iOS and Mac development are contained in Xcode itself.

Most of the documentation *isn't* installed. Xcode will download it the first time you run it. It's not practical to bundle it into the Xcode download: It runs hundreds of megabytes, it changes more frequently than the developer tools, and you may not want it all. The **Downloads** panel of the Preferences window controls the downloads.

One advantage of MAS distribution is that once the App Store application knows it has installed Xcode, it can alert you to updates. When you accept an update, the App Store sends only the components that changed, greatly reducing the download time. One update in the 4.3 series was only 98 MB.

Command-Line Tools

If you're running Xcode 5 on Mountain Lion, Xcode will offer to install command-line tools, the fundamental programs that turn source code into executables. Open-source projects expect those programs to be in standard locations (/usr/bin and related directories), and in a stock installation of Mountain Lion, they aren't there. If you want to do development on the command line, you should accept the offer.

Mavericks is different. Executable files of those names exist in /usr/bin. But they aren't the actual programs that go by those names. They are trampolines; when you run them, they hand off to the real programs elsewhere in the system:

- To the tools embedded in the Xcode application package, if Xcode is present.
- To the tools in /Library/Developer, if present. This is where the contents of the command-line tools package go.
- If none can be found, the trampoline program will offer to download and install the command-line tools package. You can also do this by executing sudo xcode-select --install.

In any case, the executable files in /usr/bin will always be trampolines.

So if you're running Xcode 5 and Mavericks, you don't need a separate package of developer tools. The system will act as though they were there already—and your Xcode and command-line builds will use the same tools, which should make most developers a lot less nervous.

If you're running Mavericks and don't want Xcode 5, don't install Xcode. Run one of the tools, or go to http://developer.apple.com/downloads and grab an installer; be sure to get the version that goes with your version of OS X.

Removing Xcode

Your life has changed. The honeymoon is over. You've had your look, and you're done. You've decided to edit a theatrical feature and you need the space. You're giving your Mac to your daughter in art school. For whatever reason, you're done with Xcode. How do you get rid of it?

This was a complicated process before Xcode 4.2; it involved uninstall scripts and directory deletions. Now, you just drag Xcode into the Trash, and you're done. Almost.

The reason uninstallation was so complicated in earlier Xcodes was that you had to get rid of the tools, libraries, headers, and frameworks that Xcode would infiltrate throughout the system. The scripts ran down the inventory and rooted out each item.

But remember what I said earlier about the command-line tools: The tools and other files are all inside Xcode. Everything else out in the system is a trampoline to those files. Throw away Xcode, and you'll have gotten rid of what previously had been infiltrations...

...unless you installed the stand-alone Command Line Developer Tools package. You can find those in `/Library/Developer/` along with some large documentation libraries. Delete that directory. Do the same with `~/Library/Developer/`.

Apple Developer Programs

Anyone can pick up Xcode 5 for free and start developing OS X and iOS software. If your interest is in distributing Mac software on your own, your preparation is done: Build your apps, burn them to CDs, put them on the Net, and God bless you.

However, if you want to distribute your work on the Mac or iOS App Store; assure users with Gatekeeper that your Mac apps are safe; or even test your iOS app on a device, you have to go further. You'll need to pay for a membership in the Mac or iOS Developer Program. (If you need to, you can join both.)

Apple's policies and methods for joining developer programs are subject to change, so the best I can do for you is to give an overview. Start by browsing to `http://developer.apple.com/`. Prominently featured will be links to join the iOS and Mac developer programs. The programs will give you:

- Access to prerelease software, including operating systems and developer tools.
- Access to the parts of the developer forums (`http://devforums.apple.com/`) that cover nondisclosed topics.
- Two incidents with Developer Technical Support (DTS), Apple engineers who can advise you on development strategies and help you with troubleshooting. This is the only official, guaranteed way to get help from Apple. If you have the time, by all means go to a developer forum or mailing list first (you'll find lots of leads in Appendix B, "Resources"), but if that fails, DTS is the best choice.
- The right to submit your applications for sale in the Mac or iOS App Store.
- In the case of iOS, the right to load your app into a device for debugging purposes (see Chapter 17, "Provisioning," for details).
- In the case of OS X, a Developer ID certificate that enables users who use Gatekeeper to install your app.

Make your choice (whichever you choose, you'll be offered both programs), and you will be taken to a page with an **Enroll Now** button, citing the cost of a year's membership ($99 in the United States as I write this).

The next step is to establish your status as a "registered Apple developer." Registered developers have few privileges beyond having a persistent record with Apple that can be used to sign up for developer programs. (There are a limited number of resources to which your assent to terms and conditions entitles you, such as access to the released-product sections of the developer forums.) If you're already registered, say so, and skip to the signup process. If you're not, present your Apple ID (such as you might be using with iTunes) or get one, fill out marketing and demographic questionnaires, and assent to the terms and conditions of Apple programs. They'll send you an email you can use to verify your contact information.

Once that's done, you're given your choice of programs. Select all you are interested in and can afford; the iOS and Mac programs are separate charges, and there's no discount. There's also a free Safari program, which allows you to develop and sign extensions for the desktop Safari web browser.

Next you'll have program-specific licenses to agree to. When that's done, you're a member.

Downloading Xcode

The App Store download is convenient, but it's not for everybody. New versions of Xcode—even point releases—may drop features on which you may have relied. Xcode supports keeping more than one copy of the application on your computer, but the App Store *doesn't*. When you accept an update from the App Store, it seeks out older versions, wherever they may be, and deletes them. You'll have to take control of the process yourself.

> **Note**
>
> See Chapter 26, "The Xcode Build System," for the `xcode-select` and `xcrun` command-line tools that support using multiple versions of Xcode.

If you're a developer program member (even a member of the free program), you have access to `http://developer.apple.com/downloads`. Use the checkboxes to narrow the listing to developer tools. You will find every Xcode toolset going back to 1.0 (a 584-MB CD image for OS X 10.3). The currently released version of Xcode will be near the top. Download it.

If you want a prerelease version, you'll have to go to either the iOS or OS X developer center, log in with your paid developer-program credentials, select the prerelease section, and receive a Mac App Store redemption code. This will get you the first prerelease version of Xcode, which the Mac App Store application will update.

You'll end up with a compressed disk-image (`.dmg`) file. Double-click it to reveal the Xcode application. Drag it into `/Applications`, or wherever you like. If you want to preserve an earlier version, rename that copy first.

Updates carry two penalties compared to the MAS method: You'll have to keep track of their availability yourself, and you'll have to download the whole toolset again. No incremental updates for you.

> **Warning**
>
> Apple's official position is that Xcode 5 is the only version it will support on Mavericks. Historically, Apple has been very conservative with the word "support" as it applies to previous versions of developer tools on newer operating systems. My interpretation is that Developer Tools had enough on its hands building a major version of Xcode without exhaustively testing and revising the version they were making obsolete. Maybe it works, maybe it doesn't, but Apple isn't going to stand behind it.

Additional Downloads

Download files for earlier versions of Xcode topped out at 3 GB. The Xcode 4.3 image was just over half that size, 1.8 GB.

One way Apple keeps download sizes down is to provide only stubs for OS X and iOS documentation. The first time you run Xcode, it triggers a download of the full documentation sets. This annoys people who want 100% functionality after installing Xcode aboard airplanes, but there's really no alternative: Not everybody needs every documentation set. Further, Apple updates its documentation much more often than it updates Xcode, so even if the download included full documentation, you'd have to pull in the current docs anyway.

Another trick for reducing download size is to recognize that not everybody needs every development tool. Apple has broken seven toolsets out into downloadable archives. Not only does this keep these files out of the main download, it allows Apple to free them from the release cycle of Xcode itself.

Here are the available packages as I write this:

- Accessibility—Tools for auditing and testing accessibility support of your Mac applications.

- Audio—Applications for examining Core Audio units, plus headers and sample code.

- Auxiliary—PackageMaker (construct Installer packages for OS X), Help Indexer (create Mac application help books), and tools for auditing your source for legacy code.

- Command-line tools—Commands you can use from the Terminal application for classic-style development; this how you'd get the tools without needing Xcode even to install them.

- Dashcode—Apple's visual editor for HTML5/CSS/JavaScript to be used as OS X Dashboard widgets, and for iOS-like web applications.

- Hardware IO—Probes for USB and Bluetooth, as well as the Network Link Conditioner, which allows you to degrade network performance and reliability to simulate mobile connectivity in the iOS Simulator.

- Graphics—OpenGL development tools, and the Quartz Composer builder for chains of image and video filters.

If you want one of the supplemental toolsets, open Xcode and select **Xcode** → **Open Developer Tool** → **More Developer Tools. . . .** Your default browser will be directed to the developer downloads site, with the search string set to `for Xcode`, which will show you what's available.

When you find what you need, click the disclosure triangle to show a description of the package and a link to download it. You'll be asked to read and accept the general license for Apple's developer tools. Agree, and the download will start.

What you'll get is a `.dmg` disk image containing applications and installers. Drag the apps into `/Applications`, or wherever else you find convenient—they will not appear under the **Xcode** menu.

In addition to the specialized toolsets, there are other components like device-debugging software and simulators for back versions of iOS. Use the the Preferences window, **Downloads** panel, **Components** section to download and install them if you need them.

Summary

Apple has tried to strike a balance between making Xcode easily available to everybody, and providing choices about what and how much to install. The free installation from the Mac App Store will get you everything you need to get started with iOS and OS X development. If your needs are more specialized—if you need older versions, or customized toolsets—the developer downloads site has it all.

2

Kicking the Tires

Now you have Xcode. It's time to start it up and see what it looks like.

Starting Xcode

You'll find Xcode in the /Applications directory, just like any application. You'll be using it constantly, so you'll want to keep it in the Dock at the bottom of your main screen. Drag Xcode to the Dock—take care to drop it *between* icons, and not *on* one.

Now click on the Xcode icon. It bounces to show Xcode is being launched. The first time you run any of Apple's developer tools—even through the command line—you'll be asked to read and accept a license agreement for the tools and SDKs. It's no different from any other click-through license process.

Next, Xcode will ask you for permission to install "additional components" it needs. Permit it, and present an administrator's credentials. Those components overlap the iTunes frameworks, so you may be asked to close iTunes.

Once the progress window clears, you are greeted with the "Welcome to Xcode" window (see Figure 2.1).

If this is the first time you've ever run Xcode, the table on the right will be empty ("No Recent Projects"); as you accumulate projects, the table will contain references to them, so you have a quick way to get back to your work. When you accumulate projects in this list, you'll be able to select one, but Xcode doesn't reveal any way to open it. The trick is to double-click the item, or press the Return key.

You have three other options:

- **Create a new Xcode project.** This is obvious enough; it's how you'd start work on a new product. You're about to do this, but hold off for the moment. You could also select **File →New →New Project. . .** (⇧⌘N).

- **Check out an existing project.** Xcode recognizes that source control management is essential to even the most trivial of projects. Your development effort might start not with your own work, but with collaborative work pulled in from a source repository. Use this link to get started.

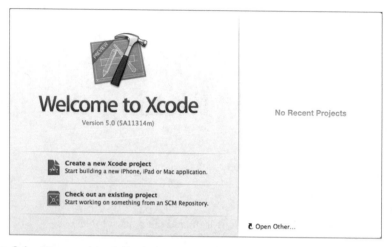

Figure 2.1   When you launch Xcode, it displays a "Welcome" window with options for creating a new project, reopening a recent one, or fetching a project from a source-control repository.

- **Open Other. . .** (at the bottom of the "recents" list). This will get you the standard get-file dialog so you can select any Xcode project file you want. You can do the same thing with the **File → Open. . .** (⌘ O) command.

If you need to get back to the Welcome window, select **Window → Welcome to Xcode** (⇧ ⌘ 1). If you're tired of seeing this window, uncheck **Show this window when Xcode launches**.

> **Note**
>
> "Show this window when Xcode launches" is not quite accurate. If you had a project open when you last quit Xcode, it will reopen automatically when you start it up again, and the Welcome window won't appear.

Hello World

Just to get oriented, I'm going to start with the simplest imaginable example project—so simple, you won't have to do much coding at all.

A New Project

Click the **Create a new Xcode project** link. Xcode opens an empty Workspace window, and drops the New Project assistant sheet in front of it (see Figure 2.2). Select **OS X → Application** from the list at left, and then the **Command Line Tool** template from the icons that appear at right. Click **Next**.

The next panel (Figure 2.3) asks for the name of the project and the kind of command-line tool you want.

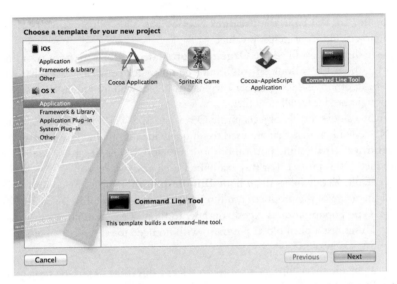

Figure 2.2   The New Project assistant leads you through the creation of an Xcode project. First, you specify the kind of product you want to produce.

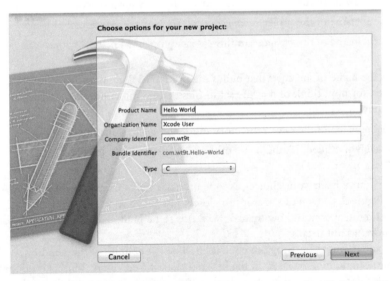

Figure 2.3   The **Options** panel of the New Project assistant lets you identify the product and what support it needs from system libraries.

1. Type **Hello World** in the **Product Name** field. This will be used as the name of the project and its principal product.
2. Xcode should have filled the **Organization Name** in for you, from your "me" card in the Address Book. If you listed a company for yourself, that's what will be in the field; otherwise, it's your personal name. Xcode will use this as the name of the copyright holder for all new files.
3. Virtually all executable objects in the OS X and iOS world have unique reverse-DNS-style identifiers that are used to uniquely identify them. The **Company Identifier** is the leading portion of those reverse-DNS names, to be used by every product of this project. For this example, I used com.wt9t.
4. By default, Xcode infers the unique **Bundle Identifier** from the company identifier and the name of the product. You'll see later how to change this if you have to.
5. The **Type** popup prompts Xcode on how to fill in the system libraries the tool will use. This is just a plain old C program, with no need for C++ or Apple-specific support, so choose **C**.

Finally, a put-file sheet appears, so you can select a directory to put the project into. For this example, select your Desktop. One more thing—*uncheck* the box labeled **Create local git repository for this project**. Source control (Chapter 7, "Version Control") is a Good Thing, but let's not deal with it in this trivial example. Click **Create**.

If you look on your Desktop, you'll find that Xcode has created a folder named Hello World. The project name you specified is used in several places.

- It's the name of the project *directory* that contains your project files.
- It's the name of the project *document* (Hello World.xcodeproj) itself.
- It's the name of the *product*—in this case a command-line tool named Hello World.
- It's the name of the *target* that builds the product. I'll get into the concept of a target later; for now, think of it as the set of files that go into a product, and a specification of how it is built.
- It's the name of the *target's* directory inside the *project's* directory.
- Suitably modified, it's the name of the man-file template for the tool (Hello_World.1).

When you've made your choices, Xcode unmasks the workspace for the Hello World project (Figure 2.4). Don't look at it too closely just yet. Xcode starts you off with a view of the settings that control how Hello World is to be built. This is useful information, but for now, it's just details.

More interesting is the program code itself. The left column of the window is called the *Navigator area*. Find main.c in the list, and click it (see Figure 2.5). The Editor area, which fills most of the window, now displays the contents of main.c. This is the code for the canonical simplest-possible program, known as "Hello, World."

The Navigator area displays many different things in the course of development—it's not just a file listing. It can display analyses, searches, and build logs. Which list you see often depends on what Xcode wants to show you; you can make the choice yourself by

Figure 2.4   Once set up, the Hello World project window fills in with a list of source files and a display of the options that control how the application will be built.

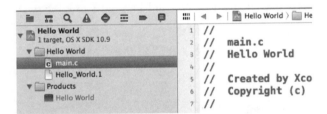

Figure 2.5   Clicking the name of an editable file in the Project navigator displays its contents in the Editor area.

clicking the tiny icons in the bar at the top of the Navigator area. Hovering the mouse pointer over them will show you the names of the various views.

As this book goes on, you'll meet all of them. For now, you care only about the "Project" navigator, the file list Xcode starts you out with. Feel free to click the other icons, but to keep up with this example, be sure to return to the Project navigator, as shown in Figure 2.5.

Quieting Xcode Down

But first.

Xcode is a toolset that contains everything its creators could think of to provide a powerful, helpful environment for writing iOS and OS X applications. Often, you barely need to begin a task, and Xcode will offer to finish it for you. It will usually be right. I use these features all the time. I recommend them.

You're going to turn them all off.

Automatic completions and indentations and code decorations and code fixes are great, once you know what's going on, but an automaton that snatches your work out of your hands, however helpfully, is straight out of *The Sorcerer's Apprentice*. Better to start with what *you* want to do; once you're confident of what that is, then you have the discretion and control to direct Xcode as it helps you.

So you're going to damp Xcode down a bit. You'll do all of this in Xcode's Preferences window, which you can summon with **Xcode → Preferences...** (⌘ **comma**). The Preferences window is divided into panels, which you select with the icons at the top of the window.

To start, make sure the **General** panel is visible. Under **Issues**, uncheck **Show live issues**.

Next, select the **Text Editing** panel, which has two tabs. Select the **Editing** tab, and uncheck **Show: Code folding ribbon**, and all the options under **Code completion:**.

In the **Indentation** tab, turn off **Line wrapping: Wrap lines to editor width** and the **Syntax-aware indenting** section.

Now Xcode will mostly stay out of your way as you explore.

Building and Running

The program in `main.c` would run as is, but we have to trick Xcode into keeping its output on the screen long enough to see it. Add a few lines after the `printf` call so it looks like this:

```
int main(int argc, const char * argv[])
{

    // insert code here...
    printf("Hello, World!\n");

    /*********************************************
     *   Pause, so the console doesn't disappear
     *********************************************/
    char    dummy[128];
    fgets(dummy, sizeof(dummy), stdin);

    return 0;
}
```

Now we can run it. Select **Product → Run** (⌘ **R**).

In the ordinary course, Xcode would then build and run `Hello World`. However, if this is the first time you've run any application, there is a security problem: Running an app from Xcode puts it under the observation of a debugger, which will have access to the internal data and running state of the app. Crossing process boundaries like that is technically a security breach, and you have to authorize it.

Xcode posts an alert, **Enable Developer Mode on this Mac?**. It explains that you could be asked for an administrator's password every time you run the debugger (**"Developer Tools Access needs to take control of another process. . . "**), or, with Developer Mode, you could do the authorization once and forget about it. Click **Enable**, enter an administrator's credentials, and carry on.

> **Note**
> You can turn Developer Mode off, or on again, from the Devices organizer (⇧⌘ **2**). Select your Mac and click the button **Disable Developer Mode**.

With authorization taken care of, a heads–up window ("bezel") appears almost instantly, to tell you "Build Succeeded." (If Xcode is in the background, a notification banner will appear saying the build succeeded, and identifying the project and product involved.)

So. What happened?

Hello World is a console application; it just writes out some text without putting up any windows. Xcode captures the console of the apps it runs in the Debug area, which popped into view when you ran the program (Figure 2.6). The Debug area includes a console view on the right. It says Hello, World! (Figure 2.7).

Click in the console to make it ready for text input, and press the Return key. Hello World exits, and the Debug area closes.

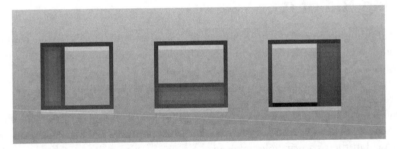

Figure 2.6   The **View** selector in the toolbar shows and hides the Navigator, Debug, and Utility areas (left to right) of the project window. Clicking a button so it is highlighted exposes the corresponding area. Here, the Navigator and Debug areas are selected.

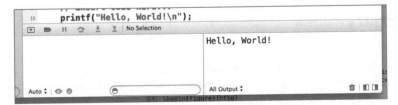

Figure 2.7   Opening the Debug area after running Hello World shows the eponymous output.

> **Note**
>
> If the Debug area didn't hide itself as soon as an application terminated, we wouldn't have had to add that `fgets()` call. That's easy to change; see the "Behaviors" section of Chapter 4, "Active Debugging."

The Real Thing

What Xcode just produced for you is a real, executable application, not a simulation. To prove it, open the Terminal application (you'll find it at `/Applications/Utilities/Terminal`, and you'd be well advised to add Terminal to your Dock). In Xcode, find the `Hello World` product in the Project navigator by clicking the disclosure triangle next to the Products folder icon. Drag the `Hello World` icon into the Terminal window, switch to Terminal, and press the Return key. (The path to a file deep in a directory for build products is remarkably long, but Terminal takes care of the necessary escaping.) "Hello, World!" appears.

If you want access to the executable file itself, select it in the Project navigator, then **File → Show in Finder**—also available in the contextual menu you get by right-clicking the `Hello World` icon. A window will open in the Finder showing you the file.

You're done! You can close the Workspace window (**File → Close Project**, ⌥⌘W) or quit Xcode entirely (**Xcode → Quit Xcode**, ⌘Q).

Getting Rid of It

There is nothing magical about an Xcode project. It's just a directory on your hard drive. If you don't want it any more, close the project, select its enclosing folder in the Finder, and drag it to the Trash. It's gone. It won't even show up in the Recents list in the Welcome to Xcode window, or in the **File → Open Recent** menu.

That's it.

Okay, yes, the build products of the project will still stick around in a warren of directories inside `~/Library/Developer/Xcode/DerivedData`. They aren't many or large in this case, but there's a principle involved.

If you want them gone, the best way is to close the project window, open the Organizer window (**Window → Organizer**, ⇧⌘2), select the **Projects** panel, select the "Hello World" project, press Delete, and confirm the deletion in the ensuing alert sheet. All trace of the build products is gone.

Summary

In this chapter, you had your first look at Xcode, and you discovered that it doesn't bite. You saw how to create a simple project, one you didn't even have to edit. You saw what happens when you run a project in Xcode, how to close a project and quit Xcode, and at last how to get rid of the project entirely.

Next, we'll start doing some real work.

3

Simple Workflow and Passive Debugging

This chapter begins your use of Xcode in earnest. Here's where I introduce the problem that is the basis for all of the example code in this book.

The problem is the calculation of *passer ratings*. In American/Canadian football, quarterbacks advance the ball by throwing (passing) it to other players. The ball may be caught (received, a good thing) by someone on the quarterback's own team, in which case the ball is advanced (yardage, more is better), possibly to beyond the goal line (a touchdown, the object of the game); or it may be caught by a member of the opposing team (intercepted, a very bad thing).

But those are four numbers, and everybody wants a figure-of-merit, a single scale that says (accurately or not) who is the better passer. The National Football League and the Canadian Football League have a formula for passer ratings, yielding a scale running from 0 to (oddly) 158.3. A quarterback who rates 100 has had a pretty good day.

Creating the Project

As in Chapter 2, "Kicking the Tires," you'll start with a command-line project. Start Xcode and click **Create a new Xcode project**, or select **File → New → New Project. . .** (⇧⌘N). In the New Project assistant sheet, select an OS X Command Line Tool, and name the tool `passer-rating`; for **Type**, once again choose **C**.

Another difference: When you are shown the get-file sheet to select the location for the new project, check the box labeled **Create git repository on**, and select **My Mac**. Git is a *version-control system*, an essential part of modern development. You'll learn all about it in Chapter 7, "Version Control," but now is the time to start.

> **Note**
>
> Are you ever going to change anything in a project? Get it under version control. Seriously. Your work will be safer, and you'll do it faster.

Again, you'll be shown target settings, which you can ignore for now. Instead, mouse over to the Project navigator at the left side of the Workspace window, and select `main.c`.

Delete everything in the `main()` function but its outer braces, and replace the body of the function so the file reads thus (keep the comments at the top of the file):

```
#include <stdio.h>
#include "rating.h"      // Yet to create; initially an error

int main(int argc, const char * argv[])
{
    int         nArgs;
    do {
        int         comps, atts, yards, TDs;
        printf("comps, atts, yards, TDs: ");
        nArgs = scanf("%d %d %d %d %d",
                    &comps, &atts, &yards, &TDs);
        if (nArgs == 5) {
          float  rating = passer_rating(comps, atts, yards, TDs);
            printf("Rating = %.1f\n", rating);
        }
    } while (nArgs == 5);

    return 0;
}
```

You'll notice that as you type closing parentheses, brackets, and braces, the corresponding opening character is briefly highlighted in yellow.

The rating calculation itself is simple. Put it into a file of its own: Select **File → New...** (⌘ N). You'll be presented with the New File assistant sheet; see Figure 3.1. Navigate the source list on the left, and the icon array on the right thus: OS X → C and C++ → C File.

Click **Next**, and use the save-file sheet that appears to name the file **rating** (Xcode will append `.c` automatically).

The save-file sheet has two custom controls. The **Group** popup lets you place the new file in the Project navigator (the source list at the left of the project window). Roughly, groups are simply ways to organize the Project inspector list; they have no influence on how the new file will be placed on-disk. Make sure the passer-rating group is selected.

Second is **Targets**, a table that for now has only one row, **passer-rating**. A target is a group of files and settings that combine to build a product. A file that isn't part of a target isn't used to build anything. Make sure that **passer-rating** is checked.

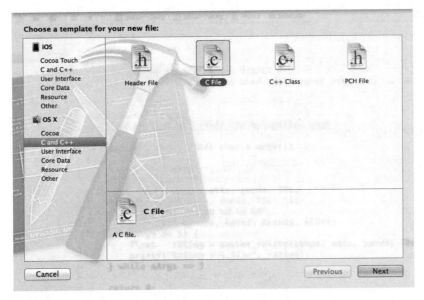

Choose a template for your new file:

Figure 3.1   The New File assistant sheet offers many templates you can use to start a new file. Select the category from the source list on the left, and pick the template from the array of icons on the right.

Note

It's easy to miss the target assignment. Xcode 5 sets no targets for files as they enter projects. If you don't remember to select the targets, you won't know about it until your app fails to build or mysteriously crashes because a needed resource wasn't included.

Here's what goes into `rating.c`:

```
#include "rating.h"

static
double pinPassingComponent(double component)
{
    if (component < 0.0)
        return 0.0;
    else if (component > 2.375)
        return 2.375;
    else
        return component;
}
```

```
float
passer_rating(int comps, int atts, int yds, int tds, int ints)
{
    //  See http://en.wikipedia.org/wiki/Quarterback_Rating

    double     completionComponent =
                    (((double) comps / atts) * 100.0 - 30.0) / 20.0;
    completionComponent = pinPassingComponent(completionComponent);

    double     yardageComponent =
                    (((double) yds / atts) - 0.3) / 4.0;
                    //  intentional bug
    yardageComponent = pinPassingComponent(yardageComponent);

    double     touchdownComponent =
                    20.0 * (double) tds / atts;
    touchdownComponent = pinPassingComponent(touchdownComponent);

    double     pickComponent =
                    2.375 - (25.0 * (double) ints / atts);
    pickComponent = pinPassingComponent(pickComponent);

    double retval =  100.0 * (completionComponent +
                             yardageComponent +
                             touchdownComponent +
                             pickComponent) / 6.0;
    return retval;
}
```

> **Note**
>
> You see a few bugs in this code. Well done. Throughout this book, I'm going to give you some buggy code to illustrate debugging techniques. Just play along, okay?

By now, you've missed a couple of braces, and you are tired of tabbing to get the extra level of indenting. Xcode can do this for you—it's among the features I had you turn off in the last chapter.

Open the Preferences window (**Xcode → Preferences, ⌘ comma**) and select the **Text Editing** panel. In the **Editing** tab, check **Code completion: Automatically insert closing "}"**. In the **Indentation** tab, check **Syntax-aware indenting: Automatically indent based on syntax**.

Now type an open brace in your code, at the end of a line. So what, it's a brace. Now press Return. Xcode adds two lines: Your cursor is now at the next line, indented one level, and a matching closing brace appears on the line after that.

Finally, you've noticed that both `main.c` and `rating.c` refer to a `rating.h`, which notifies `main()` of the existence of the `passer_rating` function. Press ⌘ N again, and choose Header File from the available C and C++ files. Name it **rating**, and put this into it:

```
#ifndef passer_rating_rating_h
#define passer_rating_rating_h

float passer_rating(int comps, int atts, int yds,
                    int tds, int ints);
#endif
```

> **Note**
>
> Place header files wherever you like among the project groups, but don't add them to any targets. There are exceptions; if you need to do it, you'll know. Chapter 6, "Adding a Library Target," has more.

Click **Create**.

Building

That's enough to start. Let's try to run it. It's easy: Click the **Run** button at the left end of the toolbar, or select **Product → Run** (⌘ R). It doesn't matter if you haven't saved your work; by default Xcode saves everything before it attempts a build. Xcode chugs away at your code for a bit... and stops.

- A heads-up placard flashes, saying "Build Failed."
- The Navigator area switches to the Issue navigator (fourth tab), which shows two items under `main.c`. One is tagged with a yellow triangle (a warning), and the other with a red octagon (an error). These include descriptions of the errors (Figure 3.2, top).
- The editor highlights two lines in `main.c` (click a line in the Issue navigator if `main.c` isn't visible). The line that triggered the warning is tagged in yellow, with a banner describing the warning; the error line in red, with a banner of its own (Figure 3.2, bottom).

It seems the only place where I remembered about interceptions was the format string of the `scanf` call. The compiler was smart enough to match the number of format specifiers to the number of arguments of the `scanf` and complain. Similarly, I left off the last parameter to `passer_rating`, which is an outright error.

> **Note**
>
> For a compiler, an *error* is a flaw in your source that makes it impossible to translate your code into executable form. The presence of even one error prevents Xcode from producing a program. A *warning* indicates something in your source that *can* be translated but will

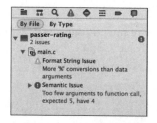

Figure 3.2   (top) When Xcode detects build errors, it opens the Issue navigator to display them. (bottom) Clicking an issue focuses the editor on the file and line at which the issue was detected.

probably result in a bug or a crash when you run it. Experienced developers do not tolerate warnings; there is even a compiler option to make a build fail upon a warning just as though it were an error. Don't ever ignore a warning.

Note

Need a reminder of what `passer_rating` does with its parameters? Try this: While `main` is visible in the Editor area, hold down the Command key and point the mouse at the symbol `passer_rating`. You'll see it turns blue and acquires an underline, as if it were a link on a standard web page. Click it: The editor jumps to the declaration of `passer_rating`. You can jump back by clicking the back-arrow button in the upper-left corner of the editor; by pressing ⌃ ⌘ ←; or by swiping right across the editor area with two fingers, if you've enabled the gesture in System Preferences. (Option-clicking the name gets you a popover that tells you `passer_rating` was declared in `rating.h`. More on this in Chapter 25, "Documentation in Xcode.")

You can dash off a fix very quickly:

```
do {
    int          comps, atts, yards, TDs, INTs;
    printf("comps, atts, yards, TDs, INTs: ");
    nArgs = scanf("%d %d %d %d %d",
                    &comps, &atts, &yards, &TDs, INTs);
    if (nArgs == 5) {
        float    rating = passer_rating(comps, atts, yards,
                                            TDs, INTs);
        printf("Rating = %.1f\n", rating);
    }
} while (nArgs == 5);
```

To be conservative (I don't want Xcode to run the program if a warning remains), **Product → Build** (⌘ B) will compile and link `passer-rating` without running it. You needn't have worried: It compiles without error, displaying a "Build Succeeded" placard.

Note
The Issues navigator will show two warnings. Let's play dumb and carry on.

Running

Now you have something runnable. Run it (**Run** button, first in the toolbar; or ⌘ R).

There is a transformation: The Debug area appears at the bottom of the window; and the **View** control in the toolbar highlights its middle button to match the appearance of the Debug area (Figure 3.3).

The right half of the Debug area is a console that you'll be using to communicate with the `passer-rating` tool. If all has gone well, it should be showing something like this:

`comps, atts, yards, TDs, INTs:`

...which is just what the `printf()` was supposed to do. `passer-rating` is waiting for input, so click in the console pane and type:

`10 20 85 1 0 <return>`

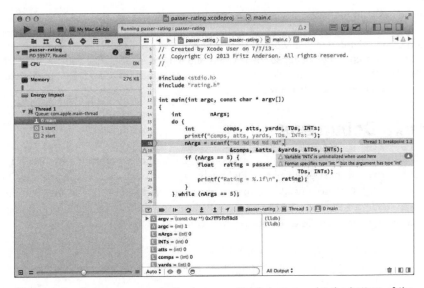

Figure 3.3   Running an app in Xcode opens the Debug area (at the bottom of the project window).

Something went wrong. `passer-rating` crashed. `lldb`, the debugging engine, takes control, and the debugging displays fill up.

- In the Navigator area, the Debug navigator appears, showing the status of the program when it crashed. The upper part of the navigator contains performance bar charts that will be useful when you get to more complex projects. Ignore them for the moment.

  What's left is a *stack trace*, showing the chain of function calls that led to the crash. The top line, labeled 0, is the name of the function, `__svfscanf_l`, where the crash occurred; if you click it, you can see the assembly code (the source isn't available) focused on the very instruction that went wrong. The next line is `scanf`, which you recognize as the function you called from `main`, the function on the next line.

  Xcode identifies `main` as your work by flagging it with a blue head-and-shoulders icon. Click that line to see what your code was doing when the crash occurred.

- In the Debug area at the bottom of the window, the left-hand pane fills with the names of variables and their values. You see, for instance, "**atts** = (int) 20," which is just what you entered. Chapter 4, "Active Debugging," discusses this more.

- The Editor area has the most interesting change: A green flag at the left margin and a green banner at the right of the call to `scanf`. The banner says, "Thread 1: EXC_BAD_ACCESS (code=1, address=0x0)." The message may be truncated; you can see the full text in a tooltip that appears if you hover the mouse cursor over the banner.

Note

Xcode has a lot of these banners; often they are the only way it will convey important messages. You will probably set your editor fonts to the smallest you can comfortably read so you can see more of your work at once. The banners are one line high, and their margins take up some space, so the text in them may be *smaller* than you can comfortably read. The only solution is to select larger fonts for everyday use; see the **Fonts & Colors** panel of the Preferences window.

Simple Debugging

EXC_BAD_ACCESS entails the use of a bad pointer, perhaps one pointing into memory that isn't legal for you to read or write to. (The 64-bit virtual-memory management on OS X and modern iOS is set so any address that might be derived from a 32-bit integer is illegal, making it harder to cross `int`s and pointers.) Reexamine the line in `main` that crashed the application and allow a scale to fall from your eyes:

```
nArgs = scanf("%d %d %d %d %d",
              &comps, &atts, &yards, &TDs, INTs);
```

`scanf` collects values through pointers to the variables that will hold them. This call does that for all values except `INTs`, which is passed by value, not by reference. One of the warnings I had you ignore said exactly that: "Format specifies type '(int *)' but the argument has type 'int'." Simply inserting an &

```
nArgs = scanf("%d %d %d %d %d",
              &comps, &atts, &yards, &TDs, &INTs);
```

should cure the problem. Sure enough, running `passer-rating` again shows the crasher is gone:

```
comps, atts, yards, TDs, INTs: 10 20 85 1 0
Rating = 89.4
comps, atts, yards, TDs, INTs: <^D>
```

With the **^D** keystroke, the input stream to `passer-rating` ends, the program exits, and the Debug area closes.

You ordinarily wouldn't want to run or debug a program under Xcode if another is running. Instead, you'd like the incumbent app to clear out. There are four ways to do this.

- Simply let the app exit on its own, as you did when you used **^D** to stop `passer-rating`, or would by selecting the **Quit** command in an OS X application. But this doesn't work for iOS apps, which in principle never quit. You'll have to use one of the other techniques.
- Click the **Stop** button in the toolbar.
- Select **Product → Stop** (⌘ **period**).
- Tell Xcode to run an application, the same or a different one, and click **Stop** in the alert sheet that appears. See Figure 3.4.

That alert sheet also offers an **Add** button, which will run and debug the new process without quitting the old one. Xcode will start a new execution context: You can switch

Figure 3.4   When you tell Xcode to run an application while it already has an application running, it displays a sheet asking what you want to do with the existing app. Normally, you'd click **Stop**, but there is also the option to **Add** the new instance to run concurrently with the old one.

between them using the jump bar at the top of the Debug area, and the **Stop** button in the toolbar becomes a menu you can use to select which instance to stop.

> **Note**
>
> Don't check the **Do not show this message again** box. There will come a time when you want to continue the execution of a program you are debugging, and rather than clicking the tiny button the debugger provides, you'll go for the large, friendly **Run** button in the toolbar. That time comes to me frequently. The add-or-stop sheet is the only thing standing between you and the ruin of your debugging session.

For the moment, you're done: The `scanf` call will return fewer than five inputs if the standard input stream ends. You end it as you would in a terminal shell, by pressing **^D**.

> **Note**
>
> **M** and **A** badges are accumulating in the Project navigator. These have to do with version control. Nothing is wrong. Patience! I'll get to it in Chapter 7, "Version Control."

Summary

This chapter stepped you up to writing and running a program of your own. It introduced the first level of debugging: what to do when your program crashes. It turns out that Xcode offers good facilities to help you analyze a crash without you having to do much. You accepted Xcode's guidance, quickly traced the problem, and verified that your fix worked.

But we're not done with `passer-rating`. There are still bugs in it, and this time you'll have to hunt for them.

## 4

Active Debugging

In passer-rating, you have a program that runs without crashing. This is an achievement, but a small one. Let's explore it a little more and see if we can't turn it into a program that works. This entails a small test, and maybe some probing of the inner workings.

A Simple Test Case

Run passer-rating again. Give it the old data set if you like, for a short, mediocre game; but also try a rating for a quarterback who didn't play at all:

```
comps, atts, yards, TDs, INTs: 10 20 85 1 0
Rating = 89.4
comps, atts, yards, TDs, INTs: 0 0 0 0 0
Rating = nan
comps, atts, yards, TDs, INTs:
```

H'm. Not what you expected. It doesn't crash, but it's wrong. A performance in which a passer never passed should be rated zero. passer-rating gave a rating of "nan," which is a code for "not a number." That indicates a logical error in how the math was done.

Now is the time to use the Xcode debugger to examine what is actually happening in passer-rating. Don't stop passer-rating—the debugger lets you instrument your application without changing it.

Going Active

In your previous encounter with the debugger, it took control over passer-rating when a fatal error occurred. This time, you want the debugger to take control at a time of your choosing. By setting a *breakpoint* at a particular line in passer-rating, you tell the debugger to halt execution of the application at that line, so that the contents of variables can be examined and execution resumed under your control.

Setting a Breakpoint

The easiest way to set a breakpoint is to click in the broad gutter area at the left margin of the source code in one of Xcode's editors. Select **rating.c** in the Project navigator to bring that file into the editor. Scroll to the first line of the passer_rating function if it isn't visible, and click in the gutter next to the line that initializes completionComponent (see Figure 4.1, top). On the screen, a dark-blue arrowhead appears in the gutter to show that a breakpoint is set there. You can remove the breakpoint by dragging the arrowhead to the side, out of the gutter; you can move the breakpoint by dragging it up or down the gutter.

You can also set a breakpoint at whatever line the editor's insertion point or selection is on by selecting **Debug →Breakpoints →Add Breakpoint at Current Line** (⌘ \).

> **Note**
>
> If you're keyboard oriented, you can select among the navigators by pressing ⌘ *n*, where *n* is the number of a tab in the Navigator area. Of course, you'll still need the mouse to use the navigator.

There are three ways to avoid a breakpoint. The first is simply to drag it out of the gutter, but if you'll want to restore it, you won't have a marker for the line you were interested in. If you just want to turn off a breakpoint, click on the dark-blue arrow; it will turn pale, and the debugger will ignore it (see Figure 4.1, bottom).

Finally, there is a button in the Debug area's control bar (use the middle segment of the **View** selector at the right end of the toolbar to expose the Debug area) shaped like a breakpoint flag. It's a toggle: When it's blue, the debugger will honor all active breakpoints. When it's gray, the debugger will ignore all breakpoints. Even if the master breakpoint control is off, the debugger will take control if the program crashes.

> **Note**
>
> The Breakpoint navigator (the seventh tab in the Navigator area) lists all of the breakpoints in your project. You can disable or delete breakpoints, or navigate to the corresponding code.

```
25    // See http://en.wikipedia.org/wiki/Quarterback_Rating
26
27    double      completionComponent =
28                    (((double) comps / atts) * 100.0 - 30.0) / 20.0;
29    completionComponent = pinPassingComponent(completionComponent);
30
```

```
25    // See http://en.wikipedia.org/wiki/Quarterback_Rating
26
27    double      completionComponent =
28                    (((double) comps / atts) * 100.0 - 30.0) / 20.0;
29    completionComponent = pinPassingComponent(completionComponent);
30
```

Figure 4.1   (top) Clicking in the gutter at the left edge of the editor sets a breakpoint at that line of code. When the application reaches that line, execution will pause, and the debugger will display the state of the program. (bottom) Clicking an active breakpoint will preserve its place in your code, but the debugger will ignore it. The breakpoint arrow dims to show it is inactive.

You don't have to stop and relaunch a program to start debugging it actively: Setting a breakpoint doesn't change your code, and it doesn't change the executable that was compiled from it. Now that the breakpoint is set, return to the debugger console, where passer-rating still awaits your input, and enter that line of five zeroes again.

Xcode hits the breakpoint, and responds much as it did for that EXC_BAD_ACCESS error: The Debug navigator shows a stack trace from main to passer_rating, the variables pane in the left half of the Debug area displays the variables in their current state, and a green banner appears in the editor with the label "Thread 1: breakpoint 1.1." At the left margin, just outside the gutter, is a green arrowhead; as you go along, the arrowhead marks the line currently being executed.

> **Note**
>
> The Debug area consists of two panes: variables on the left, and console on the right. A control to show either or both is at the bottom-right corner of the Debug area.

The Variables Pane

Turn your attention to the variables pane. There will be five lines flagged with a purple **A** to designate function arguments and one flagged with a blue-green **L** for the local variable completionComponent. The arguments are all shown as "(int) 0," as you'd expect from the numbers you supplied. The local variable, completionComponent, is also a zero, but typed double.

But wait a minute, there's more than one local variable. Where are the rest? The debugger tries to narrow the list of variables to the ones that are interesting at the moment. yardageComponent is uninteresting because it hasn't been set yet. You don't need to see the garbage value. If you do want to see everything, use the popup menu at the bottom left of the variables pane and select **Local variables** (Figure 4.2, top).

Expose all of the local variables so we can set the values to something that will make it easier to see when they change: Click the line for each one and press Return (double-clicking works as well). Type -1 and press Return again (Figure 4.2, bottom).

> **Note**
>
> There's another way to examine the values of variables as they are displayed in the editor view. Hover your mouse pointer over a reference to the variable, and Xcode will show a popover view containing at least the value, and in the case of complex types like structs and objects, some accounting of the contents. In the case of graphical values, the QuickLook (eye) button will even show you the graphic. It's very powerful and will probably be your first resort as you debug. I'm using the variables pane because it shows all variables continuously and allows you to change them.

Stepping Through

You're ready to watch passer-rating execute. Just above the variables pane is a bar containing a series of controls (Figure 4.3). All controls have menu equivalents, most of them in the **Debug** menu.

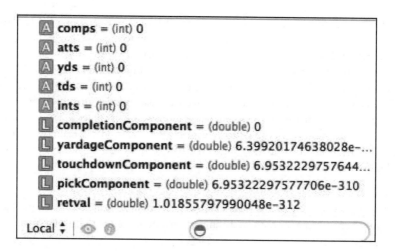

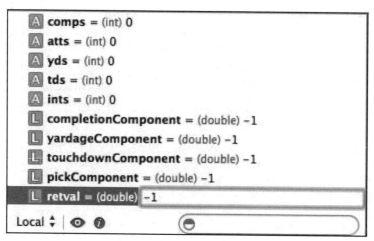

Figure 4.2   (top) When you set the scoping popup at the bottom left of the variables pane to **Local**, you can see all of the arguments and local variables in the current function. (bottom) Double-clicking the value portion of a variable's line allows you to change values on the fly.

Figure 4.3   The bar at the top of the Debug area provides controls for advancing the execution of the program and navigating through its state.

1. The **Hide/Show Debug Area (⇧⌘Y)** button reduces the Debug area to just the debugging bar, and expands it again.
2. The **Activate/Deactivate Breakpoints (⌘Y)** button enables or disables all of the breakpoints in your project.
3. **Continue (^⌘Y)** lets the program run until it hits another breakpoint or crashes.
4. **Step Over (F6)** executes the current line and stops at the next one.
5. **Step Into (F7)** proceeds with execution until it enters the next function called on this line; you'll resume control on the first line of that function.
6. **Step Out (F8)** proceeds with execution until it leaves the current function; you'll resume control in the caller.
7. **Simulate Location** sets the location your app will see when it uses Core Location. This is a popup menu with a selection of common locations throughout the world. You can specify a location of your own by providing a JSON GPX file describing it.
8. A jump bar traces the state of the program from the process to the thread to the current location in the stack trace. Each step allows you to examine a different process, thread, or level in the call stack, and each step presents a submenu so that you can set all three levels with one mouse gesture.

> **Note**
>
> Your Mac may be set up so that the F-keys are overridden by hardware-control functions like volume and screen brightness or intercepted at the system level for other functions. Review the settings in the **Shortcuts** tab of the **Keyboard** panel in System Preferences if you want to clear these keys for Xcode's use. Holding down the **fn** key switches the function keys between the two uses.

You're interested in seeing what `passer_rating` does, line by line. Click the **Step Over** button (the arrow looping over an underscore). The green arrowhead jumps to the next line, and something changes in the variables pane: `completionComponent`'s value changes to `NaN`. This is a new value, so Xcode highlights it by italicizing it and coloring it blue. So now you know: The result is poisoned from the first calculation. Even if the other values are good, a `NaN` in any part of a calculation makes the result a `NaN`, too.

The next line calls `pinPassingComponent`; does that cure the error? Click **Step In** (the arrow pointing down into an underscore). The arrowhead jumps up the page to the first line of `pinPassingComponent`. Step through. You'll find that as `component` fails each of the tests in the `if` statements (`NaN` doesn't compare to anything), the arrow follows execution, jumping over the lines that don't get executed. Stepping through the final `return` jumps execution to the exit point of the function, and then to the next line of the caller.

Fixing the Problem

The problem in `passer-rating` was obvious: I never accounted for the possibility of zero attempts. Time to get back to `rating.c` and make the fix.

Behaviors

But if you've been following along, you'll find some annoyances:

- When `passer-rating` finishes, the Debug area goes away, and you can't inspect its output. You'll have to go to the toolbar and expose it again. A slight pain, but still a pain.

  It was worse in the case of `Hello World`, because without the `fgets()` call, the program would have exited so quickly the debugger console would have closed before you could see it had opened.

- If `passer-rating` were slightly different, and didn't display a prompt before `scanf()` accepted input, you'd never see the debugger at all. The debugger bar would appear at the bottom of the window, but the program would hang until you expanded the debugger and typed something in. Xcode displays the debugger only when the program prints something.

- Xcode does open the debugger in response to output, the Debug *navigator* doesn't show, unless it had been showing before.

- *But*, stopping for a breakpoint *does* switch to the Debug navigator.

Opinions may differ on these points, and maybe there's a majority for each separately. But it's unlikely that most users will be satisfied with the combination.

Xcode provides a solution. What I've just described is the default, but you can replace the default. Xcode lets you set *behaviors* to control what it does when certain events occur.

Examine the **Behaviors** panel of the Preferences window (Figure 4.4). You'll see the available events listed on the left, divided into building, testing, running, OpenGL analysis, searching, integration builds, and file unlocking. You're interested in the **Running →Starts** event—what happens when your application runs under the debugger.

What you'd like is for the Debug area to appear whenever you run your application for debugging. By default, Xcode does nothing special when you trigger a run: However your project window is configured is how it will stay, and you won't get any sort of notification.

If, instead, Xcode presented the full debugging interface without waiting for breakpoints or output, you'd get your full application status from the start. Here's how you do this.

1. Check the box next to the **Show/Hide. . . navigator** item.
2. Be sure the first popup menu says **Show**.
3. Select **Debug Navigator** in the second popup.
4. Check the box next to the **Show/Hide. . . debugger** item.
5. Select **Show** from the first popup, and **Current Views** from the second. You can also force the debugger to show either or both of the variables and console panes.

The **Starts** row in the behaviors table now has a check next to it. Its actions now match the ones for the **Pauses** and **Generates output** actions, but there's no harm in it,

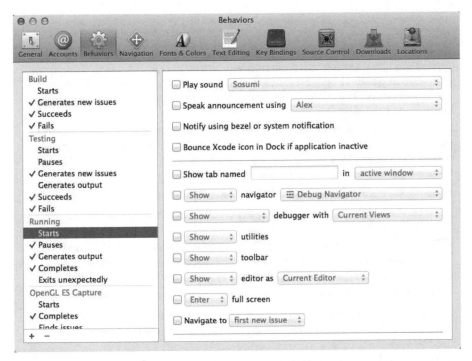

Figure 4.4   The Behaviors panel of Xcode's Preferences window lets you determine what Xcode will do in response to certain events.

and if you change your mind about **Starts**, you won't have to do anything to get back to where you were.

At the end of the run, I'd like to hide the Debug area and resume the use of the Project navigator. If I need to refer to the app's messages, I can bring the debugger back with a click on the **View** control at the right end of the toolbar; and once debugging is complete, the Debug navigator goes blank. Leave the **Completes** behavior as it is by default: **Show** navigator **Project Navigator**, and **Hide** debugger.

> **Note**
>
> There's another way to refer to the debugger output of a program. The last tab of the Navigator area, labeled with a speech balloon, opens the Log navigator. It contains the results of every major operation you've performed recently, including debug sessions. If there are more than one, you can examine and compare each of them.

Try it: Run passer-rating one more time, enter some data, get a result, then press ^D to terminate it. The Debug area appears when the run starts and reverts when it ends. Success.

Tabs

You also see an option in the **Behaviors** panel labeled "Show tab named," and it's tempting. True to the notion that Xcode is a browser for your project, you can add tabs to the window, each of which provides a different perspective on your work. Other editors can put separate files in each tab, but that misconceives Xcode's model. The feature is much more powerful but, in a way, also fragile.

Select **File** → **New** → **New Tab** (⌘ **T**) to switch to a new tab. It starts with the same content you had when you issued the command. Try selecting a different file in the Project navigator, and use the toolbar's **View** control to expose the Utility area (on the right). Now switch back to the original tab: Not only does it show the original file, but the Utility area is closed.

Imagine another use. You might have tabs for three different purposes:

- One for straight text-editing: Nothing but the Editor view and the Project navigator.
- One for Interface Builder, which takes up a lot of horizontal space: Navigator hidden (you'd use the jump bar to navigate); Assistant view (the middle button of the **Editor** control that's second-to-last in the toolbar) to show the header for the view's controller; and the Utility area shown for access to the component library.
- One for debugging, with the Debug navigator and Debug area displayed.

You can name tabs: Double-click on the tab's label (by default it shows the name of the file being displayed). It becomes editable, so you can name the tabs "Edit," "Interface Builder," and "Debugger," respectively.

With *that*, you can open the **Behaviors** panel to set the **Completes** action to **Show tab named**, with the name of your "Edit" tab. Just remember to uncheck the **Show navigator** and **Debug Navigator** actions; the tab is already set up for that. The effect is that you can set changes in the window's appearance and function that are much more complex than the simpler options in the **Behaviors** panel.

This is great, as far as it goes, but it's unstable. The same freedom that lets you set each tab as you like doesn't prevent your changing that tab, losing the effort you put into arranging it and focusing it on the right type of file. If you have any behaviors lingering (such as exposing build issues or showing the Debug area), a simple build-and-go could ruin your carefully constructed Interface Builder tab, unless your system of tabs and behaviors changes to a separate context at every event.

The Fix

At last, we get around to repairing `passer_rating`. After all this business with behaviors and tabs, the fix is an anticlimax. Just add this to the start of `passer_rating`:

```
if (atts == 0)
    return 0.0;
```

⌘ **R** runs `passer-rating` one more time. Enter 0 0 0 0 0 at the prompt, and sure enough, you are rewarded with **Rating = 0.0**. Press ^**D**; the Debug area goes away, and the Navigator area returns to the Project navigator. Just what you wanted.

Summary

In this chapter, you used Xcode's debugger to take charge of `passer-rating` to track down a bug. You set a breakpoint, stepped through, into, and out of functions, examining and changing variables as you went.

You also picked up a couple of skills—setting behaviors and tabs—that make it easier to get control of Xcode's habit of changing its windows on its own initiative. On the way, you came to a crucial insight: Xcode isn't meant to be just a source editor; it is a browser on the whole flow of your development effort.

Now I'm going to take a break from that flow to have our first, focused view on what the Xcode tools are doing.

5

Compilation

Before continuing, let's review how computer programs get made. If you're coming to Xcode from long experience with GNU Make or another development environment, this discussion will be very familiar to you. Bear with me: I'm going back to basics so every reader will be on a par for what they know about the build process.

Programmers use *source code* to specify what a program does; source code files contain a notation that, although technical and sometimes cryptic, is recognizably the product of a human, intended in part for humans to read. Even the most precise human communication leaves to allusion and implication things that a computer has to have spelled out. If a passer-rating tool were to refer to the local variable `yardageComp`, for example, you'd care only that the name `yardageComp` should consistently refer to the result of a particular calculation; the central processor of a computer running an application, however, cares about the amount of memory allocated to `yardageComp`, the format by which it is interpreted, how memory is reserved for the use of `yardageComp` and later released, that the memory should be aligned on the proper address boundary, that no conflicting use be made of that memory, and, finally, how the address of `yardageComp` is to be determined when data is to be stored or retrieved there. The same issues have to be resolved for each and every named thing in a program.

Compiling

Fortunately, you have a computer to keep track of such things. A *compiler* is a program that takes source files and generates the corresponding streams of machine-level instructions. Consider this function, that calculates two averages and sends them back to the caller through a results `struct`:

```
void calculate_stats(Results * results)
{
    int     n = 0, nScanned = 0;
    double  sum_X, sum_Y;
    sum_X = sum_Y = 0.0;
```

```
    do {
        double     x, y;
        nScanned = scanf("%lg %lg", &x, &y);
        if (nScanned == 2) {
            n++;
            sum_X += x;
            sum_Y += y;
        }
    } while (nScanned == 2);
    Results     lclResults = { .avg_X = sum_X/n
#if CALCULATE_AVG_Y
        , .avg_Y = sum_Y/n
#endif
    };
    *results = lclResults;
}
```

CALCULATE_AVG_Y is defined as 1 or 0, depending on whether the function is to calculate the average of the y values it reads. With average-y included, these 22 lines translate into 54 lines of assembly code (the human-readable equivalent of the bytes the processor would execute):

```
_calculate_stats_100000e40:
    push      rbp
    mov       rbp, rsp
    push      r15
    push      r14
    push      r13
    push      r12
    push      rbx
    sub       rsp, 0x28
    mov       r14, rdi
    lea       rdi, qword [ds:0x100000f82] ; "%lg %lg"
    lea       rsi, qword [ss:rbp-0x50+var_32]
    lea       rdx, qword [ss:rbp-0x50+var_24]
    xor       al, al
    call      imp___stubs__scanf
    xorps     xmm1, xmm1
    cmp       eax, 0x2
    jne       0x100000ecb
    xor       ebx, ebx
    lea       r15, qword [ds:0x100000f82] ; "%lg %lg"
    lea       r12, qword [ss:rbp-0x50+var_32]
    lea       r13, qword [ss:rbp-0x50+var_24]
    xorps     xmm2, xmm2
```

```
nop         word [cs:rax+rax+0x0]
addsd       xmm1, qword [ss:rbp-0x50+var_24]
```

. . .

Note

For the record, this code was produced by the Xcode 5 version of the clang compiler with optimization set to -O3.

I've cut this off at the first 25 lines; you see the kind of output involved. It's not very instructive unless you live with assembly every day. Fortunately, I have the useful Hopper Disassembler, which can reconstruct a C-like function from the byte stream:

```
function _calculate_stats_100000e40 {
    r14 = rdi;
    rax = scanf("%lg %lg");
    xmm1 = 0x0;
    if (rax == 0x2) {
        rbx = 0x0;
        r12 = &var_32;
        r13 = &var_24;
        xmm2 = 0x0;
        do {
            xmm1 = xmm1 + var_24;
            var_16 = xmm1;
            xmm2 = xmm2 + var_32;
            var_8 = xmm2;
            rax = scanf("%lg %lg");
            xmm2 = var_8;
            xmm1 = var_16;
            rbx = rbx + 0x1;
        } while (rax == 0x2);
    }
    else {
        xmm2 = 0x0;
    }
    asm{ divsd    xmm1, xmm0 };
    asm{ divsd    xmm2, xmm0 };
    *r14 = xmm2;
    *(r14 + 0x8) = xmm1;
    return rax;
}
```

You lose the variable names, but you can see the outline. Even at this level, you notice a difference between the machine code and the source: The compiled function calls scanf() *twice*. The read-and-calculate loop in the original function is controlled by whether `scanf()`, in the loop, returned two values. That determination is made at the bottom of the loop, but that's *after* the input is added to the sums, so the original code guards the calculations in the middle of the loop by testing whether there are two inputs. The compiler simplified the loop by making an extra call to `scanf()` before the loop starts, eliminating the need for the big `if` block in the middle.

By now you've seen an important point: Your source is *your* expression of what your code does, but if you let it, the compiler will substantially rearrange (*optimize*) it to meet some criterion—usually speed, but sometimes size or memory pressure. Its only obligation is to ensure that the emitted code has the same effect. But in the line-by-line details, if you were to step through optimized code, the program counter would jump apparently randomly around the lines of your code.

There's more. Let's set the CALCULATE_AVG_Y macro to 0, which does nothing more than remove the final use of sum_Y. The inner loop (while `scanf()` returns 2) becomes:

```
do {
    var_16 = xmm1;
    var_8 = var_32;
    rax = scanf("%lg %lg");
    xmm1 = var_16;
    xmm1 = xmm1 + var_8;
    rbx = rbx + 0x1;
} while (rax == 0x2);
```

If you puzzle this out, you'll see that sum_Y *isn't there at all*. The compiler saw that, even though the variable was used to accumulate a sum, nothing else used it. There's no point in doing the sum, so it removed sum_Y completely. If you were to trace through this function in the debugger, you wouldn't be able to see the value of sum_Y, because there is no value to see.

Fortunately, you can turn optimization off completely, and the reconstructed loop would look almost identical to what you wrote, including the summing of the sum_Y value that will never be used:

```
function _calculate_stats_100000e70 {
    xmm0 = 0x0;
    var_56 = rdi;
    var_52 = 0x0;
    var_48 = 0x0;
    var_32 = xmm0;
    var_40 = xmm0;
    do {
        rax = scanf("%lg %lg");
        var_48 = rax;
        if (var_48 == 0x2) {
            var_52 = var_52 + 0x1;
            var_40 = var_40 + var_24;
```

```
        var_32 = var_32 + var_16;
    }
} while (var_48 == 0x2);
asm{ divsd      xmm1, xmm2 };
var_0 = var_40;
var_8 = 0x0;
rax = var_56;
*rax = var_0;
*(rax + 0x8) = var_8;
return rax;
}
```

This setting (-O0) is what Xcode uses for debugging builds.

When imagining the tasks a compiler must perform in producing executable machine instructions from human-readable source, the first thing that comes to mind is the choice of machine instructions: the translation of floating-point add operations into addsd instructions or expressing the do/while loop in terms of cmpl, je, and jmp. Even this simple example shows that this isn't the whole story.

Another important task is the management of *symbols*. Each C function and every variable has to be expressed in machine code in terms of regions of memory, with addresses and extents. A compiler has to keep strict account of every symbol, assigning an address—or at least a way of getting an address—for it and making sure that no two symbols get overlapping sections of memory. Here's how the assembly for the unoptimized version begins:

```
push        rbp
mov         rbp, rsp
sub         rsp, 0x40
xorps       xmm0, xmm0
mov         qword [ss:rbp-0x40+var_56], rdi
mov         dword [ss:rbp-0x40+var_52], 0x0
mov         dword [ss:rbp-0x40+var_48], 0x0
movsd       qword [ss:rbp-0x40+var_32], xmm0
movsd       qword [ss:rbp-0x40+var_40], xmm0
```

In its analysis of calculate_stats, the compiler budgeted a certain amount of memory in RAM for local variables and assigned general-purpose register rbp to keep track of the end of that block. The 8-byte floating-point number x (var_40) was assigned to the memory beginning 40 bytes into that block; y was assigned to the eight bytes before that. The compiler made sure not to use that memory for any other purpose.

In the optimized version, the sums don't even get stored in memory but are held in the processor's floating-point registers and used from there. Register xmm1, for instance, holds the value of the sum_x variable. Once again, the compiler makes sure that each datum has something to hold it, and that no two claims on storage collide.

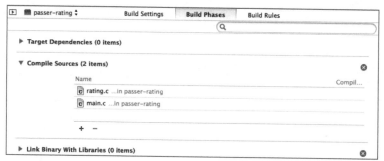

Figure 5.1   Selecting the project icon in the Project navigator displays an editor for the project and its targets. The **Build Phases** tab of the Target editor is a table showing the steps in building the target. Click the disclosure triangle in a phase's header to display the files that go into that phase. Even a simple build has a "Compile Sources" phase (upper) containing every file to be transformed into object files; and a "Link Binary With Libraries" phase (lower) to designate precompiled system and private code to bind into a finished product.

In an Xcode project, files that are to be compiled are found in the Target editor: Open the Navigator area on the left side of the window and select the first tab to display the Project navigator. The item at the top represents the project and all its targets. Select your product's name from the **TARGETS** list.

The files to be compiled in the build of the target are listed in the "Compile Sources" build phase under the **Build Phases** tab. See Figure 5.1.

Linking

The accounting task does not end there. The assembly code includes this instruction once or twice:

```
call        imp___stubs__scanf
```

This line is the translation of the call to the scanf() function. What sort of symbol is imp___stubs__scanf? Examining a full disassembly of an application using scanf() won't tell you much: It traces to a location named imp___la_symbol_ptr__scanf, which is initialized with a 64-bit number. The compiled application does not contain any code, or any memory allocated, for scanf().

And a good thing, too, as scanf() is a component of the standard C library. You don't want to define it yourself: You want to use the code that comes in the library. But the compiler, which works with only one .c or .m file at a time, doesn't have any way of referring directly to the starting address of scanf(). The compiler has to leave that address as a blank to be filled in later; therefore, in building a program, there has to be an additional step for filling in such blanks.

The product of the compiler, an *object file*, contains the machine code generated from a source file, along with directories detailing what symbols are defined in that file and what symbols still need definitions filled in. Objective-C source files have the suffix .m; object files have the same name, with the `.m` removed and `.o` (for object) substituted. Libraries are single files that collect object files supplying useful definitions for commonly used symbols. In the simplest case, a library has a name beginning with `lib` and suffixed with `.a`.

The process of back-filling unresolved addresses in compiled code is called *linkage editing*, or simply *linking*. You present the linker with a set of object files and libraries, and, you hope, the linker finds among them a definition for every unresolved symbol your application uses. Every address that had been left blank for later will then be filled in. The result is an executable file containing all of the code that gets used in the application. See Figure 5.2.

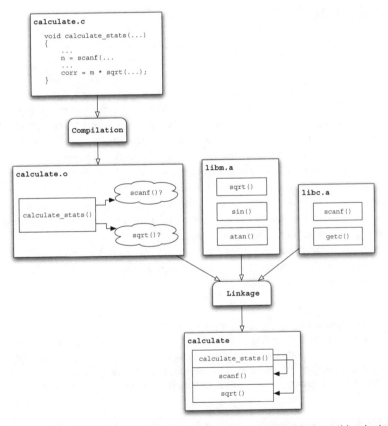

Figure 5.2   The process of turning source code into an executable binary, ruthlessly simplified. You provide source code in `calculate.c` (top left); compiling it produces an object file, `calculate.o`, that contains your translated code, plus unresolved references to functions `calculate.c` doesn't define. Other libraries (the notional `libm.a` and `libc.a`) contain machine code for those functions. It's the job of the linker to merge your code and the other functions you requested into a complete executable program (bottom).

This process corresponds to the "Link Binary With Libraries" build phase in the application's target listing. This phase lists all of the libraries and frameworks against which the application is to be linked.

> **Note**
>
> Sharp-eyed readers will have seen that the linkage phase shown in Figure 5.1 contains no libraries at all. There are two reasons: First, most C compilers will link programs against the standard C library without being told to. Second, with Xcode 5, `clang` implements the *modules* extension to C-family languages, which can add libraries to the linkage task whenever one of their headers is used. See the "Precompilation" section later in this chapter for details.

Dynamic Loading

Actually, it's one step more complicated than that. Standard routines, such as `scanf()`, will be used simultaneously by many—possibly hundreds—of processes on a system. Copying the machine code that implements `scanf()` into each application is a pointless waste of disk space. The solution is *dynamic loading*: The application leaves the addresses of common library functions unresolved even in the final executable file, providing the partial executable code along with a dictionary of symbols to be resolved and the system libraries to find them in. The operating system then fetches the missing code from a library that is shared system-wide, and links it into the executable when the application runs.

Dynamic loading saves not only disk space, but RAM and execution time. When a dynamic library—a collection of object files set up for dynamic linking and having the prefix `lib` and the suffix `.dylib`—is loaded into physical memory, the same copy is made visible to every application that needs it. The second and subsequent users of a dynamic library won't incur memory or load-time costs.

Also, dynamic libraries can be updated to fix bugs and improve performance. Installing a new version of a library will improve all of the applications that use it, without any need to change the application code itself.

> **Note**
>
> You can't produce your own dynamic libraries for iOS. Dynamic linking still happens—everything the OS does for you is provided through dynamic libraries—but iOS does not allow applications to load or execute anything but main application code (exceptions: interpreted scripts that are embedded in the app, or JavaScript executed in WebKit). On OS X, third-party dynamic libraries are common. See Chapter 23, "Frameworks," for an example.

64- and 32-bit Applications

Apple has been shipping desktop computers that express numbers and pointers as 64-bit integers for quite a while, and its 64-bit libraries get all the new features and almost all the maintenance effort.

However, some Mac applications need 32-bit compatibility, because they rely on the old Carbon human-interface framework or must support older systems. OS X keeps 32-bit versions of all the libraries those applications are eligible to use. This means that when you run an application built for 32 bits, it will force the loading of what is practically a second copy of the operating system. The user never sees it directly, but it reduces the capacity of her computer. If you don't have to, don't deliver 32-bit applications, or at least build a "fat" version that includes 64-bit code for systems that can use them.

Further, though modern Macs are 64-bit, the ARM processors in Apple's mobile devices before 2013 were 32-bit. If you want to share code across platforms, look up the 64-bit porting guide in the documentation to learn about width-safe programming.

If dynamic libraries don't get linked with the application's executable code until run-time, why do they figure in the linkage phase of the build process at all? There are two reasons. First, the linker can verify that all of the unresolved symbols in your application are defined somewhere and it can issue an error message if you specified a misspelled or absent function. Second, the linker-built tables in the dynamically linked code specify not only the symbols that need resolving but also what libraries the needed definitions are to be found in. With files specified, the dynamic loader does not have to search all of the system's libraries for each symbol, and the application can specify private dynamic libraries (in OS X) that would not be in any general search path.

Xcode and Clang

A traditional compiler sticks to what I've just described: It's a command-line tool that starts, reads your source code, writes some object code, and then stops. That's what gcc, the Free Software Foundation's widely used compiler, which Xcode at least made available through Xcode 4, does. In Xcode 3.2, Apple began to introduce a new compiler technology called llvm. llvm is a library that reads and analyzes source code. It has these advantages:

- It is a library. It can be used to build a compiler, but it is linked into Xcode itself to provide on-the-fly indexing and syntax-checking using essentially the same compiler as will be used to build the object code.

- The llvm library is linked into lldb, the debugging engine under the Xcode debugger. llvm lets you enter C-family statements on its command line. It will compile them—compatibly with the code being debugged, because it's the same compiler—and inject them into the code being debugged.

- OpenCL, the OS X facility that harnesses graphics-chip computing power for massively parallel computation, relies on storing C-like source code in the client program. It has to; GPUs are all different. The OS uses llvm to convert the source text into the binary for the system's GPU.

- Vendors providing bridges between Cocoa and "managed" or interpreted languages link the llvm library to their own compilers to translate relatively slowly interpreted code to CPU-native code.

- The Xcode text editor links to llvm to get continuous information on the state of your code from the same parser that will translate it into your product. Open the Preferences window (**Xcode →Preferences. . . ⌘ comma**) and set **Issues: Show live issues** to display warnings and errors as you enter your code.

- And, of course, llvm can form the core of a compiler, such as clang, the C-family compiler that Xcode uses.

Also, gcc had become hard to live with. gcc is. . .mature. Apple has been extending gcc for years, and publishing its contributions, but making significant changes to a code base with many stakeholders and dependencies is wearisome. Since moving to llvm, Apple has been able to rapidly introduce new features for the Objective-C programming language, faster compilation, better analysis for optimization and warnings, and (to cut the list short) a C++11 compiler with a reputation for being the fullest implementation in the industry.

Local Analysis

The insight the previous generation of compilers have into source code is confined to a certain scope, no finer than a single line, no broader than a fairly large function. They can tell you what line an error occurred on; clang can specify the *token*. They can tell you that a symbol you used isn't known; you can ask them to flag certain coding practices for you to double-check. clang can offer to correct the spelling, and recode expressions that it *knows* are problematic in the context, which can be very broad.

clang can be made to know about conventions and other constraints on your code. A common idiom in Cocoa programming is for a method to accept a pointer to the pointer for an NSError object. If an error occurs, the method can fill the reference with an error object, thus passing it back to the caller. However, such methods always offer to accept a NULL pointer, in case the caller wants to ignore the error detail.

Consider this Foundation command-line program, which implements a simple class with three methods:

```
#import <Foundation/Foundation.h>

static NSString * const MyErrDomain = @"MyErrDomain";

@interface MyClass : NSObject
- (void) doSomething;
- (BOOL) methodWithErrorRef: (NSError **) error;
@property(nonatomic, assign) BOOL   somethingWrong;
@end
```

```objc
@implementation MyClass

- (instancetype) init
{
    self = [super init];
    if (self) {
        _somethingWrong = NO;
    }
    return self;
}


- (void) doSomething { self.somethingWrong = YES; }

- (BOOL) methodWithErrorRef: (NSError **) error
{
    NSError *   justInCase =
            [NSError errorWithDomain: MyErrDomain
                                code: -1 userInfo: nil];
    *error = justInCase;        //  Line 29

    [self doSomething];
    if (self.somethingWrong)
        return NO;
    else
        return YES;
}

@end

int main(int argc, const char * argv[])
{
    @autoreleasepool {
        MyClass *       object = [[MyClass alloc] init];
        NSError *       error;
        if ([object methodWithErrorRef: &error]) {
            NSLog(@"Method on %@ succeeded", object);
        }
        else {
            NSLog(@"Method on %@ failed", object);
        }
    }
    return 0;
}
```

Note

Notice that `methodWithErrorRef:` fills the `error` output with a catchall error object before it knows whether an error occurred. Methods that accept `NSError*` references are allowed to do that. Callers *must not* try to determine whether something went wrong by examining the returned `NSError`. It may be present, but not valid. Only the method's return value can tell you whether it failed.

`MyClass` is about as simple as it can be, just enough to have a method that appears to do something, and accepts a pointer to an `NSError*` pointer. Make `clang` take a really close look at it: Select **Product → Analyze** (⇧ ⌘ B). Soon the Issues navigator appears with one blue-flagged entry, which in the log appears as:

```
main.m:29:9: warning: Potential null dereference.
    According to coding standards in 'Creating and
    Returning NSError Objects' the parameter may be null
        *error = justInCase;
        ~~~~~~~~~~~~~~~~~~~~
```

So that's a nice feature—Apple taught `clang` about one of its coding standards, and `clang` alerts you when you violate one. It will even identify the character position (the = assignment operator) where the error occurred. (The editor will show a red caret at that position.)

Cross-Function Analysis

It goes beyond nice. In `main()`'s call to `methodWithErrorRef:`, replace `&error` with `NULL`. Repeat the analysis.

The coding-convention error flag is joined by a "logic error." Click the disclosure triangle in the Issues navigator, and step through the details it contains:

1. In `main()`, "Passing null pointer value via 1st parameter 'error'"
2. "Calling 'methodWithErrorRef:'"
3. In `methodWithErrorRef:`, "Entered call from 'main'"
4. Dereference of null pointer (loaded from variable 'error')"

The original flag was for an in-place violation of a coding convention. This is a warning of an *actual* programming error arising from an *actual* execution path that `clang` traced across two methods. See Figure 5.3.

Note

Between the banners and the Issues navigator, it can be hard to see the full text of error, warning, and analysis messages. The banners often run out of room, even with the tiny font they use, and the Issues items show only the first few words of the messages. You can do better: Open the **General** panel of the Preferences window, and set **Issue Navigator Detail:** to **Up to Ten Lines**. That should be plenty of room.

```
int main(int argc, const char * argv[])
{
    @autoreleasepool {
        MyClass         object = [[MyClass alloc] init];
        if ([object methodWithErrorRef: NULL]) {    ⊟ 1. Passing null pointer value via 1st parameter 'error' ▲
            NSLog(@"Method on %@ succeeded", object); ⊟ 2. Calling 'methodWithErrorRef:'
        }
        else {
            NSLog(@"Method on %@ failed", object);
        }
    }
    return 0;
}
```

```
⊟ ─ (BOOL) methodWithErrorRef: (NSError **) error                    ⊟ 3. Entered call from 'main'
   {
     NSError *justInCase =
       [NSError errorWithDomain: MyErrDomain
                          code: -1 userInfo: nil];
⊟   *error = justInCase;                        ⊟ 4. Dereference of null pointer (loaded from variable 'error') ▲
                                                ⊟ Dereference of null pointer (loaded from variable 'error')
     [self doSomething];
     if ([self somethingWentWrong])
         return NO;
     else
         return YES;
   }
```

Figure 5.3   `clang` can warn of programming errors that arise from program flows as they actually occur, even between functions. Expanding a logic error message will show arrows demonstrating exactly the path that will lead to the error.

Indexing

Project indexing was a marquee feature of Xcode 1, and remains at its core. In the background, Xcode examines your code base, and all of the system files you use, to collect the type and place-of-definition of every symbol. That information is used so:

- The editor can give a unique color to each construct on the screen.
- You can jump directly to the declaration of a symbol by command-clicking on it. The gesture works on the semantic unit—command-clicking the first part of `fileExistsAtPath:isDirectory:` will pick up the whole method name and won't bounce you to `fileExistsAtPath:`.
- You can click in a symbol, and then on the indicator that appears next to it, to command **Edit All in Scope**; editing the one symbol will change all other instances, but only those that refer to the same object.
- The Symbol navigator (second tab in the Navigator area) can show you a directory of the symbols defined in your project, jumping you to the definition of each. This works even for `@property` directives: They normally create hidden methods to set and examine the property. The Symbol navigator shows the implicit methods.
- The new facility for changing documentation comments into live help text can choose which documentation among identically spelled methods it should show.
- The refactoring feature can operate on all instances of a complex symbol (like a multipart method name), and only those, without the limitations of a search for text or patterns.

- The Assistant editor can be set to display all callers or callees of the method selected in the main editor. This makes possible the trick of moving callers of an obsolete method over to a new one by simply stepping through the callers and converting them until the caller list is empty.

Before the transition to `llvm`, Xcode had to fall back on its own parser, which could be made to match the behavior of the `gcc` compiler only with difficulty. With a slower indexing parser (and, yes, slower computers), it was common to have re-indexing interrupt your workflow. Creating an index for a large project still takes time (though you can continue work while it happens), but after that, you won't notice it. `llvm` guarantees that the indexer and `clang` work from the same sophisticated code model.

Compiler Products

Object files are the principal products of the compilation process: You're most often interested only in building something you can run and test. But sometimes, the compiler will identify issues or produce results that, with all diligence, you can't make sense of. In such cases, it's useful to see what the compiler did on the way to translating your code.

Also, the build process will produce files that encapsulate repetitive tasks, like compiling common header files. These, too, are compiler products.

Intermediate Products

When you are tracing bugs—or are just curious—you may need to see what the compiler has done in the steps between your source and the executable product. Xcode provides a way to do this.

C-family compilers were originally run in three stages, each feeding the next. Modern compilers merge the steps to gain a better understanding of how to generate the best code, but notionally the steps are still there, and you can get the products of each:

1. The *preprocessor* takes your code and outputs the "real" source after making simple string substitutions. When it finds `#include` and `#import` directives, it inserts the contents of the included files into the output stream. Macros from `#define` directives are expanded and substituted into the stream. Conditional directives admit or block sections of code in the input file.

   You can see the results of the preprocessor by clicking on the **Related Items** menu (at the left end of the jump bar above the editor) and selecting **Preprocess**. The editor shows the full interpreted stream of the current source file. This can be long, but you can track down bugs by making sure that the code you thought you were compiling, and the symbols you thought you were using, are really there.

   Choosing **Preprocess** from the root item in the jump bar of the Assistant editor will display a preprocessed version alongside the file you are editing. Also, you can issue **Product → Perform Action → Preprocess**.

2. The parser/generator takes the "simplified," preprocessed code, reduces it to logical constructs (parsing), and produces the assembly source for a machine-language program that does what the original source directs (code generation).
There are three ways to call for an assembly listing.

- Selecting **Assembly** from the **Related Items** menu, which drops down from the small array-of-rectangles button at the left end of the jump bar (Figure 5.4), replaces the editor's contents with the translated code.

- The **Product** → **Perform Action** → **Assemble** command does the same thing.

- Selecting **Assembly** from the Assistant editor's jump bar will show the assembly for whatever file is in the Standard editor.

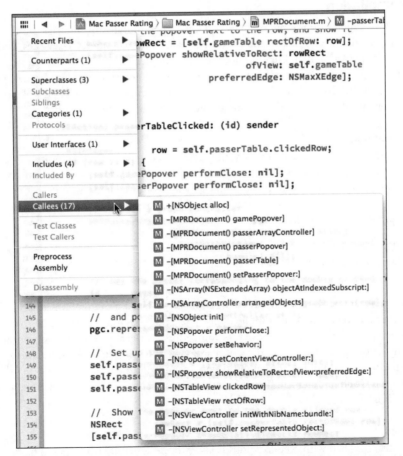

Figure 5.4   The small item at the left end of the jump bar above any editor view is the anchor for the **Related Items** menu, offering many alternative views of the file displayed in the editor.

> **Note**
>
> This is not a disassembly like the one I began this chapter with. It is not derived from the final executable stream of the completed product. It is a representation of the compiler's understanding of your code, and features annotations that relate back to `clang`'s knowledge of your source.

3. An assembler reads the assembly source and reduces it to executable bytes in an object file, with references to be filled in by the linker. The `otool` command-line tool has a plethora of options for examining object files and libraries, with disassemblies and file layouts, and limited options for editing. The nm tool is useful for examining the symbol tables in a library. See man `otool` and man nm for details.

Precompilation

Mac and iOS applications draw on *frameworks*, packages of dynamic libraries, headers, and resources that define and link to the operating systems, human interface services, and other services. Frameworks entail huge numbers of large header files. In early days, it made sense for programmers to speed up builds by carefully choosing the system headers they included, but the Cocoa frameworks are so interdependent that that isn't possible. (In fact, Apple emphatically warns against trying to pull pieces out of frameworks.)

Prefix Headers

Framework headers are usually the first things an implementation file imports, either directly or through headers of its own. You can set a *prefix file* to be injected automatically into the source stream of all your files; in fact, when you instantiate an iOS or OS X project, Xcode automatically generates a `.pch` file and sets up the build settings to inject it. A typical prefix file looks like this:

```
#ifdef __OBJC__
    #import <Cocoa/Cocoa.h>
#endif
```

That's convenient, but doesn't solve the problem of speed if the prefix is to be read and converted every time you compile a file. The `.pch` extension gives a clue to the solution: The file's intended purpose is as source for a *precompiled header*; if you opt for precompilation, `clang` will read the `.pch` and save its parsing state. All subsequent uses of the prefix header will reload that saved state, saving you the time that repeating the compilation would have taken. There is another build setting for precompilation, and by default, it is on.

Modules

The `clang` supplied with Xcode 5 adds *modules* to the C-family languages. The designers saw a problem: Notionally, the `#include` and `#import` directives that have been a part of C since its inception are nothing more than commands for pouring the uninterpreted text of one file into another. The included file defines symbols and macros that the compiler applies in the order it sees them. If you reorder the includes in your source files, the reordering of the definitions could change their meanings. Further, because you could insert defines among your includes, there is no way to be sure you can share precompiled inclusions among implementation files; even the same sequence of includes could yield completely different code.

Beyond that, if you were to #include <Foundation/Foundation.h> in a file, your source files will come out of the preprocessor with line counts in the five figures. Computers are fast, but you have work to do. You need quick turnaround on your builds, and having to load and parse repeated inclusions of declarations, most of which you will never use, gets in the way. Precompilation helps, but what remains is not good.

The llvm engineers' response is a system of modules, to be added to the C-family programming languages. Unlike header files brought in by the preprocessor, each module is a discrete unit and can come into the compilation state as completely parsed units.

There is a price: For the full benefit, you can't modify the effects of included headers by interleaving your own macro definitions. (It forces the compiler to generate a unique module file for just that case.) If you ever found it a good idea to do that, it's because bad design in the headers forced you. If you deliberately exploited order dependencies among your header files, you were insane, and should have stopped.

For a concrete instance, the C standard libraries might be encapsulated into an umbrella module called std, and you could request only the parts you want by asking for sub-modules like std.io or std.strings. You can invoke the module feature directly by replacing your framework includes and imports with the @import Objective-C directory, so

#import <Foundation/Foundation.h>

becomes

@import Foundation;

Command-clicking the module name will take you to the framework's umbrella header.

Unfortunately, none of the living authors of the many billions of C/C++/Objective-C source files are going to amend them to replace preprocessor directives with @import directives. For legacy code, when clang sees an #include or #import, it tries to build a module on the fly and use the module from then on.

Apple has modularized the Mavericks system libraries, so the worst of the #include-and-recompile cycle has already been eliminated. If you examine the preprocessed version of your source, you'll find that the contents of the system headers have been replaced with "implicit imports." If you want to pre-build modules of your own, you can describe the structure by providing a module.map file.

The module.map file does something else: It associates libraries with each module. If you #include/#import a header from a modularized framework, you don't have to add the framework to the "Link Binary With Libraries" build phase.

Xcode 5's new-project and -target templates are set to use modules by default. If you want the automatic linking feature as well, set "Link Frameworks Automatically" to **Yes**—that's the default, as well.

I've left many of your questions unanswered; visit `http://clang.llvm.org/docs/Modules.html` to learn more.

Summary

This chapter was a short but essential review of what happens when you compile and link a program. You saw how compilation not only translates your code into machine-executable code, but also transforms it. The biggest task in building an executable is not translation, but the bookkeeping involved in allocating space to data and code and how it culminates in the linkage phase. Linkage can be done all at once, as in a static linker, but iOS and OS X rely heavily on dynamic linkage, where much of the heavy work is done as the program starts running.

6

Adding a Library Target

The `passer_rating` function is a tremendous achievement—and hard-won. It plainly has applications beyond that simple command-line tool, so let's encapsulate its services for use in other programs.

All right, no, you won't, but doing so will introduce some important skills. So you can create a static library (an archive of reusable code) for `passer_rating`. You can move its code from the `passer-rating` tool into the new library and link it back into the tool.

Adding a Target

You don't need to start a new project to create a library—it's better if you don't. Open the `passer-rating` project in Xcode and click the top entry, representing the project, in the Project navigator. This brings up the Project/Target editor.

Like all editors, it has a jump bar at the top. The next bar contains the tabs that organize the target's settings. At the very left end is a button with a triangle on it. This opens the master list of the objects the Project/Target editor can work on. If you don't see the master list on the left side of the editor, click this button to disclose it. The list contains listings for the project itself, and for the sole target, passer-rating (Figure 6.1).

The last item in the master list is **Add Target. . . .** Click it.

This produces a New Target assistant sheet, which organizes the available templates in the way you've already seen for projects and files.

1. In the column on the left, select **OS X → Framework & Library**.
2. You're given a choice of linkable targets. Pick **C/C++ Library** (`passer_rating` doesn't involve anything more than standard C), and click **Next**.
3. Name the product. You may be aware that Unix static libraries have names of the form `libname.a`. Don't worry about that; just provide the base name **passer**, and the build system will take care of naming the file.
4. Select **Type: Static**, and accept **Project: passer-rating**.
5. Click **Finish**.

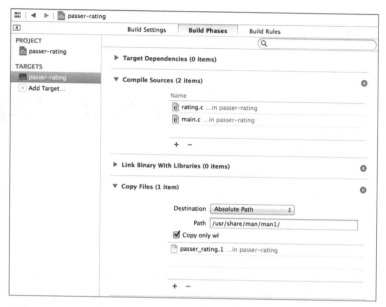

Figure 6.1   Click the button on the left end of the Project/Target editor's tab bar to disclose the master list of objects the editor can work on.

The Editor area is filled with a Target editor for the new "passer" target. For simple targets like C libraries and tools, the editor has three tabs:

- **Build Settings** lets you set all the options that control how the target is to be built. Even for so simple a library, there are quite a few of these. You can cut down by selecting the **Basic** and **Combined** filters. There are several all-caps settings that Xcode calls "User-Defined." These refer to clang. Xcode treats them this way because the passer library doesn't contain any source files yet, and Xcode doesn't know about clang until something in the build process uses it.

- **Build Phases** is something you saw before, in Chapter 5, "Compilation." It describes the components of the target and how they will be converted for use in building it. This is the first thing Xcode will show you when you create a target.

- **Build Rules** allow you to change the tools the Xcode build system uses to process files into the target. You can define rules of your own so you can add custom files and processes, but most developers never bother with it. You can learn more in Chapter 26, "The Xcode Build System."

Select the **Build Phases** tab.

Targets

What have you done? What is a target? Let's step back from the details of the Target editor.

A *target* describes a single build process in Xcode: It has a specific product, a specific set of files that go into the product, and a specific set of parameters for the build process.

Targets are organized into *build phases*. A build phase accepts files that are members of its target and processes them in a particular way. Source files (`.c`, `.m`, and `.cpp` files, most commonly, but other files for other compilers, as well) go into a "Compile Sources" phase; libraries, into a "Link Binary With Libraries" phase; and so on.

> **Note**
>
> Chapter 26, "The Xcode Build System," covers build phases and their role in the Xcode build system in detail.

You can change the files and settings as much as you like, but the type of the product, which determines what build process will be used, can't change. If you've started a static library, for instance, and then decide you need a dynamic library instead, you're out of luck. You have to create a new target for a dynamic library and add the source files again.

Target Membership

Targets consist of a product (which you specified), build settings (which you've accepted), and member files, of which the passer target has none. You'll have to add something—specifically `rating.c`.

Adding Files to a Target

There are three ways to do this.

- Click the project item in the Project navigator, and select the library target, passer, from the Targets list. Select the **Build Phases** tab. Find `rating.c` in the Project navigator, and drag it into the "Compile Sources" phase. The label will show that there is one item in the phase, and the phase will open to show `rating.c` in the list (Figure 6.2).

- Undo that by selecting `rating.c` in the Compile Sources table, and clicking the − button at the bottom of the table (or pressing the Delete key), so you can try another way.

  > **Note**
  >
  > Removing a file from a build phase, even all build phases, won't delete the file or remove it from your project.

  Now click the **+** button at the bottom of the Compile Sources table. A sheet containing the project outline drops down. Click `rating.c`, and then the **Add** button. If you click **Add Other...**, you can add files to the build phase and the project in one step.

- The third way is to come at it file-to-target: Click `rating.c` in the Project navigator. Then expose the Utility area by clicking the right-hand segment of the **View** control at the right end of the toolbar. Make sure the first tab, the File inspector, is selected. The File inspector lets you control the way Xcode treats the selected file (or files; if you select more than one in the Project navigator, the

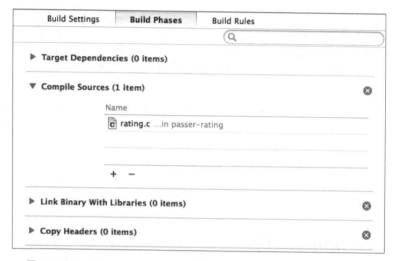

Figure 6.2 You can add a source file to a target by dragging it from the Project navigator into the "Compile Sources" phase. This gives you the most control of the role the file will play in the build process.

settings will affect all of them). One of the sections is **Target Membership**, listing all the targets in the project. For rating.c, click the checkbox for the passer target (Figure 6.3).

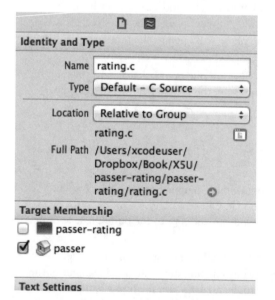

Figure 6.3 A table in the File inspector lets you select which targets a file is to contribute to.

The advantage to working from the build-phase end is that you have control over which phase a file goes into. Yes, .c files should almost always be compiled, but suppose you were creating a programmer's editor for OS X that has file templates embedded in it. Your TemplateFile.c file *looks* like C source—it is—but you want it bundled as a text file, not compiled as source. The phase you want is "Copy Bundle Resources" (available only for application and bundle targets), not "Compile Sources." If you start from the build phase, there's no ambiguity.

Working from the file's end of the chain has an advantage of its own: If your project has many targets, the checkboxes allow you to set all memberships at once, without having to visit the Target editors and hunt for the files. Xcode will guess which build phases they should go into, but its guesses are usually correct.

When you create a new file, using **File → New → File...** (⌘ N), you get a shortcut to assigning targets from the file end: The save-file dialog for the new file includes a picker for the targets to which you want to add it. Similarly, when you add files, **File → Add Files to...** (⌥ ⌘ A), you're given a target picker. Again, Xcode will guess at the build phases (Figure 6.4).

Warning

The target picker may not be set for the targets you expect. This is easy to miss, and the resulting errors will puzzle you.

However you added `rating.c` to the `passer` library, remember to *remove* it from the passer-rating target. The whole point of having a library is that clients don't have to include the source for the services it provides.

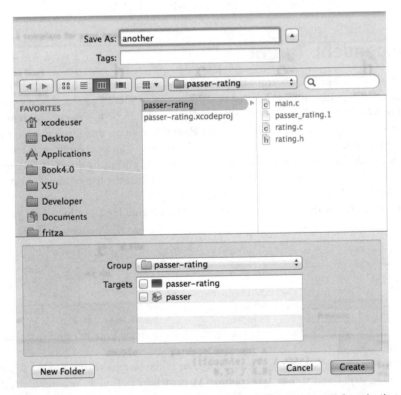

Figure 6.4 The save-file sheet for creating a new file includes a table for selecting the targets the file is to contribute to. The table is always set so the file won't belong to any targets.

Headers in Targets

What about `rating.h`? You can't add it to an application target from the file end: Headers themselves aren't compiled—they merely contribute to implementation files. If you want them inside an application bundle for some reason, you can drag them into the "Copy Bundle Resources" phase.

`rating.h` *can* be added to a *library* target. You can choose the role the header plays in your product:

- **Project**, if it's to be visible only inside your project, as an element in a build.
- **Public**, if it's to be installed somewhere like `/usr/local/include`, or the `Headers` directory of a framework.
- **Private**, if it's to be installed in the `PrivateHeaders` directory of a framework.

Select `rating.h` in the Project navigator, and open the Utility area to expose the File inspector (first tab). There you'll find the by-now-familiar **Target Membership** panel. Check the passer target, and select the role from the popup menu in that row of the table.

If we're serious about `libpasser.a` being a public utility, `rating.h` should be installed in a globally visible location. Set its visibility to **Public**.

A Dependent Target

Next to the **Run** and **Stop** buttons in the toolbar is the **Scheme** control, which sets the target and CPU architecture to be used for actions like running a product. Select **passer – My Mac 64-bit**, then click **Run**. (If the leftmost button in the toolbar isn't a right-facing triangle, hold down on that button and select **Run** from the list that drops down.) `passer` is a library, so it doesn't run anything, but the library builds, and the build succeeds.

Now switch the scheme popup to **passer-rating – My Mac 64-bit**. Click **Run**. The build fails. Let's see why. Select the Log navigator (last tab at the top of the Navigator area), where you'll see a table with two items carrying a red **!** icon. Click the first line, and the Editor area fills with a description of the problem highlighted in a log of the failed build:

```
Undefined symbols for architecture x86_64:
  "_passer_rating", referenced from:
     _main in main.o
ld: symbol(s) not found for architecture x86_64
clang: error: linker command failed with exit code 1 (use -v to see invocation)
```

In other words, `main()` uses `passer_rating`, but the linker couldn't find that function. See Figure 6.5.

This makes sense: You removed `rating.c`, and therefore `passer_rating`, from the passer-rating target, and you haven't told that target where to find it. Yes, the file and the library product are still in the project, but it's the passer-rating target, not the project, that determines what files go into the `passer-rating` tool.

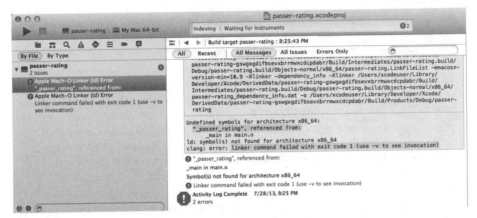

Figure 6.5   The Log navigator lists all of the problems that arose in your build. Clicking on an issue presents an editor displaying the location of the problem. In this case, the error came at the link phase, so the editor displays the link command and the error messages it printed.

Adding a Library

So you need to correct the passer-rating, which means going to the Target editor. You know the drill: In the Project navigator, select the passer-rating project at the top of the list. In the targets list, select passer-rating, and then the **Build Phases** tab.

You want to link `libpasser.a`, the product of the passer target, into `passer-rating`. It's straightforward: Open the "Link Binary With Libraries" build phase, and click the **+** button. A sheet appears with a two-section list. The first section, titled "passer-rating Project," lists the libraries the project produces—in this case, only `libpasser.a`. Select it and click **Add**.

> **Note**
>
> A popup containing **Required** and **Optional** appears next to the name of `libpasser.a`. Always use **Required** until you have enough experience to know why you wouldn't.

> **Note**
>
> If you're building a Cocoa (iOS or OS X) application, you can also add libraries in the Linked Frameworks and Libraries section of the **General** tab in the Target editor.

Now click **Run**. The build succeeds, `passer-rating` runs, and when you enter some test data, it works. Everything is great.

Implicit Dependencies

In a more traditional build system, your work would not be finished. Suppose you added a `printf()` call to `rating.c`. The change in the file would cascade to a rebuild of `libpasser.a`.

And there the changes would stop. Such build systems have to be told when a product (such as passer-rating) must be updated in response to a change in a constituent library. Changing rating.c would not get the updated library linked into passer-rating, and when you run it, there would be no call to printf().

Xcode 5 is subtler than that. When it sees the product of a library target used in another target, it knows to bring the library up-to-date, so the target that uses it gets the latest version. This is almost always what you want.

If it's not what you want (usually because you have to keep compatibility with an Xcode 3 project), use the Scheme editor. Open it by selecting **Product → Scheme → Edit Scheme...** (⌘ <). (On U.S. keyboards, this amounts to ⇧ ⌘ **period**.) The Scheme editor controls the environment in which targets are built and run.

Make sure passer-rating is selected in the popup at the top of the editor sheet that slides down, and select **Build** from the master list. Uncheck **Find Implicit Dependencies**. Click **OK** when you're finished.

Now you can choose which targets (dependencies) will be rebuilt when the consumer target is rebuilt. In this example, click the top item in the Project navigator to open the Target editor for the passer-rating target, and disclose the "Target Dependencies" phase. Click the **+** button to select the passer target, and **Add** it to the dependency list.

Then remove it, go back to the Scheme editor, and enable implicit dependencies again. There's no point in making yourself crazy.

Debugging a Dependent Target

One more thing. Suppose you develop a new interest in libpasser.a and want to debug it as it is called by the command-line tool. The tool and the function are produced by different targets; does that matter?

See for yourself: Set a breakpoint at the assignment to completionComponent. Run passer-rating.

Sure enough, the debugger stops the application at the breakpoint. Xcode will consolidate the debugging information across the targets that go into the current executable.

Summary

You've divided the passer-rating application into a main executable and a static library. It hardly deserves it, but it's just an example.

On the way, you created a target to assemble and build the files needed for the new library, and distributed files between the library and the main program. You added the libpasser.a library product to the main passer–rating target.

You saw that Xcode does right by you in two important ways: Adding the library to the application target not only linked the library into the application, it ensured that the library is always brought up-to-date when the application is built. And, it incorporated the debugging information from the library so you can examine the working of the library while the application is running.

Next, a chapter about hygiene.

7

Version Control

There isn't much to the passer-rating project—less than a hundred lines of source, plus the contents of the project file and the boilerplate man page—but you have already invested time and trouble in it. So far, you've only created three files, but soon you will be moving on from *creation* to *change*. If you're like most programmers, you are conservative of the code you've written. An old function may no longer be required, but it may still embody an insight into the underlying problem.

One solution might be simply to keep all of the obsolete code in your active source files, possibly commented out or guarded by #if 0 blocks, but this bloats the file and obscures code that actually *does* something. Once the revisions get more than one layer deep, it can be difficult to track which blocked-out stretch of code goes with which.

A *source-control* (or *version-control*) system is a database that keeps track of all of the files in a project and allows you to register changes to those files as you go. Version control frees you to make extensive changes secure in the knowledge that all the previous versions of each file are still available if you need to roll back your changes.

You may have heard of version control and concluded that it's only for large projects with many developers. It is true that it makes it much easier to manage large code bases and to coordinate the efforts of large teams. But even if you work alone:

- You will still make extensive changes to your source.
- You will still need to refer to previous versions.
- You will still need to revert to previous versions to dig yourself out of the holes you dug with those extensive changes.
- You will find it easier if you can make changes cleanly, rather than trying to make sure you caught all the obsolete code in comments and #if 0 blocks.
- You will likely need to work on more than one computer, each of which will contribute different changes to your code base.

As I said in Chapter 3, "Simple Workflow and Passive Debugging," if you are going to change your code, *ever*—if you save a file more than once—you ought to put it under version control. Xcode 5 makes it easy.

> **Note**
>
> Xcode 5 supports two version-control systems: Subversion and Git. Subversion is in wide use, but it has been overtaken by distributed systems like Git. Most open-source projects are now shared through public services like GitHub, or private repositories on the Net. Xcode's workflow has centered on Git since Xcode 4. I regret it, but for simplicity's sake, I'm only covering Git.

Taking Control

So I've convinced you. You want to get your project under source control. How do you start?

If you took my advice in Chapter 3, you've started already. When you place a new project on disk, Xcode offers a checkbox, **Create git repository on**, followed by a pop-up menu that defaults to **My Mac** (Figure 7.1). You checked it. The `passer-rating/` directory contains a hidden `.git/` directory that indexes the project, and Xcode tracks the files you add and edit.

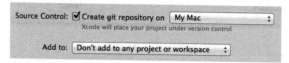

Figure 7.1   When you create a project, Xcode offers to create a local Git repository to control it.

If you used the Welcome window (**Window → Welcome to Xcode**, ⇧⌘1), you may have chosen **Check out an existing project**, which would have led you through the process of cloning a remote repository into your local storage. The cloning process creates a `.git` directory, and the copy is under the control of the local repository.

There is a third option. If you've registered an Xcode server in the **Accounts** tab of the Preferences window, the **Create git repository on** popup will include the name of that server. If you select it, Xcode will still create a `.git` directory for a local repository in your project directory, but it will also negotiate with your server to set up a remote repository on that machine. Other developers (or your other computers) will then be able to coordinate their work with a central copy of the project.

> **Note**
>
> Xcode Server is a feature of Mavericks Server. The server-management application includes a configuration panel for Xcode, just as it does for mail and the web. Mavericks Server is a simple add-on (early versions of OS X Server were pricey replacements for the retail OS) costing about $50 in the Mac App Store. As a paid member of the Mac Developer Program, you can download the current version for free.

Creating a Git Repository by Hand

Most of the time, you'll use the automated methods for creating or retrieving a local repository, and you don't have to think about it. Still, you must know how to bring an existing project under control if Git had never touched it.

There's one optional step I recommend: Create a `.gitignore` file to tell Git that certain files and directories are off limits. They won't be included in mass additions to the repository, and they won't be listed in status messages as unmanaged. It's simple. Open the Terminal application (/Applications/Utilities/Terminal) and get busy:

```
$ # Focus on the project's directory:
$ cd /path/to/my/project
$
$ # Enter the contents of the file, closing with control-D
$ cat > .gitignore
xcuserdata/
.DS_Store
^D
$ # Want to add other files?
$ # Include them in that last command,
$ # or append them to the existing .gitignore
$ # with "cat >> .gitignore" (two carets).
$
```

> **Note**
>
> Apple's distribution of Git already knows to ignore some files and directories.

> **Note**
>
> Xcode 5 and Mavericks do a bit of legerdemain with command-line developer tools like `git`. See "Command-Line Tools" in Chapter 1, "Getting Xcode."

```
$ # Add a Git repository to this directory:
$ git init
Initialized empty Git repository in
    /Users/xcodeuser/Desktop/MyProject/.git/
$
$ # Tell Git you want to control everything in "." (this
$ # directory tree), except for what's in .gitignore:
$ git add .
$
$ # Tell Git to record the files you added,
$ # logging it as "Initial commit"
$ git commit -m 'Initial commit'
[master (root-commit) f0d59bf] Initial commit
 9 files changed, 819 insertions(+)
 create mode 100644 .gitignore
 ...
```

This is all you need do so far as Git is concerned, but if the project was open while you did it, Xcode won't notice. You'll have to quit and restart Xcode before the **Source**

Control menu recognizes your project, and source-control status flags appear in the Project navigator.

Part of the metadata Git attaches to the files it tracks is the name and email address of the person who made each change, line by line. The first time you try to commit to a Git repository, if you have not configured your name and address, Git will balk and demand that you make the settings. It will give you examples of the commands you will have to issue.

If your first-ever repository was created by Xcode, this presents a problem. The first thing Xcode does with a new project is to commit almost all the files it instantiates from the project template. That commit will fail if you haven't set your Git identity. Xcode will display Git's message in an alert sheet, and the commit will not have gone through. You'll have to fix it in Terminal:

```
$ # Focus on the project directory (use your own path)
$ cd /path/to/my/project
$
$ # Set your metadata (your own address and name)
$ git config --global user.email "xcodeuser@example.com"
$ git config --global user.name "Xcode User"
$
$ # Do the commit Xcode couldn't
$ git commit -m 'Initial commit'
```

> **Note**
>
> Once the local repository is in place, you can also make up for the lack of a link to a remote repository. See the "Working with Remote Repositories" section later in this chapter.

The State of Your Files

Xcode presents a model of source control that is close to that of the version-control system you chose. Subversion and Git are different; I'll show you how Git sees files, and how Xcode reflects that view.

In Git's world, a file can be in one of six states:

- **Ignored**—The file's name matches a pattern in the .gitignore file. Git will never attempt to manage it, unless you explicitly add it to the repository.

- **Untracked**—Git sees the file, but it's neither in the repository nor staged for adding to the repository. There is no history of its previous contents. The git add command *stages* it for entry into the repository.

- **Modified**—In a way, a modified file isn't much different from an untracked one: Its contents won't go into the repository until it is staged. However, its previous contents *are* in the repository and can be compared against the current version, or restored. It, too, can be readied to commit its contents with the git add command.

- **Staged**—The file has been designated (with git add) for inclusion in the next commit. Why doesn't the add command simply put the modified/new contents into the repository? Because you usually make logical changes to your project in more than one file—a method in an .m file, its declaration in a header, and its use in other .m files—and it doesn't make sense to register or roll back changes that are only partway made. When you stage a file, you're assembling it into a conceptual group that will arrive in the repository all at once.

- **Unmerged**—You changed the file and attempted to pull in changes from another repository, and the two sets of changes couldn't be reconciled. Git marks the file to highlight the conflicts, and warns you if you attempt a commit without resolving the conflict. When you modify and restage the file, Git takes it that the conflicts are resolved and stops complaining.

- **Unmodified**—The file's current state, as registered with git commit, is what's in the repository. So far as Git is concerned, there's nothing more to be done with it unless you want to inspect or restore an earlier state. When you edit and save the file, it becomes "modified," and the add/commit cycle begins again.

If you delete a file, that counts as a modification. git rm will stage the deletion for the repository. If you move or rename a file, that's equivalent to a git rm of the file at its old location or name, and git add at the new one. git mv will do it all in one step. However you do it, Git will notice that the "old" and "new" files are identical, and the file's track in the history will be unbroken.

How Xcode Works with Git

Xcode's view of a Git repository is slightly different, because its demands as an IDE require another layer of abstraction. As Xcode presents them, files have five states:

- **Unmodified**, with no badge on the file's entry in the Project navigator. The file's history is in the repository, and you haven't saved any changes.

- **Modified**, with an **M** badge. The file is in a repository, but you've changed your working copy since it was last committed. Git will see these files as "modified," but not "staged." Xcode's version-control model has no "staged" status. When you commit a revision, Xcode lets you choose which files to include in the commit, and stages and commits them at the same time.

- **Added**, with an **A** badge. You've created a new file in the project (**File → New → File...**, ⌘N), or added an existing one and copied it to the project directory (**File → Add Files to...**, ⌥⌘A). Xcode *will* automatically stage added files, but will still let you withhold them from a commit.

- **Conflicted**, with a red **C** added to any other status indicator. When you merge changes from another repository into your own, it may not be possible to determine which lines from which files are to survive the merge—more on this soon. Xcode flags these with a **C** and will refuse further commits until you use **Source Control → Mark Selected Files as Resolved** to clear the conflicted state. Git's approach is slightly different: It tracks conflicted files, but clears the conflicts automatically when you edit and stage them.

See "Merges and Conflicts," in this chapter, for how you can resolve conflicts in a file.

- **Unknown**, marked **?**. The file is in the project directory, but not in the repository. This is equivalent to Git's "untracked" state.

Your First Commit

If you created a Git repository along with your project, Xcode has already done your first commit—all of the source files, and all of the configurations that aren't one-user-only are already in the repo.

But what about the first commit *you* do? Set up an experiment:

1. If you didn't have Xcode create a repository for the passer-rating project, use the techniques I just showed you to add one.
2. Open the passer-rating project.
3. If you just now created the local repository (and possibly restarted Xcode), the Project navigator will be full of files marked **M**. Otherwise, make a change to one of the files and save it; the file will pick up the **M** badge in a few seconds.
4. Select **Source Control** → **Commit. . .** (⌥ ⌘ C). A sheet will appear (Figure 7.2) showing your changes and offering a text-editing area for your notes on what you changed.

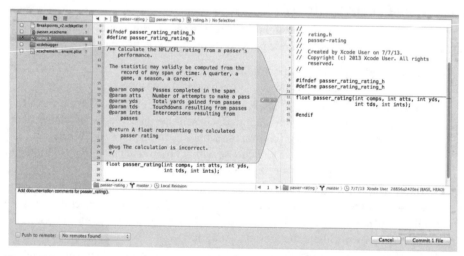

Figure 7.2   The Commit editor sheet contains a variant on the Comparison editor. It highlights the changes made in each file. The source list on the left side of the window allows you to withhold files by unchecking them. The file to be committed can still be edited. The area at the bottom receives your message describing the new revision. Xcode will not permit you to complete the commit without a message.

> **Note**
>
> The Commit editor, which shows the changes you're committing in a file, is a real editor. You can make last-moment changes, and those will be a part of the file as it is committed.

Working with Remote Repositories

Git is a *distributed* source-control system. To simplify, every developer has a repository containing the whole history of the project. The repositories are peers; in principle, none of them are authoritative. The concept that Subversion has of a single repository feeding the truth to clients in the form of snapshot copies of the project has no *inherent* expression in Git.

However, it's common to have such a central repository for a project, one on a machine that is continuously available, is backed up, and has a stable hostname and IP address. That way, multiple developers, or a single developer with more than one computer, can keep each other current.

Usually these are "bare" repositories, `cloned` or `inited` with the `--bare` option so they do not include the literal set of controlled files that developers would have in their working copies.

> **Note**
>
> A local working copy may be associated with more than one remote repository, but let's keep it simple.

Xcode has three ways to deal with remote repositories.

Cloning an Existing Repository

The remote is known to exist. You can clone it by selecting **Check out an existing project** from the Welcome window (⇧⌘1). The **Source Control →Check Out. . .** command has the same effect. Obviously, the remote repository was there; you wouldn't have a clone otherwise.

Creating a Repository with Xcode Server

The remote does not exist, but Xcode can make it exist. If you have an Xcode server registered in the **Accounts** tab of the Preferences window, you can ask the server to create a bare repo for you.

If your project has a local repository in its working copy, you can select the working copy in the **Source Control** menu, and then **Configure. . . .** The Configure Repository sheet will drop down; select the middle tab, **Remotes**.

Click the **+** button at lower left and select **Create New Remote. . . .** You'll be asked to identify the Xcode server from a list of the ones you registered in the **Accounts** preferences and to give it a name for local reference. (The name has to be usable by the Git tools; Xcode will reject names that don't fit the need.) See Figure 7.3, top right.

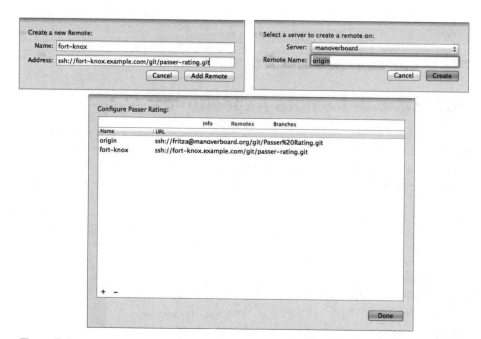

Figure 7.3   Using the Configure Repository sheet (bottom) available for a project in the **Source Control** menu, you can add an existing repository as a remote (left), or negotiate a completely new repository with an Xcode server (right).

Xcode logs into Xcode Server and negotiates the creation of the repo, and the server does the rest. Push your working copy onto the remote (**Source Control →Push. . .**, and select the remote and branch). You're done. On the server, the Server control application's **Xcode** panel shows the new repository (Figure 7.4).

Adding a Reference to a Repository

Selecting **Add Remote. . .** from the **+** button in the Configure Repository editor shows a simple dialog sheet that asks you for a local name and a URL for a repository (Figure 7.3, top right). Xcode updates your working copy's configuration with the pointer to the remote. Xcode will show the remote and its branches whenever you push or pull files with it.

Add Remote. . . has exactly the same effect as the most common variant of `git remote add` on the command line. That includes the fact that this is only a local, named *reference* to a remote repository. Creating the reference in Xcode does not ensure that the repo exists or is reachable.

Setting Up a "Remote"—Locally

You don't need a fancy purpose-made server to work with a remote repository. You don't even need another machine. You can do everything I'm going to show you in this chapter using a "remote" that's nothing more than a local file directory.

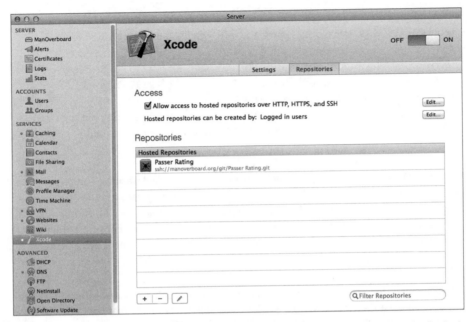

Figure 7.4   Adding a repository to an Xcode server from Xcode adds the new repo to the list in the control application on the server.

You're going to create a "bare" (no working files) repository in /Users/Shared/, marked as "shared," where all users can get at it. Open the Terminal, and do this:

```
$ # Work on the "Shared" user
$ cd /Users/Shared
$
$ # Create a directory for Git repositories...
$ mkdir git
$
$ # ... and work on that
$ cd git
$
$ # Create a shareable, bare repository named passer-rating.git
$ git init --bare --share=all passer-rating.git
Initialized empty Git repository in
    /Users/Shared/git/passer-rating.git/
$
$ # The directory contains just the repository infrastructure
$ ls -al passer-rating.git/
drwxrwxr-x  10 xcodeuser  wheel   340 Aug 19 12:12 .
drwxr-xr-x   3 xcodeuser  wheel   102 Aug 19 12:12 ..
```

```
-rw-rw-r--    1 xcodeuser   wheel    23 Aug 19 12:12 HEAD
drwxrwxr-x    2 xcodeuser   wheel    68 Aug 19 12:12 branches
-rw-rw-r--    1 xcodeuser   wheel   172 Aug 19 12:12 config
-rw-rw-r--    1 xcodeuser   wheel    73 Aug 19 12:12 description
drwxrwxr-x   11 xcodeuser   wheel   374 Aug 19 12:12 hooks
drwxrwxr-x    3 xcodeuser   wheel   102 Aug 19 12:12 info
drwxrwxr-x    4 xcodeuser   wheel   136 Aug 19 12:12 objects
drwxrwxr-x    4 xcodeuser   wheel   136 Aug 19 12:12 refs
$
```

With this, /Users/Shared/git/ includes a repository named passer-rating.git.
It's a "bare" repository because there is no working directory containing files you can edit
and check in, and there never will be. Its sole purpose is to hold work from other clients.
The --shared flag tells Git that whenever it makes changes to the repository, they should
be given filesystem permissions that preserve other users' access to the repo.

> **Note**
>
> Readers have felt cheated that this "remote" repository isn't on a different machine, but
> that's not what the term means in Git. A remote repository is one that isn't your local
> repo. It doesn't matter where it is—it could even be another subdirectory of your home
> account. Simply add an item to the Repositories list in the **Accounts** panel of the
> Preferences window, and enter a URL—file, ssh, http, whatever—giving the host and
> path for the repo, and your credentials to access it. Once the link is established, Git hides
> the details of where the remote actually is. As I write this book, I'm using a repo on an
> Xcode server because it fits my workflow and I want to demonstrate some other features,
> but you can follow along with a file remote and see no difference.

> **Note**
>
> What, by the way, is a Git server? Git transactions can take place over HTTP or HTTPS,
> but the most common setup for small teams is a Unix box running an ssh server, on which
> the stock Git package has been installed. That's it. There is no software package that is a
> "Git server." And not every remote repository is a server, anyway—all repos are peers,
> and it's perfectly legitimate to push and pull revisions with another developer's local
> repository. There are far too many variants to cover in this book; I'll recommend complete
> guides later in this chapter and in Appendix B, "Resources."

Return to your passer-rating project in Xcode, and from the **Source Control** menu,
select your local repository and branch, and then **Configure passer-rating...** (or
whatever your local is named). The Configure Remote editor appears as I showed earlier
in this chapter. In the **Remotes** tab, select **Add Remote...** from the + popup menu.
Name the remote **origin** (the expected name for the primary remote) and enter the
URL **file:///Users/Shared/git/passer-rating.git**.

You're now ready to use the origin repository using exactly the same techniques no
matter where it's located.

Pushing to the Remote

New bare repositories have absolutely no content, and if you try to clone (retrieve a new copy) from one, you'll get an error message from Git. You have to push your files into the remote, thus filling its database with your files and the history they accumulated back to the creation of your local repo.

Select **Source Control** → **Push.** . . . Your project may be associated with many remotes, each remote may hold many branches, and you may want to add one of your local branches to the remote. (More about branches soon, in the "Branching" section.) So Xcode presents a dialog sheet (Figure 7.5) for you to specify exactly what you want.

Figure 7.5 Selecting **Source Control** → **Push.** . . drops a concise dialog with which you can designate what remote, and branch within the remote, you want to push to. If you have a local branch that the remote does not, the popup menu will include the option of creating the branch on the remote.

If you got here by adding a regular remote repo by hand, you weren't sure the remote existed or was reachable—that's not how Git works, it's just a convenience name for a URL. When the push dialog appears, Xcode pauses briefly before filling the remote/branch popup. In that period, Xcode *does* verify that the remote exists and accepts connections; if it doesn't, Xcode won't add it to the popup.

Click **Push**. The dialog will show an activity spinner as the push is negotiated with the remote and your changes are transferred. When it's done, a green checkmark badge appears briefly, and the sheet retracts.

Merges and Conflicts

All your work so far has been done under one user account on your Mac; call that "User A." Let's imagine that User A is working with User B. For the sake of example, User B will be played by a second account on the same Mac. In practice, your collaborators will be other people—or you—using different computers.

User B doesn't have a copy of the passer-rating project, but we've already seen how easy it is for her to get one. She can

- Open the Welcome to Xcode window (⇧⌘1), and select **Check out an existing project**; or
- Select **Source Control** → **Check Out.** . . .

Xcode will present a window that lists some repositories it already knows about, plus a text field for the URL of any other. Xcode knows about some repositories because you registered them in the **Accounts** panel of the Preferences window. And, of course, it knows about remotes you added to other projects.

But User B is a stranger to all of that. She'll have to enter the URL for the passer-rating repository and click **Next**. The checkout window shows progress bars as it goes through the process of gaining access to the remote, and then offers a get-file sheet for her to select a directory to receive the project folder.

> **Note**
>
> Or, User B might be given a window telling her that whatever is at the other end of the URL she entered "doesn't appear to be a git repository," which could mean anything. It covers bad credentials, bad connection, bad URL... but the usual explanation is a bad URL. Consult whoever gave you the URL and a Git tutorial for the formats Git expects for remote URLs.

With that, User B has a complete copy of the master branch of the passer-rating directory, including the complete revision history. The remote from which she checked out is linked to the local repo as `origin`, and pushes and pulls go through it by default.

User A

User A has definite ideas about code style. In particular, he doesn't like the long identifiers in `rating.c` for the components of the passer rating. He does a search-and-replace to change all instances of *Component* to *Comp*.

Change: Replace All in File

He did this by selecting **Find →Find. . .** (⌘ F), and typing `Component` into the text field that slides down into the editor. As he typed, the editor highlighted its contents to show the matching text. He has a choice of options from a popover window he can summon by clicking the magnifying-glass icon in the search field and selecting **Edit Find Options. . .**

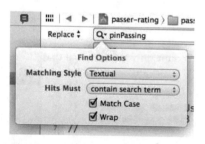

Figure 7.6   Selecting **Edit Find Options. . .** from the drop-down menu attached to the search badge brings up a popover box to adapt in-file searches to your needs.

from the drop-down menu (Figure 7.6). He can search by literal text or regular expression, whether the match must be at the beginning, at the end, anywhere in, or all of a word. He can make the search case sensitive, and let it wrap around to the start of the document when it reaches the end.

He definitely wants to make the search case sensitive, so as not to disturb the `component` parameter to `pinPassingComponent`.

If he wants more flexibility, but doesn't want to bother with regular expressions, he can stick with a text search, set the insertion point in the search field, and select **Insert Pattern** (^⌥⌘P). This will show a drop-down with common wildcard patterns, like word characters, various kinds of whitespace, and even email, IP, and web addresses. Selecting one adds it to the search text.

> **Note**
>
> You'll wish it did more. The great thing about wildcard patterns in regular-expression searches is that you can pick out the actual content the wildcard matched and use that to refine the search or build the replacement. When you use the simplified find patterns, once the pattern matches, you have no access to the details.

To replace, he clicks the popup menu at the left end of the search bar, and changes it from **Find** to **Replace**. (Or he could have selected **Find → Find and Replace...**, ⌥⌘F, in the first place.) Another field appears to receive the replacement text. It offers three actions: **Replace** substitutes the replace-field contents for the last-found text in the document. **All** does the replacement for every instance of the match. And if he holds down the Option key, **All** will become **All in Selection**. He wanted to cover the whole file, so he released the Option key and clicked **All**.

> **Note**
>
> If User A wanted to do a replace-in-selection, he'd have to do a dance that other editors don't require. The usual way is to make your selection, enter the find and replace strings, and call for in-selection replacement. It can't work that way for Xcode because in-file searches are incremental: You can't set up a search-and-replace without losing your selection in favor of the search results. So User A would have had to enter his search and replacement text first, then select the range he wanted to operate on.

Change and Conflict: The Copyright Claim

Also, he's noticed that Xcode has copyrighted all the files to Xcode User (see the sidebar). That's not right; all the work is being done by hire for me. He uses the Find navigator to replace every instance with "Frederic F. Anderson." I'll show you how User B did the same thing later in this chapter.

Selective Commits

Ideally, Git revisions represent coordinated changes to the project. Each commit serves a discrete purpose, even if more than one file is changed. User A has made edits for two purposes—fixing the copyright and cleaning up the variable names. If you followed the ideal of conceptual revisions, that's now a problem because `rating.c` embodies both. On the other hand, it's against human nature to expect a programmer to edit a file, accomplish one task, commit it, and only then make changes for the other task.

Git accommodates this with a "cherrypicking" option to its `add` command, and Xcode takes it further. The marker between the last-committed and uncommitted versions of a group of lines has two controls (Figure 7.7). The right end of the marker drops down a menu allowing you to exclude the change from the planned commit or to remove the change from the uncommitted file entirely. The left end of the marker is a toggle: If it is a checkmark, the change will be checked in; if it's a prohibition mark, the change ribbon

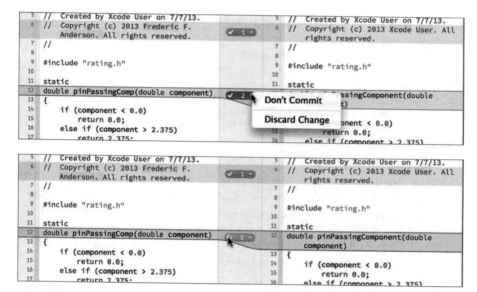

Figure 7.7   (top) Xcode's Commit sheet offers two ways to manage multiple changes to a file. The drop-down menu disclosed from the right end of the change marker lets you withhold a change from this commit, or even abandon the change for good. (bottom) The check/prohibit toggle button is a more convenient way to withhold a change. The second range of lines has turned gray, showing they will not be committed.

will turn gray, and the commit won't include that change. This is another example of how Xcode's version-control support puts a wrapper on the technical details of the underlying system.

User A does two commits, unchecking the copyright changes for the first, and letting every remaining change go through in the second. Eventually, he'll push his accumulated commits into the shared repository.

Whose Project Is It?

Xcode's templates for source files include a standard comment at the beginning showing the name of the file (which it knows because it created and named the file), the date it was created (because it knows when it created it), the name of the person who created the file, and a copyright notice (the year of which it knows from when it created the file). The names of the creator and copyright holder may surprise you. How did it get those?

Like any modern operating system, OS X has user accounts under which all user applications run. When you set up your Mac on its first run, you gave a short user name and longer natural name to the first, administrative user of the computer. If you added accounts, you provided natural names for those users, too. Xcode fills in the "Created by" line of the comment from that natural name.

The copyright claim includes a copyright holder and a year, as by law it must. Xcode *could* fill this in from the user's natural name, but that's almost never necessary. When you create a project or target, Xcode asks you for an **Organization Name**, which it uses for the copyright holder. For your own work, you'd enter your name (Fritz Anderson), but if it's work for hire, you'd enter the name of the owner of the project (The University of Chicago).

Failing that, Xcode will use the company name on the "Me" card in the Contacts application. Failing *that*, it will use the full name on the "Me" card.

If you don't set an organization name at the start, you can always select the project itself in the Project navigator (top item in the list), open the File inspector (expose the Utility area on the right, and select the first tab, which looks like a sheet of paper), and edit the **Organization** field.

User B

User B is a stickler for copyright, too. She replaces all of the claims by "Xcode User" in her copy with "Fritz Anderson." Also, she sets the **Organization** name in the Project inspector, so the problem won't come up again.

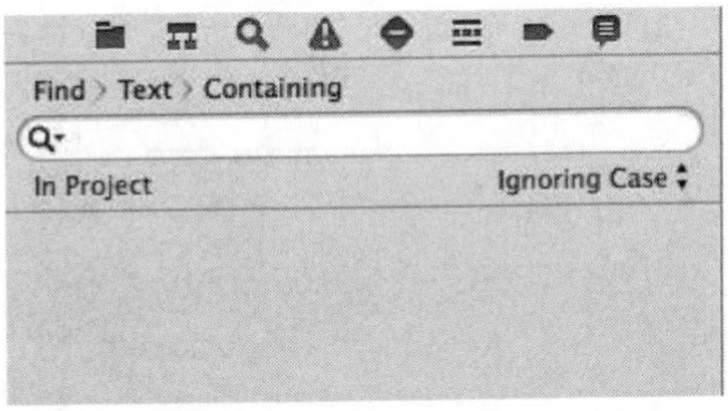

She makes her changes to the copyright notice using a global search-and-replace. She starts by selecting the Find navigator (third tab), or **Find →Find in Project. . .** (⇧ ⌘ F).

The Find navigator contains a search field and some options (Figure 7.8).

Figure 7.8   The Find navigator presents a search field and affordances for configuring the search.

We'll get back to the options in detail, but what she sees is

- At the top, a path control cascading from the action (**Find**) through the search type and word-boundary selections (**Text** and **Containing** by default). She wants to do a replace, not just a find, so she clicks the first segment and changes it to **Replace**.

- A button that says **In Project**, to select the file set the search is to cover. She clicks it to see the options, and the provision for creating her own, then clicks it again; an in-project search is just what she wants.

- A popup menu to choose case sensitivity. It doesn't matter now, but she should remember to look, or she'll get more or less than she expects.

- The magnifying-glass drop-down in the search field itself gives a history of recent searches, and the same character-pattern palette the in-file search field offers.

User B types **Xcode User** in the search field and presses Return. The list below it fills with all the matches, organized by file, showing each match in context. It's only a single line, but it's better than nothing, and it's not much trouble to click an entry to get the whole story. See Figure 7.9.

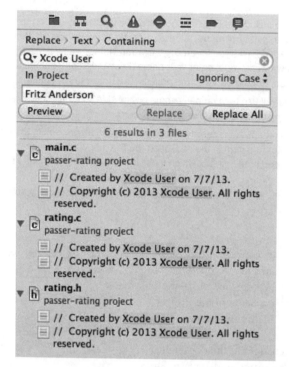

Figure 7.9   The results of a find-in-project come in the form of a table grouped by file, showing the matches in a one-line context. The Find navigator has been switched over to Replace mode and is ready to replace all instances of "Xcode User" with "Fritz Anderson."

> **Note**
> The buttons that execute a global replace won't be active until a search has been done. You're not allowed to fly blind.

User B has a problem: She wants to correct the copyright claim, but the files should still identify Xcode User as the creator. She has more matches than she wants. She has two ways to deal with this:

- She can command-click on each instance she wants to replace, and then click **Replace** (which is now active, because there would be a difference between replacing just the selections and doing a **Replace All**, which would replace all instances, selected or not).

- She can click **Preview**.

If she opts for a preview, a variant of the familiar Comparison editor drops (Figure 7.10) containing a source list of all the matches, and the after-and-before contents at each match. Click the toggles to accept or reject each replacement. She rejects the creator credits, and clicks **Replace**.

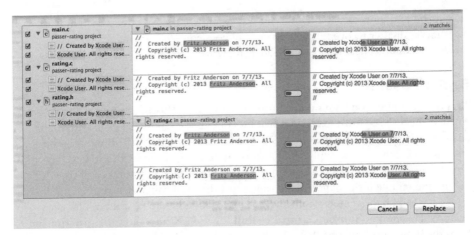

Figure 7.10   Clicking the **Preview** button in the multi-file replace view displays a comparison of each match, after and before the replacement. A toggle at each match lets you accept or reject the changes.

This being the first time she issues a command with project-wide effects, Xcode will drop a sheet offering to take a *snapshot* of the project (Figure 7.11). A snapshot is an archive of the whole project that provides a last-resort way to revert to the state of the project before the change.

You can recover the snapshot through the **Projects** panel of the Organizer window (⇧ ⌘ 2); select your project and a snapshot, and a button below the snapshot list will offer to **Export Snapshot**. Xcode uses the word "export" advisedly—the result will be a separate directory with the contents of the snapshot, not a reversion of the project you're working on.

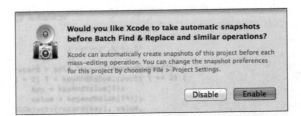

Figure 7.11   The first time you attempt a project-wide change, Xcode offers to create a snapshot that preserves the current state of the project.

You can change your mind about snapshots by selecting **File** → **Project Settings...** and editing the **Snapshots** tab.

Snapshots mimic the habits of developers who don't practice version control, but they aren't a replacement. It's awkward to do them frequently, there is no way to segregate changes by their purpose, and there is no way to browse the back versions. Think of snapshots as disaster recovery if version control goes completely wrong.

User B commits her changes to the local repository, and then pushes it.

Back to User A

This is where User A does his push (**Source Control** →**Push. . .**). And it doesn't work. An alert sheet slides down to tell him that his copy of the repository, even without his changes, had fallen behind the one he's trying to push to. ("Behind" in the colloquial sense is a difficult word to apply to a network of developers whose files, as here, are actually newer than the remote repository reflects. In version control, a local copy is behind the remote if the remote has changes that the local hasn't seen yet.)

He has to pull the remote's contents into his local set before he can push his own changes. He chooses **Source Control** →**Pull. . .** (⌥⌘X); he selects **origin/master** from the popup (it should be the only choice) and clicks **Pull**. An activity indicator spins while Git retrieves the remote's content, and then a progress pie says Xcode is "detecting conflicts" in what it found.

And it found some, in all three of the files he was trying to push. If this were command-line Git, this would be tedious, because you'd have to refer to the list of conflicts, then hunt down the markup Git adds to the conflicted files, remember which versions of the conflicted lines you want to keep, save your decisions, and use `git add` to put them in the staging list.

Merging Revisions

Xcode reduces this to the point where your only headache is in deciding what version is to prevail. Immediately upon detecting the conflicts, it tells you that you can't proceed with your push until you've examined them all and made your choices. The source list at the left side of the comparison sheet that appears lists every file that would be altered by the pull (Figure 7.12). Some of these are benign—Git could figure out how to merge the changes line-by-line—but if there is a line that was changed by the two contributors after their versions split from their common ancestor, Git can't make a choice. You have to resolve it.

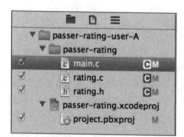 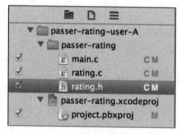

Figure 7.12   (left) When you pull a version of the working files that conflicts with your own, Xcode's Merge editor lists the conflicted files with a red **C** marker. (right) Once the conflicts are resolved, the **C** markers turn gray, and you can complete the pull.

`rating.c` is the most interesting file—it contains a conflicted line, but also some lines Git had no trouble choosing. User A's local version is more or less on the left, and the version that would be pulled is on the right. A control at the bottom of the editor (Figure 7.13) lets him pick which version he wants of each group of lines.

Figure 7.13 The control at the bottom of the Merge editor gives you four choices for resolving differences between the local and remote versions of a group of lines: The local version followed by the remote; the local version; the remote version; or the remote followed by the local. The options to use both versions are available only for conflicts.

> **Note**
>
> I say "more or less" because there are three things to show—your version, the remote's version, and the result of your choices between them—and Xcode makes do with only two views. The view on the left shows the result of your choices. You can see your lines, but only if you opt to use them in the final merge. The control implies you'd be choosing the version "on the left," but it's not visible on the left until you choose it.

Lines without Conflicts

Let's start with the easy part: the lines that don't conflict. By default, command-line Git does unconflicted merges automatically: If only one version has changed a line since the common ancestor of the two, the change wins.

Xcode gives you more control. The Merge editor draws blue ribbons to highlight each group of changed lines, with a marker in the middle that looks like a sliding switch. The local version is on the left, and the remote is on the right. The slider points to the version that wins. You can't use the marker directly. Instead, select the ribbon for a change group (look for the outline a selected group picks up—it's easy to miss), and use the control at the bottom of the editor sheet to make your choice. See Figure 7.14. The options to use both versions, one after the other, aren't available for unconflicted lines.

```
29                                                    29
30    double        completionComponent =             30    double        completionComponent =
31                  (((double) comps / atts) *        31                  (((double) comps / atts) *
                    100.0 - 30.0) / 20.0;                            100.0 - 30.0) / 20.0;
32    completionComponent = pinPassingComponent        32    completionComponent = pinPassingComponent
      (completionComponent);                                 (completionComponent);
33                                                    33
34    double        yardageComp =                      34    double        yardageComponent =
35                  (((double) yds / atts) -           35                  (((double) yds / atts) -
                    0.3) / 4.0;                                          0.3) / 4.0;
36                  // intentional bug                 36                  // intentional bug
37    yardageComp = pinPassingComp(yardageComp);       37    yardageComponent = pinPassingComponent
38                                                           (yardageComponent);
39    double        touchdownComponent =               38
```

Figure 7.14 Git doesn't let you pick and choose groups of lines to be merged from a pull, but Xcode displays all the potential changes and lets you choose whether to accept them.

Conflicted Lines

That leaves the conflicts. User A and User B started with a common version that claimed copyright for Xcode User. Independently, they changed the claims, using different names. Git has no way to prefer one over the other, so it reports a conflict and forces you to decide. Conflicted lines are joined by red ribbons, again with a lozenge in the middle. But this time, there is no slider: With no way to choose, the lozenge contains a question mark (Figure 7.15, top).

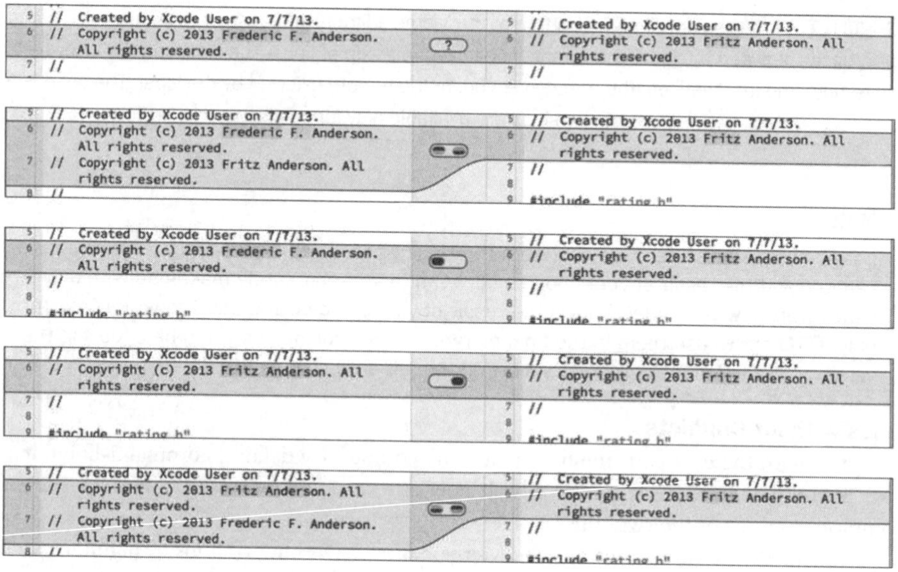

Figure 7.15   (top) When part of a file has picked up independent edits since the last common revision, it's a conflict, which Xcode highlights in red. Because it can't choose between them, the marker in the middle of the highlight ribbon contains a question mark. The control at the bottom of the Merge sheet lets you choose among (second through last) local-before-remote, local, remote, and remote-before-local.

It's up to User A to resolve the conflict, using the control at the bottom of the sheet. In this case, he'll concede User B's use of "Fritz Anderson" and select the third segment (use remote) of the control. For the rest, the no-conflict lines, he's adamant about those shortened variable names. He picks the second segment (use local) to keep his changes.

With all the conflicts cleared (see the source list on the right side of Figure 7.12), Xcode enables the **Pull** button, and only then does User A's working set reflect the results.

Committing the Choices

Deconflicting edits are no different from any other kind of edit. They're present on disk, but not in any repository. As with any other modified files, the Project navigator flags them with **M** badges. User A must commit the merged files to his local repository (providing a commit message explaining the merge), and then push the state of his repo out to the remote. Assuming the remote hasn't picked up any more changes from User B, the push goes through.

He can send an email to User B to let her know there are changes for her to pull. Or he could just let her discover them for herself, but that says something worrisome about how A and B are getting along.

The Version Editor

Checking files into version control, or even merging them, is not much use if you can't see what you changed. Xcode's Version editor (third segment of the **Editor** control in the toolbar) lets you do just that. Click the Version editor segment and hold the mouse button down (Figure 7.16). The Version editor has three views:

- You'll use the **Comparison** editor most frequently; you've already seen it, in specialized forms, whenever refactoring or version-control actions require a side-by-side display of changes.

- **Blame** displays files broken up to reflect which commit was responsible for the current version of a line.

- The **Log** view lists all commits that affected the current file.

I'll cover each, starting with the Comparison view.

Figure 7.16   The right segment of the **Editor** control anchors a drop-down menu to select the three version-control editing styles.

Comparison

If you've been following along, the passer-rating project has accumulated a few revisions by a couple of authors. Select one of your source files and switch the editor to the Version view. It splits into two panels: The left side shows your file in its current state, saved or not. The right side shows what it looked like the last time you committed it. See Figure 7.17.

Just now, they're probably identical, but try editing the current copy of the file. A blue band appears across the editor, stretching from your changes to the equivalent position in the committed version. If you made changes within a line, the differences are highlighted in a muted yellow.

The editor panes are real editors: You can make any changes you want, though any changes you make to a committed version won't stick. Between the columns, in each of

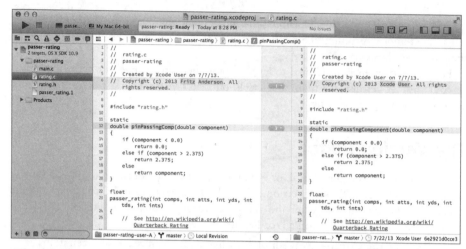

Figure 7.17   The Comparison view of the Version editor puts two versions of a file side by side, with a highlight connecting the changes you made between the two versions. The jump bar at the bottom lets you select among versions and branches.

the change ribbons, is a numbered marker. Clicking it selects that change; once a change ribbon is selected, you can move rapidly among them with the Up- and Down-Arrow keys. The triangle at the right end of the marker signals a drop-down menu with the single command **Discard Change**, letting you wind those lines back to their form in the earlier revision.

> **Note**
>
> If you just want to abandon all the changes you made to a file since the last revision, there's no need to do it piecemeal. Right-click the file in the Project navigator and select **Source Control** →**Discard Changes...** from the contextual menu. If you expose the File inspector in the Utility area, a section will give the full details of the file's version-control status, including a **Discard...** button. If you want to abandon the changes to all your files, there's **Source Control** →**Discard All Changes....**

The editor isn't confined to the last two versions. You'll find a jump bar at the bottom of each pane, with segments representing the repository, branch, and revision the pane displays. Each segment is a popup menu; you can set the halves of the editor to any revision you like, and you'll be shown the differences between them.

There's an even easier way to select revisions. Click the clock icon at the bottom of the gutter between the panes. You'll be rewarded with a timeline, a black bar with hash marks; the shorter marks represent the revisions that affect this file, the longer ones dates. See Figure 7.18. Move your mouse pointer over the timeline; Xcode displays a popover showing the date, the revision ID, the committer, and the description for that version.

There are arrowheads on either side of the timeline. Clicking the timeline moves the arrow on that side to the click location, and that side of the editor is filled with that revision of the file.

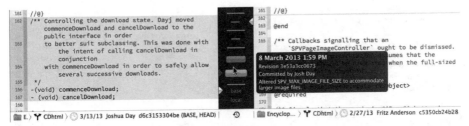

Figure 7.18 Clicking the clock icon at the bottom of the center column of the Comparison editor reveals a timeline of revisions for the current file. Hovering the mouse cursor over a tick displays information about that revision. Clicking to either side of a tick will display the corresponding version in the editor view on that side.

The graphical Comparison editor is a great way to visualize the changes in your code, but it's not usable if you want to communicate the differences to others. You could give them full access to your repositories, urge them to buy Macs, sign up as Apple developers, and install Xcode; or you could select **Editor → Copy Source Changes**, which will put a listing of the differences, in the style of the `diff` command-line tool, onto the clipboard.

Blame

The Comparison view shows your revisions along one axis, the accumulated changes between two revisions. The Blame view lets you see another: who wrote what parts of your current file, when, and why. Choose **Blame** from the Version-editor segment in the toolbar to expose the Blame view.

> **Note**
>
> "Blame" is the technical name for this perspective on a version-control system and probably reflects the mood of developers when they want to track down the perpetrator of this or that change. Subversion tactfully offers "credit" as a synonym.

The right-hand panel in the editor goes away, to be replaced by a column of annotations. Each note matches up to lines in your code. At minimum, it shows the author and date of the last commit that changed those lines; if room permits, the annotation will include the commit message. See Figure 7.19. You can get the full details of any commit by clicking the information button in the annotation box.

As always, you can select any revision from the jump bar at the bottom of the editor to see how contributions arrived and were overwritten over the history of the file.

Log

The Log view gives a third perspective on the history of a file. Select **Log** from the Version editor's drop-down menu in the toolbar. Again, you see a single view of the file, in the revision you select from the jump bar. The column to the right shows the full information for every revision that affected that file, and only those revisions.

Revisions that have files uniquely associated with them (merges don't) include a notation like **Show 2 modified files**. Clicking the notation drops a comparison-browser

Figure 7.19   (top) The Blame column annotates each group of lines in a file with the details of the commit that was responsible for them. Bigger blocks of lines permit more information to be shown. The bars at the right margin are more intense for more recent revisions. (bottom) Clicking the information button in an annotation pops up the full details of the commit, including address-book information about the person responsible, so you can render your compliments at the click of a mouse.

sheet with a source list containing every file in that revision and a side-by-side comparison of the selected file after and before the commit.

> **Note**
>
> The `git` command-line tool will give you something similar that might suit you better: `git log –name-only` will print every revision in the current history, with the commit messages and a list of the files that were changed in each.

Branching

One more thing. Programming is not a linear activity. I've gone through the revision process as though it were a unitary march of progress with every step leading surely to a bigger, better program. That's not real life. In real life, you have ideas that may or may not be useful in your product, and you shouldn't pollute the often-parallel progress of your "good" revisions while you play with them.

You do this with *branching*, which lets you accumulate revisions along separate lines (branches) of development and merge them as you need. passer-rating (so far) is too simple to provide a good example, so I'll just explain how it works; you can follow along with Figure 7.20.

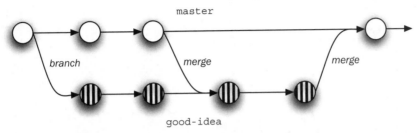

Figure 7.20   The main line of development of this project goes along the revisions in the `master` branch. A developer has an idea she wants to try out, so she creates the `good-idea` branch, occasionally merging in the improvements from `master`. When she's done, the `good-idea` changes can be folded back into `master`.

Every project in Git or Subversion starts with one branch, which Git calls `master`. This example begins with just the one branch. Our developer comes up with a good idea and creates a branch she calls `good-idea` (the quality of her ideas doesn't extend to the names she makes up). She does this by selecting **New Branch...** from her working copy's submenu in the **Source Control** menu. A sheet appears so she can give the branch its name, and she clicks **Create**. The sheet shows an activity spinner, reports success, and goes away. The local repository is now focused on `good-idea`.

She then does the normal work of revising and testing her program. In the mean time, she also needs to maintain the program on the `master` branch, which reflects what has gone out to users, and which other developers are using as the common meeting point for their own revisions. She switches back to the `master` branch using the **Source Control** →**working copy** →**Switch to Branch...** command. The command summons a sheet displaying all branches, local and remote, that are available to her; she selects `master`, clicks **Switch**, and gets busy. See Figure 7.21.

In Figure 7.20, both branches progress by a couple of revisions, and she decides her work on `good-idea` can't proceed without taking account of changes made to `master`. She can do this by selecting **Source Control** →**working copy** →**Merge from Branch...** if she is on the `good-idea` branch; she selects the source branch (`master`) from the picker sheet, and clicks **Merge**. Or, if she is on the `master` branch, she selects **Merge into Branch...** and selects `good-idea`.

Either way, she'll be presented with the merge-comparison sheet so she can review the changes and approve them one by one.

She makes a few more revisions to `good-idea` before she is satisfied that her idea really was good and it's ready to go into the main branch. She selects **Merge into Branch...**, chooses the `master` branch, and completes the final merge.

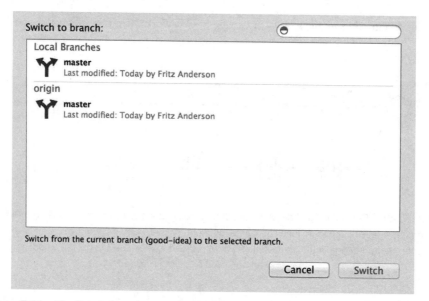

Figure 7.21   The Switch-Branch sheet displays all available branches, local and remote. (Remote branches may take a few seconds to appear if getting a list entails a network transaction.) Selecting a branch and clicking **Switch** checks the files on that branch out into the working copy.

Summary

This was a long chapter, but there's a lot to version control, and the benefits of mastering it are immense. When you created your first project, Xcode provided a Git repository automatically, just by your checking a box. If you had registered an account on an Xcode server, you could even have Xcode hook you up with a fresh remote repository. In this chapter, you began to use it, committing your work step by step. Then you were able to compare versions of your work to see what was done when, and to get a measure of forgiveness, of which there is not enough in this world.

Xcode's support for Git and Subversion is good enough for day-to-day work, but it's not comprehensive. You dipped into the command line to round out repository management. There is much more to Subversion and Git than I can cover in one chapter. The command-line interfaces to those packages are very powerful, and you should at least look at them to learn what's available. The best resources are:

- **Git**—*Pro Git*, the best beginner-to-advanced treatment of Git. You can read it online for free at `http://git-scm.com/book`, but consider supporting Scott Chacon, the author, by buying a physical or electronic copy.

- **Subversion**—*Version Control with Subversion*, written by (some of) the authors of Subversion and revised with each release of the tool. Find it at `http://svnbook.red-bean.com/`.

In particular, seek out and understand the idea of tagging a revision, which allows you to mark the place in your project's history that corresponds to (for instance) a release. Tagging is the biggest gap in Xcode's version-control support.

This takes me to the end of my generic introduction to Xcode. Now that you have a background, you can proceed to the tasks Xcode was really built for: producing graphical applications for iOS and OS X.

Part II

The Life Cycle of an iOS Application

## 8

Starting an iOS Application

Now that you have the basic skills down, let's move on to a real project. You'll build an iPhone application that manages a list of quarterbacks and displays their game and career statistics.

Planning the App

Before coding, it's best (though not customary) to know what you're doing. Specifically, what are you going to present to the app's user, what data do you need to keep to make that presentation, and how do you translate between the data and the presentation?

Model-View-Controller

The Model-View-Controller (MVC) design pattern formalizes those questions into an architecture for graphical applications. The Cocoa Touch application framework is designed to implement applications that follow the MVC pattern. If you don't follow it, you will find yourself "fighting the framework": Winning through to a finished application would be difficult, and maintaining it would be miraculous. The Xcode development tools are designed to support Cocoa programming and therefore the MVC pattern. MVC divides the functionality of an application into three parts, and each class in the application must fall into one of them:

- Model objects embody the data and logic of a particular problem domain. Models tend to be unique to each application. You can create your own subclasses of NSObject or NSManagedObject to give life to your models.

- View objects handle user interaction, presenting information and enabling the user to manipulate data or otherwise influence the behavior of the program. Views are usually drawn from a repertoire of standard elements, such as buttons, tables, scrollers, and text fields. Views ideally know nothing about any problem domain: A button can display itself and report taps without needing to know what tapping means to your application. In iOS, views are instances of UIView or its many subclasses.

- Controller objects mediate between the pure logic of the model and the pure mechanics of the views. A controller object decides how views display and how user actions translate into model events. In iOS, controllers are almost always instances of subclasses of `UIViewController`.

Okay, in practice some classes won't fall exactly into model, view, or controller. If you have a view custom-built to display your particular data, making that view completely independent of your data model makes no sense. Still, MVC is an important discipline: If you fudge on it, you should be aware that you're fudging and consider whether you can restore the MVC separation.

The Model

From the nature of a passer rating, all you need is one model class: a `Passer` to carry one passer's name, and the total attempts, completions, yards, touchdowns, and interceptions. Let's make this a little more interesting: Ratings can be calculated over as many attempts as you like and are usually calculated per-game as well as in a career aggregate. So `Passer` should "own" any number of `Game` objects, with details of the game (who played, what date, and so on) as well as the passing statistics for that game.

The model then looks like the diagram presented in Figure 8.1.

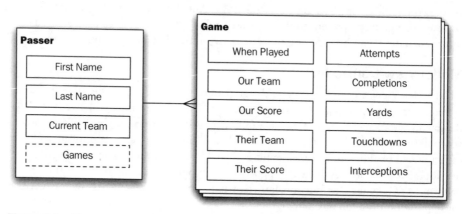

Figure 8.1   The summary description of what data a passer-rating app would need leads to the plan shown in this diagram: A `Passer` object serves only to identify a single player; his career statistics are in a set of `Game` objects that `Passer` "owns."

What about a passer's aggregate statistics—the career yards, touchdowns, and rating? Those can be pulled out of his `Games`—it will turn out not to be hard at all.

The Views

iOS applications don't usually have a concept of documents, but even simple ones acquire many screens' worth of views. You'll deal in passers and their games, and you need to view and edit both.

You need a list of passers, who can be created or edited in a separate view; and a view devoted to a selected passer, with a list of games that need a view of their own to create or edit them. A sketch of the flow appears in Figure 8.2.

> **Note**
>
> That's what a full version of Passer Rating should look like, and getting it down on paper is an essential step. Alas, this book will run out of Xcode examples before we complete the app.

Typically, each phase of an iOS application displays a view object—a UIView—that fills the screen. That main view usually contains a hierarchy of other views. For instance, the

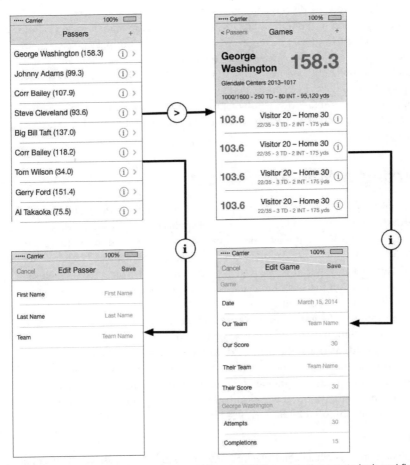

Figure 8.2   A rough sketch shows how we'd like the iOS Passer Rating app to look and flow. It starts (top left) with a list of passers. Tapping a row shows the detailed record for that passer (top right). The user can add or edit passers (bottom left) and games (bottom right).

`Passer` editor at the lower-left corner of the sketch (refer to Figure 8.2) consists of a wrapper `UIView`; it contains a navigation bar (`UINavigationItem`, at the top), which in turn contains two buttons (`UIBarButtonItem`, at either end). It also contains a table (`UITableView`) with three rows (`UITableViewCell`), each containing a label (`UILabel`) and a text-entry field (`UITextField`).

The Controllers

iOS applications are organized around a sequence of view controllers, objects derived from `UIViewController`. Each view controller mediates between model objects and the views that fill the device's screen. For each full-screen view you see in the sketch, you must provide a `UIViewController` subclass to link the data in the model to the views on the screen. In the life cycle of a view, the controller comes first; when it is initialized, it creates or loads the view objects and sets them up to reflect the model.

Now, even a simple application like this slides four main views onto and off of the screen, according to a precise hierarchy. Managing the relationships between them—which to slide in, which to slide back to—would seem to be an involved task, and it is. But, thankfully, it is not a task you need to worry much about. UIKit, the user-facing part of iOS, provides umbrella view controllers (such as `UINavigationController`) that manage the navigation tasks for you by taking ownership of your controller objects. All you need to do is request a transition between the views, and the umbrella takes care of the rest.

Starting a New iOS Project

Start by creating a new Xcode project, selecting **File → New → Project...** (⇧⌘N). Select **Application** under **iOS**, and from the array of application types, select Master-Detail Application. Passer Rating follows the common pattern of presenting a progression of lists and detail views, under a navigation bar that provides a "breadcrumb" trail back up the tree. The Master-Detail Application template is a skeleton for such an app. Click **Next**.

The next panel in the New Project assistant lets you name the project **Passer Rating**. That much is obvious.

The next item is **Organization Name**; whenever Xcode creates a new text file, it includes a copyright notice, and this is to be the name of the holder.

Company Identifier is the next field. Every application in the iOS (and OS X) universe has a string that uniquely identifies it. The Passer Rating app needs one. The customary way to produce a unique identifier is to reverse the order of your domain name, add a dot, and then give the application name, suitably encoded for the OS. I own the `wt9t.com` domain, so I'd fill in `com.wt9t`.

> **Note**
>
> You don't have a domain name of your own? Next you'll be telling me you don't have a T-shirt for the project. Get one (a domain name). They're cheap, and you don't have to do anything else with them.

Xcode generates an identifier for you and displays it just under the company ID: com.wt9t.Passer-Rating.

The **Class Prefix** is a string that Xcode's file templates will offer to prepend to names for the classes it generates automatically, and for new classes. This is necessary because Objective-C doesn't have namespaces, so you have to observe a convention to keep your names from colliding with others'. Apple recommends the prefix be three characters long. I dare to use two: **PR**

Device Family determines whether the template should include UI setups for iPhone, iPad, or both. Select **iPhone**; it's easier to fit on the screen.

Last of all, check the **Use Core Data** checkbox. Core Data is Cocoa's object-persistence and relational framework, and will be very handy for keeping the database organized. The project template will add a number of convenient housekeeping methods for getting a Core Data–based application running. We'll be using Core Data for this sample project.

Click **Next**, and you'll be shown a get-folder sheet like the one you first saw in Chapter 2, "Kicking the Tires." Pick a spot, and be sure to set **Source Control** to create a local (**My Mac**) Git repository.

Clicking **Create** unmasks the project window as before, and once again, you see the Target editor.

Target Editor

The Passer Rating project consists of two targets: "Passer Rating," which produces the app, and "Passer RatingTests," which will contain the application test suite. Xcode will initially show you the **General** editor for the Passer Rating target. (Click the Passer Rating project item at the top of the Project navigator to bring it up yourself.) It provides an interface for the basic settings that identify your project—its identifier, target environment, orientations, and where it can find the images that are the face UIKit puts on your app. It also keeps a list of the libraries the target will link to.

You won't have to do much about the **General** tab—or any of the others—for a while, but there is one thing that may bother you:

In the first section, "Identity," you may find a yellow warning badge with a label like "No matching code signing identity found" or "No matching provisioning profile found." This is your first encounter with provisioning (see Chapter 17, "Provisioning," for an exhaustive treatment).

The short of it is that for not particularly greedy reasons, Apple wants to thwart the installation of applications from outside its App Store. It does so by requiring crypto-graphic signatures. If you want to install your app for testing, you have to register the devices you'll be using, and in many cases the app itself, with Apple. *Provisioning* is the name for this process.

If you're a member of Apple's iOS Developer Program, Xcode will take care of most of this automatically. Just select your team from the **Team** popup above the notice. If that doesn't work, click **Fix Issue**, and Xcode will take care of applying for and downloading all the necessary permissions.

If you're not a member of a developer program, don't worry about it. You can still work on iOS apps, you just won't be able to put them on a device.

Do take note of the **Deployment Target** field in the "Deployment Info" section: This is where you designate the *minimum* version of the operating system your app will accept. It won't run on anything less, and you can be assured that you can use all of that OS's features freely. The project template set this to the latest version (7.0 as I write this). We'll be exploring features unique to iOS 7, so leave the setting alone.

There is another concept, the *SDK*, which you can find in the **Build Settings** tab. In Xcode's parlance, an SDK is a tree of headers, libraries, and other resources that let your app use the features of a particular version of an OS. In the past, Xcode came with a library of development kits for back versions of OS X, but now you'll get only the latest iOS and the one or two versions of OS X that the Xcode can run on.

Even though you no longer have a choice of SDKs, you should remember the rule: The target version is the *earliest version on which you will run*, and the SDK version is the *latest version from which you can draw functionality*. If you want to be compatible back to iOS 5.1, set the target to 5.1, use the current SDK, and be careful not to use any features from later OSes. The build system will link your app so it does not require the newer API in order to run.

> **Note**
>
> Also, if you target an OS that is earlier than the SDK, the build system will give you the behavior of the older OS, even if the later one fixes bugs and adds features—you'll be given the behavior you developed for and expected.

What's in the Project

The project template you chose for Passer Rating includes a lot:

> **Note**
>
> If you don't see the Navigator area, highlight the button near the right end of the toolbar that shows a bar at the left side of the window rectangle; the Project navigator is the first tab.

- **Class PRAppDelegate:** The application itself is represented by an object of class UIApplication, which you should never have to subclass or replace. True to the delegation pattern used throughout Cocoa, all of the unique behavior of the application comes through the methods of a delegate object, which the application object calls into. PRAppDelegate is declared as a subclass of UIResponder, and an implementor of the UIApplicationDelegate protocol (it promises to include the methods UIApplication needs from its delegate). The template for the implementation (.m) file contains a good starter for managing the application life cycle, including setting up the Core Data database.

- **Main.storyboard:** A storyboard is a graphical representation of the layout of your user interface, plus the top-level flow between the screens in your program. We'll be living with this one throughout this project.

- **Class PRMasterViewController:** This is, as the name says, the controller for the master (root-level) view of Passer Rating, which the design says will be a table of passer names and ratings. Because navigation-based applications almost always start with a table, the template makes PRMasterViewController a subclass of UITableViewController, which is suited for running a table view. The implementation file includes skeletons of the methods you'll need to fill in the table. It also provides an instance of NSFetchedResultsController, which does a lot to bridge Core Data data stores with tables.

- **Class PRDetailViewController:** The controller for the next layer of Passer Rating, the one that will be seen when the user taps a passer's name. The template declares it a simple subclass of the generic UIViewController.

- **Images.xcassets** is a catalog of the minimum set of images iOS will require in order to run an application. It starts with two categories: LaunchImage, for the image—don't call it a splash screen—that displays in the hopefully tiny period between launch and being ready for work; and AppIcon, which is what you'd think. As screen sizes, UI conventions, and resolutions have proliferated, and human nature being what it is, Xcode 4 projects accumulated a large number of such images, many of them long-since obsolete. The media-assets catalogs wrap them all up in a single project entry, with a slot for each variant. Applications seeking an asset need only ask for it by name, and the asset-catalog mechanism will provide the best fit for the environment.

- **Passer_Rating.xcdatamodeld:** Core Data isn't a full-service database, but if you have a background in SQL, there are helpful analogies. The Data Model file is the equivalent of an SQL schema. It defines the entities (think "tables") that will hold the data, and the attributes (think "columns") those entities will have. It also sets up one-to-many and many-to-many relationships between entities (think "never having to look at a join table again"). Xcode provides a graphical editor for data models.

- In the Supporting Files group, **Passer Rating-Info.plist**: This is the source file that yields an Info.plist file to be embedded in the application. It provides basic information on what the application can do, what data it can handle, and how it is presented to the user in the Home screen. Some of that information is presented to the user as text, so its content is merged with the application's InfoPlist.strings for the user's language. (Chapter 21, "Localization," covers localization in OS X, but most of the concepts apply to iOS, as well.)
  There are a couple of Objective-C source files in the Supporting Files group: main.m is the standard container for the main() function where the program starts; you usually won't change it. Passer Rating-Prefix.pch contains common initialization for the compiler.

- The "Passer RatingTests" target has a class file and Info.plist support similar to the app target's.

- **Frameworks:** The Frameworks group contains UIKit, Foundation, CoreData, CoreGraphics, and XCTest (which is used only by the unit-test target).

They provide links into the iOS system software, and Passer Rating won't run without them. If you open the **Build Phases** tab of the Project editor for the Passer Rating target, you'll find the frameworks in the Link Binary With Libraries phase.

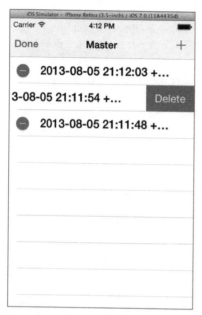

Figure 8.3   The skeletal code that comes with the Core Data + Master-Detail Application project template is enough to produce an app that will run in the iOS Simulator. It will add rows to its table, and, as shown here, respond to the **Edit** button by offering to delete rows.

Xcode's template for the project also includes a panoply of build settings, specifying how Passer Rating is to be compiled, linked, and organized.

The project is fully functional, as far as it goes. Run it: **Product → Run** (⌘R). Xcode builds the app, and in a few seconds, the iOS Simulator starts up and launches Passer Rating. Out of the box, the app is the iOS/Core Data equivalent to "Hello World": It shows an empty table under a navigation bar with **Edit** and **+** buttons. Tapping the **+** button adds a row with the current date and time; tapping the new entry pushes the "detail" view into view; the **Edit** button in the root list (or swiping across a row) lets you delete rows. You can close and reopen the app to find that the rows you added are still there. See Figure 8.3.

Note

As to whether Passer Rating is actually saving those dates and times, make sure there's nothing up your sleeve. Closing an iOS app usually doesn't stop it: The OS just puts it to sleep in the background, and its data won't be disturbed. To see a real, fresh restart, go back to Xcode and click the **Stop** button in the project toolbar, and then click **Run**.

One More Thing

Passer Rating is supposed to calculate passer ratings, which is a problem you've already solved. Let's add your solution to the project. Select **File → Add Files to "Passer Rating "…** (⌥⌘A). Xcode opens a modified get-file sheet (Figure 8.4). (The command will be available only if you've selected the project item at the top of the Project navigator, or one of the other project files.) Track down `rating.h` and `rating.c` from the old `passer-rating` project, and command-click on them to select both. Don't click **Add** yet, because there's more to do.

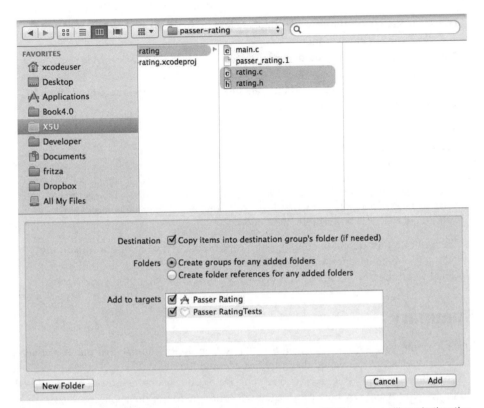

Figure 8.4   When you add files to a project, you are given some options controlling whether the files are to be used in place and how they are to be used.

Check the box labeled **Copy items into destination group's folder (if needed)**. That will add copies of the files to Passer Rating's project directory. It sometimes makes sense not to do this, as when you want to share a common copy of files across projects, but for now, this is the least complicated way to go. You'll see a better way to do the same thing later on.

Under **Folders**, you can decide how Xcode will treat any directories you add. It can represent them in the Project navigator by group folders, as an organizational aid; or it can have the project refer to the directories *themselves* as the objects the finished app will contain. The latter makes sense if you want to include a whole directory of data files in your product. You're not adding any directories, so this isn't an issue, but it's a good idea to make sure the setting is **Create groups for any added folders**, as it's the safer action to take by accident.

The **Add to targets** table allocates the added files to the targets in your project. If none of the boxes are checked, nothing you add will have any effect on any of your projects. Check the boxes for the targets that should use the new class. Xcode will remember your selection for the next class you add.

For this project, both the Passer Rating app and the Passer RatingTests need `passer_rating`, so check both.

Now you can click **Add**. Xcode will insert the files into the Project navigator immediately after the item that was selected when you added them. I never remember to plan this in advance, so I always end up dragging them elsewhere in the list, or into a group, afterward.

> **Note**
>
> Figure 8.4 suggests a quandary. I'm lazy. I want to add both files to my project, but I also know better than to have Xcode add a header file to a target (the build system will copy the file into the app). Being lazy, I select both, ask for both targets, and click the **Add** button, expecting that I'll have to clear `rating.h`'s target settings. I expected wrong: Xcode is smart enough to know that if you're adding a `.c/.h` pair, you probably don't want to put the `.h` in any targets. So it doesn't.

The `rating` files were copied into your project directory, so Xcode automatically added them to the Git repository (they're badged **A**); and the project file itself was modified to list the new files (and so is badged **M**). You should commit your work.

Summary

In this chapter, you began work on an iOS application. Before doing anything in Xcode, we decided what the app would do and what it would look like.

Once that was done, you knew enough to have Xcode create the project. You explored the Project editor and saw how it managed the configuration of the application itself. Then you explored the files Xcode's template provided.

The "empty" application Xcode provided was runnable; you found that running it launched the iOS Simulator, which allowed you to use the app.

Finally, you prepared the app for your own work by adding the `passer_rating` function from the `passer-rating` project.

Now you're ready to make the empty app your own, to start implementing the design we put together in this chapter. We'll start with the model.

9

An iOS Application: Model

It's time to put some flesh on Passer Rating's data design. The Core Data framework for iOS and OS X provides a powerful system for managing object-relational graphs and persisting them in an SQLite database.

> **Note**
>
> SQLite (you will make it a gentler world if you tolerate both "ess-cue-light" and "see-kwel-light") is the full-featured SQL database library and command-line tool at the foundation of Core Data. The Core Data API is agnostic about its bottom layer (on OS X, there are two alternatives) and affords no direct access to the underlying database. The library is a standard component of both iOS and OS X. See `http://sqlite.org`.

Xcode includes essential support for Core Data. In this chapter, you'll see how to use Xcode's graphical editor to turn a data design into an executable data model.

Implementing the Model

Core Data is going to store the model objects for you and track their relationships to each other. To do that it needs a *managed-object model*, which specifies what *entities* are in the data store, and what *properties* and *relationships* they have. In the completed application, this is kept in a `.mom` file, which is efficient but not human-readable. For development, you will be editing an Xcode data-model file (`.xcdatamodel`) that displays all this information graphically, in a format not too different from the model sketch in Figure 8.1.

> **Note**
>
> As your application evolves, so will your data model. Data files created with one managed-object model are not compatible with another. Core Data provides techniques for migrating data stores to later models, if it has the full sequence of models available to it. The aggregated versions are kept in directories—`.momd` for use at runtime, and `.xcdatamodeld` in Xcode.

Entities

Select `Passer_Rating.xcdatamodeld` in the Project navigator. The Data Model editor comes in two parts. The column on the left lists the top-level contents of the model, the main ones being entities. Entities describe individual records in the Core Data database. If you're familiar with SQL databases, these are roughly like tables.

The model supplied from the template is very simple: There is one entity, `Event`. If you select it in the editor, you'll see its properties in three tables. (If you don't see tables, make sure the **Editor Style** control at the lower right has the first segment selected, for the tabular layout.)

- **Attributes** hold simple data like strings, dates, or numbers. `Event` has one attribute, `timeStamp`; you see in the top table that this attribute is of type `Date`.

- **Relationships** link entities one-to-one, one-to-many, or many-to-many. Core Data maintains relationships without your having to deal with keys or joins.

- **Fetched Properties** define fetch requests (queries for objects matching search criteria). These amount to relationships that are not continually updated as the database changes; to get a current object set, you'd have to refire the fetch yourself. Fetched properties have their uses, but you won't have any of those uses in this project.

Click the right half of the **Editor Style** control to have a look at the other view of the model. This gives you a diagram of the whole model, in which each entity is represented by a box that contains its attributes and relationships. With only one entity, having only one attribute, the diagram is unprepossessing.

Let's make something to see of it. Switch back to the Table style. Select the `Event` entity and press the Delete key. You want to add entities of your own. Going by Figure 8.1, you need two: `Game` and `Passer`. `Game` has some interesting content, so let's start with that.

1. The bar at the bottom of the editor has two circled + buttons, and if you look carefully, you'll see the tiny triangle that tells you it is an anchor for a drop-down menu; each can add more than one kind of thing. The thing you want to add is an entity for games.
   Hold the mouse button down on the + button on the left and select **Add Entity**. An entity named `Entity` appears in the entities section of the editor. Double-click the entity's name in the list to make it editable; name it **Passer**.
2. Click **Add Entity** again (the most recent use of the button sticks), and name the resulting entity **Game**.

Attributes

So now you have `Game` and `Passer` entities, but they don't hold any data. Entities are aggregates of simple data; these are *attributes*.

3. With `Game` still selected, click the + button at the bottom of the Attributes list. A new attribute appears in the table with its name ready for editing.

4. Name the new attribute `whenPlayed`. You'll notice that the Type column for `whenPlayed` says it is of **Undefined** type. That's undesirable, but you'll take care of that soon.

5. Instead, create some more attributes: `attempts`, `completions`, `interceptions`, `ourScore`, `ourTeam`, `theirScore`, `theirTeam`, `touchdowns`, and `yards`. You'll find you have to chase the attributes around. When you change the name, Xcode sorts the new attribute into alphabetical order. That's easy to miss, and you may find yourself editing the wrong row as the one you were working on is swapped out from under you.

> **Note**
>
> Remember to press Return when you're finished editing a name; if you add another attribute before doing so (depending on how you do it), Xcode will abandon the edit and leave the name as `attribute`.

6. You're running up the score on the errors reported in the status area in the toolbar, because none of those attributes have types. Let's take care of that. Start with `whenPlayed`: Select **Date** from the popup in the Type column.

7. Scalar type is not everything there is to say about an attribute. Click the right end of the **View** control (rightmost in the toolbar) to expose the Utility area. The Utility area is divided into an upper section, the Inspector, and a lower one, the Library. Drag the bar at the top of the Library down to make the Inspector as large as possible, and click the third tab to show the Data Model inspector.

8. Select `yards` in the Attributes list; this loads the properties of that attribute into the inspector. See Figure 9.1.

The inspector has four sections, the first of which, **Attribute**, is the most interesting. The name, `yards`, is right. The **Properties** checkboxes reflect how Core Data stores the attribute. Leave **Transient** (the attribute would be in the model, but not persisted) and **Indexed** (Core Data would efficiently retrieve `Game` objects by `yards`) unchecked. Uncheck `Optional`: The record of the game isn't complete unless it counts the yards gained.

In the next part of the section, set the **Attribute Type** to **Integer 32**—an integer in the range of plus-or-minus two billion. When you do that, **Validation** fields appear to receive a **Minimum**, **Maximum**, and **Default** for the attribute. Core Data will refuse to save an object with an attribute out of range; and if you make an attribute mandatory, it's wise to have Core Data initialize it to something legal. Zero is a good choice for a new record. To enable a default (which we want for this project) or a validation (which we don't), check the respective checkboxes.

> **Note**
>
> There is an argument to be made that you shouldn't make an attribute mandatory, or set validation conditions, until late in the development process. Core Data will raise an error if

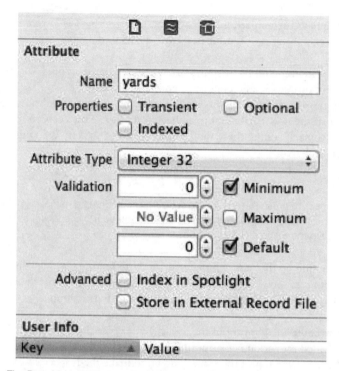

Figure 9.1   The Data Model inspector, focused on `Game`'s `yards` attribute. This is another way to set the type of the attribute, and it allows you to set detailed information on how Core Data is to treat it.

you try to save an object in which a mandatory attribute isn't set or any attribute isn't in range. If your code isn't finished, you might not have gotten around to setting everything.

The next part, **Advanced**, has to do with paralleling the Core Data store in a directory that has one file for each record in the store. This is a convenience for OS X's Spotlight global-search service to find objects (like individual emails) that can be extracted from your database. You aren't going to do anything like that, and this is an iOS application anyway.

The **User Info** section lets you add any information you like, in key-value form, to the description of this attribute. You won't be introspecting the database's metadata, so you can ignore this section. "Versioning" gives hints to Core Data if you revise the schema for your database—it will migrate your data to the new schema automatically *if it can*. Ignore it.

That's `yards` taken care of, and six more integer attributes to go. This looks tedious. There's a better way. Click `attempts`; then hold the Command key down and click `completions`, `interceptions`, `ourScore`, `theirScore`, and `touchdowns`. Now all six to-be-integer attributes are selected.

Turn your attention to the Data Model inspector, and change the properties as before: not optional, integer 32, default, and minimum zero. You've just set the properties of all six attributes.

`ourTeam` and `theirTeam` should be non-optional strings; check the **Min Length** box and set a minimum-length validation of ten characters or more.

And that sets up the attributes for `Game`. Do the same for `Passer`, with three mandatory string attributes, `firstName`, `lastName`, and `currentTeam`. Use your judgment on defaults and validations.

Relationships

The data model so far is not very useful. You can store and enumerate `Passers`, and you can do the same with `Games`, but quarterbacks participate in games, and `Game` is the only thing that holds a quarterback's actual performance. Core Data calls the link between two entities a *relationship*.

9. Make sure the `Passer` entity is selected. A passer may start with no games played but will eventually play in many. Choose **Add Relationship** from the drop-down on the right-hand **+** button; click the **+** button under the Relationships table; or select **Editor → Add Relationship**. A new entry appears in the Relationships list.

   > **Note**
   > If you don't see the new relationship, make sure the disclosure triangle next to the "Relationships" label is open.

   > **Note**
   > Whenever you're in doubt about what you can do in an editor, check the **Editor** menu. It shows different commands depending on the type of editor you are using, so it changes a lot. What's available now may be very different from what you saw the last time you opened that menu.

10. Name it **games** (it's a good idea to name a relationship the same as the related entity, plural if the relationship is to be to-many).
11. Select **Game** from the popup in the Destination column of the Relationships table. Game doesn't have any relationships yet, so there's nothing to do yet with the Inverse column.
12. Turn to the Data Model inspector, which now shows options for a relationship. The items at the top reflect your choices from the table, so you can leave them alone. **Optional** is checked, which is right, because the passer may not have played at all.
13. For the **Type**, select **To Many**, because a passer may play in more than one game. (Note that Core Data will take care of record IDs and foreign keys silently.)
14. There is an **Ordered** checkbox. Normally, an object's to-many relationship is represented as a *set*, an unordered collection of unique objects. Checking **Ordered** makes the relationship an *ordered set*; like an array, its elements have an inherent order; like a set, no element can appear more than once.

This example has no inherent or preferred ordering for related objects, and ordered relationships come with a performance penalty, so we won't be using them.

15. Don't bother with setting a minimum or maximum: The relationship is optional, so a minimum is irrelevant, and we're okay with however many Games may be linked to this Passer.

16. The **Delete Rule** is important. What happens if the Passer is removed from the database? You wouldn't want its Games to remain; there's no point in having statistics that aren't related to any Passers. You have four choices:

   - **No Action** does nothing when the Passer is deleted; the Games will be orphaned *and* they will have dangling references to the now-deleted Passer. You don't want that.

   - **Nullify** is scarcely better; the Games remain in the database, but at least their back-references to the Passer are closed off.

   - **Deny** goes too far, as it would prevent a Passer from being deleted so long as it had any Games. You'd have to unlink all of them before you could delete.

   - What you want is **Cascade**. Deleting a Passer would pursue the relationship and delete all of the objects it reaches: No Passer, no Games.

17. The rest of the inspector covers the global-search, metadata, and versioning attributes I showed you for attributes. Again, you don't care.

At this point, you can ask a Passer for all of its Games, and it can give them to you. But you can't ask a Game for its Passer. You need to establish an *inverse relationship*. Select the Game entity, and create a relationship named passer. The destination is Passer; the inverse is games.

> ### Note
>
> In fact, it's so rare not to want an inverse for a relationship that momc, the compiler that translates .xcdatamodels into .moms, will warn if you don't specify one.

Now that you have both ends of the one-to-many relationship, you can specify an inverse: In the Inverse column, specify games. In the Data Model inspector, the relationship is *not* optional: Again, a Game without a Passer makes no sense, and we'd like Core Data to enforce that. Setting the **Type** to **To One** lets Core Data know to treat passer as a direct link to one Passer, and not to a set of many. And for this relationship, the **Delete Rule** should be **Nullify**—you want the Passer to live, with its relationship to this Game removed.

The data model is complete. Click the Graph (right-hand) side of the **Editor Style** control at the bottom to see all the entities laid out in a diagram (Figure 9.2) that looks a lot like the original design in Figure 8.1. (You'll have to drag the two entity blocks apart if they overlap.)

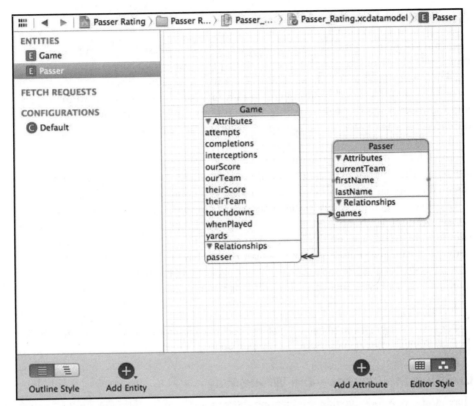

Figure 9.2   The Graph style of the Data Model editor shows all the entities in the model laid out in a block diagram. The one-to-many relationship between `Passer` and `Game` is shown by an arrow with one head at the `Passer` end and many on the `Game` end.

You can edit—even create—the data model in the Graph view if you wish; it's just a matter of using the **Add** buttons and the Data Model inspector.

> **Note**
>
> This data model would not pass muster as a design for a "real" database. The name `Game` is a misnomer, as it implies a particular event held at a particular place and time, at which at least two quarterbacks make passes; but you're using `Game` to refer to one passer's performance at that event. A more sophisticated model would make the `Game` entity describe the event and use a join to link between `Passer`s and `Game`s and hold one quarterback's performance at that game. Further, a quarterback may play for many teams during his career, and it would be interesting to list all the games a team played; the model should normalize a `Team` entity out of `Passer` and `Game`. Noted. It's just an example.

Managed-Object Classes

You could begin using the data model right away. You could ask Core Data to instantiate a Game as a generic object of class NSManagedObject that can set, store, and return its attributes when you pass it a name: [aGame setValue: date forKey: @"whenPlayed"]. You could instantiate a Passer the same way, and it would be an NSManagedObject that handled those attributes. It would work. It worked for the dummy Event entity when you ran the project template unaltered.

But. . .

You'll have noticed a lot that isn't in the data model. There is no passer-rating attribute—the point of the whole application—anywhere. Passer has no attributes for career attempts, completions, yards. . . . What are you going to do about that?

What you're going to do is to calculate passer rating and other stats while the application is running, rather than storing them. Those statistics are derived from the numbers you do store. In order to do those calculations, you'll need Objective-C methods that draw on the attributes of Passer and Game. And to have those methods, you'll need classes (subclasses of NSManagedObject, as it happens) that implement them. You need interface (.h) and implementation (.m) files for two new classes.

> **Note**
>
> For safety's sake, if you're following along, commit your project *now*. Remember the "Your First Commit" section of Chapter 7, "Version Control."

Creating the Classes—the Wrong Way

Here's the way Xcode provides for creating NSManagedObject subclasses, and it is wrong. If you want to follow along anyway, make sure you did that commit I just told you to do; when you're done with this sidetrack, revert all your files. Or if you're not using source control, copy the project directory, and work on the copy.

First: Passer and Game are fine for entity names, but Objective-C class names should follow the protocol for all of the classes in your project: PRPasser and PRGame. This is not just punctilio; classes and entities are distinct things and should have distinct names. By default, Xcode will generate classes that have the same names as the associated entities. Select each entity in the Data Model editor and fill the **Class** field in the Data Model inspector with the class names you want.

Select **File → File. . .** (⌘ N). Navigate the New File assistant to **iOS → Core Data → NSManagedObject subclass**. The description says that this is "An Objective-C NSManagedObject subclass, with a header," but that undersells it. Click **Next**.

> **Note**
>
> You can get to the same place without the template picker by selecting **Editor → Create NSManagedObject Subclass. . .** while the Data Model editor is visible, so long as at least one entity is selected.

The next two pages are unique to creating NSManagedObjects. The first shows you a list of the data models in your project (only one in this case). Check the boxes next to each one from which you want to draw classes. The next page lists all of the entities defined in those models; check those off to select the classes you want to generate. You want to create custom classes for Passer and Game, so check both and Click **Next**. (Don't worry about being shown the entity names and not the class names—Xcode will do the right thing.)

A get-file sheet appears for you to select a directory to receive the source files. To be tidy, create a directory just for the model objects: With the Passer Rating source directory selected, click **New Folder**, and name it **Model**. Make sure the new directory is selected in the file browser by clicking on it.

In addition to the pickers for the Project-navigator group (put it into the group for the Passer Rating target) and targets (just the app target, not the tests), the get-folder sheet presents a checkbox labeled **Use scalar properties for primitive data types**. NSManagedObject is a container for object values—numbers like completions must be wrapped in NSNumber objects.

This is true to the way Core Data works, so this exercise will leave the box unchecked; but boxing and unboxing the numbers is more work for you. If you check this box, your new subclasses will expose numbers in their native forms, doing the translation for you.

Click **Create**. You'll see four new files in the Project navigator for the PRPasser and PRGame code. They should have **A** badges to show they have been added to the local repository, but have not yet been committed. Because you want to keep the Project navigator tidy, select all the new files (shift- or command-clicking as necessary) and then **File → New → Group from Selection**. They'll be wrapped in a group named "New Group," which you can rename (for instance, to **Data Model**) by clicking on it and pressing Return.

As part of the conversion, Xcode gives the new classes property declarations that make it easy to get attributes and relationships directly from classes that represent your stored objects.

> **Note**
>
> The Project navigator represents groups by yellow folders, and you probably associate folder icons with filesystem directories. That isn't so in this case. At the first approximation, Xcode's yellow group folders are simply a convenient way to organize your files. Files stored in the same directory can be in different groups; moving a file to another group doesn't move it on disk.

If you were working with the real copy of the Passer Rating project, you'd commit your changes now. But you're not—or if you are, use **Source Control → Discard All Changes. . .** to wind back to a version created before you generated the class files. No matter how you do it, if you pursued the "wrong way" option, get it out of your project, including any generated files, so you're back where you were.

Why Doing It Xcode's Way Is a Mistake

Now, a thought experiment: You created the PRPasser and PRGame classes because you want to go beyond the simple accessors Core Data provides you. You'd want to add methods like this:

```
/// Fetch an array of all games played on a certain date.
/// @bug As implemented, the games must have been played
///        at the same instant.
+ (NSArray *) gamesOnDate: (NSDate *) aDate
                inContext: (NSManagedObjectContext *) context
{
    NSArray *        retval = nil;

    //  Ask for all Games...
    NSFetchRequest *    req = [NSFetchRequest
                            fetchRequestWithEntityName: @"Game"];
    // ... that match the given date.
    req.predicate =
        [NSPredicate predicateWithFormat: @"whenPlayed = %@", aDate];
    NSError *          error;
    //  Do the fetch:
    retval = [context executeFetchRequest: req
                                    error: &error];
    if (! retval) {
        //  Not just no matches; the fetch errored-out.
        //  Log it, and let the nil come back.
        NSLog(@"%s fetch failed; error = %@",
            __PRETTY_FUNCTION__, error);
    }
    return retval;
}
```

All is well. Next, add a string property, weather, to the Game entity. And...now what?

If you want a reliable way to keep PRGame up with changes in your data model—and some day they will be a lot more complex than this—you'd want to repeat the process of generating it from the data model. When you try this, Xcode will give you fair warning:

The following files already exist and will be replaced:
/Users/xcodeuser/.../Passer Rating/Game.h
/Users/xcodeuser/.../Passer Rating/Game.m

And the warning will come with the **Cancel** button highlighted and throbbing. If you do it the automatic way, you will lose work. If you try to keep the class in sync by hand, you will miss something, and the resulting bugs may not be easy to track down.

You're in a corner.

The Right Way—mogenerator

Xcode's treatment of Core Data isn't history's first instance of the problem of enhancing automatically generated code. In object-oriented programming, the solution is almost always to let the generator have sole control over the class it creates, and subclass that for your customizations. Unfortunately, Xcode's managed-object class generator isn't quite flexible enough to do this for you—you're left to cobble the subclasses by hand.

Jon "Wolf" Rentzsch has created mogenerator, a command-line tool that does exactly that. Download and install the tool from http://rentzsch.github.io/mogenerator/; the installer will put mogenerator into /usr/bin, which makes it available from the command line.

> **Note**
>
> As I write this, the mogenerator installer package was not signed with a Developer ID. If you have Gatekeeper running, you can unblock the installation by right-clicking on the package icon and choosing **Open**. You'll be given the option to open it without interference from Gatekeeper.

This time, you will be using the "live" copy of the project, which you've already restored. As before, set the class names for the Game and Passer entities to PRGame and PRPasser—Xcode's generator will take the entity names by default, but mogenerator insists on your setting them.

Open the Terminal application, jump to your project-source directory, and run the tool:

```
$ #   Substitute the path to your own project
$ #   "..." is for space; enter the full path
$ cd /Users/xcodeuser/.../Passer Rating/Passer Rating
$ #   Verify you're in the same directory as the data model:
$ ls
...
Passer_Rating.xcdatamodeld
...
$ #   Run mogenerator:
$ mogenerator --model Passer_Rating.xcdatamodeld \
> --output-dir mogenerated \
> --template-var arc=true \
> --includeh PRDataModel.h
4 machine files and 4 human files generated.
Aggregate header file was also generated to PRDataModel.h.
$ ls mogenerated/
PRGame.h     PRPasser.h    _PRGame.h _PRPasser.h
PRGame.m     PRPasser.m    _PRGame.m _PRPasser.m
$
```

As you see, a new mogenerated/ directory contains eight files: For each entity, there is a header and an implementation file for the classes that belong to you (PRPasser and

PRGame) and to `mogenerator` (_PRPasser and _PRGame). This is the last time you'll care about the "machine" classes and files. When you make a change to your model, run `mogenerator` again, and it will re-create the "machine" files without touching the work you did in the "human" files.

Simply entering **mogenerator - -model Passer_Rating.xcdatamodeld** would have done a fine job, but `mogenerator` has many options. Type **mogenerator- -help** to see most of them.

The options I show here create a directory, `mogenerated/`, to receive the results, and ask for an umbrella header, `PRDataModel.h`, for convenient reference to all the headers in the data model. One option that isn't mentioned in the help is `- -template-var arc=true`. `mogenerator` was written well before automatic reference counting, and for backward compatibility, it won't generate ARC-compliant code unless you ask for it.

Add the new files to your project: Select **File → Add Files to "Passer Rating"...** (⌥ ⌘ A). A get-file sheet descends that is familiar to you from the "One More Thing" section of Chapter 8, "Starting an iOS Application." This time the **Folders: Create groups for any added folders** radio button is significant—be sure to select it, because you'll be adding the contents of a whole directory.

- Click the `mogenerated/` directory.
- Hold down the Command key and click `PRDataModel.h`.
- Make sure the Passer Rating item in the **Add to targets** table is checked, and Passer RatingTests is not.
- Click **Add**.

A new group appears in the Project navigator, `mogenerated`, containing the generated class definitions. Once again, Xcode is smart enough to add only the `.m` source files to the target; the headers are added to the Project list without being marked for copying into the finished Passer Rating package.

Extending the Classes

`mogenerator` puts a number of convenience properties and methods into the machine-owned classes. In _PRGame, for instance, you find this:

```
@property (nonatomic, strong) NSNumber* attempts;
@property (atomic) int32_t attemptsValue;
- (int32_t) attemptsValue;
- (void) setAttemptsValue: (int32_t) value_;
```

But we have `PRGame.h` and `PRGame.m` all to ourselves. Let's add our first extension to the header—what the app is supposed to be all about:

```
@property (nonatomic, readonly) double   passerRating;
```

...which is to say, a `double`-precision number that is the calculated passer rating for this PRGame. You can read it, but you can't change it.

Implement the @property in PRGame.m, between the @implementation and @end:

```
- (double) passerRating
{
    double  rating = passer_rating(self.attemptsValue,
                                   self.completionsValue,
                                   self.yardsValue,
                                   self.touchdownsValue,
                                   self.interceptionsValue);

    return rating;
}
```

You can see the calculation is no different than it was in the passer-rating tool. Now any reference to someGame.passerRating will produce the passer rating for that game, as drawn from the Core Data database.

Do the same thing in PRPasser.h and PRPasser.m. It's the same @property declaration, but Passer doesn't have any passer-performance statistics; all of those come through its to-many games relationship. The implementation reflects that. At the top of _PRPasser.m, add

```
#import "rating.h"
```

to let the compiler know about the passer_rating function, and then implement PRPasser's passerRating @property:

```
- (double) passerRating
{
    int attempts = [[self.games
                    valueForKeyPath: @"@sum.attempts"] intValue];
    int comps = [[self.games
                    valueForKeyPath: @"@sum.completions"] intValue];
    int yards = [[self.games
                    valueForKeyPath: @"@sum.yards"] intValue];
    int tds = [[self.games
                    valueForKeyPath: @"@sum.touchdowns"] intValue];
    int ints = [[self.games
                    valueForKeyPath: @"@sum.interceptions"] intValue];

    double rating = passer_rating(attempts, comps,
                                  yards, tds, ints);
    return rating;
}
```

This method works through the games relationship. It uses the key-value coding method valueForKeyPath: to pull (for instance) the attempts of each game from the games set, and then to sum (@sum) the results.

You can use aggregate keypaths to derive some other interesting facts about a passer—for instance:

```
- (int) sumOfGameAttribute: (NSString *) attribute
{
    NSString *      keyPath = [NSString stringWithFormat:
                                @"@sum.%@", attribute];
    return [[self.games valueForKeyPath: keyPath] intValue];
}


- (int) attempts
{
    return [self sumOfGameAttribute: @"attempts"];
}


- (NSDate *) lastPlayed
{
    //  The date of the last game the passer played
    return [self.games valueForKeyPath: @"@max.whenPlayed"];
}


- (NSArray *) teams
{
    //  The name of every team the passer played for
    return [[self.games valueForKeyPath:
                @"@distinctUnionOfObjects.ourTeam"]
            allObjects];
}
```

The sample code includes read-only properties for the sum of all the raw game statistics—attempts, completions, yards, touchdowns, and interceptions—all the teams the passer played for, and the beginning and ending dates of his career.

Some Test Data

Passer Rating won't work without data. In a finished product, that would be easy: The user provides his own data. But we don't want to wait on having a full suite of editors in the app to see how it works. You need some test data to preload into the app.

This can take the form of a CSV file. I have a script, `generate-games.rb`, that will produce a good-enough data set:

```
firstName,lastName,attempts,completions,interceptions, ...
Jimmy,Carter,37,11,1,0,56,2010-03-24,Boise Bearcats,2, ...
Andy,Jackson,33,8,1,1,30,2010-03-24,Modesto Misanthropes,9, ...
James,Madison,20,15,0,4,241,2010-04-14,San Bernardino Stalkers,47, ...
Quinn,Adams,9,3,1,1,17,2010-04-14,San Bernardino Stalkers,47, ...
...
```

> **Note**
>
> The script runs to about 280 lines, so look for it in the sample code. The output is flawed—team A is recorded as playing at team B on the same day that team B is at team C, and Big Bill Taft turns out to be a much better quarterback than you'd expect. Those aren't relevant to exercising what the app does; for further information, check the Wikipedia entry for "YAGNI."

If the sample data doesn't exist, or doesn't reflect the latest version of `generate-games.rb`, it should be (re)built. Can Xcode take care of this?

Yes. First, add `generate-games.rb` to the project by the add-files command you saw before, or simply by dragging it in from the Finder. Now open the Project editor (click the top row of the Project navigator), and select the Passer Rating target. Click the **Build Phases** tab to reveal the agenda for building Passer Rating. We want that agenda to include running that script.

Do this by selecting **Editor → Add Build Phase → Add Run Script Build Phase**. A new phase, labeled "Run Script," appears as the last phase. It's no good running `generate-games.rb` *after* the "Copy Bundle Resources" phase moves the sample data into the application, so drag the new phase up so it comes before. Double-click on the phase's title and change it to **Generate Test Data**.

The Run Script editor (click the disclosure triangle if it isn't visible) comes in three parts:

- At top, you provide the script to be run. This won't be `generate-games.rb`: The script works by writing to standard output, which you'll have to redirect to a file. So for the **Shell**, specify the vanilla **/bin/sh**, and for the script, the one-liner

  ```
  /usr/bin/ruby "${SRCROOT}/Passer Rating/generate-games.rb" \
  > "${SRCROOT}/Passer Rating/sample-data.csv"
  ```

  (I've broken the line with a \ for readability, but you should put it all on one line.)

  > **Note**
  >
  > The quotes are necessary. The SRCROOT shell variable will expand to a path to your Passer Rating directory, and the space will confuse the sh interpreter.

- Next comes a table of input files. If Xcode knows what files go into and out of a phase, its build system can skip the phase if the inputs haven't changed since the last run. Click the **+** button below the **Input Files** table and enter

  `$(SRCROOT)/Passer Rating/generate-games.rb`

- For an output file, enter

  `$(SRCROOT)/Passer Rating/sample-data.csv`

This run-script phase says, "run the Ruby script `generate-games.rb`, sending the output to `sample-data.csv` in the project root directory. If the output file is already there and is newer than the script, don't bother."

Now all you have to do is make sure `sample-data.csv` is part of the Copy Bundle Resources build phase, so it will make its way inside the Passer Rating app. Click the disclosure triangle to expose the table of files to be included, click the **+** button to add the CSV file and...

There are a couple of problems. The first is that, not knowing what to do with an `.rb` file when you added it to the project, Xcode dumped it into the copy-resources phase. You don't want `generate-games.rb` to be in the product. Easy enough: Select its entry in the table and click **−**.

The bigger problem is a chicken-and-egg thing: `sample-data.csv` doesn't exist, so there's no way to put it into the table. The solution is to do a build (**Product → Build**, ⌘ B). That runs `generate-games.rb` and puts `sample-data.csv` in the project directory. Now you can click the **+** button, then the **Add Other...** button to find the CSV file. Xcode offers to add the file to the project, which is just what you want.

When they're all set up, the script and resources build phases should look like Figure 9.3.

Xcode marks both the Ruby and the CSV file for inclusion in the source-control repository, as evidenced by the **A** badges next to their names in the Project navigator.

Source Control and Product Files

Strictly speaking, `sample-data.csv` is a product file, completely reproducible from `generate-games.rb`, and there should be no point in treating every hit on the script as a significant source-control event. It shouldn't go into a repository...

...but we're going to include it anyway to demonstrate integration builds in Chapter 15, "Unit Testing."

If you were to do it the right way, you'd look around in the Xcode menu commands, and the File inspector, and the Commit editor... and find there is no way to do that from within Xcode. You'd have to break out the Terminal.

The first thing to do is to prevent Xcode from including `sample-data.csv` in the next commit. Tell Git to remove the file from the staging area:

```
$ git status
# On branch master
# Changes to be committed:
```

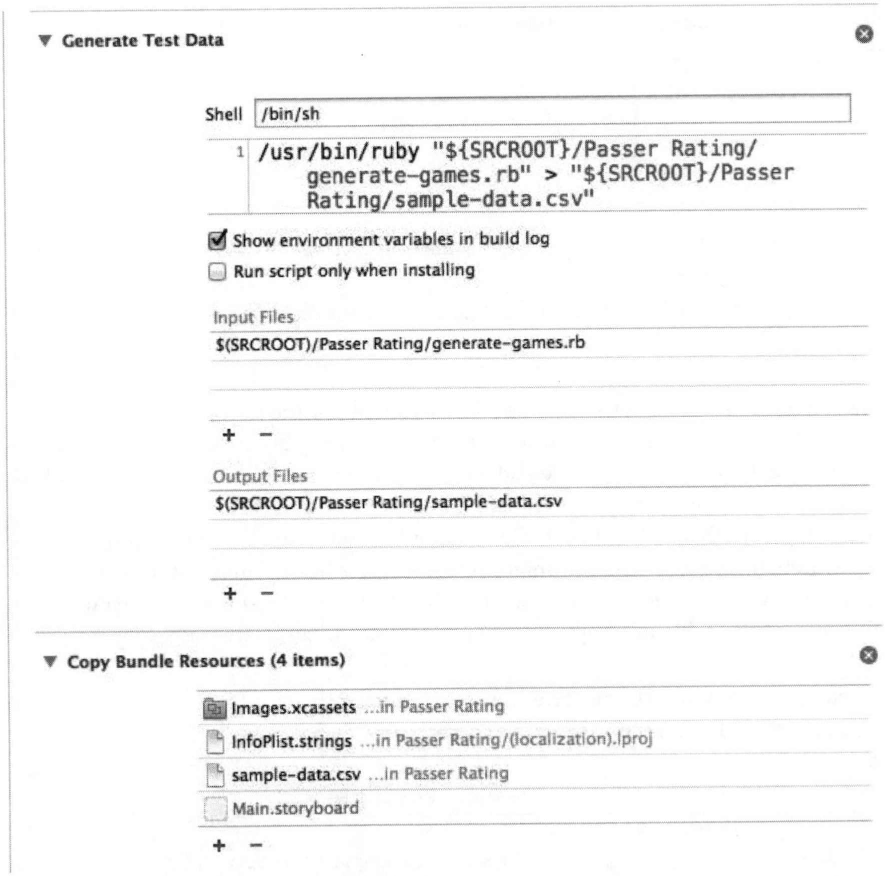

Figure 9.3   The Generate Test Data and Copy Bundle Resources build phases, set up to run the `generate-games.rb` script and produce `sample-data.csv`, which is then copied into the Passer Rating product. `Main.storyboard` is shown in red because Xcode has never been able to keep track of storyboard files. It's harmless.

```
#   (use "git rm --cached <file>..." to unstage)
...
#  new file:   sample-data.csv
...


$#    The offending file is there
$#    and Git gives a hint on how to remove it:


$ git rm --cached sample-data.csv
```

```
$#    That took care of it for now:
# On branch VersionControl
# Changes to be committed:
#    (use "git rm <file>..." to unstage)
... sample-data.csv isn't there ...
... but it is here: ...
# Untracked files:
#    (use "git add <file>..." to include in what will be committed)
#       sample-data.csv
#       ../Passer Rating.xcodeproj/project.xcworkspace/xcuserdata/
...
```

Git may be subtle, but it is not malicious. When you ask for the status of your working directory, it shows you what files will be in the next commit, but it also tells you how to withdraw a file. Once you do, Xcode badges sample-data.csv with a **?**, which at least means it won't commit it automatically, and Git calls it "untracked."

That's all you really need, but such files accumulate in the sidebar in the Commit editor, as though Xcode hoped you might relent. Clutter hides significant information, so you'd prefer never to see that file, or any .csv file, in source-control listings again. You saw the .gitignore file in Chapter 7, "Version Control," and here it is again:

```
$#    Make sure you're in the same directory as
$#    the .git local-repository directory
$ ls -a
.               .git                Passer RatingTests
..              Passer Rating
.DS_Store                           Passer Rating.xcodeproj

$#    append something to the .gitignore file
$#    (which will be created if it isn't there)
$ cat >> .gitignore
*.csv
xcuserdata/
<^D>
```

What this does is tell Git (and Xcode) not to mention any .csv files when they report on the state of source control. I added the xcuserdata/ directory as well. It preserves information particular to your use of the project, from schemes and breakpoint lists to the file you last selected in the Project navigator. You can mark the important things as "shared" if you need them to be visible to all users; and Xcode won't treat every tab selection as a significant source-control event.

Did it work?

```
$ git status
# On branch master
# Changes to be committed:
... still no sample-data.csv ...
# Untracked files:
#   (use "git add <file>..." to include in what will be committed)
#
#   .gitignore
... none here, either ...

$#   (Let's make sure the .gitignore file sticks around:)
$ git add .gitignore
```

I won't go into the details of the simple CSV parser (SimpleCSVFile) I built, and the code I added to Passer and Game to make them clients of the parser. If you need the details, they're in the sample code. The application delegate is set up so that when the app starts up, it loads its Core Data store from the CSV.

Making the Model Easier to Debug

You've already run Passer Rating with the dummy data model from the template. This has stored a Passer_Rating.sqlite file in the app's documents directory. If the contents of that file don't match up with the current managed-object model (.mom), Core Data will report an error and your application will be crippled. (The code that comes with the template actually crashes the app.)

But you've changed the model to add Passer and Game. You'll probably change it again.

What I do in the early stages of development is to delete the .sqlite data file at the start of every run. Eventually, of course, you'll want your persistent data to persist, but this is a quick, easy way to save yourself some headaches.

Find the -persistentStoreCoordinator method in PRAppDelegate.m. Add some code after the declaration of storeURL:

```
    NSURL *storeURL = [[self applicationDocumentsDirectory]
            URLByAppendingPathComponent: @"Passer_Rating.sqlite"];
#if ALWAYS_DELETE_STORE
    // For ease in debugging, always start with a fresh data store.
    [[NSFileManager defaultManager] removeItemAtURL: storeURL
                                        error: NULL];

#endif
```

and #define ALWAYS_DELETE_STORE 1 early in the file.

Summary

You've started building an iOS application in earnest. You learned how to use the Data Model editor to construct a Core Data managed-object model that embodies your design, making entities that describe the data types, and endowing them with attributes that have suitable types and constraints. You also traced relationships among the entities to express the fact that `Passers` play `Games`.

You went one step further into the model by writing its first actual code. You had Xcode build `NSManagedObject` subclasses from the entities, and made first-class objects out of the database records.

Finally, the need for test data drove you to your first encounter with the **Build Phases** tab in the Target editor. You added a script phase that generates test data, and set the phase up so that it produces it on demand.

10

An iOS Application: Controller

If I were smart, I'd start unit-testing the model as soon as the first draft was done, before adding the complexity of a human-interface layer. But I'm not smart; I'm going to put testing off until Chapter 15, "Unit Testing."

Instead, let's go ahead with the first cut at a real app. Xcode's Master-Detail Application template provides a working version of the first table. Let's convert that into a table of quarterbacks and their ratings.

You remember from the "The Controllers" section of Chapter 8, "Starting an iOS Application," that the view comprising a full-screen stage in an iOS application is managed by a *view controller*, a subclass of `UIViewController`. iOS services view controllers with a defined repertoire of method calls throughout the life cycle of the view: loading, response to events, and teardown. It is your responsibility to provide a `UIViewController` that supplies these methods. In this chapter, I'll fill out the initial controller, `PRMasterViewController`.

> ### Note
> Again, I can't supply complete listings for the files you'll be working on. The project template will provide much of what I don't show, so you'll have that in front of you already. For the rest, see the sample code you can get by following the instructions in the Introduction. Note that the sample code folders *do not* include Git repositories; use them for reference only. Switching from your own version-controlled directory to a sample will lose your repo.

Renaming Symbols

But first. In the first version of the `PRPasser` class, I have a convenience constructor, a class method named `quarterbackWithFirstName:last:inContext:`. This is wrong. By Cocoa conventions, a convenience constructor should begin with the name of the class, and I think it's bad style to say `last:` when the argument sets a property named `lastName:` it should be `passerWithFirstName:lastName:inContext:`.

Refactoring a Method Name

Well, you've done a global search-and-replace before, in Chapter 7, "Version Control;" this is just a matter of finding every instance of `quarterbackWithFirstName:last:inContext:` and substituting `passerWithFirstName:lastName:inContext:`, right?

Not so fast. You'll have to take care of the second part of the selector, and that means examining every instance of `last:` to make sure it's part of the `quarterbackWithFirstName:last:inContext:` selector. To be correct, a search would have to involve a regular expression that captures all, and only, the uses of those strings that are the selector for that method. That means accounting for the arguments that come between the parts; the possibility that a call might be spread across more than one line; interpolation of line and delimited comments; uses of the bare selector in `@selector` expressions; and preventing changes to a possible method named `quarterbackWithFirstName:last:team:inContext:`.

If you're a regular-expression hobbyist, you might be able to come up with search-and-replace expressions that work. But they would take more time to formulate and verify than it would to do all the changes by hand. Refactoring does it right the first time.

`quarterbackWithFirstName:last:inContext:` is declared in `PRPasser.h` and defined in `PRPasser.m`. Open either file, and click anywhere in the name of the method. Select **Edit** → **Refactor** → **Rename. . . .**

A sheet appears, with just the original selector shown. As you edit the selector, you'll find that Xcode will not accept the new name—it will display an error message—unless it has the same number of colons as in the original selector. That makes sense; if the number of arguments differs, there's no way to redistribute them.

Click **Preview**, and examine the changes in the comparison sheet. (Xcode will probably offer to make a snapshot of your project, as it did in Chapter 7, "Version Control.") Every use of the symbol—the declaration, the definition, and calls, whether on one line or three—are changed. Xcode can do this because refactoring doesn't rely on searching at all: It has an index of all uses of the symbol, so it can differentiate it from near-misses and ignore issues of spacing and parameters. See Figure 10.1.

Click **Save**, and commit the change to version control. (Yes, really. You should commit every time you have a group of modified files that represent a single, logical change to your project. If you commit frequently, your commit log will reflect your intentions, and not be just a list of mini-backups.)

Refactoring a Class Name

There's another naming problem, this time with the `PRMasterViewController` class. The name, provided by the project template, is descriptive in its way, but it describes the class's *role*, and not what it *does*. It's a list of passers, and the name ought to reflect it: `PRPasserListController`. This is another case for the name-refactoring tool.

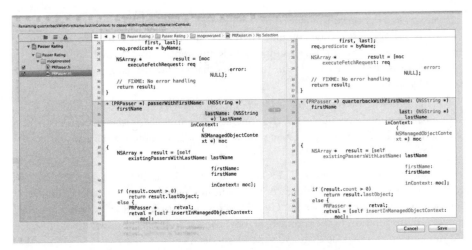

Figure 10.1   When you use refactoring to rename a method, the Comparison editor shows you the changes to be made. The result text (left) cannot be edited.

Surely this *can* be done with a search-and-replace? That doesn't quite work. For one thing, though it isn't the case here, PRMasterViewController might appear as a substring of some other symbol.

For another, the name of PRMasterViewController isn't just in text files. iOS apps are laid out in .nib and .storyboardc files—object archives—which refer to classes by name. .xib files, from which Xcode compiles NIBs, and .storyboard files, from which .storyboardcs are derived, are ultimately XML, but the XML is emphatically not human-editable. You'd have to go into a special editor, Interface Builder, and ferret out all the references.

Find the class name PRMasterViewController in either the .m or .h file, and click on it. Then select **Edit → Refactor → Rename. . .** , as before. Enter PRPasserListController, and make sure you check the **Rename related files** box. Click **Preview**, and have a look at the changes:

- Wherever PRMasterViewController had appeared in the source files, Xcode has substituted PRPasserListController. You've seen this already.

- The files whose base names had been PRMasterViewController now have the base name PRPasserListController.

- In the .m files for PRPasserListController and PRAppDelegate,

  #import "PRMasterViewController.h"

  has been changed to

  #import "PRPasserListController.h"

  so the renaming of the files carries over into the #import directives.

- `Main.storyboard` is included in the list of changed files. Look at the comparisons: You'll see some complex XML, and the class-name references are changed. You'll also see that this isn't a simple search-and-replace in the XML source; the refactoring made structural edits to the files that would not have been safe for you to do by hand.

- The names of the files in the header comments haven't changed. Refactoring renames only the symbols, not the contents of comments or strings. Xcode can't be sure which occurrences of a string in human-readable content are literal and not symbolic.

Save and commit the changes. The Commit editor will flag the `PRMasterViewController` files as **A+**, to indicate that they've been "added" under their new names. Behind the scenes, Git will record a deletion of the files with the old names, and the addition of them under the new names; and it will bridge the old histories into the new entries. Xcode spares you the messy details.

Editing the View Controller

The new `PRPasserListController` method is still set up to display the placeholder `Event` entity from the template. That's long gone, and you'll have to substitute your own code to show `Passers`. The template code is set up to use `NSFetchedResultsController`, an auxiliary class that provides many services for listing, grouping, sorting, and editing a list of Core Data objects.

`NSFetchedResultsController` is a very powerful facility, but you have to be comfortable with quite a bit of Core Data before you can use it effectively. If I were teaching Cocoa programming, I'd put it off as the advanced topic it is. But this is an Xcode book, the code is already there, and we're going to soldier on.

In Chapter 11, "Building a New View," you'll see some of the underlying mechanism, which is simpler for simple things.

Start by adding the umbrella model-class header we had `mogenerator` create, so `PRPasserListController` can pull data from the model classes:

```
#import "PRDataModel.h"
```

The Table View

`PRPasserListController` is a subclass of `UITableViewController`, itself a subclass of `UIViewController` that takes care of some of the details of views that consist solely of tables. Table views fill themselves in through the *delegate* design pattern: The table provides almost all of the user-side behavior, and calls back to the controller (or other object)—the delegate—to provide the details that make a particular use of the table special. A `UITableView` doesn't keep any data itself; it pulls it from the data-source delegate.

Table-view delegates serve up the *cells* that make up the rows of the table; they create `UITableViewCells` and fill them in with data. Typically, this is done only when the table asks for a row (in the method `tableView:cellForRowAtIndexPath:`). The controller you get from the template factors populating the cell into the custom `configureCell:atIndexPath:` method. Find that method, and substitute this:

```
- (void) configureCell: (UITableViewCell *) cell
        atIndexPath: (NSIndexPath *) indexPath
{
    PRPasser *    passer = (PRPasser *)
            [self.fetchedResultsController objectAtIndexPath:indexPath];
    NSString *  content = [NSString stringWithFormat: @"%@ %@ (%.1f)",
                                passer.firstName, passer.lastName,
                                passer.passerRating];
    cell.textLabel.text = content;
}
```

The `indexPath` indicates which section (always zero for this simple list) and row the cell is for. The method pulls the corresponding `PRPasser` from the fetched-results controller (which mediates between the database and this controller) and then formats a string with the `PRPasser`'s information. That string goes into the text content of the cell.

Setting Up the Passer List

The `fetchedResultsController` method sets up a fetch request (think of it as a `SELECT`, if you're SQL-minded) that describes and sorts the objects for presentation to the view controller. There are two changes.

- Change the lines that initialize the `NSFetchRequest` and point it at the `Event` entity to a single line that initializes the request for `Passer`:

```
NSFetchRequest *fetchRequest =
    [NSFetchRequest fetchRequestWithEntityName: @"Passer"];
```

- The fetch request can have sort descriptors (`ORDER BY`) that turn the unordered set of fetch results into a sorted array. Create `NSSortDescriptor`s for the last and first names, package them in an `NSArray`, and attach them to the fetch request in place of the template's sort on `timeStamp`:

```
NSArray *        sortDescriptors;
sortDescriptors = @[
    [NSSortDescriptor sortDescriptorWithKey: @"lastName"
                                  ascending: YES],
    [NSSortDescriptor sortDescriptorWithKey: @"firstName"
                                  ascending: YES]
                    ];
fetchRequest.sortDescriptors = sortDescriptors;
```

Creating a New Passer

The `insertNewObject` method gets called when the **+** button in the navigation bar at the top of the table is tapped; the link is made in `viewDidLoad`. The code in the middle inserts an `Event` in the database and sets its `timeStamp`. As supplied in the template, `insertNewObject` pulls the entity (table) type from the `fetchedResultsController`, and instantiates the new object from that.

That's clever, but you already have a generator for `PRPasser` instances that avoids all the filibuster. Replace the body of the method with:

```
- (void) insertNewObject: (id) sender
{
    //  Leave this in. I'll explain why.
    NSEntityDescription *entity =
        [[self.fetchedResultsController fetchRequest] entity];

    //  Create a new PRPasser.
    PRPasser *          newPasser =
        [PRPasser passerWithFirstName: @"FirstName"
                             lastName: @"LastName"
                            inContext:  self.managedObjectContext];
    newPasser.currentTeam = @"TeamName";

    // Save the context.
    NSError *error;
    if (![self.managedObjectContext save:&error]) {
        //  ...
        NSLog(@"Unresolved error %@, %@", error, [error userInfo]);
        abort();
    }
}
```

Giving every new Passer the same name and team isn't ideal, but it lets us move on and get back to it later.

Live Issues and Fix-it

I've made some substantial changes, and I'd like to see whether the compiler will accept them. In a traditional workflow—and if you followed my advice in the "Quieting Xcode Down" section of Chapter 2, "Kicking the Tires," you're in a traditional workflow—you'd run the file through a check compilation.

Xcode 5 has a command to do just that: **Product →Perform Action →Compile** will compile just the file in the current editor, without triggering a recompilation of the whole project. The command is buried two layers deep, but you could always use the **Key Bindings** panel of the Preferences window to assign a convenient key equivalent.

If you select the command, and you and I are in sync (go to the sample code if we aren't), there won't be any errors, but there will be a warning in `insertNewObject`— "Unused variable: entity."

You can see this is so. When you removed the generic Core Data methods for creating `Event` and substituted the `PRPasser` constructor, you cut out the need for an entity description (the constructor handles it)—but I asked you to leave it in, just for this example. So you can comment the line out and compile `PRPasserListController.m` again.

There's another way to do this, which most people prefer; it's a matter of taste. Back in Chapter 2, I had you go into the Preferences window, **General** panel, and uncheck **Show live issues**. Go back and check it.

What happens now? With no errors, nothing much. Try uncommenting that orphaned `entity`. The warning comes back—you didn't have to command a recompilation. Now, in the expression `[self.managedObjectContext save: &error]`, in the `if` statement in the middle of the method, delete the `t` in `managedObjectContext`. This time, an error badge appears, and the fragment gets a red dotted underline.

Click the red badge. A banner appears in the editor saying, "Property 'managedObjectContex' not found on object of type 'PasserListController *'; did you mean 'managedObjectContext'?"

Beg pardon? Did I *mean* `managedObjectContext`?

There's more: Xcode shows a popover window rooted at the misspelled symbol, with the same message, and, highlighted, the message: "Fix-it: Replace 'managedObjectContex' with 'managedObjectContext'" (Figure 10.2).

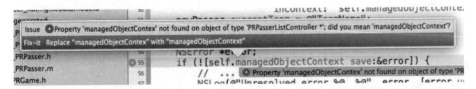

Figure 10.2   Xcode flags code issues almost immediately. Clicking the badge for an error may produce a "Fix-it" popover, offering to change the problem code to something that would cure the error. Double-clicking the fix, or pressing Return, will edit the code.

But wait—what you see in the underlying text already says `managedObjectContext`, with the `t`. That's because Xcode is showing you the fix it is offering. If you click away from the popover, it, and the proposed fix, will go away. Instead, double-click on the offered fix, or just press the Return key. Xcode makes the edit, and the error goes away.

Fix-it is not just a spelling checker. It uses the `llvm` library to gain insights into your code and to check what it finds against questionable coding practices. For instance, this sort of loop is idiomatic in C programming:

```
int     ch;
while (ch = getchar())
    putchar(ch);
```

but using an assignment (=) in a Boolean context like the condition of a `while` statement smells. Meaning an equality test (==) and doing an assignment is a very common error. When the missing-braces-and-parentheses warning is enabled, Xcode will detect that you could mean either assignment or comparison, and the Fix-it popover will offer corrections that suit either interpretation. See Figure 10.3.

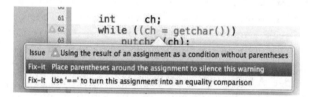

Figure 10.3   When more than one solution is possible (as in this assignment in the condition of a `while` loop), Fix-it will offer the alternatives and demonstrate what the corrected code would look like.

The Real Passer Rating

If all has gone well, you no longer have a boilerplate application: You have an app that calculates and displays passer ratings. Let's try it out. Select **Product → Run** (⌘ **R**).

Another Bug

By now you know that when I say something like "if all has gone well," the app will crash. And so it has: The Debug navigator shows a trace back through an exception handler, and the console says

```
Terminating app due to uncaught exception 'NSInvalidArgumentException',
    reason: '*** -[NSDictionary initWithObjects:forKeys:]:
        count of objects (1) differs from count of keys (12)'
```

followed by a stack trace that last touched your code at `-[SimpleCSVFile run:error:]`. It would be nice to see what was going on in `run:error:`, but after the app ran through the exception handler, that information was lost. It would be nice if it weren't.

> **Note**
>
> An *exception* is a signal by program code—your own or in the system—that something has gone wrong. When an exception is raised, execution resumes at the nearest caller that has registered to handle it. If nothing does handle it, the last-resort handler kills the application. That's what happened here. Coders in other languages often use exceptions as routine control structures; the practice in Objective-C, where exceptions have historically been expensive, is to use them only for conditions that are truly exceptional, impairing the normal operation of the app.

There is a way to do that. Open the Breakpoint navigator, which shows you a list of all the breakpoints you set in your project. It isn't confined to what you created by clicking in the margins of your source; in particular, you can set an *exception breakpoint*, which will halt execution whenever an exception is raised.

You'll find a **+** button at the bottom-left corner of the Breakpoint navigator. If you click it, you'll be shown a popup menu, from which you can select **Add Exception Breakpoint. . . .** An "All Exceptions" breakpoint appears in the list. You can configure it (right-click it, or Option-Command-click to see a popover), but the default behavior is good enough.

> **Note**
>
> One case for editing the breakpoint is to cut off C++ exceptions, which some OS libraries use routinely.

With the exception breakpoint set, run Passer Rating one more time. Now when the exception is raised, the debugger shows you the last point of contact with your code:

```
// Compose a dictionary of the fields, keyed by the headers.
NSDictionary * values =
            [NSDictionary dictionaryWithObjects: fields
                                       forKeys: self.headers];
```

and the stack trace in the Debug navigator shows you the backtrace you got in the console message before. Almost.

The main part of the Debug navigator is taken up by the stack trace, showing all of the pending functions from the crashed/breakpointed function at the top, to your root `main` function at the bottom. Your functions are highlighted in two ways: First, their names are shown in black instead of gray, to show that Xcode can display their source code.

Second, they are marked with a blue icon with the head-and-shoulders badge that Apple customarily uses for "user." The icon indicates the framework the function came from. Other examples are a purple mug for the Cocoa frameworks, an olive series of dotted lines (which may represent layers of bricks) for Foundation and Core Foundation, a dark-pink briefcase for the event-servicing frameworks, and a tan circle for the runtime library.

Not many of these are interesting. There is a lot that goes on inside Cocoa, and beyond knowing what called you, what you called, and what crashed, there's not much profit in watching Cocoa crawl around inside itself. Xcode understands. At the bottom of the

Debug navigator is a slider (Figure 10.4) that filters the stack trace. When it's at the far right, you see everything. As you drag it to the left, Xcode edits more and more of the "irrelevant" frames out of the list.

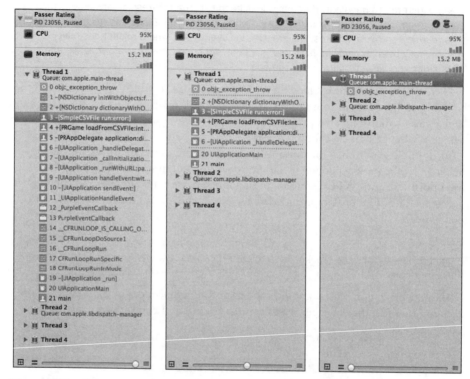

Figure 10.4   (left) When your application is stopped in the debugger, the Debug navigator shows the current stack trace of each of the app's threads. (middle) The slider at the bottom of the navigator controls the amount of detail in the stack trace, letting you focus on your own code. (right) Sliding the control too far to the left can elide more stack frames than is useful.

If you drag the slider all the way to the left, all you'll see are the first and last functions, which probably doesn't tell you anything. But somewhere in the middle, you'll get what you need: what crashed, what code of yours was running, and a frame of context to either side. In the middle of Figure 10.4, you see a stack 22 frames deep reduced to the 8 you need.

The debugger, especially the description of the exception, tells you what you need: The last of our lines to be executed was, you remember,

```
NSDictionary *  values =
        [NSDictionary dictionaryWithObjects: fields
                                    forKeys: self.headers];
```

The exception message said that there was only 1 object for 12 keys, so immediately you're interested in `fields` and `self.headers`. Have a look at the variables pane at the left of the Debug area (Figure 10.5). Click the disclosure triangles in the left margin. Sure enough, the `fields` variable holds an `NSArray` (which is the public, abstract class—what's shown is the concrete subclass `-NSArrayI`) with one element, an empty string. `_headers`, the instance variable backing the `headers` property, points to an array of 12 elements.

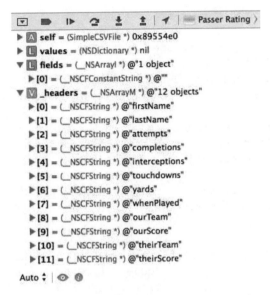

Figure 10.5   The variables pane of the Debug area can interpret the contents of many Objective-C objects.

So the question is, what would cause a line to present a single empty element? Well, if the file ends with a newline character, the "last" line, as delimited by the last newline, will be empty. Disclosing the contents of `self` in the variable display confirms this: `_lineCount` is exactly the number of lines in `sample-data.csv`.

The solution is to add one test before the assignment to `values`:

```
//  Skip blank lines.
if (fields.count <= 1)
    continue;
```

And, because the CSV parser ought to catch some errors:

```
if (fields.count != self.headers.count) {
    //  The record does not have the same number of fields as
    //  specified in the header.
```

```
    if (error) {
        *error = [self badLineFormatError: fields.count];
    }
    return NO;
}
```

...where `badLineFormatError:` is a convenience method that builds the error object:

```
- (NSError *) badLineFormatError: (NSUInteger) fieldCount
{
    NSString *      localizedDescription =
    [NSString stringWithFormat:
        @"%@:%d: Expected %d fields, got %d.",
        self.path, self.lineCount, self.headers.count, fieldCount];

    NSDictionary *  userInfo = @{
        kCSVErrorLineKey            : @(self.lineCount),
        kCSVExpectedFieldsKey       : @(self.headers.count),
        kCSVActualFieldsKey         : @(fieldCount),
        NSFilePathErrorKey          : self.path,
        NSLocalizedDescriptionKey   : localizedDescription
        };

    return [NSError errorWithDomain: WT9TErrorDomain
                               code: errCSVBadFormatLine
                           userInfo: userInfo];
}
```

Running Passer Rating

Everything is fixed now, I promise. Run the app. The iOS Simulator starts, and after a delay, you see the first cut at Passer Rating (Figure 10.6). It required a little focused effort on the controller end, but the data model seems to be holding up with some reasonable-looking results. When you swipe across a row in the table, or tap the **Edit** button, the app offers to delete a passer, and when you tap **Delete**, the passer collapses out of sight. The + button creates one passer with the name "FirstName LastName," but that's all you asked for. As far as it goes, the app works (until you tap one of the passer's entries in the list; the app will crash when it can't find the `timeStamp` attribute in `PRPasser`).

> **Note**
>
> Deleting passers in the running app is a little frightening because you can do that only so many times—at most 43, from this data set. However, you're not going to run out because I've rigged `PRAppDelegate` to reload the sample dataset every time the app is run.

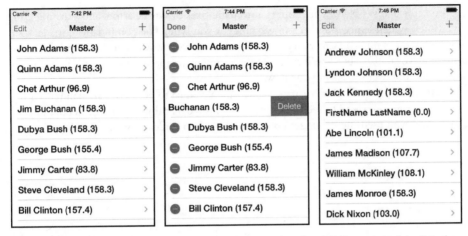

Figure 10.6 The first real version of Passer Rating, at last. It reads the sample data, lists the passers and their ratings, and responds to commands to add and delete passers.

When you're done, click the Home button at the bottom of the simulated iPhone (or **Hardware → Home**, ⇧⌘H, if your screen can't accommodate the simulated devices at a one-for-one scale), and return to Xcode. But wait: The **Stop** button in the Workspace window's toolbar is still enabled. What's going on?

Remember that iOS apps don't halt when the Home button is pressed; they go into suspension in the background, and can resume their run at any time. The **Stop** button is still active, and the debugger is still running, because Passer Rating hasn't quit. Tapping its icon on the home screen will bring it to the foreground again, still running.

This is the right thing to do, but not always what you want. If you want your app to stop, click the **Stop** button. Or, simply go on with your work, and issue the **Run** command. Xcode will present a sheet offering to stop the incumbent.

> **Warning**
>
> The alert that offers to stop the incumbent process offers to suppress this warning in the future. *Don't check that box.* Suppose you are engaged in a long debugging session, and you are at a breakpoint. You want to resume running. You're concentrating on your work, not the tool. Which button, labeled with a triangle, will you reach for? The tiny **Continue** button tucked into the lower middle of the window? Or the large, friendly **Run** button at the top left, which would ruin your debugging history if that alert didn't save you?

Summary

In this chapter, I proved the data model by turning it into a real iPhone application. On the way, I got into one of the things that the Xcode refactoring engine can do for you: intelligent renaming of Objective-C classes and methods in ways that a simple search-and-replace could not match.

You came across Fix-it, which offers automatic fixes of syntax errors and warnings, and Live Issues, which exposes errors and warnings as you type. The combination, made possible by the nimble `llvm` library, won't be enough to remove "check compilation" from your vocabulary, but you'll find that the moment-to-moment support will keep you working with fewer breaks in your flow.

A bug in Passer Rating's CSV parser gave you a chance to get better acquainted with the Debug navigator, and to see how it can do a little data mining to make debugging easier. And, you used the debugger console to get a better idea of what's going on.

11

Building a New View

The passer list works well enough now. It's not fancy, but it very nearly matches the wireframe in Figure 8.2. One thing it is lacking is a transition from a list of passers to a passer summary and a list of games. For this, you will create a new view controller and make the acquaintance of Interface Builder.

The Next View Controller

The thing to remember is that unless you are doing some custom drawing or event handling, there's little reason to create a new subclass of `UIView`. The standard views are so generic, versatile, and easy to combine that making a new one is rare. What isn't rare is the need to set the content of views and respond to the events they capture. You know already that this is the business of the controller layer of the MVC design pattern, for which you'll need a subclass `UIViewController`.

The application template you started with did this for you: `PRDetailViewController` is already in your project in the form of `.h` and `.m` files, and its scene in `Main.storyboard`. Once again, the default name is uninformative, so select the class name at the `@interface` directive in `PRDetailViewController.h`, issue **Edit → Refactor → Rename...**, and rename it to `PRGameListController`.

Version control will show the `PRGameListController` files with **A+** badges, reflecting the new-but-not-new nature of renamed files. The `PRPasserListController` files, which referred to `PRDetailViewController`, are badged **M**. Now would be a good time to commit a revision.

If You Want to Add a View Controller

This time around, it wasn't necessary to add a view controller. The master-detail project template provided a detail view, and all you had to do was a little renaming and repurposing. What would you have to do to create a new view controller?

It's not hard. First, you need interface (.h) and implementation (.m) files for a subclass of `UIViewController`. Select **File → New → File...** (⌘ N), and pick the iOS → Cocoa Touch → Objective-C class template. You'd name the class, select `UIViewController` as the superclass, find that Xcode had appended `ViewController` to the class name you'd just typed, and change your class name back. This being a view controller, there will be two checkboxes that I'll discuss shortly.

> **Note**
>
> Xcode's revision of the name you chose for your class is annoying, but the principle is sound: Pick a name that describes the role. It seems obvious, but the temptation to call a controller for editing passers `PasserEditor` or `PasserEditorView` is strong.

Click **Next**, and use the get-folder sheet as you have before, to pick a place for the files on-disk, select a project group to display them, and assign them to one or more targets.

In principle, you're done. Your controller could build its entire view tree in code by implementing the `-loadView` method.

In practice, you'd rarely do that. You would instead embody the controller's view in a layout created in an Interface Builder document—usually a storyboard so you can integrate it into the flow of your application design. If you need a stand-alone design—for instance, if you intend to use the same layout repeatedly in different contexts—you'd isolate the view in its own XIB file.

That's the purpose of the two checkboxes that become active when you create files for a view controller: **Targeted for iPad** and **With XIB for user interface**. Check the latter to have Xcode create a XIB linked to the new class. The former determines whether the view will be iPad- or iPhone-sized.

If you want to add your controller to the storyboard flow, you'll add it and its view to the canvas as a scene. Create the scene by looking for **View Controller** in the Object library in the Utility area, and dragging it into the canvas, where it will bloom to the size of a screen. Click the bar below the scene to select the controller, and use the **Custom Class** field in the Identity inspector (third tab) to identify your new class as the controller.

Back to our story. Refactor to change `PRDetailViewController` into `PRGameListController`. The refactoring will automatically change the name of the controller class for the detail-view scene.

Storyboards, Scenes, and Segues

Superficially, Interface Builder looks like a tool for drawing UI layouts. And that is *part* of what it does: More accurately, Interface Builder is a visual editor for the relationships between objects in your application. What-goes-where is just one kind of relationship.

> **Note**
>
> From the 1990s through Xcode 3, Interface Builder was a separate application. There are other editors in Xcode that are also radically different from the main code editor, but

because of its long history of being a stand-alone application, people still speak of IB as a thing apart.

You've seen UI-layout editors before, on many other platforms: Most of them emit executable code that constructs the view hierarchy described in the editor; or they work on files that the build process turns into executable code; or at least they construct data streams that script the creation of UI objects. IB is similar in that the files it works on are compiled and installed at build time for use in the target application.

That's where the similarity ends. Remember this: *There is no code. There is no script.* Interface Builder products are not executable; instead they are archives of Objective-C objects. The archives include links between objects and methods both within themselves and externally. Many newcomers who are used to other systems want code so they can "see how it's really done." The IB products *are* how it's really done. Except in trivial cases, it's hard to produce code that mimics NIB loading correctly; and in some cases (particularly on OS X) it isn't possible.

Note

That is at least where you should start your thinking. On iOS, it's often useful to instantiate, arrange, and link views dynamically—it's how many project templates start out—but code should not be the first technique you try. Interface Builder can be intimidating because it feels magical. As with most of Cocoa, it does things you may be used to controlling yourself. Relax. In the long run, if you learn to use Interface Builder effectively, you'll spend much less of your life fighting the operating system.

A storyboard goes beyond even that: It provides a *canvas* that holds *scenes*, each representing a controller that runs (roughly) a whole screen at a time; linked by *segues* running from individual controls to the next scene to be presented. When tapping a button in the running app triggers a segue, the tap goes directly to UIKit, which creates the next scene and its controller, gives the outgoing controller a chance to touch up the new one's configuration, and moves the scene onto the screen. Again: The storyboard product makes a lot happen that you may be accustomed to controlling yourself. If you can adjust your thinking to take advantage of the flow, you'll find you can do almost anything, and much more easily.

Arranging Your Tools

Interface Builder has peculiar needs for its editing space. A completed storyboard is very large—there are zoom-in and -out buttons in the bottom-right corner of the canvas view—but even if you are working on a single screen in your app, every pixel in the canvas view is precious. A Mac screen that is otherwise respectable for development probably won't show all of an iPad layout at once.

Note

At the maximum, zoomed-in scale, the canvas displays the layout to match the screen point-for-point. This is the only scale at which Interface Builder allows you to lay out views. However, you can link outlets, actions, and segues in zoomed-out views.

At the left edge, IB has a Document Outline view that you'll rarely want to close, and on the right, you need the Utility area open to create and adjust the views you insert. If you use an Assistant editor (and sometimes you must), things get tighter still. What you don't need are the Navigator area, because you'll spend most of your time on one IB document, or the Debug area.

This is a job for tabs. You probably already have your workspace window set up as you prefer for editing source files. Start from there. Select **File →New →New Tab** (⌘ T). This is where you'll do all your IB work, so double-click on the tab's name and change it to `Interface Builder`.

Now configure the tab: Use the Project navigator to select `Main.storyboard`. With the **View** control in the toolbar (three rectangles with portions highlighted), close the Navigator and Debug areas and open the Utility area. The bottom part of the Utility area is called the Library; select the Object library tab (the third one, with the cube) to show the repertoire of objects you can put into the canvas or a scene.

With the Project navigator gone, how will you get to other files? That's not a problem in this project: Passer Rating has one storyboard, and that's all it will ever need. But sooner or later you'll have a project with more than one file that needs attention from Interface Builder. How do you switch among them without shoving the Navigator area back into the window?

You've probably already noticed the bar that spans the top of the Editor area. This is the *jump bar*. It presents a number of controls for navigating your project directly. What interests you at the moment is the path control, spanning most of the bar. It takes the form of a series of arrow-shaped segments. Each segment is a link in the chain that starts with the project and goes down through the project's groups, to the file on which the editor is focused. (In the case of structured documents, it will go on through the hierarchy of functions or IB objects.) If the current file has a selection, one last link identifies the selection by name. See Figure 11.1.

Clicking a segment displays a popup menu offering a choice of the projects, groups, files, and selections available at that level in the hierarchy. The popup is itself hierarchical, so you can trace a new path for the editor. If one level of the jump bar has too many items to search by eye, you can narrow it incrementally by typing a search string—the search key isn't consecutive, so **prcon** will turn up the **PRPasserListController** and **PRGameListController** source files.

This suggests a strategy if you want to keep a dedicated **Interface Builder** tab. Open the Project navigator again. In the search field at the bottom, type **.xib** to narrow the list down to the project's XIBs. Command-click each so they are all selected. Then select **File →New →Group from Selection**. All of your XIBs are now in a common group, which means that they are all at the same level in your jump bar. You can move your storyboard files to the same group. The file segment of the path control will switch you among the design files directly. You can close the Project navigator for good. Your workspace should look like Figure 11.2.

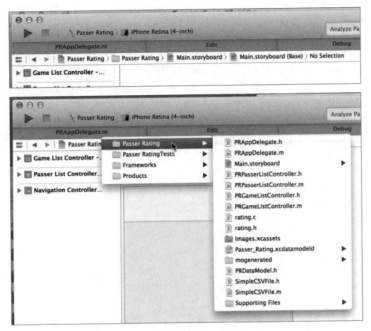

Figure 11.1   (top) The jump bar runs across the Editor area between the tabs and the editor itself. The main part of it is a path control tracing from the project through your groups to the current file and its selection. (bottom) Each level of the path control is a hierarchical popup menu that lets you set the path.

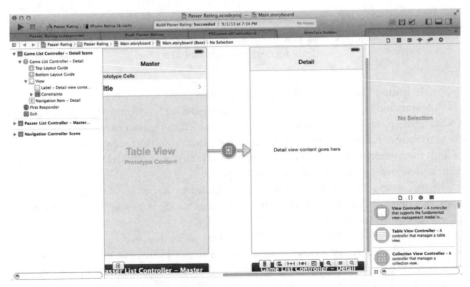

Figure 11.2   Interface Builder is easier to use if you give it its own tab, configured for the purpose.

Building a View

The Master-Detail Application template provides a detail controller class (the one we've renamed to PRGameListController) and realizes it in Main.storyboard as the third scene in the canvas (Figure 11.3). The first scene, marked with the single arrow that shows it is the initial scene in the storyboard, is for a UINavigationController. It is joined by a *root view controller* segue to its initial content, the PRPasserListController that presents the roster of passers. In turn, a *push* segue links it to the next step, the game list.

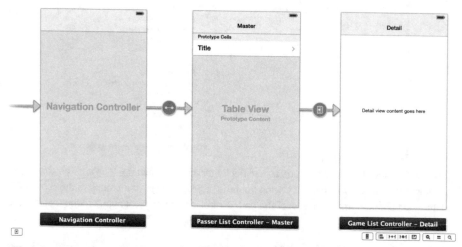

Figure 11.3   The master-detail project template fills Main.storyboard with three scenes: A navigation controller that contains a master scene (Passer List Controller), which cascades to a detail scene (Game List Controller).

The navigation controller is a wrapper on the other two; it manages a stack of views that slide into and out of the screen as the user navigates a hierarchy, such as from a passer in a list to the passer's detailed record. It also maintains a navigation bar at the top of the screen to display the current view's title and a back button so the user can step back through the hierarchy (from passer to passer list). The first scene linked to it is the *root view*, the first view the navigation controller will display.

The succeeding views in the controller stack all display navigation bars, but those controllers don't actually manage those bars: The bars are there so you can allow for the space as you work the layout out.

The last view in the chain, the "detail" view that we've renamed PRGameListController, comes from the template as a plain view, empty but for a single label; the template simply filled the label with the time-of-day held by the dummy Event entity. That's not what we want, but before we get rid of it, there's something to notice.

Outlets and Assistants, in Passing

Click the middle item in the **Editor** group in the toolbar—it looks like a formal vest and bow tie (meant to suggest the uniform of a butler). This adds an *Assistant editor* to the Editor area. This probably ruins the window layout you worked so hard to construct, so make adjustments until you have something like Figure 11.4.

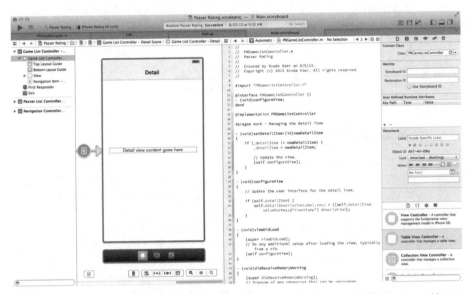

Figure 11.4   Adding the Assistant editor by clicking the middle button in the **Editor** group (the one that looks like a vest and tie) requires some adjustments to the project layout.

At base, the Assistant editor is just another editor, allowing you to see more than one file as you work on them. And that is one way you can use it. What makes the Assistant editor special is that it can automate its choice of content, adapting itself to what you do in the main editor. The jump bar in the assistant determines the relationship it will pursue. Use the first segment as a menu to set the assistant to **Automatic**, and click on the various objects in the IB canvas. You'll see that the assistant shows the source code that backs each object.

Click the black bar below the Game Controller scene. As fits the pattern, the Assistant editor fills with either PRGameListController.m or PRGameListController.h. Because two files meet the need, the control at the right end of the jump bar shows **2**, and you can click the arrowheads on either side to switch between them. (You can do the same from the keyboard by giving the code editor focus—click in it—and pressing ⌃ ⌘ **Up-Arrow**.)

Select PRGameListController.h. The template has added this line to the class @interface:

```
@property (weak, nonatomic) IBOutlet UILabel *detailDescriptionLabel;
```

So: One of the properties of the controller is a reference to the label in the middle of the view. There's something more—notice the keyword IBOutlet. In modern Objective-C, it's a keyword, but historically, the symbol was simply a macro defined to be empty. It is merely a signal to Interface Builder that this property of the view controller is eligible to receive a pointer to something in the scene.

For your first look at what this means, hover the mouse cursor over the dot you see in the gutter next to the line (Figure 11.5). That dot shows that a link has been made between an IB object and that outlet. Interface Builder demonstrates the link by highlighting the label in the canvas when the mouse hovers over the linkage dot.

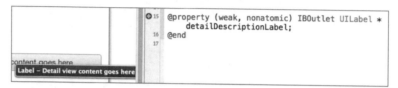

Figure 11.5   IBOutlet properties are meant to be filled with pointers to objects that will be realized when a scene is loaded. Hovering the mouse cursor over the linkage bubble next to an outlet @property directive highlights the corresponding object in the controller's scene.

That's all there is to see this time around; there will be much more later. For now, we don't need that label. Select it in the game-controller scene, and press Delete. After taking note that the connection bubble next to the @property directive is now empty, select the line and delete that, too. Now that the outlet property is no longer defined, Xcode will flag an error at every attempt to reference it; delete those lines, too.

Warning

If you go the other way around, and forget to delete the label, you're heading for a crash: When the scene loads, the storyboard still calls for linking the label. UIKit will look for the outlet property in the controller, and will throw an exception when it doesn't find it. The error message will be only vaguely helpful, and you're on your own finding the dangling reference. Make sure you clean up both ends.

The Billboard View

Now you can add content of your own. The design calls for two elements: a billboard containing overall statistics for the passer, and a table with the details of each game. Start with the billboard.

The billboard will contain labels of various sizes and styles. First, add the container itself. Click in the search field at the bottom of the Object library (third tab, bottom part of the Utility area), and type **UIView**. You'll see an entry labeled "View." Drag it out of the library and into the scene in the editor. As you drag it, it transforms into a rectangle that sizes itself to the available space in the scene. Let it go.

You don't want this view to take up the whole space. Click on it to display resizing "handles" at the sides and corners. Drag the bottom edge up until the view takes up about the top quarter of the available space on a 4-inch screen. This may be a bit tricky—IB clips the handles to the edge of the superview. It may be easier to grab the top handle, size it down, then drag the resized view up until it abuts the navigation bar.

> **Note**
>
> If you're ambitious, you could use the Size inspector (fifth tab), which will show you the location and size of the view numerically. It should be at 0, 64, width 320 points, and height 162 (you may have to vary the size to accommodate your eventual layout).

The detail view is supposed to be light gray, to match the navigation bar. In the Attributes inspector, there's a **Background** control, which has two parts: The left part is a color well, which you can click to get a color palette to edit the color. The right part is a drop-down menu containing standard colors. At the time I wrote this, the palette was still set to the iOS 6 colors, so you'll have to set it yourself. Click the color well to bring up the color-picker palette; click the magnifying-glass button and then the navigation bar that's already in the scene. The inspector should look like Figure 11.6.

Pretty nice, eh? Use the first segment of the Assistant editor's jump bar to display a **Preview** of the layout. (Select the PRGameListController scene if it isn't already selected.) You'll see something like Figure 11.7, with the scene rendered as it will be on screen.

The controls in the corner of the Preview view let you experiment with screen sizes,

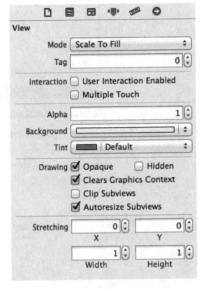

Figure 11.6 The Attributes inspector for the passer billboard view should look like this when you're done.

orientations, and UI idioms (such as iOS 6 versus iOS 7). Click the one on the right to shrink the screen from 4 inches to 3.5, as in Figure 11.8, on the left. So far, so good: The billboard shows the size and position we intended. Click the middle button, with the curved arrow, to rotate the screen, and we have work to do: The top-left corner of the billboard is still where we want it, but the view, being the same width as before, doesn't stretch across its container (Figure 11.8, top right).

But the Preview assistant didn't tell you the whole story. Run the app in the iOS Simulator with a destination of **iPhone Retina (3.5 inch)**. The preview thought the billboard would still be snug against the navigation bar, but the simulator shows that it hangs below it—the navigation bar in landscape orientation is shallower than in portrait.

There is some fixing up to do. To do it, you'll make your first encounter (brief or extended) with autolayout.

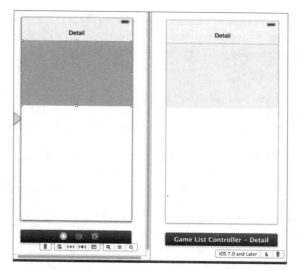

Figure 11.7   Selecting the **Preview** view in the Assistant editor's jump bar displays a straightforward rendering of the selected scene. Controls at the lower left change the presentation of the view for different screen sizes, orientations, and idioms.

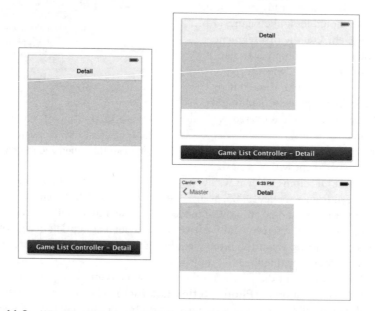

Figure 11.8   When the Preview assistant is changed to show the scene on a portrait-oriented iPhone 4 screen (left), the billboard view is placed where you would expect it to be. (top right) Turning the iPhone 4 preview to landscape orientation shows the billboard's top-left corner sticks to its original placement, but the view doesn't stretch across its container as intended. (bottom right) Running the layout in the iOS Simulator, however, shows that the Preview assistant hadn't shown the accurate layout.

Autolayout for the Nonce

Autolayout allows you to specify your *intentions* for how views are to be laid out—this view spaced 8 points from that, centers aligned, and so on. You express your intentions as a system of *constraints*, which Cocoa reconciles to lay out your views. It is versatile and effective.

The core principles are not hard to understand: Every view's size and placement on both axes should be completely specified by a chain of constraints that must not contain contradictions. Simple.

Simple to understand, but not to get right. I wasn't satisfied with the constraints system for the billboard view we're about to build until I had produced nearly 40 of them. Some conflicts are inevitable, and you have to give autolayout a way out by assigning priorities among them, and in a long chain of dependencies, there's a lot of trial and error. Doing the billboard view right would consume most of this chapter.

Which is why we're going to do it quick and dirty in this chapter, and do it right in the next. You really should read that chapter—in iOS 7, as a practical matter, autolayout is not an optional feature—but if you can live with quick and dirty, I won't be there to scold you.

This chapter will be all about building the billboard view. There are two things you must do to get over the immediate problem of the billboard disappearing:

1. Click the black bar below the `PRGameListController` scene, and select **Editor → Resolve Auto Layout Issues → Add Missing Constraints in Game List Controller**. This will put best-guess constraints on the billboard view's position relative to its nearest neighbors.
2. If you still have the Preview assistant open to show a 3.5-inch screen in portrait mode, you see that the billboard is compressed vertically, from the intended height of 162 points to 74. If you rotate the preview, the height of the billboard goes to nothing.
3. Select the billboard view, and look at the Size inspector (fifth tab): At the bottom of the panel is a list of the constraints IB added to the view. Horizontally the "leading" and "trailing" spaces (I'll get to that terminology soon) are fixed to the container, and those don't seem to be a problem; you want the sides glued to the sides of the screen.

The top and bottom edges are placed relative to the respective *layout guides*, notional lines in the screen view that represent the extent to which upper and lower bars (navigation, tab, status, toolbar) compress the usable vertical space. As I placed and sized the billboard, the top edge is one point from the upper guide, and 341 from the lower. The upper guide, allowing for the status and navigation bars, is 64 points from the top of the screen. So when the device is turned to landscape, the billboard's available height is $320 - (1 + 64)$ `(bars)` $- 341$ `(bottom margin)` $= -86$ points. The "missing constraints" did not serve us well.

On reflection, we care about the billboard's being just below the upper bars (we have a constraint for that), we don't care about its keeping a consistent distance from the bottom (but IB gave us a constraint for that); we do care about its having a consistent height (but we don't have a constraint for that).

4. Select the billboard view itself. An i-beam line extends from its bottom edge to the bottom of the view, representing the bottom-edge constraint. Click to select it. (You won't catch it the first time; if you miss, reselect the billboard and try again. You'll know you got it when the i-beam picks up a white border.) Press Delete to get rid of it.

5. At the lower-right corner of the editor, you see a palette of button groups. The one with four segments governs autolayout. With the billboard view still selected, click the **Pin** button (⊦╋⊣). A popover view appears in which you check the box marked **Height**. Click **Add 1 Constraint** at the bottom of the popover.

That's it; the billboard behaves as intended on all screen sizes and orientations, in the preview and the simulator. There will be one more step once you've populated the billboard.

Lots of Labels

The billboard view consists of 14 instances of the UIKit class `UILabel`. Some of them are labels in the colloquial sense—static text that identifies something else on the screen. Others are "labels" because even though the application will change their content, the user can't. They'll be placed in three groups:

- The *name label*, across the top
- The *left-side* group, consisting of labels and values for cumulative statistics like total attempts
- The *right-side* group, with summary information like the overall passer rating, the passer's most recent team, and the span of his career

> **Note**
> The cries of horror you will be hearing will be those of professional graphic designers. Ignore them. They're used to it.

The Name Label

This is only one label, extending across the top of the view.

Type `label` into the Library search field to turn up the label (`UILabel`) view. Drag it into the top of the billboard view. The Attributes inspector will have a **Text** field; fill it with **FirstName LastName**, and discover that most of what you typed was truncated (with an ellipsis) because the label was too narrow. `UILabels` adjust their text size (down to a limit you can set) to fit the content to the bounds of the label; if that's not enough, they truncate. Stretch the label across the top of the detail view so no shrinkage is necessary.

The passer's name is pretty important, so let's give it some emphasis. The **Font** element in the inspector shows the text to be "System 17.0." Click the boxed-T button to open the **Font** popover (Figure 11.9). Make it **System Bold** and 18 points.

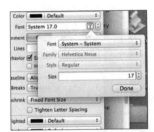  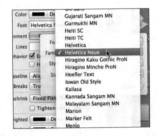

Figure 11.9   (left) Clicking the **T** button in the **Font** field in the Attributes inspector displays a popover to specify the font, style, and size for the text in a view. (middle) The **Font** popup menu offers you the "System" fonts, plus the dynamic-typography categories. (right) Selecting **Custom** from the **Font** popup enables the **Family** popup, which offers every font family available in iOS 7.

The Right-Side Group

Now a label for the passer rating, on the right side, just under the name. This is really, really important, and I have no taste, so make it big, bold, and red. Fill it with `158.3` and set the font to System Bold, 52 points (you'll need to stretch the bounds). For **Alignment**, choose right-aligned (the third segment), so numbers less than 100 will line up. Click the color well at the left end of the **Text Color** control in the inspector; that gets you the Colors palette. Use the fifth tab in the palette, and select the "Maraschino" crayon. The passer rating is now really, really red. Experiment with **Shadow** and **Shadow Offset**, if you like.

A label for a team name, System Bold, 14 points, right justified, should go under the big rating label. Set its text to `Tacoma Touchdown-Scorers`, the longest team name in the data set, so you can be sure it will fit. In the Attributes inspector, there's a stepper for **Lines**; if you set it to **2**, the team name can wrap to two lines. Resize the label so the whole name is visible.

And this is the last one, I promise: A label to show the start and end dates of the passer's career: Below the team name, System, 12, right justified. Fill with the widest plausible content, `10/29/2015-10/29/2015`.

The Left-Side Group

The statistics come next. Start with one label, `Attempts`, System, 14-point, regular, sized to fit, and positioned just under the left end of the name label. You need four more captions, and you can save some effort by duplicating the one you just set up: **Edit →Duplicate (⌘D)**, or hold down the Option key and drag. Line those up under the original, then edit each so that they read `Attempts`, `Completions`, `Yards`, `Touchdowns`, and `Interceptions`.

> **Note**
>
> You can set the text style of multiple items by selecting them all and setting the style in the Attributes inspector.

Next, the labels for the statistics themselves. Insert five `UILabels` next to the stat-name labels. Throughout the process, Interface Builder will snap your views to blue guide lines that show standard spacing, and alignment with their neighbors. In the case of views with text content, you'll also be given a dotted line when the view's baseline is aligned with its neighbors. When in doubt, align baselines.

Figure 11.10   (top) The billboard view as it comes from the hard work of filling in the constituent labels. The lines around the labels are their layout rectangles, which are the criteria autolayout uses to calculate layout. (bottom) The same view, if autolayout is fired without any work on constraints.

I suggest filling the value labels with `10000`, `20000`, etc., so you can tell them apart in listings. Make their text style the same as the stat-name labels, only right-justified.

The result should look like Figure 11.10, top. I used **Editor → Canvas → Show Layout Rectangles** for clarity. Note that I've taken care to keep the labels from overlapping. Autolayout doesn't work well if views overlap their nearest neighbors.

Just for fun, make sure the Game List Controller scene is selected, and select the **Editor → Resolve Auto Layout Issues → Update All Frames in Container** command, which you can also find in the third button (◗●◖) of the autolayout group in the canvas. (The last part of the command name will adjust to that of the scene.)

No. Unless you're aiming at a Dadaist commentary of the predicament of the modern citizen in an era of information overload, that's not what you want (Figure 11.10, bottom). Autolayout will attempt to lay out your views, like it or not, so you have to give it some constraints so it won't wreck your display. Undo (**Edit → Undo** (⌘ Z), did I need to tell you?) the layout.

Again making sure the game list scene is selected, select **Editor → Resolve Auto Layout Issues → Add Missing Constraints in Container**. (Xcode will adapt the command name to refer to the selected scene.) Once again, Interface Builder will take its best guesses at what you intend for the layout and create constraints accordingly. If you click around among the labels, you'll see blue i-beams and alignment strokes representing the constraints.

It's good enough for now.

The Table View

It's almost an afterthought—we don't yet have a table view to hold the individual game performances, taking the form of a `UITableView`. Typing **table** in the Library search field should show you a "Table View." Drag it into the lower part of the main view. (Take care not to use the "Table View Controller" instead.) You'll have to expand it to fit the available space. This isn't too hard at the sides and bottom, because Interface Builder "snaps" the edges to the bounds of the main view, but it won't give you any help with the top edge.

This is something that autolayout actually makes easier. Place the table view in the lower part of the scene, and size it so it is clear of all neighbors. Click the ▐╈▌ button in the autolayout group at the bottom right of the canvas to expose the **Pin** popover. Set all four spacing fields to 0, making sure the drop-down menu for the upper spacing makes it relative to the billboard view.

Set the **Update Frames** menu in the popover to **Items of New Constraints**, and click the acceptance button at the bottom, which now has the label **Add 4 Constraints**. The table view will snap to exactly the position and size you want, with the added benefit that it will resize in sync with the rest of the scene.

Outlets

Nine of the 14 labels in the billboard view display names, dates, and statistics that are taken from the Passer Rating data store. There has to be a way to get them from the model onto the screen. In the Model-View-Controller design model, that's the job of a controller—in this case `PRGameListController`. The question then becomes, how does the view controller get to the labels?

When an Interface Builder product is loaded into a running program, an object in the program is designated as the owner—in this case it will be a `PRGameListController`. The file carries in it a list that pairs objects (your choice) to *outlets* in the owner. In modern practice, the outlets take the form of declared properties. The `@interface` flags the outlets it wants to make available with the keyword `IBOutlet`:

```
@property (weak, nonatomic) IBOutlet UILabel *datesLabel;
```

Every NIB, and every Storyboard scene, has an owner. This is an object that is external to the scene (or NIB); the loading mechanism then fills the `IBOutlet` properties with pointers to objects in the scene. Storyboards and XIBs have different treatments for owners:

- Interface Builder's editor for XIBs includes an "object" in the document outline named "File's Owner." This object does not literally exist in the XIB; Interface Builder shows it in a section of the Document Outline for placeholders. It stands in for the owner object that will load the XIB (actually its NIB product) at runtime.

- In a storyboard, each scene belongs to a `UIViewController` subclass. The controller's placeholder appears in the Document Outline, and in the bottom bar when the scene is selected, as a yellow circle with a "view" in the middle.

When you create a subclass of UIViewController, NSWindowController, or NSViewController, Xcode enables a checkbox marked **With XIB for user interface**. If you check it, Xcode will create a XIB in addition to the new class's .m and .h files. Xcode knows what the owner class will be, so it sets the class of File's Owner accordingly.

If you create a XIB alone, Xcode does not know what the class of File's Owner should be, and you have to set it yourself. Select the File's Owner icon in the Document Outline and the Identity inspector (third tab in the Inspector view in the Utility area). The first field will be a combo box to enter the name of the owner's class. The box will auto-complete as you type.

It's the same with view controllers in a storyboard: After you drag a view controller into the canvas to create a scene, the owner is identified as a plain UIViewController. You must edit the class name in the Identity inspector to point the scene at the right controller.

Back to the specifics of PRGameListController. We have to hook the controller's IBOutlets to objects in its scene. You could type in @property declarations for all the labels you'll be using. Try it: In the **Editor** control in the toolbar, click the middle segment to display the Assistant editor. This splits the Editor area in two. The left half is still Main.storyboard. Select **Automatic** in the assistant's jump bar. The Assistant view fills with the header or implementation file for PRGameListController. (If it doesn't, click the icon for the controller object, either in the outline or in the bar below the scene.) The Assistant editor can be made to track the "appropriate" counterpart of any file you are editing.

IBOutlets must be in an @interface for the controller class. You have two choices for an @interface section: The one in PRGameListController.h is the main one—it is the "official" declaration of the class. But it's not the one you want. That @interface is for a public API, and other classes have no business knowing how PRGameListController runs its views.

Instead, you want the *class extension* at the top of PRGameListController.m. It declares a supplemental API for the class, and is usually kept in the .m file so it is private to the class. The template for the detail controller included a short class extension for what is now PRGameListController. At the right end of the assistant's jump bar is a control with what ought to be a **2** between two arrowheads. Click either to cycle through the "Automatic" file set.

Somewhere before the @end of the extension, type the @property for datesLabel:

```
@interface PRGameListController ()
- (void)configureView;

@property(nonatomic, weak) IBOutlet UILabel *   datesLabel;
@end
```

Save `PRGameListController.h`. Now go back to the Document Outline sidebar at the left edge of the canvas (click the button in the lower-left corner if it isn't visible), and right-click on "Game List Controller," the Englished name of the scene's owner. A small black heads-up display (HUD) window appears, containing a table of outlets, among them `datesLabel`. There's a bubble at the right end of that row in the table. Drag from it to the label you set up with a range of dates, and release; the adjoining column in the HUD fills with a reference to the label (Figure 11.11). Now, when the scene is loaded, the owning `PRGameListController`'s `datesLabel` property will contain a pointer to that label.

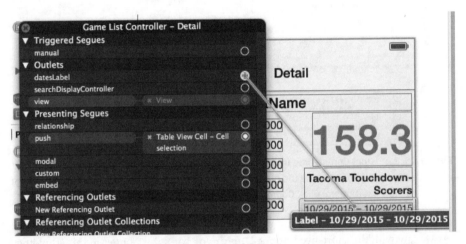

Figure 11.11   Right-clicking the "Game List Controller" entry in the Document Outline opens a heads-up display window that includes the controller's outlets. Drag from an outlet's linkage bubble to a view in the controller's scene, and the outlet's `@property` will be filled with a pointer to that view.

You could repeat this with each `IBOutlet` you will need for the data labels: Declare the property, make sure it has the right type, open the HUD, and drag out the connections. Not too bad, but there is a better way.

In the HUD, click the **x** next to the outlet to clear the link. In the header, delete the `datesLabel` `@property`. Now control-drag from the date-range label into the class-extension `@interface`. As you drag within the `@interface`, a horizontal insertion bar appears. Let go of the drag. Xcode displays a popover window. This window offers to declare a `@property` where you let go of the drag. All you have to do is type **datesLabel** into the **Name** field, click **Connect**, and the declaration appears. See Figure 11.12.

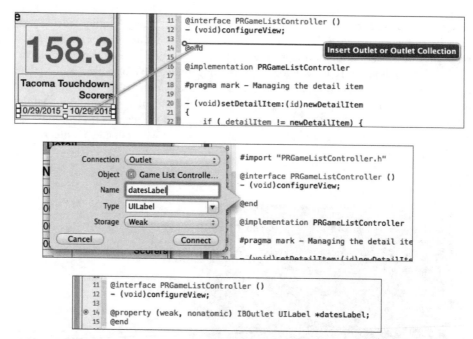

Figure 11.12   (top) Control-drag from a view in a scene into its owner's `@interface` in the Assistant editor. (middle) Releasing the drag produces a popover offering to declare an `IBOutlet` to the view. (bottom) Click **Connect** to declare the outlet and link it to the view.

As we saw with the short-lived `detailDescriptionLabel` outlet in the "Building a View" section earlier in this chapter, the connection bubble for the new outlet is filled both in the source code and in the Connections inspector, and if you hover the mouse over them, the dates label will highlight in the storyboard.

Hooking Up the Outlets

Before you go on a spree of making outlet connections, taking a little care will pay off: There is a **+** button next to the right end of the assistant's jump bar. Click it. The Assistant area is now divided into two editors. Use the lower editor's jump bar to navigate to _PRPasser.h. You want the names of the new outlets to match up with the names of the _PRPasser properties they display, and the new editor will give you a reference for the property names.

Now control-drag from the variable labels to make new properties in `PRGameListController`. Use this convention in naming the outlets: Take the name of a Passer property, and add **Label** to it. The team name label goes into the controller interface as **currentTeamLabel**, attempts as **attemptsLabel**, and so on.

> **Note**
>
> Interface Builder can also link controls to action methods, declared with the `IBAction` tag in the class `@interface`. When you trigger a control that you've linked to an `IBAction`, the action method is executed. See the "Wiring a Menu" section of Chapter 18, "Starting an OS X Application," for an example.

`PRGameListController` needs to know about the table view, as well. Control-drag a link from the table to the `@interface`, and name it `tableView`.

Checking Connections

Do one last pass to verify that everything is connected to what it's supposed to connect to: With the storyboard in the main editor, and the `IBOutlet` declarations for `PRGameListController` showing in an Assistant editor, run your mouse down the connection dots, and make sure every view gets highlighted in turn.

If an outlet isn't connected, or is connected to the wrong view, drag from the connection bubble to the correct view. An `IBOutlet` can refer to at most one view—it's just a single pointer. A view can be connected to many outlets because it has no reference back to the outlets. Checking the outlets, one by one, and reconnecting them as needed will be enough to get you out of any tangles.

Connecting `PRGameListController`

Interface Builder is great, but you still have to write code to get data from the model into the view. You'll make some changes to `PRGameListController`.

The template provides a setter for `detailItem`, `setDetailItem:`, that calls through to a `configureView` method. That's where you'll move the statistics in Passer to the labels in the view.

The `configureView` Method

Here's `configureView`. It's a little long, but there's a point I want to make:

```
- (void)configureView
{
    if (self.detailItem) {
        PRPasser *   thePasser = self.detailItem;
        NSArray *  integerProperties = @[
                       @"attempts",
                       @"completions",
                       @"yards",
                       @"touchdowns",
                       @"interceptions"];
        for (NSString * prop in integerProperties) {
            // Get the property from the PRPasser
            // valueForKey: will wrap it as an NSNumber object
```

```
        NSNumber *  statObject;
        statObject = [thePasser valueForKey: prop];

        // Find my label by name
    NSString *  labelName = [prop stringByAppendingString: @"Label"];
    UILabel *   label = (UILabel *) [self valueForKey: labelName];

        // Put the stat's formatted string into the label.
    label.text = [intFormatter stringFromNumber: statObject];
    }

    // Passer rating
    NSString *      ratingString;
    ratingString = [NSString stringWithFormat: @"%.11f",
                    thePasser.passerRating];
    self.passerRatingLabel.text = ratingString;

    // Team name
    self.teamNameLabel.text = thePasser.currentTeam;

    // Start and end of career
    NSString *      startString, * endString;
    startString = [shortDateFormatter stringFromDate:
                    thePasser.firstPlayed];
    endString = [shortDateFormatter stringFromDate:
                thePasser.lastPlayed];
    self.datesLabel.text = [NSString stringWithFormat:
                        @"%@ - %@", startString,
                        endString];

    // Name label and controller (nav bar) title.
    self.title =
    self.fullNameLabel.text = [NSString stringWithFormat: @"%@ %@",
                thePasser.firstName, thePasser.lastName];
    }
}
```

Supporting `configureView`

You'll get a cluster of error flags from clang, as it has never heard of PRPasser or the formatter objects configureView uses. Let's patch them up. These are excerpts, with a few lines to give them context:

```
#import "PRGameListController.h"
#import "PRDataModel.h"
    // Loads the declaration PRPasser and PRGame

// Declare the formatters.
// Formatters work better than passing values through
```

```
//  +[NSString stringWithFormat:] because the resulting
//  strings will always match the user's locale and
//  preferences.
static NSDateFormatter * shortDateFormatter;
static NSNumberFormatter * intFormatter;
static NSNumberFormatter * ratingFormatter;

// ...

@implementation PRGameListController

//  The runtime calls +initialize before the first use
//  of a class. This is simplified here; look +initialize
//  up in the documentation for the problem of it being
//  called more than once.

+ (void) initialize
{
    if (! shortDateFormatter) {
        intFormatter = [[NSNumberFormatter alloc] init];
        intFormatter.numberStyle = NSNumberFormatterDecimalStyle;
        intFormatter.minimumIntegerDigits = 1;
        intFormatter.maximumFractionDigits = 0;

        ratingFormatter = [[NSNumberFormatter alloc] init];
        ratingFormatter.numberStyle = NSNumberFormatterDecimalStyle;
        ratingFormatter.minimumIntegerDigits = 1;
        ratingFormatter.maximumFractionDigits =
        ratingFormatter.minimumFractionDigits = 1;

        shortDateFormatter = [[NSDateFormatter alloc] init];
        shortDateFormatter.timeStyle = NSDateFormatterNoStyle;
        shortDateFormatter.dateStyle = NSDateFormatterShortStyle;
    }
}
```

How configureView Works

Here's where the care in naming the label outlets pays off: You can loop through the property names; use those to get the PRPasser values by key-value coding (an Objective-C technique that gives access to object properties through string paths); add Label to get the names of the matching labels; and use Key-Value Coding (KVC) to set the labels' content from the PRPasser values. You don't have to get each property name right, and if you change your suite of labels, you only have to change the property-name array.

`configureView` uses `NSNumberFormatter` and `NSDateFormatter` for conversion of numbers and dates into strings. The advantage is that you only need to state your intention for the format—a short date, for instance—and the formatter object will render them according to the conventions of the user's locale.

`passerRatingLabel`, `datesLabel`, and `fullNameLabel` have one-off formats. Those can be done individually.

Code Completion and Snippets

You probably fumbled a bit as you filled in all this code. Cocoa Touch is a huge API, and nobody remembers every symbol and method name. `NSString` has more than 130 methods in its basic interface. If you don't have a crib, you might be pausing to look up spellings all the time. Here is where you turn on another feature I had you turn off in the "Quieting Xcode Down" section of Chapter 2, "Kicking the Tires."

Open the Preferences window (**Xcode →Preferences. . .**, **⌘ comma**), and turn to the **Editing** tab of the **Text Editing** panel. Check **Suggest completions while typing**.

Now try the line `labelName = [prop stringByAppendingString: @"Label"];` again, typing **stringB**. Xcode pops up a window offering to complete the symbol and shows the proposed completion in gray in the editor (Figure 11.13). There are a lot of methods beginning with `stringB`, so you can scroll the popup through all of them. Pressing the Up- or Down-Arrow key lets you choose.

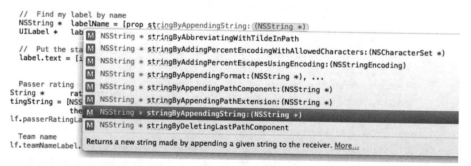

Figure 11.13   With autocompletion on, typing a partial symbol will yield a list of possible completions, including a brief description of each. Select one and press Return to accept a completion.

Automatic completion is surprisingly good. It's context sensitive, and I've found that when I've recently used one symbol from an enum list, the next suggestions for the same prefix will prefer other members of the same enum.

Continue typing to refine the completion list. When the selected completion shares a prefix with other suggestions, pressing the Tab key will advance the cursor through the common prefix, narrowing the completion list. If you're satisfied with the current suggestion, press Return and continue editing.

Completion is sometimes perverse, offering suggestions that have nothing to do with what you want. This is particularly painful when you want to type a symbol (e.g., `completion`) that shares letters, but not case, with another (e.g., `COMPLETION`). You can type to the end of your desired spelling, but Xcode will insist on the other one. If this happens to you (or if you simply want to suppress the popup), press Escape, and the completions will go away.

> **Note**
>
> Don't like automatic completion at all? If **Escape key shows code completions** is checked, you can summon the code-completion window whenever you want it. Even with escape-completion turned off, you can still invoke completion with ^**Space**.

Code completion doesn't stop at spelling. Xcode supports *code snippets* (see the second tab, marked with braces, in the Library section of the Utility area), which are blocks of code you can insert and edit for your purposes.

`+initialize` creates three `static` formatter objects the traditional way—rely on the fact that static pointer variables start out as `nil`, so when the method is first run, it fills in the objects, the pointers will never be `nil` again, and the initialization will never be repeated.

This is not thread-safe. (Ignore for the moment that, in this app, we don't care.) If `+initialize` is run on two threads at once, it's anybody's guess which of them, if not both, will see the `nil`s. If you're experienced in multithreading, the fact that the object creation is guarded only by `shortDateFormatter` will make you uneasy.

Grand Central Dispatch, the OS facility for managing separate queues of operations, includes a function, `dispatch_once`, that guarantees a block of code will be executed only once: The first comer will take a lock, any others will be blocked out of it, and when the first completes the block, no threads will ever execute the block again. Select the body of the `if (! shortDateFormatter)` statement, cut it, and remove the remainder of the `if` entirely. Now type **disp**. Autocompletion will show you a number of symbols beginning with `dispatch_`. Tab twice to get through the common prefix, and type **o**. That will get you `dispatch_once`, which is what you want. Press Return.

What you'll see is

```
static dispatch_once_t onceToken;
dispatch_once(&onceToken, ^{
    <#code to be executed once#>
});
```

You get a complete, self-contained code block with a highlighted placeholder for your customization. It there were more than one placeholder, the Tab key would select them in turn. Paste the initializer code back into the placeholder, and you have a correct

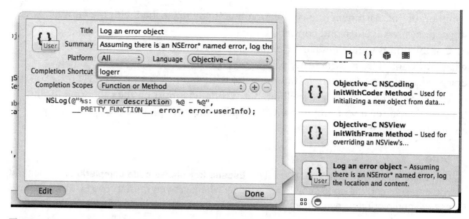

Figure 11.14   Drag code of your own into the Code Snippet library to create a new snippet. Click on the badge to open an editor in which to refine it (for instance, surrounding some text with <##> changes it into a placeholder), describe it, and restrict it to a particular context. In this case, typing **logerr** will trigger code completion for the snippet.

single-dispatch initializer for your formatters. You can create snippets of your own; see the example in Figure 11.14.

```
+ (void) initialize
{
    static dispatch_once_t onceToken;
    dispatch_once(&onceToken, ^{
        //  Cache integer and date formatters
        intFormatter = [[NSNumberFormatter alloc] init];
        intFormatter.numberStyle = NSNumberFormatterDecimalStyle;
        intFormatter.minimumIntegerDigits = 1;
        intFormatter.maximumFractionDigits = 0;
        //  ...
    });
}
```

Testing the Billboard View

Everything should be in place now. Run Passer Rating. Xcode builds the app and installs it in the iOS Simulator, which launches it. (The app takes a long time to load that CSV file—long enough that you might worry that iOS would kill it for being nonresponsive, but there are things you can do about that. See Chapter 16, "Measurement and Analysis.")

Select a passer from the initial view. Something like the view in Figure 11.15 should appear. All of the labels are filled in. It works. The game table is still empty, but you've made progress in making the data available to the user.

Figure 11.15   Running Passer Rating and selecting a passer shows that the passer-detail view works.

Summary

This was a long chapter, but you got a lot done. The passer table at the root of the application came almost fully implemented from the project template; all you had to do was change some formats and data-table names. This time, you took a view from practically nothing to a display of the unique data Passer Rating manages.

You provisioned the screen with a table and a container view for the summary billboard. After that, it was all labels, but you learned how to lay them out and how to use the Attributes editor to fit them to their purposes. And, I showed you how to finesse the problem of autolayout, at least for a while.

Data displays need data, and controller objects move data from the model to the views. Using Interface Builder with an Assistant editor, you gave `PRGameListController` direct access to the data labels and filled them in from the `PRPasser` object.

And, at least through the billboard display, it works. The rest, the table of games, will come in Chapter 13, "Adding Table Cells," later on. But first I will (and you should) take a closer look at laying out that billboard view.

12

Autolayout in a New View

Chapter 11, "Building a New View," was about creating scenes in Passer Rating. To preserve that focus, I finessed the issue of autolayout with a quick workaround. For the purpose of an exercise, you don't need to do more; Passer Rating is not a professional-grade product.

You'll need to know more sooner or later, and this chapter is a closer look at auto-layout. You can put it off, or even skip it entirely. I won't know.

> **Note**
>
> If you attempted autolayout in Xcode 4, you found it was a nightmare, and I wouldn't blame you if you were a bit phobic on the subject. *It's better in Xcode 5.* Much better. However, the new workflow is available only if you select **Xcode 5.0** in the **Opens in** popup in the File inspector. If you choose **Xcode 4.6** compatibility—maybe you or a coworker have to open the file in Xcode 4, perhaps to link the project against the iOS 6 SDK—you're back to the horrible old workflow.

Why Autolayout?

For decades, NeXTStep, Cocoa, and Cocoa Touch used *autosizing* to automatically adapt the layout of views to changes in geometry—the resizing of a window or the rotation of a device. Autosizing was very simple: Notionally, each view had "springs," which would permit it to be resized on one or both axes, and "struts," which governed whether an edge of the view would rigidly maintain its distance from the corresponding edge of its container. As the superview resized, the subviews would adjust according to the spring-and-strut rules.

Limitations of Autosizing

This worked. Mostly. But there were some things it couldn't do, things that would have been common had they been easy. Application code would have to intervene for special cases, and some requirements had to be met by trial-and-error.

Ultimately, layout can't be a matter of the window pushing or pulling on its contents, which push or pull on theirs, and so on down the line. Suppose you have a label that absolutely must be readable in full, and it's three layers down in the containment hierarchy. Its container must not become so small that the full label can't be shown; so the container above must not become small enough for that to happen and so on to the container above that, up to the root view of the window. The only place to enforce that must-not-shrink requirement automatically is in the size limits for the window itself: Experiment, see how small the window can get without pressuring the label, write that dimension down, and set it in the parameters for the window.

Now translate the label from English to German: Pour your translations into a duplicate XIB file, see how the widths work out, and repeat the experiments to determine how to constrain the window.

You have ten international markets. And there's another label that must be readable at all times, and its content is determined programmatically. This entails some math.

We have computers to do math. In the real world, constraints on size and layout propagate up and down—and even across—the containment hierarchy. There have to be compromises and priorities: "I want this label to be centered and wide enough to show its contents (I don't need it wider), but it has to be at least 8 points away from the controls on either side, and to preserve that distance, respond first by moving it off-center, and if you must, by narrowing the label, but never narrower than 120 points. Stop the window (three layers up) from resizing if it means making the label any narrower. And I have similar ideas for ten other views..."

Autolayout

This is completely expressible with *autolayout*. And while autolayout has a reputation for complexity, it's a lot simpler than writing code to implement that description.

> **Note**
>
> Apple does not have a consistent spelling for autolayout. Sometimes it's one word, sometimes two; sometimes capitalized, sometimes not. For simplicity's sake, I'm going to treat it as a one-word common noun unless I have to refer to a label in Xcode.

Internally (meaning: don't think too hard about this), any two views can be related to each other by *constraints*. A constraint applies to a specific property in each view (such as location of edge, center, or baseline; height, width) and specifies gaps and alignments by an offset, a multiplier, and a priority. Views may have "inherent" sizes, and some views (usually ones containing text) can resist being drawn wider or narrower than their contents. Autolayout takes all of these constraints and reconciles them to produce an overall layout that satisfies as many as possible, sacrificing lower-priority ones to meet higher priorities.

The Thing to Remember

"Satisfying all constraints" imposes a duty on you: For each view, on each axis, the chain of constraints should fully specify the view's location and size (*sufficiency*). And, the constraints must not contradict (*consistency*). If those conditions are not met, autolayout will raise exceptions, and Interface Builder will post warnings.

The Player Billboard, Revisited

In Chapter 11, "Building a New View," I had you put together the billboard view at the top of the `PRGameListController` view with little thought of declarative/automatic layout. You switched a couple of constraints to get a bug out of the way, and asked Interface Builder to do the rest.

Why You Should Do More

It's good enough for a start, but there are flaws. Unless you were very careful about alignments, the generated constraints might be a little off of your intention, and when you turn the billboard to landscape, you get a portrait-sized information block in a landscape-sized view (Figure 12.1).

Figure 12.1   The automatically generated constraint system you can get from Interface Builder is workable, but it doesn't make the best use of the area available in landscape orientation.

Start by examining the constraint system you have now. There are a few ways to explore: If you select a view in the canvas editor, it will display lines to show the constraints that apply to it; the Size (fifth) inspector will include a list of those constraints. The constraint objects themselves stand alone in **Constraints** categories you'll find throughout the Document Outline. (You may have to dig.) Selecting one will highlight it in the editor.

Whose Constraint Is It, Anyway?

The way Interface Builder displays constraints makes it tempting to say that a view that is subject to a constraint somehow "owns" it. In the sense you're probably thinking about, that isn't so. A constraint is an independent object in its own right—you can even point an `IBOutlet` at it. Except for size constraints, they point to two views; neither view is privileged, neither is an owner. That you can get at a constraint through one of its views is a convenience.

However, each constraint *is* owned by a view. A constraint between two views is held by their first common container.

Once a constraint is selected, you can delete it or use the Attributes (fourth) inspector to edit it. Selecting one in the editor requires some dexterity, but the other two methods are easy. If you go through a view's Size inspector, you'll have to use the gear menu attached to each to delete or edit one.

> **Note**
>
> The **Editor → Canvas** menu contains a number of options for what information Interface Builder will show, particularly as relates to constraints. What interests us now are **Show Bounds/Layout Rectangles**, which frame views according to either the `.frame` property of the `UIViews`, or, what may be different, the bounds that autolayout uses to measure spacing and alignment. Also, there are options that expose constraint relationships—some essential, and some useful as debugging aids.

One thing to notice: When you ask Interface Builder to add missing constraints, it can only guess at your intentions, but the guesses aren't too bad. One thing is particularly good: Most of the constraints cascade. Usually, the most important thing about the layout of one view is how it lines up with another.

Consider a partial calendar view that consists of a row of day-of-week labels, and below it a few rows of buttons representing the days. You don't care about the x-and-y location of a day-of-month button; you care that it be centered on its day-of-week label, and a certain distance below it depending on the week.

A good autolayout system gives absolute locations to as few views as possible. The strategy for the calendar view is to provide absolute locations for the day-of-week labels, and let relative (centering, spacing) constraints do the rest. If you move the day-of-week labels, the rest of the layout takes care of itself.

Constraints for Real

Now we'll replace the patchwork constraints in the billboard view with the real thing: Select the billboard view in the game-list controller scene. At the bottom right of the storyboard editor is a group of controls that adjust the display and offer tools for autolayout. The third group, with four segments, is the autolayout group (Figure 12.2).

> **Warning**
>
> I'm going to lead you through a complete layout of the billboard view, and I'm going to comment on the automatically generated constraints I got in the last chapter. The constraints you got will probably be different. My remarks will be useful to you as

Figure 12.2   The controls at the lower-right corner of the storyboard canvas editor govern how the canvas is displayed and provide your primary tools for managing autolayout constraints. The groups: Show and hide the Document Outline; switch iPhone layouts between 3.5- and 4-inch screens; menus and popovers for work with constraints; and zoom between whole-storyboard and single-scene views.

comments on the sort of things you'll have to do, but if you're following closely on your own you may be better served by starting from zero: Select the billboard view, and select the command **Editor →Resolve Auto Layout Issues →Clear Constraints**.

Click the second segment, marked ⊦✚⊣; it's an elaboration of the **Editor →Pin** submenu. Xcode presents a popover that sets distance, size, and simple alignment constraints (Figure 12.3). On the horizontal axis, the billboard's size and placement will be completely determined if it keeps each edge at a distance of zero from the corresponding edge of the scene; its width follows from the need to span the distance. On the vertical axis, the top of the billboard must be zero distance from the top of the container; and the height must be exactly 162 points (as I have it). The placement of the bottom edge follows from there.

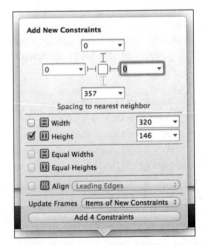
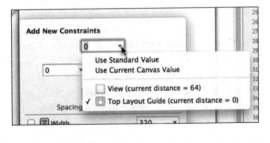

Figure 12.3   The **Pin** popover set up to keep a constant-height billboard view at the top of its container. Clicking the menu indicator on the spacing field for an edge lets you choose the other view the spacing is to be measured from.

Note
You must select two or more views before the alignment constraints will become available.

The upper half of the **Pin** popover represents the selected view, joined by i-beams to numeric fields representing the "neighbor" in that direction. The neighbor could be another view (near or far), or the edge of the containing view. Click the menu triangle in the "up" field (Figure 12.3, right); this menu allows you to choose which neighbor to measure against; you also get a couple of convenience setters for the current gap or the one specified by the iOS human-interface standards. Select **Top Layout Guide** and release. (The position of the "edge" of the scene's container varies depending on the presence of status, navigation, and tool bars, and whether you want your view to extend under them. The layout guide lets you lay out relative to whatever that position might be.)

If the set gap isn't zero already, enter **0** in the "up" field. When you make the setting, the corresponding i-beam changes from dashed to solid, showing that the constraint will be added if you accept the changes you made.

Do the same for the left and right edges, setting them to zero distance from the sides of the container. Also, check the **Height** box, setting it to **162** points (or whatever your version of the billboard requires). That's it: top specified, height specified; left specified, right specified (and therefore width specified).

> **Note**
>
> It appears you are setting the left and right edges for the view, and in this case it doesn't matter; but in fact, you are setting the *leading* and *trailing* edges, as determined by the language your app is currently using. A text label with a leading gap of 8 points will be 8 points from the left of the container in a Latin script like French, but 8 points from the right in a right-to-left script like Arabic. Autolayout will reorder leading/trailing edge views to suit the locale. If you really mean literal left and right, select the constraint and use the Attributes inspector to change the **Direction** popup.

Setting constraints doesn't immediately change the placement of the views you're constraining. You wouldn't want it to: You're setting them one at a time, and autolayout executes them all at once. If a view's constraints don't add up to a determinate width (or height), and you let autolayout evaluate the constraint system, it will usually crush that axis to zero, making the view invisible and unselectable in the canvas. (If this happens, find the view in the Document Outline, the sidebar you can show and hide with the button at the lower left of the canvas, select it, and use the Size inspector—fifth tab—to give it any size and location that will put it back in reach.)

So you need to see how your constraint system works out, but only on demand. The **Update Frames** menu next to the bottom of the **Pin** popover lets you fire just the constraints attached to the view you focused on (**Items of New Constraints**) or every constraint in the selected view's container (**All Frames in Container**). Select **Items of New Constraints**, and click the acceptance button at the bottom, which now has the label **Add 4 Constraints**.

Nothing much should change in the scene, but look at the Preview assistant: No matter how you turn or resize the simulated screen, the billboard stays where you mean it to be.

> **Note**
>
> Note the language of the button: "*Add* Constraints." The **Pin** popover isn't an editor—it has no effect on existing constraints. If you select the billboard view again, and type another number (or even the same number) in the top field, the view will now have *two* top constraints, and they may contradict, which is trouble. My advice for now: Select the view, and look at the Size inspector (fifth tab); it will include a list of the constraints affecting the view. Check for duplicates, and select **Delete** from the gear menu for the ones you don't want. There are other uses for that list, and better ways to handle this problem, but that's for later.

The Label System

Now for the labels inside the billboard. The constraints Interface Builder gave you cascade, but its choices aren't perfect. Our task now is to make sure the cascade reflects what we intend.

Start from the layout in Figure 12.1. I'd like the layout to be about the same in portrait, but in landscape, I'd like it to take advantage of the whole width of the billboard.

My concern is how the billboard lays out in landscape orientation, so let's work for a while in landscape. Select the Game List Controller (the yellow icon in the black bar below the scene) and the Attribute inspector (fourth tab). The first items in the attributes for a view controller, **Simulated Metrics**, control the geometry of the view: whether to make room for navigation and tool bars, and orientation. Normally these are **Inferred**, and Interface Builder picks them up from containers like navigation controllers. Change **Orientation** to **Landscape**. The scene lays out in the wide aspect.

By exploring the constraints Interface Builder provided, I found that the horizontal layout cascades from the name label at the top: The respective edges of the left and right columns are aligned on the leading and trailing edges of the name label; the name label is centered; and its width is dictated by the interelement spacing within and between the columns.

The first step would be to take advantage of the cascade, and give the name label an intrinsic width of its own, 4 points in from the leading and trailing edges of the billboard. Select the name label. You've seen the **Pin** popover, from the second segment of the autolayout control in the canvas, before. Select the left and right constraints and set them to 4.

Set **Update Frames** to **Items of New Constraints**, and click the **Add 2 Constraints** button. You asked to update only the frame of the name label, but the other labels' horizontal placement depend on the edges of the name label. They're now out of place, and Interface Builder flags the problems (Figure 12.4).

The flags show i-beams spanning the discrepancies between the actual locations and the ones that would result from executing the current set of constraints. Interface Builder leaves the discrepancies in place because you didn't ask it to adjust anything other than the name label.

If you look in the Document Outline, you'll see that IB has put a yellow marker on the entry for the game-list controller. Click it; a list slides in showing all the misplacements

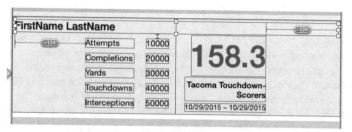

Figure 12.4   Changing the placement of the name label's edges left the other labels, whose position depends on those edges, out of place. Interface Builder flags the discrepancies, marking them with the number of points between the expected and actual positions.

caused by the reframing of the name label. There are many because, directly or indirectly, many labels depend on alignment with the name label for their placement. If you select a row, the corresponding view is highlighted on the canvas.

Click the yellow badge on one of the rows. This brings up a popover (Figure 12.5) that offers three fixes for the misplacement of the label.

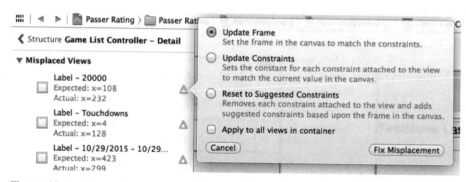

Figure 12.5   Clicking the badge on a Misplaced Views item yields a popover offering options for correcting the misplacement.

- **Update Frame** returns the view to compliance with the constraints as they are.
- **Update Constraints** lets you keep the view where it is and correct the existing constraints to make that possible.
- **Reset to Suggested Constraints** lets you bail out. Interface Builder will strip the view's constraints and replace them with its suggestions for a new set.

The problem here is that the constraints are (as far as we know) just fine, but the other views haven't been moved in conformance to them. Select **Update Frame**, and check **Apply to all views in container**—you want to update all the views in the list. Click **Fix Misplacement**.

What you see next makes a kind of sense, if you examine the label frames and click around to examine the constraints. What it looks like is that both columns have been hauled over to the margins—except that the Yards number (30000) has been pulled over against the right column. Your exploration tells the story: That label is aligned at its leading edge with the other statistics labels, but it is unique in that it has a fixed-spacing constraint with the team-name label. To satisfy both, it stretches to span the two, and because the content is right-aligned in the label, the number appears next to the team label.

This isn't inconsistent—the integer labels don't have constraints aligning their trailing edges; it's a part of IB's admirable minimalism in adding its own constraints.

But, you notice that while the other integer labels have leading edge placement set, they don't have a specified width. Isn't that insufficient to lay them out horizontally? Not all views need explicit size constraints; they may have *intrinsic sizes*. Some, like standard controls, are simply fixed-size. Text containers' intrinsic size is determined by the size of the text they contain.

This could be trouble. The integer labels look good, but they all have five digits as content. If autolayout depends on the intrinsic size of the labels, what happens if they aren't all five digits? Try it: Change the 10000 label to **1**. The edit changed the layout: You get a misplacement warning in the Document Outline, saying "Expected: width=8 Actual: width=40." In the canvas, the label's current frame is shown with solid lines, and the frame as it should be, in dashed lines (Figure 12.6).

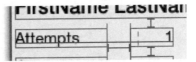

Figure 12.6   When a view is out of place according to the current constraint system, Interface Builder draws a dashed frame to show where the view ought to be. (**Editor →Canvas →Show Resize Knobs** was turned off to make the effect visible.)

Allow IB to redo the layout, and it's confirmed: The integer labels are all set to right-justify their contents, but their inherent sizes make them no wider than their contents. And if the labels are all aligned at their leading edges, all of the numbers are laid out as though they were all left justified—except for 30000, whose anchor to the right column made it wide enough that right justification is visible.

We *intend* that the labels line up at their trailing edges. Make it so: Select all the integer labels and use the **Align** segment of the autolayout control to set a trailing-edge constraint on all of them.

Better: All the integers are aligned, even 30000, which now has a high-priority directive to set its trailing edge; the fixed gap to the team name is satisfied by stretching that label. This has the nice side effect that the name is shown on two lines when the billboard is narrow, and on one when the billboard gives it some room. Use the simulated metrics control to switch between landscape and portrait, and it looks pretty good. You'll have to tell Interface Builder to adjust frames when you go to portrait, but the effect will be the same as you'd get from autolayout if it ran the system all the way through. (The Preview assistant editor does the complete layout without interruption.)

Our work here is done, right? No. The landscape version of the billboard makes full use of the greater width, but now the center is vacant. This bothers me. Let's try to line up the integers near the center.

The first thing to do is to cast the integer column off from the labels on their left. There's only one spacing constraint, between **Attempts** and what is now 1. Select it and delete it. There's nothing to stretch out the team name label, so it snaps back to the minimum for a single line of content, and pulls the integers with it (Figure 12.7).

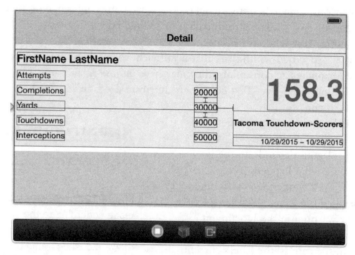

Figure 12.7   Cutting the integer column away from the labels at the left draws them across to the right column.

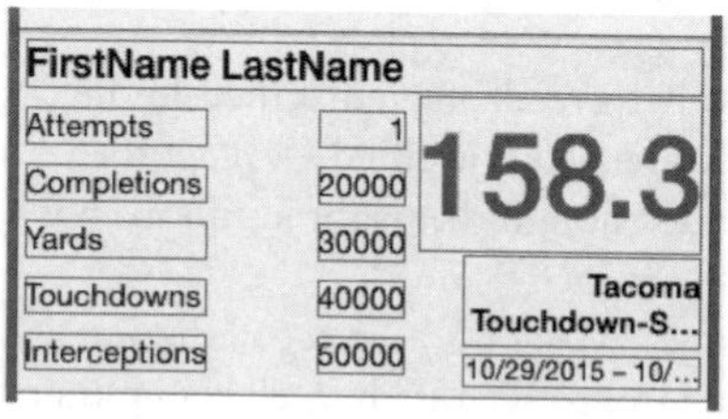

Figure 12.8   Insisting on placing the integer column in the center of the billboard forces the team-name label to compress enough that its contents are truncated.

This isn't too bad a look, but I've heard that insane pickiness is the key to success in this business. I want them to color the center of the billboard. Because the placement of the integers is carefully cascaded, you only have to set the constraint on one of them to move the whole column. Select the top integer (1), click the **Align** segment in the autolayout control, check **Horizontal Center in Container**, ask that all frames in the scene be updated, and click **Add 1 Constraint**.

Better still, until you return the layout to portrait. The integers stick to the center of the billboard; because the spacing between 30000 and the team name is fixed, the centering compresses the name until part of it is truncated (Figure 12.8).

We have to be cleverer. We want the integers to be in the center of the billboard, but we don't care so much about that if it means losing visible information. Centering is a lower priority than keeping the team label uncompressed.

Fortunately, the idea of priority is central to autolayout. Text containers use their contents to set their inherent sizes, but by default that sizing is given less importance than enforcing spacing and alignment. Out of 1000, "Content Compression Resistance Priority" (select the team label and look in the Size inspector) is 750. If we indicate that the centering constraint is less important than showing the whole contents of the team label, we can get centering when we can, but concede it if we must.

The goal is to bring the centering priority below 750. The centering constraint is on the top integer label (1). Select that label, and either be so deft as to click on the constraint on the canvas and select the Attributes inspector; or find it in the label's Size inspector and choose **Select and Edit. . .** from the attached gear menu. The **Priority** slider, and the field next to it, show that centering has a priority of 1000. Slide it left; a popover will show you a description of how the selected priority relates to other default priorities (Figure 12.9).

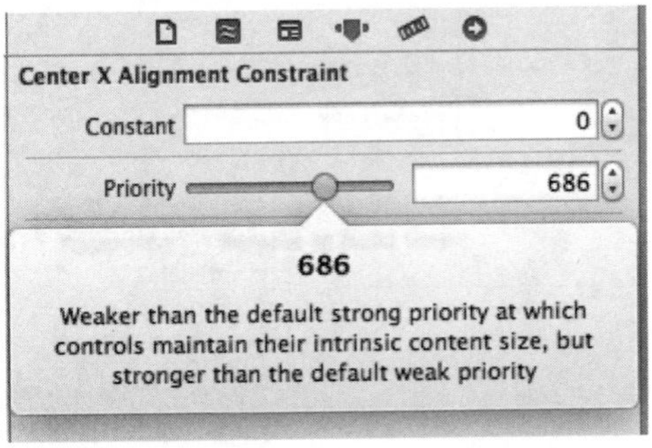

Don't concede more than you have to—set the centering constraint's priority just below 750. In fact, for this sort of work, you really should edit the number field rather than use the slider, so you don't end up with a confusing scatter of priorities, which is very hard to debug.

Figure 12.9 When you drag the **Priority** slider in the Attributes inspector for a constraint, Xcode displays a placard describing how the selected priority compares to standard priorities.

> **Note**
>
> When a constraint has gone below 1000 priority, Interface Builder represents it on the canvas with a dashed line.

As soon as the centering gives way to showing the full content of the team label, the integers get out of the way and there's no more truncation (Figure 12.10, top). Turn the scene to landscape, and the integers are back at the center of the view (Figure 12.10, middle). Turn it back. . . and there's a problem (Figure 12.10, bottom).

Apparently, once a text label has gone from two lines to one, there's no going back. The intrinsic size of the team label is wider, and with centering at low priority, the integer column can't resist being shoved into its labels.

So we've discovered another intention we have for the billboard: The labels shouldn't collide with the integers. Undo the effects of that rotation (**Edit →Undo**, ⌘ **Z**), which will bring you back to landscape orientation. Let's continue to use the first integer label as

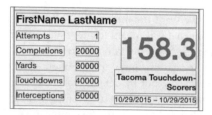

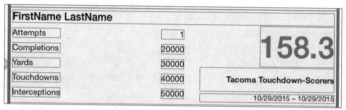

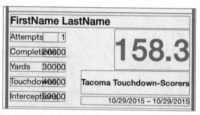

Figure 12.10   (top) Making the center placement of the integer column lower priority than the integrity of the team name moves the column out of the way so the name is rendered in full. (middle) When the billboard is in landscape, the two goals don't conflict, and the column goes back to the middle. (bottom) But once the team name has been laid out in a single line, it doesn't go back, and it shoves the integer column into its labels.

the clearinghouse for the layout of the column. Select it, and use the **Pin** popover to set 4 points' spacing to its nearest neighbor to the left (the **Attempts** label). Ask that the change be applied to all frames, and click **Add 1 Constraint**.

Between the new constraint and the rule that the stats-label labels should align their trailing edges, this has the effect of stretching out those labels. Try rotating the view again, and tell IB to let the constraint system work itself out. Now, when you rotate to portrait, the integers will still be pushed off-center, but the pushback from the labels on the left makes the team label compress to use two lines. This is what we wanted.

Almost. Now that the integers are in the exact center of the billboard, I feel they aren't adequately associated with their labels. They should be biased to the left of center.

You can do that. Remember that every constraint has a constant associated with it: Spacing, dimension, and the like. Centering constraints have a constant, too, to bias the alignment of the inner view off of center.

The integer labels (in my experiment) are 40 points wide, and if we offset them that much from center, they'll shift to leave half of their width between their trailing edges and the center line. Select the centering constraint and change the **Constant** to **40**. If the frames in the view don't show the change immediately, use **Editor →Resolve Auto Layout Issues →Update All Frames in Game List Controller** (or its equivalent in the third segment of the autolayout control) to settle them down.

Now I'm satisfied (Figure 12.11).

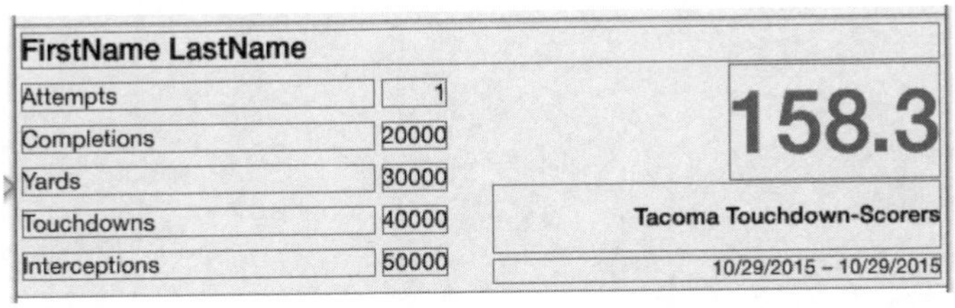

Figure 12.11   The "finished" layout for the billboard: The integer column is laid out relative to the centerline of the view, but the constant on the centering constraint offsets the column so that it falls to the left of center.

Summary

That was a lot of work. Maybe there's something to the belief that autolayout is hard enough that there are better, simpler choices. I've made the general argument against that at the beginning of this chapter. Specifically, about our work on this example, consider these points:

We were fooling around. We started with a ready-made constraint system, and tinkered with it, step by step, until we got it to do something like what we wanted. As if it were an example in a book.

In real life, your intentions will come before the constraint system. Draw the layout by hand. Decide what the relationships have to be—you saw how effective the strategy of placing just a few objects, and using alignments and spacing to cascade your layout to the rest of your view. If you're lucky, you'll be able to approach autolayout knowing what you want to accomplish. From there, it's just a matter of setting up the cascade, and flowing with it.

So long as there are managers and clients in this world, you will have to overhaul existing work, including constraint systems. Even so, you will have two advantages: You know enough about constraint design that what you already have can accept changes; and you know enough that if you have to strip the whole system out of the view, and start again with placement and cascade, it won't intimidate you.

13

Adding Table Cells

You've filled the game-list view with everything but...a list of games. In this chapter, you'll hook up the game table, produce a custom view for the table cells, and pick up some techniques along the way.

The Game Table

The master-detail project template provided the root-controller class that became `PRPasserListController`. That was a subclass of `UITableViewController`. It was preconnected to its table, and was provided with an `NSFetchedResultsController` that needed little modification to deliver `PRPassers` to the table.

`PRGameListController` is not a table-view controller; it's just a `UIViewController` for a view that happens to include a table. Table-view controllers are already connected to their tables; you'll have to do the connecting yourself.

The first thing to do is to modify the `@interface` for `PRGameListController` to promise that it will implement the methods the table needs to display cells and respond to events:

```
@interface PRGameListController : UIViewController
    <UITableViewDelegate, UITableViewDataSource>
```

Outlets in the Table View

You have to connect the table view to the controller. That's been done at the controller's end—you set the `tableView` property when you built the view in Interface Builder. But the table view has to know where it can get its data (its `dataSource` property) and what will handle its events (the `delegate` property). Return to the storyoeard, focus on the Game List Controller scene, and control-drag connections from the table to the yellow controller icon in the bar below the scene. Select `dataSource` from the heads-up menu that will appear; repeat the process for `delegate`.

> **Note**
>
> Earlier, you created and linked IBOutlets in PRGameListController from views in its scene; this time you're linking a view outlet to the controller.

> **Warning**
>
> It's common for UIKit objects to rely on delegates and data sources. Unless they are connected, they do nothing. Despite their importance, Interface Builder doesn't make it obvious that you should connect them. Forgetting to do so is one of the most common causes of bugs, no matter how experienced you are.

Adding Required Protocol Methods

Once the parser catches up to the change, the activity view in the middle of the toolbar will flag two warnings. The error/warning icon with arrowheads, at the right end of the jump bar, will offer quick navigation to the sites of the issues, but to see them all at once, select the Issues navigator (fourth tab). Both warnings are tagged "Semantic Issue." Once you declared PRGameListController as implementing UITableViewDelegate and UITableViewDataSource, you promised that you would provide the methods those protocols mandate.

The warnings have disclosure triangles next to them that mark your source with the particulars. For each, they are "Method declared here" / "Required for direct or indirect protocol 'UITableViewDataSource'." Clicking on the declared-here item opens UIKit's UITableView.h header, and highlights a method in the UITableViewDataSource protocol: tableView:numberOfRowsInSection: in one case, tableView:cellForRowAtIndexPath: in the other. Copy the declaration of tableView:numberOfRowsInSection:, paste it into PRGameListController.m, and fill it out:

```
#pragma mark - UITableViewDataSource

- (NSInteger) tableView: (UITableView *) tableView
  numberOfRowsInSection: (NSInteger) section
{
    PRPasser *      passer = self.detailItem;
    return passer.games.count;
}
```

...a mark directive puts the text in the rest of the line into the function popup
...gment of the jump bar. If you prefix it with a hyphen, the label will be
... dividing line.

...mplain that it doesn't know what a PRPasser is; add

...ser.h"

to the top of the file.

```objc
- (UITableViewCell *) tableView: (UITableView *) aTableView
        cellForRowAtIndexPath: (NSIndexPath *) indexPath
{
    static NSString *cellIdentifier = @"Basic Game Cell";

    UITableViewCell *   cell =
        [aTableView dequeueReusableCellWithIdentifier: cellIdentifier];

    // Pull data from this row's Game.
    PRGame *        game = [self.arrangedGames objectAtIndex: indexPath.row];
    NSString *      content;
    content = [NSString stringWithFormat: @"vs %@ %@ - %@",
            game.theirTeam,
            [shortDateFormatter stringFromDate: game.whenPlayed],
            [ratingFormatter stringFromNumber: @(game.passerRating)]];
    cell.textLabel.text = content;
    // Why box the passer rating in an NSNumber when it could go into
    // %.11f? The float formatter doesn't automatically localize the format.

    return cell;
}
```

> **Note**
>
> I'll lead you through three variants on the layout of the game cell in this chapter, showing you each as a single block of code. The sample code is different; it contains all three variants, which you can select by #defineing CELL_TO_USE to designate the one you want. The table in Main.storyboard contains a prototype for each variant.

Adding Model-to-View Support

The compiler has never heard of arrangedGames, so it flags an error. Time to correct that. It's common to back a list in the human interface with an "arranged" data structure—usually an array for relatively small data sets, but you've already seen how NSFetchedResultsController performs the same service—that secures the data, puts it in the current order for presentation, exposes the count, and returns items by index. The obvious way to do this is for PRGameListController to keep an array of PRGames in the proper order.

The template put a *class extension*—an @interface qualified by " ( ) "—that defines a private API for PRGameListController. Edit it so it adds an instance variable to hold the cached array, and then write arrangedGames:

```objc
@interface PRGameListController () {
    NSArray *   _arrangedGamesCache;
}
// ...
@end
```

```
//  ...
@implementation PRGameListController
//  ...

- (NSArray *) arrangedGames
{
    static NSArray *     sByDate = nil;
    static dispatch_once_t onceToken;
    dispatch_once(&onceToken, ^{
        sByDate = @[
            [NSSortDescriptor sortDescriptorWithKey: @"whenPlayed"
                                          ascending: YES]
            ];
    });

    if (! _arrangedGamesCache) {
        PRPasser *      passer = self.detailItem;
        _arrangedGamesCache = [passer.games
                        sortedArrayUsingDescriptors: sByDate];
    }
    return _arrangedGamesCache;
}
```

When you get a new passer, in the setDetailItem: method, clear the cache out before reloading the views:

```
- (void) setDetailItem: (id <NSObject>) newDetailItem
{
    if (_detailItem != newDetailItem) {
        _detailItem = newDetailItem;
        _arrangedGamesCache = nil;

        //  Update the UI
        [self.tableView reloadData];
        [self configureView];
    }
}
```

A Prototype Cell

You've noticed that the placeholder for UITableView is labeled "Table View / Prototype Content." Prototype cells are important to building tables in Storyboard, and if you needed another reason to use Storyboard, this is a big one.

Prototypes allow you to create and lay out custom cells in the table itself; when UIKit calls your tableView:cellForRowAtIndexPath: method, you ask the table to instantiate a cell. With tables derived from NIBs, if you have a custom cell, you have to create one yourself, loading a separate NIB for just that cell.

Search the Object library (at the bottom of the Utility area, third tab) for `cell` to find "Table View Cell," and drag it into the table, where it becomes a prototype instance of `UITableViewCell`. For the first pass at the game table, we're sticking to a simple, single-string format: Use the **Style** popup in the Attributes inspector, and select **Basic**.

The `tableView:cellForRowAtIndexPath:` method we have now asks the table view for a cell with the identifier "Basic Game Cell". Enter that in the **Identifier** field.

We don't yet have an editor for game instances, but let's be prepared: Select **Detail** from the **Accessory** popup to put a circled-i button in the cell, which will eventually lead to the editor. The finished cell should look like Figure 13.1.

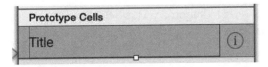

Figure 13.1   The prototype for the simple "starter" cell for display in the game table.

The Game Table: First Run

Now go back to your code-editing view, because you're about to run the app.

Run it, and select a passer. So far, so good. The table fills with cells for each game the passer played. The detail button is there as expected. The strings overrun the width of the cells, but it's just a prototype to see whether the table works at all (Figure 13.2).

Have a look at the Debug navigator. The application isn't halted, so the area for the stack trace is empty, but at the top of the navigator you'll find two bar graphs, one labeled CPU, the other Memory (Figure 13.3).

This is a new feature in Xcode 5. Xcode has always come with Instruments, a sophisticated tool for capturing event-by-event performance data and displaying it on a time scale. It's a powerful debugging tool, but it requires a special build, and then some setup. (Hold the mouse button down on the toolbar's **Run** button to see that there is a **Profile** action that runs your app under Instruments.)

> **Note**
>
> You'll learn more about Instruments in Chapters 16, "Measurement and Analysis," and 27, "Instruments."

The incentives work out that profiling with Instruments is a special occasion—special enough that most developers never run it at all until their applications get into obvious performance trouble. By that point, you don't have just one problem; you will have to shuttle between Xcode and Instruments as you hunt down each problem in turn.

Further: The iOS Simulator is not an emulator. It is an OS X application that floats on top of hardware that is ten times as fast as an actual device, and, with paged memory, has practically unlimited memory, not a hard gigabyte.

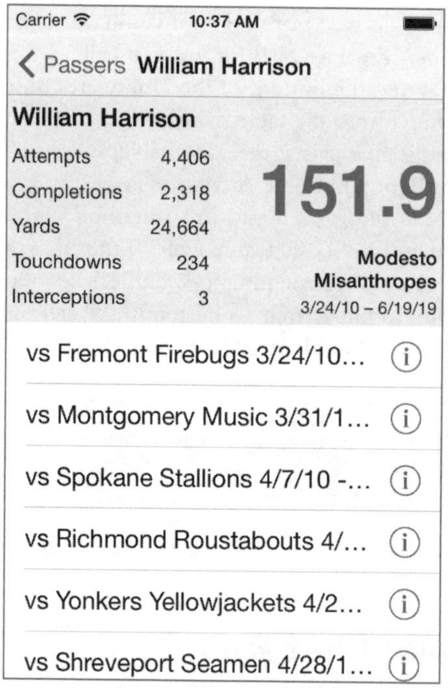

Carrier 📶   10:37 AM   ▬

< Passers **William Harrison**

William Harrison

Attempts	4,406
Completions	2,318
Yards	24,664
Touchdowns	234
Interceptions	3

151.9

Modesto Misanthropes
3/24/10 – 6/19/19

vs Fremont Firebugs 3/24/10... ⓘ

vs Montgomery Music 3/31/1... ⓘ

vs Spokane Stallions 4/7/10 -... ⓘ

vs Richmond Roustabouts 4/... ⓘ

vs Yonkers Yellowjackets 4/2... ⓘ

vs Shreveport Seamen 4/28/1... ⓘ

Figure 13.2   The new mechanism for filling in cells for a `PRPasser` record works first try.

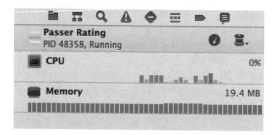

Figure 13.3   Bar graphs at the top of the Debug navigator show trends in the processing and memory performance of your application.

The debug-time graphs aren't high-precision, but the sampling imposes very little burden on the process being examined, and you can see trends. Even if your app doesn't run into visible trouble on a Mac, the absolute numbers in the graphs will warn you when you approach the actual limits of a device.

In this case, the only appreciable hit on the CPU comes when you scroll the game table, as the app fetches new data and fills in recycled cells for display. It's not a big hit, and you don't see any persistent demand. The same for memory: Usage escalates as the data is loaded, and a little more when you first scroll the list and cause OS caches to fill, but in my case, it settled in around 19.1 MiB. In a 1-GiB machine, that's nothing. No worries so far.

> **Note**
>
> In previous versions of this book, Passer Rating suffered an instructive crash related to memory management, and I could lead you through the basic techniques for prosecuting such bugs. I can't do that any more. Automatic Reference Counting (ARC) makes orphaned objects and dead pointers virtually impossible in any but edge cases. Memory crashes are now an advanced topic.

A Custom Table Cell

The default table cell leaves practically no room for information about games. If you want to see your data, you'll have to make a cell of your own.

A new table cell calls for a new prototype cell in the game table. Drag a new `UITableViewCell` from the Object library into the table. This time we'll go far beyond UIKit's standard cells, so set the **Style** popup to **Custom**, and its identifier to `Custom Game Cell`.

A prototype cell is a view like any other; you drag views into it and customize them as you need. It's a standard-size table-view cell, 320 points wide (the width of an iPhone screen) and 44 points high (the recommended minimum size of a tappable object). That's not tall enough to accommodate what we want to do. You want a custom cell because the standard size can't accommodate all of the information you want to show. So drag the top or bottom edge of the cell (or use the Size [fifth] inspector) to make it taller; my experiment left me with a cell 85 points high.

Now you go through much the same drudgery as for the passer-detail view in Chapter 11:

- A large label for the game rating. I used `158.3` (the maximum rating), System Bold, 30 points, blue. Put it in the upper-left corner. The initial size of the label is too small to accommodate the content, but dragging a resizing handle will make it snap to a large-enough size.
- At the top right, a label for the teams, scores, and the date of the match. For size, fill it with

  `Tacoma Touchdown-Scorers 88`
  `Tacoma Touchdown-Scorers 88`
  `12/12/12`

  Use the **Lines** stepper/field to make the field accommodate three lines; the easiest way to enter multi-line text is to use the **Text** field and use Option-Return for line breaks. Make it System Italic, 11 points, right justified.
- Across the bottom, a label in System 14 points, left justified. Size it with `999/999 - 999 yd - 99 TD - 99 INT`.

When you're done, you should have something like Figure 13.4.

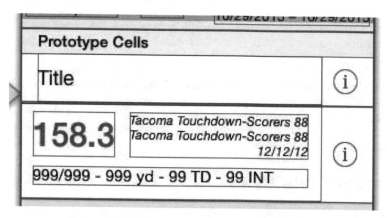

Figure 13.4   The finished layout of the game-list cell.

> **Note**
>
> I also added autolayout constraints to the labels, but let's not revisit that process.

What about connecting the cell to `PRGameListController`? For the passer-detail view, you used `IBOutlets` for the connections, but the controller manages only one of those views at a time. For the game cell, it will be reloading the prototype cell over and over again. There can't be a single outlet for the cell or its labels. What the controller *will* have at any moment is a pointer to the cell it is working on right then. It can pull pointers to the labels from that.

This is done by setting the *tags* of the labels. Every `UIView`—cells and labels included—can have an integer associated with it. You can retrieve the view from its hierarchy if its tag is unique by sending `viewWithTag:` to any ancestor view with the subview's tag.

By default, the tag is **0**. Use the Attributes inspector to set the rating label's tag to **1**, the scoring label to **2**, and the statistics label to 3. You'll find the **Tag** field low in the inspector, in the "View" section.

Finally, with the cell selected, expose the Size inspector. Take note of the height (85 points in my case). `UITableView` normally doesn't measure the rows it presents; there's one height for all of them, and by default it's 44 points. Select the game table in the Game List Controller scene. Tables put a "Table View Size" section at the top of the Size inspector. Set **Row Height** to the height of your cell (85). The basic cell will also grow to 85 points, but that doesn't matter any more.

Save all your work, and check it in.

Now modify `tableView:cellForRowAtIndexPath:` in `PRGameListController.m` to load the compiled `GameTableCell` NIB whenever it needs a fresh cell. The method can then find the labels, and format the game data into each.

```objc
// Tag values for the labels in the game cell
#define CELL_RATING_LABEL    1
#define CELL_SCORE_LABEL     2
#define CELL_STATS_LABEL     3
// More on this later:
#define CELL_REACTION_IMAGE 4

- (UITableViewCell *) tableView: (UITableView *) aTableView
         cellForRowAtIndexPath: (NSIndexPath *) indexPath
{
    NSString *              cellIdentifier;
    cellIdentifier = @"Custom Game Cell";

    // Get the cell with the identifier "Custom Game Cell"
    UITableViewCell *      cell;
    cell =
        [self.tableView dequeueReusableCellWithIdentifier: cellIdentifier];
    PRGame *       game = [self.arrangedGames objectAtIndex: indexPath.row];

    // Get the rating cell and format the rating into it
    UILabel *    currentLabel;
    currentLabel = (UILabel *)[cell viewWithTag: CELL_RATING_LABEL];
    currentLabel.text = [ratingFormatter stringFromNumber:
                                        @(game.passerRating)];

    // Get the score cell and format the teams,
    // scores, and dates into it
    currentLabel = (UILabel *)[cell viewWithTag: CELL_SCORE_LABEL];
    NSString *  content;
    content = [NSString stringWithFormat:
                @"%@ %d\n%@ %d\n%@",
                game.ourTeam, game.ourScore.intValue,
                game.theirTeam, game.theirScore.intValue,
                [shortDateFormatter stringFromDate: game.whenPlayed]];
    currentLabel.text = content;

    // Get the statistics cell and format
    // the summary stats into it
    currentLabel = (UILabel *) [cell viewWithTag: CELL_STATS_LABEL];
    content = [NSString stringWithFormat:
                @"%d/%d - %d yd - %d TD - %d INT",
                game.completions.intValue, game.attempts.intValue,
                game.yards.intValue, game.touchdowns.intValue,
                game.interceptions.intValue];
    currentLabel.text = content;

    return cell;
}
```

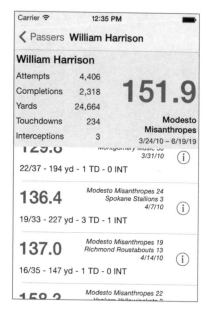

Figure 13.5   The text-based custom cell displays complete game-by-game information in a readable form.

Run Passer Rating one more time. When you tap a passer, his full record appears, including the complete statistics on every game. The display portions of the app behave as specified, as you can see in Figure 13.5.

> **Note**
>
> The tagged-label approach worked well for this simple case. However, if your needs were more complex—more intricate data, or even custom drawing—tagged subviews won't be enough. You'd need to create a new subclass of `UITableViewCell`. Such a subclass would have outlets of its own for its labels and would expose a `@property` that would accept a `PRGame` object as its represented object. Setting the `PRGame` would cause the custom cell class to fill its labels from it. `table-View:cellForRowAtIndexPath:` could simply set the game property and not worry about the details of the cell view.

Adding Some Graphics

I'm never satisfied. Football is an emotional sport, its fans alternating jubilation with despair. The game list should reflect this. There should be a graphic in each row expressing how the passer's performance feels.

A Cell with an Image in It

This calls for yet another custom cell. Fortunately, all the contents of the previous cell can carry over with little change. Select the custom game cell, and duplicate it (by **Edit →Duplicate**, ⌘D—don't choose **Duplicate. . .** in the **File** menu).

1. In the Attributes inspector, change the new cells **Identifier** to `Graphical Game Cell`.
2. Resize the cell to a height of 96 points. This should also change the table's general row height.
3. Change the statistical-summary label to two lines, and use Option-Return to put a line break between "yd" and the number of "TD"s.

4. Search the Object library for **Image**, which will show you an image view (UIImageView), Drag it in, put it into the lower-left corner of the cell, and resize it to 30 × 30 points.
5. If you're doing constraints, center it vertically on the stats label, set its leading edge to align with that of the rating label, and fix its height and width to 30.
6. Give the image view a tag of **4**.

The result should be like Figure 13.6.

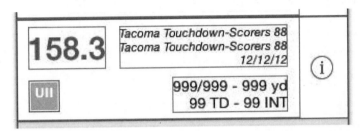

Figure 13.6   The last iteration of the game cell adds a UIImageView to the lower-left corner.

Hooking the Image View to the Images

You have to amend `tableView:cellForRowAtIndexPath:` (excerpts):

```
#define CELL_REACTION_IMAGE 4
// ...
- (UITableViewCell *) tableView: (UITableView *) aTableView
        cellForRowAtIndexPath: (NSIndexPath *) indexPath
{
    NSString *              cellIdentifier;
    cellIdentifier = @"Graphical Game Cell";
    // ...

    //  Changing the format for the stats label:
    currentLabel = (UILabel *) [cell viewWithTag:
                        CELL_STATS_LABEL];
    content = [NSString stringWithFormat:
            @"%d/%d - %d yd\n%d TD - %d INT",
            game.completions.intValue, game.attempts.intValue,
            game.yards.intValue, game.touchdowns.intValue,
            game.interceptions.intValue];
    currentLabel.text = content;

    //  Get the image view
    UIImageView *   reactionView;
```

```
reactionView = (UIImageView *)[cell viewWithTag:
                                CELL_REACTION_IMAGE];
// Fetch the reaction image for the rating
UIImage *      reactionImage;
if (game.passerRating < 122.0) {
    reactionImage = [UIImage imageNamed: @"Despondent"];
}
else {
    reactionImage = [UIImage imageNamed: @"Elated"];
}
// Set the image.
reactionView.image = reactionImage;

return cell;
}
```

The Assets Catalog

That leaves the images themselves. I drew up a couple of badge images (PNG, with transparency) and produced single-resolution and double-resolution (60 × 60 pixels) versions (find these in the `icons` and `images` folder in the sample code):

- `Despondent.png` - 30 × 30 pixels
- `Despondent@2x.png` - 60 × 60 pixels
- `Elated.png` - 30 × 30 pixels
- `Elated@2x.png` - 60 × 60 pixels

Note

If you can, draw up at least your simple images in a vector-drawing application, and let it take care of scaling the images for single- and double-resolution sizes.

Image Sets

Before Xcode 5, if you had images to embed in your application, you simply dragged them into the Project navigator and did the usual negotiation about whether it should be copied, its target memberships, and its place in the group hierarchy. Keeping a rigorous group hierarchy, giving each functional group its own folder in the navigator so you know what images are being used for each purpose, would keep the image zoo under control.

Not every human does such things. I've seen projects that evolved through adding, replacing, and discarding images to the point where the great majority of the `.png`s in the project navigator were orphans. Clearing out the deadwood is nearly impossible, because there's no way to be certain which are still in use.

In Xcode 5, that's gone. You no longer have to keep references to image files in the Project navigator. When you create a new iOS application target, the template includes an *asset catalog*, a container with the .xcassets extension. Its entry in the Project navigator looks like a folder, but it doesn't open in the navigator. Instead, it presents an editor for the catalog—select Images.xcassets.

An asset catalog contains *image sets*, each of which contains representations of what is notionally a single image, adapted for the resolutions and devices on which they will be displayed. Images in image sets can be retrieved by the name of the set; UIKit will do the work of selecting the suitable representation without your having to specify it.

The sets keep the many representations out of the Project navigator, and automatically group them by function. When you have to replace an image, there's only one place you have to go, and the catalog editor will take care of cleaning up the obsolete representations.

By default, the catalog includes an AppIcon set for the application's icon, and a LaunchImage set for the image that iOS displays while your app is launching.

Note
An OS X application can keep its icon set in an asset catalog, as well.

The editor is divided into a "Set list," a source list of image sets on the left side, and the "Set viewer," the main view. Select a set from the source list, and the Set viewer will show all the representations in that set. The Utilities area adds an Attributes inspector (third tab) for each image and image set.

Adding Images to the Assets Catalog

Drag the four image files into the Set list of the assets catalog. That's it. Xcode will infer the set grouping and resolutions from the names and the actual sizes of the images (Figure 13.7).

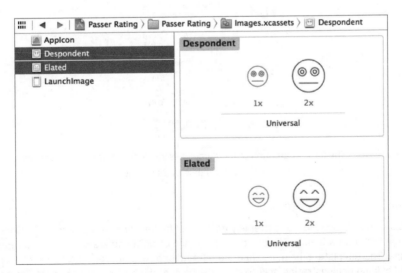

Figure 13.7   Dragging image files at single- and double-resolution into the Set list of an assets catalog sorts them by name into image sets and displays each resolution of each set.

The new code for `tableView:cellForRowAtIndexPath:` already uses `+[UIImage imageNamed:]` to retrieve images by name from the asset catalog. Run Passer Rating again; the build process compiles the catalog into a single binary file that UIKit can efficiently use, and the app launches. (You can still use asset catalogs in projects targeted for iOS versions earlier than 6. For compatibility, catalogs are not compiled; their contents are placed separately in the application's bundle.)

Note

The first time Xcode 5 opens an older project, it adds an asset-catalog file. This is harmless—you don't have to use it—but the **General** tab of the Target editor will help you migrate your icons and launch images into the catalog. That's harmless, too, and a very good idea.

Select a passer and scroll through the game list. Games in which the passer earned a rating of 122 or above are greeted with elation; lesser performances, with despondency (Figure 13.8).

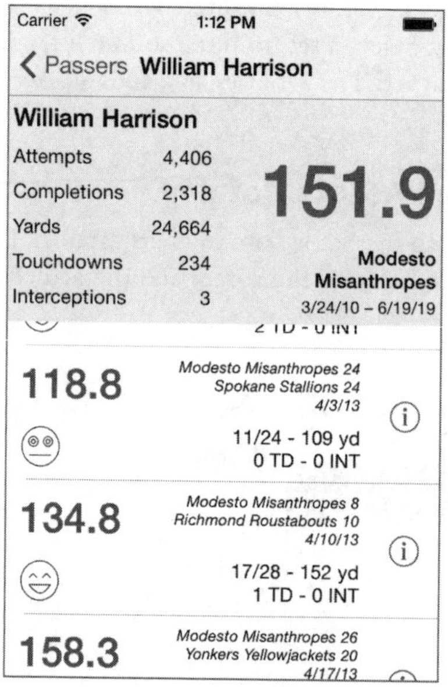

Figure 13.8   The final incarnation of the game cells includes a graphical assessment of the passer's performance in that game.

Note

Class `UIImage` provides an extremely useful tool for handling resizable images. Consider a button for an OS X dialog. The button's shape and background are provided by a template image. The template is no more than the left end cap (with its rounded corners), a one-pixel column demonstrating how to color the body of the button, and the right end cap. Applying `-[UIImage resizableImageWithCapInsets:]` to the template yields a special `UIImage` that, when rendered in a wider rectangle, fills the space by preserving the proportions of the end caps, and stretching that single pixel across the width between them. The Image Set editor lets you slice a managed image into three or nine segments. Expose the feature with **Editor →Show Slicing**. There isn't room in this book for a full discussion, but it's well worth your time to look into it.

Icons and Launch Images

While we're here, it's time to fill in the icons and launch images. In the asset catalog, select the AppIcon image set. If you've dealt with icons for iOS applications before, what you see may come as a pleasant surprise: the set carries wells for only three double-resolution images for iPhone Spotlight and Settings (29 points—58 pixels—on a side); iPhone/iOS 7 Spotlight (40 points); and an iOS 7 icon for the Home screen (60).

The repetition of "iPhone" and "iOS 7" should be a clue: The Passer Rating application is an iPhone-only app targeted at iOS 7. The Attributes inspector for an icon image set carries checkboxes for iPhone and iPad icons for iOS 7 and iOS 6, plus a box for Mac icons.

The checkbox labeled **iOS icon is pre-rendered** is a convenience for setting the flag in the app's `Info.plist` file that tells iOS that the "gloss" effect iOS put on application icons in versions 6 and earlier is not wanted.

Adding iOS 6 slots for iPhone gives you three more images to fill for the smaller application icon at two resolutions and a single-resolution Spotlight/Settings icon.

Note

Note that the icon wells are labeled in *points*, not pixels. An iPhone application icon, pre-iOS 7, is 57 points on a side, and that's how it's labeled. That's 57 *pixels* at single resolution, but at 2×, it's 114. You're expected to do that math yourself.

Check all the iOS boxes. To cover every icon style for two devices running two operating systems, you'd have to provide 16 icon images. If you were building a Mac icon set instead, you'd have to fill 10 spaces.

Let's not get crazy; uncheck all but the iPhone/iOS 7 option. I've drawn Passer Rating's icon in the three sizes required, and I dropped each image file into its respective slot. Done (Figure 13.9).

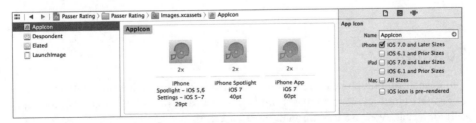

Figure 13.9   The complete repertoire of application icons can be covered in three images if you set the Attributes inspector's checkboxes to limit the set to iOS 7 on iPhone.

Now the launch image. Assuming it isn't running already, an application launches when the user taps its icon on the Home screen. The launch process concludes when the app is ready to respond to user actions. Both the OS and the app will have to do some work before the app is ready for service. This can take some time even now—it took more on the iPhone as it was in 2007.

Apple resorted to some stagecraft. In the period before an application is running, iOS pulls a *launch image* from the app's bundle and displays it until the app can present its first active screen and respond to user actions. This is a user-experience trick: Showing the user something that *looks* like the app's main screen assures the user she's running the app she intends and gives her the impression that the device is responding to her more quickly than it really can.

> **Note**
>
> Your management will speak of the launch image as a "splash screen." It isn't. A real splash screen has to block the user's access to her data for a certain amount of time. A launch image goes away as soon as the app is ready for use. Ideally, the interval between tapping your application's icon and its being ready for service is zero, and the launch image should never be seen at all. That ideal will be tested in Chapter 16, "Measurement and Analysis."

Select the LaunchImage image set. Once again, the available slots are refreshingly few, portrait-only for 3.5- and 4-inch screens in double resolutions. Again, the Attributes inspector offers many more options for iPad (portrait and landscape), and the same for iOS 6 and earlier (including iPad images that don't cover the status bar). Taking into account the single-resolution variants supported by iOS 6, there are 17 possible images (the status-bar variants mean that the practical maximum is 13).

Uncheck everything but iPhone **Portrait, iOS 7.0 and Later**, and give thanks. I took screen shots of the passer-list screen and stripped out the text. Launch images should not have anything that looks like data or reflects the locale. Seeing data other than her own would disconcert the user. There is only one set of launch images for all locales. A transition from an image of an English-language button to the live button is smooth; but if you're using a German localization, the appearance of foreign-language text that is replaced by the local text is jarring.

I darkened the navigation bar for this example. The screen is never darker than 96 percent white, and you'd never see the images when reduced to the tiny thumbnails in the Set viewer.

Summary

This chapter told the story of how Passer Rating fills its game table from a `PRPasser`'s games set. This took us to another feature of Storyboard, the ability to specify prototype cells for a table. We advanced through three stages:

- A simple text-only cell as provided by iOS, just to test the mechanism

- A cell with a custom layout that can display the full information about a game in a compact and interesting (or you could make it interesting) format
- A development of the full-information cell that supplemented the contents with a `UIImageView`

The image was silly, but it yielded an in-depth look at the asset-catalog feature, which makes it much easier than before to manage the explosion of system images an iOS application might have to carry.

14

Adding an Editor

The last substantive change we'll make to Passer Rating is to add an editor for passers. The task itself will be very quick—you know how to add a scene, and the concepts of the editor are not difficult. But it'll give us the chance to take a deeper look at Storyboard.

The Plan

We already know roughly what we want to do—the layout is already there in Figure 8.2 in Chapter 8, "Starting an iOS Application." It's a modal view (it slides up from the bottom), containing a table with rows for editing a passer's first and last names and the name of his current team. **Save** and **Cancel** buttons allow the user to exit the editor one way or another.

Adding a Modal Scene

Bring `Main.storyboard` into the editor, and use the minus magnifying-glass button in the group in the lower-right corner of the editor to zoom out to give you room to drag in a new view. Find "View Controller" (`UIViewController`) in the Library portion of the Utility area (make sure the third tab, for the Object library, is selected), and drag it in just below the game-list controller (the segue arrow will be easier to follow that way).

Select the new scene, and the Identity inspector (third tab, top of the Utility area). Name the **Class PRPasserEditController**. Make a mental note to actually build such a class.

The scene consists of two parts: A toolbar at the top, and a table below it. It would be tempting to control this scene with a `UITableViewController`, but if you do that, the whole scene must be a `UITableView`. We don't want that.

Contrariwise, we don't want to drop a `UITableView` directly into the scene, either. We're going to take advantage of *static table cells* for the editing form, and you can't have those without a `UITableViewController`. It seems we're stuck.

While pondering this, drag a `UIToolbar` in, and put it at the top of the scene—you'll have to click the = button in the zoom control. Set the constraints to be zero from the leading and trailing edges of the superview, and zero from the Top Layout Guide (the imaginary line below any bars at the top of the screen—you may have to start the top well below any top bars before you get the top guide as an option).

The toolbar already contains a button labeled **Item**. Toolbars don't have any vertical layout, and they take care of their own horizontal layouts: Drag in a "Flexible Space Bar Button Item" (yes, it's technically a button, but inert) to the right of it, and another `UIBarButtonItem` to the right of that.

Now you have two buttons labeled **Item**. There is a time to be enigmatic, but human-interface design is not it. Select the button on the left. If this were a `UIButton`, you'd edit a **Title** field in the Attributes inspector. Bar-button items are different, because very often they have standard titles or icons. Look at the "Bar Button Item" section of the Attributes inspector.

- Set the **Style** popup to **Bordered**. Putting borders around buttons is out of style in iOS 7, but that's the historic name for what we want, and if you run on iOS 6, you'll get the dark-gray sunken appearance.

- Have a look at the **Identifier** popup. It starts at **Custom**, which allows you to set the title, as you'd expect. But there are many items offering the standard button types. Some of them correspond to icons—a **Stop** button carries a large saltire—but some get rendered as strings, like **Save**. What's the good in that? iOS renders "acceptance" buttons in a heavier font, and because the title is standard, it will localize the title automatically. Choose **Save** from the **Identifier** popup.

- Select the left-hand button in the bar and set its identifier to **Cancel**.

These buttons should do something. They will, soon.

Toolbars don't have a way to label themselves the way navigation bars can. Cheat: Drag in a `UILabel`, title it `Edit Passer`, set it in System Bold, 17. Select the label and the bar (you can't put the label *in* the bar), and use the alignment control to align the horizontal and vertical centers. The content will run off the end of the label, but if you have the **Resolve Auto Layout Issues** menu redo the layout for the scene, the label's content will push it out so the full text is visible.

An Embedded View Controller

To review: We can't have a `UITableViewController`, because we need that toolbar. But if we simply drop a `UITableView` in, we can't have the static table cells that will make our lives so much easier.

> **Note**
>
> Other developers might solve this by putting the editor in the same `UINavigationController` chain as the other scenes; or embed a table-view controller in a navigation controller all its own. I'm having you do it this way so I can show how you can break out of the navigation-controller stack and still have control; and how you don't have to fall prey to dilemmas like this.

So we're going to have our `UITableViewController`. And our toolbar. Without compromise. The trick is the *embedded view controller*, in which the editor view cedes a container for another controller to run.

Type **contai** into the search field at the bottom of the Library panel, to find and place "Container View" into the Passer Edit scene. This doesn't look good. It's too small, but some constraints will take care of that (zero to bottom, leading, and right edges of the container; zero to the bottom of the toolbar).

The container seems to have brought another view controller with it. Probably Interface Builder has placed it inconveniently, but that, too, is easy to deal with: Zoom the canvas out so you can drag it to the right of the editor. You find that the new scene has sized itself to match the container. Good. You also find that the new scene has assigned itself a `UIViewController`. Bad. See Figure 14.1.

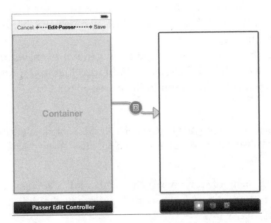

Figure 14.1 The editor view has its toolbar and a container for its table, but the container view brought in a plain `UIViewController`, when we need a `UITableViewController`.

The reason it's bad is that we need a `UITableViewController`. That's ultimately a subclass of `UIViewController`, but if you simply set the class of the existing controller, Interface Builder won't correct its presentation to include the tools for building a table. This is the wrong scene for the wrong controller.

Bring in the right controller. Find the Table View Controller object and drag it into the canvas. As far as Interface Builder knows, this is a stand-alone scene, so it is shown at the screen size you're currently using for the storyboard. Not a problem.

Control-drag from the container view in the editor scene to the new table-controller scene. A heads-up window will appear so you can set the type of segue you want. Click **embed**, which is the only choice you have. The container can have only one embedded controller, so the embed segue to the interloping `UIViewController` is broken. Select its scene and press Delete.

Select the new table controller, and use the Identity inspector to set its class name to `PRPasserEditTableController`. It's unwieldy, but a stranger (including you, next month) will need every part of the name to understand what the class does.

Segues should always have names. Select the embed segue and use the Attributes inspector to set the **Identifier** to something like **Passer Edit Embed**.

Linking the Editor to the Passer List

We need a way to get from the root list of passers to the editor. This is complicated—but only slightly—by the fact that there will be two uses for the editor: to work on the content of an existing `PRPasser`, and to populate a new one.

We can do most of the jump from an existing `PRPasser` in Interface Builder.

`-[PRPasserListController viewDidLoad]` hasn't changed since the project template gave it to us. Part of what that method does is to set the right button of its navigation item to the standard **Add** button. We need to use that button as the root of a segue, and code isn't the way to do it.

Drag a bar button from the Library into the right end of the navigation bar in the passer-list controller scene. Select the standard **Add** identifier in the Attributes inspector. Control-drag from the new **Add** button to the passer-editor scene.

> **Note**
>
> I bet your editor scene and the **Add** button can't fit on the screen at the same time. Good news: You can't do much with the zoomed-out view of the canvas, but you *can* drag segues.

You'll be offered a menu of segue types; choose **modal**. The segue is to be triggered by a tap on the accessory, and it should present the editor modally (sliding up from the bottom over the `PRPasser` list).

> **Note**
>
> With its bigger screen, the iPad offers other modes for presenting modal views. Consult the documentation for `modalPresentationStyle`.

Provide an identifier for the new segue: **Edit passer**. The Attributes inspector for the segue offers other **Transition** styles, but let's not get fancy; experiment with them yourself.

> **Note**
>
> It's an identifier, not a coding symbol. There's no compiler to tell you the identifier should not be comfortable for a human to read.

Now for editing an existing `PRPasser`. `UITableViewCells` can display one of five standard accessories at the right end of the row:

- Disclosure, a right-facing caret to indicate that tapping the cell will disclose the next-lower layer of the hierarchy.

- Detail, a circled **i**, which will summon an editor for the object the cell represents. You have to tap the accessory itself to get the editor. (In iOS 6 and earlier, this was a chevron in a blue circle.)

- Detail Disclosure, which shows both the caret and the circled **i** to show that tapping the detail button will show an editor, and tapping anywhere else in the row will navigate to another screen.

- A checkmark.

- No accessory at all.

The passer table's prototype cell has the disclosure accessory because we've been using the cell to advance to a display of one passer's record. Now that we want to edit it, we need a detail-disclosure accessory. Select the cell in the Passer List Controller table, and use the Attributes inspector to set **Accessory** to **Detail Disclosure**.

The detail-disclosure accessory is a button. As such, it can trigger a segue. You will be tempted to drag an additional segue from it to the editor controller. That will work, as far as it goes, but there is a problem: In order to edit an existing passer, the `prepareForSegue:sender:` method has to know which passer it is. By the time control gets to that method, that information is lost; one accessory tap looks like any other.

Leave the question aside for the moment.

Static Table Cells

Now we can build the editing form from the table embedded in the Passer Editor scene. Zoom in on the table in that scene and select it. You will make these changes:

- Change **Content** from **Dynamic Prototypes** to **Static Cells**.

- Notice that **Sections** is set to **1**. That's what we want.

- Change **Style** to **Grouped**. **Plain** style is better for sectioned data—it keeps the section header on screen even when you scroll far down in the section—but a grouped table is better for a static presentation.

- **Selection** should be **No Selection**.

Now move on to that one section. To select the section, either find it in the Document Outline, which you can expand with the arrowhead button at the lower-left corner of the canvas, or by control-shift-clicking on the section in the scene, and selecting the section.

You'll make two changes: Set **Rows** to **1**, and set **Header** to `Passer`. (IB will force it to all-caps, but that's okay.) The form will have three rows, but if you lay out one, and duplicate it twice, you'll have three identical layouts without more trouble.

You're down to one cell. Drag a label into it (vertically centered in container; fixed leading margin; width 120 points), and set the title to `First Name`. Drag in a `UITextField` and put it at the right end of the cell (fixed trailing edge, width 150 points, baseline aligned with the label).

Select the section again, and set it to have three rows; as I promised, the three have the same layout. Set the label titles to **First Name**, **Last Name**, and **Current Team**. Just to be stylish, set the **Placeholder Text** in the text fields to **First**, **Last**, and **Team**.

The Editor View Controllers

We've worked up quite a debt in unimplemented code, and now we must pay off.

Create the promised classes, PRPasserEditController (a subclass of UIViewController) and PRPasserEditTableController (subclass of UITableViewController).

The last two lines of -viewDidLoad in PRPasserListController set up an **Add** button for the passer list's navigation bar. Remove them. This obsoletes insertNewObject:, but it's harmless, and it would be a distraction to remove it.

The Editor Table

The editor table doesn't have to do much. It must keep track of its text fields and their contents; and it has to accept and return the strings the fields edit. If we choose the names of the fields and the properties that back them, we can automate much of the task of running the data from field to controller to PRPasser properties. The PRPasser values are firstName, lastName, and currentTeam. The names of everything else will be, or be derived from, those names.

Now that we have class files, we can link the fields to PRPasserEditTableController. Rig your Interface Builder tab so the Assistant editor is visible and the first segment of its jump bar set to **Automatic**; and the Navigator and Utility areas are hidden to make room. The assistant will show the controller's source files when its scene is selected. Control-drag from each field into the @interface block in PRPasserEditTableController.h. (I'd prefer to use a class extension in the .m file, but the template didn't give me one, and I'm lazy).

Add one more @property, making the @interface look like this:

```
@class PRPasserEditController;

@interface PRPasserEditTableController : UITableViewController
@property (weak, nonatomic) IBOutlet UITextField *firstNameField;
@property (weak, nonatomic) IBOutlet UITextField *lastNameField;
@property (weak, nonatomic) IBOutlet UITextField *currentTeamField;

@property(strong, nonatomic) NSDictionary *          values;
@property(weak, nonatomic) PRPasserEditController * parent;
@end
```

The controller's API uses a dictionary to pass the editor's values in and out. One might think the best way to get the values into and out of the editor would be to call out each in an `NSString` property, but this technique has the advantage of removing the structure of the data from the API, and providing a single way to pass the data back and forth regardless of whether it's for an existing or new record. Also, there are Key-Value Coding (KVC) methods that make it easy to get and set object properties through dictionaries. The dictionary keys will be `firstName`, `lastName`, and `currentTeam`.

Here's how you'd back that `values` property:

```
#import "PRPasserEditTableController.h"
#import "PRPasserEditController.h"

static NSArray *    sPropertyNames;

@implementation PRPasserEditTableController

+ (void) initialize
{
    static dispatch_once_t onceToken;
    dispatch_once(&onceToken, ^{
     sPropertyNames = @[@"firstName", @"lastName", @"currentTeam"];
    });
}

- (void) viewDidLoad
{
    [super viewDidLoad];
    [self.parent childReadyForValues];
}

- (NSDictionary *) values
{
    NSMutableDictionary *    retval = [NSMutableDictionary dictionary];

    for (NSString * propName in sPropertyNames) {
        UITextField *      field;
        field =
            (UITextField *) [self valueForKey:
                    [propName stringByAppendingString: @"Label"]];
        retval[propName] = field.text?: @"";
    }
    return retval;
}

- (void) setValues: (NSDictionary *) values
{
    for (NSString * propName in sPropertyNames) {
```

```
        UITextField *        field;
        field =
            (UITextField *) [self valueForKey:
                    [propName stringByAppendingString: @"Label"]];
        field.text = values[propName] ?: @"";
    }
}

@end
```

If the editor table is simple, the container does practically nothing. Here's the header:

```
@class PRPasserEditTableController;

@interface PRPasserEditController : UIViewController

- (void) childReadyForValues;

@property(nonatomic, weak) PRPasserEditTableController *    childEditor;
@property(nonatomic, strong) NSDictionary *                editValues;

//  As a convenience to the client, hold a reference to
//  whatever we're editing. We don't do anything with it.
@property(nonatomic, strong) id <NSObject>  representedObject;

@end
```

And here's the implementation:

```
#import "PRPasserEditController.h"
#import "PRPasserEditTableController.h"

@implementation PRPasserEditController {
    //  A place to hold the editor contents until the child is ready
    NSDictionary *      _savedValues;
}

//  The embed segue is like any other: It has a source (the parent)
//  and a desination (the child). Capture the link between them;
//  there is no way to do it before now.
- (void) prepareForSegue: (UIStoryboardSegue *) segue sender: (id) sender
{
    if ([segue.identifier isEqualToString: @"Passer Edit Embed"]) {
        self.childEditor = segue.destinationViewController;
        self.childEditor.parent = self;
    }
}
```

```
//  The child exists and has fields it can fill
- (void) childReadyForValues
{
    self.childEditor.values = _savedValues;
}

//  The child's .values property is the "real" data,
//  but when the client sets them, the parent has to remember
//  them until the child can accept them.
- (NSDictionary *) editValues { return self.childEditor.values; }
- (void) setEditValues: (NSDictionary *) editValues
{
    _savedValues = editValues;
    self.childEditor.values = editValues;
}

@end
```

The embed segue is like any other: It has a source controller and a destination controller. When it is triggered (by loading the edit controller from the storyboard), it gets a `prepareForSegue:sender:` message, as it would for any other segue. From that, it can get a pointer to the embedded controller (there's no way to link an outlet to the child in Interface Builder).

However, at that moment, the views haven't been instantiated in either the parent or the child; and while the parent can rely on its own views' existence when `-viewDidLoad` is called, it can't be sure about the child. Therefore, the transaction of handing the values to be edited off to the child has to wait until it is ready. `PRPasserEditController` takes care of this by publishing a `childReadyForValues` method to receive the signal.

Passing the Data to the Editor

You may ask yourself how the edited data gets between the editor and the `PRPasser` model object. The editing classes we just wrote do everything we need at their end. In the past, the editor would declare a delegation protocol for its client (the passer list) to implement so it could receive the news that one way or another, the editing session ended. That's not necessary any more.

But first to get the data into the editor. We have an entry to the editor in the form of the `Edit passer` segue, but we have two uses for it. For one of them, adding a `PRPasser`, it's straightforward: Have the **Add** button trigger a segue; there's only one **Add** button.

The other use, for editing an existing passer, is trickier. There is no one origin; you have to know which passer triggered the transition. If you hooked up the detail button directly to the segue, that information would be lost. So you have to do some processing ahead of time, while you still can identify the passer.

The most straightforward way to do this is to add an old-fashioned
UITableViewDelegate method to PRPasserListController:

```
// Remember to put this before any @interfece or @implementation!
#import "PRPasserEditController.h"

...

// Add an instance variable to the class
// Was: @implementation PRPasserListController
// Now:
@implementation PRPasserListController {
    PRPasser *      _passerToEdit;
}

...

// Remove the in-code setup for the add button so
// the one connected to the editor segue is used:
- (void)viewDidLoad
{
    [super viewDidLoad];
    self.navigationItem.leftBarButtonItem = self.editButtonItem;
}

...

- (void) tableView: (UITableView *) tableView
accessoryButtonTappedForRowWithIndexPath: (NSIndexPath *) indexPath
{
    // What passer is represented by the accessory's cell?
    // Save it in _passerToEdit
    _passerToEdit = [self.fetchedResultsController objectAtIndexPath: indexPath];
    // Trigger the "Edit passer" segue in-code
    [self performSegueWithIdentifier: @"Edit passer"
                              sender: _passerToEdit];
}

- (void)prepareForSegue:(UIStoryboardSegue *)segue sender: (id)sender
{
    if ([[segue identifier] isEqualToString:@"showDetail"]) {
      NSIndexPath *indexPath = [self.tableView indexPathForSelectedRow];
      NSManagedObject *object = [[self fetchedResultsController]
                                  objectAtIndexPath:indexPath];
        [[segue destinationViewController] setDetailItem: (PRPasser *) object];
    }
    else if ([segue.identifier isEqualToString: @"Edit passer"]) {
      PRPasserEditController *   editor = segue.destinationViewController;
        if (_passerToEdit) {
          editor.editValues = [_passerToEdit dictionaryWithValuesForKeys:
                    @[@"firstName", @"lastName", @"currentTeam"]];
```

```
        editor.representedObject = _passerToEdit;
    }
    else {
        editor.editValues = @{@"firstName"    : @"",
                              @"lastName"      : @"",
                              @"currentTeam"   : @""};
        editor.representedObject = nil;
    }
}
_passerToEdit = nil;
}
```

It's been a long time since we've run Passer Rating. Do it now; tap on the detail-disclosure button on one of the rows, or on the **Add** button. The new editor slides up from the bottom, populated correctly. You can edit the fields (see Figure 14.2).

Getting the Data Back

What you can't do is close the editor, nor get your work back into the model. Up through iOS 5, the most straightforward way to get this done was to declare a `@protocol` in `PRPasserEditController.h` that `PRPasserListController` could implement. When the **Cancel** or **Save** button is pressed, the editor would use the delegate methods to signal the results to the list controller, its delegate.

But why do this, when Storyboard can eliminate the editor-side code entirely, and free the client from setting a delegate outlet and conforming to a strict API?

You can't dig out of a view controller with an ordinary segue. If you control-dragged a segue from the **Cancel** button back to the `PRPasserListController`, you'd get a segue that creates a new passer-list controller. That's what most segues do—they create view controllers.

Figure 14.2   The new editor fills itself from exiting `PRPasser`s as hoped. You just can't close it.

What you want is an *unwind* segue. An unwind (or exit) segue shops itself up the chain of view controllers until it finds one that can handle the transition. (If you think of that chain as simply the sequence of modal and navigation presentations that arrived at the scene where the segue was triggered, you've got a workable idea, but it's a bit more complex, and you can modify it in code.)

A view controller declares its readiness to handle an unwind segue by implementing an `IBAction` method with one argument of type `UIStoryboardSegue`. clang and the runtime don't care about those properties—the information is basically lost by then.

Interface Builder *does* care about them. Even as IBAction in a method declaration tells IB that a method is a candidate to handle control events, the combination of IBAction and the argument type adds the method to IB's candidates for unwind handlers.

By definition, the target for an unwind segue is undefined. The undefined target of a control action is represented by the First Responder placeholder. The undefined handler for an unwind is represented by the green **Exit** icon in the bar beneath the scene that contains the sender. Start as you would for any segue: Control-drag from the control that triggers the segue. Bring it down to the green **Exit** icon below the scene (Figure 14.3). Release the mouse button and choose from the list of declared unwind handlers (Figure 14.4).

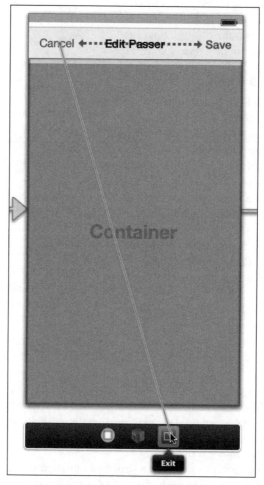

Figure 14.3   Link a control to an unwind segue by control-dragging from it to the **Exit** placeholder in the scene's bottom bar.

Figure 14.4   When the control-drag is released, a heads-up menu shows the selectors of declared handlers for unwind segues.

Before you can do that, you have to provide the handlers. There are two exits from the editor: **Cancel** and **Save**. PRPasserListController needs a handler for each:

```
#pragma mark - Editor results

- (IBAction) editorDidSave: (UIStoryboardSegue *) sender
{
    //  An unwind segue, presumably representing an exit
    //  from an editor, accepting the contents, has arrived.
    //  The segue provides the source controller, which is the editor.
    PRPasserEditController *   editor = sender.sourceViewController;

    //  The editor gives back the pointer to the PRPasser (if any)
    //  it was editing. It did _not_ change its values; the editor
    //  was just holding the pointer so we could get it back.
    PRPasser *              passer = editor.representedObject;

    if (! passer) {
        //  It's a new passer. Create it.
        passer = [PRPasser insertInManagedObjectContext: self.managedObjectContext];
    }

    //  Set the new/changed passer's attributes directly from
    //  the editor's values.
    [passer setValuesForKeysWithDictionary: editor.editValues];

    NSError *              error;
    if (! [self.managedObjectContext save: &error]) {
        NSLog(@"%s: Could not save edited passer %@ - %@",
            __PRETTY_FUNCTION__, error, error.userInfo);
    }
}


- (IBAction) editorDidCancel: (UIStoryboardSegue *) sender
{
    //  If the edit was canceled, there's nothing to do.
}
```

That works. You can create a new passer (albeit without a link to any games, and therefore no career dates or ratings), or edit an existing one, and the changes show up in the passer list and in the passer-detail view. If you cancel, nothing happens. That's how it's supposed to be.

Segues

By now we've seen four kinds of segue that can appear on the storyboard canvas: Push (to advance through a navigation controller); Modal (to slide up a view for a one-screen sidetrack for something like an editor); Embed (container-child relationship); and the Root View Controller relationship (not a segue) between a navigation controller and its initial view.

There are three others: Popover (presents the destination controller in an iPad popover view); Replace (the destination controller becomes the detail part of a split view); and Custom (your own UIStoryboardSegue subclass). See Figure 14.5.

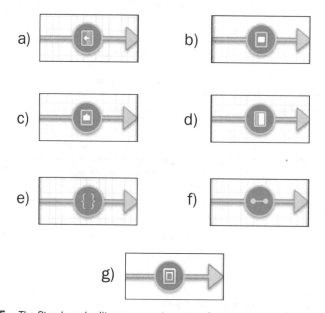

Figure 14.5   The Storyboard editor represents segues by seven types of arrows: a) Push, for pushing the next controller onto a navigation stack. b) Modal, to present the next controller as a modal view. c) Popover, a UIStoryboardPopoverSegue to present the destination controller as an iPad popver. d) Replace, to set the content in the detail half of an iPad split-view controller. e) Custom, representing a UIStoryboardSegue class you write yourself. f) Relationship, which shows that the container view on the left, such as a navigation-controller scene, dynamically manages content scenes, of which the scene on the right is the first. g) Embed, showing that the controller on the left sets a portion of its view aside for the single controller on the right.

> **Note**
>
> Unwind segues don't appear on the canvas at all—by their nature, they don't have predetermined endpoints, and therefore no graphical representation.

Summary

In the course of adding a modal editor for Passer Rating, we decided we wanted a presentation like that of an ordinary `UIViewController`, but with a `UITableView` showing static cells. If you want static cells, you have to use a `UITableViewController`, which we didn't want.

We solved the problem by employing the embed segue, to set aside a portion of the editor controller's view to be run by a table-view controller.

With the table view in hand, we added static cells to create the form we needed for the editor. You saw how to take advantage of the Key-Value Coding technique to move the edited data between three controllers and the model with the minimum of fuss.

You arranged a modal segue to get into the editor; on the way, I showed you how to solve the problem of a segue that might come from a source that could be lost by the time you saw it.

Having gotten the data in, we had to get it out. This was an opportunity to set unwind segues by creating handlers for the transitions we needed and linking the **Cancel** and **Save** buttons to an **Exit** placeholder attached to their scene.

And last, you saw a gallery of the kinds of segues you'll see in your work with Storyboard.

You also learned something that you may have to explain to your managers: Storyboard saves a lot of effort, and cuts the opportunities for errors down dramatically, but it's not magical. You can't build an application "just by drawing." Every scene has to be backed by a controller object you provide, at least as a skeleton, in advance. The demos that look magical (and seduce nontechnical managers) hand-wave the significant coding effort you'll still have to put in.

With three of the four views we planned in Figure 8.2 squared away, the Passer Rating app looks to be well in hand. There's one thing, though.

I don't trust those ratings.

15

Unit Testing

All of your development so far on the passer-rating projects has left out one essential consideration—one that I worried about at the end of the last chapter:

How do you know it works?

Yes, you know generally what to expect, and you've used the Xcode debugger to verify that what the application does makes sense, but you don't have the time, and most people don't have the discipline, to monitor for every possible error. Ideally, for every change to your application, you'd verify that everything still worked. With a prompt warning, you can isolate the problem to the last thing you did.

This discipline of verifying that each little part of your application works is called *unit testing*. The meticulous search for errors is the sort of mind-numbing, repetitive, per-fectionist task that you bought a computer to do.

This is a well-enough understood problem that solutions have been devised in the form of testing frameworks. Such frameworks make it easy to take your code, more or less in the actual context in which you use it, present it with known inputs, and compare the results with what you expect. If everything is as expected, the test succeeds; otherwise it fails. The framework provides a way to run all the tests, record the results, and issue a report on them.

Unit testing is a first-class part of Xcode. Any product template you choose will include a target for the product, and a parallel target constitutes a *test suite*, linked against the XCTest framework.

The suite consists of subclasses of XCTestCase, which implement tests as methods whose selectors begin with test. The code in the test methods exercises a small, manage-able part of the product's functionality and challenges the results with *assertions*. An XCTest assertion macro checks the results against its criterion—Boolean true or false, scalar equality, object equality, and the like—and if the criterion fails, it records the failure and a message you provide to describe it.

Although the test suite is a separate target, it can't be run independently. It is bound to the product target and is treated as the implementation of the product's Test build action. You remember that Xcode recognizes five goals for a build: Run, Test, Profile, Analyze, and Archive. You're already familiar with Run—it's how you execute an application for debugging—and Analyze. We'll get to Profile in Chapter 16, "Measurement and Analysis," and Archive in Chapter 17, "Provisioning." This chapter is about Test.

Selecting the Test action (**Product → Test**, ⌘ U):

- Builds the product
- Builds the test target
- Launches the product
- Injects the test suite into the project, runs the tests, and collects the results
- Closes the product

If any test failed, the failure message is attached to your code and the Issue navigator in the same way that syntax errors are.

> **Note**
>
> You'll probably never need any test suite but the one Xcode gave you at the start, but you might if you're working with a project that was created before Xcode 5. Select the project file, which is the top line in the Project navigator, to display the Project/Target editor. Click the **Add Target...** item in the source list, or if you've collapsed the source list, select it from the jump bar. Xcode will drop the familiar New Target assistant sheet. You'll find a "Unit Testing Bundle" target in the Other category. *Be very sure* that you select the target from the list for the platform you intend; if your product is iOS, and the test is OS X, things become confusing very quickly. In addition to the usual details, you'll be allowed to choose a **Type** for compatibility with the old OCUnit framework and a Target to designate the product target the test suite should be attached to.

The Test Navigator

Xcode 5 confers its highest honor to unit testing by giving it its own navigator (Figure 15.1). The navigator lists every test case (XCUnitTest subclass) in the project, and every test method in those classes. The status of the last run of a test is shown by a green-check or red-X diamond badge next to it.

Those badges are not merely informative: Clicking a test or a whole test case runs just those tests. If you are working on just one test, you don't have to run the entire test suite just to get the results you need.

Those badges also show up in the margins of the test code. See Figure 15.2. Again, clicking the badge repeats just that test. If a test has never been run (or never run since the project was open), there will be no mark, but if you hover the mouse over the row, a "play" button will appear.

> **Note**
>
> Xcode 5 makes it much easier to select tests than it ever was in Xcode 4, but in the Scheme editor, the **Info** tab for the Test action lets you select and reject tests as it did in version 4. This is not redundant. The Test navigator is for running a test or a test class as you work on bugs. The list in the Scheme editor governs the tests and classes that will be

run when you select the full-up Test action. This is important for your day-to-day work, but you can also share those settings with others: Select **Product** →**Scheme** →**Manage Schemes...**; the Manage Schemes editor will drop down, showing a list of all the schemes in your project. Each has a checkbox for sharing the scheme. If a scheme is shared, it is removed from your personal settings and exposed to everyone who works on the project. If they select your shared scheme, they can duplicate your running configuration.

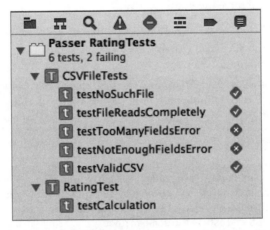

Figure 15.1   The Test navigator lists every XCUnitTest class in the test target, and every test method in those classes. Flags in the right column indicate the result of the last run of those tests: A red-X diamond for failures, a green-checkmark diamond for successes. Tests that haven't been run have no mark at all, but hovering the mouse pointer over their names gives you a "Play" button to click.

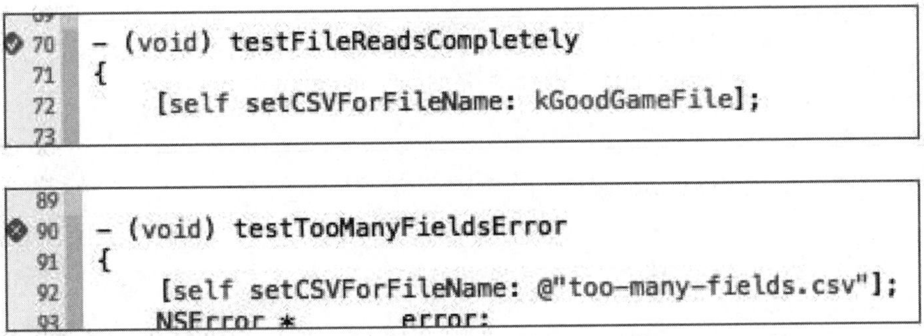

```
 70    - (void) testFileReadsCompletely
 71    {
 72        [self setCSVForFileName: kGoodGameFile];
 73
```

```
 89
 90    - (void) testTooManyFieldsError
 91    {
 92        [self setCSVForFileName: @"too-many-fields.csv"];
 93        NSError *      error;
```

Figure 15.2   The success and failure flags are repeated in the margin next to the code for test methods. Clicking a badge reruns just the one test.

Testing the CSV Reader

Let's see how this works by constructing some tests of `SimpleCSVFile`, the primitive parser for `.csv` data files. We already have a `Passer_RatingTests.m` file. There's no need for a header: The class has no clients other than the `XCTest` framework itself, and it picks up the class's API from analysis at runtime. Use the **Edit → Refactor → Rename...** command you remember from the "Refactoring a Class Name" section of Chapter 10, "An iOS Application: Controller," to change the class and file name to `CSVFileTests`.

The file comes with three methods.

- `setUp` is run before each test (selector beginning with `test`) method.
- `tearDown` is run after each test. Together with `setUp`, you can create fresh, consistent conditions for each test.
- `testExample` is just that: An example method that's a test, because its selector begins with `test`, containing only an `XCTFail` macro, meaning that if you run the Test action without doing anything else, Xcode will report one test and that it failed.

> **Note**
>
> Remember that you can't rely on the order in which tests will be run. If a test needs a specific starting condition that isn't covered by `setUp`, the test will have to configure the conditions itself. If you really need a test to use the end-state of a previous test, your best bet is simply to put both tests in the same method.

The CSV Test Code

We can do more with our tests than reflect unremitting despair. Replace `testExample` with something better, as well as some housekeeping code (these are excerpts, with some of the existing code left in for context):

```
#import "SimpleCSVFile.h"

@interface CSVFileTests : XCTestCase
@property(nonatomic, strong) SimpleCSVFile *    csvFile;
@property(nonatomic, strong) NSMutableArray *   records;
@end

@implementation CSVFileTests

- (void)setUp
{
    [super setUp];
    _records = [NSMutableArray array];
}
```

```objc
- (void) setCSVForFileName: (NSString *) fileName
{
    //  Common utility; almost every test will load a named .csv file

    //  The use of +bundleForClass: is explained later in the chapter
    NSBundle *  bundle = [NSBundle bundleForClass: [self class]];
    NSString *  csvPath = [bundle pathForResource: fileName
                                           ofType: @""];
    //  Catch the data file's being absent.
    XCTAssertNotNil(csvPath, @"Could not find %@ in main bundle", fileName);

    self.csvFile = [[SimpleCSVFile alloc] initWithPath: csvPath];
    //  Catch the parser's being unable to use the file.
    XCTAssertNotNil(self.csvFile, @"file should initialize");
}

- (void) testFileReadsCompletely
{
    [self setCSVForFileName: @"2010-data-calculated.csv"];

    NSError *   error;
    BOOL        success;
    success = [self.csvFile run: ^BOOL(SimpleCSVFile *file,
                                    NSDictionary *values,
                                    NSError *__autoreleasing *error) {
        [self.records addObject: values];
        return YES;
    }
                          error: &error];

    XCTAssertTrue(success, @"File should be valid");
    XCTAssertEqual(328U, self.records.count,
                @"%@ should return 328 records, returns %u",
                @"2010-data-calculated.csv", self.records.count);
}

- (void) testTooManyFieldsError
{
    //  Assert that if the parser is given a file with more
    //  data in its records than appear in the header line,
    //  it reports a failed parse, with a correct description in
    //  the returned NSError object.
    //  See the sample code for the end of this chapter for the full method.
    //  ...
}
```

```
- (void) testNotEnoughFieldsError
{
    // Assert that if the parser is given a file with less
    // data in its records than appear in the header line,
    // it reports a failed parse, with a correct description in
    // the returned NSError object.
    // See the sample code for the end of this chapter for the full method.
    // ...
}


- (void) testValidCSV
{
    // Spot-check the results of parsing a good .csv file,
    // verifying that the values in those records are as expected.
    // See the sample code for the end of this chapter for the full method.
    // ...
}


- (void) testNoSuchFile
{
    // When handling a nonexistent file, asserts that the parser
    // doesn't run the parser, and reports the correct error.
    // See the sample code for the end of this chapter for the full method.
    // ...
}
```

As I said, it's mostly housekeeping. What's most interesting are the functions (actually macros) whose names begin with XCT. These come from XCTest. Here, they verify that the requested test file exists and can be read (XCTAssertNotNil), that it could be parsed (XCTAssertTrue on the success of run:error:), and that the number of records matched the count I made in advance (XCTAssertEqual). A full list will come later in this chapter.

You can see the obsessiveness that goes into a good test; in fact, these tests are probably not obsessive enough. It's tedious, but once it's written, the test harness does the hard work, and you won't be single-stepping through every line of the parser as it plows through hundreds of records.

Test Data

The CSVFileTests class relies on three data files, 2010-data-calculated.csv, a known-good data file; too-many-fields.csv, which has more record fields than headers; and not-enough-fields.csv, which doesn't have enough. The last two were constructed for the sole purpose of verifying that SimpleCSVFile catches the error and refuses to continue work.

Later in this chapter, we'll be testing the accuracy of the passer_rating function, and we'll need a typical game-data file and another file of ratings independently calculated from the same records.

For that, you'll need a data set that is fixed, not the one that periodically regenerates itself as a part of Passer Rating's build process, so take the current edition of `sample-data.csv`, and copy a year's worth of games—328 in the toy league I created, covering 32 passers—into a separate file (`2010-data.csv` in my tests). `2010-data-calculated.csv` is the "gold standard" version of the file, an input for the test methods, containing known-correct results for all of the calculations. `2010-data.csv` is the "normal" data file to be used by Passer Rating as it makes those calculations for itself.

Drag the test data files into the Project navigator under the test-target group or use **File** →**Add Files to...** (⌥⌘ A) to select them from the get-file sheet. In either case, make sure they go into the test target only.

> **Note**
>
> To ensure that the tests are reproducible, the test data should be checked into source control.

Running the Tests

Let's execute the test by holding the mouse button down on the **Action** button at the left end of the toolbar and selecting **Test**, or by selecting **Product** → **Test** (⌘ U). Xcode builds Passer Rating and then the test bundle. The first thing that happens is that Xcode reports the build succeeded (if it didn't, clean it up; I'll wait).

When the build finishes, you'll see the iOS Simulator launches and opens Passer Rating. This is normal: `XCTest` works by injecting your test code into your running application. Your tests will run under actual operating conditions, not in an isolated test-bench environment. That's why it was not necessary to link `SimpleCSVFile.m` into the test target.

Passer Rating closes as swiftly as it appeared, and the next thing you see is the Issues navigator, which (if you've been keeping up) has two red flags. See Figure 15.3. Except for

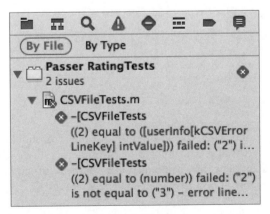

Figure 15.3 Two of the tests of `SimpleCSVFile` failed. The locations and messages from the failures appear in the Issues navigator.

the red badges being diamonds instead of octagons, test failures are no different from the errors you'd get from a compilation: Click one, and you'll be shown the assertion's message spread in a banner in your test code.

One of the failures comes in `testTooManyFieldsError`, where `SimpleCSVFile` is deliberately fed a file with more record fields than headers. The parser refuses the file, which is good, and returns an `NSError` object with all the expected information...

```objc
- (void) testTooManyFieldsError
{
    [self setCSVForFileName: @"too-many-fields.csv"];
    NSError *      error;
    BOOL success;
    success = [self.csvFile run: ^BOOL(SimpleCSVFile *file,
                                       NSDictionary *values,
                                       NSError *__autoreleasing *error) {
        XCTFail(@"CSV file with the first data line bad should not call out");
        return YES;
    }
                        error: &error];
    XCTAssertEqualObjects(WT9TErrorDomain, error.domain,
              @"Field-count error should be in WT9TErrorDomain, was %@",
              error.domain);
    XCTAssertNotNil(error, @"Error object after error should be non-nil.");
    // expect = 16
    // actual = 17
    NSDictionary *  userInfo = [error userInfo];
    int             number = [userInfo[kCSVExpectedFieldsKey] intValue];
    XCTAssertEqual(16, number,
              @"expected fields should be 16, are %d",
              number);
    number = [userInfo[kCSVActualFieldsKey] intValue];
    XCTAssertEqual(17, number,
              @"expected fields should be 17, are %d",
              number);
    number = [userInfo[kCSVErrorLineKey] intValue];
    XCTAssertEqual(2, number,
              @"error line should be 2, is %d",
              number);
}
```

...except for that last one. This was the assertion that the error should have occurred at line 2, the line after the header, containing the first game data; that's where the mismatch should become apparent. The `userInfo` dictionary of the returned `NSError` should say so. Instead, the test reports it occurred at line 3. That's wrong.

Testing and the Debugger

What's going on? You need to see what the parser is doing on those lines. Fortunately, the debugger works in unit tests. Set a breakpoint at the start of `-[SimpleCSVFile run:error:]`, and run just `testTooManyFieldsError` by clicking the red diamond next to its name in the Test navigator or as it appears in the margin of the definition of the method.

The breakpoint at `run:error:` fires, but look at the stack trace in the Debug navigator: The call came from `PRAppDelegate` via `PRGame`. This isn't the test run; because you're running the test in the full context of Passer Rating, you're seeing the parsing run from the initialization of the app. Click the **Continue** button in the debugger bar, and wait for the second call to `run:error:`.

Now you're at the test run, and you can step through the method. It checks that the file exists and can be read into a string, then bursts it into an array of lines:

```
NSArray *   lines = [contents componentsSeparatedByCharactersInSet:
                    [NSCharacterSet newlineCharacterSet]];
```

...then it steps through the array, bursting each line at the commas to get fields.

If you're watching the variables display in the Debug area, you see something on the second pass through the loop that you'd expect should be the first line of the data: The string for that line is empty! The first line of data doesn't come through until the *third* pass through the loop, and the method reports the error line as number three.

With a little thought, it should come to you: This is the CSV file that was exported from the spreadsheet of precalculated statistics. CSV has its origins in Microsoft Excel, and to the extent that CSV has any standards at all, it can be expected to have Windows line endings—carriage-return, line-feed. The `componentsSeparatedByCharactersInSet:` method burst the file at each occurrence of a character in the `newlineCharacterSet`, not caring that in this file, the CRLF pair represents a single line separator.

Fight down the temptation to simply open the file in a text editor that will convert the line endings. `SimpleCSVFile` is supposed to work with real CSV files (so long as they don't have any commas or quotes in the fields); it may have a life beyond this one project; and it really ought to handle a line delimiter that will probably appear in most of the files it sees.

So replace the simple line-bursting code with a category on `NSString` that parses line endings more carefully, and try again.

> **Note**
> You can make the switch in the sample code by changing the `#define` of NAIVELINEBREAKS to `0`.

```
@interface NSString (LineBreakingExtensions)
- (NSArray *) componentsBrokenByLines;
@end

@implementation NSString (LineBreakingExtensions)
- (NSArray *) componentsBrokenByLines
{
    NSScanner *        scanner = [NSScanner scannerWithString:
                                    self];
    NSCharacterSet *   lineEnders = [NSCharacterSet
                                       newlineCharacterSet];
    NSMutableArray *   retval = [NSMutableArray array];

    [scanner setCharactersToBeSkipped: nil];
    while (! [scanner isAtEnd]) {
        NSString *      token;
        [scanner scanCharactersFromSet: lineEnders intoString:
          NULL];
        if ([scanner scanUpToCharactersFromSet: lineEnders
             intoString: &token])
            [retval addObject: token];
    }
    return retval;
}
@end
```

This time all of the methods in CSVFileTests come through clean.

Now that you're sure the data is coming in as you expect it, you can build a RatingTest class to read the CSV that contains the precalculated values for the rating and its completion, yardage, touchdown, and interception components, and compare their presumably correct (or at least independently calculated) values against the values the passer_rating function produces. The function doesn't export those intermediate results, so I created a little support method that would do those calculations just the way that passer_rating did:

```
//  At the top of the file:

typedef enum {
    kCompletion,
    kYardage,
    kTouchdown,
    kInterception
} ComponentKey;
//  ...
```

```objc
@implementation RatingTest
//  ...

- (double) calculateFromRating: (ComponentKey) key
                      attempts: (int) atts
                          stat: (int) stat
{
    double      retval = 0.0;

    switch (key) {
        case kCompletion:
            retval =  (((double) stat / atts) * 100.0 - 30.0) / 20.0;
            retval = pinRating(retval);
            break;

        case kYardage:
            retval = (((double) stat / atts) - 3.0) / 4.0;
            retval = pinRating(retval);
            break;

        case kTouchdown:
            retval = 20.0 * (double) stat / atts;
            retval = pinRating(retval);
            break;

        case kInterception:
            retval =  2.375 - (25.0 * (double) stat / atts);
            retval = pinRating(retval);
            break;

        default:
            break;
    }

    return retval;
}
//  ...
@end
```

...and then I wrote a very dense `testCalculation` method that goes through every record in the CSV, reworks every statistic, and compares it all to the precalculated results. In part, the tests look like this:

> **Note**
>
> By now you know you can find the changes made in this chapter in the sample code for the end of this chapter.

```
yards = [game[@"yards"] intValue];
component = [self calculateFromRating: kYardage
                                attempts: attempts
                                    stat: yards];
accum += component;
expectedComponent = [game[@"yComp"] doubleValue];
XCTAssertEqualWithAccuracy(component, expectedComponent, 0.01,
                          @"Yardage for game %d (%d / %d)",
                          index, yards, attempts);

component = (100.0 / 6.0) * accum;
expectedComponent = [game[@"rating"] doubleValue];
XCTAssertEqualWithAccuracy(component, expectedComponent, 0.051,
                          @"Rating for game %d", index);

rating = passer_rating(completions, attempts,
                       yards, touchdowns, interceptions);
XCTAssertEqualWithAccuracy(rating, expectedComponent, 0.051,
                          @"passer_rating for game %d", index);
```

... and if you looked up the passer-rating formula on Wikipedia, you wouldn't be surprised that the three assertions you see here—that the yardage component and the rating, calculated two ways, should match the "right" answers—generated more than 800 test failures. The calculation in `calculateFromRating:` that says:

```
retval = (((double) stat / atts) - 0.3) / 4.0;
```

and similarly in `passer_rating`, was wrong. The subtrahend should be 3.0, not 0.3. My unease about the ratings I was seeing was right, and now I have a test of 328 games to make sure that if it ever goes wrong again, I'll know right away.

> **Note**
>
> When you program a Cocoa application, you get used to referring to embedded files through [NSBundle mainBundle]. This doesn't work for test classes because the main bundle for testing is the application, not the test suite. The right frame of reference is [[NSBundle bundleForClass: [self class]].

Application Tests

In earlier versions of Xcode, Apple emphasized a distinction between *logic tests*, in which elements of an application are linked into the test bundle and exercised on their own, and *application tests*, which are run in the context of the application. Now, all testing is done in the application context.

It's not hard to gain insight into an application's state: Because Passer Rating is completely initialized before it's turned over to your tests, you can ask the

UIApplication singleton for the application delegate (PRAppDelegate), get the application's managedObjectContext, and have complete access to the game database. Your code can edit the store, and, for instance, delete a PRPasser and verify that the deletion cascades to its PRGames. If you're ingenious, you can send PRPasserListController (the top item in the UINavigationController that is the root controller for the app delegate's window property) a message indicating that a passer editor (coming soon) has returned with new data.

But the things that most need reproducible tests in an application are the human interactions and network transactions, and those depend on delayed returns from the run loop or completion callbacks. This isn't easy at all; among other things, it's possible that the entire test suite may exit before the callback comes.

The solutions are beyond the scope of this book, but basically involve preventing the test method from proceeding until the asynchronous process returns. Many such processes depend on the main run loop to service their events, so the test method would loop on -[NSRunLoop runUntilDate:] until the callback clears a flag to indicate it has finished.

Human-interface elements present another problem: A UISlider control, for instance, sends a continuous stream of messages to its view controller with its changing value as the user drags its indicator. XCTest has no solution for this, but Instruments (see Chapter 27, "Instruments") has an instrument that accepts JavaScript to manipulate the UI for performance profiling.

Still, application testing has limitations.

- For *unit testing*, if you're testing a view controller's response to an IBAction call, your test will have to set the control's value itself, or (if the IBAction uses the "sender" parameter) pass in a "mock" object that returns the values the handler expects.

- A test can't do much to verify the actual appearance of your views.

- Tests occur in an unpredictable order, and the application will accumulate state from each. In logic tests, the setUp and tearDown methods guarantee a "clean" state for each test. Application test methods can't assume the application is in a "clean" state when they run.

TestKit Assertions

Assertions—statements that test for expected conditions—are the core of unit testing. If the condition is not met, XCTest logs it as a test failure. Assertions are made through preprocessor macros that begin (with one exception) with XCTAssert. The initial parameters to the macros vary as necessary, but you are always allowed a format string (as an NSString literal), followed by values to fill the format in. Hence:

```
XCTAssertEqualWithAccuracy(component, expectedComponent, 0.01,
                    @"Yardage for game %d (%d / %d)",
                    index, yards, attempts);
```

If the assertion fails, it would produce an error message like

```
'1.8096 should be equal to '1.135' + or - '0.01':
                        Yardage for game 97 (98 / 13)
```

Notice that your annotation only has to describe the circumstances of the test; XCTest will print out the particulars of any mismatch.

Here are the available assertions. See XCTestAssertions.h for the exact details of how to call them and what they do. The easiest way to get at the header is to use the Project navigator, and open Frameworks → XCTest.framework → Headers.

Simple Tests

These are the simplest assertions—true or false, nil or not.

- XCTFail—This is the simplest of them all. XCTest logs a failure, plus your formatted message.
- XCTAssertTrue / XCTAssert—Fails if the Boolean expression you test is false (zero). Use this or XCTAssertFalse if you have complex conditions that the more specific assertions don't handle.
- XCTAssertFalse—Fails if the Boolean expression you test is true (non-zero).
- XCTAssertNil—Fails if the object pointer you test is not nil.
- XCTAssertNotNil—Fails if the object pointer you test is nil.

Equality

These assertions test for whether two things are equal, in three senses of the word. XCTest is very picky about the values you pass for comparison, as it uses the Objective-C @encode directive to check *at run time* that the expression types match. If you use XCTAssertEqual to test the count of an NSArray, the test value had better be unsigned (e.g., 230U and not just 230), or the test will fail every time.

- XCTAssertEqual—Fails if the values you test are not equal. XCTest applies the == operator to make the test.
- XCTAssertNotEqual—The complement of XCTAssertEqual.
- XCTAssertEqualWithAccuracy—Never test floating-point values for exact equality; you have to assume there will be rounding errors with anything but trivial calculations on trivial values. Instead, decide on an *epsilon* value—how close the two can be for you to call them equal—and test whether the values are within that margin. Pass the two values and your epsilon to the macro; it will fail if they differ by more than that.
- XCTAssertNotEqualWithAccuracy—The complement of XCTAssertEqualWithAccuracy.

- XCTAssertEqualObjects—Fails unless [value1 isEqual: value2]. This is equality of the values of two objects, and not just their pointers (for which you'd use XCTAssertEqual). Take care for the order of the objects, as isEqual: doesn't have to be reflexive.

  Remember that messages to nil objects are zero-valued, and isEqual: returns NO if the argument is nil; so the assertion fails if either argument of the macro is nil.

- XCTAssertNotEqualObjects—The complement of XCTAssertEqualObjects.

Exceptions

Cocoa will throw exceptions if it is called under improper conditions, like being on the wrong thread or receiving illegal parameters. You might throw some exceptions of your own. You'll want to verify that code that should give rise to an exception does so; and if your code has triggered exceptions in the past, you'll want to keep up a test to verify that your fixes have suppressed them.

A further advantage of these macros is that they catch the exceptions. Ordinarily, if a test method triggers an exception, the whole method exits without attempting its remaining tests. Because they trap the exceptions within the method, these macros allow the test to continue.

These assertions can be a little tricky. With XCTAssert, you can do a long calculation, distill it into one value, and pass that to the macro. You can then use the value for calculations later in the test.

Exception assertions deal with expressions that have two effects: Some sort of calculation as well as the presence or absence of a throw. The expression parameter to the macros will be more elaborate. Bear in mind that assignments and comma expressions are legal, so you can still capture values while you test for exceptions. You can encapsulate complex expressions in helper methods; exceptions thrown inside them will propagate up to the assertion macro.

The XCTest macros evaluate the expressions only once.

- XCTAssertThrows—Fails if the expression you submit does not raise an exception.
- XCTAssertNoThrow—Fails if the expression you submit raises an exception.
- XCTAssertThrowsSpecific and XCTAssertNoThrowSpecific—Fails if an exception of a specific class is not (or is) thrown. This way you can test that your code is doing what you expect with your own subclass of NSException, while distinguishing different exceptions thrown by other libraries.
- XCTAssertThrowsSpecificNamed and XCTAssertNoThrowSpecificNamed— Some exceptions (usually NSExceptions) aren't distinguished by class, but by a subtype indicated by the exception's name. These assertions fail upon the absence or presence of an exception of the given class and name.

Summary

Automated testing is a liberating discipline for a programmer. Any change you make *probably* doesn't have any effect on on anything else, but most bugs live in the space between "probably" and "actually." A good testing régime relieves you of obsessive audits that never answer the question: Does it all still work? You'll know; and with that confidence, you'll be free to make bold changes to your application.

In this chapter, you learned about XCTest, the Xcode framework for unit-testing applications, and how to build tests from the XCTestCase class. I walked you through part of the exhaustive task of producing a test suite that would verify that the process of reading a CSV and pulling accurate statistics from it works correctly. In the course of it, you found a couple of bugs that would be at least tedious to discover by checking the whole application by hand. Now that you have this test, you won't have to worry that something you do in the future will bring those bugs back.

Finally, I ran through the assertions that XCTest makes available to verify that what you expect is what actually happens.

Now, let's move on from *whether* Passer Rating works, to *how well*.

16

Measurement and Analysis

Passer Rating has quite a way to go before it's useful for the general public, but you've run it several times, and begun a testing régime, and you're pretty confident that to the naked eye, it works.

As usual, the qualifier ("to the naked eye") means more than "it works." There are issues in Passer Rating of speed and memory performance. Before you can act, you have to know what's going on—you have to profile the app. The Instruments application is the tool for profiling applications.

> **Note**
>
> If you follow along with me—I recommend starting from the sample code for the end of the previous chapter—you will find different statistics than I show here. You and I have different computers, different devices (if your developer-program membership permits it), different operating systems, background loads, free RAM and storage... all of which can have big effects on how exactly a measurement run will turn out. If you don't get exactly the results I show, neither of us is doing anything wrong. It's in the nature of the task.

Speed

The sample code has been changed so that `generate-games.rb` produces a league history from 2010 to 2059—16,438 games, 1.4 MB in size. You'll find the product, `sample-data.csv`, in the same directory. Substitute them into your project, and run the app in the simulator.

Passer Rating takes an appreciable amount of time to start up; with the enlarged data set, if you ran the app on a device, it wouldn't start at all: When you launch, the screen stays black for 21 seconds, and then you're back to the home screen. It takes too long: If your app doesn't respond to user actions for more than 20 seconds, the system watchdog timer kills it. It has to be faster.

> **Note**
>
> In crash dumps, you'll know that the watchdog killed the app if the exception code is `0x8badf00d`.

To analyze speed, I'll be working with Passer Rating on an iPhone 5. The iOS Simulator provides a lot of insight into how an app will work, but it is only a simulator: It has multiples of the RAM available to a device, and if it should run out, it can page memory to disk. It exposes the OS X API, and the shared API is optimized for a completely different processor. And, especially, the simulator has a much faster processor.

> **Note**
>
> Again, you may have a different device to test on, or if you aren't an iOS Developer Program member, you won't be able to test on a device at all. If you can't participate, just read along. You can find the details of getting permission to load an app into an iOS device, and how to do so, in the next chapter, Chapter 17, "Provisioning."

To install Passer Rating on a device for testing, you have to be a paid member of the iOS Developer Program, register the device, and obtain a signing certificate. All of the details are in Chapter 17, "Provisioning."

The **Code Signing Identity** that authorizes Xcode to install your app on a device can be set on a per-configuration basis. Typically the "Debug" configuration would use your developer certificate and "Release," the distribution certificate. But we're not at the point of distribution, so set the identity to **iOS Distribution** for both.

Plug the device in, and use the second segment of the scheme control (next to the **Run** and **Stop** buttons) to direct the next build to it. If you've already enabled the device for development, Xcode will already have arranged for a development profile that includes Passer Rating and your device. (Again, see the Provisioning chapter if this isn't clear.)

The Debug Navigator

Click the **Run** button; Xcode will do a fresh build targeted at a device and install the product in your phone. When that's done, it launches Passer Rating.

> **Note**
>
> If the phone is locked with a passcode, you'll have to unlock it before Xcode will let you proceed.

The Debug navigator gives us the first clue: During initialization, the performance bar graphs show the app is saturating one of the cores in the device—100 percent CPU. See Figure 16.1. (An iPhone 5 has two processor cores, so potentially a process could take 200 percent, but Passer Rating isn't threaded yet and uses one core at a time.)

Click on the CPU bar graph in the Debug navigator, and you'll see more of the story: a detailed running history of how much processor time Passer Rating is soaking up currently, over time, and as a proportion of the available resources (Figure 16.2).

My first guess was that `SimpleCSVFile` was so simple that it was inefficient. My temptation was to dive into the parser code, audit it, tinker with the works, introduce "speed optimizations" and maybe a little assembly, and try again.

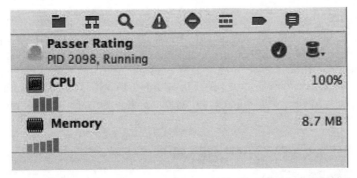

Figure 16.1   The first clue that something is wrong with Passer Rating's performance at startup is the CPU bar graph in the Debug navigator, which shows it taking up 100 percent of the time on one of the device's processor cores.

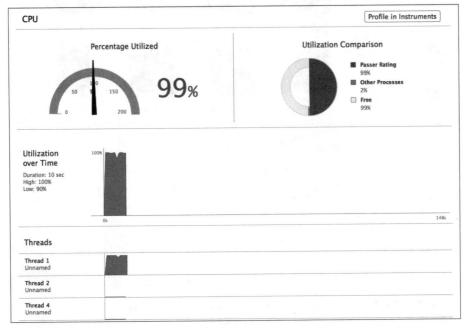

Figure 16.2   Clicking one of the bar graphs at the top of the running Debug navigator presents the details of the Passer Rating's resource usage currently, over time, and as a percentage of available resources.

Don't do this. Don't guess. Instruments will tell you *exactly* where your app is spending its time. That's the "low-hanging fruit"; make those parts of your code faster, and you've done more to solve the problem than if you'd nibbled around the periphery.

Use the **Stop** button to halt the app.

Instruments

Profiling an application is easy. Xcode provides an action for it. Trigger the **Profile** action by holding down on the **Run** button and selecting **Profile** from the menu that drops down. (When you choose an action using the button's menu, the button continues to display the icon for that action.) Or, select **Product → Profile** (⌘I). The profiling application, Instruments, will launch and offer you a choice of what kind of profiling you want to do. See Figure 16.3.

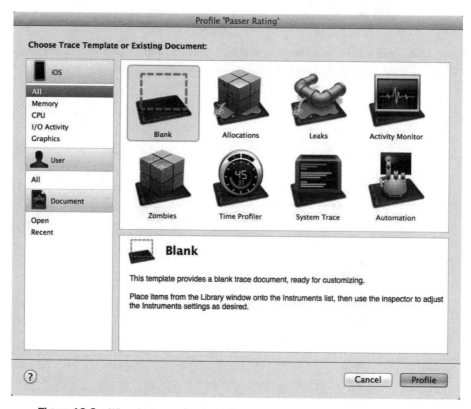

Figure 16.3   When Instruments starts, it presents a template picker for the profiling suites it offers.

Note

You may be asked for administrator's credentials to permit Instruments to probe another process's internal state.

In the new-template sheet, select **iOS → CPU → Time Profiler**, and click **Choose**. After a brief pause, Passer Rating launches on the phone, and the Instruments window begins to fill with the record of what the phone was doing from moment to moment.

Note

Xcode has a shortcut for selecting Instruments templates. Open the Scheme editor
(**Product** → **Edit Scheme…**, ⌘ <) and select the **Profile** action. Select **Time Profiler** from
the **Instrument** popup, and click **OK**. Even more convenient, if you hold down the Option
key while triggering the **Profile** action, the Scheme editor will drop down for you to select
an instrument, and then proceed.

iOS and Instruments give you some grace when you're measuring performance: The
watchdog timer does not fire, and Passer Rating is allowed to run as long as you need,
even though it is unresponsive. In my setup, It took a minute and five seconds to present
the initial passer list—three times the limit. Embarrassing. See Figure 16.4.

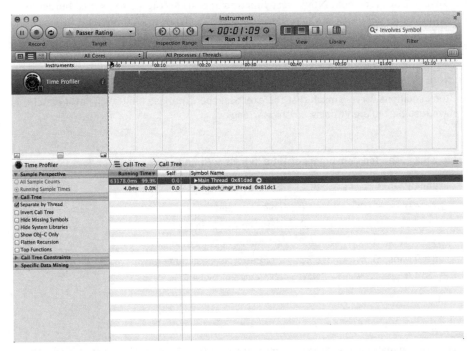

Figure 16.4 The trace of Passer Rating paints a discouraging portrait of the CPU being nearly
saturated for more than a minute. The top part of the window is the Trace area, with a track showing
CPU usage over time. Below it is the Detail area, for cumulative stack traces of the code
that was executing.

Your business with Passer Rating is done for the moment, so click the **Stop** button at
the left end of the Instruments toolbar. Turn your attention to the *Detail area*, the lower
half of the trace window. This is the Call Tree listing of your session. Instruments' time
profiler does "statistical profiling" of your code: At very short intervals, it records what
part of your code is executing, and what the call stack is at the time.

Instruments gives you the call tree from the bottom up: It starts with `main()`, with 99.8 percent of the application's running time spent there, or in some routine called from it. The **Self** column shows the proportion of time spent in `main()` itself, which, as you'd expect is 0 percent—it calls `UIApplicationMain` almost immediately, and that function never ends.

You can click the disclosure triangles at each line to expose the functions and methods that branched from that function. Often, if you trace down far enough, you'll find the same function at the far end, usually `objc_msgSend`, which dispatches Objective-C method invocations.

It's usually more interesting to see how much time a function takes, total—not just in individual calls, but throughout the app. In the column to the left of the Detail area, check the **Invert Call Tree** box. Now every function appears according to its total burden on the application—and sure enough, the app spent 37 percent of its time in `objc_msgSend`.

The call tree in the Detail area summarizes the samples; Table 16.1 shows the first few lines.

> **Note**
>
> Run conditions vary so much that the exact numbers in these tables will never match your own results. You aren't doing anything wrong.

Table 16.1   The Top Consumers of Time in Passer Rating

Running Time		Self	Symbol Name
23394.0 ms	37.0%	23394.0	objc_msgSend
6997.0 ms	11.0%	6997.0	CFBasicHashGetBucket
5454.0 ms	8.6%	5454.0	-[NSManagedObjectContext...
3169.0 ms	5.0%	3169.0	_CFBasicHashFastEnumeration
814.0 ms	1.2%	814.0	objc_msgSendSuper2

> **Note**
>
> Always use Instruments' **Stop** button to close out a profiling session. Just closing an app in iOS doesn't end its run—it may be preserved in the background indefinitely, and profiling will continue with it.

This doesn't seem to leave much scope for improvement. Every call tree is rooted in a function or method deep in the runtime, Foundation, or Core Data. You're not responsible for the performance of those functions. `objc_msgSend`, the hottest function, accounts for a bit more than a third of the app's business, but again, if you're using Objective-C, you have to expect to call some methods. Where's the low-hanging fruit?

You can find your own code further up the call tree; if you click on the disclosure triangles down from `objc_msgSend`, you find an entry for Passer Rating (Table 16.2):

Table 16.2   Tracing Down to Application Code

Running Time		Self	Symbol Name
23394.0 ms	37.0%	23394.0	objc_msgSend
20080.0 ms	31.7%	0.0	-[NSManagedObjectContext...
20078.0 ms	31.7%	0.0	+[PRPasser existingPassers...

Again, where's the low-hanging fruit? In the worst branch of the call tree, your code, `+[PRPasser existingPassersWithLastName:firstName:inContext: ]`, accounts for so little of what Passer Rating was doing that its in-self time rounded to zero.

Not so fast. In the options area to the left of the Detail area, click **Hide System Libraries**. This removes from the tree every function that isn't in your code, and charges those system functions' time to the methods in your code that called them (Table 16.3).

Table 16.3   Charging Time Spent to Application Code

Running Time		Self	Symbol Name
52521.0 ms	83.1%	52521.0	+[PRPasser existingPassers...
6007.0 ms	9.5%	6007.0	__44+[PRGame load..._block_invoke
1597.0 ms	2.5%	1597.0	-[_PRGame objectID]

Oh. 83.1 percent of the startup time—more than 52 seconds of the minute—was in one method, `existingPassersWithLastName:firstName:inContext:`. That *is* your problem.

Double-click on that top line of the call-tree list. Instruments fills the Detail view with the source for `existingPassersWithLastName:firstName:inContext:`. What's more, some of the lines in that method are highlighted, showing what proportion of the CPU samples occurred at what lines (Figure 16.5).

Optimization: First Try

Here's the method:

```
+ (NSArray *) existingPassersWithLastName: (NSString *) last
                             firstName: (NSString *) first
                             inContext: (NSManagedObjectContext *) moc
{
    NSFetchRequest *    req = [NSFetchRequest
                              fetchRequestWithEntityName: @"Passer"];
    NSPredicate *    byName;
    byName = [NSPredicate predicateWithFormat:
            @"firstName = %@ AND lastName = %@",
            first, last];
```

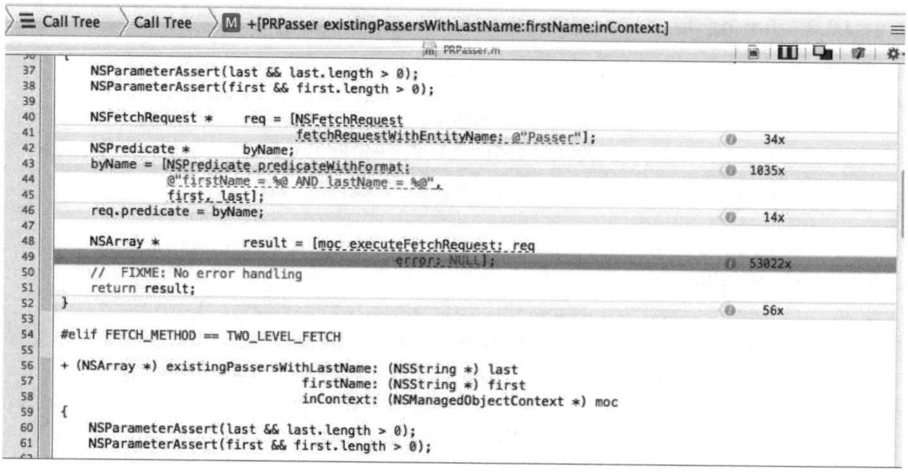

Figure 16.5   When you double-click on a line in the call tree that points to your code, Instruments displays the source to that method in the Detail view. "Hotspots," where the CPU spent the most time, are highlighted. The banners show how many times a line was hit in the sampling process; you can change it to percentages from the gear menu at the top right.

```
    req.predicate = byName;

    NSArray *              result = [moc executeFetchRequest: req
                                                       error: NULL];
    return result;
}
```

The listing shows the hotspot, at nearly 98 percent of the time spent in the method, is the call to `executeFetchRequest:error:`. So now you know: Speeding up the database search for a `Passer` with a given last and first name will relieve the problem.

Maybe it's simple: The data model doesn't call for any indices for `Passer`. It would be easy to go back to Xcode's Data Model editor, focus on `Passer`, and check the **Indexed** boxes on `lastName` and `firstName`; then make a side trip to Terminal to rerun `mogenerator`.

Issue the **Profile** action again. The binding between Passer Rating and Instruments' time-profiling document guarantees that it won't try to open a fresh trace document. Instruments can store more than one session in a document.

The new profile doesn't look good. Stop Passer Rating when it finally displays the passer table, and look at the time trace. If you click and drag in the time-scale ruler at the top of the Time Profiler track, you'll find you're dragging a "playback head" through the record. A tooltip near your mouse pointer shows you the time, and another down in the track shows the CPU usage at that moment. Initialization took 1:05.25. No difference, and `existingPassersWithLastName:firstName:inContext:` takes up 83.4 percent of the execution time—no change.

Selecting **Instrument → Compare Call Trees...** adds a bar to the top of the Detail area that replaces the Running Time column with the difference between the two runs, both as absolute time and as a percentage. It's less than half a percentage point.

> **Note**
>
> The activity view in the middle of the toolbar gives you a way to navigate among the runs without opening the stack of runs: It shows "Run 2 of 2," and you can use the arrowheads to either side to step from run to run.

Indexing isn't the answer. Time for something more radical.

Optimization: Second Try

Maybe the compound search predicate is the problem. If you specify the first name of a Passer, you narrow the list down considerably; you could pull the results in and filter them in-memory:

```
+ (NSArray *) existingPassersWithLastName: (NSString *) last
                            firstName: (NSString *) first
                            inContext: (NSManagedObjectContext *) moc
{
    // Ask Core Data for a first-name match ONLY:
    NSFetchRequest *    req = [NSFetchRequest
                                fetchRequestWithEntityName: @"Passer"];

    NSPredicate *       byName;
    byName = [NSPredicate predicateWithFormat: @"firstName = %@", first];
    req.predicate = byName;

    NSArray *           result = [moc executeFetchRequest: req
                                            error: NULL];

    // Once you have the first names, filter by last name:
    result = [result filteredArrayUsingPredicate:
            [NSPredicate predicateWithFormat: @"lastName = %@", last]];
    return result;
}
```

...and profile again. You can't say it didn't help; initialization is down to 1:02.77, still three times the amount of time the watchdog timer will tolerate.

> **Note**
>
> The sample `PRPasser.m` contains the code for every variant in this chapter. Just set the `#define` of `FETCH_METHOD` to select the one you want.

Optimization: Third Try

Enough of the suspense. Here's a radical step—if executeFetchRequest:error: is a big time sink, don't call it at all:

```objc
static NSMutableDictionary *   sAllPassers;

+ (void) initialize
{
    static dispatch_once_t onceToken;
    dispatch_once(&onceToken, ^{
        sAllPassers = [NSMutableDictionary dictionary];
    });
}


+ (NSArray *) existingPassersWithLastName: (NSString *) last
                              firstName: (NSString *) first
                              inContext: (NSManagedObjectContext *) moc
{
    NSString *   key = [NSString stringWithFormat: @"%@|%@", last, first];
    PRPasser *   passer = [sAllPassers objectForKey: key];
    NSArray *    result;

    //  Conform to the promise to return an array
    if (passer)
        result = @[passer];
    else
        result = @[];
    return result;
}
```

And when you create the passer in passerWithFirstName:lastName:inContext:, after insertion and setting the first and last names:

```objc
    NSString *    key = [NSString stringWithFormat:
                        @"%@|%@", lastName, firstName];
    sAllPassers[key] = retval;
```

Profile it again. It worked: Initialization takes just under 8 seconds. The watchdog timer won't kill Passer Rating.

Warning

This is an outrageous hack made possible because Passer Rating happens to use only one managed-object context. With only one table of Passers, I could write a version of existingPassersWithLastName:firstName:inContext: that *ignores* the context parameter and uses a single global lookup table instead. Once I get to Chapter 18,

"Starting an OS X Application," where there will be a separate managed-object context per document, I'll have to fall back on the original, Core Data–based version.

Can you go back to the well? Table 16.4 shows the call tree as it stands after inserting the hack.

Table 16.4   Time Distribution after the `PRPasser` Hack

Running Time	Self	Symbol Name
3839.0 ms 58.1%	3839.0	__44 +[PRGame load...._block_invoke
966.0 ms 14.6%	966.0	-[SimpleCSVFile run:error:]
576.0 ms 8.7%	0.0	main
532.0 ms 8.0%	0.0	-[PRPasser sumOfGameAttribute:]

The new champion is the block that processes the CSV records in `loadFromCSVFile:intoContext:error:`. Examining it shows that it spends nearly half of its time using an `NSDateFormatter` to translate the CSV file's dates into `NSDates`. That's an avenue worth exploring—the date format in the data file is in our control, so there's no need to consider localized date formats. But you've seen enough.

You've relieved the problem for this particular 50-year CSV, but it's not a general solution. It's unlikely that this league would want to keep track of more seasons than that, but no programmer likes to leave code that has only a sporting chance of behaving correctly. I tested on an iPhone 5; in *Xcode 4 Unleashed*, this exercise used an iPhone 4, and it choked on a database of only ten years. There are still a lot of iPhone 4s out there.

The mere speed of the CSV load is not the real issue; the real issue is that the user doesn't get control soon enough. The real solution is to put the load on a background thread, and display the passer table, updating it as data comes in. This book isn't going to do that; Core Data is thread-safe, but you have to divide your code very carefully between the background and foreground tasks. It's kind of fun, but it's beyond the scope of a book about development tools.

Memory

You're not done with Instruments. iOS devices have a limited amount of memory, and while the OS does have virtual memory (it remaps the address space, shares read-only data between processes, and doesn't use actual RAM for unwritten addresses), it does not page memory out to permanent storage. iPhones and iPads have only a fraction of the RAM that a desktop machine has, and once you've run it out, iOS will kill your app. (Experiments on the 1–GB iPhone 4 have shown you get your first warning at about 150 MB, and will be evicted at 400 MB.) Instruments provides powerful tools for monitoring your memory usage and diagnosing problems.

> **Note**
>
> The iOS Simulator uses the OS X virtual-memory system, so a runaway app won't likely be killed for exhausting memory. But if you're just looking for bad behavior, the simulator gives you useful information on a quick turnaround. The rest of this chapter switches back to the simulator; click the destination segment of the scheme selector in the toolbar to select it.

Allocations: First Look

Close the Instruments document you've been using for time profiling and bring the Passer Rating project in Xcode to the front. Save yourself some trouble by preselecting your Instruments template: Open the Scheme editor (**Product** → **Scheme** → **Edit Scheme…** ⌘ <) and select the **Profile** action. In the **Info** tab, select **Allocations** from the **Instrument** popup.

> **Note**
>
> All the build actions take their cues from their associated Scheme panels. If you need to tune the scheme before taking an action, you can save a step by holding down the Option key while triggering the action. The Scheme editor for the action will drop down, and the button at the lower right takes the name of the action—in this case, **Profile**.

Trigger the **Profile** action, and let Instruments run Passer Rating. Scroll the passer list a bit, select a passer or two, scroll the game lists—give the app a workout—and then tell Instruments to **Stop** the app.

Once again, you see a document window with timelines on the top and a Detail area at the bottom. This time there are two tracks in the timeline for the Allocations instrument and the VM Tracker instrument. Ignore VM Tracker; it's useful only when you're testing on a device, as the simulator's virtual memory system doesn't behave the same as a device's.

The Allocations track shows an area graph that traces how much memory your app has allocated. The shape of the graph isn't surprising: For a few seconds, memory plateaus just short of 3 MB, followed by a sharp spike above 26 MB, then back down 8.8 MB. Exercising the list controllers bumps the total a bit as the app and the OS fill some caches, and then it goes up and down according to demand. See Figure 16.6.

> **Note**
>
> Instruments assumes your runs will last more than a few seconds, so this short run will be jammed into a narrow space at the beginning of the timeline; you may find it difficult to drag the head along the actual run to read times and sizes. **View** → **Snap Track to Fit** (^ ⌘ **Z**) will usually do what you need to get the track to a usable scale. The best way to zoom into an area of interest is to hold down the Shift key while you drag across the track area. The interval you swipe is scaled to fit the width of the window.

Click on the Allocations track to make sure the Detail area contains the statistics the Allocations instrument collected. The statistics take the form of the number of objects of various types that were allocated any time during the run, the total amount of the memory

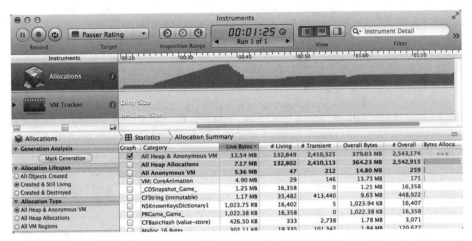

Figure 16.6 Running the Allocations instrument against Passer Rating produces an area graph showing the total active memory held by the application as time goes by.

they took up, and the number and size of the objects that were "still living"—had not been released—by the end of the run. Table 16.5 shows what the first few lines look like.

Table 16.5   The Largest Consumers of Application Memory

Category	Live Bytes	# Living	# Transient	Overall Bytes	# Overall
All Heap & Anonymous VM	12.54 MB	132849	2410325	379.03 MB	2543174
All Heap Allocations	7.17 MB	132802	2410113	364.23 MB	2542915
All Anonymous VM	5.36 MB	47	212	14.80 MB	259
VM: CoreAnimation	4.90 MB	29	146	13.73 MB	175
_CDSnapshot_Game_	1.25 MB	16358	0	1.25 MB	16358
CFString (immutable)	1.17 MB	35482	413440	9.63 MB	448922
NSKnownKeysDictionary1	1,023.75 KB	16402	5	1,023.94 KB	16407

What you see is that Passer Rating allocated 2,543,174 objects of all types (the top line), totaling 379.03 MB. 2,410,325 of these were "transitory"—they had been deallocated by the end of the run—and 12.54 MB, in 132,849 objects, persist. To repeat: Once Passer Rating settled down, it held about 3 percent of the bytes it had churned through.

> **Note**
>
> The third row, "All Anonymous VM," refers to virtual-memory allocations related to services like Core Animation and Core Graphics. As you process images and render them

to the screen, those frameworks may allocate large image buffers, particularly if you're working in a pixel format that doesn't match the device hardware. The greatest part of the total was the Core Animation heap, shown on the fourth line. These are the numbers that will tell you whether, and where, you're getting into trouble. Passer Rating doesn't do anything fancy, and we can ignore it.

The rows that follow list each kind of object that was allocated. The most common allocation in the application's heap was of "_CDSnapshot_Game_," 1.25 MB persisting out of 1.25 total, presumably related to Core Data internals. Then come strings, dictionaries, simple blocks from `malloc`—all the things you'd expect to find in an application's memory.

The last column of the object-category rows show the transitory and living object counts graphically, with the number of living objects shown in a dark color and the number of transitory ones shown pale. If the proportion of living objects is very small, Instruments will color the bar red/pink. If you have control over how your objects and buffers are allocated, you should consider reusing them instead of churning through allocation and deallocation.

Focusing on One Object Type

If you click on one of the category rows, you'll see a small arrow button next to the category name. Click the row for "CFString (immutable)." The Detail area fills with a table of every allocation of that type in the time span you are examining. There will be a lot of them—Table 16.6 shows an excerpt from the "CFString (immutable)" category.

Table 16.6   Allocation History of CFStrings (excerpts)

#	Address	Timestamp	Live	Size	Responsible Caller
0	0xabc07d0	00:19.617.343	*	160 bytes	NSStringFromClass
1	0xabc08a0	00:19.617.403		176 bytes	NSStringFromClass
2	0xabc0950	00:19.617.428		160 bytes	NSStringFromClass
3	0xabc09f0	00:19.617.434		144 bytes	NSStringFromClass
4	0xabc0a80	00:19.617.436		32 bytes	NSStringFromClass

Of these objects, only number 0 was still alive at the end of the time span. All the rest were later deallocated. We know that in the course of this profiling run, 448,922 CFStrings were allocated, and 413,440 of them were deallocated. There has to be a way to filter them. The first way is to confine the list to whether the object is alive or deallocated at the end of the span you're looking at. The **Allocation Lifespan** radio buttons at the left side of the Detail area gives you the choice.

- **All Objects Created** lists all the objects that had been created in the span you're examining, whether they survived or not.

- **Created & Still Living** lists only the objects (or categories) that were created during the span and were still in memory at the end. In the excerpt in Table 16.6, only object 0 would remain in the list.

- **Created & Destroyed** focuses on transient objects that were created during the span, but did not survive to the end. In Table 16.6, 0 would be removed.

There's a further way to filter the list: by time interval. There are two ways to focus the object list on a portion of the profiling run. The easiest is to hold down the Option key and drag your mouse across the span that interests you. It's easy, but imprecise. The precise way is to drag the head to the beginning of the interval, and click the left segment in the **Inspection Range** control in the toolbar; then drag the head to the end of the interval, and click the right segment. Clicking the middle segment clears the selection.

Either way, the segment you selected will be highlighted in the timeline, and the object list will be reduced to objects that were created in that interval. Figure 16.7 gives an example: Instruments is focused on the up slope of the memory spike in the initialization of Passer Rating. Selecting **Created & Still Living** restricts the list to the objects that contributed to the spike. Each row shows where the allocation was made. If you expose the Extended Detail area on the right (use the **View** control in the toolbar), you can see the full stack trace at the moment of creation. It appears that most of them were allocated in NSScanner's scanUpToCharactersFromSet:intoString: and NSPlaceholderString's initWithFormat:locale:arguments:, and componentsSeparatedByString: from NSString. And that the common element above them in the stack is run:error: from SimpleCSVFile. H'm.

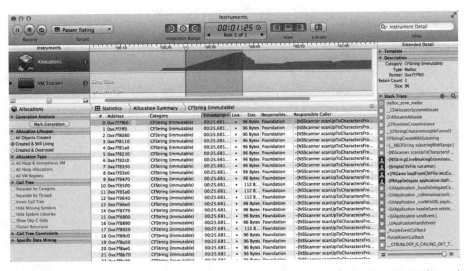

Figure 16.7 By selecting the time span from the beginning of the spike in allocations to its peak and restricting the list to objects "Created & Still Living," you get a complete listing of CFString objects created in the spike. Opening the Extended Detail area (left segment of the **View** control) shows a stack trace for each allocation in the table.

There's more. If you hover the mouse pointer over a row, you'll see an arrow button next to the object's address. Click it, and the Detail table will show you the complete history of the object, when it was allocated and freed, and what the stack trace was at the time.

The bar at the top of the Detail area is a hierarchical jump bar; click on a segment to back out to that level.

Allocations, too, has a Call Tree option—select it from the menu that pops up from the first segment of the jump bar. Select the **Invert Call Tree** and **Hide System Libraries** options, and if you're still focused on the memory spike, you'll see 36.6 percent of your allocations had their last contact with... `run:error:`. You can ask for a source listing by double-clicking the row, and see that the hotspot was the call out to the block that was passed into the method by `PRGame`.

Cleaning Up the Transients

The spike is only 26–MB high, but the fact that we find `run:error:` in so many samples suggests that we can do some good by examining it closely and seeing whether we can improve matters.

Select the **Allocations** list from the Detail area's jump bar to see a table of every allocation in the selected time span (which should still be on the up slope of the allocated memory for initialization). Select **Created & Still Living**. Type **CFString** in the search field, and the table narrows down to all the entries that contain `CFString`; there are 490,000 as I'm doing this. Browse around. You'll see a lot of invocations of `componentsSeparatedByString:`. Follow that lead: Press Return to turn `CFString` into a separate search token, and type **componentssep**; the list now contains only 196,307 strings. (More or less; setting the bounds of the time span is not a science.)

The `sample-data.csv` file I'm working on contains 16,486 lines of data, with 12 fields each...197,832 strings. I call that a match. All of those strings go unused after their record is read and assimilated. Cocoa turns their memory over to an *autorelease pool*, a kind of broker holding memory to be released later; but the default autorelease pool doesn't get drained until control is turned over to the main event loop, which you have painfully learned doesn't happen until all of the initialization is done. No wonder almost all of those strings are still alive.

So let's put an autorelease pool of your own into the CSV-read loop:

```
- (BOOL) run: (SimpleCSVRecordBlock) block
      error: (NSError **) error
{
    NSString *  contents = [NSString stringWithContentsOfFile: self.path
                                              encoding: NSUTF8StringEncoding
                                                 error: error];
    // ...
    NSArray *  lines = [contents componentsBrokenByLines];

    self.lineCount = 0;
    NSError *  returnedError = nil;
```

```
    for (NSString * line in lines) {
        //  Wrap the contents of the loop in an autorelease pool.
        @autoreleasepool {
            self.lineCount++;
            NSArray *      fields = [line componentsSeparatedByString: @","];
            if (! _headers) {
                //  ...
            }
            else {
                //  ...
                if (fields.count != self.headers.count) {
                    //  The record does not have the same number of fields as
                    //  specified in the header.
                    returnedError = [self badLineFormatError: fields.count];
                    goto return_no;
                }
                //  ,,,
            }
        }
    }

    return YES;
return_no:
    if (error) *error = returnedError;
    return NO;
}
```

...and profile yet again. Now, when you survey the same stretch of the initialization, most of the strings allocated are transitory, leaving their memory free for reuse. Peak memory falls by 14 MB to 12.35 MB. Any day you can reduce your peak memory demand by more than half is a good one.

> **Note**
>
> That may be the first `goto` statement you've seen in years. Here's why: `run:error:` detects some errors inside the `autoreleasepool` block, and in response allocates `NSError` objects. But those objects are in the autorelease pool, which gets drained as soon as control gets out of the block. The caller gets a pointer to a deallocated object, which is one of the few ways that can happen nowadays. So any `NSError` that gets created is assigned into `returnedError`, which has a life outside the autorelease block. The assignment into the caller's error pointer has to be made outside the block, so instead of an inline `return`, the in-pool code branches to the code that makes the assignment and returns `NO`.

Summary

In this chapter, I showed you two tools for testing performance and memory bugs in Cocoa applications: the summary graphs and displays in the Xcode Debug navigator, and the time-base profiling application, Instruments.

Instruments served well in tracking down a fatal performance bug in Passer Rating. It relieved you of trial-and-error fixes to code that wasn't the problem, by pointing you to the exact parts that were the problem. It provided the tools to measure what you did, and the courage to take radical steps when they were needed.

Likewise with the memory-management instruments: The Allocations instrument showed how the app was using memory from moment to moment, block by block. It showed peak memory usage, and what code was causing it. By reading the subtle clues, you found a buildup of temporary objects, and a simple fix cut peak usage by half.

There is a *lot* more to Instruments, and I'll cover it in depth in Chapter 27, "Instruments."

## 17

Provisioning

Here's the short of it: Apple does not want any app running on any iOS device that isn't written by someone it trusts. It doesn't want any apps in general circulation that it doesn't curate through its App Store. At each stage of the life cycle of your app—from testing on your desktop, to circulating it among beta testers, to final distribution—you have to jump through some hoops.

For the first several years, the process was straight out of Lovecraft: You had to manage two signing certificates by generating requests on your Mac, upload them to Apple's provisioning portal, wait for the portal to issue the certificates, download, and install them in your keychain. You had to register a unique identifier for every product. You had to register every device you wanted to debug on. For each application, you had to request a "provisioning profile" for each purpose of debugging, beta testing, and shipment to the App Store, and install them into Xcode. Change any of the certificates or devices? Reissue the profiles.

The potential for error was enormous. Nobody got it right.

As Xcode has developed, more and more of the burden has shifted from the portal web site to Xcode itself. In Xcode 5, the process is *almost* transparent. You'll still need to understand the underlying principles, but until it comes time to circulate your app, Xcode does it all for you.

This chapter will show you the triangle of identities—signing, application, and device—that go into provisioning an iOS app for installation on a device, and how to turn those identities into provisioning profiles. I'll start with the process for iOS applications, then explain the differences for OS X.

Apple Developer Programs

To get your app onto a device, Apple has to trust you (or if it can't, it at least has to be able to identify you and track you down). It needs your name and address, your assent to the licensing terms, and a payment that both defrays its costs and verifies you are who you say you are. Early on, you'll have to pony up for a paid iOS developer program ($99 in the United States as I write this).

To join, visit `http://developer.apple.com/`, click the large image for the iOS (or Mac) Developer Program, and proceed from there. A shortcut to the same process is to open the **Accounts** panel of Xcode's Preferences window, hold down on the **+** button, and select **Add Apple ID....** A sheet will drop down asking for the Apple ID and password associated with your developer registration, but it will also have a **Join a Program...** button that takes your browser straight into the application process.

There are two kinds of registration for the general iOS and Mac developer programs.

Organizations

Organizations (companies) are entities with credentials like a DUNS number from the Dun & Bradstreet credit-rating organization. Apple allows them to have more than one developer working on the company account; these are organized into a hierarchy of actors, with different levels of privilege.

- **Team Members** may install apps for development purposes, subject to the authorization of senior members of the team. Members can't authorize anything; they can only post requests to Admins or the Agent.

- **Team Admins** can invite others to the Organization account, approve devices for use in development, manage signing identities, issue distribution profiles, approve requests from Team Members, and do all the things Team Members can do.

- There can be only one **Team Agent** because the Agent represents the legal authority and identity of the Organization. She is responsible for keeping the program membership in good standing and reviewing and accepting contracts.

Individuals

The story is much simpler for developers registered in the Individual program: Access is available to only one person, who acts as Team Agent. No permissions, no restrictions.

The Enterprise Program

Apple has a separate "Enterprise" developer program for organizations wishing to develop apps for in-house use. Member organizations can distribute apps, like expense trackers, strictly within themselves, without having to publish them through the App Store. The apps can be installed on an unlimited number of devices, subject to a provisioning profile that must be renewed every three years. Enterprises have Members, Admins, and Agents, as with the Organization account.

Apple's B2B program offers another way to distribute an application, even a custom version of an application, to an organization. The organization doesn't have to qualify for or maintain an Enterprise membership, and there is no awkwardness about allowing outside developers access to Enterprise credentials. A B2B release is distributed through the App Store, but it is not visible to the general public. The organization makes a bulk purchase of the custom app for its employees, who are given claim codes for use on their App Store accounts. That's only a snapshot of the B2B program; see `http://developer .apple.com` for the current details.

Provisioning for iOS

Here is what happens in the iOS provisioning process—the process of getting an application from Xcode to a device. Xcode (usually) hides the details from you, but there are always corner cases that will be hard to deal with if you don't know what's really going on.

> **Note**
>
> The process for OS X provisioning is closely analogous, except that you must apply both a distribution certificate and an installation certificate when you submit applications to the Mac App Store.

Authorization to install an app *always* consists of three identities.

- A **signature**—The app must be cryptographically signed by a developer (or in the case of general distribution, a Team Admin or Agent) to identify it with the developer-program membership. The certificate represents a *signing identity*. Apple issues the signing certificates.

- An **application ID**—This identifies the particular app. It's a simple string, made unique through the reverse-domain convention, that you register to your program membership through Apple. This is the same as the bundle ID set in the application's `Info.plist`. For Passer Rating, this is `com.wt9t.Passer-Rating`.

- An **authorized device**—App Store and Enterprise applications can be installed on any iOS device in the world. For development and beta, the device has to be registered with Apple for your program membership. Your program has 100 registrations, and each lasts a year; you can unregister a device, but its slot won't be available to you until the anniversary of your membership.

> **Note**
>
> Some developers report that Apple offers them 200 device slots. Perhaps this represents a change in policy, but at the time I write this, most see only 100.

> **Note**
>
> Ad hoc (beta) distribution may pose a political problem if you develop for an organization. The 100-device registry is a finite resource of the organization and must be managed. You can't develop if you can't register new devices, but there will be pressure to authorize copies for the CEO, your boss's boss, your boss's boss's committees. . .all of whom will "test" your app by running it once to show to their friends. Before the question arises, make sure your organization establishes a policy that conserves the device registry for testing and development.

On the basis of these, Apple will issue a *provisioning profile*. It binds your app ID, one or more authorized signers, and one or more devices together into a cryptographic bundle that assures your iOS device that it's permitted to accept the app. There are development profiles for tethered debugging, ad hoc profiles for beta testing, and distribution profiles for forwarding to the App Store.

Apple maintained the iOS Provisioning Portal web application to handle all the identity and registration business, with an upload and download at nearly every step.

What You'll See

Xcode 5 does almost all of this automatically. The portal site, renamed "Certificates, Identifiers & Profiles," is still there, but it mostly serves as a dashboard for your provisioning information, as an additional interface for performing registrations, and as the only interface for obtaining distribution profiles and certificates. You can reach it by logging into `http://developer.apple.com/membercenter/`.

> **Note**
>
> "Certificates, Identifiers & Profiles" is a cumbersome name, so I'll keep calling it the "portal."

Registering Your Team Membership

Before you do any developer-program-related work with Xcode 5, open the Preferences window and select the **Accounts** panel.

The **Accounts** panel gathers the addresses and credentials for three kinds of network services: Source-code repositories; Xcode Server accounts; and, what interests us here, the Apple IDs for a registered developer. My own setup is varied enough to make a good example—see Figure 17.1.

To add an Apple ID, hold the mouse down on the **+** button at the bottom left of the source list, and select **Add Apple ID...** from the menu that drops down. You'll be asked for the Apple ID you use for development, the account password, and a description of the account so you can identify it in the list.

With the credentials in hand, Xcode logs into your developer account, identifies all the teams you belong to, and downloads all of the provisioning profiles associated with your team memberships. If you don't have all of the signing certificates you're entitled to, Xcode will apply for them and install them automatically. If you don't have Apple's intermediate signing-authority certificates, Xcode installs them. Figure 17.1 shows what my entry looks like.

If you find you still lack a signing certificate you need, click the **+** under the certificate list in your team-member detail sheet (Figure 17.1, bottom), and select the type of certificate you need. Xcode will apply for the certificate, download it, and install it. You can hold more than one of some distribution certificates—the idea is that in the middle of one cert's term, you obtain another so you can spend the last part of certificate A's validity using certificate B, which will survive beyond A's expiration.

This opens up a risk: In an idle moment, you may find you've accidentally applied for and received an additional distribution certificate. Stay calm, visit the portal, and revoke the newer certificate (double-check the expiration dates before you commit yourself).

Registering Your App

When you create an iOS project, the **General** tab of the Target editor will protest that Xcode doesn't know of any provisioning profiles for the product. To get a profile, you have to be on the team of a developer-program member. You'll be invited to select one of your team memberships from a popup menu. You can also decline to select a team (**None**), possibly because you don't have a membership, nor work for anyone who does. Or, Xcode

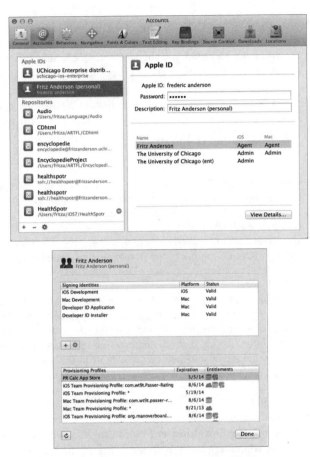

Figure 17.1   When an Apple ID account is added to the **Accounts** panel of the Preferences window, (top) Xcode fetches all developer-program teams that ID is associated with. (bottom) Selecting a team membership and clicking **View Details...** displays all certificates and provisioning profiles available to that team member.

may not be aware of your registration as a developer with Apple. **Add an Account. . .** will open the **Accounts** panel of the Preferences window to take care of that.

> **Note**
>
> The terminology can get a bit tangled. A *program member* is a person or organization that has paid $99 to have access to the App Store, provisioning profiles, prerelease software, and the like. Each program member has a *team*. Individual-program members have themselves as a one-person team. Organizations can have the hierarchy of team members I discussed at the beginning of this chapter. A *registered developer* hasn't paid a dime to Apple; he's merely clicked the **Register** link tucked into the corner of the `developer .apple.com` web page. Apple collected an Apple ID from him and got his assent to a terms-of-service agreement. A mere registered developer doesn't belong to any team, but organizational program members can invite him.

Selecting the team gives Xcode another opportunity to serve. Now that it knows which program membership owns the product, it registers the Bundle Identifier it synthesized from the company identifier and the target name. Xcode and Apple know the signing identities for all the team members, the application ID, and your team's roster of registered devices. That's all three of the prerequisites to issuing a provisioning profile: Xcode asks Apple for a *Team Provisioning Profile*—one that recognizes the developer certificates of everyone on your team—for the app, and installs it. By the end of all this, your whole team is authorized to load your app into any registered device for debugging.

Note

There are two kinds of team provisioning profile. The *generic* one has an application ID of *, meaning it will authorize any application. For a while, that was the one-and-only team profile. In the Xcode 5 era, different apps have different entitlements for access to (mainly) cloud services; each app has to have its own development profile that matches its entitlement set. These are still called team profiles because they carry the developer identities and registered-device rosters of the whole member organization.

Note

You remember that if you're a mere Member of a team, you don't have the authority to register devices or application identifiers, or even to issue yourself a development signing certificate. Instead of delivering them to you immediately, the provisioning system will email the Admins and Agent asking them to approve your requests. When they do, have Xcode refresh your information by clicking the circular-arrow button in the team-member details sheet (Figure 17.1, bottom).

You say your device isn't registered? Plug it in, assure it that it can trust your computer, and find it in the Devices organizer (⇧⌘2, first tab). Select the top line of the device's entry, and click the **Enable for Development** button in the main view. Xcode will ask you which of your teams should register the device (you can choose more than one). Xcode installs (or exposes) some performance-debugging facilities on the device itself (**Settings → Developer**, just above the panels for applications); downloads the symbols for your device's version of iOS, if Xcode hadn't seen that version before; and registers the device with the teams you selected. A change in the authorized-device list means a change in the provisioning profiles, so Xcode repeats the download of all of the affected profiles.

Note

In some cases—for beta (ad hoc) users particularly—it's not practical or desirable to plug the device into Xcode. Those devices have to be hand-entered in the portal. Enter the site, select the iOS section (if you have a choice), and select the **Devices** section from the source list on the left. Click the **+** button and enter a convenient name for the device, and its *UDID*. This is a 40-character hexadecimal string that uniquely identifies the device. The Devices organizer displays the UDID prominently; nontechnical users should plug the device into iTunes, select it, and click the serial number to reveal the UDID. The text is not selectable, but the usual **Copy** gesture will put the string onto the clipboard so the user can mail it to you.

Protecting Your Assets

This is a lot of work, even if you didn't have to do much of it yourself. You can get most of it back, or retrieve it on another machine, just by adding the same accounts to the **Accounts** panel and reentering your credentials.

But there is one part Apple and Xcode can't restore for you: your signing identities rely on public/private key cryptography. Xcode generates a private key for each certificate it applies for. As the name says, it's private. Apple never sees it. It exists only in your keychain: Look for it in the **login** → **Certificates** section of the Keychain Access application; if a certificate has a disclosure triangle next to it, opening it will reveal the private key—in fact, this is a good way to diagnose a missing private key, which is a common cause of code-signing problems.

It it's lost, it's gone. Irrecoverable. The only remedy is to revoke that certificate and apply for a new one, which makes all applications that rely on it, and aren't already in the App Store, stop working.

So back it up. You can preserve just the key pairs by selecting the certificates in Keychain Access and selecting **File** → **Export Items. . .** (⇧⌘E), but Xcode can do better for you. In the **Accounts** panel, select **Export Accounts. . .** from the menu attached to the gear button at the bottom of the source list. Xcode will lead you to a password-protected archive of all your assets. Keep it somewhere safe, away from your development machine.

> **Note**
>
> If you distribute signing certificates to support a consortium of developers on an "open" project, expect Apple to revoke the certificates and ban you from its developer programs. Personal accountability for the use of developer credentials is part of the deal.

Submitting an iOS Application

Apple draws a line between installations of applications on an iOS device.

Development is the process of loading an app for debugging. It's an interaction between the device, the developer, and the debugger. It requires a development signing certificate for the person of the developer.

Distribution refers to any dissemination of an application for nontethered use by other devices. This includes beta (ad hoc) distributions, which must be made to registered devices identified in the provisioning file; in-house (Enterprise) distributions, which are unrestricted except for the contractual obligation not to let them out of the developer's organization; and sales through the App Store, which are likewise free of device restrictions.

> **Note**
>
> The word "distribution" has picked up synonyms over the years in serial attempts to make the purpose clear. The signing identity for the purpose has the common name "iPhone Distribution." The portal refers to those certificates as "Production." The build config-uration for the purpose (actually, you'd probably have more than one) is "Release." The

usual way to create a distribution package is with the Archive build action, the result of which is an archive, so the process may be called "archiving."

Ad hoc (beta) and in-house (Enterprise) distribution are virtually identical to each other, and the concepts are similar to those of App Store submission. You can find the exact procedures in the Apple documentation; the docs for in-house distribution can be found only on the web. For simplicity, I'll just cover the path to the App Store.

Apple promises that developers who use ad hoc distribution for purposes other than testing, or in-house distribution for use outside of the licensed organization, will be terminated. Bear it in mind.

If you use any of the cloud services for which Apple demands a unique identity from the client application—in-app purchase, push notifications, Game Center—you must register the full application ID for your app. If you don't need them—if your app is *generic*—Apple doesn't need the ID. The provisioning system recognizes "wildcard" identifiers, in which the tail of the identifier is replaced with an asterisk (*). Anything that matches the part before the asterisk matches the provisioning profile. If the ID is just an asterisk, that profile can authorize any app you sign.

The Capabilities Editor

What I've described covers the bare minimum of the registrations and certifications you'll need to distribute an application. There are additional capabilities that need continuing support from Apple, such as servers for iCloud, Game Center, and push notifications. Your app has to be registered for the services, and some require additional cryptographic signatures. Others don't need any Apple support at all, but you must declare your need for them in an *entitlements* claim that is sealed into your app. Still others have to be advertised in the app's `Info.plist` file (see Chapter 22, "Bundles and Packages").

Xcode 4's Target editor wrapped some of this—the Mac sandboxing entitlements—into a simple checkbox interface. Xcode 5 provides a unified editor for the most common capabilities in the Target editor's **Capabilities** tab. Each facility has an on/off switch. Clicking the disclosure triangle describes what the facility is and what Xcode will do to enable it for your product. Some capabilities have further options.

Capabilities for Both iOS and OS X

In keeping with the convergence of OS X and iOS, some capabilities are common to the two.

- **iCloud** is the shared-storage service for a user's Apple devices. Turning on the capability will register the requirement with Apple and put the store identifier into your entitlements file.

- **Game Center** is the Apple-hosted mediator for leaderboards and player challenges. Xcode will register your app as using Game Center; note the need for GameKit in your `Info.plist`, and link `GameKit.framework` to the app. iOS apps are automatically registered for Game Center, but you must still turn the capability on

to use it. Additionally, you must log into iTunes Connect (`itunesconnect`
`.apple.com`) to obtain the necessary credentials for your app.

- **In-App Purchase** lets you sell application services from your app. There are
  restrictions on what you can sell—see the review guidelines and the IAP documentation for details. Flipping the switch links `StoreKit.framework` and adds
  IAP to the app's registration with Apple. You will still have to register your IAP
  products with iTunes Connect.

- **Keychain Sharing** lets your applications share credentials through a common
  keychain. Each app must list each shared keychain's identifier in its entitlements file.
  This option lets you manage that list.

iOS Capabilities

- For iOS targets, selecting the **Maps** capability alone simply links `MapKit`
  `.framework`. However, beyond simply displaying maps, an iOS app may provide
  routing information. In that case, it has to publish what kind of routing it
  provides—automobile, foot, bus—and that it accepts routing-request documents.
  The Capability editor gives you checkboxes to select the routing options.

- **Inter-App Audio** is a specialized service that allows one app to exchange MIDI
  commands and audio streams with another. Activating it registers the entitlement
  with Apple, adds it to the application entitlements file, and links `AudioToolbox`
  `.framework`, with which you are about to share a long adventure.

- **Background Modes** exposes checkboxes for your app to claim the privilege of
  running periodically while it is not the frontmost application. iOS permits only
  limited operation in the background, and your app must declare the services you
  want in its `Info.plist`. Apple's reviewers will check to see that your app is doing
  what you claim with its background privileges.

- **Data Protection** indicates that all document-file access by the app should be
  encrypted to one degree or another. The protection levels are Complete (locking
  the device cuts off all access to a file, even if you had it open); Complete Unless
  Open (your app can keep access to a file if the file was open when the device was
  locked); or Complete Until First Login (the file becomes readable the first time the
  user unlocks the device after startup).

  However, you can only specify those levels in the portal's listing of your app's
  privileges. You can always specify encryption options on individual files and data
  blocks in your code.

OS X Capabilities

- Activating **Maps** for a Mac application registers the entitlement with Apple and
  links `MapKit.framework`.

- **App Sandbox** is a long story. See the next section, "OS X Sandboxing."

OS X Sandboxing

iOS has a strict security régime that keeps each app in a "sandbox," an environment in which an app has no access to files outside the application package or that it did not create, nor to device services except as permitted by the OS.

OS X 10.7 Lion introduced sandboxing to the Mac as an opt-in for most applications, and mandatory for all apps sold through the Mac App Store. You can't get access to Apple services like iCloud or Game Center without selling through the App Store, and you can't get into the App Store without sandboxing.

The idea is to make it harder to attack the user's Mac by having the operating system block any service the developer didn't declare. If you didn't say you need to operate a socket for incoming network connections, and your app suddenly attempts to do that, the change must (the theory goes) have come from malware that exploited a weakness in your app.

By default the sandbox is completely closed to everything but direct interaction with the user. It can't even read or write files. Everything else is an exception, which you must claim through the app's entitlements file. You must sign (and, for the App Store, Apple must countersign) the app to seal it against alteration. You declare your requested entitlements in an .entitlements file (in the property list format; see Chapter 24, "Property Lists"). The build process embeds them in the signed application binary.

The **Capabilities** tab of the Target editor gives you checkbox access to the most common entitlements. The repertoire is:

- Network
  - Incoming connections (Server)
  - Outgoing connections (Client)
- Hardware
  - Camera
  - Microphone
  - USB
  - Printing
- Apps
  - Contacts
  - Location
  - Calendar
- **No Access, Read Access,** or **Read/Write Access** to
  - User-selected file
  - Downloads folder
  - Pictures folder
  - Music folder
  - Movies folder

Note

There are many more possible sandbox entitlements. Some are obscure (deservedly or not), such as access to AppleScript, shared preferences, or files that have the same base names as files the user had authorized in the same directory. Some are *temporary exceptions*, which could mean that Apple is still working out how to implement the privileges they represent; or it could mean that Apple means eventually to close off those privileges, and is giving developers time to figure out workarounds. And some you may have to invent for yourself, in the (usually forlorn) hope that Apple's reviewer will open the sandbox to some privilege that your app absolutely needs. Search the Documentation organizer for the *Entitlement Key Reference*, ask around in the developer forums at `http://devforums.apple.com/`, and comb through WWDC videos. This is one of the few instances where the forums are of more use than Stack Overflow.

Take special note that if you want to read and write files outside your app's sandbox directory, you must ask for the privilege. Even then, you will gain access only to files that your user has explicitly designated. These could be dragged and dropped onto your app's icon in the Finder or the Dock, or into one of your windows (if you handle file drops); or through PowerBox (so named because it's...like a box), the secure OS X process that replaces the open-file and save-file sheets.

If you submit your app for App-Store review, be sure to include a justification for every entitlement you claim—common, uncommon, or exceptional—in the review notes. For example, "MyEditor is an editor for document files and must have read and write access to user-identified files. It needs to make outgoing network connections to download templates and to validate user-entered URLs."

Why Sandbox?

The most powerful incentive for adopting sandboxing is that you can sell your app through the App Store. This isn't just a matter of having a convenient way to distribute your work and handle payments. App Store access enables your app to use a number of OS X features that require the use of Apple servers:

- iCloud
- In-app purchase
- Push notifications
- Game Center

But there is another reason. Sandboxing is intended to prevent an application from being an attack vector. Even if the app gets pwned, it can't erase a user's files, send her contacts to an identity thief, or operate a spam SMTP server. (Always granting that the latter two could still happen if the app originally asked for the necessary privileges.) A sandbox error that crashes your product is embarrassing, but embarrassments happen, and people will wait (briefly) for a fix. A breach that ransacks the user's system will ruin you.

Why Not Sandbox?

If sandboxing doesn't fit your application's needs, don't use it. The only costs are that you won't be able to sell through the Mac App Store, and thus make use of Apple-served features.

What needs would interfere with sandboxing? Basically, if you want general-purpose access to resources that belong to the system or other applications, you can expect sandboxing to pinch. Common trouble spots are

- Gaining privileged access to system resources or access-restricted files. If you've written an editor for system-configuration files, you're out of luck.

- Writing an assistive application. The sandbox will let you expose your UI through the accessibility API, but if you want to send accessibility events *to* another application—a technique that many developers use as poor-man's inter-application communications—the sandbox will stop you.

- You can receive and respond to Apple events (most commonly from AppleScript), but you can send them only to applications you list in a temporary exception entitlement. An Open Scripting Architecture script editor won't work in the sandbox.

- You can't access other apps' preferences unless, under a temporary exception, you list the domains you want to access. Also, you can share data among apps in a suite by having each declare themselves to belong to an "application suite" keyed to your development team ID.

- You can't load kernel extensions. Are you surprised?

These are all useful, reasonable things to do; you just can't do them and work in the sandbox.

Gatekeeper and Developer ID

OS X 10.8 Mountain Lion introduced Gatekeeper, another way to reassure your users about the security of your apps, without the limits the sandbox imposes. When Gatekeeper is in effect, all downloaded applications (or executable documents like scripts) are on a blacklist, and users will not be permitted to open them. Only apps that come from "identified" developers are on the whitelist.

You become "identified" by obtaining a *Developer ID* cryptographic signing identity from Apple and applying it to your app. Signing with a DevID clears it for execution, with only a one-time warning that it had been downloaded from the Internet.

Getting a Developer ID

Developer ID is available to any member of the $99 Mac Developer Program. In fact, once you're in the program, DevID is almost impossible to avoid: When you enter your developer account in the **Accounts** panel, the DevID certificate is automatically created and installed. This is another public/private key pair, so secure it either by creating a developer-account archive or exporting it from Keychain Access.

As a paid member of Apple's Mac Developer Program, you will have five signing identities; be careful to keep them straight in your mind and in your keychain.

- **Developer ID Application** is the certificate you'll apply to get your app past Gatekeeper. Don't bother to set any certificate in the "Code Signing Identity" build setting; Xcode asks you to choose your Developer ID certificate when you click the **Distribute...** button in the Archives organizer.

- **Developer ID Installer** is used to assure Gatekeeper about non-application products like installer packages and `.xip` archives. Xcode never touches the DevID installer certificate; you use it with the `productsign` and `xip` command-line tools.

  > **Note**
  > `xip` is pronounced "chip."

- **3rd Party Mac Developer Application** sounds similar to the Developer ID Application certificate, but the closer analogue is the "iPhone Distribution" identity on the iOS side: In a build to be uploaded to the Mac App Store, you select this identity in the "Code Signing Identity" build setting. As with the iOS distribution certificate, the certificate has to match up with the application's ID through a provisioning profile you get from Apple.

- **3rd Party Mac Developer Installer** is *not* an analogue to the Developer ID Installer certificate. Unlike with iOS packaging, you use separate signing identities to prepare an application for validation and submission to the Mac App Store. The Developer Application certificate is used in the build process. The Developer Installer certificate is applied when you click **Validate...** or **Distribute...** in the Archives organizer. You'll be presented with a choice of installer certificates; choose the default Xcode offers you unless you are *positive* you need something else.

- The **Mac Developer** certificate is different from the two "3rd Party Mac Developer" certificates, for all that it has nearly the same name. The concept is most similar to the "iPhone Developer" identity you use for iOS development. It is the build-time signing identity you apply to debug builds when you're testing identity-sensitive features like sandboxing, Developer ID, and access to Apple cloud services. This, too, matches to a provisioning profile, in this case a *development* profile.

Using Developer ID

Open an Xcode project containing a Mac application target, and select **Product →Archive**. All going well, Xcode will show you the Archives organizer with your application archive displayed. Click **Distribute....** A sheet drops down presenting your options (Figure 17.2). The middle choice, **Export Developer ID-signed Application**, is the one you want. Click **Next**.

Figure 17.2   The sheet that appears when you click **Distribute...** on a Mac archive offers the choice of creating a Developer ID-signed application.

Once you've chosen the distribution method, Xcode examines the archive, the provisioning profile, and your keychain. It then gives you a popup menu to select the signing identity you want to apply—the one it selects automatically is usually correct.

An activity spinner turns for a while as the cryptographic signatures are assembled, and at last you are given a put-file sheet so you can save the completed application.

That's it. Xcode gets you a certificate, it signs your app with it, it puts the app on disk. It's actually more trouble to save an unsigned application. You're free to distribute the app however you like; any method—.zip archives, disk images, CD-ROMs, email attachments, paper tape—that a Mac application can survive. The only difference is that when a user of Gatekeeper downloads it, OS X will let her run it.

Note

Once you start embedding frameworks or helper tools in your app, things get complicated; each needs its own signature independent of the application's. This should be easier than it is, and it may have become so by the time you read this. Until then, have a look at Jerry Krinock's solution on GitHub at https://github.com/jerrykrinock/DeveloperScripts/blob/master/SSYShipProduct.pl.

Limitations

Developer ID is not a panacea. It doesn't guarantee that the application is secure. It does not prevent an app from doing something malicious. It detects the app's signature only the first time it is launched from download quarantine; if something injects malicious code at runtime, the OS won't detect it. It doesn't apply to any file that wasn't downloaded or was downloaded by means other than the usual browsers or mail applications. Unlike App Store products, it does not attest that someone has reviewed the app for security or quality.

> **Note**
>
> Gatekeeper will restrict downloaded documents, as well, if they are of a "dangerous" type, like scripts or installer packages. The `productsign` tool can apply your "Installer" Developer ID to packages, and `xip` can produce archives of "dangerous" files that can be expanded safely by double-clicking them. See the respective man pages.

The only assurance that Gatekeeper gives—and the UI is careful to say so—is that the developer of an app is "identified." When you signed up for the Mac Developer Program, you gave enough information that Apple can find you. If it discovers you've been distributing malware, it can revoke your Developer ID, and your applications won't run any more. Want to continue distributing malware? Come up with another identity and bank account, and pay another $99. Cheap if you're an evil mastermind, but most scammers won't bother.

Which is why you can't get a Developer ID without paying for the Mac Developer Program.

Developer ID and sandboxing are separate concepts. If you want your app to be in the Mac App Store, sandboxing is mandatory and DevID is pointless. Outside the App Store, neither excludes or requires the other. DevID says only that an app came from a (so far) reputable source. It does not say that the app is safe, or secure. You might want to consider sandboxing as a backstop to your secure-coding practices.

Distribution Builds

Once your project goes from development to distribution (you remember this is any dissemination of an app to be run untethered), Xcode is still friendly, but it's a bit higher maintenance.

If Xcode has a distribution profile on-hand that matches your application ID, it will match the profile to your app, and the profile will specify the necessary signing certificate. Good.

Basic Build Settings

The build settings for your product are the key to the selection of the profile and the signing identity.

The (`INFOPLIST_FILE`) setting is the name of the precursor for your product's `Info.plist` file. The precursor, which has a name like `PasserRating-Info.plist`, is almost a complete `Info.plist`, but it has some build-setting references that have to be resolved, and it's missing some keys. The build process finishes up the file and installs it in the product as `Info.plist`.

> **Note**
>
> `Info.plist` is at the core of most OS X and iOS products; learn more about property list files in Chapter 24, "Property Lists," and the content of `Info.plist` in the "The `Info.plist` File" section of Chapter 22, "Bundles and Packages."

`Info.plist` is where your app specifies its application ID (`CFBundleIdentifier`), which is how the build system can identify the matching provisioning profile.

At least that is how it could go, and did until recently. Now, it has been recognized that release builds could be ad hoc or for publication, and provisioning profiles may be issued with wildcard application IDs. So the build settings now include a key, `PROVISIONING_PROFILE`, that you set to precisely identify the profile you mean; the popup list will include every profile Xcode knows about. It's optional now, but Apple warns that it will be required soon.

The profile knows what signing identity it requires. If you leave the signing identity build setting (`CODE_SIGN_IDENTITY`) to accept a generic "iPhone Developer" or "iPhone Distribution" identity, the build system will pick the right one. You *can* select a different identity, but if it's one that Xcode doesn't match to your app, it's probably the wrong one.

If all those ducks are in a row, you're ready to do an Archive build. Barring special circumstances.

Adjusting the Build Settings

It may not be so simple. In my work, we've had to work on the same basic product, using three means of distribution:

- A straightforward article that's headed for the App Store, as I showed you. It needs development profiles, and a final App Store distribution profile.

- A beta version, perhaps of the current App-Store product, perhaps of the next generation. It needs an ad hoc distribution profile.

- An in-house version, distributed under our Enterprise license. It *must* have its own application ID, because it has to be provisioned out of our Enterprise account, and Apple won't let us reuse the App Store version's ID. It needs a distribution profile of its own, issued under that developer program membership.

Let's tease out the Enterprise-versus-App Store issue first: Two developer-program memberships means two different teams, each with its own distribution signing certificate and its own source for provisioning profiles. Xcode 5's integration with the provisioning process weds each target to a single team membership. Our product must have two targets, one for App Store–related builds, and one for Enterprise. There are two products, each following its own path to distribution independently, and we don't have to worry about both at once.

> **Note**
>
> Projects, of course, can have many targets, each with its own team membership. There's nothing wrong with keeping the App Store and Enterprise targets in the same project.

Let's proceed with the other two products: the App Store article and its beta counterpart.

We don't *have* to treat the beta as a separate product. It can share its application ID, icons, and versioning progression with the release article. If so, the two can share an `Info.plist`. It's easy; all you have to do is clone a "beta" build configuration from the Release configuration that simply selects the "ad hoc" (beta) distribution profile.

> **Note**
>
> Chapter 26, "The Xcode Build System," covers build configurations in exhaustive detail, but here's the short of it: The process of building an application invokes many separate tools, each with many options to configure its behavior and identify its inputs and outputs. A build configuration is a package of those settings. You can have more than one—by default, you get Debug and Release—to tailor the process to the purpose of a build.

Generating the beta product then becomes a simple matter of choosing the configuration. If you duplicate the App Store target's scheme and name it something like **MyApp beta**, and select the beta configuration for the Archive action, you can switch between the release methods just by selecting a scheme from the popup menu in the toolbar.

Apple doesn't recommend this for serious development. If your product is already in the App Store, your beta product is going to be an early version of the next release. If the beta and the released version share application IDs, the beta will overwrite the public release app on your testers' devices. Few people will volunteer to beta-test software if it means losing the working version. So `CFBundleIdentifier`, the app ID, has to be different.

`CFBundleVersion`, what Apple is calling the "build number," will probably be different, too. You'll have many betas for *MyApp 1.1*, all of them with the same "marketing" `CFBundleShortVersionString` (1.1). If the `CFBundleVersion` is also 1.1, you'll find that iOS (and the OS X installer) won't replace the beta app with new betas—the OS refuses to install an application package that has the same `CFBundleVersion` as the incumbent. For an example of a build number, select **Xcode →About Xcode** to see the difference between a "marketing" version number (5.0.2) and a "build" number (5A3005).

If the identifier and the bundle version have to be different, then the beta and final products must each have its own `Info.plist`, the file that sets those properties (and others) for an application bundle. Your project does not contain a literal `Info.plist`; instead, it contains precursors with names like `Passer Rating-Info.plist` that are processed into the `Info.plist` to be installed in the application package.

Select your product's precursor file in the Project navigator, and then select **File** →
Duplicate. . . (⇧⌘ S). Give the new file a suitable name reflecting the target name and its
purpose as a beta. Edit the new file:

- Give the file its own `CFBundleIdentifier` (bundle ID), because you don't want
  to overwrite the release article on your testers' devices. You'll have to register the ID
  with the portal, and (for a beta product) have Apple issue an "ad hoc" provisioning
  profile for that ID.

- Create names for the betas' own icon files—your testers would like to be able to tell
  the beta apart from the production app. You'll have to add the icon keys by hand:
  The build system creates the icon records automatically from your settings in the
  target editor, but for a custom plist, you'll have to do it yourself. See Chapter 22,
  "Bundles and Packages," for the keys and their meaning.

- Set `CFBundleVersion` to conform to the build-versioning scheme you've chosen.

- You'd want a beta to have a distinctive name, but leave **Bundle name**
  (`CFBundleName`) alone. By default, it's set to `${PRODUCT_NAME}`, which is taken
  from the **Build Settings** for the current configuration.

Create such a configuration: Create an "Ad Hoc" build configuration by cloning the
Release configuration in the Project editor. That will add an Ad Hoc variant to all of the
settings in the Target editor's **Build Settings** tab. Adjust the settings for the Ad Hoc
variant as needed by clicking the setting's line and clicking the disclosure triangle to
expose the Ad Hoc configuration: At least, select your cloned `Info.plist` precursor file,
set **Product Name** to something that distinguishes the beta version, and select the ad hoc
provisioning profile.

Then create a new scheme for building the beta version: Use **Product** → **Scheme**
→ **Manage Schemes. . .** to reveal the list of the project's build schemes. Duplicate the
default scheme for your product, give it a name (`My App Ad Hoc`) and click **Edit. . . .**
For the Archive action, set the **Build Configuration** to your custom ad hoc
configuration. The scheme will appear in the popup menu in the project window's
toolbar. You can switch between the beta and final releases instantly.

The Build

The goal is to produce an archive from which you can generate a distributable product.
To produce an archive you must have

- The necessary distribution (and in the case of OS X, installation) identities, with
  both the public and private keys, in your keychain.

- A provisioning profile that authorizes the kind of distribution you intend.

- A build configuration that selects the proper profile, and an `Info.plist` that
  declares a matching bundle ID.

- A scheme, the Archive action of which designates the correct build configuration.

- The scheme, and a target-device (not simulator) destination, selected in the scheme popups at the left end of the project window's toolbar.

Select **Product → Archive**. Wait. Assuming there are no build errors, the Archives organizer will appear with your product selected.

> **Note**
>
> This is another of those "if all goes well" situations. If there's a regular compilation, linkage, or resource error, you know what to do. If it's a provisioning problem—the profile, the identifier, the certificates—every unhappy build is different. In the Documentation browser, look up the Troubleshooting chapter of the App Distribution Guide, and work from there.

If you're headed for an App Store, you'll have to have registered the app with iTunes Connect, providing all the necessary marketing, legal, and technical information—including your application ID. And you must have told iTC that the app is "Ready for Upload." (It's then up to you to get the application ready.)

With that done, you can click the **Validate. . .** button to subject your app to some automated tests. Then you can click **Distribute. . .**, and tell Xcode to submit the binary to the App Store.

And that takes you into review and, we hope, to release.

Summary

Provisioning applications for development and release has always been intricate, but over the past couple of years, it's gotten much better. Xcode 5 and Apple Developer Programs do what they can to make the process as painless as possible for as many developers as possible.

But you should understand the underlying principles—what the provisioning system expects, and how Xcode wraps the process—in case your needs are atypical or if something just goes wrong. I reviewed the three prerequisites to installing an app on an iOS device: signature, application ID, authorized device. Everything else is a variation on the common theme.

With that in mind, the magic Xcode performs with your developer privileges should have been clearer to you. You saw the interplay of identities, entitlements, and permissions come together to produce an application you can distribute, whether through an App Store, or (in the case of OS X applications) by your own means, with at least some assurance to your users that you are doing no harm.

Part III

Xcode for Mac OS X

## 18

Starting an OS X Application

Now you can advance to Xcode skills that apply to OS X development. If you're a Mac developer, I hope you haven't skipped Part II, "The Life Cycle of an iOS Application." Most of what I showed you in the iOS part of this book applies to Mac projects as well, and I won't be repeating them in these chapters.

By the same token, if your interest is in iOS, *don't stop reading*. You aren't done yet! Bundles and property lists aren't the priority for you that they are in OS X, but you have to know about them and their place in Cocoa development. In particular, have a look at the section on `Info.plist` in Chapter 22, "Bundles and Packages."

What you're going to do now is to port the Passer Rating iPhone app to OS X. Because you kept a good separation in the Model-View-Controller design, the model layer of the application could come through unchanged (though you're going to expand it a bit). The view and controller layers will be all new; the human-interface layers for the two platforms, UIKit on iOS and AppKit on the Mac, share some concepts but are very different.

> **Warning**
>
> This chapter builds upon the work in the iOS Passer Rating application. The narrative concentrates on the workflow of setting up an OS X application, at the expense of complete transparency about everything that was needed for the adaptation. After you have Xcode instantiate the project template, you *must* download the sample code (if you haven't already), or you won't be able to follow along. The tradeoff was not easy for me to make, but the alternative was to drown the Xcode techniques (the subject of this book) in code listings and diffs. I'll guide you through the process, but have the finished code for this chapter handy so you can fill in the gaps.

The Goal

A desktop application is a different sort of thing from a mobile app. Desktop apps present their information in windows, and users expect data-handling windows to be *documents*, each of which stores its data in its own file. Mac Passer Rating *could* present only one window for only one data set, but as you'll see, it's not much more trouble to work with

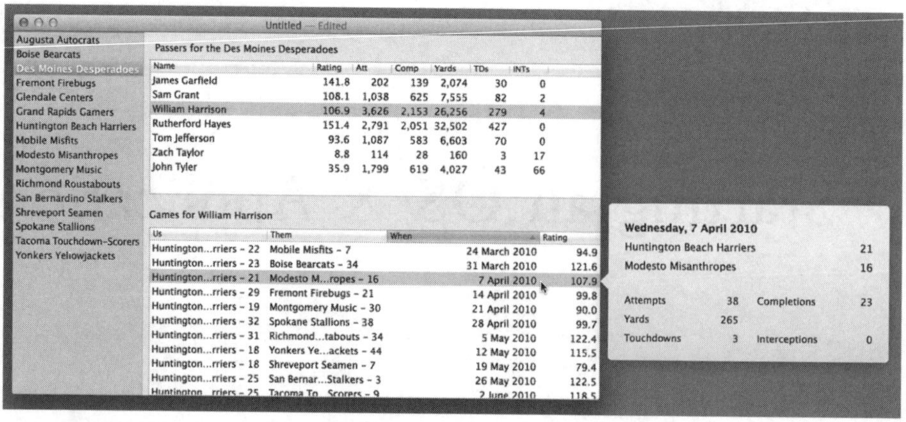

Figure 18.1   Mac Passer Rating as we want it to look, at least for the purpose of this example. A document represents a "league" composed of teams (left table). Selecting a team fills the upper table with the passers who have played on it. Selecting a passer lists all of his game performances in the lower table. Clicking on a game brings up a popover window with the details.

documents. That way, the user can organize passer statistics into leagues, which he can exchange with others.

The top level of the iOS Passer Rating app was a list of passers. Does that make sense if you have more than one document? If you have documents for discrete leagues, it may be better if you take *teams* as the root of the data set. This will entail a slight rework of the data model, which I'll get to presently.

So a league (the document) has a list of teams. Each team has a list of passers that have (at least for a time) played for it. Each passer has a list of game performances. When you were working on the iPhone screen, you were restricted to showing only one level of the hierarchy at a time. On the desktop, you can make it all visible. Something like Figure 18.1 is what you'll be shooting for.

Getting Started

Starting a Cocoa application project is scarcely different from what you saw in Chapter 2, "Kicking the Tires": Select **File → New → New Project** (⇧ ⌘ N), which will give you an empty workspace window and a New Project assistant sheet. Select **OS X → Application** from the master list at the left, and the Cocoa Application icon from the array at the right. Click **Next**.

Now you come to the panel of project options, and there are quite a few of them.

- **Product Name** will be `Mac Passer Rating`. It's a dumb name for an application—the user knows she's using a Mac, and probably doesn't care that there are other versions—but it helps you keep track of things if the project has a distinctive name. You can rename the product later by seeking out "Product Name" in the **Build Settings** tab of the Target editor.

- The **Organization Name**—the copyright holder—is probably your name (Fritz Anderson).

- **Company Identifier** forms the prefix for the application ID. For my purposes, this is `com.wt9t`. Enter your own.

- The **Bundle Identifier** concatenates the company identifier and the product name. This is how the application will be identified to the system and (if you intend to sell through the Mac App Store) to Apple. The field isn't editable; it's just for your information.

- **Class Prefix** is insurance against your class names' colliding with those of classes from Cocoa or third-party libraries. We'll use `MPR`.

- You're given an opportunity to choose an **App Store Category** from a popup list. Apple allows more than one category, so if you want more, or if you change your mind, you can edit `Mac Passer Rating-Info.plist` later. **Sports** fits this app.

- Check **Create Document-Based Application** because the app will produce documents. The document options in this panel have big effects on the boilerplate code Xcode's template will produce for you.

- OS X relies on filename extensions to regulate which files go with which applications. Mac Passer Rating won't be sharing any common document types, so fill **Document Extension** with something distinctive like `leaguedoc`—you shouldn't include a dot. Don't feel you have to restrict yourself to three or four characters: The people who use Mac Passer Rating won't ever have to type the extension.

- You used Core Data for iOS Passer Rating, and you'll use it here. Check **Use Core Data**.

- If you check **Include Spotlight Importer**, the template will add a target that produces a plugin for the Spotlight system-wide search utility. One could imagine making league documents searchable by team and player names, but this is just an example. Leave it unchecked.

Now click **Next**, which drops a select-directory sheet for you to place the project directory (which will be named `Mac Passer Rating`, like it or not). Make your choice, check **Create git repository on**, select an Xcode server if you have one, **My Mac** if not, and click **Create**. The Workspace window now fills with the skeleton of the application.

- `MPRDocument.h` and `MPRDocument.m` define the class that loads and stores the league data, and presents it for display and editing. `MPRDocument` is the controller class in the Model-View-Controller pattern. AppKit, the Cocoa framework for Mac applications, encompasses a sophisticated scheme for managing documents, centered on the `NSDocument` class. `NSDocument` responds to requests to read, save, present, or edit its data; your document subclass merely customizes the standard behavior.

Because you asked for a document that uses Core Data, MPRDocument is a subclass of NSPersistentDocument, which does even more for you. It takes care of loading and saving data, and it handles undo and redo events.

> **Note**
>
> It would be better to leave MPRDocument to the tasks of reading and writing the document data (as a *model controller*), and provide an NSWindowController subclass for running the details of the document window (as a *view controller*), but I'll do everything in the document class for simplicity.

- MPRDocument.xcdatamodeld is an empty data model for MPRDocument. Throw it away by selecting it in the Project navigator and pressing Delete; when Xcode asks what you want to do with it, click **Delete**. You're going to replace it with a copy of the model from the iOS Passer Rating app. The name of the model file doesn't matter; by default NSPersistentDocument loads all the compiled .mom files and merges them into a single model.

- Images.xcsasets is a container for icons and the images you will use in your application. Image sets relieve the burden of tracking the ever-proliferating gaggle of images in various sizes and resolutions that go into a modern application. See the "Image Sets" section of Chapter 13, "Adding Table Cells," for the details.

- Mac Passer Rating-Info.plist is a precursor to the Info.plist file that describes the properties and behavior of the application to the Finder and Launch Services. The **General** and **Info** tabs of the Target editor provide a (relatively) simple way to customize this file. Again, the "Bundles and Packages" and "Property Lists" chapters will tell you more about Info.plist. InfoPlist.strings provides a dictionary that matches Info.plist entries to translated versions.

- Mac Passer Rating-Prefix.pch is a *prefix* file, and the source for the project's precompiled header. Review the "Precompilation" section of Chapter 5, "Compilation," for a review.

- MainMenu.xib and MPRDocument.xib will be compiled into NIB files. They specify the human interface for the application and MPRDocument, respectively. There are no storyboards in OS X.

- Unless you build one of your own, AppKit will compose an About box from information in Info.plist. If a Credits.rtf file is part of the application bundle, its contents will appear in a scrolling subview. Don't let the application get out the door without reviewing the credits file.

- main.m is the entry point into the application. All it does is call the AppKit NSApplicationMain function. You will never edit main.m.

As with the iOS template, Mac Passer Rating is runnable as is. Select **Product →Run** (⌘ **R**). In a moment, you'll be running the application, which won't look like much—just a menu bar with **Mac Passer Rating** in it. Select **File →New** (⌘ **N**), and you'll see a

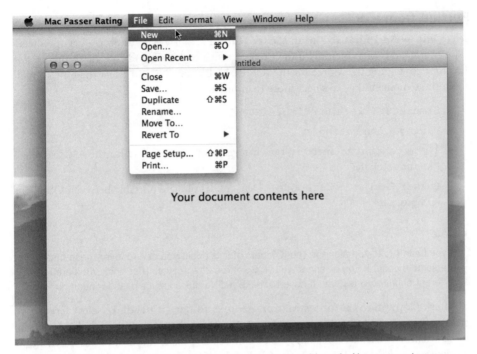

Figure 18.2   The document-application template is runnable as is. You can create a new document and save it to a file that you can reopen in the Finder.

document window that you can close, resize, and even save to a file that will reopen if you double-click it in the Finder. See Figure 18.2.

> **Note**
>
> If you save a document file at this stage, be sure to delete it. You'll be changing the data model for Mac Passer Rating. Once upon a time, Core Data would simply crash and leave you guessing, but now it throws an exception with the description, "The autosaved document. . .could not be reopened. The managed object model version used to open the persistent store is incompatible with the one that was used to create the persistent store." Watch the debugger console.

Once the novelty has worn off, you'll want to turn this application into something about football.

Model

As I said, adding a third level to the hierarchy—the team—requires a rework of the model. The data model and supporting classes from the iOS Passer Rating app are a good place to start.

Porting from iOS

Select **File** → **Add Files to "Mac Passer Rating"...** (⌥⌘A) to drop a get-file sheet. (The command is available only if the Project navigator is visible.) Navigate to the directory containing the source for the iOS Passer Rating app, and select these files (hold down the Command key to select more than one file):

- `SimpleCSVFile.h` and `SimpleCSVFile.m`
- `rating.h` and `rating.c`
- The `mogenerated` directory, or whatever container you had for the `PRGame` and `PRPasser` classes.
- `Passer_Rating.xcdatamodel`. Data-model files are portable between OS X and iOS projects.

> **Note**
>
> If you hadn't followed along in the iOS part of this book, you can recover these files from the sample code. If you arranged your iOS source directory so that some files are in different subdirectories, you'll have to make a different add-files pass for each directory.

Check **Copy items into destination group's folder (if needed)**; select **Create groups for any added folders** so the `mogenerated` class files come in individually, and not as whatever their directory happens to contain; and make sure **Mac Passer Rating** is checked in the **Add to Targets** table. Click **Add**. The files appear in the Project navigator; you'll want to select them all, issue **File** → **New** → **Group from Selection**, and rename the resulting group something like `Model`.

> **Note**
>
> This would be a good time to commit the project to the local repository.

Adding an Entity

The next step is to factor (database-savvy developers would say *normalize*) `ownTeam` out of `Game` and into a new entity, `Team`. Click on `Passer_Rating.xcdatamodel`, and (using the skills you picked up in Chapter 9, "An iOS Application: Model") create the `Team` entity, with one attribute, `teamName`. `teamName` should be a string, indexed, not optional, and with an obviously bogus default name like **UNASSIGNED_NAME**. Add a relationship, `games`, tracing to many of the `Game` entity; deletion should cascade.

Game can lose the `ourTeam` attribute, and gain `team`, a to-one relationship to `Team`, nullifying on delete. Be sure to set up this relationship as the inverse of `Team`'s `games`. When you're done, the diagram view of the data model should look like Figure 18.3.

As with `Passer` and `Game`, you will want to add a convenience method that will generate a `Team`; that will require an Objective-C class to wrap the `Team` entity.

At this point, we'd go to the Terminal and invoke `mogenerator` to build human and machine classes for the entities. However, we did a lot of work on the "human" `PRPasser` and `PRGame` during the iOS Passer Rating project, and we should carry it over to this one.

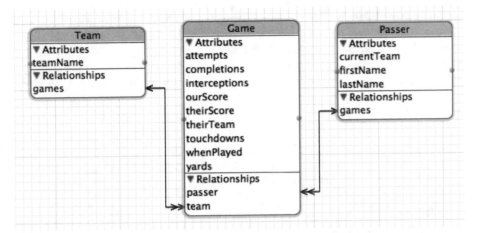

Figure 18.3   For the Mac, the Passer Rating model adds a `Team` entity. Each `Team` relates to many `Games`. `Game`'s `ownTeam` string attribute goes away, as its purpose is served by `team.teamName`.

Dig up the `mogenerated` directory from the iOS project and drop it into the Mac project directory, next to `Passer_Rating.xcdatamodeld`.

> **Note**
>
> Or, if you haven't kept the old code around, you can find the directory in the sample code for the end of this chapter.

You'll still have to create the `Team` class, and you'll need to bring the existing machine classes up-to-date with the changed model. Select the `Team` entity in the Data Model editor, expose the Core Data inspector (third tab at the top of the Utility area), and set **Class** to `PRTeam`. (Shouldn't that be `MPRTeam`? That's a good point, but once we've accepted all the `PR*` classes from the iOS project, this is less confusing.)

Now open Terminal, and regenerate the class files:

```
$ # cd to the same directory that includes
    Passer_Rating.xcdatamodeld.
$ cd 'whatever/Mac Passer Rating'
$ # Run mogenerator.
$ mogenerator --model Passer_Rating.xcdatamodeld \
    --output-dir mogenerated --template-var arc=true \
    --includeh mogenerated/MPRDataModel.h
3 machine files and 1 human files generated.
Aggregate header file was also generated to
    mogenerated/MPRDataModel.h.
$
```

Use **File → Add Files to "Mac Passer Rating"...** (⌥ ⌘ A) to add the `mogenerated` directory to the project. It should go into the Mac Passer Rating target and be added as a group of files, and not a reference to a living folder.

We were going to add a convenience method to `PRTeam` so we can find and create Teams. Turn to `PRTeam.m`, and create the method and a couple of derived properties:

```objc
@implementation PRTeam

+ (PRTeam *) teamWithName: (NSString *) aName
                inContext: (NSManagedObjectContext *) moc
                   create: (BOOL) doCreate
{
    //  Look for a Team with the given name
    NSFetchRequest *    fetch;
    fetch = [NSFetchRequest fetchRequestWithEntityName: @"Team"];
    fetch.predicate = [NSPredicate predicateWithFormat:
                        @"teamName = %@", aName];

    NSError *           error;
    NSArray *           result;
    result = [moc executeFetchRequest: fetch error: &error];
    if (! result) {
        NSLog(@"%s: Bad query for Team %@, %@",
              __PRETTY_FUNCTION__, error, [error userInfo]);
        return nil;
    }

    //  If there is at least one, return one of them.
    if (result.count > 0) {
        return [result lastObject];
    }

    //  None found, and we're not asked for a new one?
    //  Return nil.
    if (! doCreate) {
        return nil;
    }

    //  If there was no existing Team, create a new one.
    PRTeam *            retval =
    [NSEntityDescription insertNewObjectForEntityForName: @"Team"
                                 inManagedObjectContext: moc];
    assert(retval);
```

```
    retval.teamName = aName;
    return retval;
}


- (NSUInteger) ownTotalScore
{
    NSNumber *     total =
            [self.games valueForKeyPath: @"@sum.ourScore"];
    return total.unsignedIntegerValue;
}

- (NSUInteger) oppTotalScore
{
    NSNumber *     total =
            [self.games valueForKeyPath: @"@sum.theirScore"];
    return total.unsignedIntegerValue;
}
```

@end

and declare them in the header file. That's it.

The model has changed, and PRPasser and PRGame should change accordingly. Where you create a new PRGame, in csvFile:readValues:error:, use teamWith Name:inContext:create: to link up to a PRTeam rather than recording the ourTeam string directly:

```
    newGame.team = [PRTeam teamWithName: values[@"ourTeam"]
                             inContext: moc
                                create: YES];
```

Elsewhere, wherever a team name was referenced through ourTeam in PRGame, refer to team.teamName. For instance, in PRPasser.m:

```
- (NSArray *) teams
{
    return [[self.games valueForKeyPath:
            @"@distinctUnionOfObjects.ourTeam"] allObjects];
}
```

becomes

```
- (NSArray *) teams
{
    return [[self.games valueForKeyPath:
            @"@distinctUnionOfObjects.team.teamName"] allObjects];
}
```

And remember to revert `passerWithFirstName:lastName:inContext:` to the version that looked up `PRPassers` in a particular `NSManagedObjectContext`, instead of keeping one in-memory table for the whole app:

```
+ (NSArray *) existingPassersWithLastName: (NSString *) last
                              firstName: (NSString *) first
                              inContext: (NSManagedObjectContext *) moc
{
    NSParameterAssert(last && last.length > 0);
    NSParameterAssert(first && first.length > 0);

    NSFetchRequest *    req = [NSFetchRequest
                              fetchRequestWithEntityName: @"Passer"];
    NSPredicate *       byName;
    byName = [NSPredicate predicateWithFormat:
             @"firstName = %@ AND lastName = %@",
             first, last];
    req.predicate = byName;

    NSArray *           result = [moc executeFetchRequest: req
                                                    error: NULL];
    //  FIXME: No error handling
    return result;
}


+ (PRPasser *) passerWithFirstName: (NSString *) firstName
                          lastName: (NSString *) lastName
                         inContext: (NSManagedObjectContext *) moc
{
    NSArray *    result = [self existingPassersWithLastName: lastName
                                                 firstName: firstName
                                                 inContext: moc];
    if (result.count > 0)
        return result.lastObject;
    else {
        PRPasser *      retval;
        retval = [self insertInManagedObjectContext: moc];
        assert(retval);

        retval.firstName = firstName;
        retval.lastName = lastName;

        return retval;
    }
}
```

> **Note**
> You'll want to refer to the sample code for the end of this chapter for all the details.

Wiring a Menu

Let's get this thing doing *something* before we go much further. Will MPRDocument load up some sample data (yes, the same .csv sample you labored with on iOS) and display at least some team names?

The first thing to do is to add a menu item to Mac Passer Rating's **Edit** menu to load up a document. Select MainMenu.xib in the Project navigator; Interface Builder will appear with a menu bar at the top of the Editor area (if the bar isn't there, click on the menu icon in IB's sidebar).

If you click a title in the menu bar, the corresponding menu appears. What you want to do is to add an item to the **Edit** menu that will trigger the load. Click **Edit**; you'll find a lot of items having to do with searching and speech that don't fit Mac Passer Rating. Click on each, and press Delete.

While you're at it, delete the **Format** and **View** menus, too; but take care to close the menus before pressing Delete: In the peculiar hierarchy of AppKit menus, the menu bar is a menu; it contains menu *items*, whose contents may themselves be menus. If you try to delete an open **Format** menu (for instance), Xcode will delete the *menu*, but not the menu *item* that contained it. You can tell by the fact that a gap remains in the menu bar where the menu was. Select that and delete it; or close the menu so the Delete key will kill both the item and the menu it contains.

You add a menu item by dragging it from the Object library (in the lower part of the Utility area, third tab) into the menu. Type **menu** into the library's search field. Find "Menu Item," and drag it to the bottom of the open **Edit** menu. See Figure 18.4.

Double-click in the **Item** label, and replace the name with **Fill with Test Data**; and in the blank area at the right end of the menu item, double-click, hold down the Command key, and press **t** to make the key equivalent ⌘ **T**.

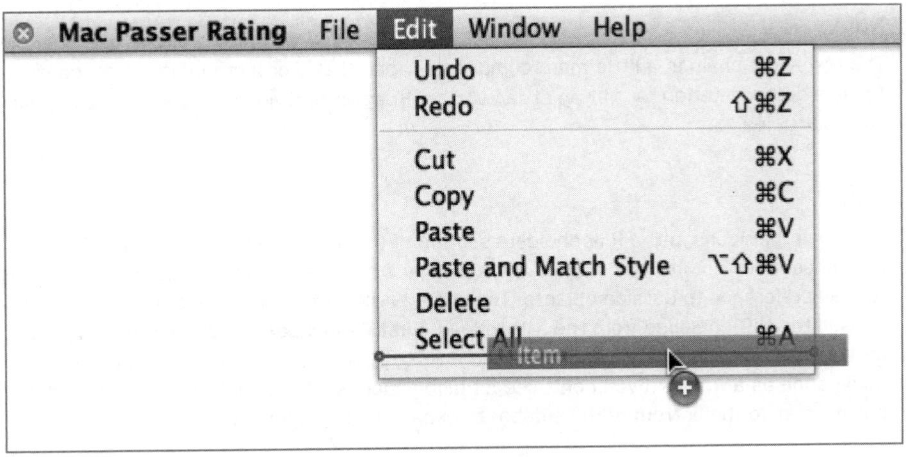

Figure 18.4   Dragging a new menu item into a menu.

> **Note**
>
> When I did this, I held down the Shift key to get what I thought would be a capital T. This resulted in a key equivalent of ⇧⌘T; not what I wanted. I reselected the field and hit Delete; this made the key equivalent **Delete**. This is a good time to make friends with the Attributes inspector, the fourth tab in the upper part of the Utility area. When you have a menu item selected, the top two fields are **Title** and **Key Equivalent**, and the latter has an **x** button to clear it.

Target/Action

Now you want the menu item to do something. As in the iOS app, user-interface elements direct a message (an *action*) at an object (the *target*) when they are triggered. You haven't written the action method yet, but you can make up a name for it: `fillWithData:`.

What about the target? You'll search `MainMenu.xib` in vain for a reference to `MPRDocument`—that's a class that's associated with individual documents, not the application as a whole. To what Cocoa object will you assign the task of responding to `fillWithData:`? *I don't know*, says a stubborn part of your subconscious, *anything that wants to respond to it, I guess.*

This turns out not to be a stupid answer in Cocoa. AppKit keeps a continually updated *responder chain*, a series of potential responders to user actions. The chain begins at the "first responder," which may be the selected view in the front window, and then proceeds to the front window, the window's document, and finally to the application itself. You have probably noticed that the second icon in the Interface Builder sidebar, a red cube, represents the **First Responder**. A user interface control can designate the **First Responder**, whatever it may be at the time, as the target of its action, and AppKit will shop the action up the responder chain until it finds an object that can handle it.

> **Note**
>
> The responder chain is a little more complicated than that. For more information, consult Apple's documentation for `NSApplication`, `NSResponder`, and the related Programming Topics articles.

> **Note**
>
> Like the other icons in the Placeholders section of the Interface Builder sidebar, First Responder does not literally exist in the XIB. It is a *proxy*, a way for objects within the XIB to make reference to outside objects. These are **File's Owner**, which is the object that caused the NIB compiled from the XIB to load; **First Responder**, the current starting point for the responder chain; and **Application**, the `NSApplication` object that embodies the application as a whole. If you don't see a Placeholders section, click the boxed-triangle button next to the bottom of the sidebar to expand it to labeled icons.

First Responder

If you try control-dragging an action link from the new menu item to the **First Responder** icon, you're balked. Interface Builder presents a HUD for the link, asking you to choose the method selector for the desired action. The list it presents does not include `fillWithData:` because you just made that up. Before you can make the link, you have to tell Interface Builder that `fillWithData:` is a possible action.

Interface Builder allows you to do this by editing the properties of the **First Responder** object in the Attributes inspector (fourth tab). Select the **First Responder** icon. The Attributes inspector shows an empty table for user-defined actions that a responder might answer to. Click the **+** button, click the new row to put focus on the table, press Return to make the **Action** label editable, and type `fillWithData:`. The "Type" column presents a popup menu of possible control types that might send that action; you can leave it as `id`, the generic object type, unless you want IB to offer to originate the action from senders of that type only. We don't care. Interface Builder now knows that in this NIB, `fillWithData:` is one of the actions a first responder might perform.

> **Note**
>
> In AppKit, action methods must take one argument: `fillWithData:`, with a colon, not `fillWithData`, without—the names are distinct. If you leave the colon off, IB will supply it.

Now you can control-drag from the new menu item to First Responder, and the HUD will contain `fillWithData:`. The display will even be scrolled close to it, as a rough match for the item's label. Make the connection. See Figure 18.5.

> **Note**
>
> The Connection inspector (sixth tab in the inspector portion of the Utility area) affords another way to make the connection—and to break it. Select First Responder and the Connection inspector. The "Received Actions" section fills with the same long list of actions you saw in the connection HUD when you control-dragged to the FR icon, but it's larger and easier to scroll. Next to each selector is a bubble; dragging from it to the menu item would make the connection, and a label would appear showing where the connection went to. An **x** button next to the connection label lets you break the connection.

Loading Data into `MPRDocument`

Importing the `.csv` file is simple—most of the work was done on the iOS side. Add `sample-data.csv` to the project, declare

```
- (IBAction) fillWithData: (id) sender;
```

in `MPRDocument.h` and put

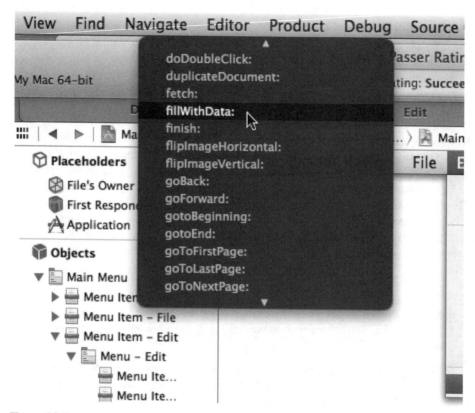

Figure 18.5   Control-dragging from a menu item to First Responder produces a heads-up window that includes `fillWithData:`, the method we had added to the First Responder's repertoire of action methods.

```
#import "PRGame.h"
     .
     .
     .
- (IBAction) fillWithData: (id) sender
{
    NSString *  dataPath =
    [[NSBundle mainBundle] pathForResource: @"sample-data"
                                   ofType: @"csv"];
    [PRGame loadFromCSVFile: dataPath
             intoContext: self.managedObjectContext
                  error: NULL];
}
```

into MPRDocument.m.

Note

Action methods, which respond to triggers from user-interface elements, are by convention given the return type IBAction, rather than void (for which IBAction is a synonym). This signals to Interface Builder that the method should be listed among the actions the class handles. Xcode will put a connection bubble next to any declaration or definition of an IBAction, so you can link it to a control action in Interface Builder.

This is enough for you to see whether the menu command works. Set a breakpoint at the beginning of fillWithData:. Run Mac Passer Rating. With Mavericks' state-restoration feature in place (you can turn it off in the **Options** tab of the Scheme editor's **Run** panel), you'll probably see the document window from your first run; if not, make a new one with ⌘ N. Save the document (anywhere, any name). Then select **Edit → Fill with Test Data (⌘ T)**.

Note

If the command is dimmed (inactive) check MainMenu.xib to see if it's connected to First Responder. AppKit will activate a menu item only if something in the responder chain implements its action method.

Three things will happen. First, the breakpoint you set at the beginning of fillWithData: will trigger, so you know the menu item worked. Second, if you continue, the title bar will add the gray **Edited** flag, to show that the command resulted in a change of the document's contents—even if you can't see it.

The third thing is that the bar graphs for CPU, memory, and energy impact are going wild. I altered sample-data.csv to have tens of thousands of lines, enough to keep Mac Passer Rating busy for a while. Clicking each bar graph gets you a running history on the three scales. See Figures 18.6 through 18.8. They are intended to be lightweight: Unlike Instruments, they don't keep complete statistics for every tick of the clock or event, and you can see only recent history, but it's enough to give you an idea:

- The CPU report (Figure 18.6) shows Mac Passer Rating taking up all of the capacity of one of the cores of the Mac that hosts it. The gauge at upper left shows the current demand on a logarithmic scale, with an arc extending to the maximum observed demand. The pie chart compares its demand to other processes' and the idle time of the other core. The chart at the bottom of the display breaks the demand out into the threads in the application, reflecting that the data load is done on the main thread only.

- The memory report (Figure 18.7) shows a spike in memory demand as data comes in, but it's nothing compared to the capacity of the Mac the application is running on.

- The energy-impact report (Figure 18.8), at least at this stage of execution, is a disaster. The transient gauge is pinned limit-high. Mac Passer Rating has had no recent CPU wakes (though there were ten in the previous second), probably because the continuous running of the app blocked sleep.

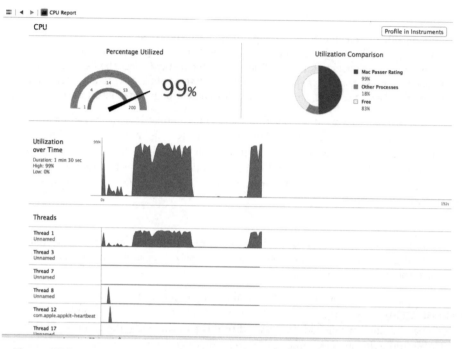

Figure 18.6   As `MPRDocument` is commanded to load a large data file, its demand on the processor essentially saturates it. The allocation pie chart at top right shows Mac Passer Rating consumes half the available capacity (not being threaded, it is confined to only one of the two processor cores).

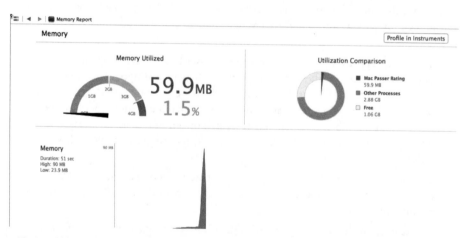

Figure 18.7   Loading a large data set into `MPRDocument` spikes the memory usage of Mac Passer Rating, though it does not take up a significant amount compared to what is available on a MacBook Air, which has much more RAM than an iOS device.

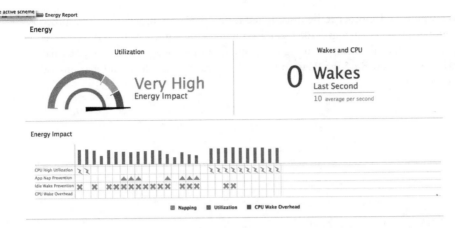

Figure 18.8   The Energy Impact display shows that Mac Passer Rating consumes as much power as an OS X application can. The chart at the bottom of the display demonstrates all the ways the app defeats Mavericks' energy-saving strategies. Not seen are the explanations of the strategies and buttons that will attach Instruments to your app to diagnose exactly these issues.

The chart at the bottom confirms this: All of the bars but one show no significant power drain from waking up the CPU—it's all resource utilization. App Nap, the feature in which Mavericks suspends and reschedules application demand to save energy, never happens. The triangles in the chart show that the app prevented napping several times.

These are summary displays, and lightweight—the data is collected so as to interfere with the operation of the app as little as possible. If you need details, such as millisecond-level assessments of processor demand or event-level memory transactions, with stack traces attached, you need Instruments. (See Chapter 16, "Measurement and Analysis," and Chapter 27, "Instruments.") The reports include a button to relaunch the app in Instruments, using the related template for the trace document.

Summary

This chapter started you off on some new Xcode skills, against the background of an OS X version of the passer-rating project. To do this, you had to go through some conversions: You created a document-based Core Data application, and you imported existing code. On the way, you discovered that Automatic Reference Counting requires changes from a non-ARC code base; I showed how to get Xcode to make those changes itself, and how you can direct and refine the process.

You saw that document-based Mac applications are different from iOS applications in that they are based on at least two separate NIBs, one (`MainMenu.xib`) for the application as a whole, and another to be instantiated for each document window. This posed a conundrum when an app-wide facility—a menu command—had to communicate with a document-specific facility: editing the content of one document among potentially many. You learned how the First Responder proxy in Interface Builder, and the responder chain, bridge the gap.

## 19

Bindings: Wiring an OS X Application

If you have another look at Figure 18.1, you'll see that even in the abbreviated form Mac Passer Rating will take, there will be more than 20 pieces of information distributed across 4 displays, to be filled in, edited (in some cases), and coordinated across updates. This is going to involve some tedious, repetitive code and a lot of communications infrastructure through the network of objects, isn't it?

No. AppKit (the Mac-specific part of Cocoa) offers a facility called *bindings*, supplemented by NSController classes, which are subtle when you first encounter them, but once you master them, they can cut your coding burden by an order of magnitude.

> **Note**
>
> Experienced Mac programmers—and Apple itself—will warn you: Bindings are an advanced topic. If this were a book about AppKit, I'd be taking you through an initial round of doing it the "easy," though verbose, way. My purpose in this book is to show you how to take advantage of Interface Builder's support of bindings, which is a major feature.

We'll start in Interface Builder, to adapt the window for MPRDocument to its purpose in the application. We do this through MPRDocument.xib. OS X has no equivalent to iOS's Storyboard feature, and it would be hard to add it—a mobile application mostly works one full screen at a time, whereas a desktop application can have a complex of windows to manage; the flow is rarely as tree-like as it is in iOS. We'll be working with XIB files, which are well-suited for single windows and views.

Laying Out the Document Window

The skills you'll use in this chapter are much the same as you learned in Chapter 11, "Building a New View," but now you'll go beyond that, to adding and configuring objects that run the links between your data and the screen automatically.

A Table View

First, Mac Passer Rating should have something that can display some data—a simple table to display the names of teams and the total points they and their opponents have scored.

Select `MPRDocument.xib` in the Project navigator; you'll need the Editor area for the window, and the Utility area for the Object library.

For reasons that will become apparent very soon, we *won't* be using autolayout in this XIB. (No, I have not seen the light. Autolayout is almost always the way to go, but there's an alternative.) Select the File inspector (first tab in the Utility area), and uncheck **Use Autolayout**.

Select the **Your document contents here** label in the middle of the document window and press Delete to be rid of it. Type **table** in the Object library's search field, and drag a Table View into the document window you're editing. Make sure you put the table *inside* the window: You want to contain it, not make it a top-level object.

Drag the table to the upper-left corner of the window; it will "snap" to the corner when it's aligned. Next, drag its lower-right corner so it snaps to the lower-right corner of the window. This is more than you need, but it's just to get something working.

This table is going to list team names with their total scores for themselves and their opponents. This will require three columns, and the canned table from the library has only two. With the table still selected, turn to the Attributes inspector (fourth tab), and find. . . attributes for a scroll view.

Many of the views in Interface Builder's library are not simple objects. They represent a hierarchy of views; in this case, a scroll view that contains two scrollers, a table header view, and a table view that contains two columns, each of which has a text-field cell attached to it. (See Figure 19.1.)

There are four ways to navigate this hierarchy. The first is to move your mouse pointer to the object you want to select, and press the mouse button repeatedly until your intended object is highlighted. Each click goes one level deeper. The second is to expand the sidebar to an outline view by clicking the expand/collapse button next to its lower end. You can then click disclosure triangles to expand the view hierarchy to reveal the view you want. Third, you can navigate the whole XIB hierarchy with the jump bar. Finally, you can hold down the Control and Shift keys, and click at the location you're interested in. A popup window will give you a selection of the views under your click. See Figure 19.2.

Pick your method and go one level down from the scroll view to select the table.

The Attributes inspector gives you three levels of settings, for each level in `NSTableView`'s place in the class hierarchy: first as a table view, then as a control view, and finally just as a view. Make these changes to the "Table View" section.

- This table will use cells to draw its contents, not views. Select **Cell Based** from the **Content Mode** popup.
- For **Columns**, set **3**.
- You want columns to have **Headers**, **Resizing** (you can adjust the width by dragging the edge of a header), and **Reordering** (moving columns left and right through the display). Check them all.

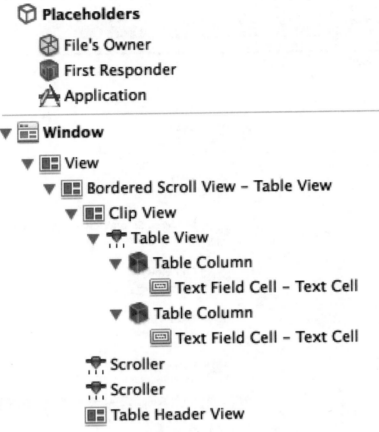

Figure 19.1   The "table view" you dragged into the document window is not as simple as it looked.

- For **Column Sizing**, set **Sequential**. That way, when resizing the table makes it wider, the first column will grow wider until it reaches a maximum width you set, and then the second up to its maximum, and then the third.

Everything else can remain as it is.

So you've set three columns—where's the third? When you resized the table to fill the window, the second (and then-last) column resized to fill the available space. The third column was added to the right, out of sight. Click at the second column—below the header—until it highlights, grab the graphical handle that appears on its right edge, and set it to the size you'll want (remember it only has to accommodate a four- or five-digit total score). That should bring the third column into sight, which you can resize the same way. You should also adjust the first column so it can accommodate team names.

Figure 19.2   Shift-control-clicking on a view in Interface Builder produces a popover window showing all the views that cover that point. Click a row in the window to select a view.

While you're selecting columns, you'll see that the Attributes inspector offers a **Title** field. Name the columns **Team Name**, **Own**, and **Opp**, respectively. The Size inspector (tab 5) is also of interest: You can set the starting, minimum, and maximum widths there.

Note

I made the Team Name column's width 250, with limits of 175 and 400. The two score columns are 100/50/200.

Let's get an idea of how this window will work practically. It's not necessary to run Mac Passer Rating to do this—not much of a consideration now, when the app is so small that it builds and shows a window quickly; but in a big project, you'd like to test the window just on its own.

Select **Editor** → **Simulate Document**. You'll get the window you've been building, with the minimal behaviors the contents can show without being connected to an application: The header titles appear; you can drag at the edges of the column headers to resize them, and they observe their minimum and maximum widths; if you add to the total width of the columns, you can scroll the table from side to side; you can drag columns to reorder them; you can resize the window. . .

Autoresizing

Wait. This isn't right (Figure 19.3). The window resizes, but the table doesn't. It just sits in the upper-left corner of the window, at the same size it had when you created it.

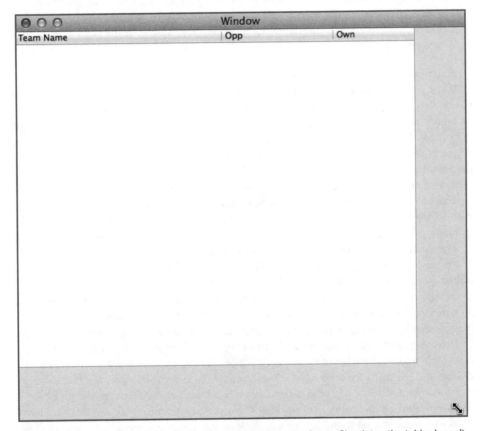

Figure 19.3   When you resize the document window in the Cocoa Simulator, the table doesn't resize with it.

Cocoa has two ways to manage sizing problems like this: You've lived through autolayout, in exhaustive detail, in Chapter 12, "Autolayout in a New View." The other is autoresizing, which has been available on the Mac and iOS from the beginning.

> **Note**
>
> If you quit the Cocoa Simulator and then reopen it, you'll find OS X's state restoration gives you the same window with the same dimensions—and misalignments—you left it with. Close the window before quitting the simulator to have a fresh view of your work.

Autoresizing adjusts the size of a view in relation to its superview (the view that contains it). When the superview changes size, the view is moved and resized automatically. How this is done, on the horizontal axis, is determined by answering three questions:

1. Does the view change its width at all?
2. Does the left edge of the view stick to its position relative to the left edge of the superview?
3. Does the right edge of the view stick to its position relative to the right edge of the superview?

A similar three questions must be answered on the vertical axis.

What you want is for the table to grow or shrink along with the window (so the answer to question 1 is "yes, both horizontally and vertically"); you want it to remain flush with each edge of the window (so the answers to questions 2 and 3 are also "yes," for both ends of both axes).

Select the scroll view enclosing the table view (*not* the table view itself), and bring up the Size (fifth) inspector. The upper part of the inspector contains what you might expect—fields to set the location and dimensions of the view inside its container.

The lower part is graphical: It has an **Autosizing** control with red lines and a square, with which you answer the three questions, and an **Example** view that does a trippy animation showing the effects. See Figure 19.4.

The **Autosizing** control consists of an inner box representing the view, and an outer box representing the superview. The view's box contains two double-headed arrows (called *springs*, for historical reasons); these answer question 1 in each direction. Click an arrow, and it turns from dotted pink to solid red, indicating that the view should resize on that axis. Click on both arrows, and see that the **Example** view shows the view (represented by a red rectangle) resizes in both directions as its animated superview varies.

Surrounding the inner box in the **Autosizing** control are four I-bar lines, extending from each edge to the edge of the superview box. (These are called *struts*.) By default only the top and left struts are solid red—you can see by the **Example** animation that the view stays a constant distance from the superview's top-left corner, while the other distances change proportionally, rather than tracking the superview's edge. Click on the other two struts to require that all four edges should stick to the superview, and see that the view in the **Example** animation resizes in unison with its container.

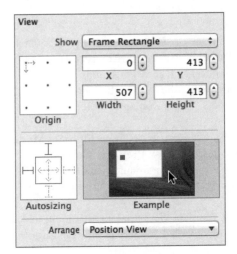
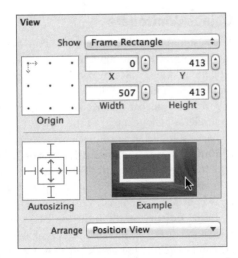

Figure 19.4 The **Autosizing** control determines whether a view can be resized on the horizontal and vertical axes (the inner arrows), and whether each edge keeps a constant distance from its superview's edges (the outer struts). (left) By default, views don't resize, and keep their distances relative to the top-left corner. (right) The scroll view containing the Team table should resize and stick to the window's edges, so the table will always fill the window.

Now run the XIB in the Cocoa Simulator: The table (strictly speaking, its scroll view) resizes along with the window, and (if you set minimum and maximum sizes for the columns) the column widths adjust to fit.

> **Note**
>
> UIKit, on iOS, offers the same autoresizing mechanism as OS X's AppKit, but carefully consider autolayout, especially in light of dynamic typography's disruption of views that depend on text.

Filling the Table—Bindings

The league table is in place, and AppKit has provided some useful services for it, but that does nothing for the actual display. NSTableView supports delegate and data-source methods much like those of UITableView, and for an application like this, we should prefer to use those methods.

But *Xcode 5 Start to Finish* has never let good sense stand in the way of demonstrating an Xcode feature, and it's not beginning now. We're going to use *bindings*, a merger of Key-Value Coding (KVC), Key-Value Observing (KVO), and subclasses of NSController, which will automatically track changes in the model and the view, and propagate the changes between them.

Object Controllers

You're still in MPRDocument.xib. Type **array** in the Object library's search field, which should narrow the list down to "Array Controller," an instance of NSArrayController, which is a kind of NSController that provides automated access to groups of objects. Drag the icon into the Editor view. The controller won't show up in the view, but it will appear in the sidebar under a new category, **Objects**. This is not a placeholder—the controller is literally a part of the XIB.

Make sure the array controller is selected, and use the Attributes inspector to set **Mode** to **Entity Name**, and the **Entity Name** field to Team. Check **Prepares Content**, which tells the array controller that it is responsible for loading instances of the entity. (If we weren't using Core Data, it would authorize the array controller to start off with a new array containing one newly created object.)

In the **Editor** control in the toolbar, select the Assistant view (the one that looks like a formal shirtfront). (The window is probably getting crowded; try hiding the Navigator area and switching the window to full-screen.)

Click the File's Owner icon in the sidebar (MPRDocument is the owner), and make sure the first segment of the Assistant editor's jump bar is set to **Automatic**. This should put either MPRDocument.m or MPRDocument.h in the Assistant view. We want MPRDocument.h. Click one of the arrowhead buttons (or press ∧⌘**Up Arrow**) to step among the candidates.

We want to create an IBOutlet for the array controller. You've seen this before, in the "Outlets and Assistants, in Passing" section of Chapter 11, "Building a New View." Hold down the Control key and drag from the Array Controller icon into the header file, just above the @end directive. When an insertion bar appears where you want it, release the drag, and fill out the resulting popover with the name of the outlet, **teamArrayController**. Click **Create**. See Figure 19.5.

> **Note**
>
> Nobody but MPRDocument cares about the array controller, and we wouldn't ordinarily publish its existence in the public @interface section, but the document template doesn't put the alternative @interface for a class extension into the .m file, and there's no point in creating one just for a demo.

This will not be the only NSArrayController in this XIB; eventually you'll have tables for passers and games, each with their own array controllers, and if you don't do something they will all be listed in the sidebar as "Array Controller." With the array controller selected, turn to the Identity (third) inspector, and type **Team Array Controller** in the **Label** field in the Document section. Be sure to press Return or Tab to commit the change. The outline shows the new label.

Now we start getting into bindings. Bindings rely on Cocoa's *Key-Value Observing* (KVO) protocol. Any object can ask to be notified when any specified property of another object changes. There are many details, conditions, and caveats to that—look up KVO in the Documentation organizer for the authoritative information—but the short of it is that properties of objects, and attributes of Core Data objects, can be observed for changes.

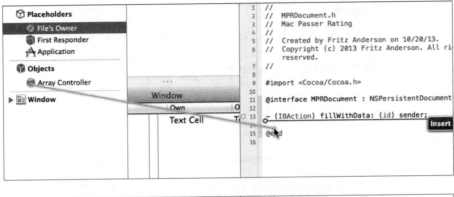

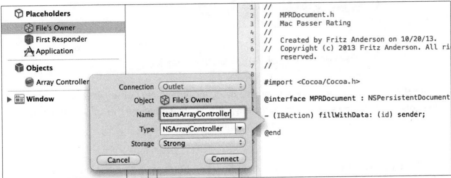

Figure 19.5 (top) Control-dragging from the Array Controller icon into the header file in the Assistant view shows an insertion bar in the class's interface. (bottom) Releasing the drag produces a popover window to create an outlet `@property` holding a reference to the controller.

`NSController` and its specializations, like `NSArrayController`, use KVO to link the values of the objects they manage to user-interface elements. The links go both ways—a model object's values get propagated to the screen as they change, and editing a value on the screen updates the model, automatically. These links are called *bindings*. (Again, this is a gross oversimplification, but it's enough to get you through Interface Builder's support for bindings.)

You've set up what is now Team Array Controller so that it observes objects of the `Team` entity. Where are those objects to be found? In the managed-object context (`NSManagedObjectContext`) of the current document. The array controller has to be told what the context is, and this will be your first binding.

With Team Array Controller selected, go to the Bindings (seventh) inspector. You'll see a list of properties of the array controller that it can take from bindings. You're interested in the last one, "Managed Object Context." Click the disclosure triangle to open it. What you'll see (Figure 19.6) is a relatively simple binding editor; all other binding editors build on these elements.

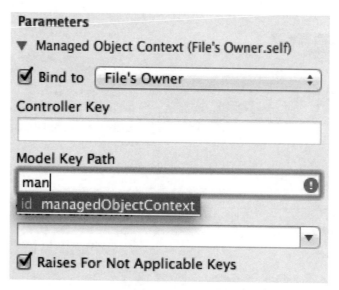

Figure 19.6   The Managed Object Context binding for Team Array Controller shows the common elements of all binding subeditors. Xcode suggests completions from the known names of the properties of the object to be bound to.

- The **Bind to** checkbox determines whether a binding is active at all. Check it.
- The popup next to it gives you a choice of sources for bindings. This will include **File's Owner**, the **Shared User Defaults Controller** (so you can control preferences directly), and any NSController objects in the XIB. Team Array Controller will be pulling its managed-object context from the MPRDocument, so pick **File's Owner**.
- If you had chosen an object controller, you'd specify a **Controller Key**. This setting points to the specific property of the controller that provides the data for this binding. In this case, ignore it.
- **Model Key Path** is the interesting one. You want to draw on MPRDocument's managedObjectContext property. Type that in—Xcode should offer to complete the name before you're finished.
- **Value Transformer** is used for user-interface bindings. A value transformer is like an adapter between one form of data (e.g., whether a property is nil) to another (whether a button should be enabled). It saves having to create additional properties in model objects just to accommodate particular views. You want managedObjectContext to come through unchanged, so leave this blank.
- Check **Raises For Not Applicable Keys**. If it is checked, and the property (model key path) you bind to can't be accessed through Key-Value Coding, AppKit will raise an exception at run time. It's imaginable that you wouldn't want that condition flagged, but usually it's an error, and you'll want to halt when it happens.

Binding the Team Table

Team Array Controller is now set up and ready for use as a broker between Team objects and the user interface. Select the first (Team Name) column of the Team table. You'll see any number of attributes that could be bound for this column, but for the moment, the only thing you care about is how to fill in the names.

> **Note**
>
> Xcode treats these bindings as though they were to the columns themselves, but that isn't true. Few of these properties are properties of table columns. The real links are between individual Team objects in the array controller's array of Teams and each row in that column. Because the bindings are uniform, it's more convenient to treat them as being to the whole columns.

Disclose the "Value" binding, and bind it to Team Array Controller. By default, the **Controller Key** is set to `arrangedObjects`, which is what you want: It's the *controller* outlet that contains all the Teams, net of sorting and filtering. The **Model Key Path** should be `teamName`—that's the Team property the column is to display. If Team Array Controller is hooked up properly (and you're lucky—the feature has always been iffy), Xcode will know the property keys for Team, and it will offer `teamName` as a completion. If the completions don't work, just type in the name of the `@property` or Core Data attribute you want. The rest of the binding editor controls the details of how the column acts as a display and editor for `teamName`. The details are beyond the scope of this book.

Now do the same thing for the second ("Own") column, binding its value to `ownTotalScore`; likewise the third column, to `oppTotalScore`.

Running Bindings

Make sure all the bindings are set up, the **Fill with Test Data** menu item points at `fillWithData:`, and `sample-data.csv` is part of the project, and select **Product →Run (⌘R)**. You should see something like Figure 19.7: A blank window fills with team names and scores at your command. The table sorts when you click a column header. Save the document, then double-click on a team name, and edit it. The gray **Edited** badge appears in the title bar, and if you click it and select **Browse All Versions...**, you're shown the current version alongside the one you saved.

Mac Passer Rating still has a way to go, even for this early milestone, as you'll find if you try to edit one of the scores. The console side of the Debug area will fill with a lusty exception trace, the gist of which is:

```
2013-10-21 15:40:09.397 Mac Passer Rating[7703:303]
    Exception detected while handling key input.
Mac Passer Rating[7703:303] Error setting value for key path
    ownTotalScore of object <PRTeam: 0x6080000b38c0>
    (entity: Team;
    .
    .
    .
    teamName = "Fremont Firebugs";
```

```
})  (from bound object <NSTableColumn: 0x60000009b120>
    identifier: (null)):
    [<PRTeam 0x6080000b38c0> setValue:forUndefinedKey:]:
    the entity Team is not key value coding-compliant
    for the key "ownTotalScore".
```

meaning that ownTotalScore is backed only by a getter (it's a computed property, after all), and not a setter (which is what would have been needed to save the edited value).

It's likely you'll be left hanging with the score cell still open for editing—handling the exception jumped the portion of the code that would have closed it. The application isn't hung; you can, for instance, **Edit → Undo** your typing. But the document is unusable. Use the **Stop** button in the project window's toolbar to kill the app.

The immediate thing to do is go to MPRDocument.xib, select the score columns, and uncheck **Editable** in the Attributes inspector. But the larger question is: How can you get

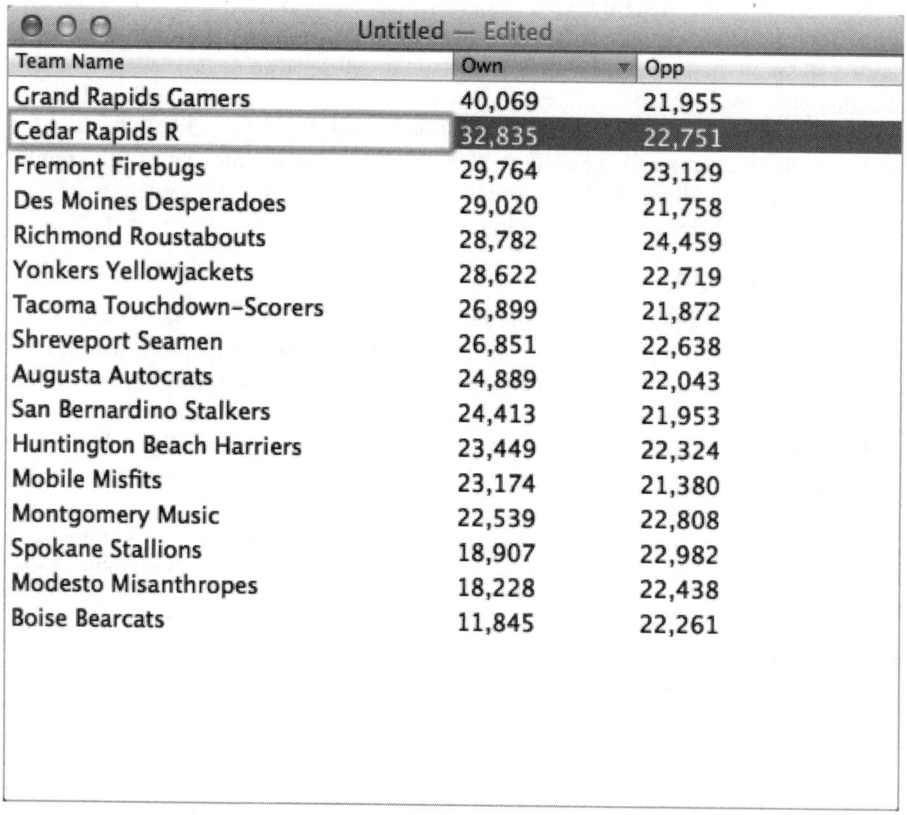

Team Name	Own	▼ Opp
Grand Rapids Gamers	40,069	21,955
Cedar Rapids R	32,835	22,751
Fremont Firebugs	29,764	23,129
Des Moines Desperadoes	29,020	21,758
Richmond Roustabouts	28,782	24,459
Yonkers Yellowjackets	28,622	22,719
Tacoma Touchdown–Scorers	26,899	21,872
Shreveport Seamen	26,851	22,638
Augusta Autocrats	24,889	22,043
San Bernardino Stalkers	24,413	21,953
Huntington Beach Harriers	23,449	22,324
Mobile Misfits	23,174	21,380
Montgomery Music	22,539	22,808
Spokane Stallions	18,907	22,982
Modesto Misanthropes	18,228	22,438
Boise Bearcats	11,845	22,261

Untitled — Edited

Figure 19.7   The first iteration of Mac Passer Rating reads the sample data and displays the Teams. Clicking on column headers sorts the table, and it is possible to edit team names.

a better handle on this kind of error? The technique I'm about to show you is useful, not just for bindings, but for many other breakdowns your app may encounter.

Select the Breakpoint navigator (seventh tab), and click the **+** button at the bottom. Select **Add Exception Breakpoint. . .** from the popup menu. A breakpoint appears—not associated with any part of your code—that will drop you into the debugger, and stop, whenever an Objective-C or C++ exception is thrown. With this, Xcode will interrupt execution at the point at which it happened.

> **Note**
>
> Holding the Option and Command keys down while clicking the new breakpoint will summon a popover offering various options for the breakpoint. Given that some libraries in OS X and iOS rely on the C++ convention of using exceptions as routine flow control, you'll often want to set the **Exception** popup to **Objective-C** only. More on editing breakpoints in Chapter 28, "Debugging."

If you retry this bug, Xcode will jump to the foreground. The stack trace doesn't go through any of your code—bindings are handled completely within AppKit—but the stack trace will be full of references to the binding system. (Move the detail slider at the bottom of the Debug navigator to the right to show more frames from the call stack.)

Use this moment to glean the context of the bug, then click the **Continue** button in the debugger bar until the exception dump appears in the debugger console. Unfortunately, the dump can't be had at the point at which the exception was thrown, which is where you really need it.

> **Note**
>
> Before Mavericks, setting the `NSBindingDebugLogLevel` preference to 1 would get you a more helpful error message than the exception backtrace Core Data would ordinarily throw at you. The easiest way to do this is to add a row to the **Arguments Passed On Launch** table in the **Arguments** tab in the Scheme editor (**Product** → **Edit Scheme. . .** , ⌘ <), and set it to `-NSBindingDebugLogLevel 1`. Mavericks gives you the feature without your having to ask.

> **Note**
>
> An easy way to get a "not key value coding-compliant" exception is to rename a property out from under a binding. If you do the renaming without using refactoring, your XIB still contains a binding that refers to the old name. When you load the NIB, the controller looks for the value in the model object; it isn't there, and you get the exception. Refactoring will automatically edit your XIBs to match the new name. If you must rename by hand, be sure to audit your bindings. The same problem can occur with `IBOutlets`.

Layering `NSControllers`

This is progress, but it's only about a quarter of the way to the app you saw in Figure 18.1. Mac Passer Rating has a cascade of tables, from Team to Passer to Game.

The Team table has shown you're on the right track, and now you can repurpose it into a "source list" at the left side of the window. Select the table in MPRDocument.xib and expose the Attributes inspector. Drop the column count to 1, uncheck **Headers**, and set the **Highlight** style to **Source List** (a blue-gradient background). Click the color well at the left end of the **Background** control, and in the color picker use the gray-scale slider (second tab, pick **Gray Scale Slider** from the popup) to set the table's color to about 80 percent white.

Sizing requires a little work. Select the enclosing scroll view and resize it to a width of about 180 points. Unset the flexible-width spring, and clear the right-edge strut; this will park the view on the left side of the window, resizing vertically with the window, but always keeping its width.

Now drag two labels (type `label` in the Object library's search field) and two tables into the window to the right of the Team list, as shown in Figure 19.8. (I used **Editor →Canvas → Show Layout Rectangles** to highlight the bounds of each element. **Show Bounds Rectangles** would have done the same thing, but it would have shown the actual view boundaries, instead of the visual extents, which is what the Aqua layout standards use.)

Here are a few points you'd keep in mind as you built this window up on your own. Work on them, and then copy the XIB in from the sample code, so you can get back in sync with the book.

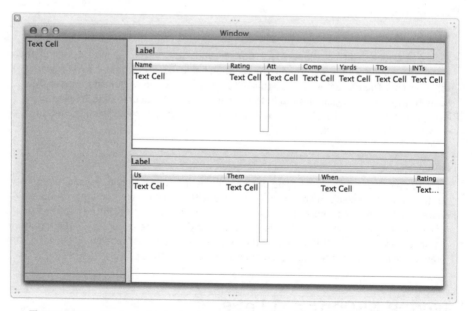

Figure 19.8   The next step in developing Mac Passer Rating is to resize the Team table (on the left) and add labels and tables for Passers and Games. Set **Editor →Canvas → Show Layout Rectangles** to have Interface Builder draw rectangles around the visible extent of the views.

- As you drag and resize the elements, Xcode will pop up blue alignment guides showing where they align with each other, and suggesting offsets and insets to suit the Aqua layout standards. By default, your drags will snap to these guides; use **Editor →Canvas →Snap to Guides** to control it.

- Once your layout is mature, you can turn on **Editor →Canvas →Live Autoresizing** so your general layout is preserved if you have to resize a superview.

- You'll now have three scroll views (one for each table) in the main view, all bearing the same name in the outline sidebar. Select each, and use the Identity inspector, Document section, to set the **Label** to something that will identify each.

- The Passer table (the upper one) is to have one column for the passer name, and then six numeric columns. Use the outline sidebar: Fully expand the items under the Passer table, hold down the Command key, and select those six columns. Now you can use the Size inspector to set the initial, minimum, and maximum widths. (I used 50, 40, and 80.)

- For all columns, uncheck **Editable** in the Attributes inspector.

- Similarly, select the text-cell objects inside each numeric column, and in the Attributes inspector use the Alignment control to set them right-justified (fourth segment).

- The principle is the same for the four columns of the Game table, at the bottom.

- For both the Passer and Game tables, set **Column Sizing** to **Sequential** in the Attributes inspector.

- Set up autoresizing for the Passer table's enclosing scroll view: fixed to left, top, and right, *but not bottom*; flexible in both directions. For the Game table's scroll view, it's fixed left, bottom, and right, *but not top*; flexible in both directions. When a view is flexible on an axis, but not fixed, the unfixed edge will float so that it maintains the same proportion from the corresponding edge of the superview.

- The Passer label should be flexible in width and fixed left, top, and right. The Game label should be the same, but floating both top and bottom.

Note

This is a fair presentation of the *skills* you'd pick up in building this window, but it's terrible as a step-by-step walkthrough of the whole process. By the fifth time I led you through setting the attributes of a text cell, you wouldn't be learning anything new about Xcode. Once you feel you've seen enough, go ahead and copy the completed XIB over from the sample code.

The Passer and Game Array Controllers

You have two tables that display objects based on Core Data entities. You need array controllers. Find "Array Controller" in the Object library and drag two of them into the editor. Use the Identity inspector (Document: **Label**) to give them distinctive names like **Passer Array Controller** and **Game Array Controller**.

The Team Array Controller picked up every `Team` in the `MPRDocument`'s managed-object context. The point of these tables is to display only the passers for the selected team and only the games for the selected passer. The Passer and Game controllers will be focused on very specific collections. How do they know what collections to use?

How Object Controllers Chain

You can start thinking about this by remembering that bindings are two-way streets. The Team Array Controller supplies information to the Team table, but the Team table also sends information back to the Team controller. Specifically, when you select a `Team` in the table, the Team controller records the selection in its `selection` property.

What would the Passer array controller want to know? First, it wants to know that it's handling instances of the `Passer` entity. Second, it wants to know how to get the collection it is supposed to be displaying. You need to tell it that it is to watch the `selection` object of the Team controller, and pull the `passers` set from that object. This is another binding.

First, you have to take care of the fact that in the simple data model I've set up, there is no `passers` relationship in the `Team` entity—it relates to a set of `Games`, and nothing else. So edit `PRTeam.m`, and add a method to provide a `passers` relationship:

```
- (NSSet *) passers
{
    return [self.games valueForKeyPath:
                @"@distinctUnionOfObjects.passer"];
}
```

which will go through all the `games`, find all the `passers`, and report each `Passer` only once. Be sure `Team` publishes the new relationship in `PRTeam.h`:

```
@property(nonatomic, readonly) NSSet *        passers;
```

Select the Passer Array Controller, and open the Utilities area.

1. Start with the Attributes inspector (fourth tab). Set the Object Controller properties to **Entity Name Passer**; check **Prepares Content**. Uncheck **Editable**.
2. Switch to the Bindings inspector (seventh tab), disclose **Controller Content → Content Set**, and bind it to **Team Array Controller**. You're taking your content through the Team controller's **selection** (Controller Key), and from the **passers** attribute (Model Key Path). Turn off **Conditionally Sets Editable**; it overrides the editability setting of the associated UI elements, yielding big surprises as properties inexplicably become editable or not.

   An object controller has a "selection," the single object it currently points to. In the case of NSObjectControllers, which deal only with single objects, this isn't very interesting. NSArrayControllers, though, deal with sets of objects (like a list of teams), and it can be made to present one of them as its selection (such as when you click on a team in a list). Changing the selection changes the team presented to the

Passer Array Controller; because the passer controller draws its list of passers from the selected team's `passers` relationship, its own content list of passers has changed. The passer controller, in turn, has a selection that the user can change; each change propagates down the line of controllers as they are pointed to new sources for their content.

3. Also, bind Managed Object Context to **File's Owner**, key path `managedObjectContext`. (File's Owner isn't an object controller, so it doesn't take a controller key.)

The process for the Game Array Controller is the same, with different values: It controls Game entities. For its content set, it binds to the Passer Array Controller, key **selection**, and pulls the selection's games as its content set. It, too, takes its managed-object context from File's Owner. Conceptually, the controller stack should look like Figure 19.9.

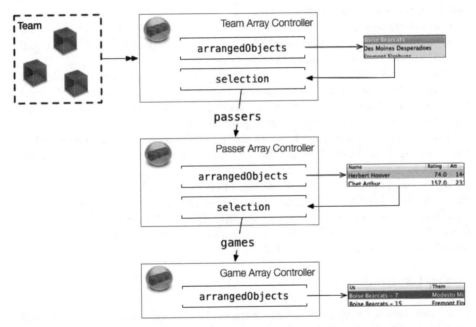

Figure 19.9   The completed network of array controllers. **Team Array Controller**, at top, feeds directly from the Team objects in the document's managed-object context. It sorts and filters the list into `arrangedObjects`, which populates the Team table. Selecting a row in the Team table sets the Team controller's `selection`; the selected Team's `passers` are what **Passer Array Controller** pulls in and assorts into its own `arrangedObjects`, and so on.

Binding the Passer Table

It's time to wire the Passer table to the Passer Array Controller. Start by binding the numeric columns. This isn't much different from what you did for the first draft of the

Table 19.1   **Property Names for the Numeric Columns in the Passer Table**

Column Head	Property
Rating	passerRating
Att	attempts
Comp	completions
Yards	yards
TDs	touchdowns
Ints	interceptions

Team table—bind the Value of each column to Passer Array's controller, through its arrangedObjects, at the key path corresponding to the column. Table 19.1 shows the matchups, which shouldn't surprise you.

I've held out on the first column, the passer's name—one column for a full name, not separate columns for firstName and lastName, which are the attributes defined for the Passer entity. How are you going to fill this column?

The solution the iOS Passer Rating used was to have a computed read-only property, fullName, that concatenated firstName, a space, and lastName. That's simple, and it's probably the right answer; it generates a full name in one place, in code. But I'm going to do it another way to demonstrate another feature of bindings.

Select the Name column, and bring up the Bindings inspector. *Do not* bother with the Value binding. Instead open "Display Pattern Value1." Bind to Passer Array Controller → arrangedObjects → firstName.

When you completed the Value1 binding, a new binding became available: "Display Pattern Value2." Bind to Passer Array Controller → arrangedObjects → lastName.

In both binding editors, you saw a unique field, **Display Pattern**. It is a formatting string; the value that comes from the Value1 binding is substituted into %{value1}@, Value2 into %{value2}@, and so on. Fill the field with

%{value1}@ %{value2}@

which will get you firstName-space-lastName. Don't worry about which editor you should put the format string into; setting one sets them both.

Do the same trick with the label above the Passer table: Bind it to Team Array Controller → selection → teamName, with the format string **Passers for the %{value1}@**.

> **Note**
>
> Bindings even automate special cases for you. Suppose no Team were selected, or the selected Team had no teamName set. You might enter **Passers** in both the **No Selection Placeholder** and **Null Placeholder** fields, and the bindings mechanism would fill the label with that string.

Data Formatters—Numbers

Check your work on the Passer table by running the app. Everything is as expected, but there's a problem. Passer ratings should come with one digit (always) after the decimal point, and the Rating column shows values like 158.3333.... At least the formatter is courteous enough to put in an ellipsis to mark the truncation. See Figure 19.10.

If a bound value is numeric, and you don't specify a format, the bindings mechanism will render it in a generic format. This is fine for the integer stats, but you'd be more particular about the floating-point rating. You want 158.3, not 158.3333.... The solution is to attach a *formatter* object to the Rating column's text cell.

> **Note**
>
> Before Lion (10.7), you'd have gotten into formatters a lot sooner than this. The bindings mechanism did not have a default formatter for numbers; if the bound cell did not have a formatter, and the binding delivered a number (or NSNumber), AppKit would give up and throw an exception.

Type **number** into the Object library's search field to find "Number Formatter." Drag it onto the "Text Cell" label under the header of the Rating column—the cell is

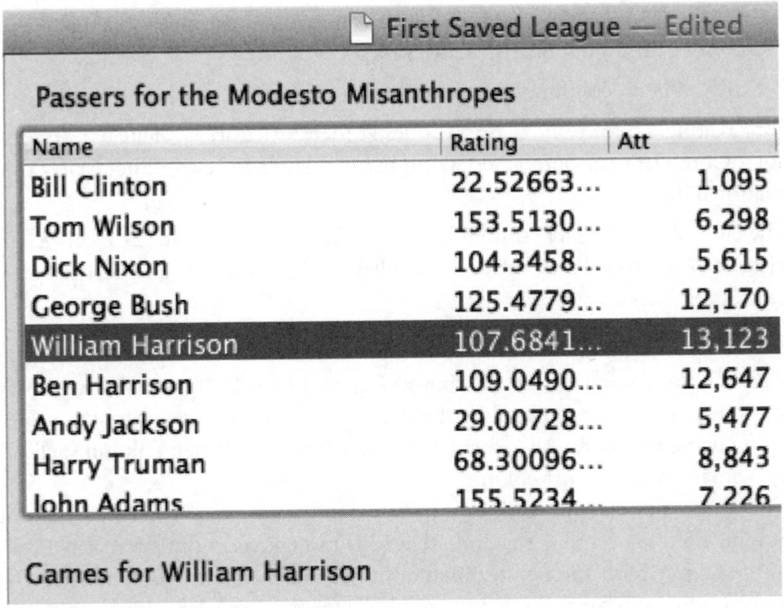

Figure 19.10   The bindings for the Passer table work, but there's a formatting problem with the passer rating.

represented only there, so just dragging into the column won't do. When the cell highlights, drop the formatter on it. The cell label changes from "Text Cell" to "123."

You must now edit the formatter so it renders numbers as you wish. It is not obvious how to do this; the formatter is not represented in the graphical editor. You have to use the outline sidebar, where you'll find the formatter indented under the cell, or the jump bar.

Select the formatter and the Attributes inspector. For **Behavior**, you want **Mac OS X 10.4+ Custom**, because you want to specify the format precisely. You don't have to bother with format strings; just scroll down to **Fraction Digits** and set both **Minimum** and **Maximum** to 1. At the bottom of the editor is a **Sample** view. Type some trial numbers in the **Unformatted** field (you'll have to press Return to commit it), and satisfy yourself that everything that shows up in the **Formatted** field is what you want.

Data Formatters—Strings and Dates

If you got through the Passer table, the Game table is going to be a breeze.

- The first two columns (Us and Them) should each use a display pattern for the team name and the game score: **%{value1}@- %{value2}@**. For the "Them" column, `value1` should be the team name—`theirTeam`—and `value2` should be `theirScore`.
  For the "Us" column, `value2` should be `ourScore`. What about the team name? Game doesn't have a direct reference to it. But that's why the Bindings inspector asks for a "Model Key *Path*." You can trace through relationships and at-sign aggregators, so the key path should be `team.teamName`.

- For the "When" column, use `whenPlayed`.

- For "Rating," `passerRating`. (It doesn't matter that it's a calculated @property, not a Core Data attribute.) Add a number formatter to restrict the display to one fractional digit.

- The label above the table should be the display pattern **Games for %{value1}@ %{value2}@**, from Passer Array Controller → `selection`, `firstName` and `lastName`.

Run Mac Passer Rating to check your progress. There are a couple of problems yet remaining. See the Us and When columns in Figure 19.11: If the team name is very long, the team-and-score value can overflow the column; the column truncates the value with ellipses, obscuring the score. Also, the default format for the When column spells the date out fully, which overflows that column.

For the team columns, the significant parts are the team name (even a part of one) at the beginning, and the score at the end. Text cells can take care of that automatically: Drill down to the text cells for the two team columns (again, the ability to command-click them in the outline sidebar really helps), and look for the **Line Break** popup in the Cell category; select **Truncate Middle**. That will make the columns look like the Them column in Figure 19.11.

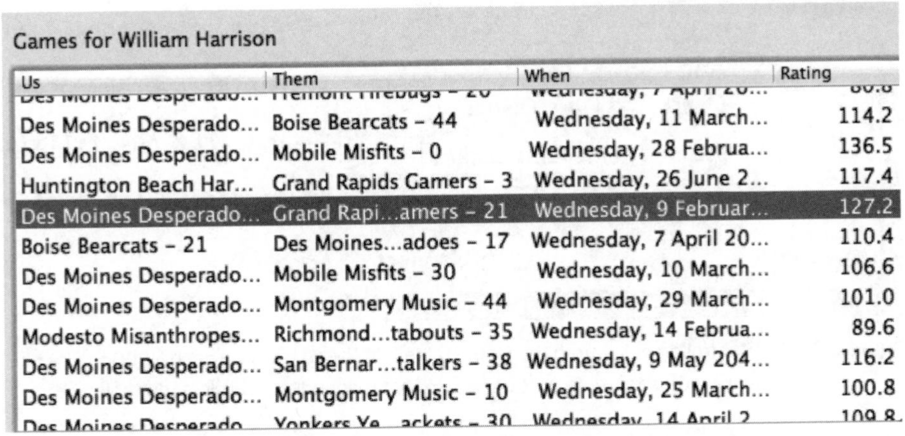

Figure 19.11   The table cell for the Us column was left at its default **Line Break** setting of **Truncate Tail**. When the column gets too narrow, the end of the team name, and the score, are replaced with ellipses. The Them column sets line breaks to **Truncate Middle**, which preserves the score and puts the ellipses where the omission is less significant. Also, the default format for dates is full-text, which is too wide for the When column.

Next select the text cell for the When column. You used a number formatter for the Rating cells, so you've probably guessed there is a date-formatter object as well. Find it in the Object library by typing **date** in the search field, and drag it onto the cell for that column. The **Mac OS X 10.4+ Default** behavior will do because you can select **Long** from the **Date Style** popup.

Running a Popover with Bindings

The plan from Figure 18.1 shows a popover window attached to a row in the Game table. I'm going to run through this quickly—mostly it involves binding work that you know how to do by now—but there are a couple of points to take note of: Setting an `IBAction` to detect a click on the table, and using `NSObjectController` to mediate single objects.

An `NSTableView` is a very complex apparatus, but it descends from `NSControl`, which is very simple. Like a menu item, a control has a target (where to send commands) and an action (the name of the method that handles the command). Different controls trigger their actions on different events—text fields send their action messages when you finish editing them—but tables, like most controls, trigger when you click them.

`MPRDocument.xib` should still be open. You'll need `MPRDocument.h` open in the Assistant editor, which you'll open with the middle segment of the **Editor** control in the toolbar. If the first segment of the Assistant editor's jump bar is set to **Automatic**, you should see `MPRDocument.h`; if you don't, click on File's Owner to get its attention. (For this step, you can hide the Utility area.)

Figure 19.12   Control-dragging from the Game table into the `@interface` in `MPRDocument.h` pops up a window to create an `IBAction` that responds to a click in the table.

You've already created an `IBOutlet` by control-dragging from a UI element to an `@interface`. You're going to do the same thing with an `IBAction` for a table click. Select the Game table (use the outline sidebar—it's easier), hold down the Control key, and drag into the header file so an insertion bar shows just above the `@end` directive. Release, and fill in the popover to describe an `IBAction` named `gameTableClicked:`. See Figure 19.12.

> **Note**
>
> By default, Xcode's linking popover offers an **Outlet**, not an **Action**. Remember to set the **Connection** popup.

A connection bubble, filled, should appear next to the new `IBAction` declaration. (Don't worry about the empty bubble next to `fillWithData:`; remember it's connected by the search up the responder chain for an object to handle the **Fill with Test Data** menu item, and not directly.) Xcode will add a stub for `gameTableClicked:` to `MPRDocument.m`; fill it out like this:

```
@interface MPRDocument ()
@property(strong) NSPopover *    gamePopover;

//  Use IB to link these outlets:

@property(nonatomic, weak) IBOutlet
                    NSArrayController * passerArrayController;
@property(nonatomic, weak) IBOutlet
                    NSTableView * passerTable;
```

```objc
@property(nonatomic, weak) IBOutlet
                    NSArrayController * gameArrayController;
@property(nonatomic, weak) IBOutlet
                    NSTableView * gameTable;
@end
    .
    .
    .
- (IBAction) gameTableClicked: (id) sender
{
    NSInteger      row = self.gameTable.clickedRow;
    //  row is -1 if the click was outside any row

    if (row >= 0) {
        //  Close the popover if one was already visible
        [self.gamePopover performClose: nil];

        //  Create a view controller for the popover's content
        NSViewController *    gvc =
            [[NSViewController alloc]
            initWithNibName: @"MPRGameViewController"
                    bundle: nil];
        //  Ask the array controller for the row'th game
        id      aGame = self.gameArrayController
                        .arrangedObjects[row];

        //  Tell the view controller what game it's to show
        gvc.representedObject = aGame;

        //  Create a popover and fill it with the view controller
        self.gamePopover = [[NSPopover alloc] init];
        self.gamePopover.contentViewController = gvc;
        self.gamePopover.behavior = NSPopoverBehaviorTransient;

        //  Place the popover next to the row, and show it
        NSRect  rowRect = [self.gameTable rectOfRow: row];
        [self.gamePopover showRelativeToRect: rowRect
                                    ofView: self.gameTable
                                preferredEdge: NSMaxXEdge];
    }
}
```

The method picks up three properties. You can figure out how to use Interface Builder to create the gameArrayController and gameTable IBOutlets; and gamePopover is a simple @property.

What about that NSViewController? View controllers are analogous to their counterparts in iOS, though they run single views within a window's hierarchy, rather than a single window-filling view as is typical in iOS. NSPopover is built to support an NSViewController.

For this purpose, everything you need to do can be handled by bindings. There is no need to subclass NSViewController.

First, create a XIB file to describe the popover's view. Use **File** → **New** → **File. . .** (⌘ N), the **User Interface** panel, to create a View XIB, named MPRGameView Controller.xib. Put the file in the Base.lproj directory in the Mac Passer Rating project directory—you'll see why in Chapter 21, "Localization."

Edit the new XIB: Select File's Owner and set the class in the Identity inspector to NSViewController. An NSViewController has a view outlet for the view it controls—make the connection, and when the view controller loads the view's NIB, the loading mechanism will fill view with a pointer to the incoming view.

Add an NSObjectController; you've dealt with NSArrayController before, and this is its superclass, which manages single objects. In the Attributes inspector, the mode is **Class**; the class is **PRGame**; it **Prepares Content**, but is not **Editable**.

The object controller needs an object to manage. In the Bindings inspector, bind Content Object to **File's Owner**, with the model key path representedObject. View controllers come with a generic object pointer, representedObject, that holds the object the view is to display.

The base view is already in the XIB; if you don't see it, click it in the editor's sidebar. This is an instance of NSView, the root class for things that know how to draw and lay themselves out. You're going to use it simply as a container for a group of labels. Drag in labels to match the layout shown in Figure 19.13.

The date is set to System Bold 14; the team names and scores, System 14; and the other labels, System 13.

Don't bother creating any outlets. The whole thing will be done with bindings. The labels and contents in the Figure 19.13 layout should tell you what labels need to be bound to what properties. All of them need to be bound to the appropriate key path for the selection key of the object controller. Remember that the first team name has to be bound to the path team.teamName! See Figure 19.14.

Another Excursion into Autolayout

This time, I *am* using autolayout, in preparation for the Localization chapter.

1. Fix the top line, the date, relative to the left, top, and right edges of the superview. That's your anchor. It defines the top layer of the layout, and the leading and trailing edges are an alignment reference for everything below them.

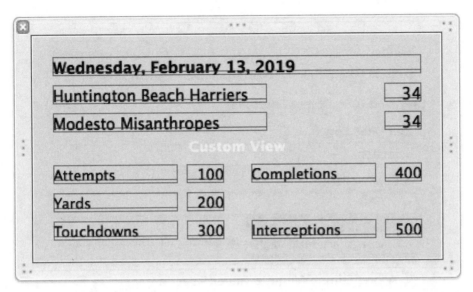

Figure 19.13 The completed layout for `MPRGameViewController.xib`. It's all labels.

2. Go down the left column of labels, aligning their leading edges. The date label has a fixed distance from the leading edge, and the alignment fixes the whole column—if you move the date label, the others will follow it. Fix the vertical space between the labels at the left side of the view, and between the last one (Touchdowns) and the bottom edge of the view.

3. Go down the right column of the date, score, completion number, and interception number labels and align their trailing edges. The date is fixed at a gap from the right side, so the horizontal positioning of all of the other labels is fixed.

4. Across every row of the view, align baselines. That, and the fixed spacing between the labels in the left column, completely determines the vertical placement of all the views.

5. Fix the horizontal spacing between Attempts and 100. Likewise between Completions and 400.

6. Fix the horizontal spacing between 100 and Completions. This determines the gap between the two columns.

7. Align the leading and trailing edges of the number labels (the ones with numeric content).

8. For width, gather the labels in the lower half of the view into two classes:

   - Make all the numeric labels in the lower half of equal width (**Editor →Pin →Widths Equally**).

   - Make all the textual labels (Attempts, Yards, Touchdowns, Completions, Interceptions) of equal width.

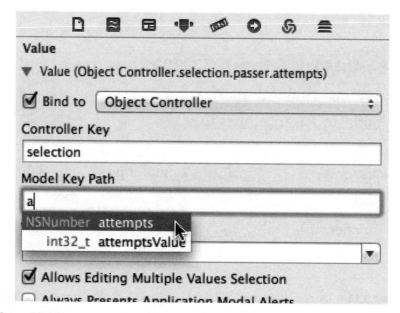

Figure 19.14   With the popover XIB's `NSObjectController` set to handle the `Game` entity, select the numeric label next to "Attempts." The Bindings inspector (seventh tab) offers a **Value** binding. Once you hook it to the object controller, the **Model Key Path** field will lead you through the `Game` keys and even let you trace through the `passer` relationship to the `Passer` attributes.

9. Find all of the width constraints by typing **width** into the search field below the Document Outline. Most of the matches will be those equal-width constraints, but you're looking for absolute-width settings. There should be one on *one* team name, *one* statistics label, and *one* number. That's the width that all the others in their class will assume. Select each of these, and in the Attributes inspector, change the **Relation** from **Equal** to the stated width to **Greater Than or Equal**.

The result is a network of constraints that rigidly determines the placement of the labels and the bounds of the enclosing view. But there is one flexibility: The width of the three classes of label won't go below the greater-than-or-equal size; but if something pushes them out—such as longer contents—they will expand and push the enclosing bounds out.

> **Note**
>
> Once again, the repetition goes on long after it did you any good in learning Xcode. Once you've seen what you've come to see, feel free to pull in the XIB from the sample code.

Running the Near-Final App

Run Passer Rating one more time. You should see the application we plotted out at the start of Chapter 18. As a bonus, if you left the name column of the Team table editable, you can edit the team name and see it propagate through the labels and Game stats (at least the ones that trace through Game's `team` attribute; editing the team has no effect on Game's `theirTeam`).

It's annoying that the tables start in random order. As with many database systems, to-many relationships have no inherent ordering (current versions of Core Data offer it, at the cost of some performance). Array controllers have a `sortDescriptors` property that lets you specify an initial ordering of their contents. This method, added to `MPRDocument.m`, assigns sort descriptors to the controller objects:

```
- (void)windowControllerDidLoadNib:(NSWindowController
                                     *)aController
{
    [super windowControllerDidLoadNib:aController];

    // Sort teams by name
    self.teamArrayController.sortDescriptors = @[
                    [NSSortDescriptor
                        sortDescriptorWithKey: @"teamName"
                                    ascending: YES]
                                                    ];

    // Sort passers by last name, first name
    // If you don't have a passerArrayController property,
    // go to MPRDocument.xib and control-drag from Passer
    // Array Controller and establish the link.
    self.passerArrayController.sortDescriptors = @[
        [NSSortDescriptor sortDescriptorWithKey: @"lastName"
                                     ascending: YES],
        [NSSortDescriptor sortDescriptorWithKey: @"firstName"
                                     ascending: YES]
    ];
    // Sort games by date
    self.gameArrayController.sortDescriptors = @[
        [NSSortDescriptor sortDescriptorWithKey: @"whenPlayed"
                                     ascending: YES]
        ];
}
```

The user can still re-sort the table by clicking on column headers.

Summary

Bindings are a tremendous convenience in OS X programming, and even this long chapter can't cover everything. In this chapter, I gave you an introduction to what bindings can do for you, but more to the point, I showed what Xcode can do to support them. It is *possible* to set up bindings in code, but Interface Builder is indispensable to getting them right, easily (comparatively) and quickly.

I showed you how bindings and formatters can render your data in forms that your model classes don't directly support, saving you from having to alter your model to accommodate per-view variations in presentation.

You also saw how to set up autoresizing, the original, simple (but inflexible) technique for adjusting the size and placement of views as their superviews are resized.

You used number and date formatters, and truncation controls, to control how information is presented in table cells and labels.

Finally, you created a XIB for a complex data view that, thanks to bindings, didn't need any code at all.

## 20

A Custom View for OS X

Let's extend Mac Passer Rating by one more step, and in the process see how to handle custom classes in Interface Builder. In this chapter, I'll add another popover, to be shown when you double-click a row in the MPRPasser table. The popover will show a simple scrolling bar graph comparing MPRPass attempts and completions, by game.

You already know how to create and populate an NSPopover. The popover needs an NSViewController. It turns out that the view controller will have to do a little bit of work, so you'll need to use **File → New → File...** (⌘ N) to create an Objective-C subclass of NSViewController named MPRPasserGraphController. (Be sure to use the OS X section of the New File assistant, so you can get the benefit of the view-controller template.) Check the box labeled **With XIB for user interface**; OS X development entails a lot of XIBs.

> **Note**
>
> Xcode 5's Interface Builder has its own format for XIB and storyboard files that's incompatible with Xcode 4 and earlier. If you must share a project with someone who is still using Xcode 4, you should go to the File inspector (first tab in the Utility area) and set the **Opens in** popup to **Xcode 4.6**. And if you're still using Xcode 4, it's probably because you need an SDK earlier than iOS 7. The **Build for** popup follows to whatever the project's deployment system is. Change it to the specific OS you're targeting. It's a shame, because falling back to the Xcode 4 format forces you back to the nearly unusable system for managing autolayout constraints.

This gets you header and implementation files, and a XIB. Select MPRPasserGraphController.xib to find that you already have an empty custom view. The template is smart enough to set the class of File's Owner (select it and choose the Identity inspector) to MPRPasserGraphController.

Drag another custom view (search the Object library for **custom**) inside the root view, and snug its edges against the root's sides. (This will make sense soon.) Use the Identity inspector to set its class to MPRPassCompletionView. Xcode won't offer to complete the name for you because you haven't defined it yet.

With the `MPRPassCompletionView` still selected, issue **Editor →Embed In →** **Scroll View**. The `MPRPassCompletionView` is now wrapped in a scroll view—expand the sidebar to the outline view (or navigate in the jump bar) to see it, as it's hard to make out visually with all three views being the same size. Select the scroll view and, in the Attributes inspector, uncheck **Show Vertical Scroller**.

> **Note**
>
> The origin (**X**, **Y**) settings for the views in the Size inspector (fifth tab) may be confusing. The scroll view, and most of the views it contains, fill their superviews. In iOS, this meant an origin of {0, 0}. OS X traces its origins to the Display PostScript engine used for NeXT displays, and PostScript uses mathematical Cartesian coordinates: Positive x and y are in the upper-right quadrant, and the origin is at lower-left. The **View** panel in the Size inspector includes an **Origin** control; select any of the dots to measure the **X** and **Y** placement of that point in the view. Imagine a view that fills its 100-by-100 superview. Clicking the dot for the view's origin corner will show the **X** and **Y** coordinates as zero-by-zero; but if you click the dot in the middle, it shows the middle is at 50-by-50 relative to the origin of the superview. See Figure 20.1.

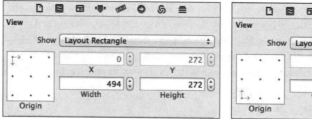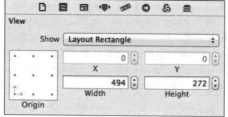

Figure 20.1   The **X** and **Y** coordinates of a view's origin are calculated relative to the bottom-left corner of the superview in OS X. If the **Origin** control in the Size inspector is set the way it would be for iOS (left), the **Y** origin will be shown as equal to the height of the view (assuming the view is set to fill its superview). Clicking the bottom-left corner of the **Origin** control shows the {0, 0} coordinates you'd expect.

Choose the Assistant editor and click on File's Owner to focus it on `MPRPasserGraphController.m`. Control–drag from the `MPRPassCompletionView` into the class–extension `@interface` to create:

```
@interface MPRPasserGraphController ()
@property (weak) IBOutlet MPRPassCompletionView *completionView;
@end
```

`clang` will complain that it has never heard of `MPRPassCompletionView`. Add

```
#import "MPRPassCompletionView.h"
```

to the top of `MPRPasserGraphController.m`. It won't help—you've just traded the undefined-class error for a missing-header error—but now's the time to do it, while it's on your mind.

That's the end of the first cycle with `MPRPasserGraphController`.

A Graphing View

I've begged the question of what `MPRPassCompletionView` is. Create a new Objective-C subclass of `NSView` with that name. You get header and implementation files. `MPRPassCompletionView` will use the delegate pattern to pull its data from the model. That requires a `@protocol` to define the method through which the delegate will provide the data. Put this in `MPRPassCompletionView.h`:

```
#import <Cocoa/Cocoa.h>

@class MPRPassCompletionView;

@protocol MPRPassCompletionDelegate <NSObject>

- (NSManagedObject *) MPRPassCompletion: (MPRPassCompletionView *) view
                       gameAtIndex: (NSUInteger) index;

@end

@interface MPRPassCompletionView : NSView

@property(nonatomic, assign) IBOutlet id<MPRPassCompletionDelegate>  delegate;

@property(nonatomic, assign) CGFloat        cellWidth;
@property(nonatomic, assign) NSUInteger     attRed;
@property(nonatomic, assign) NSUInteger     attGreen;
@property(nonatomic, assign) NSUInteger     attBlue;
@property(strong) NSColor *                 attColor;
@property(nonatomic, assign) NSUInteger     compGreen;
@property(nonatomic, assign) NSUInteger     compRed;
@property(nonatomic, assign) NSUInteger     compBlue;
@property(strong) NSColor *                 compColor;

@property(nonatomic, assign) NSUInteger     gameCount;

@end
```

> **Note**
>
> That's a lot of properties. I'll get to them soon.

`MPRPassCompletionView.m` involves a lot of detailed drawing and preparation. I'll just summarize it here; the complete file is in the sample code:

```objc
//  ... Incomplete; see the sample code for the full implementation ... //

- (id) initWithFrame: (NSRect) frame
{
    self = [super initWithFrame: frame];
    if (self) {
        NSColor *      theColor;
        // Default colors:
        // Attempts in a pale blue
        theColor = [NSColor colorWithCalibratedHue: .67
                                        saturation: 0.6
                                        brightness: 1.0
                                             alpha: 1.0];
        self.attColor = theColor;

        // Completions in a darkish red
        theColor = [NSColor colorWithCalibratedHue: 0.0
                                        saturation: 1.0
                                        brightness: 0.5
                                             alpha: 1.0];
        self.compColor = theColor;
        self.cellWidth = 15;
    }
    return self;
}


- (void) awakeFromNib
{
    //  If the completion or attempt colors are set, capture them.
    if (self.compRed || self.compGreen || self.compBlue) {
        self.compColor =
            [NSColor colorWithDeviceRed: (self.compRed / 255.0)
                                  green: (self.compGreen / 255.0)
                                   blue: (self.compBlue / 255.0)
                                  alpha: 1.0];
    }
    if (self.attRed || self.attGreen || self.attBlue) {
        self.attColor =
            [NSColor colorWithDeviceRed: (self.attRed / 255.0)
                                  green: (self.attGreen / 255.0)
                                   blue: (self.attBlue / 255.0)
                                  alpha: 1.0];
    }
    //  A cheat:
    //  Have Interface Builder set up autoresizing,
    //  and have autolayout convert those settings into constraints.
    self.translatesAutoresizingMaskIntoConstraints = YES;
}


//  Distance between cells:
#define CELL_PADDING    2.0
```

```
//  Margin around the graph:
#define GRAPH_PADDING    6.0
//  Height limit for attempt bars:
#define MAX_ATTEMPTS      50

- (void) recalculateFrame
{
    NSUInteger  cellCount = self.gameCount;
    if (cellCount < 10)
        cellCount = 10;

    NSRect        workingFrame = self.frame;
    workingFrame.size.width = 2 * GRAPH_PADDING +
            cellCount * (2 * CELL_PADDING + self.cellWidth);
    self.frame = workingFrame;
    [self setNeedsDisplay: YES];
}

- (void) setCellWidth: (CGFloat) newCellWidth
{
    if (cellWidth != newCellWidth) {
        cellWidth = newCellWidth;
        [self recalculateFrame];
    }
}

- (void) setGameCount: (NSUInteger) newGameCount
{
    if (gameCount != newGameCount) {
        gameCount = newGameCount;
        [self recalculateFrame];
    }
}

//  Distance between cells:
#define CELL_PADDING     2.0
//  Margin around the graph:
#define GRAPH_PADDING    6.0
//  Height limit for attempt bars:
#define MAX_ATTEMPTS      50

- (void) drawRect: (NSRect) dirtyRect
{
    CGFloat      maxBarHeight =
    self.bounds.size.height - 2 * GRAPH_PADDING;
    NSRect       backgroundRect = self.bounds;
    [[NSColor lightGrayColor] setFill];
    [NSBezierPath fillRect: backgroundRect];

    backgroundRect = NSInsetRect(backgroundRect,
                        GRAPH_PADDING, GRAPH_PADDING);
```

```
[[NSColor whiteColor] setFill];
[NSBezierPath fillRect: backgroundRect];

CGFloat       pixPerAttempt = maxBarHeight / MAX_ATTEMPTS;

for (NSUInteger index = 0; index < self.gameCount; index++) {
    //  For each of the MPRPasser's games...
    //  get this column's game from the delegate
    NSManagedObject *       game;
    game = [self.delegate MPRPassCompletion: self
                                gameAtIndex: index];
    NSRect  barRect;
    NSUInteger  stat;
    //  Calculate the bounds of the attempts bar
    barRect.origin.x = GRAPH_PADDING +
                index * (CELL_PADDING + self.cellWidth);
    barRect.origin.y = GRAPH_PADDING;
    barRect.size.width = self.cellWidth;

    //  Use Core Data to pull in the number of attempts
    stat = [[game valueForKey: @"attempts"]
            unsignedIntegerValue];
    stat = MIN(stat, MAX_ATTEMPTS);

    barRect.size.height = stat * pixPerAttempt;

    //  Fill the bar with the "attempt" color
    [self.attColor setFill];
    [NSBezierPath fillRect: barRect];

    //  Put a (shorter) bar with the {"completion" color in front of it.
    NSUInteger      completions;
    completions = [[game valueForKey: @"completions"] unsignedIntegerValue];
    stat = MIN(completions, MAX_ATTEMPTS);
    barRect.size.height = stat * pixPerAttempt;
    [self.compColor setFill];
    [NSBezierPath fillRect: barRect];
}
}
```

The result can be seen in Figure 20.2. Not fancy, but good enough for a demo.

Back to the View Controller

With MPRPassCompletionView defined, you can fill the gaps in
MPRPasserGraphController. As an NSViewController, it has a
representedObject property to refer to a model object that supplies its content. As a
controller, it acts as an intermediary between the represented model object and its views.

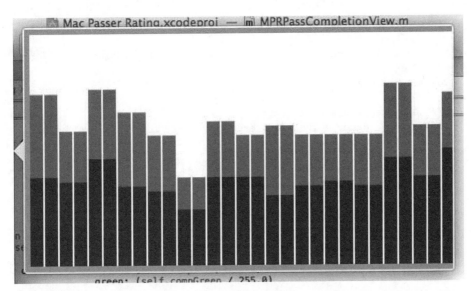

Figure 20.2 The `MPRPassCompletionView` graph is not elaborate, but it does the job of comparing one quantity as a fraction of another.

It should keep a reference to an `MPRPassCompletionView` and be that view's delegate, supplying it with `PRGames`.

All of which is to say that `MPRPasserGraphController.h` should look like this:

```
#import <Cocoa/Cocoa.h>
#import "MPRPassCompletionView.h"

@interface MPRPasserGraphController : NSViewController
                                <MPRPassCompletionDelegate>
@end
```

`MPRPassCompletionView.h` has to be `#imported` to tell `clang` about the `MPRPassCompletionDelegate` protocol, which the declaration of `MPRPasserGraphController` promises to implement.

`MPRPasserGraphController.m` is nearly as simple; notice that now you've promised to implement `MPRPassCompletionDelegate`, `clang` posts a warning to complain that you haven't done it yet:

```
#import "MPRPasserGraphController.h"

@interface MPRPasserGraphController ()
@property (weak) IBOutlet MPRPassCompletionView *completionView;
@property (nonatomic, strong) NSArray *              gameArray;
@end
```

```
@implementation MPRPasserGraphController

//  ... incomplete; see the sample code for the full listing ...  //

- (void) awakeFromNib
{
    //  Get the MPRPasser's games
    NSSet *     games = [self.representedObject valueForKey: @"games"];
    //  Sort them by date
    self.gameArray =
        [games sortedArrayUsingDescriptors: @[
            [NSSortDescriptor sortDescriptorWithKey: @"whenPlayed"
                                          ascending: YES]]];
    //  Let the graph view know how many games there are
    self.completionView.gameCount = self.gameArray.count;
}


#pragma mark - MPRPassCompletionDelegate

- (NSManagedObject *) MPRPassCompletion: (MPRPassCompletionView *) view
                            gameAtIndex: (NSUInteger) index
{
    return self.gameArray[index];
}

@end
```

...just enough to set up a list of games and parcel them out to the graphing view.

Complete the completion-graphing package by returning to
MPRPasserGraphController.xib. You've defined MPRPassCompletionView's
delegate and MPRPasserGraphController's completionView to be IBOutlets,
so you can hook them up in Interface Builder.

- Control-drag from the graph view to File's Owner, and select **delegate** from the
  HUD. The MPRPassCompletionView is buried pretty deep in the hierarchy;
  you'll find it easiest to drag from its entry in the Document Outline.

- Make sure File's Owner's completionView outlet is connected to the graph view;
  that's the view MPRPassCompletionView will use to access the specific methods
  of the subclass.

Using MPRPasserGraphController

The pass-completion graph package is finished. Here's how you use it.

1. In MPRDocument.m, add a passerPopover @property to the class extension
   (the abbreviated @interface at the top of the file). The extension should now
   look like:

```
@interface MPRDocument ()
@property(strong) NSPopover *              gamePopover;

// Use IB to link these outlets:
@property(nonatomic, weak) IBOutlet
            NSArrayController *      passerArrayController;
@property(nonatomic, weak) IBOutlet
                                    NSTableView * passerTable;

@property(nonatomic, weak) IBOutlet
            NSArrayController *      gameArrayController;
@property(nonatomic, weak) IBOutlet
            NSTableView *           gameTable;

@property(strong) NSPopover *    passerPopover;
@end
```

2. Turning to `MPRDocument.m`, add to the top:

   ```
   #import "MPRPasserGraphController.h"
   ```

3. The `-windowControllerDidLoadNib:` method already sets up the sort descriptors for the Passer and Game tables. Add these lines to the end:

   ```
   // You can't wire the double-click action in Interface Builder,
   // so you have to do it in code:

   self.passerTable.doubleAction = @selector(passerTableClicked:);
   self.passerTable.target = self;
   ```

4. ...which obliges you to supply a `passerTableClicked:` method (clang has already posed a warning on the undefined `@selector`):

   ```
   - (IBAction) passerTableClicked: (id) sender
   {
       NSInteger      row = self.passerTable.clickedRow;
       if (row >= 0) {
           [self.gamePopover performClose: nil];
           [self.passerPopover performClose: nil];

           // Create a graph controller
           MPRPasserGraphController *    pgc =
                   [[MPRPasserGraphController alloc]
                       initWithNibName: @"MPRPasserGraphController"
                           bundle: nil];

           // Get the passer corresponding to the double-clicked row
           id      passer =
                   self.passerArrayController.arrangedObjects[row];
   ```

```
    // and point the graph controller at it
    pgc.representedObject = passer;

    // Set up the popover
    self.passerPopover = [[NSPopover alloc] init];
    self.passerPopover.contentViewController = pgc;
    self.passerPopover.behavior = NSPopoverBehaviorTransient;

    // Show the popover next to the double-clicked row
    NSRect      rowRect = [self.passerTable rectOfRow: row];
    [self.passerPopover showRelativeToRect: rowRect
                                    ofView: self.passerTable
                             preferredEdge: NSMaxXEdge];
    }
}
```

Run Mac Passer Rating, and find that if you double-click on a passer in the Passer table, a lovely scrolling game-by-game graph of completions appears in a popover window. See Figure 20.3.

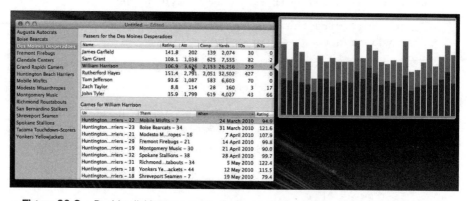

Figure 20.3   Double-clicking on a row in the Passer table reveals a popover window with a scrolling bar graph comparing passing attempts to completions for that passer.

QuickLook in the Debugger

If you looked closely at the -initWithFrame: and -awakeFromNib methods for MPRPassCompletionView, you saw that I did something a bit strange with the colors for the attempt and completion bars. In this section and the next I'll show you why, using the QuickLook feature to inspect the colors directly.

In Xcode 4, with the currently executing method in the Editor window, you could hover the mouse pointer over a variable and see a *data tip* showing the value the variable held. Scalars were displayed directly, and structs and objects got disclosure triangles so you could examine the member variables. Xcode 5 adds *QuickLook* to the data tips.

The data tip view now consists of the same display of type, value, and disclosure triangle. In some cases, such as NSRect, there might be a formatted summary. The two new features are QuickLook, offered though an eye button, and info, shown as an *(i)* button.

> ### Note
> QuickLook is also available in the Variables view; the eye and *(i)* buttons are at the bottom of the view. Select a variable, or the members of structs and objects, and click one of those buttons.

Info is straightforward: It reveals a popover window containing what you'd see in the debugger console if you used expression or po to examine it. In fact, the same output appears in the console when you use the feature. The info button in the variables pane prints to the console without a popover.

In most cases, QuickLook is less useful. Click the eye button, and you'll see a popover with the name of the variable, its type, and a badge indicating what kind of variable it is (local, global, etc.).

For some values, however, QuickLook is something special: For NSRect or CGRect, color objects, Bézier paths, and images, the QuickLook popover will show a graphical representation of the value (Figure 20.4). In the case of the color setting in

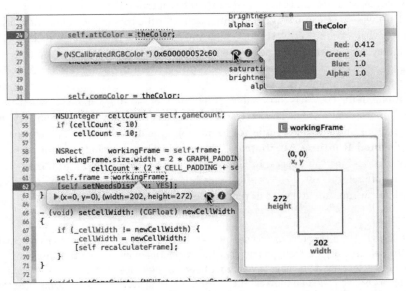

Figure 20.4   For some values, the QuickLook button in the data tip popover will provide graphical representations of a variable's value, such as a swatch for a color object (top), or a layout of the extent of a rectangle (bottom).

-initWithFrame:, it meant breaking the color value out into a local variable (you can't inspect the results of getters), but being able to visualize a color *before* it is drawn is invaluable.

Custom View Properties

Before Xcode 4, Interface Builder supported plugins: Because NIBs are archives of Objective-C objects, they aren't restricted to views—you've already seen that they can carry NSController objects. The plugin architecture allowed developers of custom views to load, display, edit, and save those views directly from Interface Builder. It was a great feature.

Xcode 4 was a top-to-bottom rewrite, and in 2010, the culture had changed: In 1995, allowing third-party code into the same execution space as critical software allowed for some nifty tricks. Plugins did not make it into Xcode 4.

As Xcode 4 developed, it gradually restored Xcode 3 features that had been lost, but there are good reasons not to include plugins: Apple has become sensitive to admitting arbitrary code to its software. It's a security hole, it commits them to an application architecture they want the freedom to change, and it adds to their support burden. Don't expect Xcode plugins to return. If you want to add a custom view to your application, get used to seeing it as a gray rectangle.

The door was not completely shut: Thanks to Key-Value Coding, it's not hard for the NIB-loading mechanism to initialize object variables from values carried in the NIB. That's why MPRPassCompletionView exposes properties like attRed, attGreen, and attBlue, which we can use as color components for the bars in the completion history.

That's what -awakeFromNib does. Like any instance variables of an Objective-C object, they start at zero. If any component of the attempt (or completion) color is non-zero, -awakeFromNib instantiates an NSColor from them and sets attColor (or compColor) accordingly.

Nothing in the code sets those values. They are there so they can be set when MPRPasserGraphController.xib is loaded. Select the completion-graph view in the XIB, and look at the Identity inspector (third tab). One of the sections in the inspector is **User Defined Runtime Attributes**, a table to which you can add rows for property keys, values, and the value types. In Figure 20.5, you see that attRed, attGreen, and attBlue are set to {200, 255, 200}, which is an unattractive pale green, but it stands out enough at run time to assure us that, indeed, the values made it through.

> **Note**
>
> The keys in the attributes, as you see, are *key paths*. You aren't restricted to properties of the selected object itself; you can set the attributes of any object that you can trace from the selection. If you have a view that keeps a reference to one of its subviews, say stopLight, you can use the key stopLight.middleLight.color to initialize the color from the NIB.

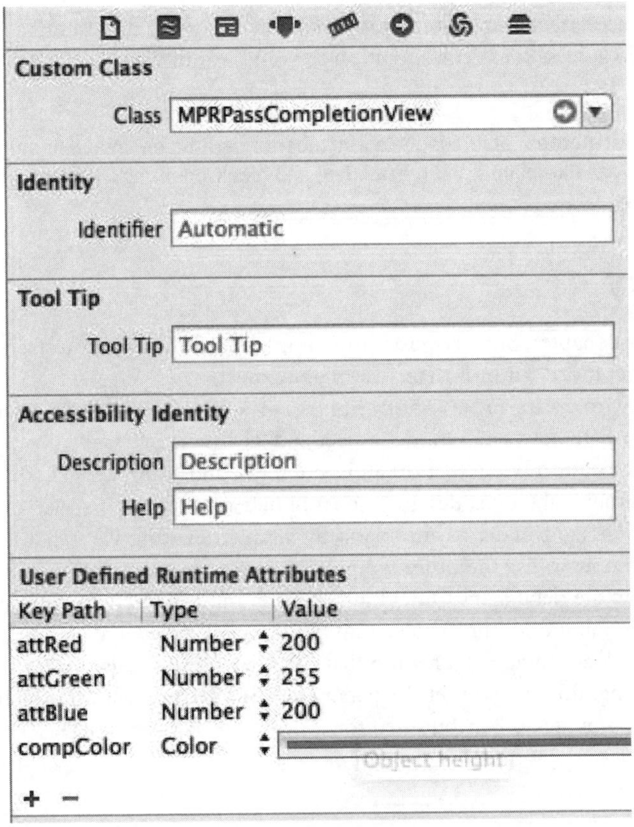

Figure 20.5   Thanks to **User Defined Runtime Attributes**, it is possible to color attempts in an unattractive viridian, and completions in a ghastly pinkish-orange.

> **Warning**
>
> Runtime attributes are one of many examples of a XIB or storyboard recording the name of one of an object's attributes. As we saw in Chapter 19, "Bindings: Wiring an OS X Application," if the attribute goes away, the references from the IB products are orphaned: When they are loaded at runtime, the loader will attempt to hook them up, find they aren't there, and throw an exception. This can be hard to debug; be on the lookout. You can mitigate this, in the case of renamed attributes, by using **Edit → Refactor → Rename...**, which is smart enough to reach into IB files.

It wasn't necessary to provide RGB outlets for the colors. The `attColor` and `compColor` properties are exposed to KVC. The user-defined attributes table accepts color values, and the NIB will set them directly when it is loaded. At the bottom of Figure 20.5, you see `compColor` set to an even less attractive pinkish-orange.

The combined effect is appalling, but it's convincing proof that Interface Builder will allow you to do at least some configuration to your custom views.

> **Note**
>
> The runtime-attributes table supports a number of data types, including numbers, basic geometric types like points and rectangles, and localized strings. The popup tells the whole story.

Summary

This was a short chapter, but I covered some important features of Interface Builder, and how you can get more out of it than you might expect.

You saw how to create an `NSViewController` subclass with a XIB for its contents and code to mediate between a model object and its views.

You created a custom view that draws its contents, and you renewed your acquaintance with the near-universal Cocoa design pattern of delegation.

You used Interface Builder to automatically wrap an existing view in a scroll view, and you considered how to use the other wrapping commands in your development.

You saw how the debugger's QuickLook feature unmasks data structures that previously you couldn't examine until they showed up (you hoped) on screen.

And, you took advantage of a feature that, while it doesn't make up for the lack of true interactive editing, does let you set the parameters of a XIB object for which Interface Builder doesn't provide an Attributes editor.

## 21

Localization

I'm pretty satisfied with Mac Passer Rating, at least as an example, but what would really make it perfect would be if I could see it in French (they play football in Québec)—an application named Quart-Efficacité. Users of OS X specify what languages they understand by setting a list of available languages in order of preference in the **Language** tab of the **Language & Region** panel of the System Preferences application. When a user's list sets French at a higher priority than English, I'd like MPR to present menus, alerts, and labels in the French language.

> **Note**
> The localization techniques I'll show you are identical to the ones you'd use for an iOS app.

How Localization Works

Cocoa applications load resources through the NSBundle class. When asked for a resource, NSBundle first searches the subdirectories of the application bundle's Resources directory in the order of the user's preferences for language. Language subdirectories are given such names as English.lproj, fr.lproj, or en-GB.lproj; plain-text language names are now deprecated; you should use ISO-standard language abbreviations, optionally suffixed with a code to identify a regional variant.

If a directory that matches the user's language and region (such as fr-CA.lproj for Canadian French) can't be found, OS X falls back to the language-only variant (fr.lproj); then so on, down the list of the user's preferred languages; then to the *base localization* (in Base.lproj); and finally to strings and layouts in unlocalized resources, not in any .lproj directory.

If you look at the Mac Passer Rating project directory in the Finder, you'll see an en.lproj directory is associated with MPR and contains Credits.rtf and InfoPlist.strings. There is also a Base.lproj directory containing MainMenu.xib, MPRDocument.xib, and MPRGameViewController.xib.

Click on those files in Xcode's Project navigator, and look at the jump bar above the Editor area. As you expect, it progresses from the project, through the enclosing groups, to the file itself. But there's one more level: It has the name of the name of the file, to which is appended (`English`) or (`Base`). So far as Xcode is concerned, what you're seeing is only one of many possible variants on that file—the one that appears in `en.lproj` or `Base.lproj`.

> **Note**
>
> There is one exception: `MPRPasserGraphController.xib`. The template for new `NSViewControllers` (at the time I wrote this) didn't put the XIB it generated into any locale directory. Even though it has nothing that requires localization, it *should* be placed in the `lproj` system—most likely at `Base`. Watch for how Xcode handles it. In the mean time *do not* try moving it to an `lproj` yourself. At the very least, the file's name in the Project navigator will turn red, meaning Xcode can no longer find it; solve that by clicking the tiny folder button in the File inspector when the red label is selected. Worse, you may confuse the localization mechanism. Experience has shown that Xcode can be fragile when resources are localized behind its back. It is getting better all the time, but don't tempt fate.

Adding a Localization

Earlier versions of Xcode (up through version 3) treated localization on a file-by-file basis: You could put files of the same name—`MainMenu.xib`, `Credits.rtf`—into separate `lproj` folders, but that was your business. Xcode took no notice of their being related.

This falls short of what a project needs on two counts. First, it's just inconvenient: If you're working on the English version of a resource, you'll want to work on the French version in parallel. Second, the point of internationalization is to produce a product that conforms to the user's locale; conceptually, you don't internationalize a file, you internationalize the whole project. Xcode now organizes the process of localization as a property of the whole project, not just file by file.

Base Localization

Xcode starts new projects with two localizations: English and Base. The idea is that the Base localization files embody the fundamental structure of the localizable resources, whereas the language/region-specific files fill in the details: `Base.lproj` contains `MPRGameViewController.xib`, which specifies the layout of the game-statistics popover.

> **Note**
>
> The strings in the XIB are all in English, but that's incidental; the XIB is in the Base localization because it is the authoritative layout.

The French localization will use the same layout, from the same XIB. You do not have to redo the layout. Instead, you supply a `.strings` file, a dictionary that provides the French text that Cocoa will substitute for French-speaking users.

> **Note**
>
> If you're working from an earlier project, you won't have a Base localization. Xcode will start you on the process if you check **Use Base Internationalization** in the **Info** tab of the

Project editor. It will present you with every file it understands to be localizable, and it asks whether you want to keep it in the English locale or move it to Base; and if you do move it to Base, whether you want to create a `.strings` file to separate the English-language content from the Base content—which in principle isn't in any language.

Localizing for French

The default setup is, strictly speaking, localized, but you could ignore it because you were dealing with only one language, and there was no need to take notice. Localization begins in earnest when you open the Project editor (select the top item in the Project navigator, and choose the whole-project icon at the top), then click the **+** button under the **Localizations** table. **Editor** → **Add Localization** will give you the same: A choice from a few common languages, and a further choice for an astonishing variety of languages and regions in which they are spoken (Figure 21.1).

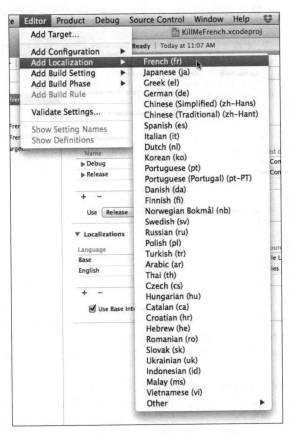

Figure 21.1   Add a localization to a project by clicking the **+** button below the **Localizations** table in the Project editor, or by selecting **Editor** → **Add Localization** and taking your pick. There are a lot to pick from.

> **Note**
>
> What you're looking at isn't just a list of languages—the dialects of French in Burkina Faso and Chad are not likely to be much different. But there is more to localization than just language. This is a list of *locales*. You could get away with the same English text throughout the Commonwealth; but if you want to depict an animal (some areas that use Commonwealth English are sensitive about some kinds of animals), or center a map on the capital city, the difference between New Zealand and India is significant, even though both treat corporate nouns as plural.

By whichever method, select **French (fr)**.

Xcode drops a sheet (Figure 21.2) listing all the localizable files it found in the Base and en.lproj directories. You can uncheck any you don't want to bring into the new locale, but we want them all.

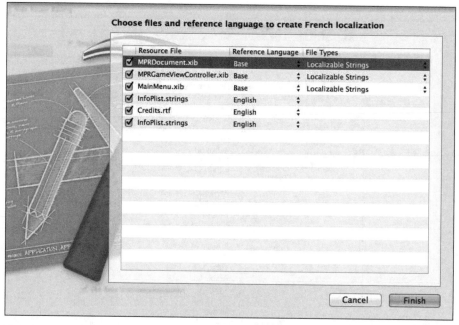

Figure 21.2   When you select the French localization, Xcode shows you the resources it found in the lproj directories, and how it proposes to generate the localization resources. A display bug in this copy of Xcode produced two entries for InfoPlist.strings.

The second column, **Reference Language**, shows the version of the file from which the French localization will be derived. These are the Interface Builder resources to be scanned for strings, or files that should be copied over for translation. If Mac Passer Rating had developed a more complex set of resources, it might make a difference whether your new locale's main XIB should be derived from the broad-layout copy you made for German, or the compact one you have for Simplified Chinese. But we're just starting out, we have only one version of each file, so the popup menus in this column have one choice each.

The third column, **File Types**, lets you choose the form the localized resource will take. In particular, for XIBs, you have a choice of a **Localizable Strings** file (the default); or **Interface Builder Cocoa XIB**, a complete duplicate of the "reference" XIB.

There are reasons you might want to keep a duplicate XIB for another language—the cultural differences I mentioned earlier are good ones—but usually you don't need to do this, and you shouldn't. Take it to the extreme: You are supporting a dozen languages in three or four scripts. (This isn't uncommon, and you want to be rich enough to have this problem.) That's 12 XIBs. Now add a row of buttons to one of them. And then to all the rest. Remember you have to link outlets and actions for each.

No. You'd rather not do that.

The classic justification for multiple XIBs was that the same idea may be expressed in only two characters in a CJK script, but require... a lot in German. Some developers solve this by laying out for German, and if that means the Japanese get tiny islands of Kanji in an expanse of dialog sheet, it can't be helped. Most developers would rather not do that, either.

And in the case of right-to-left scripts (Arabic, Hebrew), the need for duplicate XIBs seems inescapable. The **OK** button has to be at the lower left, not the lower right as it is in LTR layouts.

You remember the pain I put you through in Chapter 12, "Autolayout in a New View." That was not hazing. For almost every project, autolayout solves all of this. The same XIB can produce correct layout for Kanji and German: Remember the compression resistance of text-containing views? The longer German label will push out the enclosing view (cascading out to the bounds of the window, if necessary) to make room.

> **Note**
>
> To repeat: Autoresizing is much easier to understand, but it pushes layout only one way, down from the window edges. Autoresize if you must, but resign yourself to keeping your German IB layouts in sync manually for the lifetime of your project. In the long run, it isn't easier.

What about Hebrew? Remember how all the horizontal spacing constraints were described as "leading" and "trailing," not "left" and "right"? Autolayout knows that in Hebrew, the leading side of controls and text is on the right. If you did it right, the layout will be flopped, automatically, from the same XIB, in right-to-left scripts.

This is the long way around to my advice on the new-localization table: Leave the **File Types** column set to **Localizable Strings** unless you can articulate a *very* good reason to spin off a new **Interface Builder Cocoa XIB**. If you get autolayout right, your views will accommodate even absurdly large content. See Figure 21.3.

Click **Finish**. The obvious change is that the **Localizations** table now has a row for "French." The big changes are in the Project navigator. Type `fr` in the search field at the bottom of the navigator; you will see that the localizable files in the list aren't "files" any more, but groups with disclosure triangles. Each contains a resource of some kind tagged "(French)." Some, like `Credits.rtf`, are simply duplicates but for the added tag; others, the ones attached to XIB files, are just `.strings` files (Figure 21.4, top).

Clear out the search field and look at the entries for the XIB files (Figure 21.4, bottom). Where there had been single entries in the Project navigator for the resource

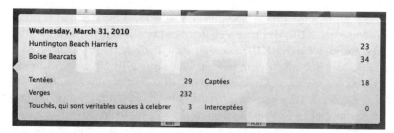

Figure 21.3   With proper autolayout, the game-view popover will present an orderly appearance even if one of its labels is pushed out by an absurdly long title.

files, there are now groups, containing the original files (now tagged as belonging to the Base localization) and the .strings files that are to adapt them to French.

Let's start simple, with the straightforward replacement of the contents of Credits.rtf. Credits.rtf appears in a scrolling view in the automatically generated About box (Figure 21.5). The file you got from the application template contains a brief, humorous list of credits (like **With special thanks to:** Mom). Brevity and humor are virtues, so I'll just translate it.

Select Credits.rtf in the Project navigator. Take the English version (with the "(English)" tag attached) or the container (the one with the disclosure triangle), which will give you the reference version, which in this case is English. It's important that we be in sync here—the French version starts out with the identical content, and it's easy to find that you're working on the wrong version.

Xcode has an RTF editor, so the credits appear in the editor as they would in the About box. (It's the standard AppKit rich-text editor, so if you want one of your own, it's about thirty lines of code.) If you look in the jump bar, you'll see the progression from the project, down the enclosing groups to Credits.rtf, and then Credits.rtf (English). The last segment will jump you between the localizations. You can jump to the other localization from that segment of the bar.

The File inspector for each version of a file includes the same **Localization** table, listing all the locales in the project. You can remove a localization for a file by unchecking the locale in the table. Or, if you visit another version of the file, you can add a localized version by checking its entry in the table (Figure 21.6).

> **Note**
>
> Have a glance at the project tree in the Finder. en.lproj and Base.lproj have been joined by fr.lproj. If you look in the language-specific folders, you'll see that both contain a file named simply Credits.rtf. Xcode's Project navigator and the jump bars add the locale, in parentheses, to the name of each file, but that's just to make it easier to distinguish versions. The parentheticals are not part of the names of the files.

It's getting to the point where, if you can imagine a way two files in a project might relate to each other, Apple can say, "There's an assistant for that." Activate the Assistant editor (middle segment of the Editor control, the one that looks like a formal shirtfront), and from the root of the jump bar, select **Localizations**.

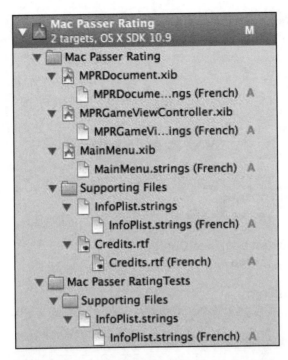

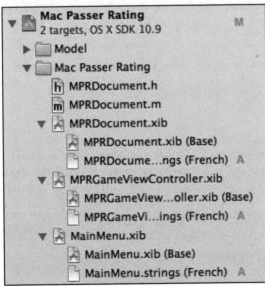

Figure 21.4 (top) When the "French" localization was added, the localizable resources picked up counterparts that were either modifiers or outright replacements for the originals. (bottom) Without the name filter, you can see that the old listings for the resource files have become disclosable groups containing both the base version and the French counterpart.

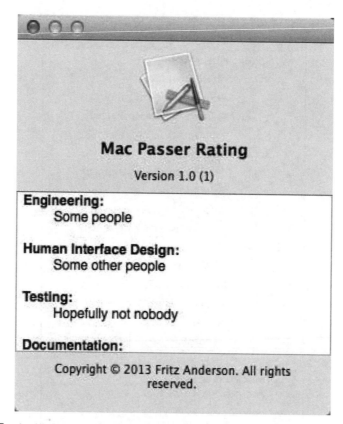

Figure 21.5   AppKit automatically generates an About box for your application if you don't supply your own. If the `Credits.rtf` file is present, it goes into a scrolling display in the middle of the window.

If there were more than one localization, you could step through them with the arrowheads at the right end of the jump bar, or by pressing ⋀ ⌘ **Left Arrow** or **Right Arrow**, but there's only one alternative this time. By now, you should have the English version in the main (left) editor and the French version in the Assistant (right) editor.

Replace the contents of each line of the French file with:

- **Les ingénieurs:** Certains gens
- **Conception d'interface humaine:** D'autres gens
- **Test:** On espère que ce n'est pas personne
- **Documentation:** N'importe qui
- **Nous remercions particulièrement:** Maman

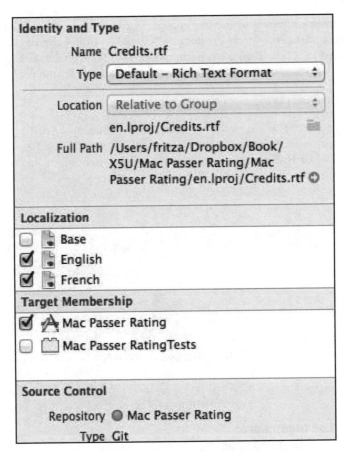

Figure 21.6   The File inspector for all versions of the `Credits.rtf` file includes a **Localization** table to enable or disable localization of the file for a locale.

Trying It Out

The obvious way to test this localization is to shuffle your language preferences in the System Preferences application, launch Mac Passer Rating, and see whether the About box contains the new text. This would, however, also make any other application you launch use the French localization until you switch the preference back. This is inconvenient unless you prefer to work in French.

> **Note**
>
> Changing the system-wide language preference *will* be necessary when you edit `InfoPlist.strings` to localize things like the display name of the application. You'll have to build the app, change the preference, and relaunch the Finder using ⌥⌘**Escape**.

A command-line option is available to change your language preference only for the application being launched. Select **Product** → **Scheme** → **Edit Scheme...** (⌘ <), and the **Arguments** tab of the **Run** panel for the Mac Passer Rating scheme. Click the **+** button at the bottom of the "Arguments Passed On Launch" table, and enter

```
-AppleLanguages (fr)
```

in the new row that appears. Run the app and examine the menus. AppKit generates some menu titles itself, and they appear in French automatically. Select **Mac Passer Rating** → **About Mac Passer Rating**; the About box shows the content of the localized `Credits.rtf`. It's a start. See Figure 21.7.

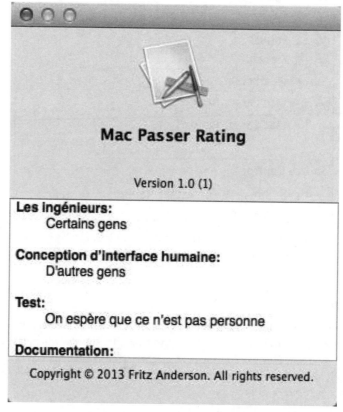

Figure 21.7   Providing a French version of `Credits.rtf` and passing `-AppleLanguages` `(fr)` as a command-line argument lead AppKit to use the localized version of the credits in the automatically generated About box.

> **Note**
>
> Some developers wonder whether it's possible to pass command-line arguments to OS X applications when users launch them from the Finder. No; command-line arguments are useful for development, but there's no way for users to specify them unless they execute an app's binary from the Terminal. If you're looking for file parameters, write handlers for open-file events in the application delegate or a custom `NSDocumentController`, or handle Apple Events.

Localizing `MainMenu.xib`

In *Xcode 4 Unleashed*, this was not a pleasant section to read, nor to write. Localizing a XIB entailed going to the command line to analyze the original, extract all the strings, generate a `.strings` file, then synthesize the original and the translated strings into a new, localized XIB. Which you must care for for life.

Things are better with Xcode 5. When you choose to localize an Interface Builder resource, Xcode takes care of extracting the strings, and AppKit reads the `.strings` file directly when it loads the resource and substitutes the translations. Select `MPRGameViewController.xib` from the Project navigator. As before, it's shown as a group, and clicking it displays the primary version—in this case, the one-and-only copy of the XIB in the Base localization—and, if you select **Localizations** in the Assistant editor's jump bar, you'll see not a duplicate of the XIB, but the extracted `.strings` file.

As provided, the file is simply a restatement of the base strings:

```
/* Class = "NSTextFieldCell"; title = "300"; ObjectID = "4Mn-jb-s5l"; */
"4Mn-jb-s5l.title" = "300";

/* Class = "NSTextFieldCell"; title = "Touchdowns"; ObjectID = "58Q-1Z-Vym"; */
"58Q-1Z-Vym.title" = "Touchdowns";

/* Class = "NSTextFieldCell"; title = "Attempts"; ObjectID = "6V4-10-0nO"; */
"6V4-10-0nO.title" = "Attempts";

...
```

It's a series of key-value pairs. The keys are Interface Builder's internal identifiers for the elements, and each is commented with the class and original content. To get a French rendering of a label, edit the strings. They're in the `fr.lproj` directory, AppKit sees from its name that it matches the XIB in `Base.lproj`, and it merges them.

> **Note**
>
> It's not likely you would, but don't give a `.strings` file the same base name as a `.xib` if you don't intend to localize it. This is a more plausible situation if you get in the habit of giving XIBs common base names like `Dictionary`.

The technical task is easy, though tedious in a large project: Replace "Touchdowns" with "Touchés," "Attempts" with "Tentées," and so on. In my experience (certainly when dealing with faculty), the social task of getting a domain expert to come up with translations is the hard part.

The preceding excerpt becomes:

```
/* Class = "NSTextFieldCell"; title = "300"; ObjectID = "4Mn-jb-s5l"; */
"4Mn-jb-s5l.title" = "300";

/* Class = "NSTextFieldCell"; title = "Touchdowns"; ObjectID = "58Q-1Z-Vym"; */
"58Q-1Z-Vym.title" = "Touchés";

/* Class = "NSTextFieldCell"; title = "Attempts"; ObjectID = "6V4-10-0nO"; */
"6V4-10-0nO.title" = "Tentées";

...
```

The equivalents are

Touchdowns	Touchés
Attempts	Tentées
Yards	Verges
Interceptions	Interceptées
Completions	Captées
Rating	Efficacité
Quarterback	Quart

Edit the French `.strings` file and check your work by running Mac Passer Rating.

It *almost* works (Figure 21.8, top). All the strings we localized through the `.strings` file are as we intend, but the date formatter is provided by OS X, and my system was still configured with English as the primary language. When I switch to French, the date falls into place (Figure 21.8, bottom).

Changing the language preference brings some other strings along: A new document is "Sans titre," marked "Modifié" when the sample data is loaded. OS X generates some commands in the **File** menu automatically if you adopt autosaving: **Save. . .** → **Enregistrer. . .** , **Rename. . .** →**Renommer. . .** , and so on.

The rest is up to you. Open `MainMenu.xib` and `MPRDocument.xib`, and repeat the process.

Apple can give you a little help here. It has a localization-support page at `http://developer.apple.com/internationalization/#resources`, where you can download tools (developer registration required). The tools, like AppleGlot, haven't been updated in some years, and in any event are meant for much bigger jobs than

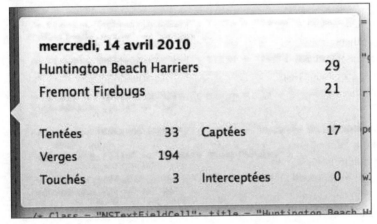

Figure 21.8   (top) Localization of a XIB through a `.strings` file is effective, except for the date format, which is provided by the system. (bottom) Making French the primary system language brings the French date formatter into play.

Mac Passer Rating. The real trove is in the glossary files that Apple used to translate its applications and system software. They're in many languages, among them French.

You'll find the equivalents in Table 21.1.

Note

I'd like to thank Bare Bones Software's BBEdit for letting me make a table out of a `.strings` file in three minutes. See Appendix B, "Resources," for more useful tools.

The results are gratifying: The menus are all in French (Figure 21.9), and so is the document window (Figure 21.10).

Table 21.1   **English-French Menu Equivalents for Mac Passer Rating**

About Mac Passer Rating	À propos de Quart-Efficacité
Bring All to Front	Tout ramener au premier plan
Clear Menu	Effacer le menu
Close	Fermer
Copy	Copier
Customize Toolbar...	Personnaliser la barre d'outils...
Cut	Couper
Delete	Supprimer
Edit	Édition
File	Fichier
Fill with Test Data	Remplissez avec les données de test
Help	Aider
Hide Mac Passer Rating	Masquer Quart-Efficacité
Hide Others	Masquer les autres
Mac Passer Rating	Quart-Efficacité
Mac Passer Rating Help	Aide Quart-Efficacité
Minimize	Placer dans le Dock
New	Nouveau
Open Recent	Ouvrir l'élément récent
Open...	Ouvrir...
Page Setup	Format d'impression...
Paste	Coller
Paste & Match Style	Coller et appliquer le style actuel
Preferences...	Préférences...
Print...	Imprimer...
Quit Mac Passer Rating	Quitter Quart-Efficacité
Redo	Rétablir
Revert to Saved	Revenir à la version enregistrée
Save...	Enregistrer...
Select All	Tout sélectionner
Services	Services
Show All	Tout afficher
Show Toolbar	Afficher la barre d'outils
Undo	Annuler
View	Présentation
Window	Fenêtre
Zoom	Réduire/agrandir

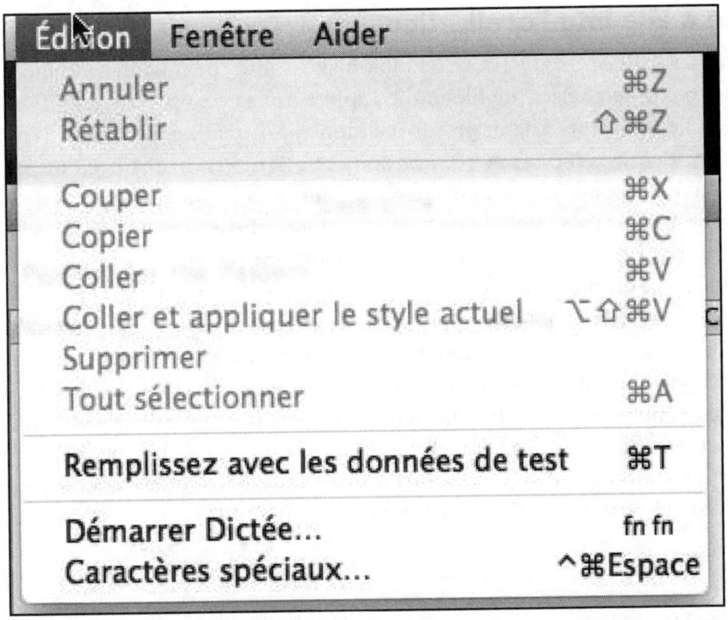

Figure 21.9   The **Edit** menu (now **Édition**) after the French `MainMenu.strings` file is complete.

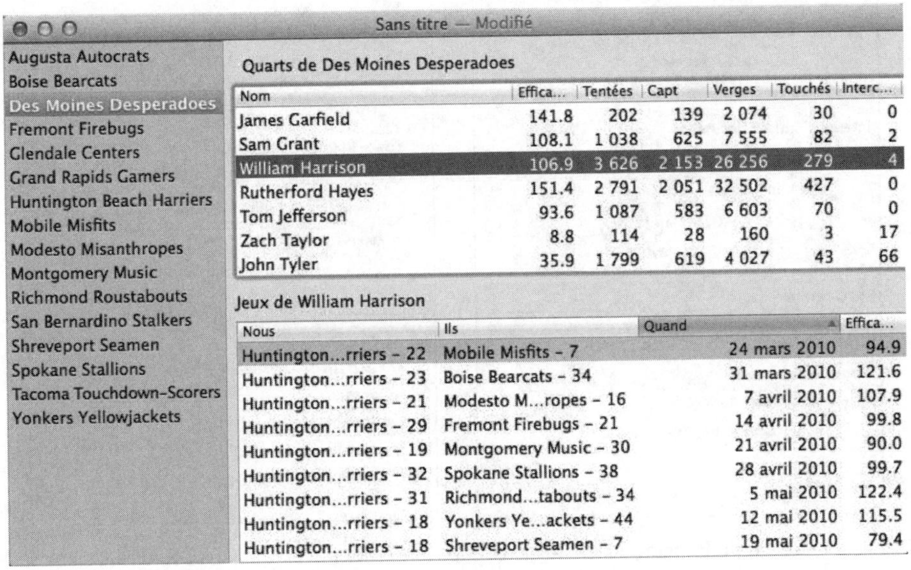

Figure 21.10   The league document window, converted to French.

Bringing a File into Localization

MPRPasserGraphController.xib didn't make it into the migration to localization. That's easy to correct. Select the file in the Project navigator, open the Utility area, and choose the File inspector. The inspector will display a **Localize...** button (Figure 21.11, left). Click it. Because MPRPasserGraphController.xib hadn't been in any lproj directory, Xcode will ask you which lproj the file is to be moved to. In this case, the XIB is the prototypical example of its view, so choose **Base**.

The inspector replaces the button with a **Localization** table, and you know what to do from here: Check off the locales you want to customize for (Figure 21.11, right). There's a difference here: MPRPasserGraphController.xib has no strings to translate. It makes no sense to offer a .strings file, and if you insist on one, you'll get an empty file. Instead, Xcode creates a duplicate XIB on the theory that what you want to localize is the layout.

Well, there's nothing about the Québequois that would make them particular about graph layouts, so give up on the French localization for this file: Uncheck the item. Xcode will confirm that you want to remove the localization file from the project, and gives you the option to delete it. Have Xcode delete the file.

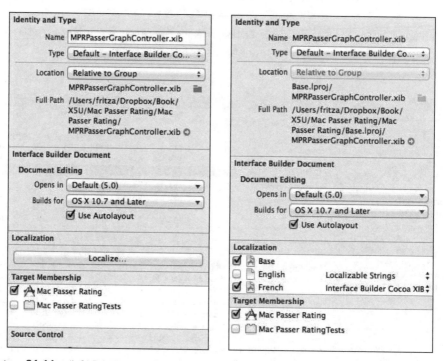

Figure 21.11   (left) Bringing a file into localization is a matter of clicking the **Localize...** button in the File inspector for the selected file. (right) Doing so adds the **Localization** table, where you can select additional localizations.

Localizing `Info.plist`

You saw earlier that localizing `MainMenu.xib` didn't take care of the application menu (**Mac Passer Rating**). There are other gaps, as well: The automatically generated About box contains the English application name and copyright notice; if you viewed MPR's icon on a French localization of the Finder, it would have the English name, and its documents would be labeled in English.

All of these strings come from `Info.plist`, which I cover in Chapter 22, "Bundles and Packages," and Chapter 24, "Property Lists." There has to be only one `Info.plist` in a bundle directory (such as an `.app` bundle), but you can change how its contents are presented through a `.strings` file in the `.lproj` directory corresponding to the user's locale.

The Cocoa Application project template starts you with the English version of the localization file, `InfoPlist.strings`. The file starts out empty, which is fine for applications running in the development region (usually `en`, but settable by the `Info.plist` key `CFBundleDevelopmentRegion`). Adding the French localization added an `InfoPlist.strings` file to `fr.lproj`.

The file has the same format as the XIB `.strings` files I showed you earlier in this chapter. There are two kinds of keys to identify the strings to be localized: If you want to set a value corresponding one-to-one with an `Info.plist` key, use that key as the key for the translation. Otherwise, use the string that appears in the base `Info.plist`.

To do what Mac Passer Rating needs, you first have to add two keys to the base source file for `Info.plist`, `Mac Passer Rating-Info.plist`. Select that file in the Project navigator, and add two rows:

- **Bundle display name** (`CFBundleDisplayName`). As a placeholder, set this to the string `${PRODUCT_NAME}`; the actual string will be pulled from the localization files.

- **Application has localized display name** (`LSHasLocalizedDisplayName`) tells Launch Services and the Finder that they must take the extra trouble of looking up the localized version of the app's name.

Next, the localized values of the `Info.plist` keys for French. This is all `fr.lproj/InfoPlist.strings` need contain (some lengthy strings are elided):

```
/* One-to-one values for Info.plist keys */
"NSHumanReadableCopyright" = "Copyright ... Toutes droits reservées.";
"CFBundleDisplayName" = "Quart-Efficacité";
"CFBundleName" = "Quart-Efficacité";

/* The file-type string is inside an array, and a single plist key
   doesn't correspond to it. Use the untranslated value as the key: */
"League File" = "Fichier de Ligue";
```

Testing the `Info.plist` localization comes in two parts. The first is easy: Run Mac Passer Rating and verify that the application menu and About box are as you expect.

Finder behavior is trickier, because you have to set your preferred language in the **Language & Text** panel of System Preferences, and then relaunch the Finder so it will pull the localized strings. System Preferences tells you to log out and log back in to see the results of the change. There's another way: Press ⌥⌘**Escape**, select Finder, and click **Relaunch**. Finder will reappear in your selected language.

> **Note**
>
> While you're in **Language & Text**, visit the **Formats** tab to be sure that the **Region:** matches the language you chose. The switch should be done automatically, but if you created a custom format set, it will stick. If it does, you won't see localized date and time formats in your applications.

If all went well with the `InfoPlist.strings` modification, Finder should present Mac Passer Rating as Quart-Efficacité. See Figure 21.12.

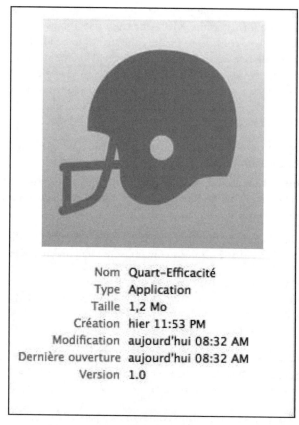

Figure 21.12   When displayed in a French Finder, Mac Passer Rating should be displayed as Quart-Efficacité.

Strings in Code

What I've done so far completes the localization of Mac Passer Rating (Figure 21.13). I've been fortunate because the application keeps all of its user-visible content in localizable resources. Not every app is so fortunate; some user-visible strings may be embedded in code. This is especially the case with alerts and other constructs that need strings formatted on the fly. Let me make a ridiculous change that illustrates the problem, and its solution.

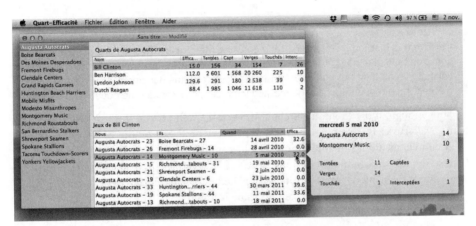

Figure 21.13   The complete localization of Mac Passer Rating (Quart-Efficacité). It reflects the XIB translations, the changed layout of `MPRGameViewController.xib`, and the `InfoPlist.strings` file. Because the app always used the standard formatters, numeric and date formats were translated automatically.

Most of the team names in the `sample-data.csv` file are alliterative—the team's name begins with the same letter as the city it represents. I have conceived the prejudice that *all* team names should be like this, and any attempt to edit a name that violates the rule should be refused.

The restriction goes into the setter for `teamName` in `PRTeam.m`:

```
- (void) setTeamName: (NSString *) newTeamName
{
    NSArray *    words = [newTeamName componentsSeparatedByString: @" "];
    NSString *   firstOfTeam = [[words lastObject] substringToIndex: 1];
    NSString *   firstOfCity = [newTeamName substringToIndex: 1];
    if (! [firstOfCity isEqualToString: firstOfTeam]) {
        NSAlert *   alert =
            [NSAlert alertWithMessageText: @"Illegal team name"
                        defaultButton: nil  // Autolocalized
                      alternateButton: nil otherButton: nil
                informativeTextWithFormat:
              @"\"%@\" must be the first letter of the team name, not \"%@\"",
                firstOfCity, firstOfTeam];
```

```
        alert.alertStyle = NSCriticalAlertStyle;
        [alert runModal];
        return;
    }

    [self willChangeValueForKey: @"teamName"];
    [self setPrimitiveTeamName: newTeamName];
    [self didChangeValueForKey: @"teamName"];
}
```

Warning

Remove this method if you intend to keep using Mac Passer Rating. The sample data contains team names that violate the constraint, and attempting to add it to a document will get you nothing but hundreds of alerts. Save a league document before adding this method, then reopen it when the method is present to exercise the code.

Sure enough, if the Fremont Firebugs move to Davenport and want to keep their team name, Mac Passer Rating objects. In English. Every time. See Figure 21.14.

A bundle, including an application bundle, can have `.strings` files of its own. In Cocoa, the `NSBundle` method `localizedStringForKey:value:table:` returns the string, from the named `.strings` table, for the best current locale for a given key. The `value:` parameter is a default in case no value is found in a `.strings` file.

Most commonly, the `localizedStringForKey:value:table:` method is wrapped in one of a family of macros. These macros have two advantages. First, they

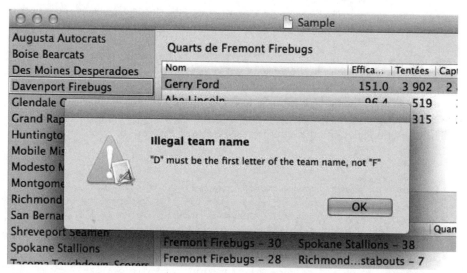

Figure 21.14   Setting alert text in code means you get the same text no matter what the locale.

provide convenient defaults for the bundle—the application main bundle—and the table file (`Localizable.strings`). Second, the `genstrings` command-line utility can scan source code for these macros and generate `.strings` files automatically.

The simplest of these is `NSLocalizedString`, which takes a key string to identify the string and a comment string to clarify, in a comment in the `.strings` file, the purpose of the string. The `NSAlert` setup then becomes:

```
NSAlert *    alert =
   [NSAlert alertWithMessageText:
    NSLocalizedString(@"Illegal team name",
                   @"alert title for non-aliterative team name")
                 defaultButton: nil  //  Autolocalized
              alternateButton: nil otherButton: nil

       informativeTextWithFormat:
    NSLocalizedString(@"\"%@\" must be the first letter of the "
                  "team name, not \"%@\"",
                   @"alert format for non-aliterative team name"),
    firstOfCity, firstOfTeam];
```

Without a localization, this code will behave the same as before. There has to be a `.strings` file to back it up. `genstrings` gets you started. In the Terminal, set the current working directory to the directory containing `Mac Passer Rating.xcodeproj`, and issue:

```
$ # Take all the .m files in this directory and its subdirectories...
$ find . -name '*.m' -print0 \
> | xargs -0 genstrings -a -o .
$ # ... and run them through genstrings, -a(ppending) each
$ # localizable item to the existing Localizable.strings,
$ # which should be -o(utput) into the current directory.
```

This will produce a `Localizable.strings` file in the same directory. It summarizes the strings you marked for localization. Add it to the project. The project doesn't carry it as localized, and that's the point of the file, so select it in the Project navigator, expose the File inspector, and click the **Localize...** button. Move the file to the `en.lproj` directory, and add it to the project.

Once again, Xcode will ask where the file is to go. This isn't a structural file—it contains assets for the English version. It should go into the English `lproj`. Then click the **French** checkbox, which will copy the file into `fr.lproj`. `Localizable.strings` now gets the same treatment as the other language-versioned files: It is shown as a group in the Project navigator, and the jump bar has a segment for switching among the versions.

Here's the entry for the alert title; the informative text is too long to fit this page:

```
/* alert title for non-aliterative team name */
"Illegal team name" = "Illegal team name";
```

The key and value are for the default string you specified; the comment appears before them. The same pair, in French, would be:

```
/* alert title for non-aliterative team name */
"Illegal team name" = "Nom de l'equipe interdit";
```

genstrings has done something strange to the format string for the alert's informative string. The %@ format specifiers have been replaced by %1$@ and %2$@. Why is this? Different languages don't have the same word ordering. What works in English may be infelicitous or ungrammatical in another language. The number *n* in a specifier says that the *n*th value in the arguments is to be used at that position, regardless of where the specifier appears in the format string. As an example that is probably infelicitous itself, the format string could be (truncated for space):

```
/* alert format for non-aliterative team name */
"\"%@\" must be the first letter of the team name, not \"%@\""
    = "... ne doit pas être \"%2$@\", il faut être \"%1$@\".";
```

Running Mac Passer Rating again, and attempting an illegal rename now shows a localized alert. See Figure 21.15.

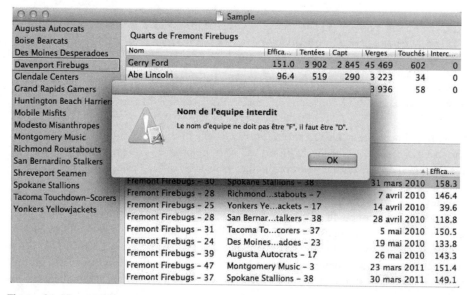

Figure 21.15   Adding a Localizable.strings file to fr.lproj, and translating the strings marked as localizable in source code, produces a localized alert panel.

Showing Mac Passer Rating in Finder

You'll have noticed in Figure 21.12 that Mac Passer Rating had picked up an icon. Now that we have the text parts of the presentation working, we can turn to bringing the correct icons and file types into reality.

Adding the Icons

OS X icons are a more complex affair than in iOS. iOS has only a few stereotyped presentations of application icons, and you need only prepare a few (for a given value of "few") PNGs for the purpose. Xcode 5 makes it easier than before to organize iOS icon sets. We went through this in the "Image Sets" section of Chapter 13, "Adding Table Cells."

The Application Icon

OS X icons have to adapt to more presentations. The Finder presents application icons in icon arrays (which the user can scale arbitrarily) and Cover Flow (in which icons have to scale as the user resizes the graphic view). The solution is the `.icns` icon-image file. An `.icns` carries bitmaps for the icon in point dimensions of 16, 32, 128, 256, and 512 on a side; also double (@2x) resolution, making 10 images total.

This is tedious to put together. There are a few things that make the load lighter:

- The `Images.xcassets` editor has slots to remind you what images to provide, and it will check that each is the proper size.
- The build system will take care of converting the assets into a single `.icns` file. Designate the icon set in the **General** tab of the Target editor by selecting the image set with the **Source** popup in the App Icons section.
- For the larger icon sizes, you can use the @2x version of the next-lower size. Apple doesn't recommend it because antialiasing should work differently in different pixel densities, but this requires a refined graphical sense that most of us don't have and can't pay for.
- If you're willing to sacrifice a little quality in rendering, you can skip some of the images. Finder will interpolate from what's there.
- If you have a good vector-drawing application, it can take a single drawing and export all the needed sizes. Again, you should really redraw the smaller images by hand—merely shrinking fine details produces a muddy bitmap that doesn't clearly show what you're trying to represent.

> **Note**
>
> The `Images.xcassets` file in the sample code contains icons for every point size up to 256 × 256. If you have appropriately sized images of your own, simply drag them into the matching slots in the AppIcon group in the assets file. If they're the wrong size, the editor will badge the errors.

Once you've assembled the images and rebuilt the app with the new `.icns` installed, the Finder will show Mac Passer Rating with its own icon.

Document Types

We haven't much cared how Mac Passer Rating handles its documents; it's a demo app, and our only interest has been how it behaves in single runs. In a real application, you'd want something more rigorous.

OS X knows what an application is. Launch Services (which takes care of matching icons and documents to applications) looks for the art in standard places with standard names. A document is a different sort of thing altogether. Each application's documents are different, with different names, icons, and associations with apps. An application has to define its document types with two keys in Info.plist: one for how the docs are to be handled, and another for defining the kind of files they are. As with most Info.plist keys, the **Info** tab of the Target editor provides a simplified editor.

Info keeps its first section, "Custom OS X Application Target Properties," open at all times; these are the settings that apply to all applications. Click the disclosure triangle for "Document Types," which will already have one entry if you told Xcode to make your app document-based when you created the project. The properties are set to defaults that are good enough to start work with, but not for a finished product.

Here's a quick rundown of what has to be done.

For the Document Types section:

1. The **Name** of the file type as displayed in the Finder should be **League File**; make sure InfoPlist.strings for French contains the pair

   ```
   "League File" = "Fichier de Ligue";
   ```

2. The **Class** associated with this document type is MPRDocument.
3. The **Extension** is **leaguedoc**.
4. The **Icon** should be **League File.icns**. We don't have that yet, but now is the time to set it.
5. The **Identifier** is a Uniform Type Identifier (UTI), which describes the kind of file this will be. Make this **com.wt9t.league**, a type we'll define in the next section of the editor.
6. **Role:** An application might create and edit this type of file (**Editor**); it might be able to import the file, but not write a file of the same type (**Viewer**); or it might not be able to handle such a file at all, but it's useful to provide the system with a label for such files in case no other app does (think of an application in a suite that can't use files created by others in the suite, but wants to brand the files (**None**). Mac Passer Rating is an **Editor** for League Files.
7. The **MIME Type** for the document. It was once thought that the ideal way to identify the content of files would be to use MIME types. Not so much, but the key is still in Info.plist. Set it to the most generic type, **application/ octet-stream**.
8. The document is not a **Bundle**, but a unitary file. See Chapter 22, "Bundles and Packages," for more about bundles.

9. In "Additional document type properties," you'll see three store types for Core Data content. On OS X, Core Data offers three file formats—you may have seen you were given a choice when you saved a league document. We want only one; delete all of them except for **SQLite**.

In addition to identifying Mac Passer Rating file types, and the application's role in handling them, you must define the data content itself. We don't intend to make any use of the data format other than as the contents of something in the filesystem, but other applications define data types that go through other conduits, such as the clipboard.

The system for defining such formats is the UTI. In the Document Types section, we said that a League File contains data of the type com.wt9t.league. Now, in the Exported UTIs section, we have to say what that is. Click the **+** button at the bottom of the table to get started.

1. Once again, you must provide a **Description**. If we had any other use for the type, we might call it **League Data**, but **League File** will do.
2. The **Identifier** for the UTI is the same as we used for the file type, `com.wt9t.league`.
3. The **Icon** is the same as for the file itself, **League File.icns**.
4. UTIs exist in a hierarchy of types, so if you had a document type that is XML internally, you could tell the system that your custom file type "**Conforms To**" XML, so if it had to interpret your file without the benefit of your app, it could fall back on handling it as XML. We don't need any fallbacks, so use the most generic type, `public.data`.
5. We aren't going to publish any details of the format, so leave **Reference URL** blank.
6. The **Extensions** field gets only one value, `leaguedoc` (no dot).
7. Again, only one item for **Mime Types**: `application/octet-stream`.
8. The data will never go on a pasteboard (clipboard), so there's no point in providing an identifier for a copy of its data in the pasteboard. Leave **Pboard Types** blank.
9. As far back as 1984, Mac OS attached four-character "type" and "creator" tags to every file, so the Finder could launch a document's creator when it was double-clicked or fall back to another application if it also claimed to handle files of that type. It was revolutionary, and is no longer used, but Apple kept it in OS X for backward compatibility. I'm sentimental, and always provide one: `Leeg`.

The result of all this work can be seen in Figure 21.16, except for the icons, which we'll get to next.

Document Icons

Xcode makes the process of getting an icon into an application pretty easy. For document icons, you're on your own. Not only do you have to compose the icons, you have to organize them in an `.iconset` directory, give them standard names, and convert them into an `.icns` file.

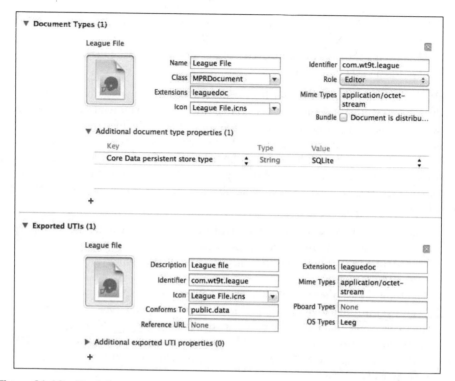

Figure 21.16   The **Info** tab of the Target editor includes sections for defining document types and Uniform Type Identifiers.

> **Note**
>
> In the end-of-chapter sample code, you'll find the `league.iconset` folder alongside the `AppIcon.appiconset` folder in the project directory's `Images.xcassets` folder. Selecting `Images.xcassets` in the Project navigator will show you all the contents of the assets catalog.

Put all of the icons for a document type into a single directory, which you can give whatever name you like, so long as you add the `.iconset` extension to it. The image files must conform to a rigid naming convention. Assuming the source image type is PNG, the full set of names would be:

```
icon_16x16.png      icon_16x16@2x.png
icon_32x32.png      icon_32x32@2x.png
icon_128x128.png    icon_128x128@2x.png
icon_256x256.png    icon_256x256@2x.png
icon_512x512.png    icon_512x512@2x.png
```

Once you have the `.iconset` directory ready, add it to the Mac Passer Rating project, by using **File → Add Files to "Mac Passer Rating"...** (⌥⌘A) or simply dropping it into the Project navigator.

Xcode will make the usual offer to move the directory into the project directory, if necessary. Do that. It will offer to incorporate the directory as a folder reference (the directory, not the files themselves, are added to the project). Don't do that. Finally, it will offer to add the files to a target, probably Mac Passer Rating. Uncheck all of the boxes in the target table. The `.iconset` directory is a source for application data, but it should not be copied into the application bundle itself.

Now for the conversion from `.iconset` to `.icns`. The developer tools provide a tool, `iconutil`, that does the conversion (and its reverse). In the Terminal application, navigate to the directory that contains `.iconset`, and type:

```
$ iconutil -c icns League\ File.iconset/
```

(assuming the `.iconset` directory has the base name `League File`). This produces `League File.icns`. You're almost there.

Add `League File.icns` to the project, this time making it part of the Mac Passer Rating target. Build the app, run it, and save a document. When you examine the document in the Finder, you should see something like Figure 21.17. (You may have to delete all copies of Mac Passer Rating and rebuild to shock Launch Services and the Finder into seeing the new `Info.plist`.)

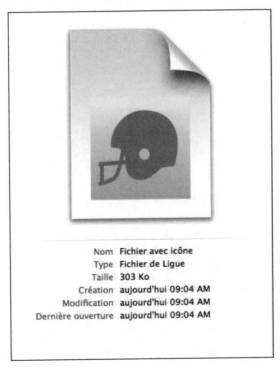

Nom	**Fichier avec icône**
Type	**Fichier de Ligue**
Taille	**303 Ko**
Création	aujourd'hui 09:04 AM
Modification	aujourd'hui 09:04 AM
Dernière ouverture	aujourd'hui 09:04 AM

Figure 21.17 Defining the League File (Fichier de Ligue) document type and providing an icon gives Mac Passer Rating data files the correct appearance in the Finder.

Summary

In this chapter, I gave you an overview of the tasks that go into localizing a Mac application; the same techniques apply to iOS.

You saw how to add a localization to a file that the application template put into the default `Base.lproj` directory, as well as how to add localizations to the project and to an unlocalized file.

I then went on to techniques for translating menus (easy) and UI layouts. Once upon a time, if you wanted localized layouts, you had to produce separate XIB files, one way or another. The `ibtool` command-line tool made it possible to extract strings from one XIB and inject them into another, but it was an easy process to get wrong. Xcode 5, and the application frameworks' acceptance of `.strings` files at runtime, have made it a matter of a few clicks (and several calls to your translator's voicemail).

Then came techniques to apply `.strings` files to the application code itself—`InfoPlist.strings` for Finder strings, and `Localizable.strings` for strings that would otherwise be hard-coded in your source.

We started caring about how Mac Passer Rating presented itself in the Finder, so we walked through the intricate process of adding icons and file types to the application package.

And, I covered how to test your localization at runtime and in the Finder.

22

Bundles and Packages

Many of Xcode's products take the form of *packages*, directory trees that the Finder presents as single files. Let's pause now to consider the problem of resources. Resources are the sorts of data that are integral to an application, but for one reason or another aren't suitable to incorporate into source code: strings, lookup tables, images, human-interface layouts, sounds, and the like.

In the original Mac OS, applications kept resources in *resource forks*, mini-databases kept in parallel with the data stream one normally thinks of as a file. The problem with the Resource Manager was that it did not scale well to sets of many, large, or changeable resources. The catalog written into each resource file was fragile, and any corruption resulted in the loss of every resource in the file. Modern apps use many more and much larger resources, and the tasks involved in managing them become indistinguishable from the tasks of a filesystem. Filesystems are a solved problem; they do their work as efficiently and robustly as decades of experience can make them. Why not use the filesystem for storing and retrieving resources?

One reason to avoid shipping application resources as separate files is that an application that relies on them becomes a swarm of files and directories, all more or less critical to the correct working of the application, and all exposed to relocation, deletion, and general abuse by the application's user. Meanwhile, the user, who simply wants one thing that does the application's work, is presented with a swarm of files and directories.

OS X provides a way to have the flexibility of separating resources into their own files while steering clear of the swarming problem. The Finder can treat directories, called *packages*, as though they were single documents.

A Simple Package: RTFD

A package can be as simple as a directory with a handful of files in it. The application that creates and reads the package determines how it is structured: what files are required, the names of the content files, and what sort of subdirectory structure is used.

A common example of an application-defined package is the RTFD, or rich text file directory. The Apple-supplied application TextEdit, in its `Info.plist` file, specifies what kinds of documents TextEdit can handle; among these is NSRTFDPboardType, which is listed as having suffix rtfd and is designated as a package file type. When it catalogs TextEdit, the Finder notes that directories with the .rtfd extension are supposed to be packages and so treats them as if they were single files, not ordinarily displaying the files within.

It is sometimes useful to look inside a package, however, and the Finder provides a way to do that. Right-clicking on a package file produces a popup menu containing the command **Show Package Contents** (see Figure 22.1). Selecting that command opens a new window showing the contents of the package directory, which can be further navigated as in a normal Finder window.

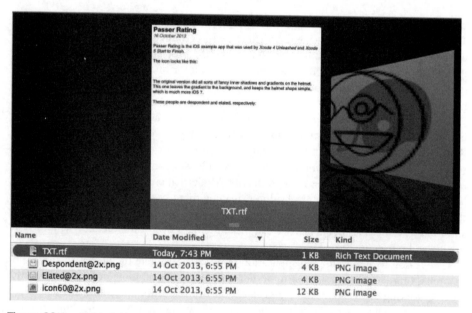

Figure 22.1   Right-clicking a package document in the Finder presents a menu that includes the command **Show Package Contents**, which shows the files within the package.

In the case of RTFD, the package directory contains one plain RTF file, TXT.rtf. The RTF file incorporates custom markup, such as

```
The icon looks like this:\
\
\pard\tx560\tx1120\tx1680\tx2240\tx2800\tx3360\tx3920\tx4480
\tx5040\tx5600\tx6160\tx6720\pardirnatural
\cf0 {{\NeXTGraphic icon60@2x.png \width2400 \height2400
}}\
```

Here, the markup refers to a graphics file—in this case, `icon60@2x.png`—that is also in the RTFD directory.

> **Note**
>
> Cocoa's AppKit application framework provides support for package-directory documents. `NSDocument` subclasses handle package reading and writing by overriding `readFromFileWrapper:ofType:error:` and `fileWrapperOfType:error:`. The `NSFileWrapper` class provides methods that assist in creating and managing complex file packages.

Bundles

A *bundle* is a particular kind of *structured* directory tree. Often, bundles are shipped as packages—the most familiar type of bundle, the application, is an example—but the concepts are separate. A directory can be a bundle without being a package, or a package without being a bundle, or it can be both. Table 22.1 has examples.

Table 22.1   Examples of Directories That Are Bundles or Packages or Both

	Not Bundle	Bundle
Not Package	Other directories	Frameworks
Package	Complex documents	Applications

There are two kinds of bundles in OS X: *versioned bundles*, which are used for frameworks—structured packages of dynamic libraries, headers, and the resource files that support them—and *modern bundles*, which are used for applications and most other executable products.

> **Note**
>
> "Modern" is a relative term; modern packages were in NeXTStep long before Cocoa.

At the minimum, a modern Mac bundle encloses one directory, named `Contents`, which in turn contains all the directories and files composing the bundle. The `Contents` directory contains an `Info.plist` file, which specifies how the bundle is to be displayed in the Finder and, depending on the type of the bundle, may provide configuration data for loading and running the bundle's contents. Beyond that, what the `Contents` folder contains depends on the type of the bundle.

Application Bundles

OS X applications are the most common type of bundle (see Figure 22.2). An application directory has a name with the suffix `.app`. The `.app` directory is a file package; even though it is a directory, the Finder treats it as a single entity. This allows the author of the

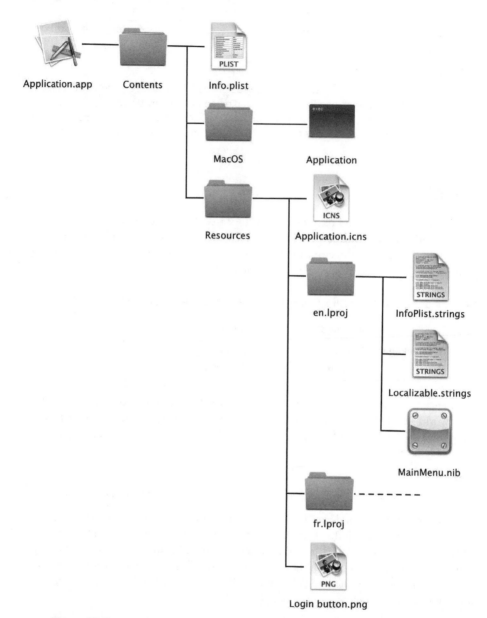

Figure 22.2   The structure of a typical application bundle. The executable file is at `Contents/MacOS/Application`. The application's human interface for English-speaking users is specified in `Contents/Resources/en.lproj/MainMenu.nib`; presumably, a French `MainMenu.strings` file is inside `Contents/Resources/fr.lproj`. The custom image for a button, `Login button.png`, is common to all languages and therefore appears in the `Resources` directory itself.

application to place auxiliary files for the application in a known place—inside the application bundle itself—with little fear that such files will be misplaced or deleted.

The `Contents` directory of an OS X application bundle most commonly contains

- `Info.plist`, an XML property list file that describes such application details as the principal class, the document types handled, and the application version. More on this file in the next section.
- `Resources`, a directory containing the application icon file, images, sounds, human interface layouts, and other parameterized content for the application. This directory may be further organized into subdirectories, according to your convenience. In addition, there may be localization subdirectories, which have the `.lproj` suffix. When an application seeks a resource, the Cocoa or Core Foundation bundle managers will look first in the `.lproj` directory that corresponds to the current language and locale.
- `MacOS`, a directory containing the executable binary for the application, along with any other executables.
- `Frameworks`, a directory of frameworks that are themselves versioned bundles, containing a dynamic library, resources needed by the library, and header files needed by users of the library. An application typically includes a framework because it links to the framework's library.

> **Note**
>
> What about iOS apps? They're packages—the Finder treats them as unitary files—but not bundles. Everything except the localization `.lproj` directories and directories you explicitly add to the application resources is in the `.app` bundle directory. Have a look: Hold down the Option key and select **Library** from the Finder's **Go** menu. Pass through `Developer/Xcode/DerivedData` and find the name of one of your iOS projects (a long hash string will follow it). In that directory, `Build/Products` is where you'll find directories for combinations of build configurations and target operating systems. Your `.app` files will be there. Right-click on any, and select **Show Package Contents**.

The `Info.plist` File

The `Info.plist` file, found in the `Contents` directory of any modern bundle and at the root of the `.app` bundle for iOS applications, is the locus of much of the information OS X and iOS need to make sense of a bundle. This file provides icon and naming information to the Finder/Home screen, flags and environment variables to Launch Services, "default" screen images in various sizes and orientations for iOS apps, and specifications for the basic structure of applications and plugins. It's a property list (`.plist`) dictionary file, a format I'll cover in Chapter 24, "Property Lists."

The Target editor's **Summary** and **Info** tabs form a specialized editor for the target's `Info.plist`. They'll give you at least a first cut at the settings you need without much trouble.

You can also edit the `Info.plist` file directly, using the Property List editor (see Chapter 24, "Property Lists"). Sort of. In point of fact, the file you'll be editing is not named `Info.plist`. If you are working on a target named `PasserRating`, the name will be `PasserRating-Info.plist`. There are two reasons. First, you may have two or more targets, producing bundles that need their own `Info.plist`s; the different files need different sources with names that identify their use.

Second, the real `Info.plist` for a product won't exist until it is installed at build time. What you're seeing is a source file that Xcode will process to generate the final property list. It's this processing phase that allows you to use build-variable references instead of literal values for some of the keys. The handling of the target-specific `Info.plist`s is special: They are *not* to be included in any build phase of your target—that will just copy the unprocessed source file into the application's `Resources` directory. Instead, the name of the file is specified in the `INFOPLIST_FILE` build variable. The build system picks it up from there.

> **Note**
>
> There are a number of build settings that control processing of `Info.plist`. Check the "Packaging" section of the **Build Settings** tab of the Target editor. Among them are the option to use C-style preprocessor directives in the source file. Unfortunately, once you use them, you are committed to editing the file as XML text because the Property List editor destroys all content that isn't property-list XML.

Localizing `Info.plist`

Some `Info.plist` properties are localizable. A file named `InfoPlist.strings` should be in the `.lproj` directory for each localization of your application. Localizable keys can then be assigned per-locale values. For instance, `InfoPlist.strings` in the `English` `.lproj` directory might include the pair

```
CFBundleName = "PasserRating";
CFBundleDisplayName = "Passer Rating";
```

The same file in the `fr.lproj` directory might include

```
CFBundleName = "Q-Effic";
CFBundleDisplayName = "Quart-Efficacité";
```

For users whose language preferences place French above English, the `Mac Passer Rating` icon will be labeled `Quart-Efficacité`. The name of the bundle directory, however, will still be `PasserRating.app`, even if the casual user doesn't see it.

The Xcode Property List editor customizes itself for `Info.plist`s. When the name of a file ends in `Info.plist`, it will fill the dictionary key column with popup menus offering the keys peculiar to that kind of property list. This means that you should avoid using Xcode to edit property lists whose names end that way (like the `DirectoryInfo.plist` file you're setting up for some names and addresses) but aren't actual `Info.plist`s.

Info.plist **Keys for Applications**

Info.plist keys have proliferated as more and more OS services need to characterize the needs and capabilities of applications. In earlier editions of this book, I was able to list practically all of the available keys—even a couple whose names appeared *nowhere* on the Internet. That's not possible any more.

What you'll see here are the most frequently used keys for application Info.plists. I've itemized the dictionary keys, followed by the plain-English labels used by the Property List editor.

Keys for Both iOS and OS X

The keys in this section apply to application bundles on both OS X and iOS.

- **Structure**
  - CFBundleExecutable (Executable file), the name of the executable file, which may be an application binary, a library, or plugin code. It corresponds to the EXECUTABLE_NAME build setting, which in turn is derived from PRODUCT_NAME (plus an optional prefix and suffix, which you'd rarely use). A bundle that mismatches this entry with the actual name of the executable file will not run. Applications must specify this key.
  - CFBundleIdentifier (Bundle identifier), a unique identifier string for the bundle, in the form of a Java-style reverse domain package name, such as com.wt9t.Passer-Rating. Xcode initializes this to the company ID you supplied when you chose the project template, followed by ${PRODUCT_NAME:rfc1034identifier}, and you can expect to leave it alone. All bundles must specify this key.
  - CFBundleInfoDictionaryVersion (InfoDictionary version), a compatibility-check version number for the Info.plist format. Xcode injects this version number automatically when it builds bundles. I've never seen a version number other than 6.0. All Info.plist files should include this key.
  - CFBundlePackageType (Bundle OS Type code), **optional on iOS**, the four-character type code for the bundle. Applications are type APPL, frameworks are FMWK, plugins are BNDL or a code of your choosing. See also CFBundleSignature. OS X applications must specify this key.
  - CFBundleSignature (Bundle creator OS Type code), **optional on iOS**, the four-character creator code associated with the bundle. OS X applications must specify this key, but it's rare for it to be anything other than ????.
  - NSPrincipalClass (Principal class), the name of the bundle's main class. In an OS X application, this would normally be NSApplication; in iOS, UIApplication.

- NSMainNibFile (Main nib file base name), the base (no extension) name of the application's main NIB file, almost always MainMenu on OS X, and MainWindow on iOS (when a main NIB is used at all). Use NSMainNibFile-ipad (Main nib file base name (iPad)) to specify a separate NIB for your app when it's launched on an iPad.
  If you're using an iOS storyboard, you want UIMainStoryboardFile.

- **User Information**

  - CFBundleGetInfoString (Get Info string), **Mac only**, a string that supplements the version information supplied by CFBundleShortVersionString and CFBundleVersion. Formerly, this key was used for copyright strings, but that is now handled by NSHumanReadableCopyright.

  - CFBundleIconFile (Icon file), the name of the file in the Resources directory that contains the bundle's custom icon, a file in .icns format for Mac, .png for iOS. You can omit the extension. An iOS application would prefer CFBundleIconFiles, an array of standardized names for the various rendering sizes of the application icon.
    All of this is moot in Xcode 5. The **General** tab of the Target editor lets you specify images for icons, either file by file or through an asset catalog. From that, the build system will inject the necessary icon references into Info.plist.

  - CFBundleShortVersionString (Bundle versions string, short), a short string with the product version, such as **4.3.4**, of the bundle, suitable for display in an About box or by the App Store. See also CFBundleGetInfoString. This key may be localized in InfoPlist.strings. Applications must specify this key.

  - CFBundleVersion (Bundle version), the build version of the bundle's executable, which may identify versions within a release cycle, such as betas: **2.1b3**, for instance. This may also be a single number, corresponding to a build number within the life of the bundle. The build version is displayed in parentheses in the About box. See also CFBundleShortVersionString.

  - CFBundleDisplayName (Bundle display name), the name for the Finder or Home screen to display for this bundle. The value in Info.plist should be identical to the name of the application bundle; localized names can then be put in InfoPlist.strings files for various languages. The OS will display the localized name *only* if the name of the application package in the file-system matches the value of this key. That way, if a Mac user renames your application, the name he intended—and not the localized name—will be displayed. Project templates will initialize this key to ${PRODUCT_NAME}. See also CFBundleName. Applications must specify this key.

- `CFBundleName` (Bundle name), the short—16-character maximum—name for the application, to be shown in the About box and the **Application** menu. See also `CFBundleDisplayName`. This key may be localized in `InfoPlist.strings`; Xcode initializes it to `${PRODUCT_NAME}`. Applications must specify this key.

- **Localization**
  - `CFBundleDevelopmentRegion` (Localization native development region), the native human language, and variant thereof, of the bundle, like `fr-CA` for Canadian French. If the user's preferred language is not available as a localization, this is the language that will be used.

- **Documents and URLs**
  - `CFBundleDocumentTypes` (Document types), an array of dictionaries specifying every document type associated with the application. Use the **Info** tab of the Target editor for the application target to edit these; you'll save yourself some headaches.

  - `CFBundleURLTypes` (URL types), an array of dictionaries defining URL schemes, such as `http:`, `ftp:`, or `x-com-wt9t-custom-scheme:`, for which the application is a handler. Use common schemes *sparingly*; if you're a web browser, you support `http:`, but if you just happen to pull some resources from an HTTP server, don't advertise yourself to the whole system as being able to service `http` URLs. It's much more useful in iOS, where your application's custom scheme can provide a handy interapplication communications method for other applications, email, and the web. See Apple's documentation, and the **Info** tab of the Target editor, for details.

  - `UTExportedTypeDeclarations` (Exported Type UTIs), an array of dictionaries that describe the types of documents your application can write, and which you want Launch Services to know about. The entries center on declaring a UTI and the chain of UTIs the principal UTI conforms to. This key is used by Spotlight to build its list of document types. UTIs take precedence over the declarations in `CFBundleDocumentTypes` as of OS X 10.5. Again, it's easier to manage this list through the **Info** tab of the Target editor. See Apple's documentation for the format of the dictionaries.

  - `UTImportedTypeDeclarations` (Imported Type UTIs), an array of dictionaries that describe the types of documents your application can *read,* and which you want Launch Services to know about. The entries are the same format as used in `UTExportedTypeDeclarations`. The **Info** tab of the Target editor provides an easy editor for this.

Keys for OS X

These keys apply only to OS X applications and cover launch configurations, help facilities, and information on the documents and URLs the application handles.

The `Info.plist` structure antedates OS X, so many keys have fallen into obsolescence, but the OS has to support them for backward compatibility. The template you instantiate for a new application target will give you everything you need to start, and the **Info** tab will help you with *almost* everything you'd ever need to fit what you want to do, but there's no substitute for following the OS release notes.

- **Structure**

  - `CSResourcesFileMapped` (Resources should be file-mapped), if `YES` or `<true/>`, Core Foundation will memory-map the bundle resources rather than read the files into memory.

  - `ATSApplicationFontsPath` (Application fonts resource path), a string. If your application contains fonts for its own use, it contains the path, relative to the application's `Resources` directory, to the directory containing the fonts.

- **User Information**

  - `NSHumanReadableCopyright` (Copyright (human-readable)), a copyright string suitable for display in an About box. This key may be localized in `InfoPlist.strings`. Applications must specify this key.

  - `LSApplicationCategoryType` (Application Category), This is a string containing an Apple-defined UTI that describes for the Mac App Store what kind of application this is—Business, Lifestyle, Video, etc. Ordinarily, you'd set this in the **Summary** tab of the application's Target editor, so you don't have to bother with the UTIs. When you submit your app through iTunes Connect, you will be allowed two categories for your listing; make sure the primary one is the same as your `LSApplicationCategoryType`.

- **Help**

  - `CFAppleHelpAnchor` (Help file), the base name, without extension, of the initial help file for the application.

  - `CFBundleHelpBookFolder` (Help Book directory name), the folder—in either the `Resources` subdirectory or a localization subdirectory—containing the application's help book.

  - `CFBundleHelpBookName` (Help Book identifier), the name of the application's help book. This name should match the name set in a `<meta>` tag in the help book's root file.

- **Launch Behavior** These keys control how Launch Services launches and configures a Mac application. iOS has a "Launch Services" framework, but there is no public interface for it.

  - `LSBackgroundOnly` (Application is background only), if it's the string 1, the application will be run in the background only and will not be visible to the user.

- `LSEnvironment` (Environment variables), a dictionary, the keys of which are environment-variable names, defining environment variables to be passed to the application upon launch.

- `LSGetAppDiedEvents` (Application should get App Died events), indicates, if `YES` or `<true/>`, that the application will get the `kAEApplicationDied` Apple event when any of its child processes terminate.

- `NSSupportsSuddenTermination` (Application can be killed immediately after launch). When you log out, restart, or shut down, OS X takes care that all running applications will be given the chance to clean up, ask the user to save files, and so on. If this key is `<true/>`, the system will shut down your application with a BSD kill signal instead. You can still use `NSProcessInfo` methods to restore the ask-first policy (such as when you are in the middle of writing a file), but the kill policy makes shutdowns much quicker.

- `LSMinimumSystemVersion` (Minimum system version), a string in the form 10.x.x, specifying the earliest version of OS X or iOS this application will run under. Under OS X, if the current OS is earlier (back through 10.4), it will post an alert explaining that the app could not be run.

- `LSMinimumSystemVersionByArchitecture` (Minimum system versions, per-architecture), a dictionary. The possible keys are `i386` and `x86_64`. For each key, the value is a string containing the three-revision version number (e.g., 10.6.3) representing the minimum version of OS X the application supports for that architecture.

- `LSMultipleInstancesProhibited` (Application prohibits multiple instances), indicating that, if `<true/>`, only one copy of this application can be run at a time. Different users, for instance, would not be able to use the application simultaneously.

- `LSUIElement` (Application is agent [UIElement]), if set to the string 1, identifies this application as an *agent application*, a background application that has no presence in the Dock but that can present user interface elements, if necessary.

- `LSUIPresentationMode` (Application UI Presentation Mode), an integer between 0 and 4, representing progressively greater amounts of the OS X UI—Dock and menu bar—to be hidden when the application is running. See Apple's documentation for details.

- **Other Services**
  - `LSFileQuarantineEnabled` (File quarantine enabled): If `<true/>`, Launch Services will regard the files your application creates as though they had been downloaded from the Internet and warn the user of the possible risk in opening them. You can exempt files from quarantine with `LSFileQuarantineExcludedPathPatterns`.

- LSFileQuarantineExcludedPathPatterns (no editor equivalent) is an array of glob wildcard patterns for files (locations, extensions, etc.) that will be exempt from quarantining even if LSFileQuarantineEnabled is set.

- NSAppleScriptEnabled (Scriptable), indicating that, if YES or <true/>, this application is scriptable. Applications must specify this key.

- OSAScriptingDefinition (Scripting definition file name), the name of the .sdef file, to be found in the application's Resources directory, containing its AppleScript scripting dictionary.

- NSServices (Services), an array of dictionaries declaring the OS X services this application performs, which will appear in the **Services** submenu of every application's application menu, subject to the **Keyboard Shortcuts** tab in the **Keyboard** panel of System Preferences. The dictionaries specify the pasteboard input and output formats, the name of the service, and the name of the method that implements the service. See Apple's documentation for details.

- SMAuthorizedClients (Clients allowed to add and remove tool), an array of strings describing the signing requirements for client applications that may install or remove a privileged tool under the launchd daemon.

- SMPrivilegedExecutables (Tools owned after installation), a list of dictionaries describing privileged helper tools for an application, to be installed by the launchd daemon. See Apple's documentation for the uses of launchd.

Keys for iOS

These tags are unique to iOS applications. *In general*, if you want to customize any Info.plist key for a particular device, create a custom key composed of the base name, followed by a hyphen, then iphoneos, a tilde, and a device specifier (one of iphone, ipod, or ipad). For example: UIStatusBarStyle-iphoneos~ipad. In practice, you can omit the -iphoneos part: UIStatusBarStyle~ipad.

- **Structure**

  - UIMainStoryboardFile, the base name of the storyboard package that is the root of the application. Use this, or NSMainNibFile, but never both.

  - LSRequiresIPhoneOS (Application requires iOS environment), whether Launch Services will refuse to launch the application except on an iOS device.

  - CFBundleIconFiles (Icon files), an array of filenames for the application icons. These are expected to be the same icon in the various sizes needed by different iOS platforms; the system will look through the files themselves to pick the proper one. If you omit the file extensions, the system will find "@2x" Retina Display variants automatically. Overrides CFBundleIconFile. (optional)

- `UIDeviceFamily`, 1 (the default) if the application is for the iPhone and iPad Touch, 2 if it's for the iPad. Or, it could be an array containing both. *Don't* set this key yourself; the Xcode build system for iOS inserts it automatically based on your setting of the device family in the Target editor.

- `UIAppFonts` (Fonts provided by application), an array of paths within the application bundle for application-supplied font files.

- `UIRequiredDeviceCapabilities` (Required device capabilities), an array of strings, like `telephony`, `wifi`, or `video-camera`, that describe what device features your application absolutely needs in order to run. This is used by iTunes and the App Store to save users who don't have those features from buying and installing your app.
  Pay particular attention to the `armv7` requirement: If present, your app will not be offered to devices older than the iPhone 3GS, even if you compile with the ARMv6 architecture. `armv7` is included in this array *by default*.

- `UIRequiresPersistentWiFi` (Application uses Wi-Fi). The Property List editor's summary is a little misleading. Ordinarily (if this key is absent or has the value `NO`), iOS will shut down the WiFi connection if you haven't used it for half an hour. If `YES`, the WiFi transceiver will be turned on as soon as your application is launched, and it will stay on as long as it is running.

- `UISupportedExternalAccessoryProtocols` (Supported external accessory protocols), for an array of strings naming all the external-device protocols your application supports. The protocol names are specified by the manufacturers of the accessories.

- **User Presentation**

  - `UIStatusBarStyle` (Status bar style), the style (gray, translucent, or opaque black) of the initial status bar. The names of the styles used in the iOS API are used, the default being `UIStatusBarStyleDefault`.

  - `UIStatusBarHidden` (Status bar is initially hidden), if `YES`, the status bar is hidden when your application is launched. Before coveting those 20 extra pixels, please consider whether you want your customers to shut your app down whenever they need to check the time or see whether they're running out of power.

  - `UIInterfaceOrientation` (Initial interface orientation), indicating the screen orientation the application starts up in. Look up `enum UIInterfaceOrientation` in the UIKit headers for the available values; the `Info.plist` entries are supposed to be the *names* of those orientations. The default is `UIInterfaceOrientationPortrait`.

  - `UISupportedInterfaceOrientations` (Supported interface orientations, Supported interface orientations [iPad], and Supported interface orientations [iPhone]), an array naming the orientations your app will support on the iOS or iPad. If you don't specify `UIInterfaceOrientation`, iOS will use the device's orientation if it is in the list; if not, it will default to one that is.

- `UIPrerenderedIcon` (Icon already includes gloss and bevel effects), if `YES`, iOS will not add a shine effect to it. This setting is obsolete in iOS 7.

- `UIViewEdgeAntialiasing` (Renders with edge antialiasing): If you draw a Core Animation layer aligned to fractional-pixel coordinates, it normally isn't anti-aliased. You can set this key to `YES` if you draw that way customarily and want to take the performance hit of making it look nice.

- `UIViewGroupOpacity` (Renders with group opacity), if `YES`, allows Core Animation sublayers to inherit the opacity of their superlayers. Cooler appearance, slower performance.

- `UILaunchImageFile` (Launch image), `UILaunchImageFile~ipad` (Launch image [iPad]), and `UILaunchImageFile~iphone` (Launch image [iPhone]), the name of the file that is shown between the time the user selects your app in the Home screen and the time when it can render its content. Prior to iOS 3.2, there was no option but `Default.png`. for the ~ipad variant, this can be a base name for an image file (such as `MyLaunchImage.png`); based on that, iOS will seek orientation-specific variants by inserting variant strings (such as `MyLaunchImage-Portrait.png` and `MyLaunchImage-Landscape.png`) and looking for those files. See the *iPad Programming Guide* in the Documentation window for details on orientation-specific keys. However, this has been made obsolete by...

- `UILaunchImages` (set through Target editor/assets catalog only), an array of dictionaries describing the launch images iOS may display when launching the app. Each dictionary specifies a filename, minimum OS version (so your launch image can match the iOS 7 appearance of your app), size, and orientation.

- **Behavior**

  - `UIApplicationExitsOnSuspend` (Application does not run in background), if true, tapping the Home button on the iOS device will shut your app down, rather than putting it into the background.

  - `UIBackgroundModes` (Required background modes). iOS typically does not allow backgrounded apps any execution time, beyond a grace period of no more than ten minutes if they request one. There are exceptions for specific cases such as audio, VoIP, and navigational apps. Provide an array of `audio`, `voip`, or `location` to be treated as such an application. Be prepared to defend your claim in the App Store review process.

  - `UIFileSharingEnabled` (Application supports iTunes file sharing), if `YES`, the contents of the app's `Documents/` directory will be visible while the device is plugged into iTunes. This allows your users to move files between their devices and their computers.

- MKDirectionsApplicationSupportedModes (Maps routing app supported modes). For an application that gives routing direction, this is an array of modes of travel, indicating, for instance, that the app provides a dictionary for road travel, foot, and subways.

Info.plist

One of the files that are automatically generated when you instantiate a bundle (including application) target is a precursor file for Info.plist, named *target name-Info.plist*. By misadventure, this file might find its way into the target's Copy Bundle Resources build phase. That would put the file into the built product, which is a mistake. It's a *source* file, and its product, Info.plist, will be built and inserted into the product automatically.

Summary

This chapter explored bundles and package directories, important concepts in both OS X and iOS development. Most of Xcode's product types are bundles. I reviewed the structure of simple packages and application bundles and examined the Info.plist file, which communicates a bundle's metadata to the operating system.

23

Frameworks

In Chapter 20, "A Custom View for OS X," you constructed a bar-graph view that is isolated from the code inside Mac Passer Rating. Yes, its method selectors refer to games, and the drawing code pulls in properties with names like `attempts` and `completions`, but the code itself doesn't link to any code in the rest of the application.

Once again I'm going to pretend that `MPRPasserGraphController` and `MPRPassCompletionView` form a package that I'd want to reuse. I did the same thing with `passer-rating` in Chapter 6, "Adding a Library Target."

But there's a difference this time: The graph view requires a non-code resource, `MPRPasserGraphController.xib`, to link the view to its controller and to set drawing parameters. If I were building a classical Objective-C library, I'd be stuck; there's no practical way to put anything but code in a linkable library.

OS X solves this problem with *frameworks*, specialized bundles (see Chapter 22, "Bundles and Packages") that incorporate dynamic libraries, headers, and supporting resource files. You're already a client of a complex set of frameworks, constituting the code and headers for AppKit, Foundation, and Core Data. In this chapter, you'll be building a framework of your own.

> **Note**
>
> This is an OS X-only chapter. iOS applications are not allowed to include loadable code, so they can't package dynamic libraries, including frameworks. They can include, but not download, script files so long as the interpreter is embedded in the application binary. JavaScript in web pages is downloadable code, but it is sequestered in the `UIWebView` that downloaded it.

Adding a Framework Target

The first step toward building a framework should be familiar to you: Go to the Project editor for Mac Passer Rating and click the **Add Target...** row at the bottom of the target list. A New Target assistant will appear. You want OS X → Framework & Library → Cocoa Framework. Click **Next**.

Name the framework **PasserGraph**, and accept the existing **Organization Name** and **Company Identifier**. Verify that you'll be adding the target to the Mac Passer Rating project, and click **Finish**.

Xcode adds a PasserGraph target, plus PasserGraphTests; a new PasserGraph group for each appears in the Project navigator. PasserGraph includes

- `PasserGraph.h` and `PasserGraph.m`. Xcode assumes you're starting your framework from scratch and provides a template for a class for the framework to vend. Select these, press the Delete key, and confirm that Xcode should move them to the Trash.

- `PasserGraph-Info.plist`. As a bundle, a framework must have an `Info.plist` file; as with application targets, the **Info** tab of the Target editor shows a basic property-list editor for `PasserGraph-Info.plist`. (See Chapter 24, "Property Lists," for more about property lists.) The template fills in everything you need. The "Principal class" entry might tempt you, but that's for plugins, which get loaded once and instantiate an object to represent the plugin. PasserGraph is a library, and it has no gatekeeper object. Leave it blank.

- `InfoPlist.strings`. It's empty. Leave it that way.

- `PasserGraph-Prefix.pch`. You'll be using Core Data as well as Cocoa. Add

  ```
  #import <CoreData/CoreData.h>
  ```

  to the file.

While you're thinking about Core Data, select PasserGraph in the Target editor, and the **Build Phases** tab. Open the Link Binary With Libraries section, click the + button, and add `CoreData.framework`.

Populating the Framework

As you did in Chapter 6, "Adding a Library Target," reallocate some files between the application and framework targets.

1. Select `MPRPasserGraphController.m` and `MPRPassCompletionView.m`, and use the File inspector (Utility view) to take them out of the Mac Passer Rating target and put them into PasserGraph.

2. Do the same for `MPRPasserGraphController.xib`. You can't change its target membership simultaneously with source files.

3. Select `MPRPasserGraphController.h`, and add it to PasserGraph (as a header, it couldn't be a member of an application target, but it can be part of a framework). In the popup menu next to the target name, select **Public**. This will embed the file in the `Headers` subdirectory of the framework, so that any project that uses PasserGraph will have access to `MPRPasserGraphController.h`.

4. Do the same for `MPRPassCompletionView.h`, but give it **Project** scope, so it won't be built into the framework at all. (**Private** scope would bundle it into a `PrivateHeaders` directory.)

5. Keep the project tidy by putting the framework files in their own group in the Project navigator. It won't affect their memberships or placement in the filesystem, but it's good organization.

Notice that the framework is more than just a library: It will also include an .h file and a NIB (compiled from the XIB file you transferred) in the single framework unit.

Using the Framework

Let Mac Passer Rating know about the new framework. In the **Build Phases** tab of the Target editor for Mac Passer Rating, open the Link Binary With Libraries phase and click the **+** button. The browser sheet that drops down includes a section for products in the project. Select PasserGraph.framework and click **Add**. Use the popup to mark the framework **Required**—you *can* make a library **Optional** if you're willing to check for the existence of its services and carry on without them if they aren't present, but PasserGraph's classes have to be there.

Because **Find Implicit Dependencies** is checked in the **Build** panel of the Scheme editor for Mac Passer Rating, there's nothing you need to do to incorporate PasserGraph in the build process for the application. Xcode sees that you're using the product of another target and makes sure it's up-to-date.

Try it: Run the application (**Product → Run**, ⌘ **R**, or select the **Run** action from the **Action** button at the left end of the toolbar). It works! You can summon up the graph view, and you can set breakpoints in the graphing code.

So why am I not ending this chapter?

Installing a Framework

Try Mac Passer Rating as a real application. Select **Product → Archive**. The framework and the application build from scratch (Archive always does; it ensures that your distribution products don't carry over any products of earlier builds). Xcode then presents you with the Archives organizer. See Figure 23.1.

An archive embodies all of the build products—and debug symbols—of a project, for sharing, installation, or submission to an App Store. Your freshly made archive is already selected, so click the **Distribute...** button in the header above the archive list. In the first sheet that appears select **Save Built Products**, and click **Next**. You'll be given a save-file sheet for you to name and place a directory containing what you've built. Put it somewhere easy to find.

Running the Application Alone

Bring the Finder forward, and open that directory. It turns out to be surprisingly complex (Figure 23.2). Ignore your misgivings, find the Mac Passer Rating application, and double-click it.

Organizer – Archives
Devices
Projects
Archives
Mac Passer Rating
Passer Rating
mogenerator
PR-Storyboard
Mac Passer Rating
Mac Passer Rating
Archive Type: Generic Xcode Archive
Creation Date: 2 November 2013 at 5:06 PM
Version: Unspecified
Identifier:
Estimated App Store Size:
Estimate Size
Validate...
Distribute...
ARCHIVE
Name
Name
Creation Date
Comment
Status
Mac Passer Rating
2 November 2013 at 5:06 PM

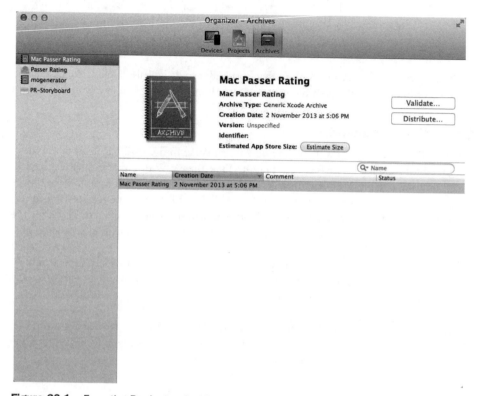

Figure 23.1 Executing **Product →Archive** opens the Archives organizer, focused on the archive you just created.

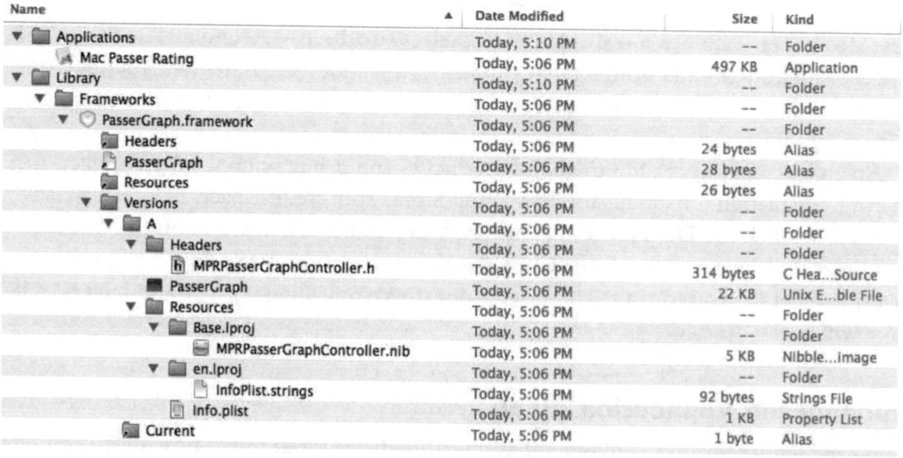

Name
Date Modified
Size
Kind
Applications
Today, 5:10 PM
--
Folder
Mac Passer Rating
Today, 5:06 PM
497 KB
Application
Library
Today, 5:10 PM
--
Folder
Frameworks
Today, 5:06 PM
--
Folder
PasserGraph.framework
Today, 5:06 PM
--
Folder
Headers
Today, 5:06 PM
24 bytes
Alias
PasserGraph
Today, 5:06 PM
28 bytes
Alias
Resources
Today, 5:06 PM
26 bytes
Alias
Versions
Today, 5:06 PM
--
Folder
A
Today, 5:06 PM
--
Folder
Headers
Today, 5:06 PM
--
Folder
MPRPasserGraphController.h
Today, 5:06 PM
314 bytes
C Hea...Source
PasserGraph
Today, 5:06 PM
22 KB
Unix E...ble File
Resources
Today, 5:06 PM
--
Folder
Base.lproj
Today, 5:06 PM
--
Folder
MPRPasserGraphController.nib
Today, 5:06 PM
5 KB
Nibble...image
en.lproj
Today, 5:06 PM
--
Folder
InfoPlist.strings
Today, 5:06 PM
92 bytes
Strings File
Info.plist
Today, 5:06 PM
1 KB
Property List
Current
Today, 5:06 PM
1 byte
Alias

Figure 23.2 The built-products directory for the Mac Passer Rating archive is surprisingly complex.

The icon appears in the Dock for an instant, and goes away. Instead, you see an OS X crash-report window. Use the disclosure triangle to expose the details (if they aren't already visible), and inspect the wreckage. The relevant message is (truncated for space):

```
Dyld Error Message:
    Library not loaded: /Library/Frameworks/PasserGraph.framework/...
    Referenced from: .../Mac Passer Rating.app/...
    Reason: image not found
```

"Image not found" means that the dynamic linker couldn't find the dynamic library in `PasserGraph.framework`, which it looked for in.../`Library/Frameworks`. Well, of course not: You never installed the framework in the global library directory.

But this explains the complexity of the built-products directory: It's a model of the final installation locations of the application (in the global `/Applications` directory) and the framework (in `/Library`). So do you have to install the framework as a system-wide resource? And why did it work at all when you ran the app from within Xcode?

The second question has a simple answer: When you're developing a framework, Xcode doesn't force you to go through an installation phase. It sets up the runtime environment so that the dynamic linker looks first in the project's derived data directory where the framework was built. That way, you always run the current development version of the framework, and no fuss.

The first question requires a little theory.

Where Frameworks Go

The core of a framework is a dynamic library—something you encountered in Chapter 5, "Compilation." The OS X dynamic linker has a search path of directories it tries when looking for a dynamic library (essentially `Library/Frameworks` in the user, local, network, and system domains). It is not wise to rely on that search, though. First, it is bad citizenship, because every library that forces a repeated search whenever it is loaded adds to the time it takes to launch applications. Second, it is bad security, because you don't know whether some other framework of the same name has come ahead of you in the search path.

> **Note**
>
> The days when frameworks could be installed in `Library` directories for sharing among applications are all but gone. It was a great idea, but the usual problem with shared dynamic libraries caught up with it: What happens when an application that relies on version n-1 of a framework is installed on a system where another application has already installed version n? The framework mechanism, with its internal versioning structure, partly solved this problem, but not fully. Nowadays, installation in a common `Library` directory is practical only for publishers of application suites that can update all their components simultaneously, which basically means Apple, Adobe, and Microsoft.

For speed and security, each time an application is built against a dynamic library, the application records the one location where it should find the correct library. That implies the framework's installed location should be known at build time. And that, in turn, implies that dynamic libraries must build their expected installation paths into themselves.

So where should the dynamic linker find PasserGraph? Hopefully, it's at the place you baked into the framework when you first built it. And the only practical place is within the .app bundle itself.

Which raises the next question: How do you bake the installation location into the framework?

Open the **Build Settings** tab of the Target editor for PasserGraph. The immediate setting for the baked-in name is "Dynamic Library Install Name" (LD_DYLIB_INSTALL_NAME)—but don't change it. If you double-click the value for that setting, you'll see it's a derived value, from DYLIB_INSTALL_NAME_BASE and EXECUTABLE_PATH. You want to go upstream from that derived name.

Instead, use "Installation Directory" (INSTALL_PATH). It, too, has a derived value, amounting to /Library/Frameworks. Change this to:

```
@executable_path/../Frameworks
```

which means "binary file that uses this library, look for it in the Frameworks subdirectory of your parent directory." The @executable_path element relieves you of having to specify an absolute directory path, which would of course change as the user moved or renamed the application. In fact, it frees the framework to be available to the developer of any application, without having to customize its installation path.

Putting the Framework in the Application

Now you've committed to putting PasserGraph.framework into the application bundle. How do you make sure it gets there?

Go to the **Build Phases** tab of the Target editor for Mac Passer Rating, and select **Editor** → **Add Build Phase** → **Add Copy Files Build Phase**. The new phase appears at the bottom of the list, which is acceptable. Click the disclosure triangle to open the phase. See Figure 23.3.

The first thing to do is to identify the file that is to be copied. Click the **+** button at the bottom of the phase's table, and use the browser to designate PasserGraph.framework. You'll find it in the Products group.

Next, determine where in the application bundle the framework is to go. The **Destination** popup offers quick settings for a number of common locations in the bundle, as well as options for an absolute path or the project's products directory. The destination you want is **Frameworks**. The **Subpath** field would allow you to designate a subdirectory of the destination directory to receive the file; this would be most useful if you were building up a directory tree in the application Resources directory. Leave it blank.

Copy only when installing controls whether the PasserGraph.framework will be put into the application bundle for non-archiving builds. Check this box; for debugging, you want to rely on the framework that is built into the project's derived-data tree.

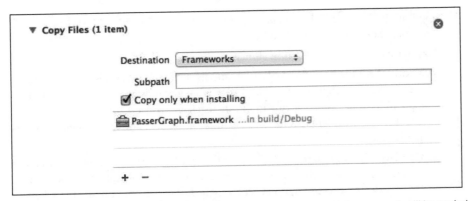

Figure 23.3   The Copy Files build phase, filled out so `PasserGraph.framework` will be copied into the `Frameworks/` directory of Mac Passer Rating's `.app` bundle.

One last step. In the **Build Settings** for PasserGraph, find the "Skip Install" setting, and set it to **Yes**. Now that the install path for the library is no longer fixed in the filesystem—in fact you just added a build phase that installs it manually—there is no point in setting up the mock installation that you got when you exported the archive directory. Setting Skip Install eliminates the creation of the separate installation tree.

> **Note**
> If you forget to set Skip Install, Xcode's build system will warn that you've set an installation location of your own, without suppressing the automatic installation. It will tell you to set Skip Install.

Building Mac Passer Rating

Select **Product → Archive** again. The Archives organizer shows you something new: Instead of the rectangular gray icon of an Xcode archive package, you're shown a new entry, with an application icon. Click **Distribute....** The export sheet is different, too. The options available to you depend on whether you are a member of the Mac Developer Program:

- **Submit to the Mac App Store Package**. If you are a member of the Mac Developer Program, this will produce an installer package to be distributed through the Mac App Store. This has to be signed, so if you choose this option, you'll have to supply a distribution signing identity.

- **Export Developer ID-signed Application**—also available only to the Mac Developer Program—saves a plain `.app` package that can be double-clicked to launch. It also signs the package with the Developer ID you will get through a Mac Developer Program membership. The signature will allow users to run the application even if they have Gatekeeper running. See Chapter 17, "Provisioning," for more about Developer ID and Gatekeeper.

- **Export as** gives you three more choices:

  - **Xcode Archive** saves the application and its debugging symbols in a form that you can keep in your records. The `lldb` debugger and other tools can find the app and its debugging information in the package, convert the addresses in bug reports into line references for that iteration of the app, and let you debug exactly that release.

  - **Mac Installer Package** creates a `.pkg` file that Installer.app can use to place your products in the user's filesystem. If you really do want to install a framework in `/Library/Frameworks`, don't set the Skip Install flag, and build an installer package. You will be required to apply a Mac Installer signing identity, available through the Mac Developer Program.

  - Apple hides **Application** from you—it would *really* prefer that you use Developer ID—but it is possible to generate a plain old app. Choose this option, click **Next**, and use the put-file sheet to save the app.

> **Note**
>
> I warned you about this in Chapter 17, "Provisioning," but it's of immediate interest, because we've embedded a framework in this edition of Mac Passer Rating. Each such component needs its own signature independent of the application's. This should be easier than it is, and it may have become so by the time you read this. Untill then have a look at Jerry Krinock's solution, on GitHub at `https://github.com/jerrykrinock/DeveloperScripts/blob/master/SSYShipProduct.pl`

Double-click Mac Passer Rating in the Finder, and test the graphing feature.

One More Thing

The graph doesn't appear. There's a bug that points up a trick in producing self-contained frameworks that maintain their own NIBs and other resources. You could launch the Console application (look in `/Applications/Utilities`), and see if there is any guidance—as it happens, AppKit prints a very helpful diagnostic message: `Mac Passer Rating[6919]: -[NSViewController loadView] could not load the "MPRPasserGraphController" nib.`, but I'll show you a different approach.

Debugging a Framework

Launch Mac Passer Rating from the Finder, and immediately turn to Xcode. Select the submenu **Debug → Attach to Process**. The submenu is very large—it lists every running process on your machine—but Xcode helpfully places Mac Passer Rating at the top, calling it a "likely target." Select it.

The Debugger and External Targets

Xcode switches to debugging mode. Double-click a passer's name, which is supposed to summon the graph. Because you set a breakpoint on exceptions (didn't you? See the "Running Bindings" section of Chapter 19, "Bindings: Wiring an OS X Application"), the debugger cuts in at the last line of the `passerTableClicked:` method of MPRDocument:

```
[self.passerPopover showRelativeToRect: rowRect
                            ofView: self.passerTable
                     preferredEdge: NSMaxXEdge];
```

Unfortunately, the debugger isn't much more help. If you type **po self**, the debugger will tell you it "Couldn't materialize struct." All of the object values in the variables display, including `self`, are `nil`. The problem is that you're dealing with an optimized release build. As you saw in Chapter 5, "Compilation," variables come in and out of existence from moment to moment, and lines are executed out of order.

> **Note**
>
> The debugger is still useful, net of two things: the information lost to optimization, and the loss of exception descriptions. You can still set breakpoints, trace execution, and get the occasional glimpse at data.

So let's kill Mac Passer Rating from the Xcode toolbar and take advantage of that `.xcarchive` package. Export one, if you haven't yet; I called it MPRArch. Open the Terminal, and set the current working directory to the archive root. Once you're there, apply the `lldb` debugger to the app:

```
$ ### Get into the archive package and see what's there
$ cd ~/MPRArch.xcarchive/
$ ls
Info.plist  Products     dSYMs

$ ### Run lldb and point it at Mac Passer Rating.
$ ### The actual executable is inside the .app package,
$ ### but lldb can figure it out.
$ lldb Products/Applications/Mac\ Passer\ Rating.app/
Current executable set to
        'Products/Applications/Mac Passer Rating.app/' (x86_64).

(lldb) ### Set a breakpoint at all Objectve-C exceptions:
(lldb) breakpoint set -E Objective-C
Breakpoint 1: no locations (pending).
(lldb) ### It's marked "pending" because the app hasn't
(lldb) ### loaded yet, and the symbol (objc_exception_throw)
(lldb) ### can't be resolved.
```

```
(lldb) ### Launch Mac Passer Rating
(lldb) process launch
Process 7736 launched: '.../Mac Passer Rating' (x86_64)
1 location added to breakpoint 1
(lldb) ### "1 location added to breakpoint 1" means the
(lldb) ### location for the exception breakpoint is now known.
```

By now, Mac Passer Rating is running inside lldb. lldb won't return to its prompt until the app hits a breakpoint or exception, or you press ⋏ C. In this case, trigger the bug. Reproduce the bug by double-clicking on a row in the passer table. This triggers the exception breakpoint:

```
2013-11-02 19:43:48.228 Mac Passer Rating[7736:303]
    unable to find nib named: MPRPasserGraphController
    in bundle path: (null)
```

```
(lldb) ### Then lldb itself reports on the stoppage: thread,
(lldb) ### location, dispatch queue, reason (breakpoint, with ID),
(lldb) ### location of top-of-stack, and a few instructions'
(lldb) ### disassembly.
(lldb) ### I've removed hexadecimal addresses for readability:
Process 7736 stopped
* thread #1: tid = 0x6993c
    libobjc.A.dylib`objc_exception_throw,
    queue = 'com.apple.main-thread,
    stop reason = breakpoint 1.1
    frame #0: libobjc.A.dylib`objc_exception_throw
libobjc.A.dylib`objc_exception_throw:
->    pushq   %rbp
      movq    %rsp, %rbp
      pushq   %r15
      pushq   %r14
```

```
(lldb) ### What's the stack look like?
(lldb) ### This is a "thread" command because each
(lldb) ### thread of execution has its own stack.
(lldb) thread backtrace
* thread #1: tid = 0x6993c, libobjc.A.dylib`objc_exception_throw,
    queue = 'com.apple.main-thread, stop reason = breakpoint 1.1
  frame #0: libobjc.A.dylib`objc_exception_throw
  frame #1: CoreFoundation`+[NSException raise:format:] + 204
  ...
  frame #4: AppKit`-[NSPopover showRelativeToRect:ofView:...
```

```
frame #5: Mac Passer Rating`-[MPRDocument passerTableClicked:]
    (self=<unavailable>, _cmd=<unavailable>,
    sender=<unavailable>) + 691 at MPRDocument.m:155
frame #6: AppKit`-[NSApplication sendAction:to:from:] + 327
frame #7: AppKit`-[NSControl sendAction:to:] + 86
...
frame #13: AppKit`NSApplicationMain + 940
frame #14: libdyld.dylib`start + 1
(lldb)
```

The last contact with Mac Passer Rating code is, as the Xcode debugger said, in frame 5 at
passerTableClicked:, and lldb can't find any variable values, either. lldb, however,
has the grace to print the exception message: "unable to find nib named:
MPRPasserGraphController in bundle path: (null)."

Out of curiosity, have a look at that frame 5:

```
(lldb) frame select 5
frame #5: Mac Passer Rating`-[MPRDocument passerTableClicked:]
        (self=<unavailable>, _cmd=<unavailable>,
        sender=<unavailable>) + 691 at MPRDocument.m:155
    152
    153     //  Show the popover next to the double-clicked row
    154     NSRect       rowRect = [self.passerTable rectOfRow: row];
->  155     [self.passerPopover showRelativeToRect: rowRect
    156                                     ofView: self.passerTable
    157                              preferredEdge: NSMaxXEdge];
    158  }

(lldb) ### What local variables are in this frame?
(lldb) frame variable
(MPRDocument *const) self = <variable not available>
(SEL) _cmd = <variable not available>
(id) sender = <variable not available>
(NSInteger) row = 1
(NSRect) rowRect = (x=0, y=19), (width=544, height=19)
(id) passer = <variable not available>
(MPRPasserGraphController *) pgc =
        <no location, value may have been optimized out>

(lldb) ### We're done. Exit lldb:
(lldb) exit
Quitting LLDB will kill one or more processes.
        Do you really want to proceed: [Y/n]
$
```

> **Note**
>
> All this time, you've probably had the Mac Passer Rating project open, and you were working with the last-built version of the app. Surely the lldb session would not have gone so well if the app had moved on to another version? Actually, it would. When an executable file is built, the linker embeds a universally unique identifier (UUID) in it, and it marks the debugger-symbols (.dSYM) file with the same UUID. When the Apple version of lldb loads the executable for debugging, it searches for the UUID in Spotlight and matches the application to the correct version of the debugging information.

There is a reference in code to a NIB named MPRPasserGraphController, and it's in passerTableClicked:...

```
MPRPasserGraphController *    pgc =
              [[MPRPasserGraphController alloc]
                initWithNibName: @"MPRPasserGraphController"
                          bundle: nil];
```

The problem is the nil that is passed in for the bundle. When a nil bundle is passed to initWithNibName:bundle:, NSViewController searches for the named NIB in the Resources/ directory of the main—the application's—bundle. But MPRPasserGraphController.xib is in the *framework's* resource directory.

There's something else wrong: As a client of PasserGraph, Mac Passer Rating shouldn't have to worry about the name of a NIB in the PasserGraph resources. So the first thing is to take the implementation detail out of passerTableClicked::

```
MPRPasserGraphController *  pgc = [[MPRPasserGraphController alloc] init];
```

and then to give MPRPasserGraphController a proper init method:

```
- (id) init
{
    self = [super initWithNibName: @"MPRPasserGraphController"
                          bundle: [NSBundle bundleForClass:
                                            [self class]]];
    //  No further initialization, so no if (self)...
    return self;
}
```

The init method shows the trick: NSBundle can identify the bundle that supplied a class—MPRPasserGraphController comes from the PasserGraph framework bundle: [NSBundle bundleForClass: [self class]], where self is an instance of MPRPasserGraphController.

Make these changes, archive, and save the application. Double-click, summon a graph popover, and find that the framework, at last, works.

Postmortem on Postmortem Debugging

The debugging sessions for Mac Passer Rating weren't completely as informative as we'd like. Were they any use at all?

Yes they were. An .xcarchive package freezes a version of your application along with its debugging information. Your users, when they report a crash, won't be able to give you a usable stack trace—all of the debugging information and symbols will have been stripped out. But you can reproduce the bug using the very code the user is running, and the debuggers can use those debugging symbols to pin the problem down to the method, probably the line, where the crash occurred.

The difficulties both in lldb and the Xcode debugger came from the fact that, by default, Archive builds are done with the Release configuration, which has clang optimize the code it emits. If you open the **Build Settings** tab for Mac Passer Rating, and set the "Optimization Level" to "None [-O0]" for the Release variant, and rebuild the archive, the problem goes away. At that point, even the Xcode debugger can attach to the app and get accurate information about the location and contents of variables. Of course, by that point, you're no longer dealing with the optimized application you got the crash report on.

Further, if your Mac application is stripped, and you get a crash report, you'll find that the only information in the stack trace about your own code is in the form of hexadecimal addresses. No method names, no source files, no line numbers. If lldb has the binary and the dSYM debugger symbols package for the version of the application that crashed—if you remembered to keep an archive of your releases and distribute them among your team members—it can symbolicate the address. That is, it can take an instruction address and translate it back to a reference to your source file:

```
(lldb) image lookup -a 0x0000000100002561
      Address: Mac Passer Rating[0x0000000100002561]
            (Mac Passer Rating.__TEXT.__text + 2273)
      Summary: Mac Passer Rating`
              -[MPRDocument passerTableClicked:] + 691
              at MPRDocument.m:155
```

> **Note**
>
> What about iOS crash reports? The process is much smoother. Apple collects all crash reports from iOS apps and makes them available to developers through their iTunes Connect accounts. Download your reports; open the Devices organizer and select the Device Logs listing; click the **Import** arrow at the bottom of the window. So long as the dSYM debugging archive is *anywhere* on your machine, Xcode will apply it to the reports, and symbolicate them for you.

Summary

In this chapter, I showed you techniques for breaking your OS X programs into reusable modules by putting them into frameworks. The technique of putting source code into a library was already familiar to you, but I showed you how frameworks could encapsulate headers and runtime resources as well.

I showed you the prerequisites for making a framework available to an application: setting the dynamic library's installation path to a relative path within the owning application, and adding a Copy Files build phase to put it there.

I finished by showing you the uses of the various products Xcode can export: Mac App Store submission packages, installers, Developer ID–signed applications, archives, installation trees, and, yes, plain old applications.

As important as the user products are, the developer product—the binary and debugging archives of your released products—is vital to tracking down bugs in locked-down copies of your app in the hands of the public. I showed you some debugging techniques that can recover the information you need from those crash reports.

24

Property Lists

Cocoa uses *property lists* (also called *plists*, after the common extension for property-list files) everywhere. They are the all-purpose storage medium for structured data, both for application resources and even application documents. Though I've put this chapter into the OS X section of this book, property lists are important to iOS developers, as well.

- Many of Apple's standard formats for configuration files are simply specifications of keys and trees for property lists. If you want a configuration file of your own, you could do much worse than a specialized plist file.

- In particular, applications on iOS and OS X alike include an Info.plist file that tells the system how the app is to be presented and what kinds of data it handles. See Chapter 22, "Bundles and Packages," for details.

- The property-list format is very mature—older than OS X itself. Cocoa can parse plist files in one line of code, directly into Foundation data types.

Property List Data Types

A property list is an archive for the fundamental data types provided by the Objective-C Foundation framework. It consists of one item of data, expressed in one of seven data types. Five property list types are scalar—number, Boolean, string, date, and data—and two are compound—ordered list and dictionary. An ordered list can contain zero or more objects of any property list type. A dictionary contains zero or more pairs, consisting of a string and an object of a property list type.

A property list can express most collections of data quite easily. A passer's performance in a single game could be represented as a dictionary of numbers with the keys attempts, completions, interceptions, touchdowns, and yards. A game could be a dictionary containing the date, team names, scores, and the performance dictionary.

Both Core Foundation and Cocoa provide reference-counted object types that correspond to the property list types (see Table 24.1). In fact, you can pass a Cocoa property list pointer to a Core Foundation routine for the corresponding type; you can also use a CFTypeRef for a property list type as though it were a pointer to the

Table 24.1   Property-List Types in Cocoa and Core Foundation

Data Type	Cocoa	Core Foundation	Markup
Number	NSNumber	CFNumber	`<integer>` `<float>`
Boolean	NSNumber	CFBoolean	`<true/>` `<false/>`
Text	NSString NSMutableString	CFString CFMutableString	`<string>`
Date	NSDate	CFDate	`<date>`
Binary Data	NSData NSMutableData	CFData CFMutableData	`<data>`
List	NSArray NSMutableArray	CFArray CFMutableArray	`<array>`
Associative Array	NSDictionary NSMutableDictionary	CFDictionary CFMutableDictionary	`<dict>` `<key>...` `plist type` `...` `</dict>`

corresponding Cocoa object. (Crossing the border between Foundation's Objective-C world and Core Foundation's pure-C world raises some memory-management issues that Automatic Reference Counting can't work out for itself. Search for "Transitioning to ARC Release Notes" in the Documentation organizer for the details of the `__bridge` family of type casts that give ARC the hints it needs.)

> **Note**
>
> The dictionary data type in Cocoa requires only that the keys in a dictionary be objects of an immutable, copyable type; Core Foundation dictionaries can be even more permissive. However, if you want to use a Cocoa or Core Foundation dictionary in a property list, all keys have to be strings.

Editing Property Lists

When you started the Passer Rating iPhone app, the first thing Xcode showed was the Target editor for the application. The third tab, **Info**, is a specialization of the Property List editor for `Info.plist`, which contains a dictionary describing to the OS how the application is to be presented. Each line of the top section represents one key-value pair at the top level of the dictionary; the **Info** editor refines the experience by wrapping some of the top-level keys (for such as document and data types) into distinct lists of convenient graphical editors. See Figure 24.1.

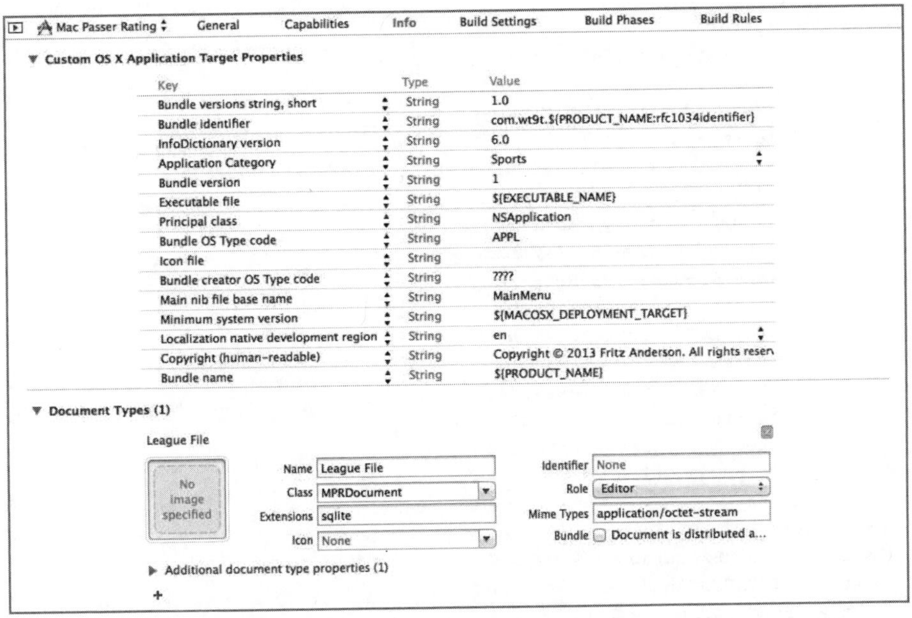

Figure 24.1 As soon as an application project is created, Xcode presents a Target editor to edit its `Info.plist` file. The first and third tabs, **Summary** and **Info** (shown here), are specialized editors to set the application's presentation and behavior.

Still, it's just an editor for a particular kind of property list. Let's have a look at the real thing. Use the search field at the bottom of the Project navigator to search for **plist**. The only file surviving in the navigator should be `Mac Passer Rating-Info.plist`. Click on it.

Not much to see. It's Xcode's generic Property List editor, which is just a little simpler than the Target editor's **Info** tab. What's the big deal? Do this: Right-click on the file's name in the Project navigator, and select **Open As** → **Source Code**. Now the Editor area fills with something like this:

```
<?xml version="1.0" encoding="UTF-8"?>
<!DOCTYPE plist PUBLIC "-//Apple//DTD PLIST 1.0//EN"
    "http://www.apple.com/DTDs/PropertyList-1.0.dtd">
<plist version="1.0">
<dict>
    <key>CFBundleDevelopmentRegion</key>
    <string>en</string>
    <key>CFBundleDocumentTypes</key>
    <array>
        <dict>
            <key>CFBundleTypeExtensions</key>
```

```
            <array>
                <string>sqlite</string>
            </array>
            <key>CFBundleTypeMIMETypes</key>
            <array>
                <string>application/octet-stream</string>
            </array>
            <key>CFBundleTypeName</key>
            <string>League File</string>
            <key>CFBundleTypeRole</key>
            <string>Editor</string>
            <key>LSTypeIsPackage</key>
            <false/>
            <key>NSDocumentClass</key>
            <string>MPRDocument</string>
            <key>NSPersistentStoreTypeKey</key>
            <string>SQLite</string>
        </dict>
    </array>
    <key>CFBundleExecutable</key>
    <string>${EXECUTABLE_NAME}</string>
    <key>CFBundleIconFile</key>
    <string></string>
    <key>CFBundleIdentifier</key>
    <string>com.wt9t.${PRODUCT_NAME:rfc1034identifier}</string>
    <key>CFBundleInfoDictionaryVersion</key>
    <string>6.0</string>
    <key>CFBundleName</key>
    <string>${PRODUCT_NAME}</string>
    <key>CFBundlePackageType</key>
    <string>APPL</string>
    <key>CFBundleShortVersionString</key>
    <string>1.0</string>
    <key>CFBundleSignature</key>
    <string>????</string>
    <key>CFBundleVersion</key>
    <string>1</string>
    <key>LSApplicationCategoryType</key>
    <string>public.app-category.sports</string>
    <key>LSMinimumSystemVersion</key>
    <string>${MACOSX_DEPLOYMENT_TARGET}</string>
    <key>NSHumanReadableCopyright</key>
    <string>Copyright (c) 2013 Fritz Anderson. All rights reserved.</string>
    <key>NSMainNibFile</key>
    <string>MainMenu</string>
    <key>NSPrincipalClass</key>
    <string>NSApplication</string>
</dict>
</plist>
```

You likely are relieved to see that the property list format is XML and that Cocoa's built-in writer for .plist files indents it nicely. The top-level element is <plist>, which must contain one property list element—in this case, <dict>, for the Info.plist dictionary. A <dict> element's contents alternate between <key> string elements and property list value elements. One of the keys, CFBundleDocumentTypes, has an <array> value. An <array> may contain zero or more property list elements, of any type, in this case, only one <dict> describing Mac Passer Rating's document type. I covered Info.plist keys at length in Chapter 22, "Bundles and Packages."

> **Note**
>
> I'm indulging in two cheats here. First, what you're looking at is not the Info.plist that will be inserted into the application bundle. It's a source file for a compiler that the build system uses to fill in variables and insert some invariant keys—you see variable names like ${PRODUCT_NAME}. Second, the Info.plist in the app bundle won't be an XML file; it will be a *binary plist*, as I show later in this chapter.

What's good about XML is that it is standard: Correct XML will be accepted by any consumer of a document type definition, regardless of the source. A .plist file generated by any Cocoa application will be treated the same as one generated by a text editor.

What's bad about XML is that it must be correct. If you forget to close an element or miss the strict alternation of <key> and values in <dict> lists, you will get nothing out of Apple's parser.

Usually, you don't have to worry about this sort of thing because you'll be using the Property List editor in its graphical form. You don't see the opening and closing tags, so you can't omit them. The editor forces you to put a key on every element in a dictionary and restricts you to the legal data types. Simple.

However, sometimes it's not practical to use the Property List editor to create or maintain property lists. Let's have a look at how the editor works, and then I can develop why it's not for every task.

The Property List Editor

We're going to create a property list that describes how to make an omelet. I'll leave to you what the file would be good for. Bring Xcode forward. Select **File** → **New** → **File. . .** (⌘ N), and navigate the New File assistant thus: OS X → Resource → Property List. (You can get the same thing from the iOS part of the assistant.) If you have a project window open, you'll be shown the usual put-file sheet. Call it **Omelet**. (Xcode will add .plist for you.) The other controls for disposing the new file in the project are now long-familiar to you.

You'll be presented with the same kind of Property List editor that you saw for the Info.plist file, only it's empty, but for a single line at the top, labeled Root. The Property List editor lets you generate <dict> or <array> plists, and the popup menu in the second column lets you choose which. Make sure it's a **Dictionary**.

But there's no obvious control for adding any content. What to do? There are two approaches.

Look at the **Editor** menu. It's dynamic, adjusting its content to the type of the active editor. Now that it's a Property List editor, you'll find the command **Add Item**. Select it, and a new row appears in the editor.

Or, hover the mouse cursor over the Root row. A + button will appear in the first column. Clicking it will add a row. See Figure 24.2, top.

The new row will be a key-value pair for the dictionary, with a *key*, represented as a text field that is open for editing; a *type*, represented as a popup listing the possible plist types; and a *value*, which is editable if the type is a scalar.

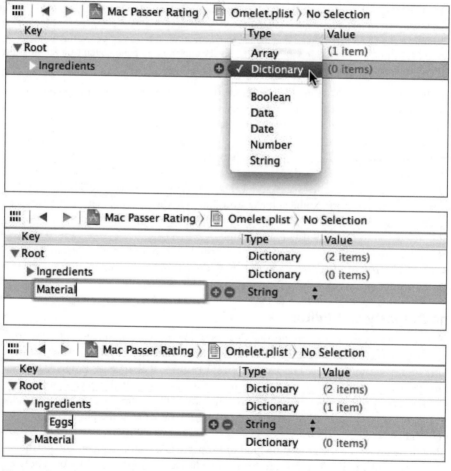

Figure 24.2   (top) Selecting **Editor →Add Item** inserts the first element in a new property list. Select from a popup menu in the Type column to indicate the data type the element represents. (middle) Pressing the Return key or clicking the **+** button when a container element is closed inserts a new element that is a sibling of the selected container. (bottom) If the container is open, pressing Return or clicking **+** inserts the new element as a child of the container.

The omelet recipe will have three sections, named `Ingredients`, `Material`, and `Method`. Ingredients should be a dictionary, with the keys naming the ingredients; the values should be dictionaries themselves, keyed `quantity` and `unit`. So name the first new row **Ingredients**, and set its type to **Dictionary**, as in Figure 24.2, top.

You want more items in the recipe. You want the `Material` and `Method` elements to be siblings of `Ingredients`, and you want to add ingredient dictionaries as children of `Ingredients`. That's two styles of adding rows to the editor.

Select the `Ingredients` row, and press the Return key (or, click the + button at the right of the Key cell, or select **Editor →Add Item**). This produces a new sibling row, which you can name **Material** and make a dictionary. See Figure 24.2, middle.

Select the `Ingredients` row again. At the left margin of the row, there is a disclosure triangle that is turned to the right, indicating that the container is closed. Click the triangle to open the container, which doesn't make much difference because a new dictionary doesn't have any contents to show.

Now press Return. A new row appears, but this time it is indented to show that the new element is *inside* the `Ingredients` dictionary (Figure 24.2, bottom). The difference is whether the disclosure triangle points closed or open. If closed, you get a sibling at the same level. If open, you get a child, enclosed in the container.

So now you have an element inside `Ingredients`. Name it **Eggs**, and make it a dictionary. Open Eggs, press Return (or click the + button) twice to create new elements named **quantity** (type **Number**, value 3—it's a generous omelet) and **unit** (type **String**, value **count**). You've completed your first ingredient.

> **Note**
>
> Make a mistake? Undo works as normal. If you want to get rid of an item, select it and press Delete, or click the – button in its Key column. Deleting a container deletes all of its contents as well.

Add more siblings to Eggs—or children to Ingredients—as shown in Table 24.2.

Table 24.2   The Remaining Ingredients in an Omelet

Mushrooms	Count	2
Salt	Pinch	1
Butter	Ounce	2

Doing this the obvious way, clicking new-sibling and new-child buttons at each step, and setting the same unit and quantity keys for each new dictionary, is tedious. There are some shortcuts.

- Once you have one dictionary (Eggs) set up the way you want it, select that dictionary by clicking on the container row (Eggs), and **Edit →Copy** (⌘ C). When you paste the row you've copied, it will be inserted as though you had clicked the + button on the selected row. So select the Ingredients dictionary while it's open, or the Eggs dictionary while it's *closed*, and **Edit →Paste**. You'll have to change the pasted element's key and change the values of the "unit" and "quantity" keys but that's the minimal work you'd have to do anyway.

- When you've finished editing a key or value, the Tab key will take you to the next visible editable string.

- The Return key will close a text-field cell if one is open. Pressing it again will create a new element (sibling or child) as though you'd clicked the + button on the selected row. The new row will have the key string (if it's in a dictionary) or the value string (if it's not) ready for editing. The initial type will be for a string, which is probably the type you'd want if you're motoring through several new rows at a time.

The Material dictionary should be simple key/string pairs, as shown in Table 24.3. The Method array should contain strings, as shown in Table 24.4.

Table 24.3   Materials for Making an Omelet

Bowl	Small
Fork	Table fork or small whisk
Crêpe pan	10" nonstick
Spatula	Silicone, high-heat
Egg slicer	Optional, for slicing mushrooms

Table 24.4   Instructions for Making an Omelet

Heat pan to medium (butter foams but doesn't burn)
Warm eggs in water to room temperature
Slice mushrooms
Sauté in 1/4 of the butter until limp, set aside
Break eggs into bowl, add salt
Whisk eggs until color begins to change
Coat pan with 1/2 the butter
Pour eggs into pan, and tilt to spread uniformly
When edges set, use spatula to separate from pan, then tilt liquid into gaps
Leave undisturbed for 30 seconds
Loosen from pan, and flip (using spatula to help) 1/3 over
Top with mushrooms
Slide onto plate, flipping remaining 1/3 over
Spread remaining butter on top

It's important that Method's strings appear in order, so it has to be an array. If it's not in the order you want, you can drag items into the order you want. See Figure 24.3.

When you've done it all, your Property List editor should look like the one in Figure 24.4.

Search-and-replace works in property lists as it does in regular text files. If you click **Find → Find. . .** (⌘ F), the find bar appears. If you type **butter**, the containers open to

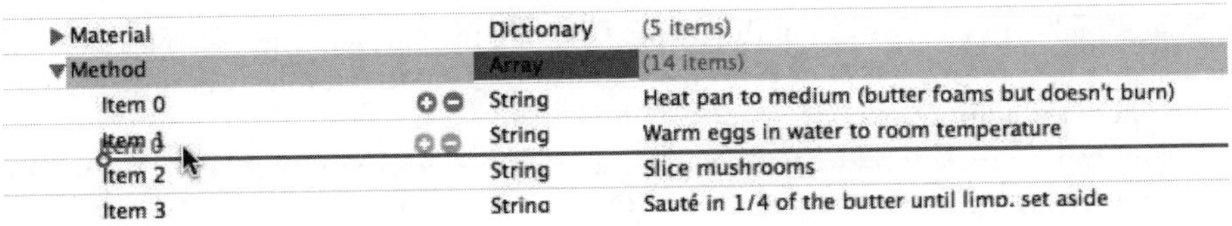

▶ Material	Dictionary	(5 items)
▼ Method	Array	(14 items)
Item 0	String	Heat pan to medium (butter foams but doesn't burn)
Item 0	String	Warm eggs in water to room temperature
Item 2	String	Slice mushrooms
Item 3	String	Sauté in 1/4 of the butter until limp. set aside

Figure 24.3   You can reorder array elements by dragging them where you want them.

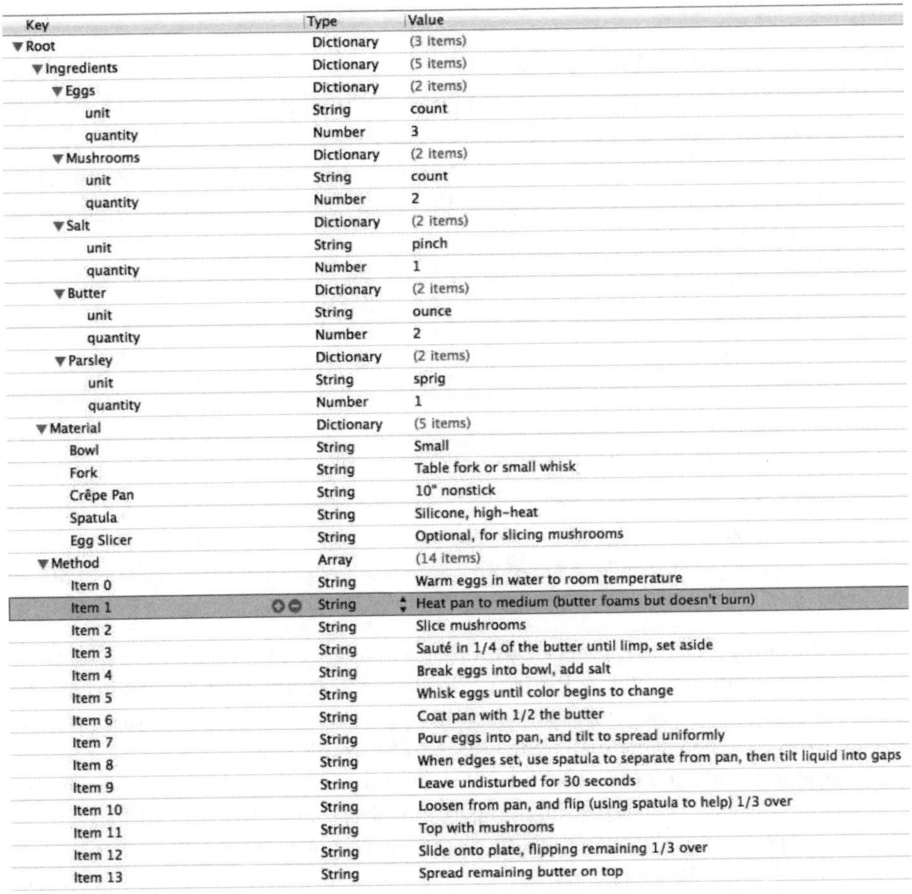

Key	Type	Value
▼ Root	Dictionary	(3 items)
▼ Ingredients	Dictionary	(5 items)
▼ Eggs	Dictionary	(2 items)
unit	String	count
quantity	Number	3
▼ Mushrooms	Dictionary	(2 items)
unit	String	count
quantity	Number	2
▼ Salt	Dictionary	(2 items)
unit	String	pinch
quantity	Number	1
▼ Butter	Dictionary	(2 items)
unit	String	ounce
quantity	Number	2
▼ Parsley	Dictionary	(2 items)
unit	String	sprig
quantity	Number	1
▼ Material	Dictionary	(5 items)
Bowl	String	Small
Fork	String	Table fork or small whisk
Crêpe Pan	String	10" nonstick
Spatula	String	Silicone, high-heat
Egg Slicer	String	Optional, for slicing mushrooms
▼ Method	Array	(14 items)
Item 0	String	Warm eggs in water to room temperature
Item 1	String	Heat pan to medium (butter foams but doesn't burn)
Item 2	String	Slice mushrooms
Item 3	String	Sauté in 1/4 of the butter until limp, set aside
Item 4	String	Break eggs into bowl, add salt
Item 5	String	Whisk eggs until color begins to change
Item 6	String	Coat pan with 1/2 the butter
Item 7	String	Pour eggs into pan, and tilt to spread uniformly
Item 8	String	When edges set, use spatula to separate from pan, then tilt liquid into gaps
Item 9	String	Leave undisturbed for 30 seconds
Item 10	String	Loosen from pan, and flip (using spatula to help) 1/3 over
Item 11	String	Top with mushrooms
Item 12	String	Slide onto plate, flipping remaining 1/3 over
Item 13	String	Spread remaining butter on top

Figure 24.4   The Property List editor showing the finished `Omelet.plist`. You can open or close all of the subelements in a dictionary or array by holding the Option key when you click the disclosure triangle.

show and highlight all instances of the string. Clicking the left- and right-arrow buttons in the find bar (or pressing ⇧⌘G or ⌘G) navigates among the found rows, but it doesn't enable them for editing.

If you want to replace butter with margarine, **Find → Find and Replace...** (⌥⌘F) will add a replacement row to the find bar. (Or, use the popup at the left end of the find bar to select **Replace** instead of **Find**.) Put `margarine` in the second field, and click the **All** button, thus sealing your status as a barbarian.

Find → Find in Workspace/Project... (⇧⌘F) works, too. The Find navigator appears, you enter `butter`, and the plist appears in the list of matches.

Why Not the Property List Editor?

The Property List editor generated a correct property list with all the data in what seems to be the most direct way possible. What more is there to say?

It isn't perfect. Right-click on the file in the Project navigator, and select **Open As → Source Code** from the contextual menu. Once again, you'll see the plist in the XML format in which it is stored.

You have doubts about your recipe. Maybe a little garnish would be nice, but you can't decide. So you add an XML comment to the `Methods` array:

```
<key>Method</key>
<array>
    .

    .


    .
    <string>Slide onto plate, flipping remaining 1/3 over</string>
    <string>Spread remaining butter on top</string>
    <!-- Should I add parsley? -->
</array>
```

Using the contextual menu, select **Open As → Property List** again. Make a tentative advance in presentation by adding Parsley (sprig, 1) to the `Ingredients` dictionary. (You'll have to open the dictionary; Xcode saves open/collapsed state, but reverts to all-collapsed if you change editors.) Switch back to **Source Code**.

The comment you added is gone. If you use the Property List editor to change a property list, it will destroy any content that isn't property-list data. Similarly, if you take advantage of the build option to apply a preprocessor pass to the compilation of `Info.plist`, so you can have `#includes` and conditional content, those directives will be lost if they pass through the Property List editor.

> **Warning**
>
> If you intend to treat property lists as normal source files, using comments for notes or to comment content out, you must *never* edit them with the graphical editor. Viewing them is okay—in fact, it's unavoidable, because Xcode puts you back in the graphical editor every time you return to the file—but don't change them.

Commenting and preprocessing aside, a text editor can just be the best tool for the job. Large and repetitive structures are a bit easier to handle in XML text, it's easier to handle programmatically generated files, and maybe you just like to work with source.

There's a way you can do this without forcing the Source Code editor every time. Select your property list file in the Project navigator, and open the Utilities area (using the right-hand button in the **View** control in the toolbar). Make sure the File inspector tab (the first one) is selected. You'll see various information about the file and its status in your project (Figure 24.5, left); the one you're interested in is the setting in the **Type** popup menu.

It starts with **Default – Property List XML**. Scroll through the menu (it will be quite a ways down) until you find the **Property List / XML** group, and select **XML**.

Nothing happens to the editor. Select a different file in the Project navigator, then go back to Omelet.plist. Now it appears as an XML file, and always will, without your having to tell Xcode to switch.

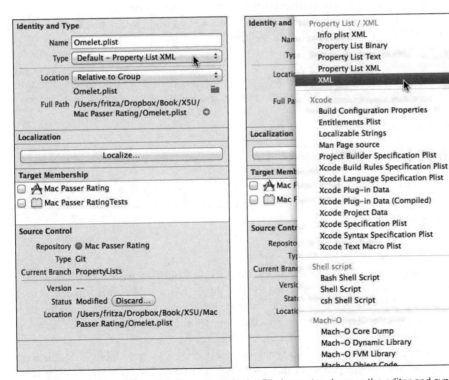

Figure 24.5   The popup under the filename in the File inspector chooses the editor and syntax that Xcode will apply to that file. You can force Xcode always to use the XML editor for a particular .plist file by selecting **XML** in the **Property List / XML** group, instead of **Property List XML**.

> **Note**
>
> That Xcode labels **Property List XML** as a default suggests that you might be able to change the default, and get the plain-XML editor all the time, without setting it for each file. In Xcode 3, you could do that. The feature was removed in Xcode 4, and it hasn't returned.

If you commit to creating and editing property lists in XML, you lose the safety of the Property List editor in keeping the syntax correct. There are a couple of ways to reduce the risk.

First, you can start your own `.plist` files by editing a known-good `.plist` file. It's difficult to omit the processing instruction or the `<plist>` skeleton if they are already in the file.

Second, you can use the macro or glossary facilities of your text editor to create a document skeleton and wrap your entries in proper tags. Bare Bones Software's BBEdit comes with a `.plist` glossary for just this purpose.

Once you have your property list file, you'll need to know if it is syntactically correct—if it isn't, you can't use it. The best way is to use the `plutil` tool. In the Terminal, type `plutil` *`pathToPropertyList`*. You will see either *`pathToPropertyList`*`: OK`, or a diagnostic message pointing to the first line that confused the parser. See `man plutil` for details.

> **Note**
>
> One of the commonest errors is forgetting that the text portions of the property list XML are parsed character data, which means that < and & must be represented by < and &.

Other Formats

If you stick to editing property lists as text, you'll find that text editors can display and edit only *most* property list files. There are two other formats a plist file may use. One is also text, the other is binary.

Text Property Lists

Property lists came to Cocoa's architecture from its ancestor framework, NeXTStep. In NeXTStep, property lists were encoded in what Apple calls a legacy format, but it is used often enough that you should be familiar with it. `defaults`, the command-line interface to the preferences system, the bundle specifications for the editor TextMate, and many of the internal Xcode configuration files use the text format.

Text property lists have only two primitive types: string and data (Table 24.5). Strings are surrounded by double-quote characters, which may be omitted if there are no spaces in the string. Number, date, and Boolean values must be stored as string representations, and the application that reads them is on its own for converting them to their respective types. The convention for Boolean values is to use the strings YES and NO.

Table 24.5   Encoding for Text-style Property Lists

Type	Coding
String	"Two or more words" *or* oneWord
Data	< 466f6f 626172 >
List	(Shirley, "Goodness and Mercy", 1066)
Associative array	{ key = value; "key 2" = < 332e3134313539 >; }

Data elements are delimited by angle brackets and contain pairs of hexadecimal digits, representing the bytes in the data. Any whitespace in the digit stream will be ignored.

Arrays are surrounded by parentheses, and the elements are separated by commas. Dictionaries are surrounded by braces, and the `key = value` pairs are *followed by* semicolons, which means that the last element must be closed off with a semicolon.

Binary Property Lists

With OS X 10.2 (Jaguar), Apple introduced a binary property list format. Binary plists are smaller and load faster. Programmatically generated plists are binary by default; Xcode, for instance, writes `Info.plist`s in binary. Property lists can be converted between XML and binary format in-place using the `plutil` command-line utility in the form

```
plutil -convert format pathToFile
```

where `format` is either `binary1`, for conversion to the binary format, or `xml1` for the XML format; and `pathToFile` is the path to the file to convert.

> **Note**
>
> Both Xcode and BBEdit will automatically translate binary property-list files into XML for editing.

The build settings `INFOPLIST_OUTPUT_FORMAT` and `PLIST_FILE_OUTPUT_FORMAT` influence how Xcode writes `Info.plist` and other-plist files, respectively, into your product. By default, these are `binary`, but you can set them to `XML`.

Specialized Property Lists

Many of Cocoa's standard "file formats" are simply property lists with stereotyped keys and enumerated values. Xcode knows about these stereotypes; you can assign a type to a plist by opening it, and right-clicking in the editor view. The contextual menu includes a **Property List Type** submenu. If Xcode encounters a stereotyped plist, such as `Info.plist` or an iOS Settings bundle, it will choose the key/value repertoire automatically.

Once a property list type is established, the Key column in the Property List editor assumes a much more active role. Xcode now knows what keys this particular plist supports and what types are appropriate to those keys.

For example: An iOS application `Info.plist` will include the key `UTExportedTypeDeclarations`. If you add a row to the plist, the key field is no longer a simple text field, but a combo field (a text field with a scrollable list of choices) in which "Exported Type UTIs" is an option. If you select it, Xcode automatically changes the type of the row to array—because the `UTExportedTypeDeclarations` element must have an array value.

If you open that array, and add a row to it, Xcode will create a dictionary—`UTExportedTypeDeclarations` must contain dictionaries—prepopulated with the three keys (and types) required of those dictionaries.

For a key that has a restricted set of scalar values, Xcode will set the element to the proper type, and instead of an editable value field, the value column will contain a popup of English-language names for the legal values.

> **Note**
>
> The values are still editable text, and if you click in most of their area, you'll get an editing field. For the popup menu, click on the arrowheads at the right end of the row.

Remember that combo fields are text fields, not menus. Xcode offers them wherever it's legal to enter a custom value. Treat that key or value as editable text, and ignore the attached list. The list isn't comprehensive or restrictive; if something you need isn't there, type it in yourself.

The combo fields' lists scroll automatically to offer presets that match what you've typed. This is handy, but the matching is case-sensitive. If you aren't finding what you expect, try typing with an initial cap.

Having English-language equivalents for all of your keys and values cuts you off from the actual content of those elements; even if XML editing isn't to your taste, you may want to audit what's going into your file. There are two strategies for this:

- Open the Utility (right) area, select Quick Help (the second tab), and click in a row. Quick Help will show the English name and the "declaration," the actual encoded key. You're out of luck for English-language values.

- Select **Editor** → **Show Raw Values & Keys** (or the same command from the contextual menu). The Property List editor will switch over to its "normal" behavior, displaying the uninterpreted keys and values.

Summary

This chapter introduced property lists, a ubiquitous data-storage format in Cocoa. You've seen how to use the Property List editor and text tools to manage them. I showed you the other ways property lists can appear on OS X and iOS, and how Xcode adapts itself to the stereotyped formats of well-known specializations of the plist format. By now, you should be pretty comfortable with the concept.

Part IV

Xcode Tasks

Documentation in Xcode

The combined documentation for developer tools and the current versions of OS X and iOS run to about a gigabyte and a half, and Apple updates it continually. Xcode incorporates an extensive help and documentation system to give you quick access to the documents while you are coding, and a browser for when you need to go into more depth. In this chapter, I'll show you how to make the most of the facilities Xcode provides, and how you can add your own documentation.

Quick Help

Quick Help is Xcode's facility for getting you information about the API with as little interruption as possible. The presentation is lightweight but thorough, and if you need to go deeper, the links are there.

Inspector

Quick Help is available on permanent view in almost every editor. Simply expose the Utility area (right-hand segment of the **View** control at the right end of the toolbar) and select the Quick Help inspector (second tab).

- If you're editing source, and the editing cursor is in a symbol for which Apple has documentation, Quick Help will show you a summary of how a method (for instance) is invoked, a description of what it does, the types and purposes of its parameters, and what it returns. It will tell you the earliest version of the OS that supports it, and it will offer you cross-references to overview documentation, related API, and the header file in which the symbol is declared. The information is drawn from the docset corresponding to the SDK you're using. See Figure 25.1, left. Quick Help works on your own symbols, too, but all you will get is a reference to the declaration—unless you provide documentation of your own. More on that later.

- When you select an object in Interface Builder, Quick Help provides documentation for the object's class.

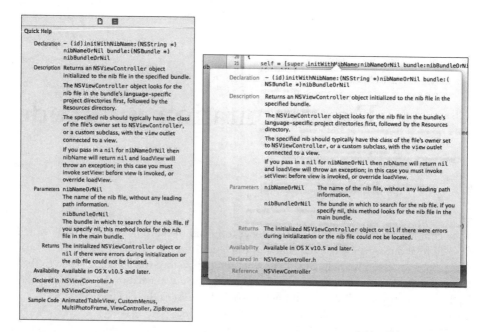

Figure 25.1   (left) When the Quick Help inspector is open, and the text cursor is in any documented symbol, the inspector displays a summary of the symbol, parameters, and other information. It includes clickable cross-references. (right) If you hold down the Option key and click on a documented symbol, Xcode displays a popover window with the same information.

- In the Project/Target editor's **Build Settings** tab, selecting a row will fill Quick Help with what will usually be the most complete documentation you can find of the setting. The description includes how the setting might get a default value, the build variable underlying the setting (see Appendix A, "Some Build Variables"), and the compiler flag, if any, the setting sets.

- In property list editors, and the **Info** tab of the Target editor, if Xcode displays an English-language equivalent of a key in the editor, Quick Help will show you the underlying key.

Popover

Holding down the Option key and mousing into a symbol will put a dotted line under it and highlight it in blue. If you click, a popover appears with most of the content you'd see in the Quick Help inspector. See Figure 25.1, right. (You can do the same thing by selecting **Help → Quick Help for Selected Item**, ⌃ ⌘ ?.)

Option-double-clicking on a symbol brings up the Documentation browser and jumps to the documentation for the symbol. It's not a search—your search settings in the

browser have no effect. The gesture takes you directly to the documentation without
any searching.

An abbreviated form of Quick Help is also available during code completion. When
the completion popup is showing, click on one of the choices, and see a couple of lines of
the symbol's description at the bottom of the popup.

Now is the time to mention command-clicking:

- Command-clicking on a symbol opens the file in which the symbol is defined and
  highlights the definition. If there's more than one definition, a popup menu offers
  you the choice. See Figure 25.2.

- Adding the Option key to a command-click shows the declaration in the Assistant
  editor; remember that adding the Option key to any navigational gesture directs the
  result to the Assistant editor.

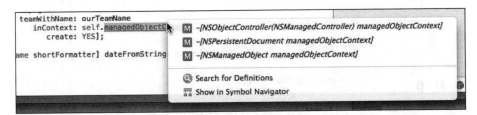

Figure 25.2   If there is more than one definition for a symbol, command-clicking will produce a
popup listing all definitions, and offering to search the project for it or to reveal symbols that contain
the string you command-clicked, in the Symbol navigator.

Open Quickly

Most programmer's editors have some sort of open-quickly or open-selection command
that lets you select a filename and have the editor find and open the file named in the
selection. Xcode's **File → Open Quickly. . .** (⇧⌘O) does the same. But that doesn't
end it.

The Open Quickly dialog has a search field that does an incremental search of the
names of the files, local and system, that your project can access. All of the possibile
matches are listed in a table, and when you select one, its location is shown in the path
control below the table.

There's more: The search extends to symbols, not just filenames. Enter
`componentsBrokenByLines`, and you'll be shown the match and its location in
`SimpleCSVFile.m`. This is not a simple incremental match. Apple anticipated that you
might want to look up a symbol or file whose name you don't quite remember; just enter
the parts you do remember: Enter `compbbl`, and it will find (among others)
`componentsBrokenByLines`. See Figure 25.3.

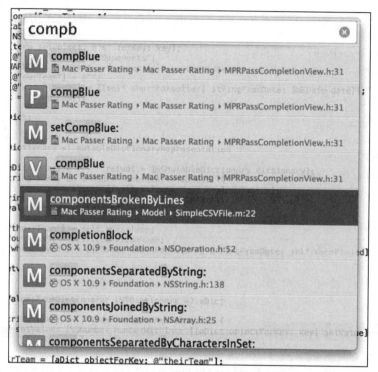

Figure 25.3   The Open Quickly dialog finds files and symbols accessible to your project based on an incremental search. It is not necessary to remember the whole name; any sequence you enter will be matched against any sequence of characters in the name, consecutive or not.

Help

Like every OS X application, Xcode has a **Help** menu. The first item in it is not a menu item at all, but an incremental search field. As you type, the contents of the menu are replaced with items in two sections:

- **Search** lists every menu item that contains the text you typed. Mousing over the listed items opens up the corresponding menu and places a pointer next to the item. Clicking on a listed item has the same effect as selecting the item itself.
  Some "hidden" items will be shown, and some will not. "Alternate" items that appear only when you hold down a modifier key (open the **File** menu and press and release the Option key to see what I mean) will be found. You will not find menu items that Xcode has removed, in particular commands in the **Editor** menu that don't apply to the current editor.

- **Documentation and API Reference**, ⌥⌘0, opens the Documentation browser. More about that shortly.

- **Xcode Overview** opens the Documentation browser on a series of articles introducing Xcode and how to use it.
- **Release Notes** are version-by-version summaries of the changes and issues in Xcode. "Release notes" doesn't sound like much, but for most Apple technologies, the notes can be as important as the "official" documentation. The Xcode notes give you details like the protocols and ports Xcode uses for version control and workarounds for issues that made it into the release.
- **What's New in Xcode** is *almost* a marketing document. It provides release-by-release feature lists.
- **Quick Help for Selected Item**, ^ ⌘ ?, is the same as option-clicking. It displays a popover with Quick Help for the selection.
- **Search Documentation for Selected Text**, ^ ⌥ ⌘ /, is the equivalent to an option-double-click: It's a menu item and key combination to bring the Documentation browser up on the contents of the selection.

The Documentation Window

Quick Help is good for focused reference, but you also need simply to read the documentation. To do this, you use the Documentation browser (**Window → Documentation and API Reference**, ⇧ ⌘ 0).

The Documentation browser consists of a large view for content, plus two sidebars you can hide or reveal using the buttons in the toolbar.

The Navigator Sidebar

The Navigator sidebar has two tabs. The first presents an outline of the entire documentation library. This will eventually reach every page in the documentation sets, but there are thousands of pages, and the tree that leads to class references is five layers deep. The first layer or two have descriptive names like "Data Management," but unless you have a miraculous sense of how Apple thinks of such things, there doesn't *seem* to be much use in the Library navigator.

The second tab is the Bookmark navigator. It's straightforward: The documentation pages, and every indexable section within the pages, carry bookmark buttons; click one, and the name of the section and article appears in the bookmark list. Clicking a bookmark returns you to that location; you can reorder the list by dragging, and a contextual menu lets you delete bookmarks or open them in new tabs.

You can hide or reveal the Navigator by clicking the third button in the toolbar, the one that looks like a disclosure triangle in a box.

The Table of Contents Sidebar

The second column is for a table of contents. Apple's documentation is organized into "books," "articles," and "sections." The table of contents lays out the structure of a major division in an outline view.

If the document on display is an API reference, the outline makes good use of Apple's standard layout for class references, with major divisions for task-grouped method lists, class methods, and instance methods.

The fourth button in the toolbar, looking like a bullet list on a page, shows and hides the table of contents.

Class Info

Another feature of class references is a header section outlining a class's superclasses and implemented protocols, its framework, the OS releases in which the class is available, a declaration header, and links to related documents and sample code. In older versions of the Documentation browser, this was simply a `<div>` at the top of the page; scroll down the page, and the summary scrolls out of view. This isn't satisfactory, because you'll need to refer to that header all the time. In Xcode 5, the header stays in its own frame at the top of the viewer, with a popover for the full content. See Figure 25.4.

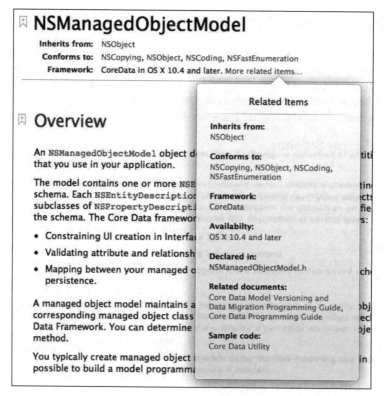

Figure 25.4   The class-summary frame at the top of class references shows the basic information for the class, including references to documentation and sample code.

And when you're looking at a class or reading an article, you may want to browse to other pages not directly cross-referenced, but on the same subject. This was impossible before Xcode 5. Select **Editor** →**Reveal in Library** to see the Library navigator with the outline opened to the current document—and the related items around it.

Searching and Navigation

The Documentation browser follows the conventions of a web browser: It has a search bar, back and forward buttons, bookmarks, tabs, and ways to share the contents.

I've already covered bookmarks, and I shouldn't have to tell you about back and forward buttons. The browser doesn't offer the common gesture of scroll-left to navigate backward and scroll-right, forward. (If you're interested in the gesture in general, it's in the **Trackpad** and **Mouse** panels of System Preferences.)

Tabs

Command-clicking on a link opens the linked page in a new tab; right-clicking on a link offers **Open Link in New Tab**. The **New** → **Tab** (⌘ T) command gets you a new, blank browsing environment.

As of Xcode 5.1, when you drag a tab out of the tab bar, Xcode shows the same drag effect as dragging a tab from a project window: A small image of the tab contents follows your mouse. That's where the similarity ends; the image disappears when you release the mouse button, and the tab remains in the browser window. You can have only one Documentation window.

Searching

The search bar is the main way you'll navigate the documentation. At the first level, it's simple: Type your search terms; as you type, the browser displays a drop-down list showing a selection of matching articles (Figure 25.5). Press Return to accept the leading result, or click in the drop-down to select another match. This is almost ideal.

If you decide you need to see another article—and this will happen frequently, because the "selected," and even the "best," matches are often not useful—the experience deteriorates. There is no way to recover the suggestion drop-down unless you back off the last character of the search field and type it again.

Try pressing Return while focus is in the search field. Nothing happens. Press Return again. Now you're in business: You get the "Show All Results" page, which is the most useful result of a documentation search. (It's also available if you select **Show All Results** in the suggested-results drop-down.)

The page shows all articles that match the search string, tabbed between API, SDK overviews, developer-tools topics, and sample code. The drop-down is one-way; the all-results page is a page with a place in the browser's history. If one result is unsatisfactory, you can go back to the results and try again. And, it contains *every* match for your search, not just a best-guess selection. The only advantage to the drop-down is that the entries display the title of the next-higher division of the documents. See Figure 25.6.

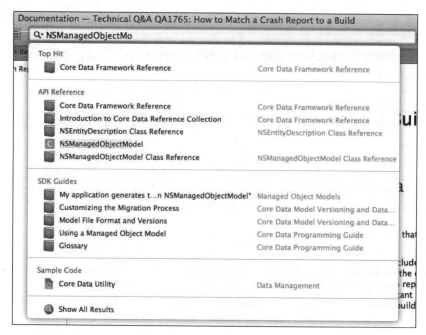

Figure 25.5   Typing in the search field produces a drop-down menu of some of the articles that match the search term.

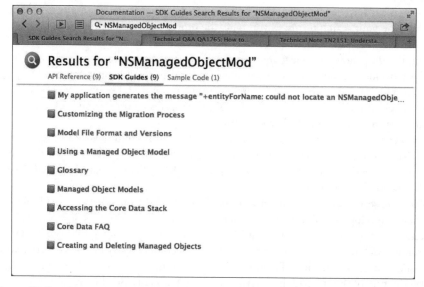

Figure 25.6   The most valuable product of a search is the all-results page, listing all matching articles by title, organized by the scope of the article. It is also the hardest product to reach.

You can restrict the search by clicking the magnifying-glass button in the search field. This will produce a popover containing a choice of **OS X** and **iOS** to search documentation for those platforms only; **All SDKs** to force the browser to search all of the available docsets; and **Automatic**, to allow it to guess the scope of the search from context, such as the currently selected target in the front project window (Figure 25.7).

Export

The **Export** button, at the right end of the toolbar, gives you options for alternative views of the current documentation page and for sharing references to it. You can bookmark the page, view its underlying HTML in Safari, or fetch the PDF document that includes the contents of the current page.

There are two other options, **Email Link** and **Message**. Each page in the documentation set can be reached by an xcdoc URL. Following an xcdoc link opens Xcode and the Documentation browser and displays the page.

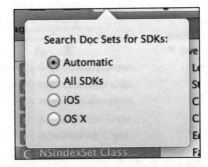

Figure 25.7 Clicking the magnifying-glass button in the search field produces a popover window for you to choose the scope of your documentation searches.

Email Link creates an email message in Mail.app containing the URL; **Message** pops up a window containing the URL and a field to receive a destination as understood by the Messages application. Click **Send**, and the recipient sees the link in Messages, a compatible instant-message service, or an SMS text.

Keeping Current

Xcode and Apple's documentation do not come out on the same schedule. They can't. Even if it were practical to halt one team while the other caught up to a release, the documents will still be extended and revised, and be ready for the public, at a much faster pace than a complex set of developer tools can.

When you first install Xcode, you don't have a complete local documentation library. What is packaged into ~/Library/Developer/Shared/Documentation/DocSets is a skeleton of a couple hundred megabytes with minimal content, filled in with references to content at developer.apple.com. The equivalent local library is an order of magnitude larger. Not including the full library makes downloading Xcode faster, and it frees Apple from providing an obsolete library (or having to rebuild the Xcode distribution every few weeks as documentation is revised).

> **Note**
>
> In earlier releases of Xcode, docsets were kept in an all-users library at /Library/Developer/Documentation/DocSets, and before that, inside the /Developer tree. Now, each user has a personal copy of the documentation.

So the first thing you're going to do when you install Xcode is to run it, need it or not. It will immediately compare its local document set with what's on Apple's servers, and it will commence a download of a gigabyte or more.

Documentation is provided in *documentation sets* (docsets), essentially large web sites plus the indexes that make Quick Help, the browsing outline, and full-text searching possible. Each docset is nearly self-contained, though it can have references out to the web.

The entries at the top level of the Documentation browser's Library navigator correspond to the current docsets. (Only the documentation for the current operating systems and developer tools is included, even if you still have older docsets installed.)

Docsets have to be downloaded and (on an irregular schedule) updated. Some, like current OSes and the developer tools, download automatically, but others, for older systems or "retired documents," are optional. You control the download process through the **Downloads** panel of the Preferences window (Figure 25.8).

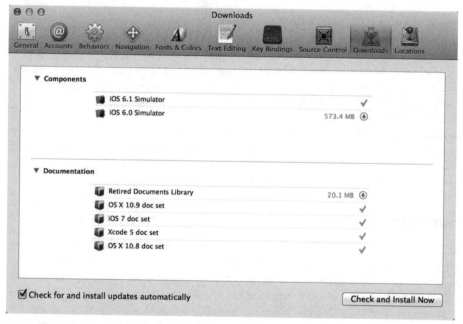

Figure 25.8   The **Downloads** panel of the Preferences window lists all of the documentation sets and other tools Xcode can install or update over the Net. Some are optional, shown with a circled down-arrow and their sizes.

Docsets (and additional development tools) are shown with checkmarks if they are present and up-to-date, and as download (circled-arrow) buttons plus estimated sizes if they are not. If you choose to download an item, its status is replaced by a progress bar showing how far the download has come.

By checking the **Check for and install updates automatically** box, you allow Xcode to download hundreds of megabytes of revised documentation at the most inconvenient moment possible—a consideration if your Internet connection is relatively slow. If you want better control over the process, there's a **Check and Install Now** button to start downloads on demand. (Remember to click this button whenever it's convenient; updates are rarely publicized.)

In previous versions of Xcode, the **Downloads** panel, or the documentation display itself, showed the location of the docset package, the version number, and other information. Xcode 5 doesn't share these any more. You needed the version number to report bugs, but the viewer now carries a floating **Provide Feedback** link, which sends the version to Apple automatically.

You still need to report the version if a docset won't load for you at all. You can find the version number by navigating to the docset in the Finder, right-clicking its icon to select **Show Package Contents**, and inspecting the Info.plist inside the **Contents** directory. You're looking for the CFBundleVersion key.

Your Own Quick Help

Xcode's documentation system is not closed. Development systems have generated documentation sets from specially formatted comments in the API for many years. The ancestor of most of these systems is JavaDoc, and the most commonly used all-purpose generator is Doxygen (http://www.doxygen.org/), which derives its vastly expanded markup language from that.

Xcode affords you two ways to expand the available documentation. One allows you easy entrée to Quick Help. The other requires more work, but gives you much more. Let's start with Xcode's direct support for documentation comments.

How to Generate Quick Help

If you know how to write documentation comments (you'll learn in the next section), getting Xcode to incorporate them in Quick Help is trivial: It just does it.

Here is the in-code declaration for SimpleCSVRecordBlock, defining the interface for the block -[SimpleCSVFile run:error:] calls to allow clients to process records:

```
/**
Receive key-value data from a line in a CSV file.

This block is called once for every line in the file
after the first by `-[SimpleCSVFie run:error:]`. The callee
can stop parsing by returning `NO.` If it does, and
`error` is not `NULL,` it must return `nil` or an
`NSError*` object in `*error.`
```

```
The dictionary will be keyed on the names found in the header
line, and the values will be drawn from the fields in the
corresponding positions.

@param      file    The SimpleCSVFile object doing the parsing.
@param      values  A dictionary of strings representing the
                    field values in the record line, keyed by
                    the field names supplied in the header line.
@param[out] error   A pointer to an `NSError` object pointer.
                    May be `NULL.` If it is not, and the callee
                    returns NO, this _must_ be set to a valid
                    `NSError` object pointer, or at least to
                    `nil.`
@return     `YES` if parsing may continue
@return     `NO`  if it may not; the callee must fill the returned `NSError`.
*/
typedef BOOL (^SimpleCSVRecordBlock)(SimpleCSVFile * file,
                                     NSDictionary * values,
                                     NSError ** error);
```

The comment begins with /** to signal that this is for documentation, followed by a one-sentence summary that will show up in high-level indexes of the API. Then comes a lengthier description, and specially marked-up annotations of SimpleCSVRecordBlock's parameters and return values.

You don't have to do anything else. Option-click any occurrence of SimpleCSVRecordBlock, and you'll get a popover containing the same formatted Quick Help as you'd get for any symbol in an Apple SDK (Figure 25.9).

The **Build Settings** tab in the Target editor includes a setting for "Documentation Comments" warnings. When the switch is on, clang will give you a running assessment of the validity of your comments, such as whether the parameter names you specify correspond to the names in the declaration.

Documentation Comment Syntax

Xcode's help parser recognizes a concise set of markup symbols to give meaning to parts of the comment—such as for parameters, return types, and special notes. The markup keywords are prefixed with either @ or \.

- @param—The first word is the parameter name; everything thereafter is a description. There can be more than one @param directive. If you follow the @param with [in], [out], or [inout], the rendered documentation will annotate it as being input-only, output-only (as it would be for pointers to NSError*), or both.

- @return—Describes the return value of a function/method.

- @exception—The first word is the name of an exception a function/method could raise; the rest is a description. There can be more than one @exception. *Doxygen only.*

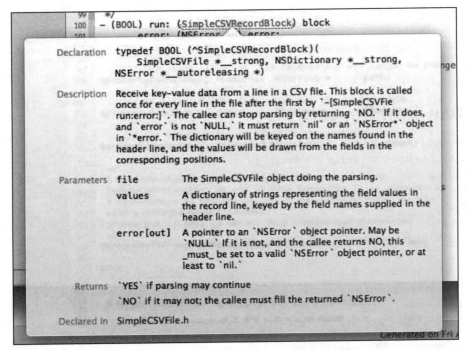

Figure 25.9 Option-click any symbol that has a documentation comment where it is declared, and you will see a popover with the formatted documentation. Xcode does not interpret style markup in the documentation.

- @bug—Commentary on a bug in the API.
- @todo—Commentary on work yet to be done for the API.
- @warning—Text that will be presented with a red bar in the margin.
- @deprecated—Flags and indexes an API as deprecated, with your notation.
- @see—An external URL or an internal symbol that Doxygen will link to.
- @author—The name, URL, or email address of the author of the annotated code. If you provide an email address, remember to escape the @ with a \.
- @c, @p—One word of "code" or "parameter" text that will be set in a monofont. Stretches of more than one word should be set out in the corresponding HTML markup.
- @em, @e, @i—One word to be set in italics.
- @b—One word to be set in boldface.

The character-style tokens are awkward to write and read. Doxygen supports Markdown style markup, so code symbols could be rendered as `symbol` and not @c symbol. Further, Markdown tokens can apply to phrases, not single words. When not using Markdown, Doxygen accepts HTML markup for phrases; Xcode ignores HTML.

Xcode doesn't interpret Markdown for Quick Help, so you have to choose between a faithful rendering and an annotation that's easier to read and write in the source, and not too bad in the rendered text, versus having Quick Help render your notes as you intend. For my part, I prefer to use Markdown.

Your Own Docsets

Doxygen (http://www.doxygen.org/) is a much more powerful system. It has an enormous repertoire of tags to generate detailed help systems, with clickable dependency and inheritance diagrams, indexes, and search. It can target languages as diverse as Objective-C, Java, and FORTRAN. It can generate HTML, LaTeX, Docbook, Xcode docsets, and many more. The variety of tags and configuration options can be confusing, but once you've settled on the subset you'll use, you don't need to think of anything more than writing your docs. The results are worth the effort; see Figure 25.10.

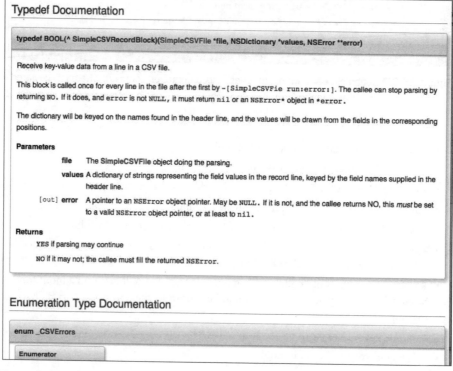

Figure 25.10   Doxygen renders the markup for `SimpleCSVRecordBlock` shown earlier in this chapter into cross-referenced and indexed HTML.

This book can't cover all the variants of markup and options Doxygen affords. If you need to know more, browse the manual at `http://www.doxygen.org/`, or download the PDF of the current edition.

Preparation

Your first step is to download Doxygen. Go to the web site, select **Downloads → Sources & Binaries**, and find the `.dmg` containing the latest version. Download it, mount the disk image, and drag the Doxygen app into the `/Applications` directory.

I recommend you install the GraphViz package of command-line graphics tools. Doxygen can use it to generate class and dependency diagrams. Find the current version at `http://www.graphviz.org/Download_macos.php`. Download the `.dmg`, mount it, and double-click the installer package (`.pkg`) you'll find there. You'll have to present an administrator's credentials. The tool Doxygen will want is called `dot`, and will be installed at `/usr/local/bin/dot`.

> **Warning**
>
> As I write this, neither Doxygen nor GraphViz carried Developer ID signatures. If you have Gatekeeper active (and you really should), OS X will refuse to run the app or the installer. The solution is to open System Preferences, choose the **Security & Privacy** panel, and click **Open Anyway**.

Configuring Doxygen: Basic Settings

`doxygen` proper is a command-line tool that processes your source code under the direction of a configuration file. The Doxygen app for OS X is mostly an editor for the configuration. Double-click Doxygen to run it. What you'll see is a "wizard" window with a list of views at the left, and a form at the right. See Figure 25.11.

`doxygen` being a Unix command-line tool, it needs a working directory. The first thing you'll do is set it, using the affordance at the top of the window. There's a text field there to enter the path directly, but use the **Select...** button to pick the `Passer Rating` project directory—that's the directory that contains the project file, not the one that contains the source.

Now let's fill out the configuration. You do this in two stages; the **Wizard** tab presents a simplified English-language interface that you can use for most of the setup. Then you round it out in the **Expert** tab, which is just a structured editor for the configuration file.

Project Panel

The **Project** panel points Doxygen at its source and destination directories and accepts project-wide settings like the title and logo.

- **Project name**—`Passer Rating iOS`
- **Project synopsis**—Something brief to explain what Passer Rating is: `iOS demo project for Xcode 5 Start to Finish`

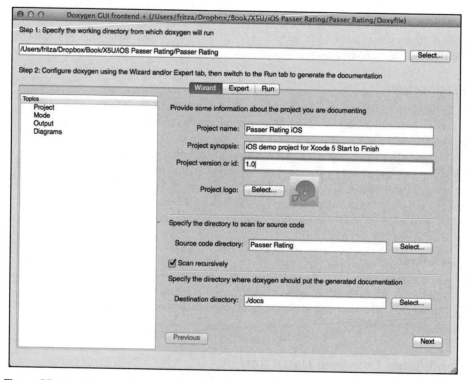

Figure 25.11   The `doxygen` command-line tool is wrapped in a graphical "wizard" for editing the configuration file for your project.

- **Project version or id**—`1.0`
- If you supply a logo image, bear in mind that it will be rendered full-size on every page of the documentation. If the image is huge, the page headers will be huge. I used the 60 × 60 icon for Passer Rating.
- **Source code directory**—Doxygen works by going through your source files, parsing and indexing them. Use **Select. . .** to choose the source directory within the project directory. Check **Scan recursively** to search subdirectories as well.
- **Destination directory**—This is where the generated documentation goes. *Do not* put it in the source directory; the version-control implications could be nightmarish. Click the **Select. . .** button, and in the select-file dialog, select the project directory, and click **New Folder**. Enter a name like **docs**. Select that new directory and click **Choose**.

Mode Panel

The **Mode** panel determines, at a rough level, how Doxygen is to interpret your source files.

- For the desired extraction mode, pick **All Entities**. Doxygen will generate documentation for all methods, constants, functions, etc., even if you haven't yet put documentation comments on them. In a production project, you might want to filter out things you've decided not to document, but for this demo, it will be fun to see what Doxygen can turn up.

- You are also asked to "optimize" for the language the project is written in. Objective-C is not on offer, but this is a radio group, so you have to pick one. Leave this option alone; you'll take care of it in the **Expert** tab.

Output Panel

Doxygen can produce documents in any or all of five different formats. Check only **HTML, with navigation panel**, and **With search function**. The **Change color. . .** button gives you hue, saturation, and value sliders to dress up the emitted pages; suit yourself.

Diagrams Panel

Select **Use dot tool from the GraphViz package**, and have fun: Check all of the available graph types.

Configuring Doxygen: Expert Settings

If you want, you can go to the **Run** tab, run Doxygen, and have it show you the results (but you haven't told it where to find GraphViz yet, so go back to the **Diagrams** panel and choose some other option). But you can get better results if you use the **Expert** tab.

To serve a multitude of needs and tastes, Doxygen has a multitude of options. They are all documented in the manual you can download from the web site. They are all in the **Expert** tab. You will need to touch very few, but it's not going to be easy: The expert settings fall into 17 panels, some of them very long. The options have been put into some order of related elements, but it's not always easy to see what that order is. You will have to pick through the items to track down the ones you need.

The **Expert** tab labels each setting with the name it has in the key-value pairs in the configuration file. If you hover your mouse over a name, an explanation will appear in the text area at the bottom left. Each setting has an editor appropriate to its data type. Settings labeled in black haven't changed from their defaults; if you change one, it will be labeled in red.

Project Panel

Check JAVADOC_AUTOBRIEF (just above halfway through the list) to emulate JavaDoc's feature in which the first sentence of a documentation block is harvested as a short description in summary tables. Otherwise, you'd have to call out brief descriptions with @brief.

In the **Mode** panel of the **Wizard** tab, you were forced to "optimize" the output to present the API for a particular language, none of them Objective-C. You get to undo this by locating all the OPTIMIZE_OUTPUT_FOR_ . . . items near the bottom of the list, and unchecking them.

Doxygen infers the language of a source file from its extension, so when it parses your .m files, it will recognize them as Objective-C. .h files remain ambiguous, which is the right thing for many projects. Relieve the ambiguity by adding a line to the EXTENSION_MAPPING table that follows the optimization checkboxes: Enter **h=Objective-C** in the text field, and click the **+** button.

HTML Panel

The HTML panel controls the formatting of the HTML Doxygen produces. This is where you set up Doxygen to index your documentation as an Xcode docset. The settings come about a third of the way down the list.

- GENERATE_DOCSET is the master setting. Check it.
- DOCSET_FEEDNAME sets a name for a grouping of documentation sets. The set you're building now is for the iOS Passer Rating app, but it might be part of a suite of docsets for *Xcode 5 Start to Finish*. Set it to **Xcode 5 Start to Finish**.
- DOCSET_BUNDLE_ID is a unique identifier for this set; it sets the bundle identifier in the docset's Info.plist. I used **com.wt9t.x5sf.docs.ios**.
- DOCSET_PUBLISHER_ID, by contrast, uniquely identifies you as the source of this and other docsets. I used **com.wt9t.x5sf.docs**.
- DOCSET_PUBLISHER_NAME is your name as presented to humans. I'm **Fritz Anderson**.

Dot Panel

Set DOT_PATH to **/usr/local/bin**.

> **Warning**
>
> If you have a legacy GraphViz and Doxygen setup, you'll find that dot will want to draw on tools from the X11 package. Because Doxygen will run dot once or twice for every @interface and file in your project, it will spawn dozens of instances of the X11 app. Because you likely don't have the X11 infrastructure installed on your Mac, each instance will wait for you to authorize it to install the X11 libraries. This is undesirable. The tools from the current GraphViz installer won't do this, so be sure to enter **/usr/local/bin**.

Running Doxygen

You've been creating a reusable configuration file, and you should save it. Select **File** →**Save** (⌘S). The default name for the file is Doxyfile, and there's no reason to change it. I recommend placing it in the proposed working directory, which is the directory that contains Passer Rating.xcodeproj.

At last you are ready to produce some documents. Select the **Run** tab and click **Run doxygen**. The text area fills with the run log, which is intimidatingly long. If you elected dot as the graphics generator, and a lot of graph types, some of the dot processing may take a while.

The doxygen tool will not halt with formatting errors, nor even call them out conspicuously. Be sure at least to skim the log for error messages. The first run may take a couple of minutes, but doxygen has the grace not to regenerate graphs for structures that have not changed.

When processing is done, click **Show HTML output**. Your preferred web browser will open the root page of the generated documentation (which will be index.html in the html subdirectory of your designated documentation folder).

This will be the designated "main," or overview, page, and if you don't specify one, it will be blank but for a navigation bar at the top. Clicking in the bar shows you more: indexes of classes and their members; files and their contents; to-dos and bugs. If you asked Doxygen for a client-side search interface, every page will include a search field that will do an incremental search of the docset.

> **Note**
>
> The contents of the docs directory are all derived data. You should not add the directory to your version-control repository. Take this moment to add docs/ to your .gitignore file.

Installing a Docset

When you set GENERATE_DOCSET, Doxygen adds a Makefile that will direct make to install the docset into ~/Library/Developer/Shared/Documentation/DocSets, where Xcode can find it. In Terminal, set the working directory to the generated HTML directory, and run make:

```
$ # Assuming you're in the project directory:
$ cd docs/html
$ make install
    . . .
Output from make
    . . .
$
```

> **Note**
>
> Don't use sudo to run make. It's not necessary—you already have write privileges for your own Library/Developer directory—and you'd be creating directories and files owned by root, which you won't be able to change or delete.

Quit and reopen Xcode, and open the Documentation browser. Your docset should show up in the Library navigator's outline. The outline will trace through all the indexes in the set.

. . . and, as I write this, that's all it will do. Apparently, Doxygen's inputs for generating a docset don't adequately specify the indexes, and the leaves in the docset tree won't appear. You can't get at your documentation.

This ought to change by the time you read this. When it works, the rest should be easy.

> **Note**
>
> Doxygen has the annoyance that its terminology and formatting aren't tailored to Objective-C; it's hard to minimize its C++ conventions. There are other options, and they have the advantage of matching the style of Apple's own docs. Apple's HeaderDoc is supplied with the Xcode tools. It is simple to generate a suite of HTML documentation—all that's involved are a couple of command-line tools and customizing some template files. However, things rapidly become difficult when you try to generate a docset; you're left to hand-code some of the indexes. Search the tools documentation for `HeaderDoc` for more information. AppleDoc, `http://gentlebytes.com/`, is an open-source generator that will produce docsets. It's not as mature as Doxygen, and while AppleDoc's narrower focus makes the configuration system less complex conceptually, the lack of a graphical editor hurts it.

Summary

This chapter took you on an in-depth tour of Xcode's documentation system. You saw how to use Quick Help to get on-the-spot guidance on APIs, Interface Builder objects, and build settings, and how to quickly access the declarations of methods and other symbols in your code.

I showed you the Documentation browser and how to navigate it and search for articles. You learned how to manage and update your document sets.

You discovered how easy it is to generate Quick Help for your own code: Add some comments with standard markup to your declarations, and you're done. `clang` will even warn you if you get the syntax wrong.

Finally, I introduced Doxygen, a system for generating thorough, indexed, and searchable documentation sets. Doxygen should be able to produce and install documentation sets you can examine in Xcode's Documentation browser, and I showed you how that it *ought* to work. Unfortunately, it doesn't work with Xcode 5 yet.

The Xcode Build System

If you're used to building software with Unix tools like make, odds are you don't quite trust IDEs like Xcode. In a makefile, you can directly set compiler options, even file by file. You can designate build dependencies, so a change to a header file will force recompilations of the implementation files that depend on it—clang even has a mode that generates the dependency trees.

At first glance, Xcode doesn't give you that control. It's "magic," and while you're proud to make magic for your users, you don't trust it for yourself.

This chapter aims to take some of the magic out of the Xcode build system. Even if you aren't a veteran of make-based projects, you'll gain a better understanding of what Xcode does for you and how you can control it.

How Xcode Structures a Build

A makefile is organized around a hierarchy of goals. Some goals, such as the frequently used clean or install targets, are abstract, but most are files. Associated with each goal is a list of other goals that are antecedents—dependencies—of that goal and a script for turning the antecedents into something that satisfies the goal. Most commonly, the antecedents are input files for the programs that the script runs to produce a target file. The genius of make comes from the rule that if any target is more recently modified than all of its antecedents, it is presumed to embody their current state, and it is not necessary to run the script to produce it again. The combination of a tree of dependencies and this pruning rule make make a powerful and efficient tool for automating such tasks as building software products.

The organizing unit of a makefile is the target-dependency-action group. But in the case of application development, this group is often stereotyped to the extent that you don't even have to specify it; make provides a default rule that looks like this:

```
%.o     :   %.c
    $(CC) -c $(CPPFLAGS) $(CFLAGS) -o $@ $<
```

So all the programmer need do is list all the constituent `.o` files in the project, and the built-in rule will produce the `.o` files as needed. Often, the task of maintaining a makefile becomes less one of maintaining dependencies than one of keeping lists.

In the same way, Xcode makes dependency analysis a matter of list-keeping by taking advantage of the fact that projects are targeted at specific kinds of executable products, such as applications, libraries, tools, or plugins. Knowing how the build process ends, Xcode can do the right thing with the files that go into the project.

A file in an Xcode workspace belongs to three distinct lists.

Projects. A file appears once in the Project navigator for each project it belongs to. This has nothing to do with whether it has any effect on any product of a project. It might, for instance, be a document you're keeping handy for reference, or some notes you're taking. If you're working with a workspace, a file might be in the workspace without being in any project; the easiest way to do this is to make sure no project is selected (command-click to undo any selections) and select **File → Add Files to. . . (⌥⌘A)**.

> **Note**
>
> To be more precise, there are no files "in" a project or workspace. Projects and workspaces keep *references* to files. Xcode makes tracking files and building easier if a project's inputs are in a tree descending from the directory that holds the project file; but if the files are *in* anything, they're in the tree. The project just knows where they are. Workspaces are even looser: A workspace is meant to be one developer's reference binder for a set of projects and maybe some other files on the side. Because workspaces have very little role in the build process, workspace files can be anywhere you want, like your desktop.

Targets. A file may belong to zero or more *targets* in a project. A file is included in a target's file list because it is a part of that target's product, whether as a source file or as a resource to be copied literally into the product. When a file is added to a project, Xcode asks you which targets in the project should include the file. You can also add files to a target through the checkboxes in the File inspector, or by dragging them into a build phase in the Target editor.

A target is identified with the set of files that compose it. There is no concept of including or excluding files from a single target on the basis of its being built with a Release or Debug configuration. If you need disjoint sets of files, make a separate target for each set; a file can belong to more than one target, and you can set preprocessor macros per-target. This does mean that the two targets have to coordinate their settings; `.xcconfig` files, introduced later this chapter, make that very easy.

Build Phases. What role a file plays in a target depends on what *phase* of the target the file belongs to. When a file is added to a target, Xcode assigns it to a build phase based on the type of the file: Files with `clang`-compilable suffixes get assigned to the Compile Sources phase; libraries, to the Link Binary With Libraries phase; and most others to the Copy Bundle Resources phase. (See Figure 26.1.)

Build phases are executed in the order in which they appear in the Target editor. You'd almost always want the Compile Sources phase to complete before Link Binary With Libraries phase—that's the way they come—but you *can* drag them into any order you like.

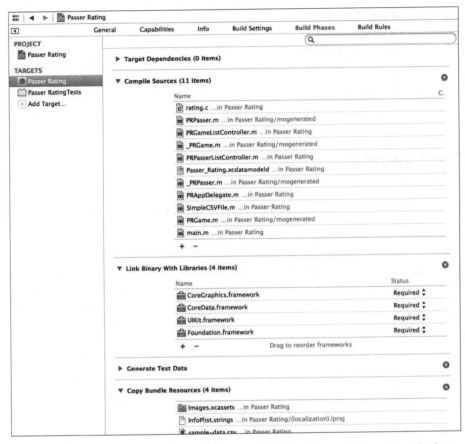

Figure 26.1 Build phases in a modest project. You gain access to build phases by selecting a project item in the Project navigator, clicking on a target, and then the **Build Phases** tab in the Target editor. The phases are represented by tables that can be expanded to reveal the files that belong to them. One of the ways to add a file to a phase is to drag it into the phase's table.

When you create a target, either in the process of creating an Xcode project or by adding a target to an existing project, you specify the kind of product you want to produce, and you can't change it except by making another target. The target type forms one anchor—the endpoint—in the Xcode build system's dependency analysis: It tells the build system what the product's desired structure (single file or package) is and how to link the executable.

The other anchor of the build system is the set of build-phase members for the target. The Compile Sources build phase, along with the sources you add to it, yield object files, which are the inputs to the linkage phase implicit in your choice of target type. The various file-copying phases and the files you supply for them yield the copy commands needed to populate the auxiliary structure of an application.

What a makefile developer does with explicit dependencies and the default rules, Xcode does by inference: It determines how new files are to be processed into a product, and how that processing is to be done. Even if you use the product of one target to build another, Xcode will detect the dependency and incorporate the build of the dependent target into the process for the composite target. All Xcode needs is for the two targets to be within the same workspace—they don't even have to be in the same project.

Build Variables

The action for the default make rule for .c files parameterizes almost the entire action. The command for the C compiler and the set of flags to pass are left to the makefile variables CC, CPPFLAGS, and CFLAGS. You set these flags at the head of the file to suitable values, and all the compilations in your build comply.

Xcode relies similarly on variables to organize build options, but at a much finer granularity. There is one variable for each of the most common settings. For instance, the variable GCC_ENABLE_CPP_RTTI controls whether clang's -fno-rtti will be added to suppress generation of runtime type information in C++. This variable is set by a popup ("Enable C++ Runtime Types") in the **Build Settings** tab of the Target editor. See Figure 26.2.

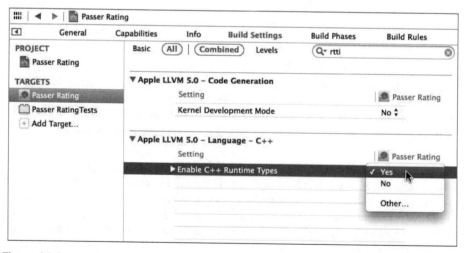

Figure 26.2   The list of settings in the **Build Settings** tab of the Target editor is extensive, but you can get it under control by typing something relevant to the setting in the search field. Typing rtti narrows the list down to a setting for C++ runtime type information, but also to a setting whose description merely refers to RTTI. The Quick Help inspector in the Utility area explains each setting, including the name of the associated build variable and the compiler flags it sets.

Let's have a good look at the **Build Settings** tab. Select a project in the Project navigator to fill the Editor area with the Project/Target editor, then select a target. Click the **Build Settings** tab. Right under the tab bar, you'll see two pairs of buttons: **Basic/All**, and **Combined/Levels**. **Basic** narrows the list down to a handful of essential elements; I'll get to the distinction between the combined and by-level presentations shortly. For now, the most straightforward presentation is **All** and **Combined**.

The list you see is a front end for most of the build variables Xcode maintains for this target. If you have the Utility area (right-hand area in the **View** control) visible, and the Quick Help (second) inspector selected, you can see a description of any setting you select. In brackets, at the end of the description, are the name of the build variable the item controls and what compiler option, if any, it affects. Both the label and the description are searchable: The list in Figure 26.2 was narrowed down to two entries by typing `rtti` into the search field at the top of the list.

> **Note**
>
> It's common for closely crafted makefiles to customize the compiler flags for some of the source files. The Xcode build system allows for this. In the **Build Phase** tab, the table for the Compile Sources phase has a second column, "Compiler Flags." Double-click an entry in that column to get a popover editor for additional flags for that file. You won't get Quick Help for what you enter, but you can explore the **Build Settings** list to see what options are available. What you type will be *added* to the flags used in compiling the file—it's not possible to override the general settings, and it's not possible to make separate per-file settings for different configurations.

Settings Hierarchy

The "Combined" list of settings shown in the **Build Settings** tab is the authoritative list of what flags and directives will be applied in building the target. However, the Xcode build system provides richer control over those settings. What's in the combined list is a synthesis of settings that come from a hierarchy of up to six layers.

- BSD environment variables
- Xcode's own default values
- The current configuration set for the whole project
- The current configuration set for the current target
- Command-line arguments to the `xcodebuild` command-line tool, if you're using it
- Added per-file compiler options

Figure 26.3 illustrates how the hierarchy works.

You'll deal most often with target and project settings; the others rarely arise. The project level allows you to set policies for every target in the project—things like the root SDK or warnings you always want to see—so a change in one place affects all. You can still exempt a product from the general policy by putting an alternate setting into its target: The target setting will override the project setting.

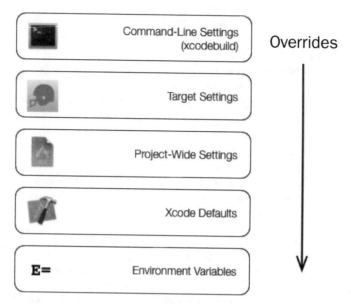

Figure 26.3   The hierarchy of build settings in Xcode and `xcodebuild`. A setting may be made at one or more of these layers, but the topmost setting in the hierarchy controls. Settings in higher layers may refer to settings from lower layers by the variable reference `$(inherited)`. The top layer, command-line settings, is present only in an `xcodebuild` invocation.

Levels

With this in mind, you can click the **Levels** button in the bar under the **Build Settings** tab (Figure 26.4). The Target editor now shows four columns for each setting, representing the default, project, and target values, and the net value that is actually effective for the target. You can edit only the middle two columns—target and project. The level that is responsible for the effective setting is highlighted in green.

> **Note**
>
> The same **Build Settings** tab is available in the Project editor, but without the target-level column.

Each level that sets (not just inherits) a value is shown in bold with a green background. The distinction between setting and inheritance is important: If, for instance, you set a string setting to empty at the target level, the effective setting will be an empty string, *not* the setting inherited from the project; if you change the project setting, the effective setting, through the target, will still be blank—watch for that green box. Likewise, setting a value to be the same as the value to the right isn't an acceptance of the inherited value; it's just an override that happens to repeat the inherited value.

If you want to remove an override from the hierarchy, select the line for that setting, and press the Delete key. The setting won't go away—it will just clear the value from the

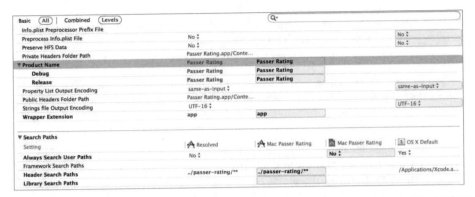

Figure 26.4   With the **Levels** view selected, the Target editor shows how each level of the settings hierarchy contributes to the settings that will be used to build the target. The chain proceeds from right to left, starting with Xcode's default for the project type at the right, through the project and target levels, and to the net setting on the left. You can edit the settings at the project or target level. The place where the operative value for a setting is selected is highlighted in green.

level (project or target) on which the editor is operating. You'll see the effect when you see the current level's value lose its boldfacing, and the green box go down to the next-lower level. When you select a different row in the table, the cells that don't carry values will be blank.

Editing Build Variables

The **Build Settings** table is intelligent about what values you can put into it.

- Some values—such as the multiple flags you can put into the "Other C Flags" setting—are logically lists. Xcode lets you edit the items individually, in a table to which you can add and remove rows.

- Some settings, such as Booleans or code-signing identities, are constrained to the few values that make sense for them. The Value column shows a popup menu with the possible values.

- Any value can be edited free-form—if you click in the value and move the mouse pointer a little, you are in a text field.

- If you are editing a value at the target level and want to supplement, rather than replace, the inherited value, include $(inherited) where you want the original setting to appear.

The **Build Settings** table is filtered for your consumption. Underlying the descriptions in the Setting column are the names of variables Xcode uses to specify the build; and the Value column displays the settings as they *effectively* are, not as they *actually* are. You'll see this when editing the text of variables whose value depends on the content of other variables: The "Architectures" setting may look like "Standard (armv6 armv7)" in the list, but if you edit it as text, you find it's $(ARCHS_STANDARD).

> **Note**
>
> If you've done shell scripting, you're used to delimiting environment variable names in braces: ${VISUAL}. Strings in parentheses are replaced by the output of the commands they contain. This is *not* so when you use Xcode build variables. Use parentheses to refer to them: $(SDKROOT).

You can change the table to display the underlying variable names and values. The command **Show Setting Names** in the **Editor** menu will reveal the names of the build variables; **Show Definitions** shows the raw text of the settings.

Configurations

So far, I've treated build settings as the product of a simple hierarchy of defaults and overrides. But build settings can be varied on another axis: A target may have different settings based on your purpose in building it, such as debugging, release, or distribution. You encapsulate these settings in *build configurations*, which you can select for each action in your product's scheme.

When it generates a new project for you, Xcode provides two configurations, Debug and Release, which it sets up with reasonable values for those two purposes. In general, the Debug configuration generates more debugging information and turns off code optimization so your program will execute line by line in the debugger, as you'd expect. Both OS X and iOS run apps on two or more processor architectures, and the Debug configuration will save time by building the target for one architecture only.

Switching between configurations is easy: The **Info** tab for each action in the Scheme editor includes a **Build Configuration** popup that lets you choose the configuration you use for that action. You can make the switch and take an action in one step by holding down the Option key while invoking the action; the Scheme editor sheet will drop down, and you can make your changes before proceeding.

If your target depends on other targets, even in other projects, those other targets will be built with the configuration you set at build time, so long as they have a configuration of the same name; otherwise they will be built in their default configurations.

Adjusting Configurations

The point of a build configuration is to have alternate settings for each purpose. This is where you get into conditional settings. As you've browsed the **Build Settings** tab, you've noticed that some settings have disclosure triangles next to them (Figure 26.5), and their values are tagged with a grayed-out "<Multiple values>." These settings have different values depending on which configuration is being used. Click the triangle, and the row opens to show subrows for each available configuration. You can make your choices there.

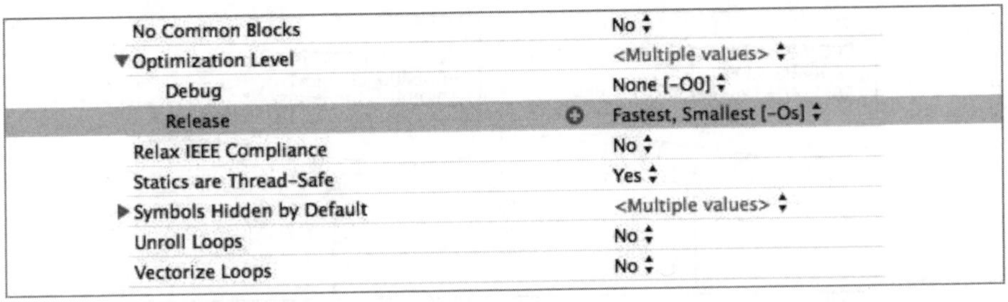

No Common Blocks	No ⏷
▼ Optimization Level	\<Multiple values\> ⏷
Debug	None [-O0] ⏷
Release	⊕ Fastest, Smallest [-Os] ⏷
Relax IEEE Compliance	No ⏷
Statics are Thread-Safe	Yes ⏷
▶ Symbols Hidden by Default	\<Multiple values\> ⏷
Unroll Loops	No ⏷
Vectorize Loops	No ⏷

Figure 26.5   When a setting has different values for different configurations, its value is displayed as "\<Multiple values\>," and Xcode displays a disclosure triangle for the row. Opening the triangle shows the configurations and their values.

If you hover the mouse pointer over a row for which there are no per-confugration settings, a temporary disclosure triangle appears. Opening that row will again show the values (identical until you change them) assigned to the setting for each configuration.

Figure 26.6 ties it all together: It shows how settings can percolate up from the defaults, through the project and target settings, and finally to the values that will direct and condition the build process. You can add configurations of your own, if you need to. The **Info** tab of the Project editor includes the list of all the configurations available to the project. You start out with Debug and Release. To create your new configuration, click the + button; this will pop up a menu offering to duplicate one of the existing configurations—it doesn't make sense to offer a new, empty configuration, because the new configuration has to include *some* settings. Make your selection, enter a name, and you're done.

Configuration Files

Configurations, too, come with disclosure triangles. Open one, and you'll see a list of the targets the project contains. This lets you select a configuration file that adjusts the settings for each target.

What's a configuration file? Here's the rationale: Say you have several projects. Perhaps you have policies for settings you must have for all of them, and the defaults supplied by Xcode aren't appropriate for you. If you just use the Project/Target editor, you will have to make those settings by hand for each configuration in each project. If your requirements vary by target type, it gets that much worse.

Configuration (.xcconfig) files are the solution. These are text files that contain key-value pairs for any settings you want to enforce.

Creating a Configuration File

You start on an xcconfig file by selecting **File → New**, and finding "Configuration Settings File" in the **Other** category (OS X or iOS, it doesn't matter) of the New File

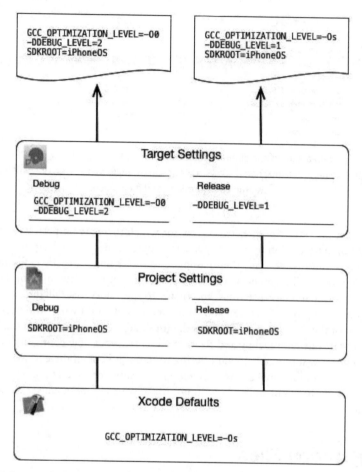

Figure 26.6   A complete example of the inheritance of build settings. By default, Xcode sets all compilations to optimize for size (bottom); that setting survives into Release builds, but for the Debug configuration, the target turns optimization off. The project sets the base SDK for all builds to `iPhoneOS`, meaning whatever iOS SDK is current (middle). The developer defines a `DEBUG_LEVEL` macro to different values depending on the configuration (top). The result is a set of build settings tailored to debugging (top left) and release (top right).

assistant. The assistant will then put you through the routine of naming and placing the file and assigning it to a project. It will offer to make the new file part of a target. You don't want your configuration file copied into your products, so make sure none of the targets are selected.

> **Note**
>
> An `xcconfig` file has to be included in a project—not a target—before the project can find and use it.

When you've done that, you find you have a text file that's empty but for a comment block with your name, copyright, and date at the top. What to do now? Open the **Build Settings** tab in either a Project or Target editor. You can copy (**Edit → Copy, ⌘ C**) rows from the editor, and paste them into the `xcconfig`, but there's a catch: You *can't* copy rows marked "<Multiple values>." You will have to use the Shift or Command key to cherry-pick the settings that interest you, and copy or drag them into the file. You can then edit the values to suit your requirements.

You can get one step closer from the command line: If you give the `xcodebuild` command the target, architecture, and configuration you're interested in, along with the `-showBuildSettings` option, it will print all the environment variables that would prevail in the course of a build:

```
$ xcodebuild -showBuildSettings -configuration Release
Build settings for action build and target "Passer Rating":
    ACTION = build
    AD_HOC_CODE_SIGNING_ALLOWED = NO
    ALTERNATE_GROUP = staff
    ALTERNATE_MODE = u+w,go-w,a+rX
    ALTERNATE_OWNER = fritza
    ALWAYS_SEARCH_USER_PATHS = NO
    ALWAYS_USE_SEPARATE_HEADERMAPS = YES
    . . .
```

But there's a problem: Not every build setting carries through into the build-process environment. Xcode consumes GCC_ENABLE_CPP_RTTI, for instance, when it constructs the `clang` build commands it will issue. The symbol never makes it out of the build system to be visible in this list. Still, it's a start. Remember that you don't have to put every setting into a configuration file—in principle there is no defined, limited set of them— and if you intend to have different settings by SDK or architecture, you'll have to get `xcodebuild` to generate each settings list separately, and merge them as shown in the next section.

Once that is done, you can return to the Project editor's **Info** tab and use the popups in the "Based on Configuration File" column to select the `xcconfig` file.

SDK- and Architecture-Specific Settings

Cocoa development often involves targeting different SDKs and processor architectures with different binaries. You may have ARMv7 assembly in your iOS app that isn't runnable on ARMv6 devices or the simulator. You may want to use the OS X 10.6 SDK for 32-bit builds, but 10.7 for 64 bits. The `xcconfig` format allows for these. For instance, the file may contain

```
(1) GCC_VERSION = com.apple.compilers.llvm.clang.1_0
(2) GCC_VERSION[sdk=iphonesimulator4.3][arch=*] =
                           com.apple.compilers.llvmgcc42
(3) GCC_VERSION[sdk=iphoneos4.3][arch=armv6] = 4.2
```

1. Use `clang` for any builds, unless a condition overrides it.
2. If the build uses the iOS Simulator SDK, use the `gcc`-fronted `llvm` compiler. (I broke the line for space; it should be all on one line.)
3. If the build is for iOS 4.3 on a device *and* for the ARMv6 architecture, use `gcc` 4.2. (This insane configuration—Xcode 5 doesn't even come with `gcc` or `llvmgcc`, and `gcc` is terrible at generating ARM code—is only an example.)

The matching to SDK and architecture is done by glob expression, which means that if you have to express a range of matches, like "any ios 6," you can match on `iphoneos6*`, as an override to an unconditional setting for other OSes.

> **Note**
>
> The graphical editor also allows you to set conditions. When you hover the mouse pointer over a configuration in a setting, a small **+** button appears; clicking it will add a condition row inside the configuration. The title of that row is a drop-down menu, in which you can select from the available conditions. See Figure 26.7. Because Xcode arranges conditional settings *within* configurations, you'll have to duplicate conditions for each configuration.

Preprocessing `xcconfig` Files

As with C-family source files, you can insert the contents of one `xcconfig` file into another with an `#include` directive. That way, you can have a base configuration file containing settings common to all your targets and build configurations, and `#include` that in files that are specific to each of them.

This enables an interesting trick. Consider the following configuration file (call it `common.xcconfig`):

```
MY_LIBS_FOR_DEBUG = -lmystuff_debug
MY_LIBS_FOR_RELEASE = -lmystuff
OTHER_LDFLAGS = $(MY_LIBS_FOR_$(WHICH_LIB))
```

There may be a `Debugging.xcconfig` file that sets:

```
WHICH_LIB = DEBUG
#include "common.xcconfig"
```

...and a `Release.xcconfig` file that contains:

```
WHICH_LIB = RELEASE
#include "common.xcconfig"
```

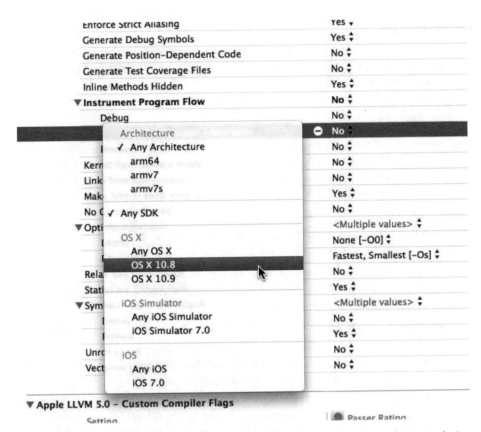

Figure 26.7   The + button next to the per-configuration label of a build setting lets you select a combination of architecture, OS, and platform to which a new conditional setting will apply.

The effect is that OTHER_LDFLAGS will be set to the value of -1MY_LIBS_FOR_DEBUG from Debug.xcconfig, and -1MY_LIBS_FOR_RELEASE from Release.xcconfig. In this simple case, it would have been easier just to set OTHER_LDFLAGS yourself, but quite sophisticated conditional configurations can be built up this way.

There are no header search paths for xcconfig files. If you #include a file, it has to be in the same directory.

Command-Line Tools

Sometimes there is no substitute for a command-line tool. The Unix command line presents a well-understood interface for scripting and controlling complex tools. Apple has provided a command-line interface to the Xcode build system and toolsets through three main commands: xcodebuild, xcrun, and xcode-select.

xcodebuild

Using xcodebuild is simple: Set the working directory to the directory containing an
.xcodeproj project package, and invoke xcodebuild, specifying the project, target,
configuration, and any build settings you wish to set. If only one .xcodeproj package is
in the directory, all of these options can be defaulted by simply entering

```
$ xcodebuild
```

That command will build the first target in the current configuration of the only
.xcodeproj package in the working directory. Apple's intention is that xcodebuild
have the same role in a nightly build or routine-release script that make would have.

In building a target, specify one of seven actions for xcodebuild:

- **build**, the default, to build the specified target out of SRCROOT into SYMROOT.
  This is the same as the **Build** command in the Xcode application.

- **test** runs the test suite for the selected scheme. You can specify a destination to
  select an attached device or a simulator configuration.

- **analyze** has the same effect as selecting **Product → Analyze**. You should specify a
  target, and you must specify a scheme.

- **archive**, to do the equivalent of the **Product → Archive** command in Xcode.
  You must specify the workspace and scheme for the build.

- **clean**, to remove the product and any intermediate files from SYMROOT. This is the
  same as the **Clean** command in the Xcode application.

- **install**, to build the specified target and install it at INSTALL_DIR (usually
  DSTROOT). The Installation Preprocessing build variable is set. There is no direct
  equivalent to this action in Xcode because there is no way to elevate Xcode's
  privileges for setting ownership, permissions, and destination directory.

- **installsrc**, to copy the project directory to SRCROOT. In Project Builder, Xcode's
  ancestor, this action restricted itself to the project file package and the source files
  listed in it, but it now seems to do nothing a Finder copy or command-line cp
  wouldn't do.

> **Note**
>
> Settings like SRCROOT can be set for a run of xcodebuild by including assignment pairs
> (SETTING=value) among the parameters.

If more than one project or workspace package is in the current directory, you must
specify which you are interested in, with the respective -project or -workspace
option, followed by the name of the package. Not specifying a target is the same as
passing the name of the first target in the -target option; you can also specify
-alltargets.

xcodebuild uses the configuration you specify in the Scheme editor panel for the build action, unless you pass a -configuration flag in the command. For the commands that require a scheme, you must name it with the -scheme option; setting a scheme is a good idea anyway.

As in the scheme selector in the toolbar of a project window, you may specify a -destination, such as a simulator configuration, operating system, attached device, architecture, or platform, all provided as key-value pairs. Find the details by typing **man xcodebuild** at a command line.

See man xcodebuild for full details.

xcode-select

It is perfectly legal to have more than one copy of Xcode on your computer. As I write this, not every developer had qualified its products for the iOS 7 human-interface idiom. If you use the iOS 7 SDK for your build, you'll get the iOS 7 appearance on compatible devices, and the iOS 7 SDK is the only one available for Xcode 5. If you want the pre-7 appearance across the board, you have to build with an earlier SDK, and for that you must use Xcode 4.6. Such developers keep Xcode 5 and Xcode 4.6.3.

> **Warning**
>
> If you need to do this, *do not* accept updates from the Mac App Store; they will remove all previous versions of Xcode. See the "Downloading Xcode" section of Chapter 1, "Getting Xcode," for details.

Each version of Xcode comes with its own set of tools—and, of course its own SDKs, which is what you're interested in. If you're invoking xcodebuild or a tool like clang from the command line, how can you be sure you're getting the right one? For command-line tools, it is not enough to trust in the version in /usr/bin: The tools in that directory are not the tools themselves. If you inspect them, you'll see that no matter how massive they ought to be, they are all about 14 KB in size. That's because they are trampoline apps that refer to the "real" ones in Xcode (or the command-line tools download directory if you downloaded them without Xcode). So you have to make those trampolines bounce to the versions you want.

You can do this with xcode-select. At its simplest,

```
sudo xcode-select --print-path
```

will tell you which Xcode is current, and

```
sudo xcode-select --switch /Applications/Xcode-4.6.3.app
```

will make a particular version of Xcode (4.6.3, in this case) current. xcode-select keeps track of the Developer directory in the Xcode package, but it will let you get by with the full path to the application, including the .app suffix.

> **Note**
>
> xcode-select changes Xcode for all users on your machine and affects system assets, so you must prove administrative privileges, such as through sudo, to make the change.

xcrun

If you have different projects requiring different SDKs and toolsets, you have a problem. Not with Xcode itself—the IDE always finds its own versions—but with scripts and makefiles. Having the same makefile produce a different product depending on the admin's mood is no way to run a business.

xcrun lets you force the choice of an SDK and a toolset. If you need to find clang, for instance, you can run

```
$ # Find the currently-selected version of clang:
$ xcrun --find clang
$ # What SDKs are installed?
$ xcodebuild -showsdks
OS X SDKs:
        OS X 10.8                            -sdk macosx10.8
        OS X 10.9                            -sdk macosx10.9

iOS SDKs:
        iOS 7.0                              -sdk iphoneos7.0

iOS Simulator SDKs:
        Simulator - iOS 7.0                  -sdk iphonesimulator7.0
$ # Run clang for the 10.8 SDK:
$ xcrun --sdk macosx10.8 clang
```

Custom Build Rules

Xcode's build system can be extended to new file types and processing tools. The default rules in the build system match file extensions to product types and process any source files that are newer than the products. You can add a custom rule that instructs the build system to look for files whose names match a pattern and apply a command to such files. See Figure 26.8, top.

> **Note**
>
> Another way to extend the build system is by adding a Run Script build phase. You've already seen it in the "Some Test Data" section of Chapter 9, "An iOS Application: Model." Run Script phases allow a lot more flexibility in how to structure the action, but they sacrifice the build rule's applicability to every file of a given type.

Create a rule by selecting **Editor →Add Build Rule** while the **Build Rules** tab is visible. A row appears at the top of the table, containing an editor for your new rule. The

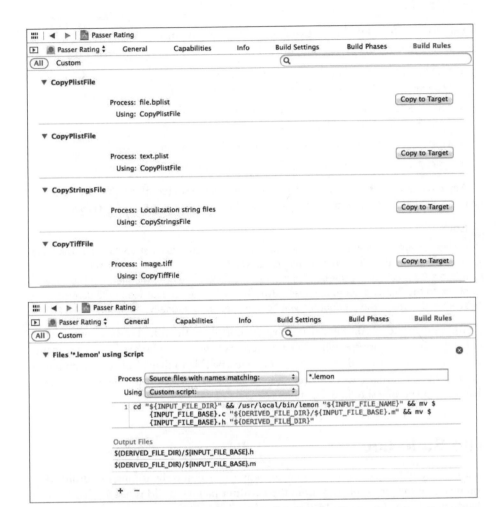

Figure 26.8   (top) The **Build Rules** tab of the Target editor lets you match up file types with the tools that will process them for a build. When you first examine the list, it contains the default suite of actions for the standard file types. (bottom) Selecting **Editor → Add Build Rule** adds a row to the table, in which you can specify a file type and the rule (possibly your own script) to process it.

Process popup menu allows you to select from some of the types of source files that Xcode knows about and includes a **Source files with names matching:** item for you to specify source files with a glob expression (like *.lemon).

The **Using** popup shows all of Xcode's standard compilers, or you can select **Custom script:** to open an editor for your own script. See Figure 26.8, bottom. Don't worry about the size of this field; it will grow vertically as you type. Remember that you can chain shell commands with the && operator.

You may use any build variable you like in the shell command. Additionally, some variables are specific to custom rule invocations:

- INPUT_FILE_PATH, the full path to the source file (/Users/xcodeuser/MyProject/grammar.lemon)
- INPUT_FILE_DIR, the directory containing the source file (/Users/xcodeuser/MyProject/)
- INPUT_FILE_NAME, the name of the source file (grammar.lemon)
- INPUT_FILE_BASE, the base, unsuffixed, name of the source file (grammar)

Apple recommends that intermediate files, such as the source files output by parser generators, be put into the directory named in the DERIVED_FILE_DIR variable.

> **Note**
>
> In this example, adding a .lemon file to the project won't do what you'd hope. The build rule recognizes the file as a source file, but Xcode doesn't: Simply adding the file will put it into a Copy Bundle Resources build phase. You'll have to drag the file from the copy phase to the Compile Sources phase. After that, with the product file in the derived-sources directory, the product file will be compiled automatically.

You can't delete or edit the defaults that are initially in the rules list, but any rule you add will override a corresponding rule that appears lower in the list. You can set priorities by dragging your rules higher or lower. You won't be able to drag a rule down among the standard rules, but that doesn't matter: Why would you add a custom rule, then specify that the standard one should override it?

The Build Log

You set the build system into motion by selecting an action or by issuing the **Build** (⌘ B) command, or one of its relatives, from the **Product** menu. (**Build** is just an alias for **Product → Build For → Build For Running**, ⇧ ⌘ R.)

> **Note**
>
> Once you've memorized the keyboard commands for actions like Run, Test, Profile, and Analyze, you can hold down the Shift key to do the corresponding build without going through with the action.

The result, if everything goes well, is a file or package embodying your product. If it doesn't, the now-familiar Issues navigator will list all the errors, warnings, and notes that turned up, and you can select an issue to jump to the place in your source that raised it.

But sometimes that isn't enough. You want to see how the build was done, right or wrong—perhaps you suspect that a step hadn't been taken. And, if you run into an error in linkage or code signing, the Issues navigator is of limited help because there is no corresponding source file. That's where the Log navigator comes in.

The Log navigator (the eighth tab in the Navigator area) contains an item for each major event in the life of your project, such as actions or source-control commands—anything that could generate text logs from tools that handle the events.

Do a build, select the Log navigator, and click the top item representing the results of the last action you took. What you'll see is a summary of the steps that went into the action. See Figure 26.9.

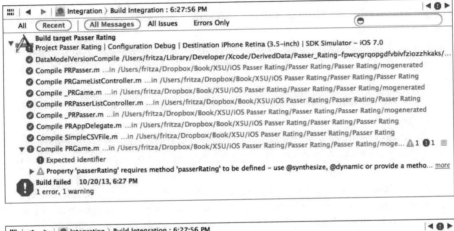

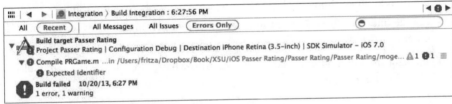

Figure 26.9 The log for a build can be filtered to narrow it to the items you want to focus on. If you select **All Messages** (not shown), you'll get a list of every action taken in the build, including the steps that succeeded. If you select **Errors Only**, the list narrows down to error messages only.

The buttons immediately below the tab bar offer the choices **All/Recent** and **All Messages/All Issues/Errors Only**. The latter group filters the list in order of importance: The all-messages setting lists everything that happened, good or not; the others eliminate the entries for successful steps and for steps that would not prevent the build from completing.

The **All** setting displays every step that contributed to the *current* state of the target. That's not the same as a list of what happened the last time you did a build: Your last build did not repeat compilations for source files that had not changed; the contributions for those files come from earlier builds. The **All** setting folds those older compilations into a complete history of the current target. If you want to restrict the list to what was done in the last build, select **Recent**.

A Simple Build Transcript

What follows is the build transcript for an iPhone project that isn't as simple as Passer Rating, but is still relatively simple: It encompasses only 39 .m files. The only unusual thing about it, for its size, is that it includes more than 50 resource files.

I ran the project through an Archive build, which processed every element of the app, including both the armv7 and armv7s architectures. When the build was done, I selected it in the Log navigator, selected **All** of the history, and **All Messages**. I selected **Editor →Copy Transcript for Shown Results (All, All Messages) as Text**, and pasted the results into a text editor.

The transcript is 535 KB of text in 1,303 lines. The commands that went into the build were in single lines that were typically above 4,000 characters, involving filesystem paths of around 274. For this book, I've made extensive edits.

- I changed the names of the product and the source files—they were confidential.
- I truncated paths ruthlessly, substituting ellipses (...). Xcode.app is the Xcode application itself. Paths beginning with Xcode/ are in ~/Library/Developer. References to a MyApp directory are in the project directory itself, containing the source files.
- Most of the command-line tools Xcode uses for builds are buried in Xcode.app itself, so their invocations burrow through to them with a long prefix path. I cut out the prefix, which should make it easier to see what tools Xcode is using.
- I broke lines with backslashes. I indented lines that continued, or were contained by, other commands.

If you want the full, undiluted experience, just do what I did, and inspect the results. Here's the edited transcript:

```
Build target MyApp

Create product structure

/bin/mkdir -p .../Xcode/DerivedData/.../MyApp.app

CpResource .../Xcode.app/.../SDKs/iPhoneOS7.0.sdk/ResourceRules.plist \
        .../Xcode/DerivedData/.../MyApp.app/ResourceRules.plist
    cd ...MyApp/project
    setenv PATH "..."
    builtin-copy -exclude .DS_Store -exclude CVS -exclude .svn -exclude .git
        -exclude .hg -strip-debug-symbols \
        -strip-tool .../Xcode.app/.../usr/bin/strip \
        -resolve-src-symlinks \
    .../Xcode.app/.../SDKs/iPhoneOS7.0.sdk/ResourceRules.plist \
        .../Xcode/DerivedData/.../MyApp.app
```

```
SymLink .../Xcode/DerivedData/.../MyApp.app \
       .../Xcode/DerivedData/.../Applications/MyApp.app
   cd ...MyApp/project
   setenv PATH "..."
   /bin/ln -sf .../Xcode/DerivedData/.../MyApp.app \
   .../Xcode/DerivedData/.../BuildProductsPath/Release-iphoneos/MyApp.app
```

The build system starts by creating the application package (remember it's just a directory with the .app extension, and copying a standard resource-rules file into it. The rules file will let codesign at the end of the process know which files in the application package might change after signing and therefore should be excluded from calculating or checking the signature.

Then it sets a symbolic filesystem link between the application directory as it will be built, to a more convenient location.

Each stage of the build begins with the "invocation" of a pseudo-command that shows the intention of the block that follows, containing the actual command-line invocations that carry out the intention. You'll see that most of the build process works through external tools, rather than methods within the Xcode IDE itself.

Note

"External" is a relative term; they're almost all located inside the Xcode.app package, but they yield independent processes, and the tools of the same name in /usr/bin are no more than trampolines to the tools Xcode uses.

```
ProcessPCH .../Xcode/DerivedData/.../MyApp-Prefix.pch.pch MyApp/MyApp-Prefix.pch \
    normal armv7s objective-c com.apple.compilers.llvm.clang.1_0.compiler
   cd ...MyApp/project
   setenv LANG en_US.US-ASCII
   setenv PATH "..."
   clang \
    -x objective-c-header -arch armv7s -fmessage-length=0 \
    -fdiagnostics-show-note-include-stack -fmacro-backtrace-limit=0 -std=gnu99 \
      -fobjc-arc -Wno-trigraphs -fpascal-strings \
      -Os -Wno-missing-field-initializers \
    -Wno-missing-prototypes -Wno-implicit-atomic-properties \
      -Wno-receiver-is-weak -Wno-arc-repeated-use-of-weak \
      -Wduplicate-method-match -Wno-missing-braces \
    -Wparentheses -Wswitch -Wno-unused-function -Wno-unused-label \
    -Wno-unused-parameter -Wunused-variable -Wunused-value -Wempty-body \
      -Wuninitialized -Wno-unknown-pragmas \
    -Wno-shadow -Wno-four-char-constants -Wno-conversion -Wconstant-conversion \
     -Wint-conversion -Wno-bool-conversion -Wenum-conversion \
      -Wno-shorten-64-to-32 -Wpointer-sign -Wno-newline-eof \
      -Wno-selector -Wno-strict-selector-match \
    -Wno-undeclared-selector -Wno-deprecated-implementations \
```

```
    -isysroot .../Xcode.app/.../SDKs/iPhoneOS7.0.sdk \
  -fstrict-aliasing -Wprotocol -Wdeprecated-declarations \
   -g -fvisibility=hidden -Wno-sign-conversion \
   -miphoneos-version-min=6.0 \
 -iquote .../Xcode/DerivedData/.../MyApp-generated-files.hmap \
 -I.../Xcode/DerivedData/.../MyApp-own-target-headers.hmap  \
 -I.../Xcode/DerivedData/.../MyApp-all-target-headers.hmap \
 -iquote .../Xcode/DerivedData/.../MyApp-project-headers.hmap  \
 -I.../Xcode/DerivedData/.../BuildProductsPath/Release-iphoneos  \
   -I.../Xcode.app/.../usr/include  \
   -I.../Xcode/DerivedData/.../DerivedSources/armv7s  \
   -I.../Xcode/DerivedData/.../DerivedSources  \
 -F.../Xcode/DerivedData/.../BuildProductsPath/Release-iphoneos  \
   -DNS_BLOCK_ASSERTIONS=1  \
 --serialize-diagnostics .../Xcode/DerivedData/.../MyApp-Prefix.pch.dia  \
 -MMD -MT dependencies -MF .../Xcode/DerivedData/.../MyApp-Prefix.pch.d \
   -c ...MyApp/project/MyApp/MyApp-Prefix.pch  \
   -o .../Xcode/DerivedData/.../MyApp-Prefix.pch.pch
```

This is the only time I'll show you the full set of options and search paths the build system provides for the clang compiler. With few exceptions, the invocations that follow are just the same.

The pseudo-command is ProcessPCH. It invokes the clang compiler to convert the .pch file in the project directory into a .pch.pch file for use as a precompiled prefix in compiling each source file.

Take special note of one of the first options: -arch armv7s. This tells clang to emit object code for the ARM armv7s CPU.

```
ProcessPCH .../Xcode/DerivedData/.../MyApp-Prefix.pch.pch MyApp/MyApp-Prefix.pch \
    normal armv7 objective-c com.apple.compilers.llvm.clang.1_0.compiler
    cd ...MyApp/project
    setenv LANG en_US.US-ASCII
    setenv PATH "..."
    clang \
       -x objective-c-header -arch armv7  \
       -o .../Xcode/DerivedData/.../MyApp-Prefix.pch.pch
```

... and here's the same thing again—but with a difference: The -arch option specifies armv7, not armv7s. The Release build configuration specifies that the product be optimized for both the v7 and the v7s architectures. The build system has to invoke the compiler and the linker separately for each architecture.

```
CompileC .../Xcode/DerivedData/.../armv7/MyStepperController.o \
       MyApp/views/MyStepperController.m
       normal armv7 objective-c com.apple.compilers.llvm.clang.1_0.compiler
    cd ...MyApp/project
    setenv LANG en_US.US-ASCII
    setenv PATH "..."
```

```
    clang \
        -x objective-c -arch armv7 \
        -c ...MyApp/project/MyApp/views/MyStepperController.m \
        -o .../Xcode/DerivedData/.../armv7/MyStepperController.o
```

```
.../MyStepperController.m:23:17: \
    warning: method definition for 'stepperValueChanged:' not found
            [-Wincomplete-implementation]
@implementation MyStepperController
       ^
```

```
.../MyStepperController.m:19:1: \
    note: method 'stepperValueChanged:' declared here
- (IBAction) stepperValueChanged: (id) sender;
  ^
```

```
1 warning generated.
```

The CompileC pseudo-command also kicks off the clang compiler, this time with the
-x objective-c option to request compilation of an Objective-C source file. This is
the armv7 pass; there will be an armv7s pass, as well.

This pass turned up a couple of warnings; MyStepperController promised a
method, -stepperValueChanged:, that didn't make it into the @implementation
section.

The compiler reports the filename, line number, and character offset; the text of the
warning, including the compiler setting that put clang on the alert for such a problem;
and an ASCII-graphic picture of the precise location of the problem. clang supplements
the warning with a note that shows where the missing method had been declared.

The Xcode IDE converts the warning text into the banners and Issues navigator entries
you see in the project window.

```
Ld .../Xcode/DerivedData/.../armv7/MyApp normal armv7
    cd ...MyApp/project
    setenv IPHONEOS_DEPLOYMENT_TARGET 6.0
    setenv PATH "..."
    clang \
    -arch armv7 -isysroot .../Xcode.app/.../SDKs/iPhoneOS7.0.sdk \
    -L.../Xcode/DerivedData/.../BuildProductsPath/Release-iphoneos \
    -filelist .../Xcode/DerivedData/.../armv7/MyApp.LinkFileList \
    -dead_strip -fobjc-arc -fobjc-link-runtime -miphoneos-version-min=6.0 \
    -framework MessageUI -framework SystemConfiguration -framework CoreData \
        -framework AVFoundation -framework MobileCoreServices \
    -framework MediaPlayer -framework UIKit -framework Foundation
        -framework CoreGraphics -Xlinker -dependency_info \
    -Xlinker .../Xcode/DerivedData/.../armv7/MyApp_dependency_info.dat \
        -o .../Xcode/DerivedData/.../armv7/MyApp
```

```
Ld .../Xcode/DerivedData/.../armv7s/MyApp normal armv7s
    cd ...MyApp/project
    setenv IPHONEOS_DEPLOYMENT_TARGET 6.0
```

```
setenv PATH "..."
clang \
  -arch armv7s -isysroot .../Xcode.app/.../SDKs/iPhoneOS7.0.sdk \
  -Xlinker .../Xcode/DerivedData/.../armv7s/MyApp_dependency_info.dat \
    -o .../Xcode/DerivedData/.../armv7s/MyApp
```

Here's the link phase, once for each architecture. The resulting, complete executable files are sent to `armv7` and `armv7s` directories in the derived-data directory.

```
CreateUniversalBinary .../Xcode/DerivedData/.../MyApp.app/MyApp normal armv7\ armv7s
    cd ...MyApp/project
    setenv PATH "..."
    lipo \
        -create .../Xcode/DerivedData/.../armv7/MyApp \
        .../Xcode/DerivedData/.../armv7s/MyApp \
        -output .../Xcode/DerivedData/.../MyApp.app/MyApp
```

The `lipo` tool was created when "universal"—multiple-architecture—binaries were called "fat" binaries. It takes libraries and executables that are identical but for their architectures, and archives them into single files from which the operating system can select the needed version.

```
CopyStringsFile .../Xcode/DerivedData/.../MyApp.app/en.lproj/InfoPlist.strings
              MyApp/en.lproj/InfoPlist.strings
    cd ...MyApp/project
    setenv PATH "..."
    builtin-copyStrings \
        --validate --inputencoding utf-8 --outputencoding binary \
          --outdir .../Xcode/DerivedData/.../MyApp.app/en.lproj
          -- MyApp/en.lproj/InfoPlist.strings
```

The localization system expects `.strings` files to be of a certain format—UTF-16 on OS X, prepared binary on iOS. This stage takes in the file in the project directory, whatever its format, converts it into the practical format, and places it in the application package.

```
CopyPNGFile .../Xcode/DerivedData/.../MyApp.app/Default.png MyApp/Default.png
    cd ...MyApp/project
    setenv PATH "..."
    copypng \
        -compress .../MyApp/Default.png \
        .../Xcode/DerivedData/.../MyApp.app/Default.png
```

A `.png` file is not just a `.png` file. The `CopyPNGFile` pseudo-command converts PNGs into a compressed format and places them in the product bundle. You should be aware that not every graphics program can read PNGs in this format, although the QuickLook view in the Finder and the Preview application can.

```
CompileStoryboard MyApp/en.lproj/MainStoryboard.storyboard
    cd ...MyApp/project
    setenv IBSC_MINIMUM_COMPATIBILITY_VERSION 6.0
```

```
    setenv PATH "..."
   setenv XCODE_DEVELOPER_USR_PATH .../Xcode.app/Contents/Developer/usr/bin/..
    ibtool \
        --errors --warnings --notices \
        --minimum-deployment-target 6.0 --output-format human-readable-text \
        --compile .../MyApp.app/en.lproj/MainStoryboard.storyboardc \
        .../MyApp/project/MyApp/en.lproj/MainStoryboard.storyboard
```

ibtool does just about everything imaginable with Interface Builder sources and products. In this invocation, it serves as a compiler that converts the app's main storyboard into a .storyboardc, and moves it into the product bundle.

```
CopyPlistFile .../DerivedData/.../MyApp.app/en.lproj/when-and-where-strings.plist \
          MyApp/en.lproj/when-and-where-strings.plist
    cd ...MyApp/project
    setenv PATH "..."
    builtin-copyPlist \
        --convert binary1 --outdir .../Xcode/DerivedData/.../MyApp.app/en.lproj \
        -- MyApp/en.lproj/when-and-where-strings.plist
```

Property lists (see Chapter 24, "Property Lists") are straightforward things, but storage and speed are at a premium on an iOS device. CopyPlistFile recodes .plists before moving them into the .app bundle.

```
CompileAssetCatalog .../Xcode/DerivedData/.../MyApp.app MyApp/Media.xcassets
    cd ...MyApp/project
    setenv PATH "..."
    actool \
        --output-format human-readable-text \
        --notices --warnings \
      --export-dependency-info .../assetcatalog_dependencies.txt \
      --output-partial-info-plist .../assetcatalog_generated_info.plist \
      --app-icon AppIcon --launch-image LaunchImage --platform iphoneos \
      --minimum-deployment-target 6.0 --target-device iphone --compress-pngs \
        --compile .../Xcode/DerivedData/.../MyApp.app \
        ...Media.xcassets

/* com.apple.actool.document.warnings */
...MyApp/project/MyApp/Media.xcassets: \
    ./AppIcon.appiconset: warning: A 60x60@2x app icon is required for \
        iPhone apps targeting iOS 7.0 and later
...MyApp/project/MyApp/Media.xcassets: \
    ./LaunchImage.launchimage: warning: An iPhone Retina (4-inch) launch \
        image for iOS 7.0 and later is required.
/* com.apple.actool.compilation-results */
.../Xcode/DerivedData/.../MyApp.app/AppIcon57x57.png
.../Xcode/DerivedData/.../MyApp.app/AppIcon57x57@2x.png
.../Xcode/DerivedData/.../MyApp.app/LaunchImage.png
.../Xcode/DerivedData/.../MyApp.app/LaunchImage@2x.png
.../Xcode/DerivedData/.../MyApp.app/LaunchImage-568h@2x.png
.../Xcode/DerivedData/.../assetcatalog_generated_info.plist
```

The `CompileAssetCatalog` phase (for a pre-iOS 7 target) explodes asset catalogs into individual graphics files and edits `Info.plist` to point to a file for each icon format. For iOS 7 targets, the operating system can use asset catalogs directly.

This app doesn't have the full complement of launch images; the `actool` compiler complains.

```
ProcessInfoPlistFile .../Xcode/DerivedData/.../MyApp.app/Info.plist \
                    MyApp/MyApp-Info.plist
    cd ...MyApp/project
    setenv PATH "..."
    builtin-infoPlistUtility \
        ...MyApp/project/MyApp/MyApp-Info.plist \
     -genpkginfo .../Xcode/DerivedData/.../MyApp.app/PkgInfo \
      -expandbuildsettings \
      -format binary -platform iphoneos \
    -resourcerulesfile .../Xcode/DerivedData/.../MyApp.app/ResourceRules.plist \
      -additionalcontentfile \
      .../Xcode/DerivedData/.../assetcatalog_generated_info.plist \
      -o .../Xcode/DerivedData/.../MyApp.app/Info.plist
```

`Info.plist` is no ordinary property list. The target-specific precursor files can incorporate any number of build-setting references, and those have to be resolved before a binary `Info.plist` file can be installed in the application. Here

- Build-setting references are expanded
- A `PkgInfo` file is created
- The file is converted from the convenient XML format to binary-plist
- Standard iOS settings are added
- The asset-catalog results are incorporated into the icon and launch-image specifications

```
GenerateDSYMFile .../Xcode/DerivedData/.../Release-iphoneos/MyApp.app.dSYM \
        .../Xcode/DerivedData/.../MyApp.app/MyApp
    cd ...MyApp/project
    setenv PATH "..."
    dsymutil \
        .../Xcode/DerivedData/.../MyApp.app/MyApp \
     -o .../Xcode/DerivedData/.../Release-iphoneos/MyApp.app.dSYM

Stripping .../Xcode/DerivedData/.../MyApp.app/MyApp
    cd ...MyApp/project
    setenv PATH "..."
    strip \
        .../Xcode/DerivedData/.../MyApp.app/MyApp
```

The debugging-symbol archive, which you can use to make sense of crash dumps, is created. The executable is stripped of every linkage and debugging symbol except for those that might be necessary at launch time for the dynamic linker.

```
SetOwnerAndGroup fritza:staff .../Xcode/DerivedData/.../MyApp.app
    cd ...MyApp/project
    setenv PATH "..."
    /usr/sbin/chown \
        -RH fritza:staff .../Xcode/DerivedData/.../MyApp.app

SetMode u+w,go-w,a+rX .../Xcode/DerivedData/.../MyApp.app
    cd ...MyApp/project
    setenv PATH "..."
    /bin/chmod \
        -RH u+w,go-w,a+rX .../Xcode/DerivedData/.../MyApp.app
```

The product file should belong to the user who created it, and others shouldn't be able to change it.

```
ProcessProductPackaging \
    ...Library/MobileDevice/Provisioning  Profiles/(...).mobileprovision \
        .../Xcode/DerivedData/.../MyApp.app/embedded.mobileprovision
    cd ...MyApp/project
    setenv PATH "..."
    builtin-productPackagingUtility \
        ...Library/MobileDevice/Provisioning\ Profiles/(...).mobileprovision \
        -o .../Xcode/DerivedData/.../MyApp.app/embedded.mobileprovision

ProcessProductPackaging .../Xcode.app/.../SDKs/iPhoneOS7.0.sdk/Entitlements.plist \
        .../Xcode/DerivedData/.../MyApp.xcent
    cd ...MyApp/project
    setenv PATH "..."
    builtin-productPackagingUtility \
      .../Xcode.app/.../SDKs/iPhoneOS7.0.sdk/Entitlements.plist \
      -entitlements -format xml -o .../Xcode/DerivedData/.../MyApp.xcent
```

There are two kinds of product-packaging tasks: First the provisioning file must be added to the package. Second, an .xcent file comes in to provide the codesign utility with the final version of the signing-entitlements file.

```
CodeSign .../Xcode/DerivedData/.../MyApp.app
    cd .../MyApp/project
    setenv CODESIGN_ALLOCATE codesign_allocate
    setenv PATH "..."
    Using code signing identity "iPhone Distribution: My organization" \
     and provisioning profile "MyAppE" (6019D454-9634-4D93-A880-83685E6E7744)
    codesign --force --sign 1045D4CF9B3B6A2430FC4713EE353A3BA1A57B3B  \
      --resource-rules=.../Xcode/DerivedData/.../MyApp.app/ResourceRules.plist \
        --entitlements .../Xcode/DerivedData/.../MyApp.xcent \
        .../Xcode/DerivedData/.../MyApp.app
```

The last step in creating the app is signing it with a signing identity. The signature incorporates an identity, a profile, the resource rules (exemptions from the signature), and the entitlement claims.

```
Validate .../Xcode/DerivedData/.../MyApp.app
    cd ...MyApp/project
    setenv PATH "..."
    setenv PRODUCT_TYPE com.apple.product-type.application
    Validation \
        .../Xcode/DerivedData/.../MyApp.app

Touch .../Xcode/DerivedData/.../BuildProductsPath/Release-iphoneos/MyApp.app.dSYM
    cd ...MyApp/project
    setenv PATH "..."
    /usr/bin/touch \
      -c .../Xcode/DerivedData/.../Release-iphoneos/MyApp.app.dSYM
```

Finally, the app is given a cursory inspection (not to be confused with the more thorough validation you can give it from the Archives organizer if it is registered with iTunes Connect), and its modification date of the `.dSYM` symbol file is updated, I assume so Spotlight will know there's a new version.

Summary

This was an important chapter if you want to know how Xcode really works. It explains how the build system built into Xcode itself takes the place of traditional `makefiles` and the effort needed to keep them current. It showed how a build is divided into phases that "contain" files to be worked on. Settings for compilers and other tools are an essential part of configuring a build, and you saw how Xcode organizes them by project, target, and configuration.

You saw how you can use the build system from a script, so your builds can be managed without having to trigger them manually from the IDE.

Finally, you examined the Log navigator, how to get a transcript of the commands that underlie the build process, and how to analyze a transcript.

## 27

Instruments

Instruments is a framework for software-measurement tools called...instruments. (Capital-I Instruments is the application, small-i instruments are components of the Instruments application.) The analogy is to a multi-track recording deck. Instruments records activity into tracks (one per instrument), building the data on a timeline like audio on a tape.

You've seen Instruments before, in Chapter 16, "Measurement and Analysis," where it helped you track down some memory and performance bugs in the Passer Rating iPhone app. It deserves a closer look. You'll learn how to navigate the Instruments trace window, and how to choose instruments to fit your needs.

What Instruments Is

The focus on a timeline makes Instruments unique. Historically, profiling and debugging tools did one thing at a time. You had Shark (available with Xcode 2 and 3), which sampled a running application to collect aggregate statistics of where it spent its time. Shark had several modes for taking different statistics; if you wanted another mode, you ran Shark again. Shark's profile data was aggregated over the whole session; if you wanted to profile a particular piece of your application, there was a hot key for you to turn profiling on and off.

Separately, there was a profiling application called MallocDebug, which collected cumulative, statistical call trees for calls to `malloc` and `free`. The results were cumulative across a profiling session, so you'd know how the biggest, or most, allocations happened, but not when.

If you needed the distribution and history of *object* allocations, by class, there was an Object Alloc application.

And if you wanted to know how the application was spending its time while it was making those allocations, you quit MallocDebug or Object Alloc and ran the target app again under Shark, because the other apps did only one thing.

Instruments is different. It is comprehensive. There are instruments for most ways you'd want to analyze your code, and Instruments runs them *all at the same time*. The results are laid out by time, in parallel. Did pressing a **Compute** button result in Core Data fetches?

Or had the fetches already been done earlier? Did other disk activity eat up bandwidth? In the application? Elsewhere in the system? Is the application leaking file descriptors, and if so, when, and in response to what? If you're handing data off to another process, how does the recipient's memory usage change in response to the handoff, and how does it relate to the use of file descriptors in both the recipient and master applications?

Instruments can answer these questions. You can relate file descriptors to disk activity, and disk activity to Core Data events, with stack traces for every single one of these, because Instruments captures the data on a timeline, all in parallel, event by event. And, you can target different instruments on different applications (or even the system as a whole) at the same time.

For events—like individual allocations or system calls—Instruments keeps a complete record each and every time. For time profiling, Instruments does statistical sampling, but it keeps each sample. That means that even if you want an aggregate, *you get to pick the aggregate.*

Say the list of passers in Passer Rating stutters when you scroll it. With Shark, you'd have to start Passer Rating, get to where you'd be scrolling as quickly as you could, do the scrolling, and then kill it at once so your statistical sample wouldn't be polluted by whatever followed the part you were interested in. And you'd be too late, because the CPU time soaked up by initialization would swamp the little spikes incurred by reloading the passer table cells.

In Instruments, by contrast, you don't have to worry about one part of the program polluting your statistics. You can select just the part of the timeline that has to do with scrolling, and you can see what your app was doing just then.

> **Note**
>
> Most of the power of Instruments lies in the analysis tools it provides after a recording is made, but don't ignore the advantage it provides in showing program state dynamically: If you can't see when a memory total or file I/O begins and settles down (for instance), you won't know when to stop the recording for analysis in the first place.

Running Instruments

In the "Measurement and Analysis" chapter (16), you started Instruments from Xcode by issuing **Product → Profile** (⌘ I), or selecting the **Profile** variant of the large **Action** button at the left end of the Xcode toolbar. You could set the trace template you wanted in the **Profile** panel of the Scheme editor; there's even a shortcut: Hold down the Option key while making any other gesture that starts profiling, and you'll be offered the **Profile** panel of the Scheme editor before you go on. With profiling integrated into the Xcode workflow, this will be the most common way you'll use Instruments.

For specialized uses, you'll want to go beyond the few templates the **Profile** action gives you. Instruments can run and attach to applications independently, and you can set up any instruments you like for the trace.

Instruments does not appear as an application anywhere in the Finder. Like all the other developer tools, it is kept inside the Xcode.app bundle. The first time you run it without

immediately doing a profile, you'll select **Xcode →Open Developer Tool →
Instruments**. Instruments will launch like any other application. Its icon will appear in
the Dock, and I advise you to keep it there by right-clicking its icon and selecting
Options →Keep in Dock.

When you start Instruments, it automatically opens a document (called a *trace document*)
and displays a sheet offering you a choice of templates populated with instruments for
common tasks (see Figure 27.1). A list of templates Apple provides can be found in "The
Templates," later in this chapter.

The Trace Document Window

The initial form of a trace document window is simple: A toolbar at the top, and a stack of
instruments in the view that dominates the window. Once you've recorded data into the
document, the window becomes much richer. Let's go through Figure 27.2 and identify
the components.

Figure 27.1   When you create a new trace document in Instruments, it shows you an empty
document and a sheet for choosing among templates prepopulated with instruments
for common tasks.

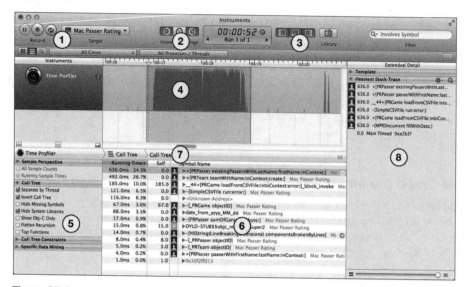

Figure 27.2   A typical Instruments window, once data has been recorded. The Extended Detail area (at right) has also been exposed. I discuss the numbered parts in the text.

The Toolbar

The toolbar comes in three sections. The controls at left ① control recording and the execution of the target applications. There is a **Pause** button for suspending and resuming data collection; a **Record / Drive & Record / Stop** button to start and stop data collection; and a **Loop** button for running a recorded human-interface script repeatedly.

> **Note**
>
> When you start recording, you will often be asked for an administrator's password. The kind of deep monitoring many instruments do is a security breach, and the system makes you show you are authorized to do it.

The **Target** popup designates the process or executable that all instruments in the document will target, unless you specify a different target for individual instruments. The choices are

- The top of the menu allows you to choose the device Instruments is to focus on. It determines what processes and targets are available for tracing.

- **All Processes**—data will be collected from all the processes, user and system, on the target device. For instance, the Core Data instruments (Mac only) can measure the Core Data activity of all processes. Not every instrument can span processes; if your document contains no instruments that can sample system-wide, this option will be disabled.

- **Attach to Process**—data will be collected from a process that is already running; select it from the submenu. Some instruments require that their targets be launched from Instruments and cannot attach to running processes. If you use only non-attaching instruments, this option will be disabled.

- **Choose Target**—This is the equivalent of the **Open. . .** and **Open Recent** items in the **File** menu. The submenu contains a list of processes you've recorded recently, and a **Choose Target. . .** item to drop a browser sheet to choose a fresh application.

- **Instrument Specific**—Each instrument can collect data from a target of its own, specified in the **Target** popup of its configuration inspector. This setting sets no target for the document as a whole and leaves the specifics to each instrument.

- **Edit Active Target**—drops a sheet for editing the arguments and environment variables to pass to the target when it is launched.

- **Options**—a submenu that directs standard I/O to Instruments or the device log; and for the iOS Simulator, selects the mode (iPhone or iPad) in which the simulator is to operate.

The **Target** popup is not selectable while Instruments is recording.

The center section ② relates to time. The clock view in the center of the toolbar displays the total time period recorded in the document. If you click the clock-face icon to the right of the time display, the clock shows the position of the triangular "playback head" slider in the time scale at the top of the Track area (Figure 27.3).

Figure 27.3 The center section of a trace document's toolbar displays a clock and controls for selecting a span of time within a recording. The clock view shows the total time in the document (or, if you click the icon at the right of the clock, the position of the "playback head") and the run being displayed if there is more than one.

The clock view also controls which run of the document is being displayed. Each time you press **Record**, a new recording, with a timeline of its own, is added to the document. The run now being displayed is shown like "Run 1 of 2," and you can switch among them by pressing the arrowhead buttons to either side.

> **Note**
>
> You can also browse among runs by selecting **View → Run Browser** (^Tab). The contents of the window will be replaced by a "cover flow" partial view of the traces in each run, along with particulars of when it was run, on what, and so on.

Most instruments will display subsets of the data they collect if you select a time span within the recording. To do so, move the playback head to the beginning of the span, and click the left segment of the **Inspection Range** control; then move the head to the end of the span and click the segment on the right. The selected span will be highlighted, and the display will be restricted to data collected in the span. To clear the selection, click the segment in the middle.

> **Note**
>
> Option-dragging across an interval in one of the traces will also set an inspection range.

The right section ③ provides convenient controls for display. **View** is the familiar three-segment control that hides and shows the Title/Options, Detail, and Extended Detail panes. **Library** shows and hides the Library window. The search field filters the Detail area by symbols or libraries that match the keywords you enter.

The Track Area

The Track area ④ is the focus of the document window and the only component you see when a document is first opened. This is the area you drag new instruments into. Each instrument occupies its own row, with a configuration block on the left, and the instrument's track on the right.

The configuration block (see Figure 27.4) shows the instrument's name and icon. To the left is a disclosure triangle so you can see the instrument's tracks for previous runs in the document. To the right is an inspector button ⓘ that reveals a configuration inspector for the instrument.

The tracks to the right of the configuration blocks display the data collected by the instruments on a timeline. The configuration inspector controls what data is plotted and how it is displayed.

> **Note**
>
> Most instruments will also put a **Configure** button in the lower-right corner for more options on how the instrument collects data. The distinction between the main and configure sides of the block is not well defined, so be sure to check both. Further, the Options view in the Detail area can contain settings that affect what data is collected. Sometimes, you won't be able to set these until after you've recorded a trace; check, and be aware that you may have to prepare the options after a throwaway run.

At the top of the timeline is a ruler matching the data to the time at which it was collected. The scale of the track can be controlled by what looks like a slider below the configuration blocks. In fact, it behaves like a joystick: The track compresses while you hold it to the left, and expands while you hold it to the right. In the ruler you will see a white triangle, the *playback head*. Drag the playback head and use the **Inspection Range** control to select intervals within the recording. As you drag the head across the track, many instruments will label their tracks with the value of their data at that time.

> **Note**
>
> Shift-dragging across a track zooms it so that the span you select will fill the width of the window.

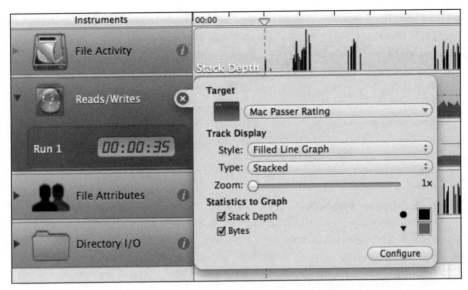

Figure 27.4   A stack of instrument tracks in a trace document. Each instrument has its own row, with a timeline extending to the right, calibrated in seconds. Clicking an instrument's configuration button (the circled **i**) opens an inspector containing settings for the instrument. Some control the style of the graph and which of its data an instrument displays, and this can be changed at any time. Instruments has done two traces on Mac Passer Rating; clicking the disclosure triangle on a track opens all previous traces for comparison.

The Detail Area

The Detail area ⑤ and ⑥ appears when you've run a trace. Click **View → Detail (⌘ D)**, and the middle segment of the **View** control in the toolbar will toggle the Detail area.

When you select an instrument in the Track view, the data the instrument collects is shown in tabular form in the Table view of the Detail area. What's in the table varies among instruments, and most instruments have more than one kind of table. The first segment of the Detail jump bar ⑦ controls which table is displayed. As you drill down into the data for a detail row, elements are added to the jump bar; click higher-level elements to return to the corresponding views.

The Options view ⑤ filters the table's contents; it may also have controls that configure an instrument or trigger an instrument's actions. The options vary by instrument and table type, but most instruments collect call trees, and will have a "Call Tree" section among the options. The call-tree display options are

- **Separate by Category**—In the Allocations instrument, the normal call tree displays all allocations of any kind. This is useful if you need to know how much memory was allocated in any one function, regardless of what the allocations were for. If you select **Separate by Category**, the call tree list is sorted by the type of the allocation. You can expand the row for the symbol name NSImage and see code paths that led to the creation of OS X image objects.

- **Separate by Thread**—Call trees are normally merged with no regard for which thread the calls occurred in. Separating the trees by thread will help you weed out calls in threads you aren't interested in.

- **Invert Call Tree**—The default (top-down) presentation of call trees starts at the runtime start function, branching out through the successive calls down to the leaf functions that are the events the instrument records. Checking this box inverts the trees, so they are bottom-up: You start at the function (usually objc_msgSend in Objective-C applications) where the event occurred, and branch out to all the successive callers.

- **Hide Missing Symbols**—Checking this box hides functions that don't have symbols associated with them. Most of the libraries in the system frameworks include symbols for their functions, and those can at least suggest what's going on. (And, of course, your code has symbols, because you've made sure your "Debug Information Format" build setting is set to "DWARF with dSYM File"—it won't inflate the size of your code.)

- **Hide System Libraries**—This skips over functions in system libraries. Reading the names of the library calls may help you get an idea of what is going on, but if you are looking for code you can do something about, you don't want to see them. Using this option along with **Invert Call Tree** will often tell a very explicit story about what your code is doing. objc_msgSend is so ubiquitous in Cocoa code that finding it in a stack trace doesn't tell you much; paring the trees down to where all those calls came from tells you everything.

- **Show Obj-C Only**—Checking this narrows the list down to calls made from Objective-C methods, whether in system libraries or not. Another way to cut out the possible distraction of calls you don't care to see.

- **Flatten Recursion**—This lumps every call a function makes to itself into a single item. Recursive calls can run up the length of a call stack without being very informative.

Note

Stack traces in the Extended Detail area also reflect your settings of these filters.

You can also add call-tree constraints, such as minimum and maximum call counts. The idea is to prune (or focus on) calls that are not frequently made. Another constraint that may be available (for instance in the Time Profiler instrument) can filter call trees by the amount of time (minimum, maximum, or both) they took up in the course of the run.

There's one feature that will do you a lot of good, but it's easy to miss: At the far left end of the Detail jump bar is what looks like a label that identifies the selected instrument. That's what it usually happens to show, but it's a popup menu. You can use it as another way to select an instrument track for the Detail view, but at the top is another item,

Trace Highlights. Many instruments can render their data as bar or pie charts, broken down by process, thread, or event type, or share of resources. When you select the highlights view, the Detail area will fill with the available charts. Often this is the best gateway to the detailed information in the trace—and clicking one of the charts will take you to the details of the responsible instrument.

The Extended Detail Area

The Extended Detail area ⑧ typically includes a stack trace when you select an item in the Detail area that carries stack information. When the selected item is part of a call tree, the Extended Detail area shows the "heaviest" stack, the one that accounts for most of whatever the instrument keeps track of. Selecting a frame in the call stack highlights the corresponding call in the call-tree outline. Double-clicking on a frame shows the corresponding source code in the Detail area, with banners showing where the instrument "hit" in the function, and what proportion of those function hits fell on which lines.

> **Note**
>
> When you double-click a stack frame to see the source code in the Detail area, the Extended Detail area fills with annotations on the function call that generated that frame. The Detail area's jump bar adds a segment for the listing (**Call Trees** →**Call Tree** →**-[SimpleCSVFile run:error:]**. You can return to the call tree in the Detail area and the stack trace in the Extended Detail area by clicking the previous segment (**Call Tree**).

A stack trace in the Extended Detail area has an **Action** (gear) menu at the top. Most commands in this menu have to do with how the calls in the trace are formatted, but a couple are of particular interest. **Look up API Documentation** acts like option-clicking on a symbol in Xcode: It opens a window showing the documentation for the selected method. **Trace Call Duration** creates a new instrument in the current document to record the stack trace whenever the function is called and how long it takes to execute.

As with Xcode's Debug navigator, the Extended Detail area has a slider at the bottom to condense the stack trace to "interesting" frames, generally defined as your functions, their callers, and the functions they call. Sliding the control all the way to the right gives you the full stack; to the left, just one (usually uninformative) call. If you don't see your code in the stack, be sure to check the slider to ensure it hasn't filtered out what you need to see.

The Library

Instruments are made part of an Instruments trace document either by being instantiated from a template or by being dragged in from the Library window.

The Library palette (**Window** →**Library**, ⌘L, or the **Library** toggle button in the toolbar) lists all of the known instruments. Initially this is a repertoire of Apple-supplied tracks, but it is possible to add your own. The palette lists all known instruments. Selecting one fills the pane below the list with a description (which has always been the same as the description in the list, but we can hope for the future). See Figure 27.5. Some descriptions include a **(?)** button, which as of Xcode 5.0.1 only takes you to the root page of the Instruments manual in Xcode's Documentation browser.

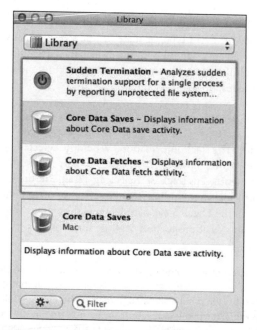

Figure 27.5   A scrolling list of available instruments dominates the Library palette. The selected instrument is described in the panel below. Selecting a category from the popup menu narrows the list down by task, and the search field at the bottom allows you to find an instrument from its name or description.

The Library gathers instruments into groups; these are initially hidden, but they can be seen if you select **Show Group Banners** from the **Action** (gear) popup at the lower-left corner of the palette. The **Action** menu will also allow you to create groups of your own—drag an instrument into your group to add it; or smart groups, which filter the library according to criteria you choose. The popup at the top of the palette narrows the list down by group, and the search field at the bottom allows you to filter the list by searching for text in the names and descriptions.

Instrument Configuration

Configuration inspectors vary by instrument, but some elements are common.

There is a **Target** popup that initially points to the document's default target (set with the **Target** menu in the toolbar). If no default target has been selected, or if the **Target** menu has been set to **Instrument Specific**, the instrument's target is active. You can select from processes already running, applications that Instruments had sampled before, a new application or tool of your choice, or, with many instruments, the system as a whole.

The ability to set a target for each instrument is important: It allows you to examine the behavior of an application *and* other processes with which it communicates, simultaneously.

In the **Track Display** section, there are three controls: A **Style** popup, a **Type** popup, and a **Zoom** slider.

The usual **Style** menu selects among graphing styles for the numeric data the instrument records. These may include

- **Line Graph.** The track is displayed as a colored line connecting each datum in the series of collected data. You can choose the color in the list of the available series.

- **Filled Line Graph** is the same as **Line**, but the area under the line is colored.

- **Point Graph.** Each datum is displayed as a discrete symbol in the track. You can choose the symbols in the list of available series in the inspector.

- **Block Graph** is a bar graph, showing each datum as a colored rectangle. In instruments that record events, the block will be as wide as the time to the next event.

- **Peak Graph** shows the data collected by an instrument that records events (like the Core Data instruments) as a vertical line at each event. Every time something happens, the graph shows a blip.

- **Stack Libraries** draws a bar for each event the instrument measures. The height of the bar depends on the depth of the call stack at the event; the bars are divided into colored segments, with a different color for each library that owns the caller at that level.

- Some instruments have graph styles of their own. The Time Profiler instrument has three custom styles:

  - **CPU Usage** is the classic format: An area graph shows the moment-to-moment time demands the application makes on all processor cores.

  - **Deepest Stack Libraries** shows a bar chart in which the height of the bars represents the depth of the call stack at each moment. The bars are color-coded to identify the libraries responsible for each call in the stack. The color code is the same as the one used in the icons in the Extended Detail area.

  - **User and System Libraries** is the same bar chart, but there are only two colors showing how much of the stack passed through system libraries.

- The Allocations instrument also has three custom styles:

  - **Current Bytes** is what we've worked with before: It's an area graph showing how much memory is in use.

  - **Allocation Density** shows how many allocations were made in each increment in time. When your app makes a flurry of allocations, it shows up as a peak in the graph.

  - **Active Allocation Distribution** filters the allocation-density graph to show where the allocations were made that were still alive at the end of the trace.

> **Note**
>
> Most instruments record events, not quantities that vary over time. In fact, the data displayed may not even be a continuous variable, but may be a mere tag, like the ID of a thread or a file descriptor. The Peak Graph style is the most suitable style for event recordings. Such displays are still useful, as they give you a landmark for examining the matching data in the other tracks. Stack Libraries would also be good, but it takes a very sharp eye to discern patterns in the call stacks of infrequent events.

The **Type** menu offers two choices for instruments that can record more than one data series. **Overlay** displays all series on a single graph. The displayed data will probably overlap, but in point and line displays this probably doesn't matter, and filled displays are translucent, so the two series don't obscure each other. **Stacked** displays each series in separate strips, one above the other.

Zoom increases the height of the instrument's track. This is especially handy in stacked displays, so you can view multiple traces without squishing them into illegibility. The slider clicks to integer multiples of the standard track height, from 1 to 10 units.

You can change the **Track Display** settings even after the instrument has collected its data. A shortcut for the **Zoom** slider can be found in the **View** menu, as **Increase Deck Size** (⌘ +) and **Decrease Deck Size** (⌘ –).

For instruments that can collect more than one series, a **Statistics to Graph** section shows a checkbox for each available series, with a popup to select the shape of points for a Point Graph, plus a color well.

Recording

There is more than one way to start recording in Instruments.

The most obvious is to create a trace document and press the **Record** button in the toolbar. Recording starts, the target application comes to the front, you perform your test, switch back to Instruments, and press the same button, now labeled **Stop**.

The first time you record into a document that contains a User Interface instrument (Mac targets only), the recording button will be labeled **Record**, as usual. Once the UI track contains events, the recording button is labeled **Drive & Record**. When you click it, no new events are recorded into the UI track; instead the events already there are *replayed* so you can reproduce your tests.

If you want to record a fresh User Interface track, open the configuration inspector (with the **i** button in the instrument's label) and select **Capture** from the **Action** popup. The recording button will revert to **Record**.

> **Note**
>
> The iOS side of Instruments gives you the same facility through the Automation instrument. Drop the instrument into the Track area, and attach a JavaScript script that will drive your application. When the Track runs, Automation will perform the UI actions you prescribed, and the other instruments will accumulate traces that you can compare directly between runs. Search the Documentation browser for "UI Automation JavaScript Reference" for details.

A second way to record is through a global hot key combination. To set the combination, Open the **Keyboard** panel in System Preferences, select the **Shortcuts** tab, and seek out the **Developer** group under **Services**. The group includes a number of profiling actions, such as collecting a time profile of the application under the mouse cursor. One of the options is **Toggle Instruments Recording**. Set the combination by clicking the **add shortcut** button in that row of the table.

> **Note**
>
> I never remember these global hot keys. Do yourself a favor and check the box next to the service, so it will show up in the **Services** submenu of the application menu. The Instruments-related command will appear with its hot key combination. If there's no combination, you'll know that the app you're running has probably taken the combination for itself.

Instruments gives you a shortcut to the System Preferences window in the **General** tab in its own Preferences window: an **Open Keyboard Shortcut Preferences** button.

With the **Toggle Instruments Recording** hot key set, set up a trace document for the app you want to record—but don't run it. Run the app, then press the key combination you chose. Instruments will start recording. Press it again, and recording stops.

If you assign a key combination for other Instruments services, such as **Allocations & Leaks**, then Instruments will create a new trace document targeting the front application and record its memory activity. The same with **File Activity**, **System Trace**, and the other services that share the names of Instruments templates.

Take special note of the three **Time Profile** commands, which target the active application, the background application that has a window under the mouse pointer, or the whole system. The option of pointing the mouse at one of the target's windows allows you to start simultaneous traces on more than one application without having to disturb their place in the window ordering.

Displaying an ongoing trace, especially for more than one application, puts a significant performance burden on the system; I'll get into the details shortly. This can be a particular problem if you use hot keys to record more than one application. If you check **Always use deferred mode** in the **General** tab of the Preferences window, you can ensure that your hot-key traces will be as lightweight as possible.

The third way to record is through the Mini Instruments window. Selecting **View →Mini Instruments** hides all of Instruments' windows and substitutes a floating heads-up window (see Figure 27.6) listing all of the open trace documents.

The window lists all of the trace documents that were open when you switched to Mini mode; scroll through by pressing the up or down arrowheads above and below the list. At the left of each item is a button for starting (round icon) or stopping (square icon) recording, and a clock to show how long recording has been going on. Stopping and restarting a recording adds a new run to the document.

Clicking the Mini Instruments window activates Instruments, and you can select **View →Mini Instruments** again to restore the trace windows. You can also return to the full display of Instruments by clicking the close Ⓧ button in the upper-left corner of the Mini Instruments window.

Figure 27.6   The Mini Instruments heads-up window. It lists each open trace document next to a clock and a recording button. Scroll through the list using the arrowheads at top and bottom.

As with the hot keys, Mini Instruments has the advantage that it's convenient to start recording in the middle of an application's run (handy if you are recording a User Interface track that you want to loop). It eliminates the overhead of updating the trace displays. Before Xcode 5, Mini Instruments floated in its own layer, so you could start a trace without sending the active application to the background. That's no longer possible.

I mentioned the burden a tracing session can put on the performance of your computer. While a trace runs, Instruments analyzes the data it collects, building up profiles and tables. Often it has to refer back to earlier data (like matching memory events to blocks and updating living-versus-transient counts) to keep the analysis current.

Computers are fast, but the process takes resources away from the target application (thus making it difficult to measure your app against real-world conditions) and can force Instruments to skip data points. You can prevent this by deferring analysis until the trace stops. **File → Record Options...** (⌥⌘R) sets parameters for tracing, like delaying data collection until a fixed time after launching the application, or limiting collection to a fixed period. The option you're interested in is the **Deferred Mode** checkbox. While it's checked, Instruments will black out the trace window until the run ends. Once the run does end, the blackout will continue as Instruments conducts the postmortem analysis, and then you'll see your trace. See Figure 27.7.

Saving and Reopening

Like any other Macintosh document, a trace document can be saved. The document will contain its instruments and all the data they've collected. There can be a lot of data—potentially, full stack traces for events only microseconds apart—so expect a trace document to be large. Tens of megabytes are not uncommon. Trace documents generally respond well to ZIP archiving.

It's likely that you will come to need a uniform layout of instruments that isn't included in the default templates provided by Apple. You can easily create templates of your own, which will appear in the template sheet presented when you create a new trace document. Configure a document as you want it, and select **File → Save as Template...**.

The ensuing save-file sheet is the standard one, focused on the directory in which Instruments looks for your templates, `~/Library/Application Support/ Instruments/Templates`. The name you give your file will be the label shown in the

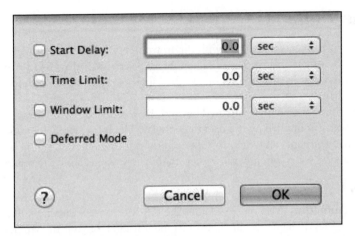

Figure 27.7   File → Record Options... (⌥⌘R) produces a sheet in which you can restrict the scope of an Instruments tracing session and improve the efficiency of the trace by deferring analysis until after the trace is done.

template-choice sheet. At the lower left of the sheet is a well into which you can drag an icon to be displayed in lists that include your custom templates. For instance, if your template is for testing your application, you'd want to drop your application's icon file here. Holding the mouse button over the well will display a popup menu so you can choose Apple-provided icons. The panel provides a text area for the description to be shown in the template-choice sheet.

- The document's suite of instruments, and their configurations, will be saved in the template.
- The template will include the default and instrument-specific targets you set.
- If you include a prerecorded User Interface track, the contents will be saved. This way you can produce uniform test documents simply by creating a new trace document and selecting the template.

As you'd expect, you can reopen a trace document by double-clicking it in the Finder, or by using the **File → Open...** command. All of the data is as it was when the document was saved. Pressing **Record** adds a new run to the document.

Note

There are three ways to run traces without having to launch Instruments. With the `instruments` command-line tool, you can select the target application and either a template or an existing trace document to capture the trace data. The `DTPerformanceSession` framework allows you to initiate traces from your source code without having to bother with the Instruments app's template and document infrastructure. And `iprofiler` provides the same lightweight profiling service from the command line. See `man instruments`, `man iprofiler`, and the `DTPerformanceSession` documentation for details.

The Instruments

There are 51 instruments that come with the Instruments application, plus any custom instruments you might create yourself. The Library palette, **Window → Library** (⌘ L), lists them all. The list in this section follows the Library's organization, adding details as I've gleaned them.

Some instruments aren't documented beyond the sentence or two they get in the Library, plus what is implied by the data they display. The listing rarely identifies which platform the instrument can target. In some cases, I can make up the gap; in others, my guess is as good as yours, often because they crash before you can see the results.

Behavior

Sudden Termination (Mac only)—Audits the OS X feature of directly killing apps that volunteer that they'd be safe to kill. This instrument flags all of your filesystem activity that happens while you've signaled the system that a sudden kill would be okay. If you're actively reading and writing files, it may not be a good idea to subject yourself to termination without notice.

Core Data

Core Data Cache Misses—A faulted Core Data object may already be in memory; it may be held in its NSPersistentStoreCoordinator's cache. If, however, you fire a fault on an object that *isn't* in the cache (a "cache miss"), you've come into an expensive operation, as the object has to be freshly read from the database. You want to minimize the effect of cache faults by preloading the objects when it doesn't impair user experience.

This instrument shows where cache misses happen. It records the thread ID and stack trace of each miss, and how much time was taken up satisfying the miss, for objects and relationships.

Core Data Faults—Core Data objects can be expensive both in terms of memory and of the time it takes to load them into memory. Often, an NSManagedObject or a to-many relationship is given to you as a *fault*, a kind of IOU that will be paid off in actual data when you reference data in the object.

This instrument captures every firing (payoff) of an object or relationship fault. It can display the thread ID and stack depth of the fault, as well as how long it took to satisfy object and relationship faults.

Core Data Fetches—Captures the thread ID and stack trace of every fetch operation under Core Data, along with the number of objects fetched and how long it took to complete the fetch.

Core Data Saves—At each save operation in Core Data, records the thread ID, stack trace, and how long the save took.

Dispatch

Dispatch (Mac only)—Records Grand Central Dispatch events, the status of queues, and the duration of dispatched tasks.

Filesystem

Directory I/O (Mac only)—Records every event of system calls affecting directories, such as creation, moving, mounting, unmounting, renaming, and linking. The data include thread ID, stack trace, call, path to the file directory affected, and the destination path.

File Activity (Mac only)—Records every call to `open`, `close`, `fstat`, `open$UNIX2003`, and `close$UNIX2003`. The instrument captures thread ID, call stack, the call, the file descriptor, and path.

File Attributes (Mac only)—For every event of changing the owner, group, or access mode of a file (`chown`, `chgrp`, `chmod`), this instrument records thread ID, a stack trace, the called function, the file descriptor number, the group and user IDs, the mode flags, and the path to the file affected.

File Locks (Mac only)—Records the thread ID, stack trace, function, option flags, and path for every call to the `flock` system function.

I/O Activity (iOS only)—Combines the functionality of all the Mac-only instruments in this category into one comprehensive instrument for iOS. By default, it only collects how long each call lasted, but click the **Configure** button to see what else is available.

Garbage Collection

Garbage Collection—Measures across the beginning and end of the scavenge phase of garbage collection. It records whether the reclamation was generational and how long scavenging took. It also records the number of objects and bytes reclaimed.

Remember that Garbage Collection was disfavored in Xcode 4 and OS X 10.8 (Mountain Lion) and Xcode 5 treats any attempt to use it as a compilation error.

Graphics

Core Animation (iOS)—Collects statistics for the current state of OpenGL, including wait times for callers, counts of surfaces and textures, and how full video RAM is, as it relates to your app's use of the high-level Core Animation framework.

OpenGL Driver (Mac) and **OpenGL ES Driver** (iOS)—collects the same statistics as the Core Animation instrument, at the lower level of OpenGL/OpenGL ES.

OpenGL ES Analyzer (iOS)—Analyzes your app's usage of OpenGL ES, flagging stalls and other errors, yielding a ranked table of problems and suggestions on how to avoid them.

Input/Output

Reads/Writes—`reads` and `writes` to file descriptors. Each event includes the thread ID, the name of the function being called, a stack trace, the descriptor and path of the file, and the number of bytes read or written.

Master Track

User Interface (Mac only), on first run, records mouse and keyboard events as you use your OS X application. You'll be asked to authorize Instruments to control your application, through the System Preferences application →**Security & Privacy** →**Privacy** →**Accessibility**. After that, running the trace plays your UI events back so you can have a uniform baseline for your program as you make adjustments.

Memory

Allocations (iOS and Mac)—Collects a comprehensive history of every block of memory allocated during the run of the trace. Every event is tagged with the block address and the current stack trace. Configuration options let you track Cocoa reference-counting events and create "zombie" objects. You learned how to use it in Chapter 16, "Measurement and Analysis."

Leaks (iOS and Mac)—Tracks the allocation and deallocation of objects in an application in order to detect the objects' being allocated and then lost—in other words, memory leaks. Leaks does not rely simply on balancing allocations and deallocations; it periodically sweeps your program's heap to detect blocks that are not referenced by active memory. If the Allocations instrument is set to monitor zombies, Leaks won't record because zombie objects, which are never deallocated, are all leaked. For an extensive example, see Chapter 16, "Measurement and Analysis."

Object Graph (Mac only)—Garbage collection, if you have it enabled in your OS X application, is not a panacea for memory management. Entire trees of objects will be collected and returned to the heap (eventually), but that requires that the collector thread see no references to any part of a tree in global or stack memory. If you forget to clear out a reference, the objects stay alive, and you have something that's as bad as a leak. The Object Graph instrument will show you what object trees are alive and how they're anchored. If the target application does not use garbage collection, you'll be alerted that the Object Graph instrument can't be used.

Shared Memory (Mac only)—Records an event when shared memory is opened or unlinked. The event includes calling thread ID and executable, stack trace, function (shm_open / shm_unlink), and parameters (name of the shared memory object, flags, and mode_t). Selecting an event in the Detail table puts a stack trace into the Extended Detail pane.

VM Tracker (iOS and Mac)—Takes a "snapshot" of the virtual-memory zones associated with your application, recording the size of each zone, and whether it is shared or private. The trace shows total usage, but the real story is in the "dirty" trace: The VM system can share things like system libraries across applications from a single chunk of physical RAM, and memory that the app hasn't written to is "clean"—the system can simulate that memory as zeroes without taking up any actual RAM. As soon as your app writes to memory, those addresses become dirty, and they must consume precious physical memory.

Don't bother with VM Tracker on the iOS Simulator; at the virtual-memory level, it's a Mac application with no relation to how memory would be used on an iOS device.

By default, you have to click a **Snapshot Now** button in the Options view to collect heap data. You can check **Automatic Snapshotting** if you want to collect data periodically.

System

Two kinds of instruments fall into the System category: instruments that actively record the state of the target machine, and those that read logs an iOS device had recorded as it had been used untethered to a Mac. I'll treat them as if they were separate.

- **Activity Monitor** (iOS and Mac)—An analogue to the Unix `top` command, with the option to focus on only one process. This instrument is too varied to explain fully here, but its features should be easy to understand if you explore its configuration inspector. It collects 31 summary statistics on a running process, including thread counts, physical memory usage, virtual memory activity, network usage, disk operations, and percentages of CPU load. Remember that you can have more than one Activity Monitor instrument running, targeting different applications or the system as a whole.

- **Connections** (iOS only)—Measures all IP networking activity for an iOS device or any of its processes, in real time.

- **Counters** and **Event Profiler** (Mac only)—Track CPU and low-level system events using hardware diagnostic counters built into each core of the CPU. The data are incredibly primitive, but if you've come to optimizing your code instruction by instruction, such as locating possibly inefficient branches, these instruments are the way to go.

  Window → **Manage Flags. . .** (⇧⌘T) controls which flags are to trigger a count in Counters. Expect a noticeable performance hit when Counters is running. For Event Profiler, **Window** → **Manage PM Events. . .** (⇧⌘P) sets the flags to audit.

- **CPU Monitor** (iOS and Mac)—The Activity Monitor with % Total Load, % User Load, and % System Load selected.

- **Disk Monitor** (iOS and Mac)—The Activity Monitor with Disk Read/Write Operations Per Second, and Disk Bytes Read/Written Per Second checked.

- **Memory Monitor** (iOS and Mac)—The Activity Monitor with Physical Memory Used/Free, Virtual Memory Size, and Page Ins/Outs checked.

- **Network Activity Monitor** (iOS and Mac)—The Activity Monitor with four of eight network statistics active: Network Packets/Bytes In/Out Per Second. It omits the absolute numbers of packets and bytes transmitted.

- **Process** (Mac)—Records thread ID, stack trace, process ID, exit status, and executable path for each start (`execve`) and end (`exit`) event in a process.

- **Sampler** (iOS and Mac)—Periodically samples the target application at fixed intervals (1 ms by default, but you can set it in the inspector), and records a stack trace each time. This instrument has been superseded by Time Profiler, except in cases, like measuring graphics performance, when it is essential to minimize the effect of CPU sampling on other measurements.

- **Spin Monitor** (Mac only)—Focuses on one OS X application, or all, and logs stack traces when they become unresponsive. An application is "unresponsive" when it has spent more than a few seconds without attempting to collect a human-interface event. This is when the multicolored spinning "beachball" cursor occurs. This is a serious fault in an application, but you can't often reproduce spins. Spin Monitor sleeps most of the time, taking up very few resources until a spin activates it.

- **Time Profiler** (iOS and Mac)—Periodically samples the target application at fixed intervals (1 ms by default, but you can set it in the inspector), and records a stack trace each time. You can then get a statistical picture of what parts of your application are taking up the most time. This is an essential tool, doing what most people mean when they speak of profiling an application. Chapter 16, "Measurement and Analysis," demonstrated the use of Time Profiler.

  When Time Profiler is in a trace document, a bar is added above the Track area that lets you refine the profile: The segment control at the left provides an overview trace (middle), or it can divide the trace among CPU cores (left) or by thread (right). A series of popup menus let you restrict the trace by processor core, process, and thread; and they let you color-code by user and kernel load. A popup at the right end of the bar shows the colors used in the chart.

System—iOS Energy Instruments

The Instruments Library puts iOS energy instruments in the "System" category, but they are different. They don't rely on Instruments to run the trace, because running them only when the device is tethered to a Mac would be counterproductive. When you designate a device for development, Xcode (or Instruments) installs a daemon on the device that can log activity that influences power drain.

You can analyze the logs when the device is plugged into Instruments again. Open Instruments and select **File →Import Energy Diagnostics from Device**.

By default, logging is off and must be turned on with the Settings app. The daemon itself can be turned off with the **Developer** panel in Settings or by an untethered reboot. If the battery runs out entirely, the daemon won't restart.

These are the instruments that analyze the usage logs:

- **Bluetooth**, **GPS**, and **WiFi**—Log when the respective radios are on.

- **CPU Activity**—This instrument is a compact version of Activity Monitor showing the total load on the CPU, with breakouts for the foreground app, audio, and graphics. Not to be confused with the active, tethered

- **CPU Monitor**, even though the Libary listing describes it as a record of CPU activity.

- **Display Brightness**—This instrument records the on/off state and brightness setting of the device's backlight. Ambient-light adjustments don't get logged.

- **Energy Usage**—Overall power drain on a scale of 20. When the device is plugged or unplugged to a power source, the event is flagged.
- **Network Activity**—Logs overall network usage in terms of bit and packet rates. Not to be confused with the
- **Network Activity Monitor**, which displays network usage in real time.
- **Sleep/Wake**—Logs whether the device is asleep, along with sleep-transition states.

Threads/Locks

Thread States (Mac only)—Represents each thread in the target application by a block, colored to indicate the state of the thread—running, waiting, suspended, etc.—at each moment. Open the configuration block ⓘ to see the color code. See Figure 27.8.

There had been a **JavaThread** instrument for working out issues with threading in Java applications, but Apple's divorce from Java is complete, and the instrument is gone.

Trace

Scheduling, **System Calls**, and **VM Operations** (iOS, Mac)—These keep a complete record of the transitions between threads; between your user code and the underlying

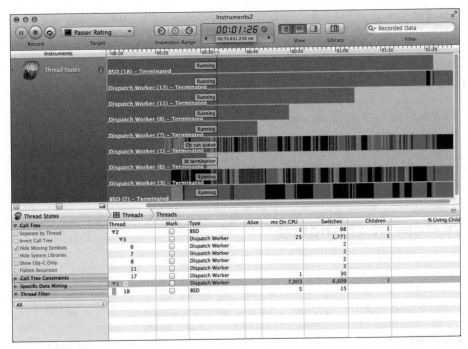

Figure 27.8   The Thread States instrument shows the state of every thread in a process as a stack of color-coded bars.

kernel; and of the layout of your working memory as managed by the virtual-memory system. You can read the duration of the time your code had to wait for kernel-level processing to complete. The track has two "strategies" for display, selectable through a segmented control at the left end of the bar these instruments will insert above the time track.

These instruments force the use of deferred mode, and they insert a bar above the time scale to select display "strategies": bar graphs of "event density," or timelines that show state and flag transitions—click a flag and get a description of the transition type, timing, and a stack trace.

The bar includes a popup to narrow the display to specific processes and threads.

UI Automation

Automation (iOS only)—Executes a JavaScript script that exercises the UI of an iOS application on a device or the iOS Simulator. Add other instruments to the trace document to produce a package that can reproduce a test and record the performance of your app as you develop it. You configure the instrument in the Options view of the Detail area. The most important part is the Scripts section, where the **Add** drop-down menu allows you to **Import. . .** a .js file to the track or **Create. . .** one in an editor within the Detail area.

UI Automation comes with an extensive class tree; consult the "Instruments User Guide" and the "UIAutomation Reference Collection" for details.

User Interface

Carbon Events (Mac only)—Monitors events returned from `WaitNextEvent`. Carbon Events records an event at every return from `WaitNextEvent` and its cousins. It captures a the thread ID, stack trace, the event code, and a string (like "Key Down") that characterizes the event.

Cocoa Events (Mac only)—Records the event objects dispatched through every call to `-[NSApplication sendEvent:]`. It captures a the thread ID, stack trace, the event code, and a string (like "Left Mouse Down") that characterizes the event.

Custom Instruments

Many of the instruments included in Instruments consist of code specially written for the task, but most involve no native code at all. They are made from editable templates: You can examine these instruments yourself—this may be the only way to get authoritative details on what an instrument does—and you can create instruments of your own.

Let's see what a scripted instrument looks like. Create a trace document from the File Activity template, select the Reads/Writes instrument and then **Instrument →Edit 'Reads/Writes' Instrument** (or simply double-click on the instrument's label). An editing sheet (see Figure 27.9) will appear with fields for the instrument's name, category,

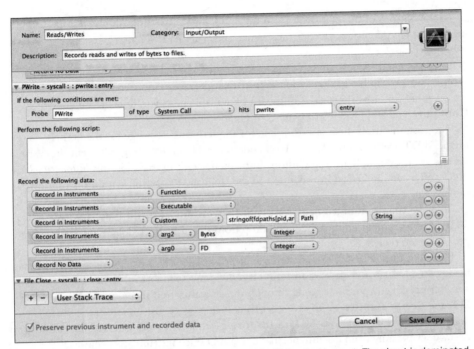

Figure 27.9   The Edit Instrument sheet for the Reads/Writes instrument. The sheet is dominated by an editable list of events the instrument is to capture. The portion that specifies how to record entries to the system pwrite function is shown here.

and description, and a long scrolling list of *probes*, handlers for events the instrument is meant to capture.

Figure 27.9 shows the event list scrolled to the condition called **PWrite**, in the domain **System Call**, for the symbol pwrite. It is to trigger when pwrite is entered. Next comes the text of a script to be executed when the probe is triggered. Instruments uses the *DTrace* kernel facility, which has its own scripting language; for instance, this event might put the time at which the event occurred into a thread variable of the probe, so that a pwrite-exit probe could calculate the duration of the call and record it. In this case, the scripting text is blank.

Then comes a series of items specifying what information is to be kept, for the trace graph or for the Detail view. In the case of Reads/Writes, this is

- The name of the function.
- The name of the executable.
- A string, to be labeled "Path," calculated from an expression in the DTrace language: a file path, derived from the file descriptor within the executable.
- The third argument (the size of the write), which is an integer to be labeled "Bytes."
- The first argument (the file descriptor), which is an integer to be labeled "FD."

At the bottom of the edit sheet is a drop-down menu that controls whether the instrument records a stack trace for its events, and whether it is a user-, system-, or Java-space stack.

Integer-valued records are included in the configuration inspector's list of **Statistics to Graph** and are eligible to display in the instrument's trace. This accounts for the odd presence of "tid" (the thread ID) in the list of available plots you'll see if you click the **Configure** button in the instrument-configuration popover.

The customization sheet is a front end for the scripting language for the kernel-provided DTrace tool; only kernel-level code is capable of detecting call events in every process. The section "Creating Custom Instruments with DTrace," in the *Instruments User Guide*, offers enough of an introduction to the language to get you started on your own instruments.

To make your own instrument, start with **Instrument →Build New Instrument. . .** (⌘ B). An instrument editing sheet will drop from the front trace document, and you can proceed from there.

If visiting `https://wikis.oracle.com/display/DTrace/Documentation` has made you a DTrace expert, you may find it more convenient, or more flexible, to write your scripts directly, without going through the customization sheet. Select **File → DTrace Script Export. . .** to save a script covering every instrument in the current document, and **File →DTrace Data Import. . .** to load a custom script. You can export DTrace scripts only from documents that contain DTrace instruments exclusively.

The stack trace in the Extended Detail view provides another way to create a custom instrument. Select one of the function frames in the listing and then **Trace Call Duration** from the stack trace's **Action** (gear) menu. Instruments will add a custom instrument to the current document that triggers on entry and exit, to record how long it took to execute the function.

The Templates

Between iOS, OS X, and the iOS Simulator, there are 24 trace-document templates built into Instruments, and as you've seen, you can add your own. The Templates assistant presents these in four sections: one for each platform, plus yours.

This section lists all of the available templates, with the instruments they contain, sorted by platform. iOS Simulator shares some instruments with both iOS and OS X; I'll call them out in the platform lists.

All Platforms

Six templates are platform independent: They appear in all three parts of the source list.

- **Blank**: a document with no instruments in it
- **Activity Monitor**: Activity Monitor

- **Allocations**: Allocations, VM Tracker
- **Leaks**: Allocations, Leaks
- **System Trace**: Scheduling, System Calls, VM Operations
- **Time Profiler**: Time Profiler

iOS Only

These seven templates are for iOS targets only, though one of them, Automation, is also available in the iOS Simulator.

- **Automation**: Automation (also on iOS Simulator)
- **Core Animation**: Core Animation, Time Profiler
- **Energy Diagnostics**: These are the analyzers for logs a device accumulates while it's untethered from Instruments—Bluetooth, CPU Activity, Display Brightness, Energy Usage, GPS, Network Activity, Sleep/Wake, WiFi
- **Network Connections**: Connections
- **OpenGL ES Analysis**: OpenGL ES Analyzer, OpenGL ES Driver
- **OpenGL ES Driver**: OpenGL ES Driver, Sampler
- **System Usage**: I/O Activity

Mac Only

Eleven templates are for OS X applications, which in a few cases includes the simulator.

- **Cocoa Layout**: Cocoa Layout
- **Core Data**: Core Data Cache Misses, Core Data Fetches, Core Data Saves (also on iOS Simulator)
- **Counters**: Counters
- **Dispatch**: Dispatch
- **Event Profiler**: Event Profiler
- **File Activity**: File Activity, File Attributes, Directory I/O, Reads/Writes (also on iOS Simulator)
- **GC Monitor**: Allocations, Garbage Collection, Object Graph
- **Multicore**: Dispatch, Thread States
- **Sudden Termination**: Activity Monitor, Sudden Termination
- **UI Recorder**: User Interface
- **Zombies**: Allocations, preconfigured to track zombie objects (also on iOS Simulator)

Summary

Instruments is a big topic, and I've put you through most of it. You started with a tour of the trace document window and moved on to populating it from the Library window. You learned general principles of how to configure an instrument track.

You saw the various ways to start and stop recordings, including human–interface recordings that can be played back to generate repeatable tests for your applications.

You walked through a partial inventory of the instruments and document templates Apple supplies and how to create your own.

As your needs and expertise progress, you'll want to consult the *Instruments User Guide*, to be found in Xcode's Documentation browser.

28

Debugging

Debugging is a natural part of the development process. The first parts of this book tell the story of a development process, and basic debugging techniques followed naturally. In this chapter, I want to call out a few subjects to provide you with a better grasp of how you can get the most out of the Xcode debugger and the lldb debugging system that underlies it.

We'll take a look at the Run action in a build scheme and how it sets the conditions for your debugging session. Then, I'll help you build the skills to make breakpoints more than mere stopping places. And we'll have a look at the command line for the lldb debugger, as it's used both in the Terminal and in the debugger console. Finally, a few short tips and techniques.

Scheme Options

Schemes have come up repeatedly in *Xcode 5 Start to Finish*, but I want to go through the scheme editor for the Run action, from which you'll do most of your debugging. It includes many options to access the OS's debugging features. The Run scheme editor has four tabs, and here they are, one by one:

Info

The options in the **Info** tab can be seen in Figure 28.1.

- For a debugger, you can choose **LLDB** or **None**.
- You have a choice of the privilege level at which the target will run.
  - You can run and debug with your user privileges (**Me**).
  - You can run with **root** privileges (so long as you can provide admin credentials).
- The timing of when the target is launched has been clarified. Ordinarily, you want to run and debug your application **Automatically** (as the label says). But sometimes you have an app that needs specific inputs and conditions from some process that launches it. The **Wait for. . . launch** radio button makes lldb wait until your app starts, and then attach once it's running.

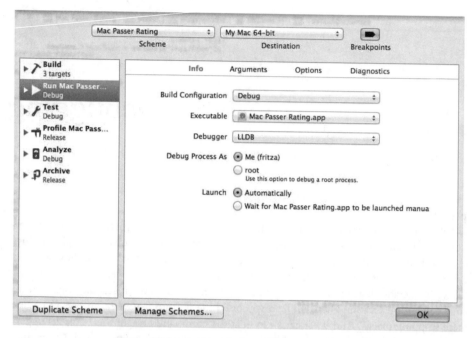

Figure 28.1   **Info** tab for the scheme's Run action.

Arguments

We worked with the **Arguments** tab in Chapter 21, "Localization." I'll summarize: The panel has two tables: one for command-line arguments, and one for environment variables. Use the **+** and **−** buttons to add and remove them. A checkbox will appear next to each item so you can choose which settings should be passed to your application on a particular run.

Argument entries can contain spaces, which will be treated as delimiters when the application is launched; that is, they will result in separate items in the traditional `argv` array. If you mean to pass an argument that contains a space, escape it with a backslash as you would on a command line.

The **Expand Variables Based On** popup menu lets you use the value of a build variable in your arguments and environment values; just include the variable's name like this: `${SETTING_NAME}`. Each target has its own set of build variables, and this menu lets you choose which set is used.

Options

The **Options** tab for the Run action is different depending on whether the target is for Mac or iOS. These controls affect runtime conditions that don't directly match up to system-defined environment variables—like location, working directories, graphics state, and whether you have to deal with potentially frustrating features like launch-time state restoration.

Mac

If you check **Allow Location Simulation**, you'll be given a choice of locations for the debug environment to report to Location Services. You can select from a menu of locations, or add a GPX file for a custom location.

In OS X, Cocoa applications are subject to automatic state restoration, wherein the OS will attempt to reopen previously open documents and configure them as they were. By checking **Persistent State: Launch application without state restoration**, you can save yourself the headaches that may come when you simply want your app to start from zero.

The Versions browser works by loading the previous versions of a document into separate document objects and having them draw themselves. Debugging a plethora of transient, near-identical documents would be...a challenge, but if you need to do it, check **Document Versions: Allow debugging when using document Versions Browser**.

The POSIX working directory is a sore point in Mac development, because when Xcode debugs an application, the working directory is set to the one that contains the executable file; whereas applications launched from Finder get /, the root of the filesystem (though this is not guaranteed). Checking **Working Directory: Use custom working directory:** sets the working directory for debugging runs. There's a field for entering the path and a button to open a get-directory sheet.

XPC services are small executables that isolate parts of an OS X application that might threaten security or make the app less stable. You're probably aware that modern web browsers do much the same thing to prevent plugins from gaining access to the browser proper.

If you check **Debug XPC services used by this application**, Xcode will attach the debugger to XPCs as they launch, as separate process objects in the lldb session.

iOS

The iOS options deal with configuring the simulator and setting up debugging on devices.

- As with Mac targets, if you check **Allow Location Simulation**, you'll be given a choice of locations for the simulator to report to Location Services. You can select from a menu of locations, or add a GPX file for a custom location.

- When you plug a development-enabled device into your Mac, you can use the Devices organizer to navigate to an application and extract its data into a data package. This is vital if you need to reproduce a bug that's dependent on the state of your application. Once you've added the data package to your project, the **Application Data** popup can select it for loading into the simulator at application startup.

- Apple expects that routing (turn-by-turn directions) applications can provide data only for parts of the globe; you'll upload a coverage (GeoJSON) file to iTunes

Connect so the App Store knows what parts of the world your app should be sold in. **Routing App Coverage File** configures the simulator to restrict your app to those regions.

- The Xcode debugger provides comprehensive tools for debugging OpenGL ES on iOS devices. **OpenGL ES Frame Capture** enables or disables the frame-capture button on the debugger's control bar, allowing you to examine your builds step by step.

- Beyond that, the debugger includes OpenGL analysis tools that examine your rendering pipeline in depth, and provide statistics and even critiques on how you're managing OpenGL performance. This involves a tremendous amount of data transfer. The **Enable Performance Analysis** popup allows you to enable or disable the feature.

- iOS 7 can launch apps in the background if they need to poll net resources for data they can download behind the scenes. Checking **Launch due to a background fetch event** simulates this kind of launch, instead of forcing the app onto the screen.

Diagnostics

The **Diagnostics** tab controls a number of diagnostic and logging options for both OS X and iOS that historically were controlled by environment variables. The most famous is detecting overreleased objects by setting NSZombieEnabled to YES. **Diagnostics** presents the most frequently used options as checkboxes. Search the Documentation browser for Technical Note TN2124, "Mac OS X Debugging Magic," for a description of them and their use. The "Debugging Magic" notes (the iOS version is TN2239) are worth reading all the way through.

> **Note**
>
> The "zombie" technique is a useful way to track down attempts to use an object that had been deallocated by Cocoa's memory-management system. Ordinarily, accessing a disposed-of object would crash, usually in objc_msgSend as your app tries to send the dead object a message. Sometimes the access would go to a completely different object that had been allocated into the same address as the dead object. Either way, it's difficult to determine what the overreleased object had been. When you enable zombies, objects' memory is never freed; they are simply replaced by "zombie" objects that remember what the class of the old object was, and halt execution whenever you try to send them a message. The result is that your app crashes at the *first* attempted access—there's no chance of a succession of accesses that turned out to be harmless—and you have at least a class name to narrow your search for the cause. Zombies are available through this panel, through environment variables, and as an option for the Allocations instrument.

Doing More with Breakpoints

Many developers, even if they regularly use breakpoints, believe logging is the only way to pull control flow and state out of their programs when it's not practical to stop dead at

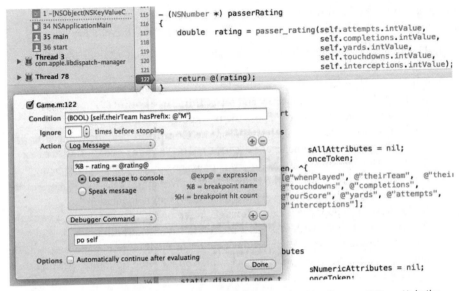

Figure 28.2   A breakpoint action can provide a more refined log than an `NSLog()` in the source code.

every pass through a segment of code. Not so. If you take nothing else away from this chapter, remember this: Almost never do you have to compile `NSLog()` or other printing functions into your application for debugging.

Use breakpoint options instead of `NSLog()`s. The options popover (Figure 28.2) is a little intimidating, but everything in it has a purpose, and once you understand what you can do, it all falls into place.

Let's start with some code from `PRGame.m` based on `NSLog()`:

```
- (double) passerRating
{
    double  rating = passer_rating(self.attempts.intValue,
                                   self.completions.intValue,
                                   self.yards.intValue,
                                   self.touchdowns.intValue,
                                   self.interceptions.intValue);
    if ([self.theirTeam hasPrefix: @"M"]) {
        NSLog(@"%s - rating = %f", __PRETTY_FUNCTION__, rating);
        NSLog(@"%@", self);
    }
    return rating;
}
```

Imagine that the problem we're tracking somehow involves passer ratings coming in PRGames in which the opponent's team name begins with "M." It could happen.

1. Delete the `if` statement, including its body. The whole point is that you don't need it.
2. Click the margin at `return...` to make a breakpoint appear.
3. Right-click the breakpoint arrow and select **Edit Breakpoint...**, or simply option-command-click it, to expose the breakpoint options popover.
4. You're only interested in "M" teams, so in the **Condition** field, reproduce the condition in the `if` statement: enter `(BOOL) [self.theirTeam hasPrefix: @"M" ]`. Breakpoint conditions can execute expressions in any language being debugged. Be sure to specify the return type of any method calls you make—`lldb` can't infer the return type of every possible method implementation.
5. In the **Action** popup, select **Log Message**, and type `%B - rating = @rating@`. Anything you bracket with @ signs is interpreted as an expression, which is substituted into the message. `%B` prints the location of the breakpoint, and `%H` prints the number of times the breakpoint has been hit. You have the option of speaking the message instead of printing it.

   > **Note**
   >
   > You also have the option of playing a sound or executing a debugger command, a shell script, or an AppleScript.

6. However, the `@ ... @` notation isn't as useful as you'd think. If you want to print an object value, this syntax doesn't help because the interpreter sees only a pointer, and prints the hexadecimal address. Your alternative is to use the `expression` debugger command, such as `expr -O -- self`, where the `-O` option tells `lldb` to print the object's description; for the comfort of `gdb` veterans, `lldb` provides the old `po` as an alias.

   So click the **(+)** button and add a **Debugger Command**. Type `po self` in the text field.
7. Or, since you have a complete Objective-C compiler embedded in `lldb`, you can simply improve on the old `NSLog()` by typing

   `expr (void) NSLog(@"opponent = %@, self is %@", self.theirTeam, self)`

   into the command field.

   > **Note**
   >
   > You may have to resort to evaluating `NSLog()` calls in breakpoints more than you'd hope. `%B` and @ expressions are still fragile.

8. In the Options section, check **Automatically continue after evaluating**. The `NSLog()`s didn't stop execution, so neither will this breakpoint.
9. Click **Done**.

> **Note**
>
> The replacement of `NSLog()` calls is complete when you check **Automatically continue after evaluating** in the options popover for a breakpoint. When the breakpoint hits, it will perform all its actions, but it won't halt the program.

Now run your app, and find that your debugger console fills with the breakpoint location, rating, opponent's name, and the contents of the `PRGame` object.

To be sure, in this simple case, it's trivial to construct logging code that does what you need—that's what we started with. But if you first notice the error only after the app had built up state for a long time, and you decide to instrument the problem, it is not practical to kill the app, insert the logging code, rebuild it, and work it to the point where it triggers the bug. Breakpoints don't need a rebuild, their presence doesn't change the state of the program itself (unless you want it to), and they can be modified on the fly.

> **Note**
>
> In earlier versions of Xcode, when you set exception or symbolic breakpoints in the Breakpoint navigator, you got a popover with breakpoint options automatically. This was useful for exceptions because the exception breakpoint can limit itself to Objective-C or C++ exceptions. Some of the Cocoa internals are implemented in C++ that makes liberal use of exceptions, which opens you up to a lot of false positives. Right-click on the new breakpoint and select **Edit Breakpoint...** from the contextual menu.

The `lldb` Command Line

The conditions and commands that you can put into a breakpoint-options popover are just a taste of what you can do with the `lldb` command line. The `lldb` command language is large but much more compact and consistent than `gdb`'s. Nobody can say for sure that it's more powerful, but one of the reasons Apple replaced `gdb` is that the complex of `gdb` settings and command options is so intricate that few users can get the maximum value out of it.

The general pattern of `lldb` commands is

```
noun verb options... arguments...
```

The *noun* portion classifies the available commands. The subsequent verbs and options refine your input to specific actions. The following is a list of built-in, permanent debugger command categories. A few of them are useful only on the command line, but most are wrapped in Xcode's debugging UI. Almost all can be used from the Xcode debugger's own console.

- **quit**—If you're using `lldb` on the command line, the first thing you'll want to know is how to get out.
- **apropos** and **help**—These are the commands you'll be using the most, at least for a while. The `lldb` web site has a good tutorial, but it can't cover every subcommand

and option you'll want to use. The command-line help system is your best resource. Enter **help breakpoint**, and you'll get a list of all the verbs for the breakpoint noun; help breakpoint set will show you the available options for setting a breakpoint.

> **Note**
>
> The documentation at http://lldb.llvm.org/ is only a promise right now (they direct you to a Doxygen tree), but the tutorial at http://lldb.llvm.org/tutorial.html is a great starting place.

- **platform**—lldb's central concept is a hierarchy of containers to organize and control a debugging session. platform is the outermost. This noun lets you examine and select the various devices and architectures that lldb can target—a single instance of the debugger can target more than one at a time—and discover the processes lldb can access.

- **target**—With target, you designate an executable as the focus of a session. You can designate more than one target, so you don't need to run a second instance of lldb to debug both a server and a client. Xcode provides this service when you run a target while another is running: It drops a sheet asking whether you want to quit the existing target, but if you choose to leave it running, the debugger will work on both simultaneously.

- **process**—This is the third layer of lldb containers. You can launch a target (thus creating a process) or attach to an existing process. The process level is where you'd interrupt execution, send POSIX signals, or kill the process.

- **thread**—Most of what you think of when you think about debugging are in this fourth container. The thread level is where you get stack traces and control execution by stepping through the program.

- **frame**—This is the innermost layer. It allows you to focus on the chain of frames—levels of the stack trace—at the point where execution is currently stopped. You can get a dump of variables at each level. The frame variables command alone gives you just the local variables (Objective-C objects will be expanded if you add the -O option). But it's much more flexible than that; type **help frame variable** for the extensive list of options.

- **breakpoint**—This category creates, deletes, lists, and attaches conditions and scripts to breakpoints. Because you can attach expression commands to a breakpoint, you can get away with executing anything you like in an application when the breakpoint triggers. **watchpoint** manages special breakpoints that trigger whenever a variable or memory region is changed—on the Mac or an iOS device.

- **expression**—The expression command is incredibly powerful. It will evaluate and print the result of any expression in the language of the file you're stopped in; lldb embeds the llvm compiler library, so it uses exactly the compiler that was used to build your application. The expression interpreter will even compile your expression into machine code before evaluating it.

It can be any kind of expression: You can do assignments and increments. You can declare local or global variables. You can execute conditionals and loops. Remember the -O option if you want to print the description of an Objective-C object.

- **command**—You'll start out with the `alias` verb to create shortcuts for commonly used commands; `lldb` comes with a set of aliases that map many `gdb` commands. `command` verbs also let you load Python modules for more sophisticated commands using the `lldb` module, which gives Python complete access to `lldb`'s internal state; `lldb` will even give Python plugins access to the target program's memory space, so you can format the internal data of an object without having to run any of the object's methods.

There are many more command categories than I can list here, useful as they are: commands for manipulating memory and registers, listing source code and disassembly, and building a custom configuration. Look for *LLDB Quick Start Guide* in the Documentation browser. In the console, the `help` command is your friend.

For daily use, however, most people find debugging a program through printing its state from a command line to be like sucking the app through a straw. Xcode's debugging UI wraps most of these commands in a much more usable presentation that puts the whole state of the program on-screen at a glance. You can even use features like summary formatters and Python-defined functions by putting them in user-, target-, or directory-specific `.lldbinit` configuration files.

Tips

Here are a few quick tips to help you in debugging your apps.

- By default, breakpoints are private to you—it's not likely that others on your team are interested in how you're working on your part of an app. But you can make a breakpoint public. Right-click on it in the Breakpoint navigator (sixth tab), and select **Share Breakpoint**. The breakpoint will move to a section marked "(Shared)," and it will be visible to users with different user names.

- Breakpoints are also private to the projects in which they were set. By default, a breakpoint applies only to the project that was active when it was set. If you share a source file among projects in a workspace, the breakpoint will trigger only during the run of its project's target. If you want it to trigger regardless of the project, right-click on it in the Breakpoint navigator, and select **Move Breakpoint To →User**.

- The variables view takes up the left side of the Debug area (so long as you select the left-side button from the two at the bottom-right corner of the Debug area. One big improvement is the "Return Value" pseudo-variable. Often you will have a (not very) complex statement like

```
labelString = [[masterObject descriptionDictionary]
                        objectForKey: @"name"];
```

where -`descriptionDictionary` is a method you had defined. Step into `descriptionDictionary`. Step out; the program counter is now just before the call to `objectForKey:`. What dictionary will `objectForKey:` be sent to? Previously, there was no way to know without digging around through the stack pointer. Now, the "Return Value" line of the variables view will show you.

> **Note**
>
> As I write this, "Return Value" didn't always show up or was easy to miss—at the machine-code level, a returned value has a very short lifetime; the bits get assigned or passed elsewhere, and the fact that they came from a function call is quickly forgotten.

- Perhaps you want a console window, just a command-line interface to see your printed output and type application input and debugger commands. Xcode 5's default appearance is discouraging, but it's more adaptable than it looks.

  Double-click any file in a navigator, or tear a tab away from the top of a project window. Either way, you'll have a separate window. Use the toolbar in that window to show the Debug area and hide the Navigator area. Drag the bar at the top of the Debug area to the top of the window, so the editor views disappear. Select **View →Hide Toolbar** to make the toolbar go away. Use the visibility control at the bottom-right corner of the window to make the variables and console view visible, according to your taste.

  You now have a console window. It's not perfect: The title of the window will show the name of whatever was in the window's editor when you started. And, as always, it's fragile. If one of your behaviors changes the format of the front window, you've lost your layout. If you close what you're going to think of as your "project" window, the "console" window will be the last surviving window, and when you reopen the project, you'll have only your console, and you'll have to get busy with the **View** menu to dig yourself out.

- You may find you have to authenticate yourself—possibly repeatedly—to enable the debugger and Instruments to breach security to the extent of permitting you to examine and change the state of another application (the one you're trying to debug). There are two ways to silence the security dialogs:

  - Open the Devices organizer and select "My Mac" from the source list. There will be a button labeled **Enable Developer Mode**. Click it and enter admin credentials. That will clear Xcode and Instruments to access other applications. Clicking the button again, now labeled **Disable Developer Mode**, disables it.

  - Or, enter `sudo DevToolsSecurity -enable` on the command line.

- The `po` (print-object) command in the `lldb` console will print the results of the object's `description` method (or `debugDescription`, which is usually the same thing). The default implementation, from `NSObject`, just prints out the object's class and address, which is of little help. If, instead, you enter `p *objectVariableName`, lldb will treat the object as a C `struct` and display all of its instance variables.

> **Note**
>
> The `print-object/po` command is just an alias for lldb's `expression -O -- objectVariable`.

- I mentioned the `watchpoint` command family in the lldb command line, which allows you to set a kind of breakpoint that triggers when a variable changes value, not necessarily at any one line of your source. Watchpoints allow you to catch bugs where a value changes, and you can't determine how.

  Xcode provides a graphical interface for watchpoints, but it's not obvious. To set a watchpoint, first set an unconditional breakpoint at the first moment the variable comes into scope—you can't work on the variable until lldb can identify it, and the variable has to be in the current scope for lldb to do that. Look for the variable you're interested in in the variables pane. You may have to use the disclosure triangle on an object to expose an instance variable, if that's what you're interested in. Right-click on the variable's row and select **Watch "*variableName*"**. The next time something changes the value of the variable, Xcode will break in.

  Watchpoints having no fixed location in the source code, there's no marker in any editor view that represents one. You can find watchpoints in a special category in the Breakpoint navigator, where you can edit, deactivate, or delete it.

  Watchpoints work on iOS devices as well as on Macs.

- When you're debugging, the top bar of the Debug area, containing all the stepping and other flow-control buttons, is visible at the bottom of the project window, even if you've hidden the Debug area. At the left end of the bar is a control that expands and retracts the Debug area. If anything has been printed in the console since you last looked at the full Debug area, this control will highlight in blue.

- The **Debug** menu provides menu and key equivalents to all the flow-control buttons in the debugger. **Add/Remove Breakpoint at Current Line** (⌘ \\) and **Create Symbolic Breakpoint. . .** (⌥ ⌘ \\) will be useful if you prefer to avoid mousing as you type.

- The **Step Over** and **Step Into** commands (both in the **Debug** menu and in the debugger bar) have two additional variants:

  - **Instruction** advances the program counter to the next machine instruction in the current function (Over) or the next instruction in the course of execution, even if that means descending through a function call (Into). The variants appear in the menu; clicking the buttons with the Control key pressed does the same thing.

  - **Thread** is a little more subtle. Cocoa applications are threaded; there's no way around it. When you do a step-over or a step-into, not only does the thread you see in the debugger advance, so does any other thread that was executing at the same time. You have no control over what thread that would be, still less what code it is executing or what effect it might have on the state you are debugging. **Step Over Thread** and **Step Into Thread** freeze all other threads while you advance the thread you're debugging. Hold down Shift and Control while clicking the buttons, or select the commands in the **Debug** menu, to get the effect.

- If you're comfortable with using lldb from the command line, you can set symbolic breakpoints that match a regular-expression pattern. Say you want to stop at entry to any method whose selector begins with passer. You can do that by using the -r option of the breakpoint set command:

```
(lldb) breakpoint set -r passer.*
Breakpoint created: 8: regex = 'passer.*', locations = 8, resolved = 8
```

lldb says you just created breakpoint 8; breakpoint list lets you examine it:

```
(lldb) breakpoint list 8
8: regex = 'passer.*', locations = 8, resolved = 8
  8.1: where = Mac Passer Rating`-[LeagueDocument passerTable] + 16 ...
  8.2: where = Mac Passer Rating`-[LeagueDocument passerArrayController] + 21 ...
  8.3: where = Mac Passer Rating`-[PRGame passerRating] + 19 at PRGame.m:117 ...
  ...
```

It turns out the command set the breakpoint at eight locations (I'm showing only three of them). lldb separates *locations* from the breakpoints that have effect at them. You can clear the breakpoint from all eight locations by deleting it: **breakpoint delete 8**.

Multi-location breakpoints don't show up in Xcode's Breakpoint navigator, nor in editor margins.

- Sometimes breakpoints get set in your code with no indication in the Xcode UI. It's not supposed to happen, but it will happen to you. You can repair this by typing **breakpoint list** at the lldb command line, finding the number of the phantom breakpoint, and listing the numbers of the breakpoints you want to clear at the end of a typed **breakpoint delete** command.

- Here's something that isn't in the menus, and I really wish it were: If you use **Step Into** enough times in a debugging session, inevitably you will find you've stepped into a function for which there is no debugging information, or no source code. If you're good enough to reliably navigate through such code on your own, you don't need this book.

  lldb has a way out: Entering **thread step-in -a true** (-a is short for --avoid-no-debug) at the lldb command line gets you past frames for which there is no debugging information, so the debugger doesn't come back to you until it hits your code again.

- If you don't remember to break on exceptions, you will inevitably find that you'll hit one, and you won't get control of the debugger until the exception stack has wound down to the run loop, or even your main function.

You can forestall this for OS X applications by setting the user default (preference) NSApplicationShowExceptions to YES in the Terminal command line:

```
$ # Set it for an app whose ID is com.yourdomain.application.id
$ defaults write com.yourdomain.application.id \
>   NSApplicationShowExceptions YES
$ # Set it for every app you run:
$ defaults write -g NSApplicationShowExceptions YES
```

Summary

Most of *Xcode 5 Start to Finish* is an examination of how to integrate Xcode's debugger into your daily workflow. That made this chapter into an opportunity to examine some details that can guide you on the way from effectiveness to mastery.

First, we'd been leaving the debugging environment to the defaults Xcode's project templates provide. The defaults are useful, but there are details—environment variables, location sensing, background processing, and cooperation with subtasks—that have to be addressed as your application becomes more sophisticated. That's the job of the Run action in the Scheme editor.

Next, we explored the power of Xcode's breakpoints. They aren't just for halting the application for you to poke around. You can set up your breakpoints so they automate the way you gather information about how your app works. With conditions and counts and prints, they can all but eliminate the need to change your code just to get a log of how the app executes, or to flick the **Continue** button time after time while you wait for a critical piece of data to arrive.

The power of breakpoints comes from the power of the lldb debugger. Xcode's debugger is a wrapper on lldb, and it's a good one. But some day, you'll need even more control and insight. lldb's command language is direct and elegant, and I showed you the outlines and the philosophy that makes sense of its design.

Finally, I passed along some small—but I hope, helpful—tricks that have helped me in my long hours of debugging.

Continuous Integration

Large software shops have been doing "nightly builds" for many years. The rationale is that team members work only on their own parts of the product. They can test their work and even fit it into the current state of the product. But the known-stable "current state" doesn't reflect the latest efforts of the team, and the members' development environment won't match the production environment that will ultimately deliver the product.

What the team wants to know is whether their work fits together in a production environment, and on a variety of target devices. It does not want to wait for everyone to agree on a "stable" version of the code base; it wants to get the real, current mismatches diagnosed and fixed as soon as they arise.

You could pick a developer out of the team whose responsibility is to maintain a production build machine; collect all the nearest-to-stable work from everyone else; attempt to build; if that succeeds, attempt unit testing on multiple devices; and prepare a report on the results compared to past results, in a form that is accessible and useful to every developer. Every day, after a reasonable deadline for the developers to chip in with their latest offerings. Good luck.

But you have a computer to do this. There are commercial integration-build services that will do your nightly build for you and send you a report. Not all of them support xcodebuild. Not all of their reports and service-configuration interfaces are tailored to the needs of Xcode developers. Fewer have suites of test devices. Fewer still have suites of test devices in every configuration you want to support. None of them have (or, at least, offer) the current prerelease tools you need to target unreleased operating systems, and an unreleased OS is probably the reason for your current project. There is a bit of expense, and a bit of trouble, which may deter smaller operations (solo developers the more so) from even bothering.

So there's a solution, but a limited one.

Xcode 5 does better, taking advantage of keeping the integration server in your hands, attached to your devices, with Apple production tools from end to end. The solution is Xcode Server, a standard service of Mavericks Server.

Xcode Server

Xcode Server is one of the services provided by OS X Server for Mavericks. OS X Server is an add-on to the consumer OS X. It lets you set up services for mail, web, DNS, XMPP (chat), wikis, FTP, calendaring, directories, mobile device management... and Xcode services. It ships from the Mac App Store as a simple OS X application. You purchase it ($50 at this writing), and open the Server application.

> **Note**
>
> If you're a paid member of the Mac Developer Program, Server is free. Log into the Mac Dev Center and download the latest version of Server directly.

When you first run the Server app, it may offer you some tutorials, but when you get down to business, it shows you a single configuration window. That's what you use to control all your services. Click **Xcode** in the source list on the left. The first thing it will do is to ask you to select the Xcode application Xcode Server is to use when it does builds. Then you are taken to the configuration panel.

There is a big **OFF / ON** switch at the top; clicking it puts Xcode Server on the air. But first, some configuration (Figure 29.1).

The Xcode panel contains two tabs, **Settings** and **Repositories**. We can make short work of the **Repositories** tab.

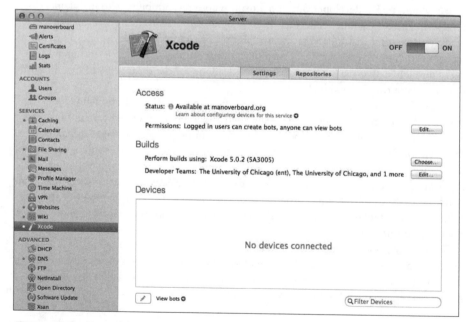

Figure 29.1   Choose **Xcode** from the Server application to start configuring the Xcode service.

Repositories

The main function of **Repositories** is to manage the Git repositories hosted by Xcode Server (Figure 29.2). The top section, "Access," sets overall rules for the Git service. There are two access rules: The first is for how the server will offer access to its hosted repositories. Click **Edit. . .** and check off your choice among **HTTP**, **HTTPS**, and **SSH**. Git service begins with the first method you check.

The second rule is for who is allowed to use Xcode to negotiate the creation of repositories with the server. As you saw in Chapter 7, "Version Control," Xcode 5 can ask Xcode Server to provision a Git repository automatically. The second **Edit. . .** button, for **Hosted repositories can be created by:**, determines who can do that. Clicking the button gives you a dialog box with three choices: **anyone** (the general public); **logged in users** (people with accounts on the Server machine); and **only some users**. The latter will expand the dialog to show a list to which you can add users and groups that will have permission to request new repositories. Click **OK** to close the access dialog.

Now we get to the management of specific repos. The "Repositories" list shows every source-control repository known to Xcode Server. The category of interest—probably the only one you'll use—is "Hosted Repositories." When Xcode IDE users negotiate repositories with Xcode Server, they appear here. You can also add repos that are hosted elsewhere; they'd appear in a "Remote Repositories" category.

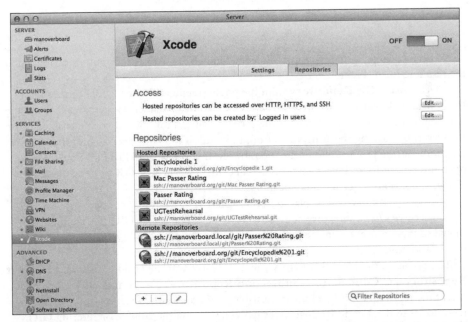

Figure 29.2 The **Repositories** tab of the Xcode Server panel sets up access rules for the server's Git service and lets you manage all the repositories the server hosts.

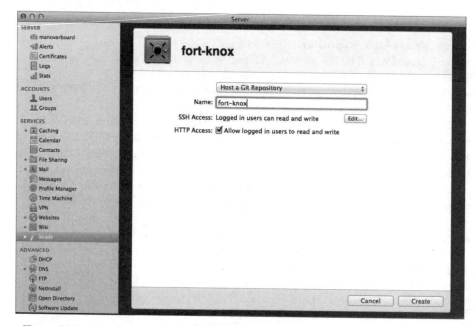

Figure 29.3   Creating a repository to be hosted on Mavericks Server is a matter of filling in a name and confirming user access.

You can create a hosted repository independently by clicking the + button and filling in the resulting form (Figure 29.3).

Select **Host a Git Repository** from the popup menu at the top of the form. Fill in the **Name:** field with the name of the repository; some characters are not allowed, and the field will not register them. Then set the access privileges for SSH (if you've enabled it for the server) by clicking the **Edit. . .** button; the result is the same access-control dialog you used for granting privileges to create repositories. If you enabled HTTP(S) access, you can open this repository to logged-in users by checking a box. Click **OK** to close the access dialog, and **Create** to create the repository.

The new repository will be placed in the `/Library/Server/Xcode/Repositories/git` directory as `repo-name.git`. The access URL for cloning is shown in the repo's entry in the Repositories list, in the form `ssh://server-name/git/repo-name.git`.

The popup in the New Repository panel also gives you the options **Connect to a Git Repository** and **Connect to a Subversion Repository**. The configuration sheet will accept the repository URL, a human-readable name, and authentication options. Adding repositories to the Xcode **Repositories** tab will save you the trouble of entering URLs and credentials when you need to create *bots*.

Settings

There is more work to do on the **Settings** tab. Click the **Edit. . .** button next to the **Permissions** label. This will drop a sheet for setting the policies for who may create and access bots, the automated processes that build and test applications. Set them to whatever will give you access.

You will need to set **Developer Teams** if you want to test or archive your products. Both require signing identities and provisioning profiles. Click **Edit. . . .** You'll be asked for your Developer Program credentials. Server will contact Apple to retrieve your team memberships. Use the **+** and **−** buttons to add the ones for whom you will be doing integration builds. Click **OK**.

Xcode Server will now register itself as a member of your team—if you have an individual program membership, you're not eligible to add members, but Server has an exemption. It will apply for development signing identities and download revised provisioning profiles for your team membership, to which Server has been added.

Turn It On

Everything is set up. Click the big switch in the **Settings** tab to start the Xcode service. It will take a minute or so, and then you're ready to go.

Bots

Now we get to the fun part.

An Xcode project maintains a *scheme* for each of its targets. (There may be more. See Chapter 17, "Provisioning," and Chapter 26, "The Xcode Build System," for examples.) A scheme gathers all the internal and external parameters for performing the five main actions (Run, Test, Profile, Analyze, and Archive) in the life cycle of a target.

Bots can be thought of as extended schemes: They carry parameters for the integration process. A bot embodies

- The repository and branch the source can be found on
- A shared scheme to set the build, test, and execution parameters
- A schedule (time of day, periodic, repository-polling, manual) for running the bot
- The services the bot is to provide (any or all of analysis, test, archive)
- The target devices and simulators for testing
- Whether, and whom, to notify when the bot's run succeeds or fails

Creating a Bot in Xcode

The easiest way to set up a bot is from Xcode.

Set up your project window to reflect the configuration you want: The bot (build-and-test task) will need to know where to find the source (a branch on a remote

repository), and how the build is to be set up (a scheme encapsulating the build settings
and execution environment).

- Switch to a source-control branch that has a remote repository the server can reach.
  The only way a bot can obtain the source for a build is by checking it out from a
  repository. Xcode can infer the remote's URL, branch, and credentials from the
  currently selected branch.

- Select a scheme that reflects the environments in which you want the bot to perform its tasks. At minimum, that means selecting the build configuration for the
  Analyze, Test, and Archive actions.

  It's likely that the scheme you want for integration builds is not the same as the one
  you need for development. Create a new scheme for the purpose in the Manage
  Schemes editor, check the box in the **Shared** column, and commit it to source
  control (at least to the branch the bot will watch, and probably to your master
  branch).

- For testing, use the **Info** tab of the scheme's Test action to select the tests you want
  to perform.

- Use **Product** →**Scheme** →**Manage Schemes. . .** to see a list of your schemes.
  Check the **Shared** box for the scheme you want the bot to use.

- The shared scheme file will be moved to a public portion of the project file. You'll
  have to put it under source control, and push it to the branch and repository you
  want the bot to pull from.

> **Note**
>
> As of November 2013, Xcode was prone to losing its ability to connect to a registered
> Xcode server. The solution is to open the **Accounts** panel of the Preferences window,
> delete the server account, and re-create it. It's not a lot of trouble, and it does no harm,
> but it shouldn't happen.

Xcode allows you to have as many schemes for a target as you like, and it follows that
you can have as many bots for a target as you like, each with its own scheme, so you can
have a bot for everyday integration and testing, and reserve another bot for release builds.

You're ready. Select **Product** →**Create Bot. . . .** A Create Bot editor sheet will slide
down to ask you all the questions I just had you answer.

- The first panel has you select the scheme, name the bot, and select the server that
  will do the integration. A checkbox lets you order the bot to run as soon as it's
  created, regardless of the schedule you set.

- Next, choose a schedule. The bot can run at set times or intervals; or only when
  manually triggered; or by polling the target's branch every few minutes and running
  when a new revision is committed.

- Finally, you can have the bot send email when it finishes. Checkboxes include all
  committers to the target's branch, and you can list additional recipients.

Click **Create Bot**. Xcode negotiates with the server, and the bot will be added to the schedule.

Create a Bot on the Web

Xcode Server runs a display and control panel for the bots it maintains at /Xcode on your server's web service (Figure 29.4). The page will show you the status of all the bots registered with the server, as well as the results of the last integration and the products of the last integration to produce any.

At the top of the page is a bar with buttons to configure the integration service. The buttons at the left end allow you to navigate backward on the path to the current screen. The controls are at the right end—these are the ones you'll see once you've logged in.

- The divided-square button changes the display over to the "Big Screen," which I'll get to shortly.
- The + button lets you create a bot.
- The gear button drops a menu for deleting or reconfiguring a bot when its detail view is on display.
- The padlock button is for signing into and out of the server; it allows you the privileges you were allowed in the **Permissions** sheet of the **Settings** tab of the Xcode server panel.

Creating a bot through the web is a little more complicated than it is in Xcode. Server doesn't have a project that it can examine for source-control information or the preferred

Figure 29.4   Browsing to /Xcode at the server's address shows you a summary of all bots registered with the server and the state of the last build, including its products, if any.

scheme. You will be taken through a four-panel assistant to enter all the information you'd have provided Xcode, plus the information Server lacks.

For the repository itself, you'll be offered a popup menu that contains all the repos known to the server—you set these up in the **Repositories** tab of the Xcode panel. Then a path from the root of the checked-out directory tree to your project (.xcodeproj) file. Xcode knows where the local-repository root and the project file are; Server has to be told.

Type in the build scheme—Xcode can see your selected scheme, Server can't. Make sure the scheme is marked "shared" in your project and that it has been pushed into the repo. Name the bot. There will be sensible defaults for all of these. Click **Continue**.

Next, schedule the builds and select the actions (Analyze, Test, Archive), and whether you want the integration to pull in the whole repo for every build. Click **Continue**.

Tell Server the platform the project is targeted for (this is another thing Xcode already knows) and what devices it's to be tested on. Click **Continue** to find the same panel for specifying who gets completion emails and when. Click **Create**.

That's it; you should be able to see the new bot in the list.

Running a Bot

This is a short section: Once a bot is installed, Server will run it on schedule, when it sees the target's repository has been updated, or when you start it manually. When it's done, it will make the results available through Xcode and the web, and it will send out any email notices you asked for. That's it.

The Xcode web service incudes a "Big Screen," which you can display by clicking the button that looks like a divided square at the upper-right corner of the display. The screen page rotates through the server's bots, showing a summary of the last integration of each. Mouse up to the top of the page to expose buttons to exit the display, or to expand it to full screen (Figure 29.5).

Figure 29.5   The web interface for Xcode Server can put up a "Big Screen," a rotating summary of the last results of all bots in the system.

> **Note**
>
> Remember that Git can never successfully check out a repository that doesn't have a Master branch, even if you're only interested in another. Be sure the repo you direct the bot to includes Master.

Seeing the Results

You can supervise bots and get their history either from the web interface or from Xcode itself. To view the history and progress of your bots, open the Log navigator (last tab). You'll have an easier time if you click the **By Group** button, which will assemble all your integration runs in one group per bot. Clicking the entry for the bot itself (the enclosing group) will give you a summary of the runs of that bot (Figure 29.6).

Inside the bot's group is a list of all the integrations it has performed. Selecting one of those gets you a detailed report on the results, a build log, the commit messages for the revisions that were new when the integration happened, and the results of the tests, for each targeted "device." "Devices" include configurations of the iOS Simulator, as well as any physical device that you've attached to the server machine and consented to use for testing in the Xcode service control panel.

Figure 29.6   Selecting a bot displays the history of integrations performed with that bot, including bar charts showing the number of errors, warnings, and passes and fails of unit tests.

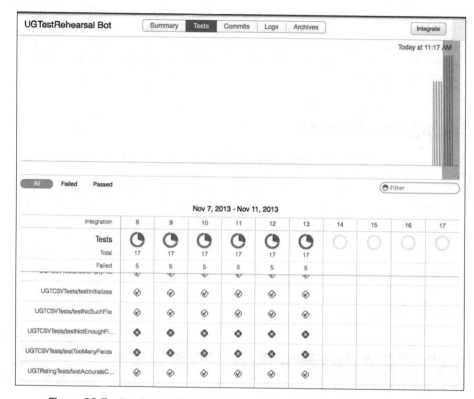

Figure 29.7   The **Tests** tab for a bot shows the test-by-test results for each build.

The **Tests** tab for the bot gives a history of the tests performed in each integration, including which tests passed and failed (Figure 29.7). If you click the integrations for the bot in the source list on the left side of the page, you can get detailed test results, device by device, test by test.

The display in the web interface is almost identical. Any authorized user can download an archive of the build products (the finished application) that can be added to Xcode's Archives organizer and used to create an App Store, in-house, or ad hoc distribution; and an application file (.ipa) that a visitor could download and install directly (given the proper device registration).

You can cancel an integration from Xcode by right-clicking it in the Log navigator and selecting **Cancel Integration**. On the web, bring up the integration's page and select **Cancel Integration** from the gear menu.

Building for Distribution

Distribution builds—which are really the most valuable use for an integration archive—are tricky. Signing certificates are divided between public and private keys, and it doesn't have access to complete distribution identities. You can take care of that by exporting the key pair from a keychain that has it, and importing it into the *system* keychain of the server. All users, including the Xcode service, will have access to that key. Plan your security accordingly.

Installing a distribution provisioning profile requires some wrenching. The Xcode service will create and download development provisioning profiles for all your team's products, but it won't download any distribution profiles. You have to copy them into the server's data directory yourself.

The target is `/Library/Server/Xcode/Data/ProvisioningProfiles/`. You have no casual access to it. You need admin privileges to list it, make it your working directory, or copy the profile into it.

```
$ ## Gain admin privileges for the entire session
$ sudo -s
Password: <your password>
# ## The hash (#) prompt signals that you are in a
# ## position to do serious harm. Be careful.
# cd /Library/Server/Xcode/Data/ProvisioningProfiles/
# ls
R3G2FGO9MM_Mac_Team_Provisioning_Profile_.provisionprofile
R3G2FGO9MM_Mac_Team_Provisioning_Profile_....provisionprofile
R3G2FGO9MM_Mac_Team_Provisioning_Profile_....provisionprofile
R3G2FGO9MM_iOS_Team_Provisioning_Profile_.mobileprovision
R3G2FGO9MM_iOS_Team_Provisioning_Profile_comwt9t.mobileprovision
...
# ## Some of those filenames are truncated for space,
# ## and the team identifier is fictitious.
# ## Do the copy (made-up filename):
# cp /Users/xcodeuser/Wildcard_ad_hoc.mobileprovision .
# ## Shed the super-privilege as soon as you can:
# exit
$
```

This isn't pretty, but it works. As I write this, Apple uses the word "profile" in its documentation *once*, to say that Xcode Server is clever about such things. This is your only choice.

Summary

Considering everything a continuous-integration server does, and especially what Xcode Server does, Xcode makes the process of configuring an integration and understanding the results very simple.

I showed you how to configure the Xcode service on OS X Server, managing developer credentials, permissions, and repositories.

Then we turned to Xcode, where you can create bots—agents that schedule, configure, and perform analyses, tests, and the creation of archives—with a few choices that are simple, because Xcode picks up most of the configuration from the project itself.

Xcode Server puts up a web application that shows the status of its bots and displays detailed reports of each target and each build/test/archive of each integration for that target. Xcode itself can track a project's integrations in its Log navigator.

Finally, I showed you how to get Xcode Server to create distribution (App Store, in-house, beta) products, which involved going behind the server's back.

Snippets

Xcode 5 Start to Finish relies mostly on narrative to take you on a tour of using Xcode for Cocoa development. I tried to cover as much as I could in the first three parts, and I mopped up the remaining big topics in the fourth. That leaves some small topics—tricks and traps—that didn't fit anywhere else.

Tricks

General

- If you're used to Unix or Linux development, you're accustomed to global macros like NDEBUG and DEBUG, and expect them to be set for you automatically.

  If the argument to the standard C assert() macro is zero, it halts the program. If NDEBUG is set, assert() does nothing, so you can publish code that may still exhibit the bug you put in the assertion for, but at least it won't crash.

  The NS_BLOCK_ASSERTIONS macro does the same with Cocoa's NSAssert family of assertion macros.

  Many developers like to define a DEBUG macro to guard logging and assertion code. It's not a standard macro, but it's very common.

  Xcode's project templates define DEBUG=1 for the Debug configuration; NDEBUG and NS_BLOCK_ASSERTIONS are never set. An easy way to cut down on the size of your released code is to open the **Build Settings** tab in the Target editor and double-click the value for the Release version of the "Preprocessor Macros" setting. You'll get a table to enter the definitions; click the **+** button to add lines. Set NDEBUG and NS_BLOCK_ASSERTIONS, and don't set DEBUG at all. Remember to include $(inherited) to preserve definitions made at other levels.

  > **Note**
  >
  > Don't prefix the symbols you put in "Preprocessor Macros" with -D, even though that's what would go into the clang command line; the setting does that automatically.

> **Note**
>
> A shorthand for setting NS_BLOCK_ASSERTIONS is to set "Enable Foundation Assertions" (ENABLE_NS_ASSERTIONS) in the **Build Settings** tab, setting **Yes** for debugging builds, and **No** for release.

- The **Editor** menu is extremely variable—it adjusts to the type of file in the active editor. If you're sure there's a feature for doing what you want, but you can't find it by typing in the field at the top of the **Help** menu, be sure to bring up a related file, and click on it to adjust the **Editor** menu.

- In a complex project, an object in a XIB may take part, as provider or recipient, in dozens of outlets, actions, and bindings, each with its own context-limited editor. You don't have to click through all the editors; select the object, select the Connection (sixth) inspector, and all of the connections will be there in one place.

- You may find some user-defined items at the bottom of the **Build Settings** table. In general, this is how Xcode preserves settings it doesn't recognize. What it recognizes depends on the context: If, for instance, you have a project that doesn't have any compilable files, Xcode won't load its list of compiler options, and those options will be shown as user-defined.

  Older projects are another source of unrecognized settings. Some options are no longer supported in Xcode 4. When you open a project, Xcode may even offer to "modernize" your project by removing them. What you do about this is up to you. Usually, it's a good idea, but if you're sharing the project file with others who are building for older Xcodes or OSes, in which those settings might still be relevant, you will want to preserve those settings for their benefit.

- One setting that I haven't mentioned is $ (inherited). Targets inherit build settings from the project, which in turn inherits settings from Xcode's defaults. Sometimes you want to add to, not replace, an inherited setting. Use $ (inherited) to include the inherited value in your setting.

- You've seen Xcode's offer to incorporate directories as "folder references" when you add files to a project. The Project navigator shows two different kinds of folder icon: What you've seen throughout this book are "group" folders. Basically, these are simply organizational tools, a way to gather files you've decided are related. Each file in a group is itself a member of the project.

  But sometimes adding a folder to a project means adding the folder itself. Suppose that you were building an educational program about presidents of the United States and wanted the Resources directory of the application to include a subdirectory containing a picture of each president. Your intention is that the application include that directory and whatever it may contain—as new administrations or replacement portraits come in—not the particular files.

  In such a case, when you add the portrait folder, you check **Create folder references for any added folders** in the add-files sheet. The folder you dragged in will appear in the list in the same blue color as folders in the Finder, not in the yellow of Xcode's file-grouping folders. The folder reference can then be dragged into the Copy Bundle Resources build phase; the folder and its contents, whatever they might be at build time, will be copied into the product's Resources directory.

- In Chapter 4, "Active Debugging," I mentioned how OS X usually supersedes the default debugger-control keys (the **F** keys) for hardware control. You aren't stuck with Xcode's choices. The **Key Bindings** panel of the Preferences window lists all of the editor functions and application commands, and allows you to set or change the key equivalents for any of them. The default set can't be changed, but click the + button to create a customizable copy.

  The **Conflicts** button in the key table's header is particularly useful. It will show you all of the Xcode assignments that are superseded by the system or by other key assignments in Xcode.

  > **Note**
  >
  > The number of text operations available in Xcode is staggering; the list in the **Key Bindings** table is worth a look. You'll find useful editing actions, like move-by-subword (underscores and internal caps) (**^ Left-** or **Right-Arrow**), you'd never have known about.

- I've made much of the fact that the Project navigator is not a directory or filesystem tool; that it reflects the way you want to structure the project, and not the placement of files in the filesystem's directories. This isn't *quite* true.

  If an Xcode project's file references were arbitrary, they'd have to be absolute paths. That would mean that all of the files would be identified by a path that ran through your home directory. Suppose you were sharing the project with another developer. The project and its files would be in *her* directory, and the reference to your home directory would be wrong.

  The solution would seem to be to keep the path relative to the project file—and indeed that is one of the options. It is not, however, the option Xcode uses by default. The default is **Relative to Group**, as shown in the **Location** popup in the File inspector. There are other choices, such as relative-to-build-products, relative-to-Xcode's internal Developer and SDK directories, and, yes, the absolute path. If you have defined source trees, you can make the path relative to one of those, too.

  But what does "relative to group" mean? If you click on a group folder, you'll see in the File inspector that groups, too, have paths (which can, in turn, be absolute or relative). Groups still aren't directories: More than one group can refer to the same file directory, and not all members of a group have to be in the same place.

  Putting a filesystem location on a group has the advantage that you can have two directories in your filesystem containing files that have the same names. Maybe the one contains live classes, and the other "mocks" for testing. Switching between the two would then be a simple matter of changing the path of the corresponding group. If the group's directory does not enclose a file in the group, that file's path will be stored as project relative.

- Renaming is another file-management service the Project navigator provides. It uses the same gestures as in the Finder: To rename a file or group, click once to select it, then again a couple of seconds later. The item becomes editable. Or, select the item and press Return.

  If the project is under version control, Xcode will do the necessary work to ensure that the change is noted in the repository.

- Suppose you've written something like this in a header file:

```
extern NSString * const    PRPFirstNameKey;
extern NSString * const    PRPLastNameKey;
extern NSString * const    PRPCurrentTeamKey;
```

  and you want to add the corresponding declarations to an implementation file. The first thing you would naturally do is to paste the declarations from the header. Stop there. Hold down the Option key, and notice that the mouse cursor has changed to crosshairs. Drag from the first letter of the first `extern` to the space after the last one.

  You have a column selection. Press Delete. The `extern`s are gone.

  It would be nice if you could type into the column and have your text appear on each line; or copy a column, click elsewhere in the text, paste, and have the column content inserted into the insertion point and the lines below. TextMate does this. Xcode does not.

- By default, the Find navigator does a straightforward search across all the text files in the project. As you saw in Chapter 7, "Version Control," global search has some simple options, readily understood. There are some deeper features:

  - You don't have to search just for text. The cascading popup menus at the top of the Find navigator offer not just text and regular expressions, but **References** (only the uses of the symbol you entered) and **Definitions** (every header declaration and function/variable definition). Later in this chapter, I'll be building a workspace to encompass the three passer-rating projects. Doing a search for **Find** → **Definitions** → **Matching passer_rating** turns up six matches, once each for the .m and .h files in the three projects. This lets you track down parallel definitions like this and look for conflicts and omissions.

  - Below the left end of the global search field is a label that says something innocuous like **In Project** or **In Workspace**. This is a button that slides in an outline of the groups in the project (and of the projects in a workspace). If you've been disciplined about keeping all of the files for a subsystem tucked away each in their groups, you have a great way to narrow your searches by subsystem.

  - There is another category in the scope outline, "Search Scopes," which starts out empty except for a placeholder named **New Scope. . . .** Clicking it triggers a popover for you to name and define a custom search scope. In Figure 30.1, I defined a "Property Lists" scope defined as files that are included in the workspace and have the `plist` extension. If I search for text containing `wt9t` in that scope, I'll be shown only the bundle and document IDs in my `Info.plist` precursors.

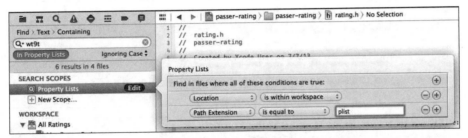

Figure 30.1   Clicking the scope button below the global-search field opens a list of potential search scopes and an affordance for defining scopes of your own—in this case, property-list files within the workspace.

Code-Folding Ribbon

When I had you abate some Xcode features in Chapter 2, "Kicking the Tires," you went to the **Text Editing** panel of the Preferences window and turned off **Show: Code folding ribbon**. The feature is useful, but "noisy"—with the ribbon visible, mousing into the left margin of the editor puts transient highlights in the content.

Many text editors implement folding: You click on a control, usually in the margin, or use a menu command or key equivalent, and the editor collapses the selected block of text. A possibly long stretch of code is elided to a single line, and you're able to see the higher-level structure of a function.

The code-folding ribbon does the same thing: Turning it on adds a stripe between the gutter and the text area of the editor. The deeper the text next to the ribbon is nested, the darker the ribbon gets. When you mouse into the ribbon, Xcode highlights the text to show the extent of the code block containing that line. Clicking the ribbon collapses that block. See Figure 30.2.

The collapsed text is replaced by a yellow bubble with an ellipsis in it. Double-clicking the bubble or clicking the disclosure triangle in the ribbon expands the text. You can find menu commands for code folding, and their key equivalents, in the submenu at **Editor →
Code Folding**.

The Assistant Editor

You've done a lot with the Assistant editor, but let me cover the basics all in one place: The Assistant editor is shown when you click the middle segment of the **Editor** control in

```
 99   // Returns the managed object model for the application.
100   // If the model doesn't already exist, it is created from the application's model.
101   - (NSManagedObjectModel *)managedObjectModel
102   {
103       if (_managedObjectModel != nil) {
104           return _managedObjectModel;
105       }
106       NSURL *modelURL = [[NSBundle mainBundle] URLForResource:@"Passer_Rating" withExtension:@"momd"];
107       _managedObjectModel = [[NSManagedObjectModel alloc] initWithContentsOfURL:modelURL];
108       return _managedObjectModel;
109   }
```

```
 99   // Returns the managed object model for the application.
100   // If the model doesn't already exist, it is created from the application's model.
101   - (NSManagedObjectModel *)managedObjectModel
102   {
103       if (_managedObjectModel != nil) {
104           return _managedObjectModel;
105       }
106       NSURL *modelURL = [[NSBundle mainBundle] URLForResource:@"Passer_Rating" withExtension:@"momd"];
107       _managedObjectModel = [[NSManagedObjectModel alloc] initWithContentsOfURL:modelURL];
108       return _managedObjectModel;
109   }
```

```
 99   // Returns the managed object model for the application.
100   // If the model doesn't already exist, it is created from the application's model.
101   - (NSManagedObjectModel *)managedObjectModel
102   {
103       if (_managedObjectModel != nil) {…}
106       NSURL *modelURL = [[NSBundle mainBundle] URLForResource:@"Passer_Rating" withExtension:@"momd"];
107       _managedObjectModel = [[NSManagedObjectModel alloc] initWithContentsOfURL:modelURL];
108       return _managedObjectModel;
109   }
```

Figure 30.2   When enabled in the **Text Editing** panel of the Preferences window, the code-folding ribbon appears as a strip at the left margin of the editor views. It shows progressively darker bands for each level of nesting in the code. Hovering the mouse pointer over the ribbon (top) highlights the lines at that level of nesting (or deeper). (middle) Moving to a deeper level dims the areas outside the highlighted scope. (bottom) Clicking the ribbon collapses the highlighted scope; its contents are replaced with an ellipsis bubble, and a disclosure triangle appears in the ribbon next to it.

the Workspace window's toolbar. It also appears when you navigate to a file while holding down the Option key.

- The wow feature of the Assistant editor is that it can track what file is displayed in the primary editor and show a counterpart, like the .h file for an .m or a .c file. If there is more than one counterpart—for instance, when there is a second header file for a private interface—the Counterpart assistant will rotate among the three when you click the arrow buttons in the assistant's jump bar or press ∧ ⌘ **Up-** or **Down-Arrow**.

The options for autofilling the Assistant editor go beyond counterparts: You can direct the assistant to related files in the class hierarchy, related Interface Builder files, files that include or are included by the primary editor, and processed content, like assembly and disassembly. As I mentioned in Chapter 5, "Compilation," the assistant can display the callers or callees of a selected function; and it can show the test methods that exercise the selected function.

- The Option-key gesture to put a destination file into the assistant pane can be modified. The **Navigation** panel of the Preferences window lets you customize how Xcode responds to navigational gestures:
  - Simple click navigation can go to the primary editor (the big one on the left) or whatever editor you're using at the moment.
  - Adding the Option key can send the selected file to the Assistant editor, an additional assistant pane, a new tab, or a new window.
  - Double-clicking can direct the file to a new window or a new tab.
  - Further, if you navigate with the Option and Shift keys, Xcode will offer you a heads-up display offering you a graphical picker for placing the file in an existing or a new view. See Figure 30.3.
- You can have more than one Assistant view; there's a **+** button at the top-right corner of the view to add another. The **x** button next to it, of course, closes the pane.
- You aren't stuck with the side-by-side arrangement of the primary and Assistant editors. The **View → Assistant Editor** submenu offers you a choice of dividing the primary and Assistant areas vertically or horizontally, or cascading all editors in coequal rows or columns. Putting the assistant below the main editor makes dragging outlet and action connections between Interface Builder and source files much easier.

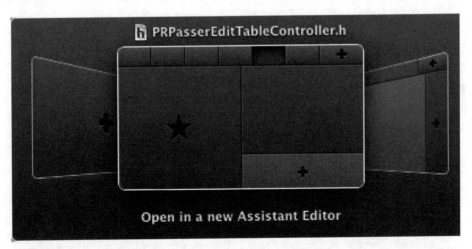

Figure 30.3   The Navigation Chooser appears when you select a file with the Option and Shift keys depressed. It is a graphical browser that lets you choose where the file is to be displayed. The menu equivalent is **Navigate → Open in. . .** (⌥⌘ <). Presented in a Cover Flow style are a new window (on the left) and a different window that is already open (on the right).

Instruments and Debugging

- It bears repeating: Apple keeps two technical notes, "OS X Debugging Magic (TN2124)," and "iOS Debugging Magic (TN2239)," continually updated with the latest techniques for making debugging easier. Search for **Debugging Magic** in the Documentation browser. It's worth 20 IQ points.

- You've probably found that when you click the **Continue** button in the debugger, and the application you're debugging reaches its run loop, the application comes to the foreground, only to hit a breakpoint and bring Xcode back. This can be distracting, so the **Debug** menu has a **Debug Workflow** submenu that lets you select **Standard Windowing** (the behavior I just described), or keeping either the app or Xcode in front at all times. The same menu lets you force assembly listings in the debugger, for when you need to step by instruction and don't want to switch to the assembly view each time.

- The Leaks and Allocations instruments take care of most memory problems, but not all of them. Sometimes, unused objects persist in memory, but because they have residual references, they aren't visible as leaks. Allocations has a button in its options area titled **Mark Heap**. Get your application started up and stable, and click **Mark Heap**. Then do something that will consume memory, but *should* return it to its original state—like opening a document, editing it, and closing it. Do it repeatedly. Mark the heap again.

  The heapshot-analysis table will show you all of the objects that were created, but not deallocated, at the end of the process. Not all will be leftovers—objects can legitimately accumulate in caches—but you should satisfy yourself that they are what they should be.

  Apple engineer Bill Bumgarner has an excellent tutorial on this. Search the web for his name and "heapshot."

Building

- Not an Xcode tip, but something every programmer should take to heart: Compiler warnings are there for a reason. llvm is very, very good at catching common programming errors and violations of the coding conventions on which Cocoa relies. Many of the questions raised on support forums (see Appendix B, "Resources") arise from novices ignoring warnings. Fix every warning. Then run the analyzer (**Product →Analyze**, ⇧⌘B) and fix those, too.

- Xcode assumes that products built with the **Run** action (or **Product →Build** (⌘B), which is a synonym for **Build for Running**) are debugging articles and not fit for release to other users; and that Archive builds, which are fit for release, are comparatively rare. Xcode therefore does not take much trouble to make build product files easy to find. For archive builds, open the Archives organizer, select the archive, and click **Distribute...**; one of the options will be to export an Xcode archive; use the Finder to break into the archive bundle and get to the executable. For run builds, do the build, find the product in the Products group in the Project navigator, and choose **Show in Finder** in the contextual menu.

- In Chapter 26, "The Xcode Build System," I said there is no way to change the set of files in a target, so if you have debug and release versions of a file, you can't switch between them in the Debug and Release configurations of your target. As applied to libraries, this isn't strictly true. The trick is to take the library *out* of the Link Binary With Libraries file, which will keep the build system from adding it to the linker command; and instead pass the name of the desired library in the "Other Linker Flags" (OTHER_LDFLAGS) build setting.

  In the **Build Settings** tab of the Target editor, search for **other** to find the setting. Open the disclosure triangle next to it, double-click the value for the Debug configuration, and click the **+** button to add an item to the list. Add the library (suppose it's named libmyname_debug.a) by typing -lmyname_debug into the new row. Do the same, for the release version of the library, in the Release item.

  At build time, those flags will be added to the command lines for linking, with either the name of the debug version or the release version, depending on the configuration.

- The linker has strong opinions on what libraries it should link into an executable. In particular, for OS X builds, it will *always* link dynamic libraries (.dylib) in preference to static libraries (.a). You can override this by making sure the full path to the .a appears in the link command line. Just add the full path to the library, including the suffix and the lib prefix, to the "Other Linker Flags" (OTHER_LDFLAGS) build setting. You can reduce the dependency on the file paths on your machine by using the BUILT_PRODUCTS_DIR build variable instead of the directory path.

- The optimization-setting flag for llvm goes in a progression from -O0 (none at all) to -O3 (everything). The temptation, when driving for the sleekest, whizziest application, is to turn the knob up full and let the optimizer fly. And yet the standard Release setting for optimization in Xcode is -Os—optimize for *size*. What's going on?

  The problem is that -O3 optimization can dramatically increase the size of the generated code: llvm will autonomously convert function calls to in-line code, so that the content of those functions will be repeated throughout the application. It will turn counted for loops into *n* iterations of the loop body, one after the other, because it's quicker to run straight through four copies of the same code than to keep a counter, test it against four, and conditionally branch.

  All of these optimizations are ingenious, but they can be short-sighted. Modern processors are much faster than the main memory buses that serve them; waiting for loads of data or program instructions can stall a processor for a substantial portion of time. Therefore, very fast cache memory is put between the processor and RAM, to make the instruction stream available at a pace that keeps up with the CPU. But cache sizes are limited. An application that has been doubled in size by unrolling and inlining everywhere will overrun the cache and hit RAM to fetch instructions at least twice as often. In the usual case, "faster" code runs slower than smaller code. Keep the Release configuration at -Os.

- The default features of Xcode's build and analysis actions only scratch the surface of what llvm and the clang analyzer can do for you. Compiler options and in-line attribute directives allow you to fine-tune the analysis and assist in optimizing your code. Look up the complete manual at
  http://clang.llvm.org/docs/UsersManual.html.

Workspaces

I've had you chasing around with three related projects throughout this book. You've probably had two project windows open much of the time, and you may have gotten to three. Given that, left to its own, an Xcode project window would consume every pixel you have, this is no way to live.

This is why Xcode has a unit of organization one step up from the project, the *workspace*. A workspace window looks like a project window, but it can contain more than one project.

Let's imagine how you could consolidate the passer-rating projects. You can start from any of them. Let's open the iOS Passer Rating project, then select **File → Save as Workspace. . . .** You'll be given a save-file sheet to name **All Ratings.xcworkspace** and place the workspace file. (Hint: Don't place it in any project folder. A workspace contains references to projects, but there is no filesystem relationship between it and any project it refers to.) The window you're looking at looks the same, except that the title bar now shows the icon and the name for the workspace file you created.

The workspace contains the Passer Rating project. Now you want to add the Mac Passer Rating project. This can be tricky. The obvious gestures for adding something to the workspace are also obvious gestures for embedding it in an existing project, which you don't want to do.

In the Project navigator for the All Ratings workspace, scroll down so that some empty space is visible. In the Finder, open a window on the directory containing the Mac Passer Rating.xcodeproj file. Drag the project file into the empty space at the bottom of the Project navigator.

Watch very closely! The Project navigator will show an insertion bar where the file will go. Drag as far down and left in the navigator as you can, so that the insertion bar is at the bottom, and the indentation bubble on the bar is at the left margin. If instead it's indented below the last item in Passer Rating, it will insert the project you're dragging into the Passer Rating project.

> **Note**
>
> It's much easier to use **File →Add Files to "All Ratings"...** (⌥⌘A), and add the project that way, but I have a point to make about dragging in files. Be sure not to check **Copy items into destination group's folder (if needed)**; the whole point of a workspace is that the

> projects it refers to don't have to move. Note well that the menu command operates on the workspace only when nothing is selected in the Project navigator. If something is selected, the add-files command will affect the project that contains the selection. Command-click the item to remove its selection, and you'll have the whole-workspace option again.

Release the drag, and see that the Mac Passer Rating project is now in the workspace. The effects are:

- You can work on and build both projects in a single window.
- In particular, you can now have Mac Passer Rating's model files in one half of an Assistant editor, and Passer Rating's in the other, making it easier to copy and paste between them.
- You can create cross-project (not just cross-target) dependencies.
- All build products are directed to a shared build tree, so projects can refer to each others' products through the standard build settings (see Appendix A, "Some Build Variables"). This means that a Mac application built by one project has the benefit of easy access to frameworks under development in the same workspace. (See Chapter 23, "Frameworks," for the details of that trick.)
- A snapshot of the workspace encompasses all projects.
- The projects and their groups appear among the search scopes in the Find navigator, so you can restrict a search to one project only.
- When the workspace is open, and you create a new project, you'll be given the option to add it to the workspace.
- New breakpoints will be kept by the workspace, though they can be moved to a project.
- The Scheme editor encompasses all targets in all projects. Schemes are kept in the workspace.
- You can still open the individual project files. The only difference is that settings stored in the workspace will not be available.

Related to this is the Projects organizer, the second tab in the Organizer window. Every project and workspace known to Xcode is listed in the source list at the left side of the window. When you select one, you are shown

- The name and location of the project/workspace file.
- When it was last opened.
- Where its "derived data" (build products) directory is; there is an arrow button to show it in the Finder, and a **Delete...** button to delete it.
- The same, for the directory that accumulates the project/workspace's snapshots.
- A list of all snapshots; buttons at the bottom of the table allow you to save a snapshot, or delete it.

> **Note**
>
> The default location for snapshots, derived data, and archives is inside your ˜/Library directory. You can change these for all projects in the **Locations** tab of the **Locations** panel of the Preferences window. If you just want to change them just for the current project or workspace, select **File → Workspace (or Project) Settings. . . .**

Each project in a workspace can be managed by a separate version-control repository or system. The commands in **File → Source Control** apply uniformly (a commit goes through one sheet for all changed files), but every action goes through the proper repos for the respective projects.

Think of workspaces as a convenience for your own work on multiple project trees, or as a way to make up for the fact that separate project windows would be too big for it to be convenient to work with more than one at a time. It's a personal resource, containing absolute paths to your personal arrangement of some unrelated directories. Projects can belong to more than one workspace—they are "in" the workspaces only by reference. Workspaces aren't readily shareable across machines or between people and are bad candidates for version control themselves.

Traps

Development is hard. Therefore Xcode is hard, both because it has to do a lot, and because any application that has to do a lot is subject to bugs and annoyances. Here are a few things to watch out for.

- When you remove an IBOutlet from your source, llvm reacts immediately, flagging errors and warnings on all references in your project—*except* for outlet connections in your XIBs and storyboards. You won't hear of it until the NIB loader starts throwing exceptions that say the target object "is not key-value coding compliant" for the missing outlet name. As soon as you change an outlet (or an IBAction), audit the related objects in Interface Builder. Most of these will be in File's Owner; select it and look in the Connection (sixth) inspector for orphaned connections.

  If you're just changing the outlet's name, use **Edit → Refactor → Rename. . . .** The refactoring mechanism will change the IB documents accurately and safely.

- Related: The Find navigator will find text in your project, and it will also turn up Core Data attributes. It will not search XIBs or storyboards, so if you're looking for bindings, outlets, or actions, you're stuck with examining the Connection inspector in Interface Builder.

- In the name of simplicity, Xcode presents a bare search field for in-document search. There are options to be had. The magnifying-glass icon at the left end of the search field anchors a drop-down menu, and the first item is **Show Find Options. . . .** Selecting it gets you a popover presenting options for case sensitivity; prefix, suffix, partial, or whole-word matching for text; or regular expressions.

Clicking anywhere else—such as to execute the search—makes the popover disappear. There is now no visible indication of what the next search will do. Your selections will persist, and you are expected either to remember them or to click on the tiny magnifying glass and select an item in a miniaturized menu. If your in-file searches yield surprising results, check the settings.

If the results are surprising, but you don't know they are (if you knew what was in the file, you wouldn't need to search it), and you ship a bug because of it, that's too bad. But you got to use an uncluttered search field.

- Most regular-expression engines use **&** in replacement fields to stand for the full string that matched the search expression. Xcode uses \0 instead.

- One big gap in Xcode's version-control support is *tags*. When your work comes to a significant milestone, like a version release, you'll want to mark the revision with a name that will allow you to return the project to that point. All version-control systems allow for this. Xcode won't set, display, or revert to tags. You'll have to go to the command line and use the git tag or svn cp subcommands.

- If you look in the AppleScript Editor application for the Xcode dictionary, you'll see what purports to be an extensive scripting interface that you could use, for instance, to create and configure Xcode projects programmatically. It might disquiet you to see many references to Xcode 3. Experiment, if you'd like—some of the commands perform as promised. Most do not.

  If you're interested in generating Xcode projects, look up the Gyp (Generate Your Projects) and cmake projects.

- One of the files that are automatically generated when you instantiate a bundle (including application) target is a precursor file for Info.plist, named *target name*-Info.plist. By misadventure, this file might find its way into the target's Copy Bundle Resources build phase. That would put the file into the built product, which is a mistake. It's a *source* file, and its product, Info.plist, will be built and inserted into the product automatically. Xcode will warn you if it sees this happening in a build.

- Xcode can't handle having a project open in more than one workspace at a time. Xcode ought to prevent you from trying, but in many cases it allows it and then behaves erratically.

- You can't have a XIB or storyboard open in more than one editor. Interface Builder products are literal archives of Objective-C objects. Concurrent access to an object network is a tremendous headache, and I don't blame Apple for allocating its resources elsewhere.

- When you drag an NSTextView into a view in Interface Builder, you're really dragging the NSTextView *inside* an NSScrollView and the clipping view that comes between them. If you attempt to connect an outlet to the text view, you may end up connecting to the scroll view (or to nothing, if your outlet is typed to accept only a text view).

The problem is that the scroll view can be larger than the text view; the text view is only as tall as the text it contains. Add some "Lorem ipsum" text to the view, drag the connector to that, and you'll connect to the text view.

- `NSTableView`, as provided by Interface Builder, is similarly complex.

- Being a dynamic language, the Objective-C compiler allows any object to receive any message. Implementations may be completely unrelated; all the compiler has to do is load the receiver, the selector, and the parameters onto the stack and call for the message to be dispatched.

This works well, but the ideal breaks down with the return value: It might be an integer, a float, a pointer, or a `struct`, and depending on the processor architecture, those results may be stored in completely different locations. The compiler has to generate the instructions to take the result from the correct place.

Things are still fine if all implementors of methods with a given signature return the same result type; so long as the compiler has seen some declaration of the method, it can proceed. Even if the compiler has seen declarations of different return types, it can still do the right thing if the receiving object's class is known.

Where it breaks down is when the receiver is declared to be `id` or `Class`, and so provides no indication of what methods it implements or how they return. In the past, the compiler would silently guess what return type you expect, an abundant source of obscure bugs. `clang` now demands that you use a cast on the receiver of the method call to remove the ambiguity.

- HFS+, the recommended filesystem for OS X, is case preserving—files will get names in the same case as you provide—but case insensitive: `Xcode.txt`, `XCODE.TXT`, and `xcode.txt` all refer to the same file. Most other Unix variants are case sensitive, so if you import code, be on the lookout for the assumption that the following two lines refer to different files:

```
#include "polishShoes.h"
#include "PolishShoes.h"
```

By the same token, make sure that your code uses filenames with consistent letter casing. Even if you don't expect to port your work, HFS+ isn't the only filesystem a Macintosh application sees, and on iOS, HFS+ *is* case sensitive. **But:** The iOS Simulator runs on the OS X filesystem. On the "iOS" that runs in the simulator, HFS+ *is not* case sensitive.

Part V

Appendixes

A

Some Build Variables

This appendix offers a brief (though you may not believe it) list of the major build variables that control the Xcode build system. Build variables determine compiler flags, search paths, installation behavior, and essential information like product names. A comprehensive explanation of Xcode's build variables can be found in the Documentation browser by searching for **Build Setting Reference**.

You can see all the build variables that are available to Run Script build phases by creating a phase that consists of only one line like echo, then checking **Show environment variables in build log**. Do a build, find the build at the top of the Log navigator (eighth tab), and select the **All** and **All Messages** filters. Click the script phase, and then the lines-of-text button that appears at the right end of the row.

You'll find there are nearly 350 variables. This appendix lists the more useful ones. For the purposes of example, assume that user "xcodeuser" is making a release build of an iOS application named MyApp out of a project named MyProject, scheme MyScheme, configuration Release; the project uses the iOS 7 SDK and Xcode 5.0.2 running on OS X 10.9.0.

Some of these settings have no corresponding interface in the **Build Settings** tabs of the Target or Project editor. You can set these—if they are not read-only—by selecting **Editor → Add Build Setting → Add User-Defined Setting**. Xcode will add a new line to the list, and you can enter the setting's name in the Setting column and the value under the level at which you want to set it. Boolean values should be entered as YES and NO.

The authoritative name for a build variable is its "setting name"—the name of the actual build variable, as visible in environment variables and substitutable into other settings and Info.plist expansions. You can find the corresponding entries in a **Build Settings** tab by typing the setting name into the tab's search field.

> **Note**
> Settings can be made conditional according to what processor architecture the product is being built for or what SDK is being used. See Chapter 26, "The Xcode Build System," for details.

The **Build Settings** tab can display setting names instead of the descriptive "setting titles." The **Show Setting Names/Show Setting Titles** item in the **Editor** menu toggles between the "real" names and the descriptive titles.

Similarly, you can control how setting values are displayed. A setting may be defined in terms of another setting, as when you specify an installation directory by `$(HOME)/Applications`. By default, Xcode displays embedded build variables by expanding them. The **Show Definitions/Show Values** item in the **Editor** menu changes the display so that variable references are shown either literally or as-interpreted.

Useful Build Variables

With no further ado, here is a list of selected build variables. I've grouped them by general function, and then by a rough general-to-specific order within those groups.

Some of these variables appear to be obsolete: Apple no longer documents them, and the target templates no longer use them by default. The build system still sets them as environment variables, presumably to preserve compatibility with old run-script build phases, but the best bet is not to use them for new development.

Environment

These are read-only variables that you can use in scripts or to build up other build settings.

- `PROJECT`—is the name of the Xcode project, without extension. Unless you override it, `PROJECT_NAME` follows this setting.
  (`MyProject`)

- `PROJECT_NAME`—is the name of the project that contains the target that is being built. Most intermediate and project paths go through a directory with this name.

- `PLATFORM_NAME`—is the name of the target platform, `macosx`, `iphonesimulator`, or `iphoneos`. This setting appears to be obsolete; Apple no longer documents it.
  (`macosx`)

- `HOME`—is the path to your home directory, just as it would be in `bash`.

- `USER`—is the user name of the person doing the build. There is a corresponding `UID` variable for the numeric user ID.

- `GROUP`—is the group name of the person doing the build. There is a corresponding `GID` variable for the numeric group ID.

- `MAC_OS_X_VERSION_ACTUAL`—is a four-digit number designating the version of OS X on which the build is being done. The first two digits will be `10`, the third `9`, and the last, the minor version. This value will be in trouble if 10.9 reaches a minor version above 9, as 10.4 did.
  (`1090`)

- `MAC_OS_X_VERSION_MAJOR`—is a four-digit number that is the same as `MAC_OS_X_VERSION_ACTUAL`, but with the last digit set to zero. (1090)

- `MAC_OS_X_VERSION_MINOR`—is a four-digit number that designates the current OS version, omitting the leading 10. In Mavericks, the first two digits will always be 09; the second two are the minor version, safe through OS X version 10.9.99. (0900)

- `MAC_OS_X_PRODUCT_BUILD_VERSION`—is the build number for the current OS. (13A603)

- `XCODE_VERSION_ACTUAL`
  (0502),
  `XCODE_VERSION_MAJOR`
  (0500),
  `XCODE_VERSION_MINOR`
  (0500),
  and `XCODE_PRODUCT_BUILD_VERSION`—This is the same version information as in the `MAC_OS_X_VERSION` settings, but for Xcode itself.

Code Signing

These settings control provisioning issues, including the selection of the provisioning profile and the signing identity.

- `AD_HOC_CODE_SIGNING_ALLOWED`—controls whether an ad hoc distribution profile will be accepted for this build.

- `CODE_SIGN_IDENTITY`—is the signing identity to be used for the build. This may be in a reduced form such as iPhone Developer or iPhone Distribution. If so, the build system will consult the provisioning profile for the full common name of the required certificate.

  You should not explicitly set the identity if you can avoid it: Otherwise, team members will force their own certificates, and then check the project into source control. The other team members get project files that require a certificate they don't have. This sets off an arms race in which developers compete to jam their own certificates into the common project file.

  Use the generic identities. Xcode will figure it out. If it can't, you have a provisioning problem that will probably get worse when you start building for distribution. It's hard to fix, but you have to do it.

- `CODE_SIGNING_ALLOWED` and `CODE_SIGNING_REQUIRED`—signify whether the code-signing step will be performed at all. The "allowed" switch must be YES before "required" is even considered.

- `CODE_SIGN_ENTITLEMENTS`—is the path to the .entitlements plist claiming permission to use certain privileged services.

- CODE_SIGN_RESOURCE_RULES_PATH—is the path to a property list that directs codesign to ignore some files in the product package, so as not to freeze files that have to be modified after signing.

- OTHER_CODE_SIGN_FLAGS—identifies any additional command-line flags you need to pass to codesign. You usually don't want to change Xcode's choice of settings for iOS builds, or for Mac builds destined for Developer ID or the Mac App Store.

- PROVISIONING_PROFILE—is the UUID of a valid provisioning profile that matches the bundle ID set in Info.plist. If you set the signing identity to **Automatic**, the build system will draw the signing identity from the specified profile. A missing or invalid profile will cause a build error.

Locations

Source Locations

- PROJECT_DIR—is the directory that contains the project file.
  (/Users/xcodeuser/Desktop/MyProject)

- PROJECT_FILE_PATH—is the full path to the project file.
  (/Users/xcodeuser/Desktop/MyProject/MyProject.xcodeproj)

- SDKROOT—is the root of the tree in which to search for system headers and libraries; this is simple for OS X SDKs, but it gets more involved once you get into the platform and OS options in the iOS SDK.
  (/Applications/Xcode.app/.../iPhoneOS7.0.sdk)

- SRCROOT—is the folder containing the source code for the project, usually the project document's directory.
  (/Users/xcodeuser/Desktop/MyProject)

Destination Locations

These are the directories to which object files, derived files, and products are directed in the course of a build. Many of these are somewhere in the "derived-data" directory for your project. You can set that directory using the **File → Project (or Workspace) Settings...** command, in the **Build** tab, but typically you'll use the default directory, within the Library folder of your home directory. The path to the default directory goes deep and involves a unique identifier string, so it's not practical for me to spell out in this list; you can depend on its beginning with the name of your target. If you see a path beginning with /Users/xcodeuser/Library, you can assume that it's the derived-data directory.

The whole idea of the derived-data directory is to locate in one place all the files—they are many and large—that Xcode generates in managing and building your projects. These files are "derived" in that they contain only information that follows from your source files and settings. They can be reconstructed completely from the contents of your project. *You do not want to put derived files in your project directory tree* if you intend to share it or put it under revision control. If you must put the derived-data directory in your project directory, make sure to give it a name you can match in the ignored-files patterns in your Subversion or Git configuration.

If you want to inspect the derived-data directory, open the Organizer (**Window →**
Organizer, ⇧⌘) and select the **Projects** panel. Find your project in the list on the left, and see the panel at the top of the detail view. The full path to the directory will be shown (middle-truncated if the window is too narrow). Next to it will be a small arrow button that will show the directory in the Finder.

- OBJROOT—is the folder containing, perhaps indirectly, the intermediate products, such as object files, of the build. Unless you override the location for intermediate files, this folder will be buried deep in your user Library directory.
  (/Users/xcodeuser/Library/Developer/Xcode/DerivedData/
  /MyProject-... /IntermediateBuildFilesPath)

- SYMROOT—is the container for folders that receive symbol-rich, meaning not-yet-stripped, versions of the product. This, too, is buried in your own Library directory.
  (/Users/xcodeuser/Library/Developer/-...
  /ArchiveIntermediates/MyScheme/BuildProductsPath)

- DSTROOT—is the directory into which the product will be "installed." For iOS targets, this is simply a holding directory. For OS X, it is usually in the /tmp tree, and the project will make and populate subdirectories in DSTROOT as though it were the root of your filesystem. It is relevant only in install builds. Nowadays, it's useful only if you're building and testing system or kernel software.
  (/Users/xcodeuser/Library/Developer/...
  /ArchiveIntermediates/InstallationBuildProductsLocation)

- BUILT_PRODUCTS_DIR—is the full path to the directory that receives either every product of the project or, if the products are scattered, symbolic links to every product. A script can therefore depend on reaching all of the products through this path. By default, $(SYMROOT)/$(CONFIGURATION), and therefore deep within your Library directory. CONFIGURATION_BUILD_DIR is a synonym.
  (/Users/xcodeuser/Library/Developer/-... /ArchiveIntermediates/
  MyScheme/BuildProductsPath/Release-iphoneos)

- TARGET_BUILD_DIR—is the directory into which the product of the *current* target is built.
  (/Users/xcodeuser/Library/Developer/... /ArchiveIntermediates/-
  InstallationBuildProductsLocation/Applications)

- DERIVED_FILE_DIR—is the directory that receives intermediate source files generated in the course of a build, such as the sources generated by the bison parser generator. This variable is paralleled by DERIVED_FILES_DIR and DERIVED_SOURCES_DIR. If you have a more general need for a place to put a temporary file, consult the Xcode documentation for PROJECT_TEMP_DIR or TARGET_TEMP_DIR.

```
(/Users/xcodeuser/Library/Developer/...
ArchiveIntermediates/MyScheme/IntermediateBuildFilesPath/-
MyApp.build/Release-iphoneos/MyApp.build/DerivedSources)
```

- `OBJECT_FILE_DIR`—is the directory containing subdirectories, one per architecture, containing compiled object files. It's in the derived-data folder, which by default is deep within your `Library` directory.
  ```
  (/Users/xcodeuser/Library/Developer/...
  ArchiveIntermediates/MyScheme/IntermediateBuildFilesPath/-
  MyApp.build/Release-iphoneos/MyApp.build/Objects).
  ```

Bundle Locations

- If the product is a bundle, like an application or a framework, `WRAPPER_NAME` is the base name of the bundle directory.
  (`MyApp`)

- `WRAPPER_EXTENSION` and `WRAPPER_SUFFIX`—is the extension and extension-with-dot for the bundle directory, if the target is a bundle.
  (`app` and `.app`)

- If `SHALLOW_BUNDLE` is `YES`, the other settings in this section are moot, because the product bundle is like an iOS application—all of the files, except for localizations, are to be found immediately inside the bundle directory, without the OS X bundle structure.

- `CONTENTS_FOLDER_PATH`—is the path, within the target build directory, that contains the structural directories of a bundle product.
  (`MyApp.app`)

- `EXECUTABLE_FOLDER_PATH`—is the path, in a bundle target in the target build directory, into which the product's executable file is to be built. Not to be confused with `EXECUTABLES_FOLDER_PATH`, which points to a directory for "additional binary files," named `Executables`.
  (`MyApp.app`)

- `EXECUTABLE_PATH`—is the path, within `TARGET_BUILD_DIR`, to the executable binary.
  (`MyApp.app/MyApp`)

- `FRAMEWORKS_FOLDER_PATH`—is the path, in a bundle target in the target build directory, that contains frameworks used by the product. This is set for iOS builds even though you can't have a framework in an iOS application. For `MyMacApp.app`, it would be `MyMacApp.app/Contents/Frameworks`. There are variables for other possible bundle directories; see the Xcode documentation for more.
  (`MyApp.app/Frameworks`)

- `UNLOCALIZED_RESOURCES_FOLDER_PATH`—is the directory, within a bundle product in the target build directory, that receives file resources that have no

localization—not even the base localization. For `MyMacApp.app`, it would be `MyMacApp.app/Contents/Resources`.
(`MyApp.app`)

Compiler Settings

These settings control how the build system produces executable code. Many of these have the prefix `GCC_`, even though `gcc` is no longer included in Apple's developer tools, substituting `clang`. They carry the prefix over for backward compatibility.

> **Note**
>
> While the build variables expose a great number of `clang` settings, bear in mind that your scripts will have read-only access to them; any changes you make won't be visible outside your script. The `GCC_` variables are primarily useful as substitutes into other build settings, including those you might create yourself. You might, for instance, assign a setting string to a preprocessor variable in `GCC_PREPROCESSOR_DEFINITIONS` so you could experiment with compiler settings and permit your code to print the build settings directly.

- `ARCHS`—are the CPU architectures for which Xcode is to generate product code. These must come from among the `VALID_ARCHS` list; by default, this is the value of `ARCHS_STANDARD`. (See Chapter 26, "The Xcode Build System," for how the build system handles multiple-architecture products.)
  (`arm64 armv7 armv7s`)

- `ARCHS_STANDARD`—is the default set of architectures Xcode will build for.
  (`armv7 armv7s`)

- `ARCHS_STANDARD_32_BIT`
  (`armv7 armv7s`), `ARCHS_STANDARD_64_BIT`
  (`arm64`), and `ARCHS_STANDARD_32_64_BIT`
  (`armv7 armv7s`)—are the standard architectures you'd use instead of `ARCHS_STANDARD` if you're particular about whether the target should be 64-bit, 32-bit, or both. On the run I did, `arm64` was not a part of `ARCHS_STANDARD_32_64_BIT`.

- `NATIVE_ARCH`—is the architecture on which the current build is taking place. This is the same as `CURRENT_ARCH` and (if the target is OS X) `NATIVE_ARCH_ACTUAL`. Note that you can't really use `CURRENT_ARCH` in a script—Run Script build phases are run only once per build, so the value you see for `CURRENT_ARCH` is only one of the architectures that will actually be built. If your script must hit every architecture being targeted, have it iterate through `ARCHS`.
  (`armv7`)

- `NATIVE_ARCH_32_BIT` and `NATIVE_ARCH_64_BIT`—are like `NATIVE_ARCH`, but refer to the 32-bit and 64-bit variants of the *development* architecture. On an iOS build, these settings are moot—they are the respective Intel architectures.
  (`i386 and x86_64`)

- GCC_VERSION and GCC_VERSION_IDENTIFIER—are the compiler version to use, which is fixed at Apple clang 1.0; there have been no backward-compatibility issues so far. The difference between the two is that the identifier uses underscores instead of dots.
(com.apple.compilers.llvm.clang.1_0)

- GCC_PREPROCESSOR_DEFINITIONS—is a space-separated list of symbols to be defined in all compilations. Items of the form *symbol=value* assign values to the symbols. Symbols defined in this way will be incorporated in precompiled headers. Related is GCC_PREPROCESSOR_DEFINITIONS_NOT_USED_IN_PRECOMPS, which specifies symbols defined in every compilation but not incorporated in precompiled headers. This allows you to share precompiled headers between build configurations, with variants in global definitions taken as options in the respective configurations.

- GCC_ENABLE_OBJC_GC—controls whether the project compiles Objective-C source with support for garbage collection.
  - If it is Unsupported, no garbage collection will be done, and no special compiler flag will be set.
  - If Required, garbage collection will be used, and anything that links with the compiled code is expected to use garbage collection itself. The compiler is passed the flag -fobjc_gc_only.
  - If Supported, the code itself will not use garbage collection, but it can link with GC binaries. This is useful only if you are writing a single library to link with both environments. The compiler is passed the flag -fobjc_gc.

> **Warning**
>
> Apple has deprecated the use of garbage collection, not just in new applications, but in maintaining existing ones. The **Build Settings** tab has not exposed this option since early in the life of Xcode 4. As of Xcode 5.1, the developer tools will not produce garbage-collected code.

- It's good practice to treat a build as failed even if the only issues were warnings, not errors: Even if an executable binary could be generated, it won't be. GCC_TREAT_WARNINGS_AS_ERRORS isn't set by default, but maybe it should be; in most cases, warnings point out logical mistakes that you'll have to debug anyway. (NO)

- GCC_WARN_INHIBIT_ALL_WARNINGS—is the inverse of GCC_TREAT_WARNINGS_AS_ERRORS. clang won't emit any warning messages. If doing this seems to you like a good idea, please warn your customers.

- OTHER_CFLAGS—is the catchall variable that receives compiler options that do not have their own build variables for C compilation.
Apple is trying to incorporate every reasonable flag in the **Build Settings** tab, so you should rarely need to use this setting. It's a good idea to type a flag into the settings tab's search field to see whether a direct setting is available. There is also an

OTHER_CPLUSPLUSFLAGS variable. For linker flags, the equivalent is
OTHER_LDFLAGS (empty).

- GCC_WARN_...—clang accepts a *lot* of warning flags, and most of them have
  equivalents in the build variables. Click around in the **Build Settings** tab with the
  Quick Help inspector (Utility area, on the right, second tab) to see what the
  warnings do and what the build-variable equivalent is.

  Many developers use -Wall as a shortcut for a comprehensive set of warnings, and
  the clang engineers provide an even stricter -Weverything, which they insist is
  mostly for debugging the compiler. The **Build Settings** tab doesn't expose those
  options, so put them in OTHER_CFLAGS if you need them.

Search Paths

- HEADER_SEARCH_PATHS—is a space-delimited list of paths to directories the
  compiler is to search for headers, in addition to standard locations, such as
  /usr/include. If you add your own paths, carry the default paths through by
  putting $(inherited) at the beginning or end of your list. If the headers in
  question are in frameworks, set FRAMEWORK_SEARCH_PATHS instead. SDKROOT is
  prepended to the paths of system headers and frameworks.
  (/Users/xcodeuser/Library/... Release-iphoneos/include,
  /Applications/Xcode.app/... /usr/include)

- LIBRARY_SEARCH_PATHS—is a space-delimited list of paths to directories the linker
  is to search for libraries. If set, SDKROOT is prepended to the paths of system
  libraries. Developers sometimes are given libraries in production and debug forms,
  as binaries, with no source; they'd like to use one version of the library in Debug
  builds and the other in Release builds. A solution is to put the two library versions
  in separate directories and specify different LIBRARY_SEARCH_PATHSes for the two
  build configurations.
  (/Users/xcodeuser/Library/...
  /BuildProductsPath/Release-iphoneos)

- IPHONEOS_DEPLOYMENT_TARGET—is the minimum version of iOS on which the
  product can run; symbols in the SDK from later versions of the OS are weak-linked.
  There is also a MACOSX_DEPLOYMENT_TARGET.
  (7.0)

Info.plist

- INFOPLIST_FILE—is the name of the file that will be the *source* for the bundle's
  Info.plist file, if the product of this target is a bundle. This should not be
  Info.plist, as a project with more than one target will need to specify more than
  one Info.plist file.
  (MyApp-Info.plist)

- If YES, InfoPlist_PREPROCESS preprocesses the INFOPLIST_FILE, using a C-style preprocessor. You can specify a prefix file with InfoPlist_PREFIX_HEADER and set symbols with InfoPlist_PREPROCESSOR_DEFINITIONS.
(NO)

- InfoPlist_EXPAND_BUILD_SETTINGS—controls whether build settings should be expanded in the generated Info.plist. This allows you, for instance, to fill the CFBundleExecutable key with ${EXECUTABLE_NAME }, and be assured that if you ever change the name of the product, Info.plist will always be in sync.
(YES)

- InfoPlist_OUTPUT_FORMAT—is your choice of the possible file formats for the Info.plist property-list file. This is binary if you want the binary format; anything else gets you an XML plist.
(binary)

- STRINGS_FILE_OUTPUT_ENCODING—.strings files map symbolic strings (usually English-language names) to strings that would be used for display in a particular language. (See Chapter 21, "Localization.") This is the encoding for the processed string, historically UTF-16, but there is now a binary format that Cocoa can use more efficiently.
(binary)

The DEVELOPER_ Variables

The settings that begin in DEVELOPER_ were a big part of the build environment in previous versions of Xcode, and the build system still sets them for the benefit of run-script build phases. This seems to be for compatibility only, because they appear nowhere in the default values in the **Build Settings** tab, and Apple no longer documents them. I'm including them in case you have no alternative.

Many of the DEVELOPER_ paths had parallel SYSTEM_ and PLATFORM_ settings, as the tool and frameworks sets may vary depending on whether you're developing for OS X or iOS.

The only survivor is SYSTEM_LIBRARY_DIR, the root of the installation path for OS X frameworks.

If you're looking for the paths to Xcode's development tools, you're better off using xcrun --find to pick out the ones that fit the current Xcode and any particular SDK you want. See man xcrun for more details.

- DEVELOPER_DIR—is the directory you chose for the Xcode installation. The DEVELOPER_ variables are important, because they track the currently selected Xcode if you have more than one installed. See man xcode-select.
(/Applications/Xcode.app/Contents/Developer)

- `DEVELOPER_APPLICATIONS_DIR`—is the folder inside `DEVELOPER_DIR` containing Xcode and the other developer applications. You may be better served by using `open -a application-name` if all you want to do is to launch a user application. (`/Applications/Xcode.app/Contents/Developer/Applications`)

- `DEVELOPER_BIN_DIR`—is the folder inside `DEVELOPER_DIR` containing the BSD tools, like `clang`, that Xcode uses. If you write scripts that execute development tools like `clang` or `yacc` directly, use this path *instead* of `/usr/bin`. The tools in this directory are the versions that correspond to the version of Xcode you're using. (`/Applications/Xcode.app/Contents/Developer/usr/bin`)

- `DEVELOPER_FRAMEWORKS_DIR`—is the folder inside `DEVELOPER_DIR` that contains development frameworks, such as for unit tests. There's also a `QUOTED` variant that you can use with the confidence that a shell interpreter won't mangle it. (`/Applications/Xcode.app/Contents/Developer/Library/Frameworks`)

- `DEVELOPER_LIBRARY_DIR`—is the folder inside `DEVELOPER_DIR` containing files (templates, plugins, etc.) that support the developer tools. (`/Applications/Xcode.app/Contents/Developer/Library`)

- `DEVELOPER_SDK_DIR`—is the folder inside `DEVELOPER_DIR` that contains software development kits. (`/Applications/Xcode.app/Contents/Developer/SDKs`)

- `DEVELOPER_TOOLS_DIR`—contains BSD tools, like `SetFile`, that are specific to OS X development and would not be expected to be in `/usr/bin`. (`/Applications/Xcode.app/Contents/Developer/Tools`)

- `DEVELOPER_USR_DIR`—is the folder inside `DEVELOPER_DIR` that you should use as a prefix for the standard `include`, `sbin`, `share`, and other directories you'd ordinarily look for in the root `/usr` directory. (`/Applications/Xcode.app/Contents/Developer/usr`)

Source Trees

A source tree provides a particular kind of build variable, a path to a directory or to the root directory of a tree with a known structure. The path can be a location to receive build results or provide access to a system of libraries and headers. When used to build source paths, a source tree provides a reliable shorthand for packages that do not belong in the directory tree of any one project.

For example, I use the eSellerate libraries in my projects. I define a source tree for the eSellerate libraries by opening the Preferences window, selecting the **Source Trees** tab of the **Locations** panel, and clicking the **+** button to add an entry. I choose `ESELLERATE_DIR` for the setting name and **eSellerate Directory** for the display name, and I type the full path name for the root of the eSellerate SDK into the path column.

Now, when I add a file reference to my project, I can use the File inspector in the Utility area to set **Location** to **Relative to eSellerate Directory**. Regardless of who copies or clones my project, so long as they have defined an ESELLERATE_DIR source tree, the project will find that file in their copy of that directory. I don't have to care about the details of the path, and I especially don't have to set up double-dot relative directory references.

Source trees are global—they span projects—but are per-user.

B

Resources

I've tried to make this book thorough, but it isn't comprehensive. Xcode is too large and subtle a system to cover exhaustively, and Apple constantly updates it. Further, your needs as a Cocoa programmer go beyond simply using the tools. This appendix is a brief reference to resources you can use to go further and keep current.

Books

Before the iOS gold rush, there were few books about Cocoa and Xcode, and they were mostly pretty good. Now, there are a lot more, and there is more...diversity. These are a selected few.

- Buck, Erik, *Cocoa Design Patterns* (2009). Cocoa conforms to a few fundamental patterns, and once you have those down, you've gone a long way toward understanding most of iOS and OS X programming. Erik Buck's book is the best survey available.

- Conway, Joe, and Hillegass, Aaron, *iOS Programming: The Big Nerd Ranch Guide*, third edition (2012). What Aaron Hillegass's *Cocoa Programming for OS X* (see below) did for Mac programmers, this book does for iOS. A stand-alone book from the ground up, it takes you from a dead start (or at least from C programming) to some advanced topics.

- Hillegass, Aaron, and Preble, Adam, *Cocoa Programming for OS X*, fourth edition (2011), and Claude, Juan Pablo, and Hillegass, *More Cocoa Programming for OS X: The Big Nerd Ranch Guide* (2013). This book was a classic from the first edition. The series is where Mac programmers have started for more than a decade. A fine introduction, and a tour by example from beginning to advanced topics. Highly recommended.

- Kochan, Stephen, *Programming in Objective-C 2.0*, fifth edition (2012). The leading book about Objective-C, teaching it as your first programming language—it does not assume you have any grounding in C or object-oriented programming. Kochan teaches the Foundation framework, but treads only lightly on the Cocoa application frameworks.

- Lee, Graham, *Test-Driven iOS Development* (2011). Test early, test every day: Lee's book shows you how.
- Napier, Rod, and Kumar, Mugunth, *iOS 6 Programming Pushing the Limits: Advanced Application Development for Apple iPhone, iPad and iPod Touch* (2012). Napier goes deep into subjects that will get beginning-plus developers well into advanced techniques.
- Neuberg, Matt, *Programming iOS 7* (2013). Matt Neuberg offers an exhaustive (800 pages) introduction to all aspects of iOS programming. Many regard this as the capstone of iOS instruction: Other books will lead you through the steps to producing applications that exhibit some advanced features of iOS. Neuberg takes a thousand pages because he explains the underlying principles step by step. You will not merely have *done*; you will have *understood*.
- Neuberg, Matt, *iOS 7 Programming Fundamentals: Objective-C, Xcode, and Cocoa Basics* (2013). This is a lighter (400+ pages) book, more a tutorial than a text.
- Sadun, Erica, *The Core iOS Developer's Cookbook,* fifth edition (2014). Or any book with Erica as the author, particularly with the word "Cookbook" in the title. She is one of the clearest and most readable technical writers in the business. Many people swear by her iOS books.
- Sharp, Maurice; Sadun, Erica; and Strougo, Rod, *Learning iOS Development: A Hands-on Guide to the Fundamentals of iOS Programming* (2013). This book starts you at the beginning of the development process and hits all of the major issues in bringing an iOS app to App-Store quality.

On the Net

Do you have a question? *Use Google.* Or whatever search engine you prefer. Somebody has probably asked your question before and gotten a satisfactory answer. Even if you intend to ask on a public forum or list, search first. Apple's documentation is on the web, and the search engines' indices are still better than the one in the Documentation browser. If you're having trouble pinning down a query, remember to include some unique symbol from the related API, or at least something like `ios`.

Then, if you can't find a good answer, consider whether the Cocoa API documentation makes the answer to your question obvious. Re-read Apple's documentation one more time. Then ask. If you can say you've made a diligent attempt to find the answer yourself, the people who can help you will be satisfied that you've done your homework, and you are worth helping.

Forums

Early editions of *Xcode Unleashed* praised mailing lists (and mailing-list archives), and even USENET groups—I'll get to them. Time has moved on. People have become comfortable getting and keeping their knowledge in the cloud. Lists that carried more than 100 messages a day a few years ago now tick along with 20 or fewer. If you want to ask a question, a web forum may be the better bet.

- I'll put the second-best first. The Apple Developer Forums *ought* to be the main resource for finding solutions to OS X and iOS problems. They were established to solve the problem that, before iPhone OS 2 went public, there was no way to discuss unpublished SDKs. As a paid developer-programs member, you can ask questions about nondisclosed topics freely. (The Developer Tools section is available to the general public with a free registration as an Apple developer.) Some Apple engineers, having started with the private forums, never branched out to public venues like mailing lists and Stack Overflow.

  The drawbacks, however, are crippling. The forums are closed to external search engines, and the internal search facilities are ludicrous. The indexer is not customized to the subject of the forums, so if you look for a symbol declared in one of the Apple frameworks, the search engine may suggest you really meant some technical term from veterinary medicine. You can narrow your search by time, but you can't go back 12 months (unless you conduct your search on New Year's Eve) because the search engine offers only the *calendar* year.

  The big, universal search engines prioritize results by the number of responses they attract—solutions usually float to the top. Not so on the Apple forums: When you enter your search terms, some encouraging result might flicker past in the Web 2.0 windowlet that pops up, but when it settles down, most of what you get are single-message threads from other hapless seekers.

  But if you're looking for solutions for NDA software, the Apple Developer Forums are the only game in town. `http://devforums.apple.com/`

- Better, much much better: *Stack Overflow*, `http://stackoverflow.com/`. It's open to search engines, the postings have usable metadata, and most of the threads you'll find will have at least one high-quality answer (though it is sometimes a trick to decide which answer that is). Very little chat, a whole lot of solutions. If your mission is problem solving, and not just reference, save yourself some trouble and prefix your search queries with `site:stackoverflow.com`.

Mailing Lists

Apple hosts dozens of lists on all aspects of developing for its products. The full roster can be found at `http://www.lists.apple.com/mailman/listinfo`. Remember that like all technical mailing lists, these are restricted to questions and solutions for specific problems. Apple engineers read these lists in their spare time, and they are not required to answer postings; they cannot accept bug reports or feature requests. Take those to `http://bugreport.apple.com/`.

These three lists will probably be the most help to you:

- `xcode-users`—covers Xcode and the other Apple developer tools. It does not deal with programming questions; if you want to ask about what to do with Xcode,

rather than how to use it, you'll be better off asking in `cocoa-dev`.
`http://www.lists.apple.com/mailman/listinfo/xcode-users/`

- **`cocoa-dev`**—is for questions about the Cocoa frameworks, for both OS X and iOS. `http://www.lists.apple.com/mailman/listinfo/cocoa-dev/`

- **`objc-language`**—handles questions about the Objective-C programming language. Questions about Cocoa programming (except for the primitive data types in Foundation) are *not* on-topic here.
`http://www.lists.apple.com/mailman/listinfo/objc-language/`

> **Note**
>
> R.I.P. **macosx-dev**, a list hosted by the Omni Group (makers of many great Mac and iOS apps) to support OS X development. It was great while it lasted, but the last traffic was a question I answered in early 2012. It was a great resource. I'll miss it.

Developer Technical Support

One resource is in a class by itself. As part of your $99 developer-program membership, you get two incidents with Apple Developer Technical Support (DTS). (You can get more in 5- or 10-packs at about $50 per incident.) If you have a critical question that needs the right answer right away, forums and mailing lists aren't the way to go. The people who really know the right answer aren't required to be there, aren't required to answer, and are not allowed the time to research your problem for you.

If you file a DTS incident, you will be assigned an engineer who will respond within three days. He will have access to OS source code and to the engineers who wrote it. He (usually) will be able to come up with a solution to your problem that works and will work even if Apple revises the OS under you.

DTS isn't a gatekeeper for insider techniques. Almost everything that has an answer has (or will have) a public answer. What you'll be getting is an engineer with good communications skills, and enough of a knowledge base to respond to your particular problem.

Sites and Blogs

- For reference problems, the first place on the web to go is `http://developer.apple.com/`, the site for Apple Developer Programs. It has everything you'll find in Xcode's documentation packages, plus more articles, downloadable examples, business resources, screencasts, and a portal to the iOS, OS X, and Safari developer pages. A good strategy for getting official (public) information from Apple is to do a Google search restricted to `site:developer.apple.com`.

  If you browse to the iOS or OS X documentation pages on your iPad, you'll find that Apple has formatted them to look *almost* like a native iPad browser, with a split master-detail interface. And it *almost* works—as I write this, it was easy to get the navigation list out of sync with the page on display and be locked into a dead end.

- If you find a bug in Apple software, or need a feature, go to `http://bugreport.apple.com` (you'll need to register with Apple as a developer, but the free program will do). Be sure to file a complete report (Apple has guidelines for you), and if you're looking for a new feature, be sure to make a concrete case for how it will improve your product or workflow. `https://developer.apple.com/bug-reporting/` will bring you up to speed on the details.

- `https://www.cocoacontrols.com`—is a clearinghouse for UI components for iOS and OS X. As I write this, its catalog listed 1,763 components.

- `http://www.cocoadev.com/`—is an active wiki encompassing tutorials, references, and links to communities. It's oriented to OS X. As with most wikis, there is a lot of information that hasn't been groomed in quite a while, but it could orient you well enough that you can find your way into the Apple documentation.

- Cocoa Literature, `http://cocoalit.com/`, aggregates Cocoa (iOS and OS X) development posts throughout the web.

- NSHipster, `http://nshipster.com/`, is a weekly blog of "overlooked bits in Objective-C and Cocoa." Each article surveys one aspect of Cocoa programming—`#pragma` directives, `UICollectionView`—and reduces it into a concise, accessible introduction. With just a *little* bit of irony.

- Mike Ash's Friday Q & A blog covers iOS and OS X topics in depth and breadth. The blog itself (updated, as you might expect, nearly every week) is at `http://www.mikeash.com/pyblog/`. You can buy it in ebook form from the links at `http://www.mikeash.com/book.html`. Send him money; he deserves it.

- `http://www.friday.com/bbum/category/science/technology/apple/mac-os-x/`—is the OS X portion of Apple engineer Bill Bumgarner's web log, providing accessible insights on Apple technologies, especially Objective-C, garbage collection, and debugging. Updated only sporadically, but the archive is eye-opening.

- `http://www.wilshipley.com/blog/labels/code.html`—is the coding portion of Wil Shipley's web log. You should especially read his "Pimp My Code" series, critical reviews of coding practices based on a deep knowledge of Cocoa design.

- Cocoa Samurai, `http://cocoasamurai.blogspot.com/`, is Colin Wheeler's blog of extended articles on intermediate-to-advanced topics in Cocoa development.

- There are many sample-code projects on GitHub, `https://github.com`. Plug "ios sample code github" (or "os x" or "cocoa" instead of "iOS") into your search engine, and browse at leisure.

Face to Face

Sitting down with a more experienced developer, and asking how you can accomplish what you want to do, can do more to get you on your way, and faster, than any book (except this one). There are user groups all over the world where you can get help and share your experiences; and there are classes you can take to get up to speed.

Meetings

- CocoaHeads, `http://cocoaheads.org/`, is an international federation of user groups for Cocoa programmers. They meet every month in more than 100 cities worldwide. The web site depends on each group's keeping its information up-to-date; my local group hasn't updated in nearly two years. You can still use the list for contacts.

- NSCoder Night, `http://nscodernight.com`, is more a movement than a user group; it has no central (and very little local) organization. Cocoa programmers gather as often as weekly in pubs and coffee houses to share experiences and code. The get-togethers occur in nearly 60 cities around the world. Unfortunately, the web site hasn't been updated since 2011. Google `NSCoder night your city`, ask around at user groups and colleges, and if all else fails, start one!

Classes

There are any number of companies and educational institutions that will teach you Cocoa programming. I'll mention two good ones, one at the high end, and one at the low, but check with your local college; you may be pleasantly surprised.

- Stanford University, CS 193, *Developing Apps for iOS*, `http://www.stanford. edu/class/cs193p/cgi-bin/drupal/downloads-2011-fall`. This is a 25-part lecture series from a course taught by the Computer Science department at Stanford University. It's available free-of-charge through iTunes U—look for the link at the bottom of the front page of the iTunes Store.

- Big Nerd Ranch, `http://bignerdranch.com/`, Aaron Hillegass's training company, provides week-long boot camps on OS X, iOS, Cocoa, Rails, Android, and OpenGL at locations in North America and Europe. Your fee (starting at $3,500) includes lodging, meals, and transportation to and from the airport.

Other Software

The Xcode tools aren't everything. There are things they can't do, and there are things they don't do well. This section examines some tools that can make your life easier. There's more to consider: You'll be using any number of productivity tools to organize your efforts and provide resources for your apps. (I recommend a good, lean bitmapped-graphics editor, for instance.) I can only survey a few programming tools.

Prices are US dollar equivalents as of late 2013, rounded to the nearest dollar (I have to round for Euro-denominated prices, so x.99 dollar amounts get rounded, too.)

Text Editors

The Xcode editor is a machine for producing Cocoa source code. It is crafted to a specific ideal of how a text editor should work. Maybe you don't share that ideal; maybe you need more direct access to text formats for which Xcode interposes a higher-level editor; maybe you need your own tools to customize your work environment.

Even if you're happy with Xcode for most tasks, as a committed Cocoa programmer you'll probably use one or more of these editors as well.

- *BBEdit*, from Bare Bones Software, is particularly good with large files and HTML. It will open anything. Its support for AppleScript, Unix scripting, and "clipping" macros make it readily extensible. This book was written in LaTeX with BBEdit. It is available from Bare Bones directly, and from the Mac App Store, but beware: Sandboxing restricts the functionality of App Store releases. The App Store version does not include a suite of command-line tools that let you do edits, comparisons, and searches from scripts; go to Bare Bones's web site for an add-on that supplies them. And, the App Store version does not allow you to read or save files that you do not own—a must if you need to edit system configuration files; there is no fix for that, other than to buy from Bare Bones directly. `http://www.barebones.com/products/bbedit/` - $50.

  > **Note**
  >
  > I should disclose that Bare Bones paid me to rewrite one of the chapters in the BBEdit manual. I'd been a happy user of BBEdit for more than a decade, and had recommended it in earlier editions of this book, before the subject was broached.

- Bare Bones provides a capable "light" version of BBEdit, *TextWrangler*. What you'll miss are BBEdit's extensive tools for web development, text completion, version-control support, built-in shell worksheet, and ponies. `http://www.barebones.com/products/textwrangler/` - Free.

- *TextMate 1.5*, from MacroMates, is a text editor with a huge capacity for customization. Syntax coloring and powerful keyboard shortcuts are available for dozens of languages and applications. TextMate has an active user community, and many developers whose products consume formatted text provide free TextMate extension bundles. I preferred TextMate for Rails projects. `http://macromates.com/` - $55.

  > **Note**
  >
  > Many of the language- and system-specific bundles that make TextMate special rely on Ruby 1.8. The transition to Mavericks includes a switch from Ruby 1.8 to 2. (It's been ten years. Get over it.)

- *TextMate 2* had been eagerly anticipated since MacroMates announced that it was 90 percent complete in mid-2009. A "pre-alpha" went public at the end of 2011, and it has attracted fans. The source was published under the GNU General Public License in August 2012. Allan Odgaard, the developer, says "the reason we still label it alpha is mainly because the manual is incomplete." `https://macromates.com/download`

- *Sublime Text 2* is a GUI editor for Mac, Windows, and Linux. You can customize it with JSON-based scripts and Python plugins. It recognizes dozens of language syntaxes, and it indexes both source and library code. Multiple selection allows you to edit common occurrences of a string simultaneously. I hear that skeptics of the future of TextMate are gravitating to Sublime Text and finding that TextMate bundles carry over. `http://www.sublimetext.com/` - $59.

- `emacs` and `vi` are supplied with every standard installation of OS X. If you have any background in the Unix command line, you probably know how to use one of these and have nothing but contempt for the other.

  There are graphical variants of both. Check Xemacs, `www.xemacs.org`, for an X Window graphical `emacs`. MacVim is the most popular Mac-native graphical editor in the `vi` family, available at `http://code.google.com/p/macvim/` as source and installable binaries. Vico, `http://www.vicoapp.com`, is an editor with `vi` key bindings that can use TextMate language bundles. All are free of charge.

Helpers

There are many, many supplemental tools for Cocoa developers—check the "Developer Tools" category in the Mac App Store for scores of choices. Here are a few of the most useful:

- *AppKiDo* and *AppKiDo-for-iPhone*. Documentation for Cocoa is getting better all the time, but the format of the documents for the core API hasn't changed in ten years. Navigation up and down the inheritance tree isn't practical—not all of the links are there. Finding a method or class by a part of its name isn't practical—a search in the Documentation browser will also turn up hundreds of matches in the overview documents. Even finding out what methods a class implements isn't practical—the class references document only the methods a class introduces, not the methods it inherits. AppKiDo provides the solution in a simple browser that shows the class tree and parses the Mac or iOS docset by section and method. One click of the mouse will show you *all* of the methods a class implements.

  AppKiDo isn't Apple software, and Apple has no obligation to keep the docsets compatible with AppKiDo's parsing methods, nor to warn when they are changing. Apple breaks AppKiDo about once a year, so be prepared to spend a painful week or two waiting for the app to catch up. `http://appkido.com` - Free

- *Dash* styles itself a "documentation browser and code snippet manager." You can start with Cocoa document sets, but you can add scores of references for Ruby on Rails, Java, jQuery, Arduino...on and on. The application is built around a search interface that leads you to matches in all the active documentation sets; you're encouraged to build task-specific groups of the docsets you need for one project. Select a page (for instance, a Cocoa class reference), and all of the categories and entries on that page are displayed in a convenient index at the left edge of the window.

The snippet manager holds code in any of dozens of languages. Select the abbreviation for one, and trigger the Dash service. The selected snippet will appear in a heads-up window so you can edit placeholders. These are more intelligent than Xcode's because editing one placeholder will edit other appearances of the same placeholder to match. Press Return to paste the completed code. Dash does a lot, and it's getting better at making everything it does accessible to an untrained user—but it still routinely posts popovers (you can suppress them) explaining fundamental uses. `http://kapeli.com/dash/`, and the Mac App Store. Free to download, $10 for full features.

- *Hopper Disassembler*, you remember, was the tool I used to produce pseudocode from a compiled C function in Chapter 5, "Compilation." If you need an analytical disassembler for your work, you're either an optimization wizard or in deep trouble with what you suspect is a compiler bug. Either way, you need it.

  You present the app with your compiled code, and it presents its best-guess partition of the byte stream into data, dynamic-linkage jump tables, and code, which it tries to break down into functions and sub-blocks within them. Then it's up to you to correct the partitions and to rename objects (including the stack offsets that define local variables) as you cycle through the task of making sense of the machine code. As you saw, Hopper will give you pseudocode, which is great for presentation and essential to solving the puzzle.

  It has hooks into the debugger. The promotional material says it works with `gdb`, but we can hope it can get by with `lldb`.

  The developer (a very patient man as he dealt with me) designed the UI for his own needs. The application is meant to be run from the keyboard, using letter (not Command-key) commands. It takes some getting used to, but it's the best game in town.

  A limited demo is available for free from the developer's web site, `http://www.hopperapp.com`. Purchase directly from the developer or the Mac App Store for $60. The MAS version can't offer the full feature set and will not be eligible for upgrade to the next major version.

- *Kaleidoscope* is a first-class file-comparison and merging editor. The first time you use it, you'll think of it as a glorified diff—a display of the differences between two files, little different from the comparison editor in Xcode. But the Xcode comparison editor goes only one way, to accept or refuse changes between versions of a file; it's a merging tool. Kaleidoscope lets you transfer divergent lines of text from one file to the other. So it's a general merge tool. It can be integrated into Versions, SourceTree, and the `git` and `svn` command-line tools.

And it does whole directories. And if you have more than two versions of a file, you can queue them up so you can select any two to compare.

And it compares images, giving you a flip comparison, a split view, or a bitmap of the changed pixels.

And that's why it's worth seventy bucks. `http://www.kaleidoscopeapp.com` - $70 from the Mac App Store or direct.

- `mogenerator`—In Chapter 8, "Starting an iOS Application," I showed you that even though Xcode's Data Model editor can generate `NSManagedObject` sub-classes from your data model, it's much better to rely on `mogenerator`. There's no reason to repeat the reasons. Use it.

> **Note**
>
> The `mogenerator` package includes the `xmod` plugin, which in Xcode 3 could monitor your data-model files and regenerate the machine-side classes automatically. Unfortunately, plugins disappeared from Xcode at version 4.

Download an installer package from the link at `http://rentzsch.github.io/mogenerator/` - Free.

- *PaintCode* is just cool. At first glance, it's a vector-based drawing application, moderately well featured. It's interesting that you can define colors by name, base other colors on variants of the plain ones, and produce gradients from the defined colors. If you have a shape filled with the named gradient, and change the base color, the derived color and gradient change to match.

  The thing is, *this is a code editor.* As you build your drawing, PaintCode generates the Objective-C code that will reproduce it. Paste the code into your drawing method, and add your own logic for dynamic elements like text or bounds sizes. I rarely use PaintCode's code unchanged—I'll want to adjust text or dimensions programmatically—but it saves me half a day's fooling around to get my arcs to go the right way. `http://www.paintcodeapp.com/` - $100 from the Mac App Store.

Package Managers

Xcode comes with most of the tools you'd need to build most free and open-source (FOSS) software. However, even if you do have all the tools you need to build everything from scratch, you don't have time to research all the dependencies among libraries and the build options necessary to make them work together. That's why most operating systems and most major scripting languages come with *package managers*, which take care of all the details and simply get you what you need to get on with your work.

OS X doesn't have a package manager, but there are four volunteer communities' projects that provide the manager software and ports of many FOSS packages. All of them work from the command line; at their simplest, it's just a matter of invoking the manager's command (`fink`, `brew`, `port`, `pod`) with the package name. There are also graphical wrappers.

Third-party package managers have a problem in that they will not be the only mechanism for installing software on a system. If you run a makefile of your own, or open an installer package that installs its own components, or even use another package manager, the installed products will interfere with each other. Each manager has its own strategy for at least protecting its products from outsiders.

- *Fink* is the oldest of the four, having been founded in 2000. It is a Mac/Darwin derivative of Debian's package-management tools like `apt-get`. Build products go into the `/sw` directory. Fink has not had a binary installation since OS X 10.5 (Leopard); you will have to bootstrap by building the source distribution. The installation instructions list PowerPC as an available platform, which is good news if you are still nursing a PPC Mac along (as I did with my PowerMac G4, 2000-2013). `http://fink.thetis.ig42.org`

- *CocoaPods* is specifically for Objective-C projects. The client software is distributed as the `cocoapods` Ruby gem. The web site consists of some background information and a search field so large, you may not realize it is one. (It's the red "SEARCH*" at the top.) Enter author, name, keyword, or other relevant information, and the incremental search shows you the matching pods. `http://beta.cocoapods.org`

- *Homebrew*, "The missing package manager for OS X," is the newest. Based on Ruby and Git, it's clean, and many new projects deliver themselves through it. Build products go into the `homebrew` directory of your home directory and are then linked from `/usr/local`. `http://brew.sh`.

- *MacPorts* (formerly DarwinPorts) is old enough that it once identified itself with Darwin, not the Mac, when Darwin was still a serious contender as an open-source Unix. The project strives to keep its packages compatible with the current version of OS X, plus the two before. Its library has grown to nearly 18,000 packages. The MacPorts tree is rooted at `/opt/mports`. `http://www.macports.org`.

Version Control

As Chapter 7, "Version Control," showed, source control is a big subject, with many subtleties, and the bare command-line interfaces for the systems are a bit tangled. I've already recommended *Pro Git* and *Version Control with Subversion* as the best guides to the command-line tools.

Xcode's Source-Control system insulates you from the worst of it, but most developers find they still get into tangles, or need functions—tagging being the leading example—that Xcode simply doesn't provide.

The people best equipped to deliver an easy way to use source-control systems are programmers. They are their own market, and this has produced a great number of finely crafted, feature-filled graphical source-control managers. Too many for me to evaluate and list here.

A few stand out.

- *Git* itself comes with some cross-platform (Tk) tools for managing repositories. I've found gitk, which you launch from the command line, to be an excellent way to visualize the branching structure of a repository. It will give you diffs between a revision and its immediate predecessor. If you've installed Xcode, you've installed all the Git tools - Free.

- *SourceTree*, from Atlassian, is a well-regarded, comprehensive application for managing Git and Mercurial repositories. When you first launch it, you give it your credentials for any of the major remote-repo providers, allow it to scan your directory for repositories, and approve the set of repos you'll allow it to manage.

  The UI is...busy, with 19 controls in the toolbar. But comprehensive management of a Git repo is a busy task, and the presentation becomes quite accessible after a few minutes. Ignoring the doc directory from Documentation was a matter of a few clicks; the feature was easy to find.

  It's compatible with OS X 10.6 and up. Atlassian promotes its own cloud software-management services, including Bitbucket, a repository service that is free to projects with up to five participants. http://www.sourcetreeapp.com - Free.

- *GitHub* is the dominant provider of public Git-repository hosting. It provides a simple interface for managing your GitHub-hosted repositories, showing version diffs and branches. It concentrates on keeping you up-to-date in synchronizing your projects with their remotes—on GitHub. GitHub means their app to be a simple, powerful interface for its product. Nothing wrong with that; it's very good at what it does. http://mac.github.com - the application is free.

- *Versions* is the leading Subversion client for OS X, having won an Apple Design award for its UI design. It provides the usual services—version comparisons, commits, branch management—and communicates with the Subversion repository using its built-in implementation of Subversion 1.7—there's no need to install anything else, and no worries about possible mismatches between the app and whatever version of svn is installed on the system.

  http://www.versionsapp.com - $59, $39 for students.

AppCode

AppCode, by JetBrains, is an evolution of the free Eclipse IDE specifically for Objective-C. Its refactoring facilities dwarf those of Xcode, and its code analysis will do everything from correcting the spelling of program symbols in your comments to detecting dead methods, to offering to implement functions and methods you've used without defining, to automated testing, and more. It is a machine for sitting down and ripping through code. If that's your priority, you should download the demo.

Xcode still does some things better. Its version-control facilities are easier to work with day to day. It has a better debugger. It supports an integration system that eliminates much of the pain of unit testing, analysis, and beta distribution. It has Interface Builder. AppCode can't build iOS distributions. AppCode can work off of Xcode projects, but Xcode is still the best way to create Xcode projects. So, frequently, developers who use

AppCode use it as a complement to Xcode—an external tool—rather than make it their primary IDE. Even Xcode fanatics (if there are such) should root for AppCode, to keep up the arms race that Apple has to run against it.

There are five tiers of licenses, including $99 for individual use and $199 for organizations. `http://www.jetbrains.com/objc/`

Alternatives to Cocoa

Xcode 5 Start to Finish teaches Xcode, and incidentally Cocoa, but there are alternatives. Here are some you should explore.

Titanium and PhoneGap are frameworks for writing cross-platform mobile applications, including iOS. Both are built around JavaScript. They provide callouts to native libraries for access to features like GPS, accelerometers, and cameras. Both are open source, with support from their parent companies—Adobe for PhoneGap and Appcelerator for Titanium.

You will still need an iOS Developer Program membership to run your apps on a device.

Adobe PhoneGap

You develop PhoneGap applications mostly with whatever web site–building tools you are most comfortable with, including Adobe Dreamweaver. UI specification comes from HTML5 and CSS. The programming language is JavaScript. To test apps, you come back to Xcode for building and running in the iOS Simulator. PhoneGap applications are wrapped in a native application that hosts the app in a `UIWebView` (in iOS).

PhoneGap is praised as good, for what it is: a "write once, run everywhere" development tool. It restricts itself to common-denominator features among the target devices (in part driven by the fact that HTML browsers vary among platforms, even if they mostly use WebKit). The communication between the HTML and native sides pass through a narrow pipe of JavaScript injection (to the HTML side) and a specialized URL scheme (to the "real" app).

`http://phonegap.com/`—Open source; no charge, premium support and training available for a fee beginning at $25, going up to $1,995 for an organization with up to 20 developers.

Wargo, John, *PhoneGap Essentials: Building Cross-Platform Mobile Apps* (2012).

Appcelerator Titanium

Titanium is more ambitious. What's common among platforms is provided in the common Titanium API, but it also provides platform-specific libraries so you can adopt native-code views and UI idioms. For the IDE, you use Titanium Studio, based on Eclipse, and complete your builds for simulation and installation with Xcode (for iOS).

You code a Titanium application in JavaScript, but that's (mostly) not what the app runs. The build process translates parts of your JS code into Objective-C (for iOS) code, which is compiled into the application. There remains a JavaScript-like interpreter in your app to handle language features that only JS can do—it's where your app gets the dynamism that JS provides. These shims call down into native code that implements most of your application. Slick.

Titanium UIs are built from JavaScript specifications. Independent developers are working on interface-building tools but, as I write this, there are none in Titanium Studio. You *can* build HTML views, but HTML is not the native form for Titanium—you simply feed your HTML source into a web view, which is the "real" view so far as Titanium is concerned. For native components—navigation bars, buttons—Titanium gives you the native objects, not images that are never quite lookalikes.

`http://www.appcelerator.com/`—Open source; no charge, premium support and training available for a fee.

Pollentine, Boydlee, *Appcelerator Titanium Smartphone App Development Cookbook* (2011).

A Biased Assessment

The opinion of a developer who has sunk decades into native development: There is a place for alternative frameworks, but not as big as some hope. If you are developing in-house applications, you are usually looking to leverage time and talent into producing an application with specific functionality, without having to commit to a single vendor, and without having to satisfy a public market. Write-once-run-anywhere (WORA) is a reasonable choice for those goals.

This strategy is a disaster when applied to commercial products. The non-captive market has paid a premium for its iPhones (and Nexuses. . .), and demands apps that pay off on the latest features and capabilities. Non-native development will never keep up, and native-code competitors will have a time-to-market advantage. The temptation is to believe that a WORA app can afford to work like one platform, or the other, or neither, and paying customers won't care; they do. WORA tools are like any modern application frameworks—they can deliver prototypes that look pretty good, and run fairly well; then comes the remaining 90 percent of the development effort, making something worth charging money for. This can involve months of chasing down special cases on each platform (even WebKit behaves differently on different phones). By that point, performance becomes a serious problem: Facebook's Mark Zuckerberg called HTML-only development "the biggest mistake we made as a company."

And even for in-house development, you have to ask the question: Are people bringing their iPhones and iPads (and Nexuses. . .) to work because they are generically portable, or because the apps on those devices are so quick, efficient, and easy to use that the devices are their preferred platform, mobile or not? If the latter, you have to deliver value on a par with those other apps, and WORA may be a waste of money.

Both frameworks tempt developers who want to avoid learning native APIs and (for iOS) a new language. It's a false economy: You end up learning a large API anyway; to the extent the API is smaller, it reflects platform features you won't have access to. A cross-platform framework is a different platform altogether, and the hope that you can just drop your web developer into a large mobile project, without a long learning curve, is likely forlorn.

Alternatives to Objective-C

One of the strengths of the Objective-C runtime and the Cocoa API is that they don't require Objective-C. If you have a dynamic object-oriented language, the whole of Cocoa is available to you. These solutions are tools for programming against the full Cocoa frameworks: They are not alternatives to learning Cocoa, and you'll still need a reading knowledge of Objective-C in order to understand the headers, examples, and documentation.

RubyMotion

RubyMotion is a framework for building iOS applications that replaces compiled Objective-C with another language in the Smalltalk family, Ruby. Everything else is the same. The advantage is that Ruby, being free of the C heritage, can greatly simplify building your own data and control structures. Foundation provides a full, safe implementation of an API for basic data structures, but it's still a *framework*, and not built into the language.

RubyMotion uses a *bridge* to the Cocoa runtime, not a library shim. There is no question of catching up to new API—if it's in the system, it's available to your code. It is an extension of the MacRuby project, started at Apple, so the underpinnings have years of maturity behind them.

The process is reminiscent of Rails development, and temperamentally anti-Xcode: "We do not believe that Xcode makes a good environment for Ruby development (or development in general)." You start with the `motion` command-line tool, which creates a project directory with template code and a `Rakefile`. Everything is done on the command line: You write your code in your favorite text editor. You build with a `rake` command and debug in the iOS Simulator using a Ruby terminal session. You even submit your apps to the App Store with `rake`. Ruby has a reputation for being slow, but that's not a worry; RubyMotion uses an `llvm`-based compiler to reduce your source to machine code.

Early demos of RubyMotion eschewed Interface Builder; all views were laid out by hand, in code. The interactive debugger allowed you to halt execution and set frames interactively, by executing code in-line, and you could take note of the corrected values. This is ingenious, but perverse. The RubyMotion project is working on support for NIBs and storyboards.

I have a soft spot for Ruby, and writing directly to the Cocoa API from code compiled from a very nice language is the right thing to do. You still need to install the iOS SDK, and you must be a member of the iOS Developer Program to install your apps on devices.

`http://www.rubymotion.com/`. $200 per developer; site and educational licenses available.

MonoTouch

To be succinct, but glib, MonoTouch is RubyMotion for C# programmers. It provides full access to Cocoa and the Objective-C runtime from a dynamic language compiled into native code. Much of your application code will have to be iOS-specific—there is no "simplifying" shim between UIKit and what you may be accustomed to—but your business logic and .NET code should carry over with little trouble. That's what they mean by "cross-platform," but not having to translate your back end between Objective-C and Java is still a win.

MonoTouch comes with its own IDE, inspired by Visual Studio. It integrates with Xcode, and you'll still need an iOS Developer Program membership and a command of Objective-C. http://xamarin.com/ios

Licenses are free for introductory-size projects, $399 for individual use, $999 for enterprises (per seat), and $1,899 per seat with priority support. Educational licensees get the business edition, without support, for $99. Xamarin will offer a volume discount (starting at the second license) once you've begun the ordering process.

C++

Many developers do cross-platform the right way, by coding their models and business logic in C++, and putting native UIs around them. Xcode's C++ compiler is excellent, and at least as of WWDC 2013, it's the most compliant with current standards. Cocoa relies on Objective-C, which has an object model completely unlike that of C++; Cocoa is inexpressible in C++. C++ can never be a complete alternative to Objective-C.

But you can bridge the two: Just as Objective-C is formally a wrapper on standard C, so is Objective-C++ a wrapper on standard C++. The ObjC++ runtime takes care of calling constructor and destructor functions on C++ instance variables of Objective-C++ objects; and of Cocoa memory management for Objective-C++ objects in C++ member variables.

The usual approach is to add your C++ code to an application project and provide a shim of Objective-C++ classes and functions to bridge to the Cocoa side of the code. clang identifies Objective-C++ source by the standard file extension .mm.

Index

C

E

G

Q

R

S

T

Addison Wesley

REGISTER

THIS PRODUCT

informit.com/register

Register the Addison-Wesley, Exam Cram, Prentice Hall, Que, and Sams products you own to unlock great benefits.

To begin the registration process, simply go to **informit.com/register** to sign in or create an account. You will then be prompted to enter the 10- or 13-digit ISBN that appears on the back cover of your product.

Registering your products can unlock the following benefits:

- Access to supplemental content, including bonus chapters, source code, or project files.
- A coupon to be used on your next purchase.

Registration benefits vary by product. Benefits will be listed on your Account page under Registered Products.

About InformIT — THE TRUSTED TECHNOLOGY LEARNING SOURCE

INFORMIT IS HOME TO THE LEADING TECHNOLOGY PUBLISHING IMPRINTS Addison-Wesley Professional, Cisco Press, Exam Cram, IBM Press, Prentice Hall Professional, Que, and Sams. Here you will gain access to quality and trusted content and resources from the authors, creators, innovators, and leaders of technology. Whether you're looking for a book on a new technology, a helpful article, timely newsletters, or access to the Safari Books Online digital library, InformIT has a solution for you.

informIT.com

THE TRUSTED TECHNOLOGY LEARNING SOURCE

Addison-Wesley | Cisco Press | Exam Cram
IBM Press | Que | Prentice Hall | Sams

SAFARI BOOKS ONLINE

Xcode 5
Start to Finish
iOS and OS X Development

Fritz Anderson

FREE
Online Edition

Your purchase of *Xcode 5 Start to Finish* includes access to a free online edition for 45 days through the **Safari Books Online** subscription service. Nearly every Addison-Wesley Professional book is available online through **Safari Books Online**, along with over thousands of books and videos from publishers such as Cisco Press, Exam Cram, IBM Press, O'Reilly Media, Prentice Hall, Que, Sams, and VMware Press.

Safari Books Online is a digital library providing searchable, on-demand access to thousands of technology, digital media, and professional development books and videos from leading publishers. With one monthly or yearly subscription price, you get unlimited access to learning tools and information on topics including mobile app and software development, tips and tricks on using your favorite gadgets, networking, project management, graphic design, and much more.

Activate your FREE Online Edition at
informit.com/safarifree

STEP 1: Enter the coupon code: EQEIZAA.

STEP 2: New Safari users, complete the brief registration form.
Safari subscribers, just log in.

If you have difficulty registering on Safari or accessing the online edition,
please e-mail customer-service@safaribooksonline.com